Data Analysis Using SQL and Excel®

Data Analysis Using SQL and Excel®

Second Edition

Gordon S. Linoff

WILEY

Data Analysis Using SQL and Excel®, Second Edition

Published by
John Wiley & Sons, Inc.
10475 Crosspoint Boulevard
Indianapolis, IN 46256
www.wiley.com

Copyright © 2016 by John Wiley & Sons, Inc., Indianapolis, Indiana
Published simultaneously in Canada

ISBN: 978-1-119-02143-8

ISBN: 978-1-119-02145-2 (ebk)

ISBN: 978-1-119-02144-5 (ebk)

Manufactured in the United States of America

SKY10031732_120121

For general information on our other products and services please contact our Customer Care Department within the United States at (877) 762-2974, outside the United States at (317) 572-3993 or fax (317) 572-4002.

Wiley publishes in a variety of print and electronic formats and by print-on-demand. Some material included with standard print versions of this book may not be included in e-books or in print-on-demand. If this book refers to media such as a CD or DVD that is not included in the version you purchased, you may download this material at http://booksupport.wiley.com. For more information about Wiley products, visit www.wiley.com.

Library of Congress Control Number: 2015950486

To Giuseppe—for twenty five years, five books, and counting . . .

About the Author

Gordon S. Linoff has been working with databases, big data, and data mining for almost longer than he can remember. With decades of experience on the practice of using data effectively, he is a recognized expert in the field of data mining.

Gordon started using spreadsheets while a student at MIT, on the original Compaq Portable, the world's first luggable computer. Not very many years later, he managed a development group at the now-defunct Thinking Machines Corporation, tasked with building a massively parallel relational database for decision support.

After Thinking Machines' demise, he founded Data Miners in 1998 with his friend and former colleague Michael J. A. Berry (who left in 2012). Since then, he has worked on a wide diversity of projects across many different companies. He has taught hundreds of classes around the world on data mining and survival analysis through SAS Institute, a leader in statistical and business analytics software. He is also an avid contributor to Stack Overflow, particularly on questions related to databases, having the highest score in 2014.

Together with Michael Berry, Gordon has written several influential books on data mining, including *Data Mining Techniques for Marketing, Sales, and Customer Support*, the first book on data mining to achieve a third edition.

Gordon lives in New York with Giuseppe Scalia, his partner of 25 years.

Credits

Project Editor
John Sleeva

Technical Editor
Michael Berry

Production Editor
Dassi Zeidel

Copy Editor
Mike La Bonne

**Manager of Content Development
& Assembly**
Mary Beth Wakefield

Marketing Director
David Mayhew

Marketing Manager
Carrie Sherrill

**Professional Technology &
Strategy Director**
Barry Pruett

Business Manager
Amy Knies

Associate Publisher
Jim Minatel

Project Coordinator, Cover
Brent Savage

Proofreader
Sara Wilson

Indexer
Johnna VanHoose Dinse

Cover Designer
Wiley

Cover Image
©iStock.com/Nobi_Prizue

Acknowledgments

Although this book has only one name on the cover, many people have helped me both specifically on this book and more generally in understanding data, analysis, and presentation.

I first met Michael Berry in 1990. We later founded Data Miners together, and he has been helpful on all fronts. He reviewed the chapters, tested the SQL code in the examples, and helped anonymize the data. His insights have been helpful and his debugging skills have made the examples much more accurate. His wife, Stephanie Jack, also deserves special praise for her patience and willingness to share Michael's time.

The original idea for the book came from Nick Drake, who then worked at Datran Media. A statistician by training, Nick was looking for a book that would help him use databases for data analysis. Bob Elliott, at the time my editor at Wiley, liked the idea.

Throughout the chapters, the understanding of data processing is based on dataflows, which Craig Stanfill of Ab Initio Corporation first introduced me to long ago when we worked together at Thinking Machines Corporation.

Along the way, I have learned a lot from many people. Anne Milley of SAS Institute first suggested that I learn survival analysis. Will Potts, now working at CapitalOne, then taught me much of what I know about the subject. Brij Masand helped extend the ideas to practical forecasting applications. Chi Kong Ho and his team at the *New York Times* provided valuable feedback for applying survival analysis to customer value calculations.

Stuart Ward from the *New York Times* and Zaiying Huang spent countless hours explaining and discussing statistical concepts. Harrison Sohmer, also of the *New York Times*, taught me many Excel tricks, some of which I've been able to include in the book.

Jamie MacLennan and the SQL Server team at Microsoft have been helpful in answering my questions about the product.

Over the past few years, I have been a major contributor to Stack Overflow. Along the way, I have learned an incredible amount about SQL and about how to explain concepts. A handful of people whom I've never met in person have helped in various ways. Richard Stallman invented emacs and the Free Software Foundation; emacs provided the basis for the calendar table. Rob Bovey of Applications Professional, Inc. created the X-Y chart labeler used in several chapters. The Census data set was created by the folks at the Missouri Census Data Center. Juice Analytics inspired the example for Worksheet bar charts in Chapter 5 (and thanks to Alex Wimbush, who pointed me in their direction). Edwin Straver of Frontline Systems answered several questions about Solver.

Over the years, many colleagues, friends, and students have provided inspiration, questions, and answers. There are too many to list them all, but I want to particularly thank Eran Abikhzer, Christian Albright, Michael Benigno, Emily Cohen, Carol D'Andrea, Sonia Dubin, Lounette Dyer, Victor Fu, Josh Goff, Richard Greenburg, Gregory Lampshire, Mikhail Levdanski, Savvas Mavridis, Fiona McNeill, Karen Kennedy McConlogue, Steven Mullaney, Courage Noko, Laura Palmer, Alan Parker, Ashit Patel, Ronnie Rowton, Vishal Santoshi, Adam Schwebber, Kent Taylor, John Trustman, John Wallace, David Wang, and Zhilang Zhao. I would also like to thank the folks in the SAS Institute Training group who have organized, reviewed, and sponsored my data mining classes for many years, giving me the opportunity to meet many interesting and diverse people involved with data mining.

I also thank all those friends and family I've visited while writing this book and who (for the most part) allowed me the space and time to work—my mother, my father, my sister Debbie, my brother Joe, my in-laws Raimonda Scalia, Ugo Scalia, and Terry Sparacio, and my friends Jon Mosley, Paul Houlihan, Leonid Poretsky, Anthony DiCarlo, and Maciej Zworski. On the other hand, my cat Luna, who spent many hours curled up next to me, will miss my writing.

Finally, acknowledgments would be incomplete without thanking Giuseppe Scalia, my partner through seven books, who has managed to maintain my sanity through all of them.

Thank you, everyone!

Contents at a Glance

Contents at a Glance

Contents

Foreword

Gordon Linoff and I have written three and a half books together. (Four, if we get to count the second edition of *Data Mining Techniques* as a whole new book; it didn't feel like any less work.) Neither of us has written a book without the other before, so I must admit to a tiny twinge of regret upon first seeing the cover of this one without my name on it next to Gordon's. The feeling passed very quickly as recollections of the authorial life came flooding back—vacations spent at the keyboard instead of in or on the lake, opportunities missed, relationships strained. More importantly, this is a book that only Gordon Linoff could have written. His unique combination of talents and experiences informs every chapter.

I first met Gordon at Thinking Machines Corporation, a now long-defunct manufacturer of parallel supercomputers where we both worked in the late eighties and early nineties. Among other roles, Gordon managed the implementation of a parallel relational database designed to support complex analytical queries on very large databases. The design point for this database was radically different from other relational database systems available at the time in that no trade-offs were made to support transaction processing. The requirements for a system designed to quickly retrieve or update a single record are quite different from the requirements for a system to scan and join huge tables. Jettisoning the requirement to support transaction processing made for a cleaner, more efficient database for analytical processing. This part of Gordon's background means he understands SQL for data analysis literally from the inside out.

Just as a database designed to answer big important questions has a different structure from one designed to process many individual transactions, a *book* about using databases to answer big important questions requires a different approach to SQL. Many books on SQL are written for database administrators.

Others are written for users wishing to prepare simple reports. Still others attempt to introduce some particular dialect of SQL in every detail. This one is written for data analysts, data miners, and anyone who wants to extract maximum information value from large corporate databases. Jettisoning the requirement to address all the disparate types of database users makes this a better, more focused book for the intended audience. In short, this is a book about how to use databases the way we ourselves use them.

Even more important than Gordon's database technology background are his many years experience as a data mining consultant. This has given him a deep understanding of the kinds of questions businesses need to ask and of the data they are likely to have available to answer them. Years spent exploring corporate databases have given Gordon an intuitive feel for how to approach the kinds of problems that crop up time and again across many different business domains:

- **How to take advantage of geographic data.** A zip code field looks much richer when you realize that from zip code you can get to latitude and longitude, and from latitude and longitude you can get to distance. It looks richer still when your realize that you can use it to join in Census Bureau data to get at important attributes, such as population density, median income, percentage of people on public assistance, and the like.

- **How to take advantage of dates.** Order dates, ship dates, enrollment dates, birth dates. Corporate data is full of dates. These fields look richer when you understand how to turn dates into tenures, analyze purchases by day of week, and track trends in fulfillment time. They look richer still when you know how to use this data to analyze time-to-event problems such as time to next purchase or expected remaining lifetime of a customer relationship.

- **How to build data mining models directly in SQL.** This book shows you how to do things in SQL that you probably never imagined possible, including generating association rules for market basket analysis, building regression models, and implementing naïve Bayesian models and scorecards.

- **How to prepare data for use with data mining tools.** Although more than most people realize can be done using just SQL and Excel, eventually you will want to use more specialized data mining tools. These tools need data in a specific format known as a *customer signature*. This book shows you how to create these data mining extracts.

The book is rich in examples and they all use real data. This point is worth saying more about. Unrealistic datasets lead to unrealistic results. This is frustrating to the student. In real life, the more you know about the business context, the better your data mining results will be. Subject matter expertise gives you a head start. You know what variables ought to be predictive and have good ideas about new ones to derive. Fake data does not reward these good ideas because patterns that should be in the data are missing and patterns that shouldn't be there have been introduced inadvertently. Real data is hard to come by, not least because real data may reveal more than its owners are willing to share about their business operations. As a result, many books and courses make do with artificially constructed datasets. Best of all, the datasets used in the book are all available for download at www.wiley.com/go/dataanalysisusingsqlandexcel2e.

I reviewed the chapters of this book as they were written. This process was very beneficial to my own use of SQL and Excel. The exercise of thinking about the fairly complex queries used in the examples greatly increased my understanding of how SQL actually works. As a result, I have lost my fear of nested queries, multi-way joins, giant case statements, and other formerly daunting aspects of the language. In well over a decade of collaboration, I have always turned to Gordon for help using SQL and Excel to best advantage. Now, I can turn to this book. And you can, too.

—Michael J. A. Berry

Introduction

The first edition of this book set out to explain data analysis from an eminently practical perspective, using the familiar tools of SQL and Excel. The guiding principle of the book was to start with questions and guide the reader through the solutions, both from a business perspective and a technical perspective. This approach proved to be quite successful.

Much has changed in the ten years since I started writing the first edition. The tools themselves have changed. In those days, Excel did not have a Ribbon, for instance. And, window functions were rare in databases. The world that analysts inhabit has also changed, with tools such as Python and R and NoSQL databases becoming more common. However, relational databases are still in widespread use, and SQL is, if anything, even more relevant today as technology spreads through businesses big and small. Excel still seems to be the reporting and presentation tool of choice for many business users. Big data is no longer a future frontier; it is a problem, a challenge, and an opportunity that we face on a daily basis.

The second edition has been revised and updated to reflect the changes in the underlying software, with more examples and more techniques, and an additional chapter on database performance. In doing so, I have strived to keep the strengths from the first edition. The book is still organized around the principles of data, analysis, and presentation—three capabilities that are rarely treated together. Examples are organized around questions, with a discussion of both the business relevance and the technical approaches to the problems. The examples carry through to actual code. The data, the code, and the Excel examples are all available on the companion website.

The motivation for this approach originally came from a colleague, Nick Drake, who is a statistician by training. Once upon a time, he was looking for a book that would explain how to use SQL for the complex queries needed for data analysis. Books on SQL tend to cover either basic query constructs or the details of how databases work. None come strictly from a perspective of analyzing data, and none are structured around answering questions about data. Of the many books on statistics, none address the simple fact that most of the data being used resides in relational databases. This book fills that gap.

My other books on data mining, written with Michael Berry, focus on advanced algorithms and case studies. By contrast, this book focuses on the "how-to." It starts by describing data stored in databases and continues through preparing and producing results. Interspersed are stories based on my experience in the field, explaining how results might be applied and why some things work and other things do not. The examples are so practical that the data used for them is available on the book's companion website (www.wiley.com/go/dataanalysisusingsqlandexcel2e).

One of the truisms about data warehouses and analysis databases in general is that they don't actually *do* anything. Yes, they store data. Yes, they bring together data from different sources, cleansing and clarifying along the way. Yes, they define business dimensions, store transactions about customers, and, perhaps, summarize important data. (And, yes, all these are very important!) However, data in a database resides on many spinning disks and in complex data structures in a computer's memory. So much data, so little information.

How can we exploit this data, particularly data that describes customers? The many fancy algorithms for statistical modeling and data mining all have a simple rule: "garbage-in, garbage-out." The results of even the most sophisticated techniques are only as good as the data being used (and the assumptions being fed into the model). Data is central to the task of understanding customers, understanding products, and understanding markets.

The chapters in this book cover different aspects of data and several important analytic techniques that are readily supported by SQL and Excel. The analytic techniques range from exploratory data analysis to survival analysis, from market basket analysis to naïve Bayesian models, and from simple animations to regression. Of course, the potential range of possible techniques is much larger than can be presented in one book. These methods have proven useful over time and are applicable in many different areas.

And finally, data and analysis are not enough. Data must be analyzed, and the results must be presented to the right audience. To fully exploit its value, we must transform data into stories and scenarios, charts and metrics and insights.

Overview of the Book and Technology

This book focuses on three key technological areas used for transforming data into actionable information:

- Relational databases store data. The basic language for retrieving data is SQL. (Note that variants of SQL are also used for NoSQL databases.)
- Excel spreadsheets are the most popular tool for presenting data. Perhaps the most powerful feature of Excel is its charting capability, which turns columns of numbers into pictures.
- Statistics is the foundation of data analysis.

These three technologies are presented together because they are all interrelated. SQL answers the question "How do we access data?" Statistics answers the question "How is it relevant?" And Excel makes it possible to convince other people of the veracity of our findings and to provide them results that they can play with.

The description of data processing is organized around the SQL language. Databases such as Oracle, Postgres, MySQL, IBM DB2, and Microsoft SQL Server are common in the business world, storing the vast majority of business data transactions. The good news is that all relational databases support SQL as a query language. However, just as England and the United States have been described as "two countries separated by a common language," each database supports a slightly different dialect of SQL. The Appendix contains a list of how commonly used functionality is represented in various different dialects.

Similarly, beautiful presentation tools and professional graphics packages are available. However, rare and exceptional is the workplace computer that does not have Excel or an equivalent spreadsheet.

Statistics and data mining techniques do not always require advanced tools. Some very important techniques are readily available using the combination of SQL and Excel, including survival analysis, look-alike models, naïve Bayesian models, and association rules. In fact, the methods in this book are often more powerful than the methods available in such tools, precisely because they are close to the data and readily customizable. The explanation of the techniques covers both the basic ideas and the extensions that may not be available in other tools.

The chapters describing the various techniques provide a solid introduction to modeling and data exploration, in the context of familiar tools and data. They also highlight when more advanced tools are useful because the problem exceeds the capabilities of the simpler tools.

How This Book Is Organized

The 14 chapters in this book fall into four parts. The first three introduce key concepts of SQL, Excel, and statistics. The seven middle chapters discuss various methods of exploring data and analytic techniques specifically suited to SQL and Excel. More formal ideas about modeling, in the sense of statistics and data mining, are in the next three chapters. And, finally, a new chapter discusses performance issues when writing SQL queries.

Each chapter explains some aspect of data analysis using SQL and Excel from several different perspectives, including:

- Business examples for using the analysis
- Questions the analysis answers
- Explanations about how the analytic techniques work
- SQL syntax for implementing the techniques
- Results as tables or charts and how to create them in Excel

Examples in the chapters are generally available in Excel at www.wiley.com/go/dataanalysisusingsqlandexcel2e.

SQL is a concise language that is sometimes difficult to follow. Dataflows, graphical representations of data processing, are used to illustrate how SQL works. These dataflow diagrams are a reasonable approximation of how SQL engines actually process the data, although the details necessarily differ based on the underlying engine.

Results are presented in charts and tables, sprinkled throughout the book. In addition, important features of Excel are highlighted, and interesting uses of Excel graphics are explained. Each chapter has technical asides, typically explaining some aspect of a technique or an interesting bit of history associated with the methods described in the chapter.

Introductory Chapters

Chapter 1, "A Data Miner Looks at SQL," introduces SQL from the perspective of data analysis. This is the querying part of the SQL language, used to extract data from databases using SELECT queries.

This chapter introduces entity-relationship diagrams to describe the structure of the data—the tables and columns and how they relate to each other. It also introduces dataflow diagrams to describe the processing of queries; dataflow diagrams give a visual explanation of how data is processed. This chapter introduces the important functionality used throughout the book—such as joins, aggregations, and window functions.

Furthermore, the first chapter describes the datasets used for examples throughout the book (and which are also available for downloading). This data includes tables describing retail purchases, tables describing mobile telephone customers, and reference tables that describe zip codes and the calendar.

Chapter 2, "What's in a Table? Getting Started with Data Exploration," introduces Excel for exploratory data analysis and presentation. Of many useful capabilities in Excel, perhaps the most useful are charts. As the ancient Chinese saying goes, "A picture paints a thousand words," and Excel charting paints pictures using data. Such charts are not only useful aesthetically, but also more practically for Word documents, PowerPoint presentations, email, the Web, and so on.

Charts are not a means unto themselves. They are one aspect of exploratory data analysis. In addition, this chapter discusses summarizing columns in a table, as well as the interesting idea of using SQL to generate SQL queries.

Chapter 3, "How Different Is Different?" explains some key concepts of descriptive statistics, such as averages, p-values, and the chi-square test. The purpose of this chapter is to show how to use such statistics on data residing in tables. The particular statistics and statistical tests are chosen for their practicality, and the chapter focuses on applying the methods, not explaining the underlying theory. Conveniently, most of the statistical tests that we want to do are feasible in Excel and even in SQL.

SQL Techniques

Several techniques are very well suited for the combination of SQL and Excel.

Chapter 4, "Where Is It All Happening? Location, Location, Location," explains geography and how to incorporate geographic information into data analysis. Geography starts with locations, described by latitude and longitude. Locations are also described by various levels of geography, such as census blocks, zip code tabulation areas, and the more familiar counties and states, all of which have information available from the Census Bureau (or an equivalent organization in other countries). This chapter also discusses methods for comparing results at different levels of geography. And, finally, no discussion of geography would be complete without maps. Using basic Excel, it is possible to build very rudimentary maps.

Chapter 5, "It's a Matter of Time," discusses another key attribute of customer behavior: when things occur. This chapter describes how to access features of dates and times in databases, and then how to use this information to understand customers.

The chapter includes examples for accurately making year-over-year comparisons, for summarizing by day of the week, for measuring durations in days, weeks, and months, and for calculating the number of active customers by day, historically. The chapter ends with a simple animation in Excel—the only use of Visual Basic in the book.

Chapters 6 and Chapter 7 explain one of the most important analytic techniques for understanding customers over time. Survival analysis has its roots in traditional statistics, and it is very well suited to problems related to customers.

Chapter 6, "How Long Will Customers Last? Survival Analysis to Understand Customers and Their Value," introduces the basic ideas of hazard probabilities and survival, explaining how to calculate them easily using the combination of SQL and Excel. Perhaps surprisingly, sophisticated statistical tools are not needed to get started using survival analysis. Chapter 6 then explains how important ideas in survival analysis, such as average customer lifetime, can be used in a business context. It continues by explaining how to put these pieces together into a forecast and for customer value calculations.

Chapter 7, "Factors Affecting Survival: The What and Why of Customer Tenure," extends the discussion in three different areas. First, it addresses a key problem in many customer-oriented databases: *left truncation*. Second, it explains a very interesting idea in survival analysis called *competing risks*. This idea incorporates the fact that customers leave for different reasons. The third idea is to use survival analysis for before-and-after analysis. That is, how can we quantify what happens to customers when something happens during their lifetime—such as quantifying the effect of enrollment in a loyalty program or of a major billing fiasco.

Chapters 8, 9 and 10 explain how to understand what customers are purchasing using SQL and Excel.

Chapter 8, "Customer Purchases and Other Repeated Events," covers everything about the purchase—when it occurs, where it occurs, how often—except for the particular items being purchased. This chapter covers RFM, a traditional technique for understanding customer purchase behavior, and various issues with recognizing customers over time. Purchases contain a lot of information, even before we dive into the details of the items.

The products become the focus in Chapter 9, "What's in a Shopping Cart? Market Basket Analysis," which covers exploratory analysis of purchase behaviors over time. This chapter includes identifying products that may be important drivers of customer behavior. It also covers some interesting visualization methods available in Excel.

Chapter 10, "Association Rules and Beyond," then moves to the formal discussion of association rules, which are combinations of products purchased at the same time or in sequence. Building association rules in SQL is rather sophisticated. The methods in this chapter extend traditional association rule analysis, introducing alternative measures that make them more useful, and show how to produce combinations of different things, such as clicks that result in a purchase (to use an example from the Web). The association rule techniques explained in this chapter are more powerful than techniques available in data mining tools because the techniques are extensible and use additional measures beyond support, confidence, and lift.

Modeling Techniques

The next three chapters discuss statistical and data mining modeling techniques and methods.

Chapter 11, "Data Mining Models in SQL," introduces the idea of data mining modeling and the terminology associated with building such models. It also discusses some important types of models that are well suited to business problems and the SQL environment. Look-alike models find things similar to a given example. Lookup models use a lookup table to find model scores.

This chapter also discusses a more sophisticated modeling technique called *naïve Bayesian models*. This technique combines information along various business dimensions to estimate an unknown quantity.

Chapter 12, "The Best-Fit Line: Linear Regression Models," covers a more traditional statistical technique: linear regression. Several variants of linear regression are introduced, including polynomial regression, weighted regression, multiple regression, and exponential regression. These are explained graphically, using Excel charts, along with the R^2 value that measures how well the model fits the data.

Regression is explained using both Excel and SQL. Although Excel has several built-in functions for regression, an additional method using Solver is more powerful than the built-in functions. This chapter introduces Solver (which is free and bundled with Excel) in the context of linear regression.

Chapter 13, "Building Customer Signatures for Further Analysis," introduces the customer signature. This is a data structure that summarizes what a customer looks like at a particular point in time. Customer signatures are very powerful for modeling.

This chapter recognizes that although SQL and Excel are quite powerful, more sophisticated tools are sometimes necessary. The customer signature is the right way to summarize customer information under many circumstances. And, SQL is a very powerful tool for this summarization.

Performance

One reason for writing SQL queries is performance—by doing at least some of the analytic work close to the data and in an environment that can exploit the resources available to a relational database. The downside to writing a book that is more generally about SQL and not specifically about a particular database is that some tricks and tips are only relevant to a single database.

Happily, many good practices for writing SQL queries improve performance across many different databases. Chapter 14, "Performance *Is* the Issue: Using SQL Effectively," is devoted to this topic. In particular, it discusses indexes and how to best take advantage of them. It also covers different ways of writing queries—and why some of them are better from a performance perspective.

Who Should Read This Book

This book is designed for several audiences, with varying degrees of technical skills.

On the less technical side are managers, particularly those with a quantitative bent who are responsible for understanding customers or a business unit. Such people are often quite proficient in Excel, but, alas, much of the data they need resides in relational databases. To help them, this book provides examples of business scenarios where analysis provides useful results. These scenarios are detailed, showing not only the business problem but also the technical approach and the results.

Another part of the audience consists of people whose job is to understand data and customers, often having a job title including the word "analyst." These individuals typically use Excel and other tools, sometimes having direct access to the data warehouse or to some customer-centric database. This book can help by improving SQL querying skills, showing good examples of charts, and introducing survival analysis and association rules for understanding customers and the business.

An important audience is data scientists who are proficient in tools such as R or Python but who discover that they need to learn about other tools. In the business world, more programming-oriented tools may not be sufficient, and analysts may find themselves having to deal with data residing in relational databases and users who want to see results in Excel.

At the more technical end are statisticians, who typically use special-purpose tools such as SAS, SPSS, R, and S-plus. However, the data resides in databases. This book can help the very technical with their SQL skills and also provides examples of using analysis to solve particular business problems.

In addition, database administrators, database designers, and information architects should find this book interesting. The queries shown in the various chapters illustrate what people really want to do with the data and should encourage database administrators and designers to create efficient databases that support these needs.

I encourage all readers, even the technically proficient, to read (or at least skim) the first three chapters. These chapters introduce SQL, Excel, and statistics all from the perspective of analyzing large quantities of data. This perspective is different from how these subjects are usually introduced. Certain ideas in these chapters, such as the example data, dataflows, SQL syntax and formatting conventions, and good chart design, are used throughout the book.

Tools You Will Need

This book is designed to be stand-alone—that is, readers should be able to learn the ideas and gain understanding directly from the text.

All the SQL in the book has been tested (in Microsoft SQL Server and, with slight variations, Postgres). The datasets and results are available at www.wiley .com/go/dataanalysisusingsqlandexcel2e. Readers who want hands-on experience are encouraged to download the data and run the examples in the book.

Most examples in the book are vendor-neutral, so they should run with only minor modification on almost any fully functional relational database. I do not recommend Microsoft Access or MySQL, because they lack window functions—key functionality for analytic queries.

If you do not have a database, several packages are available for downloading; database vendors often have stand-alone versions of their software available at no cost. Some examples: SQL Server Express, a free version of SQL Server is available from Microsoft. A free version of Oracle is available from Oracle. Postgres is available at www.postgres.org. And other database products are available at no charge.

What's on the Website

The companion website (at www.wiley.com/go/ dataanalysisusingsqlandexcel2e) contains datasets used in the book. These datasets contain the following information:

- Reference tables. There are three reference tables, two containing census information (from the 2000 Census) and one containing calendar information about dates.
- Subscribers dataset. This is data describing a subset of customers in a mobile telephone company.
- Purchases dataset. This is data describing customer purchase patterns.

This data is available for download, along with instructions for loading it into SQL Server and other databases.

In addition, the companion website has pages with additional information, such as scripts for loading the data into common databases, spreadsheets containing the SQL queries, and all the tables and charts in the book that were generated using Excel.

Summary

The idea for this book originated with a colleague's question about a reference book for SQL for data analysis queries. However, another reference book on SQL is not needed, even one focused on the practical aspects of using the language for querying purposes.

For analyzing data, SQL cannot be learned in a vacuum. A SQL query, no matter how deftly crafted, is usually not the entire solution to a business problem. The business problem needs to be transformed into a question, which can be answered via a query. The results then need to be presented, often as tables or Excel charts.

I would extend this further. In the real world, statistics also cannot be learned in a vacuum. Once upon a time, collecting data was a time-consuming and difficult process. Now, data is plentiful. The companion website for this book, for example, puts dozens of megabytes of data just a few clicks away. The problem of analyzing data now extends beyond the realm of a few statistical methods to the processes for managing and extracting data as well.

This book combines three key ideas into a single thread of solving problems. Throughout my work as a data miner, I have found SQL, Excel, and statistics to be critical tools for analyzing data. More important than the specific technical skills, though, I hope this book helps readers improve their analytic skills and gives them ideas so they can better understand their customers and their businesses.

Data Analysis Using
SQL and Excel®

A Data Miner Looks at SQL

Data is being collected everywhere. Every transaction, every web page visit, every payment—and much more—is filling databases, relational and otherwise, with raw data. Computing power and storage have grown to be cost effective, a trend where today's smart phones are more powerful than supercomputers of yesteryear. Databases are no longer merely platforms for storing data; they are powerful engines for transforming data into useful information about customers and products and business practices.

The focus on data mining has historically been on complex algorithms developed by statisticians and machine-learning specialists. Once upon a time, data mining required downloading source code from a research lab or university, compiling the code to get it to run, and sometimes even debugging it. By the time the data and software were ready, the business problem had lost urgency.

This book takes a different approach because it starts with the data. The billions of transactions that occur every day—credit cards swipes, web page visits, telephone calls, and so on—are now often stored in relational databases. Relational database engines count among the most powerful and sophisticated software products in the business world, so they are well suited for the task of extracting useful information. And the lingua franca of relational databases is SQL.

The focus of this book is more on data and what to do with data and less on theory. Instead of trying to squeeze every last iota of information from a small sample—the goal of much statistical analysis—the goal is instead to find something useful in the gigabytes and terabytes of data stored by the business. Instead of asking programmers to learn data analysis, the goal is to give data analysts—and others—a solid foundation for using SQL to learn from data.

This book strives to assist anyone facing the problem of analyzing data stored in large databases, by describing the power of data analysis using SQL and Excel. SQL, which stands for Structured Query Language, is a language for extracting information from data. Excel is a popular and useful spreadsheet for analyzing smaller amounts of data and presenting results.

The various chapters of this book build skill in and enthusiasm for SQL queries and the graphical presentation of results. Throughout the book, the SQL queries are used for more and more sophisticated types of analyses, starting with basic summaries of tables, and moving to data exploration. The chapters continue with methods for understanding time-to-event problems, such as when customers stop, and market basket analysis for understanding what customers are purchasing. Data analysis is often about building models, and—perhaps surprisingly to most readers—some models can be built directly in SQL, as described in Chapter 11, "Data Mining in SQL." An important part of any analysis, though, is constructing the data in a format suitable for modeling—customer signatures.

The final chapter takes a step back from analysis to discuss performance. This chapter is an overview of a topic, concentrating on good performance practices that work across different databases.

This chapter introduces SQL for data analysis and data mining. Admittedly, this introduction is heavily biased because the purpose is for querying databases rather than building and managing them. SQL is presented from three different perspectives, some of which may resonate more strongly with different groups of readers. The first perspective is the structure of the data, with a particular emphasis on entity-relationship diagrams. The second is the processing of data using dataflows, which happen to be what is "under the hood" of most relational database engines. The third, and strongest thread through subsequent chapters, is the syntax of SQL itself. Although data is well described by entities and relationships, and processing by dataflows, the ultimate goal is to express the transformations in SQL and present the results often through Excel.

Databases, SQL, and Big Data

Collecting and analyzing data is a major activity, so many tools are available for this purpose. Some of these focus on "big data" (whatever that might mean). Some focus on consistently storing the data quickly. Some on deep analysis. Some have pretty visual interfaces; others are programming languages.

SQL and relational databases are a powerful combination that is useful in any arsenal of tools for analysis, particularly ad hoc analyses:

- A mature and standardized language for accessing data
- Multiple vendors, including open source
- Scalability over a very broad range of hardware
- A non-programming interface for data manipulations

Before continuing with SQL, it is worth looking at SQL in the context of other tools.

What Is Big Data?

Big data is one of those concepts whose definition changes over time. In the 1800s, when statistics was first being invented, researchers worked with dozens or hundreds of rows of data. That might not seem like a lot, but if you have to add everything up with a pencil and paper, and do long division by hand or using a slide rule, then it certainly seems like a lot of data.

The concept of big data has always been relative, at least since data processing was invented. The difference is that now data is measured in gigabytes and terabytes—enough bytes to fit the text in all the books in the Library of Congress—and we can readily carry it around with us. The good news is that analyzing "big data" no longer requires trying to get data to fit into very limited amounts of memory. The bad news is that simply scrolling through "big data" is not sufficient to really understand it.

This book does not attempt to define "big data." Relational databases definitely scale well into the tens of terabytes of data—big by anyone's definition. They also work efficiently on smaller datasets, such as the ones accompanying this book.

Relational Databases

Relational databases, which were invented in the 1970s, are now the storehouse of mountains of data available to businesses. To a large extent, the popularity of relational databases rests on what are called ACID properties of transactions:

- Atomicity
- Consistency
- Isolation
- Durability

These properties basically mean that when data is stored or updated in a database, it really is changed. The databases have transaction logs and other capabilities to ensure that changes really do happen and that modified data is visible when the data modification step completes. (The data should even survive major failures such as the operating system crashing.) In practice, databases support transactions, logs, replication, concurrent access, stored procedures, security, and a host of features suitable for designing real-world applications.

From our perspective, a more important attribute of relational databases is their ability to take advantage of the hardware they are running on—multiple processors, memory, and disk. When you run a query, the *optimization engine* first translates the SQL query into the appropriate lower-level algorithms that exploit the available resources. The optimization engine is one of the reasons why SQL is so powerful: the same query running on a slightly different machine or slightly different data might have very different execution plans. The SQL remains the same; it is the optimization engine that chooses the best way to execute the code.

Hadoop and Hive

One of the technologies highly associated with big data is Hadoop in conjunction with MapReduce. Hadoop is an open-source project, meaning that the code is available for free online, with the goal of developing a framework for "reliable, scalable, distributed computing." (The SQL world has free open-source databases such as MySQL, Postgres, and SQLite; in addition, several commercial databases have free versions.) In practice, Hadoop is a platform for processing humongous amounts of data, particularly data from sources such as web logs, high-energy physics, high volumes of streaming images, and other voluminous data sources.

The roots of MapReduce go back to the 1960s and a language called Lisp. In the late 1990s, Google developed a parallel framework around MapReduce, and now it is a framework for programming data-intensive tasks on large grid computers. It became popular because both Google and Yahoo developed MapReduce engines; and, what big successful internet companies do must be interesting.

Hadoop actually has a family of technologies and MapReduce is only one application. Built on Hadoop are other tools, all with colorful names such as Hive, Mahout, Cassandra, and Pig. Although the underlying technology is different from relational databases, there are similarities in the problems these technologies are trying to solve. Within the Hadoop world are languages, such CQL, which is based on SQL syntax. Hive, in particular, is being developed into a fully functional SQL engine and can run many of the queries in this book.

NoSQL and Other Types of Databases

NoSQL refers to a type of database that, at first sight, might seem to be the antithesis of SQL. Actually, the "No" stands for "Not Only." This terminology can be used to refer to a variety of different database technologies:

   ▪ Key-value pairs, where the columns of data can vary between rows—and, quite importantly—the columns themselves can contain lists of things

- Graph-based databases, which specialize in representing and handling problems from graph theory
- Document databases, which are used for analyzing documents and other texts
- Geographic information systems (GIS), which are used for geographic analysis

These types of databases are often specialized for particular functions. For instance, key-value pair databases provide excellent performance in a web environment for managing data about online sessions.

These technologies are really complementary technologies to traditional relational databases rather than replacement technologies. For instance, key-value databases are often used on a website in conjunction with relational databases that store history. Graph and document databases are often used in conjunction with data warehouses that support more structured information.

Further, good ideas are not limited to a single technology. One of the motivations for writing a second edition of this book is that database technology is improving. SQL and the underlying relational database technology increasingly support functionality similar to NoSQL databases. For example, recursive common table expressions provide functionality for traversing graphs. Full text indexes provide functionality for working with text. Most databases offer extensions for geographic data. And, increasingly databases are providing better functionality for nested tables and portable data formats, such as XML and JSON.

SQL

SQL was designed to work on structured data—think tables with well-defined columns and rows, much like an Excel spreadsheet. Much of the power of SQL comes from the power of the underlying database engine and the optimizer. Many people use databases running on powerful computers, without ever thinking about the underlying hardware. That is the power of SQL: The same query that runs on a mobile device can run on the largest grid computer, taking advantage of all available hardware with no changes to the query.

The part of the SQL language used for analysis is the SELECT statement. Much of the rest of the language is about getting data *in to* databases. Our concern is getting information *out of* them to solve business problems. The SELECT statement describes what the results look like, freeing the analyst to think about *what* to do, instead of *how* to do it.

TIP SQL (when used for querying) is a *descriptive* language rather than a *procedural* language. It describes what needs to be done, letting the SQL engine optimize the code for the particular data, hardware, and database layout where the query is running, and freeing the analyst to think more about the business problem.

Picturing the Structure of the Data

In the beginning, there is data. Although data may seem to be without form and chaotic, there is an organization to it, an organization based on tables and columns and relationships between and among them. Relational databases store *structured* data—that is, tables with well-defined rows and columns.

This section describes databases by the data they contain. It introduces *entity-relationship diagrams*, in the context of the datasets (and associated data models) used with this book. These datasets are not intended to represent all the myriad different ways that data might be stored in databases; instead, they are intended as practice data for the ideas in the book. They are available on the companion website, along with all the examples in the book.

What Is a Data Model?

The definition of the tables, the columns, and the relationships among them constitute the *data model* for the database. A well-designed database actually has two data models. The *logical data model* explains the database in terms that business users understand. The logical data model communicates the contents of the database because it defines many business terms and how they are stored in the database.

The *physical data model* explains how the database is actually implemented. In many cases, the physical data model is identical to or very similar to the logical data model. That is, every entity in the logical data model corresponds to a table in the database; every attribute corresponds to a column. This is true for the datasets used in this book.

On the other hand, the logical and physical data models can differ. For instance, in more complicated databases, certain performance issues might drive physical database design. A single entity might have rows split into several tables to improve performance, enhance security, enable backup-restore functionality, or facilitate database replication. Multiple similar entities might be combined into a single table, especially when they have many attributes in common. Or, a single entity could have different columns in different tables, with the most commonly used columns in one table and less commonly used ones in another table (this is called *vertical partitioning*, which some databases support directly without having to resort to multiple tables). Often these differences are masked through the use of *views* and other database constructs.

The logical model is quite important for analytic purposes because it provides an understanding of the data from the business perspective. However, queries actually run on the database represented by the physical model, so it is convenient that the logical and physical structures are often quite similar.

What Is a Table?

A table is a set of rows and columns that describe multiple instances of something. Each row represents one instance—such as a single purchase made by a customer, or a single visit to a web page, or a single zip code with its demographic details. Each column contains one attribute for one instance. SQL tables represent unordered sets, so the table does not have a first row or a last row—unless a specific column such as an id or creation date provides that information.

Any given column contains the same genre of information for all rows. So a zip code column should not be the "sent-to" zip code in one row and the "billed-to" zip code in another. Although these are both zip codes, they represent two different uses, so they belong in two different columns.

Columns, unless declared otherwise, are permitted to take on the value NULL, meaning that the value is not available or is unknown. For instance, a row describing customers might contain a column for birthdate. This column would take on the value of NULL for all rows where the birthdate is not known.

A table can have as many columns as needed to describe an instance, although for practical purposes tables with more than a few hundred columns are rare (and most relational databases do have an upper limit on the number of columns in a single table, typically in the low thousands). A table can have as many rows as needed; here the numbers easily rise to the millions and even billions.

As an example, Table 1-1 shows a few rows and columns from ZipCensus (which is available on the companion website). This table shows that each zip code is assigned to a particular state, which is the abbreviation in the stab column ("STate ABbreviation"). The pctstate column is an indicator that zip codes sometimes span state boundaries. For instance, 10004 is a zip code in New York City that covers Ellis Island. In 1998, the Supreme Court split jurisdiction of the island between New York and New Jersey, but the Post Office did not change the zip code. So, 10004 has a portion in New York and a smaller, unpopulated portion in New Jersey.

Each zip code also has an area, measured in square miles and recorded in the landsqmi column. This column contains a number, and the database does not

Table 1-1: Some Rows and Columns from ZipCensus

ZCTA5	STAB	PCTSTATE	TOTPOP	LANDSQMI
10004	NY	100%	2,780	0.56
33156	FL	100%	31,537	13.57
48706	MI	100%	40,144	66.99
55403	MN	100%	14,489	1.37
73501	OK	100%	19,794	117.34
92264	CA	100%	20,397	52.28

know what this number means. It could be area in acres, or square kilometers, or square inches, or pyongs (a Korean unit for area). What the number really means depends on information not stored in the tables. The term *metadata* is used to describe such information about what the values in columns mean. Similarly, `fipco` is a numeric value that encodes the state and county, with the smallest value being 1001, for Alabaster County in Alabama.

Databases typically have some metadata information about each column. Conveniently, there is often a label or description (and it is a good idea to fill this in when creating a table). More importantly, each column has a data type and a flag specifying whether NULL values are allowed. The next two sections discuss these two topics because they are quite important for analyzing data.

Allowing NULL Values

Nullability is whether or not a column may contain the NULL value. By default in SQL, a column in any row can contain a special value that says that the value is empty or unknown. Although this is quite useful, NULLs have unexpected side effects. Almost every comparison returns "unknown" if any argument is NULL, and "unknown" is treated as false.

The following very simple query looks like it is counting all the rows in the ZipCensus table where the FIPCo column is not NULL. (<> is the SQL operator for "not equals.")

```
SELECT COUNT(*)
FROM ZipCensus zc
WHERE zc.fipco <> NULL
```

Alas, this query always returns zero. When a NULL value is involved in a comparison—even "not equals"—the result is almost always NULL, which is treated as false.

Of course, determining which rows have NULL values is quite useful, so SQL provides the special operators IS NULL and IS NOT NULL. These behave as expected, with the preceding query returning 32,845 instead of 0.

The problem is more insidious when comparing column values, either within a single table or between tables. For instance, the column `fipco` contains the primary county of a zip code and `fipco2` contains the second county, if any. The following query counts the number of zip codes in total and the number where these two county columns have different values. This query uses conditional aggregation, which is when a conditional statement (CASE) is the argument to an aggregation function such as SUM():

```
SELECT COUNT(*),
       SUM(CASE WHEN fipco <> fipco2 THEN 1 ELSE 0 END) as numsame
FROM ZipCensus zc
```

Or does it? The columns `fipco` and `fipco2` should always have different values, so the two counts should be the same. In reality, the query returns the values 32,989 and 8,904. And changing the not-equals to equals shows that there are 0 rows where the values are equal. What is happening on the other 32,989 − 8,904 rows? Once again, the "problem" is NULL values. When `fipco2` is NULL, the test always fails.

When a table is created, there is the option to allow NULL values on each column in the table. This is a relatively minor decision when creating the table. However, making mistakes on columns with NULL values is easy.

WARNING   Designing databases is different from analyzing the data inside them. For example, NULL columns can cause unexpected—and inaccurate—results when analyzing data and make reading queries difficult. Be very careful when using columns that allow them.

NULL values may seem troublesome, but they solve an important problem: how to represent values that are not present. One alternative method is to use a special value, such as -99 or 0. However, the database would just treat this as a regular value, so calculations (such as MIN(), MAX(), and SUM()) would be incorrect.

Another alternative would be to have separate flags indicating whether or not a value is NULL. That would make even simple calculations cumbersome. "A + B", for instance, would have to be written as something like "(CASE WHEN A_flag = 1 AND B_flag = 1 THEN A + B END)". Given the alternatives, having NULLS in the database is a practical approach to handling missing values.

Column Types

The second important attribute of a column is its type, which tells the database exactly how to store values. A well-designed database usually has parsimonious columns, so if two characters suffice for a code, there is no reason to store eight. There are a few important aspects of column types and the roles that columns play.

Primary key columns uniquely identify each row in the table. That is, no two rows have the same value for the primary key and the primary key is never NULL. Databases guarantee that primary keys are unique by refusing to insert rows with duplicate primary keys. Chapter 2, "What's in a Table? Getting Started with Data Exploration," shows techniques to determine whether this condition holds for any given column. Typically the primary key is a single column, although SQL does allow *composite* primary keys, which consist of multiple columns.

Numeric values are values that support arithmetic and other mathematical operations. In SQL, these can be stored in different ways, such as floating-point numbers, integers, and decimals. The details of how these formats differ are much less important than what can be done with numeric data types.

Within the category of numeric types, one big difference is between integers, which have no fractional part, and real numbers, which do. When doing arithmetic on integers, the result might be an integer or it might be a real number, depending on the database. So 5/2 might evaluate to 2 rather than 2.5, and the average of 1 and 2 might turn out to be 1 instead of 1.5, depending on the database. To avoid this problem, examples in this book multiply integer values by 1.0 to convert them to decimal values when necessary.

Of course, just because it walks like a duck and talks like a duck does not mean that it is a duck. Some values look like numbers, but really are not. Zip codes (in the United States) are an example, as are primary key columns stored as numbers. What is the sum of two zip codes? What does it mean to multiply a primary key value by 2? These questions yield nonsense results (although the values can be calculated). Zip codes and primary keys happen to look like numbers, but they do not behave like numbers.

The datasets used in this book use character strings for zip codes and numbers for primary keys. To distinguish such false numeric values from real numbers, the values are often left padded with zeros to get a fixed length. After all, the zip code for Harvard Square in Cambridge, MA, is 02138, not 2,138.

Dates and *date-times* are exactly what their names imply. SQL provides several functions for common operations, such as determining the number of days between two dates, extracting the year and month, and comparing two times. Unfortunately, these functions often differ between databases. The Appendix provides a list of equivalent functions in different databases for functions used in this book, including date and time functions.

Another type of data is character string data. These are commonly codes, such as the state abbreviation in the zip code table, or a description of something, such as a product name or the full state name. SQL has some very rudimentary functions for handling character strings, which in turn support rudimentary text processing. Spaces at the end of a character string are ignored, so the condition 'NY' = 'NY ' evaluates to TRUE. However, spaces at the beginning of a character string are counted, so 'NY' = ' NY' evaluates to FALSE. When working with data in character columns, it might be worth checking out whether there are spaces at the beginning, a topic discussed in Chapter 2.

What Is an Entity-Relationship Diagram?

The "relational" in the name "relational databases" refers to the fact that different tables relate to each other via keys, and to the fact that columns in a given row relate to the values for that column via the column name. For instance, a zip code column in any table can link (that is "relate") to the zip code table. The key makes it possible to look up information available in the zip code table. Figure 1-1 shows the relationships between tables in the purchases dataset.

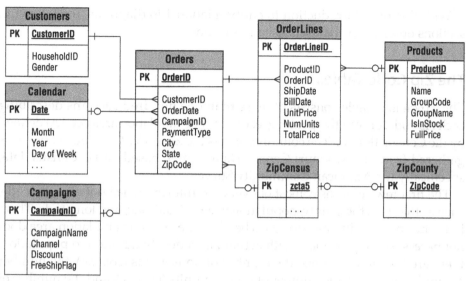

Figure 1-1: This entity-relationship diagram shows the relationship among entities in the purchase dataset. Each entity corresponds to one table.

These relationships have a characteristic called *cardinality*, which is the number of items related on each side. For instance, the relationship between Orders and ZipCensus is a zero/one-to-many relationship. This specifies every row in Orders has at most one zip code. And, every zip code has zero, one, or more orders. Typically, this relationship is implemented by having a column in the first table contain the zip code, which is called a *foreign key*. A foreign key is just a column whose contents are the primary key of another table (ZipCode in Orders is a foreign key; zcta5 in ZipCensus is a primary key). To indicate no match, the foreign key column would typically be NULL.

The zero/one-to-one relationship says that there is at most one match between two tables. This is often a subsetting relationship. For instance, a database might contain sessions of web visits, some of which result in a purchase. Any given session would have zero or one purchases. Any given purchase would have exactly one session.

Another relationship is a many-to-many relationship. A customer might purchase many different products and any given product might be purchased by many different customers. In fact, the purchase dataset does have a many-to-many relationship between Orders and Products; this relationship is represented by the OrderLines entity, which has a zero/one-to-many relationship with each of those.

An example of the one-at-a-time relationship is a customer who resides in a particular zip code. The customer might move over time. Or, at any given time, a customer might have a particular handset or billing plan, but these can change over time.

With this brief introduction to entity-relationship diagrams, the following sections describe the datasets used in this book.

The Zip Code Tables

The zipCensus table consists of more than one hundred columns describing each zip code, or, strictly speaking, each zip code tabulation area (ZCTA) defined by the Census Bureau. The column zcta5 is the zip code. This information was gathered from the Missouri Census Data Center, based on US Census data, specifically the American Community Survey.

The first few columns consist of overview information about each zip code, such as the state, the county, population (totpop), latitude, and longitude. There is a column for additional zip codes because the zip-code tabulation area does not necessarily match 100% with actual zip codes. In addition to population, there are four more counts: the number of households (tothhs), the number of families (famhhs), the number of housing units (tothus), and the number of occupied housing units (occhus).

The following information is available for the general population:

- Proportion and counts in various age groups
- Proportion and counts by gender
- Proportion and counts in various racial categories
- Proportion and counts of households and families by income
- Information about occupation categories and income sources
- Information about marital status
- Information about educational attainment
- And more

Information on the columns and exact definitions of terms such as ZCTA are available at http://mcdc.missouri.edu/data/georef/zcta_master.Metadata.html.

The second zip code table is zipCounty, a companion table that maps zip codes to counties. It contains information such as the following:

- County name
- Post office name
- Population of county
- Number of households in county
- County land area

This table has one row for each zip code, so it can be joined to zipCensus and to other tables using the zipCode column. The two tables are from different time frames and sources so not all zip codes match between the two tables—a common problem when working with data.

Subscription Dataset

The subscription data has only two entities, shown in Figure 1-2. This dataset paints a picture of a subscriber at a given point in time (the date when the snapshot was created).

The Subscribers table describes customers in a telephone company. It is a snapshot that shows what customers (and former customers) look like as of a particular date. The columns in this table describe customers as they start and as they stop. This particular snapshot table has no intermediate behavior information.

The Calendar table is a general-purpose table that has information about dates, including:

- Year
- Month number
- Month name
- Day of month
- Day of week
- Day of year
- Holiday information

This table has the date as a primary key, and covers dates from 1950 through 2050.

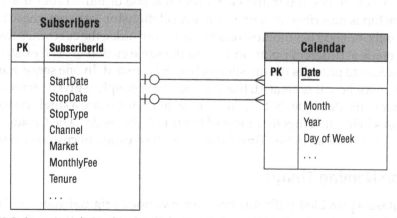

Figure 1-2: An entity-relationship diagram with only two entities describes the data in the customer snapshot dataset.

Purchases Dataset

The purchases dataset contains entities typical of retail purchases; the entities in this dataset and their relationships are shown in Figure 1-1 (page 11) :

- Customers
- Orders
- OrderLines
- Products
- Campaigns
- ZipCensus
- ZipCounty
- Calendar

This data captures the important entities associated with retail purchases. The most detailed information is in OrderLines, which describes each of the items in an order. To understand the name of the table, think of a receipt. Each line on the receipt represents a different item in the purchase. In addition, the line has other information such as the product id, the price, and the number of items, which are all in this table.

The Products table provides information such as the product group name and the full price of a product. The table does not contain detailed product names. These were removed as part of the effort to anonymize the data.

To tie all the items in a single purchase together, each row of OrderLines has an OrderId. Each OrderId, in turn, represents one row in the Orders table, which has information such as the date and time of the purchase, where the order was shipped to, and the type of payment. It also contains the total dollar amount of the purchase, summed up from the individual items. Each order line is in exactly one order and each order has one or more order lines. This relationship is described as a one-to-many relationship between these tables.

Just as the OrderId ties multiple order lines into an order, the CustomerId assigns orders made at different points in time to the same customer. The existence of the CustomerId prompts the question of how it is created. In one sense, it makes no difference how it is created; the CustomerId is simply a given, defining the customer in the database. Is it is doing a good job? That is, are a single customer's purchases being tied together most of the time? The aside "The Customer ID: Identifying Customers Over Time," discusses the creation of customer IDs.

Tips on Naming Things

The datasets provided with this book have various original sources, so they have different naming conventions. In general, there are some things that should always be avoided and some things that are good practice:

THE CUSTOMER ID: IDENTIFYING CUSTOMERS OVER TIME

The `CustomerId` column combines transactions over time into a single grouping, the customer (or household or similar entity). How is this accomplished? It all depends on the business and the business processes:

■ The purchases might contain name and address information. So, purchases with matching names and addresses would have the same customer ID.

■ The purchases might all have telephone numbers or email address, so these could provide the customer ID.

■ Customers may have loyalty cards or account numbers which provide the customer ID.

■ The purchases might be on the web, so browser cookies and logins could identify customers over time.

■ The purchases might all be by credit card, so purchases with the same credit card number would have the same customer ID.

Of course, any combination of these or other methods might be used to generate an internal customer id. And, because any one of these ids could change over time, the problem has a time component as well.

And all these approaches have their challenges. What happens when a customer browses on a tablet as well as a laptop (and different cookies are stored on different machines) or deletes her web cookies? Or when customers forget their loyalty cards (so the loyalty numbers are not attached to the purchases)? Or move? Or change phone numbers or email addresses? Or change their names? Keeping track of customers over time can be challenging.

■ Always use only alphanumeric characters and underscores for table and column names. Other characters, such as spaces, require that the name be escaped when referenced. The escape characters, typically double quotes or square braces, make it hard to write and read queries.

■ Never use SQL reserved words. Databases have their own special words, but words like `Order`, `Group`, and `Values` are keywords in the language and should be avoided.

Additional good practices include the following:

■ Table names are usually in plural (this helps avoid the problem with reserved words) and reinforces the idea that tables contain multiple instances of the entity.

■ The primary key is the singular of the table name followed by "Id." Hence, `OrderId` and `SubscriberId`. When a column references another table such as the `OrderId` column in `OrderLines` (a *foreign key relationship*) use the exact same name, making it easy to see relationships between tables.

- "CamelBack" case is used (upper case for each new word, lowercase for the rest). Hence, `OrderId` instead of `Order_Id`. In general, table names and column names are not case sensitive. The CamelBack method is to make it easier to read the name, while at the same time keeping the name shorter (than if using underscores).
- The underscore is used for grouping common columns together. For instance, in the `Calendar` table, the indicators for holidays for specific religions start with `hol_`.

Of course, the most important practice is to make the column and table names understandable and consistent, so you (and others) recognize what they mean.

Picturing Data Analysis Using Dataflows

Tables store data, but tables do not actually do anything. Tables are nouns; queries are verbs. This book mates SQL and Excel for data manipulation, transformation, and presentation. The differences between these tools are exacerbated because they often support the same operations, although in very different ways. For instance, SQL uses the GROUP BY clause to summarize data in groups. An Excel user, on the other hand, might use pivot tables, use the subtotal wizard, or manually do calculations using functions such as SUMIF(); however, nothing in Excel is called "group by."

Because this book intends to combine the two technologies, it is useful to have a common way of expressing data manipulations and data transformations, a common language independent of the tools being used. Dataflows provide this common language by showing the transformation operations fitting together like architecture blueprint for data processing, a blueprint that describes what needs to be done, without saying which tool is going to do the work. This makes dataflows a powerful mechanism for thinking about data transformations.

What Is a Dataflow?

A dataflow is a graphical way of visualizing data transformations. Dataflows have two important elements. The *nodes* in a dataflow diagram transform data, taking zero or more inputs and producing output. The *edges* in a dataflow diagram are pipes connecting the nodes. Think of the data flowing through the pipes and getting banged and pushed and pulled and flattened into shape by the nodes. In the end, the data has been transformed into information.

Figure 1-3 shows a simple dataflow that adds a new column, called SCF for Sectional Center Facility (something the U.S. Post Office uses to route mail).

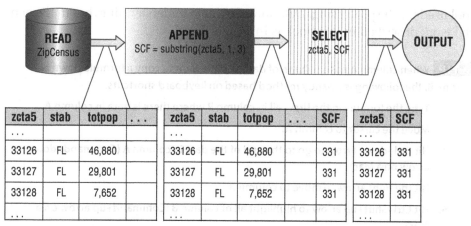

Figure 1-3: A simple dataflow reads the ZIPCODE, calculates and appends a new field called SCF, and outputs the SCF and ZIPCODE.

This column is the first three digits of a zip code. The output is each zip code with its SCF. The dataflow has four nodes, connected by three edges. The first, shaped like a cylinder, represents a database table or file and is the source of the data. The edge leaving this node shows some of the records being passed from it, records from the ZipCensus table.

The second node appends the new column to the table, which is also visible along the edge leading out from the node. The third selects two columns for output—in this case, zcta5 and SCF. And the final node simply represents the output. On the dataflow diagram, imagine a magnifying glass that makes it possible to see the data moving through the flow. Seeing the data move from node to node shows what is happening in the flow.

The actual processing could be implemented in either SQL or Excel. The SQL code corresponding to this dataflow is:

```
SELECT zc.zcta5, LEFT(zc.zcta5, 3) as scf
FROM ZipCensus zc
```

Alternatively, if the data were in an Excel worksheet with the zip codes in column A, the following formula would extract the SCF:

```
=MID(A1, 1, 3)
```

Of course, the formula would have to be copied down the column.

Excel, SQL, and dataflows are three different ways of expressing similar transformations. The advantage of dataflows is that they provide an intuitive way of visualizing and thinking about data manipulations, independent of the tool used for the processing. Dataflows facilitate understanding, but in the end, the work described in this book is in SQL or Excel.

> **TIP** When column A has a column of data and we want to copy a formula down column B, the following is a handy method based on keyboard shortcuts:
>
> 1. Type the formula in the first cell in column B where there is data in column A.
> 2. Move the cursor to column A.
> 3. Hit Ctrl+down arrow to go to the end of the data in column A (Command+down arrow on a Mac)
> 4. Hit the right arrow to move to column B.
> 5. Hit Ctrl+Shift+up arrow to highlight all of column B (Command+up arrow on a Mac).
> 6. Hit Ctrl+D to copy the formula down the column.
>
> Voila! The formula gets copied without a lot of fiddling with the mouse and with menus.

READ: Reading a Database Table

The READ operator reads all the columns of data from a database table or file. In SQL, this operation is implicit when tables are included in the FROM clause of a query. The READ operator does not accept any input dataflows, but has an output. Generally, if a table is needed more than once in a dataflow, each occurrence has a separate READ.

OUTPUT: Outputting a Table (or Chart)

The OUTPUT operator creates desired output, such as a table in a row-column format or some sort of chart based on the data. The OUTPUT operator does not have any outputs, but accepts inputs. It also accepts parameters describing the type of output.

SELECT: Selecting Various Columns in the Table

The SELECT operator chooses one or more columns from the input and passes them to the output. It might reorder columns and/or choose a subset of them. The SELECT operator has one input and one output. It accepts parameters describing the columns to keep and their order.

FILTER: Filtering Rows Based on a Condition

The FILTER operator chooses rows based on a TRUE or FALSE condition. Only rows that satisfy the condition are passed through, so it is possible that no rows ever make it through the node. The FILTER operator has one input and one output. It accepts parameters describing the condition used for filtering.

APPEND: Appending New Calculated Columns

The APPEND operator appends new columns, which are calculated from existing columns and functions. The APPEND operator has one input and one output. It accepts parameters describing the new columns.

UNION: Combining Multiple Datasets into One

The UNION operator takes two or more datasets as inputs and creates a single output that combines all rows from both of them. The input datasets need to have exactly the same columns. The UNION operator has two or more inputs and one output.

AGGREGATE: Aggregating Values

The AGGREGATE operator groups its input based on zero or more key columns. All the rows with the same key values are summarized into a single row, and the output contains the aggregate key columns and the summaries. The AGGREGATE operator takes one input and produces one output. It also takes parameters describing the aggregate keys and the summaries to produce.

LOOKUP: Looking Up Values in One Table in Another

The LOOKUP operator takes two inputs, a base table and a reference table, which have a key in common. The reference table should have at most one row for each key value. The LOOKUP operator appends one or more columns in the reference table to the base table, based on matching key values. When there is no match, LOOKUP just outputs NULL for the corresponding output columns.

   It takes two parameters. The first describes the key and the second describes which columns to append. Although this can also be accomplished with a JOIN, the LOOKUP is intended to be simpler and more readable for this common operation where no new rows are generated and no rows are filtered.

CROSSJOIN: Generating the Cartesian Product of Two Tables

The CROSSJOIN operator takes two inputs and combines them in a very specific way. It produces a wider table that contains all the columns in the two inputs, the Cartesian product of the two tables. Every row in the output corresponds to a pair of rows, one from each input. For instance, if the first table has four rows, A, B, C, and D, and the second has three rows, X, Y, and Z, then the output consists of all twelve combinations of these: AX, AY, AZ, BX, BY, BZ, CX, CY, CZ, DX, DY, and DZ. The CROSSJOIN is the most general join operation.

JOIN: Combining Two Tables Using a Key Column

The JOIN operator takes two inputs and a join condition as a parameter, and produces an output that has all the columns in the two tables. The join condition typically specifies that at least one column in one table is related to one column in the other, usually by having the same value. This type of join, called an equijoin, is the most common type of join.

With an equijoin, it is possible to "lose" rows in one or both of the inputs. This occurs when there is no matching row in the other table. A variation of the join ensures that all rows in one or the other table are represented in the output. Specifically, the LEFT OUTER JOIN keeps all rows in the first input table and the RIGHT OUTER JOIN keeps all rows in the second. FULL OUTER JOIN keeps all rows in both tables.

SORT: Ordering the Results of a Dataset

The SORT operator orders its input dataset based on one or more sort keys. It takes a parameter describing the sort keys and the sort order (ascending or descending).

Dataflows, SQL, and Relational Algebra

Beneath the skin of most relational databases is an engine that is essentially a dataflow engine. Dataflows focus on data and SQL focuses on data, so they are natural allies.

Historically, though, SQL has a somewhat different theoretical foundation based on mathematical set theory. This foundation is called *relational algebra*, an area in mathematics that defines operations on unordered sets of *tuples*. A tuple is a lot like a row, consisting of attribute-value pairs. The "attribute" is the column and the "value" is the value of the column in the row. Relational algebra then includes a bunch of operations on sets of tuples, operations such as union and intersection, joins and projections, which are similar to the dataflow constructs just described.

The notion of using relational algebra to access data is credited to E. F. Codd who, while a researcher at IBM in 1970, wrote a paper called *A Relational Model of Data for Large Shared Data Banks*. This paper became the basis of using relational algebra for accessing data, eventually leading to the development of SQL and modern relational databases.

A set of tuples is a lot like a table, but not quite. One difference between the two is that a table can contain duplicate rows but a set of tuples cannot have duplicates. A very important property of sets is that they have no ordering. Sets have no concept of the first, second, and third elements—unless another attribute defines the ordering. To most people (or at least most people who are not immersed in set theory), tables have a natural order, defined perhaps by a primary key or perhaps by the sequence that rows were originally loaded into the table.

As a legacy of the history of relational algebra, SQL tables have no natural ordering. The order of the results of a query are defined only when there is an ORDER BY clause.

SQL Queries

This section provides the third perspective on SQL, an introduction to the SQL querying language. The querying part of SQL is the visible portion of an iceberg whose bulky mass is hidden from view. The hidden portion is the data management side of the language—the definitions of tables and views, inserting rows, updating rows, defining triggers, stored procedures, and so on. As data miners and analysts, our goal is to exploit the visible part of the iceberg, by extracting useful information from the database.

SQL queries answer specific questions. Whether the question being asked is actually the question being answered is a big issue for database users. The examples throughout this book include both the question and the SQL that answers it. Sometimes, small changes in the question or the SQL produce very different results.

What to Do, Not How to Do It

A SQL query describes the result set, but does not specify how this is accomplished. This approach has several advantages. A query is isolated from the hardware and operating system where it is running. The same query should return equivalent results on the same data in two very different environments.

Being non-procedural means that SQL needs to be compiled into computer code on any given computer. This compilation step provides an opportunity to optimize the query to run as fast as possible in the environment. Database engines contain many different algorithms, ready to be used under just the right circumstances. The specific optimizations, though, might be quite different in different environments.

Another advantage of being non-procedural is that SQL can take advantage of parallel processing. The language itself was devised in a world where computers were very expensive, had a single processor, limited memory, and one disk. The fact that SQL has adapted to modern system architectures where CPUs, memory, and disks are plentiful is a testament to the power and scalability of the ideas underlying the relational database paradigm. When Codd wrote his paper suggesting relational algebra for "large data banks," he was probably thinking of a few megabytes of data, an amount of data that now easily fits in an Excel spreadsheet and pales in comparison to gigabytes of information on a mobile device or the terabytes of data found in corporate repositories.

The SELECT Statement

This chapter has already included several examples of simple SQL queries. More formally, the SELECT statement consists of clauses, the most important of which are:

- WITH
- SELECT
- FROM
- WHERE
- GROUP BY
- HAVING
- ORDER BY

These clauses are always in this order. There is a close relationship between the dataflow operations discussed in the previous section and these clauses.

Note that a SELECT statement can contain subqueries within it. Supporting subqueries provide much of the power of SQL.

A Basic SQL Query

A good place to start with SQL is with the simplest type of query, one that selects a column from a table. Consider, once again, the query that returns zip codes along with the SCF:

```
SELECT zc.zcta5, LEFT(zc.zcta5, 3) as scf
FROM ZipCensus zc
```

This query returns a table with two columns, the zip code and the SCF. The rows might be returned in any order. If you want the rows in a particular order, include an explicit ORDER BY clause:

```
SELECT zc.zcta5, LEFT(zc.zcta5, 3) as scf
FROM ZipCensus zc
ORDER BY zc.zcta5
```

Without an ORDER BY, never assume that the result of a query will be in a particular order.

WARNING   The results of a query are unordered, unless you use an ORDER BY clause at the outermost level. Never depend on a "default ordering," because there isn't one.

This simple query already shows some of the structure of the SQL language. All queries begin with the SELECT clause that lists the columns being returned. The tables being accessed are in the FROM clause, which follows the SELECT statement. And, the ORDER BY is the last clause in the query.

This example uses only one table, zipCensus. In the query, this table has a *table alias*, or abbreviation, called zc. The first part of the SELECT statement is taking the zcta5 column from zc. Although table aliases are optional in SQL, as a rule this book uses them extensively because aliases clarify where columns come from and make queries easier to write and to read.

> **TIP** Use table aliases in your queries that are abbreviations for the table names. These make the queries easier to write and to read.

The second column returned by the query is calculated from the zip code itself, using the LEFT() function. LEFT() is just one of dozens of functions provided by SQL, and specific databases generally support user-defined functions as well. The second column has a *column alias*. That is, the column is named SCF, which is the header of the column in the output.

A simple modification that returns the zip codes and SCFs only in Minnesota:

```
SELECT zc.zcta5, LEFT(zc.zcta5, 3) as scf
FROM ZipCensus zc
WHERE stab = 'MN'
ORDER BY 1
```

The query has an additional clause, the WHERE clause, which, if present, always follows the FROM clause. The WHERE clause specifies a condition; in this case, that only rows where stab is equal to "MN" are included in the result set. The ORDER BY clause then sorts the rows by the first column; the "1" is a reference to the first column being selected, in this case, zc.zcta5. The preferred method, however, is to use the column name (or alias) in the ORDER BY clause.

The dataflow corresponding to this modified query is in Figure 1-4. In this dataflow, the WHERE clause has turned into a filter after the data source, and the ORDER BY clause has turned into a SORT operator just before the output. Also notice that the dataflow contains several operators, even for a simple SQL query. SQL is a parsimonious language; complex operations can often be specified quite simply.

> **WARNING** When a column value is NULL, any comparison in a WHERE clause— with the important exception of IS NULL— always returns unknown, which is treated as FALSE. So, the clause WHERE stab <> 'MN' really means WHERE stab IS NOT NULL AND stab <> 'MN'.

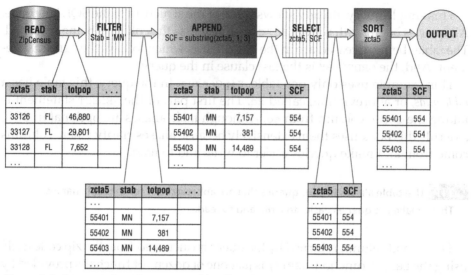

Figure 1-4: A **WHERE** clause in a query adds a filter node to the dataflow.

A Basic Summary SQL Query

A very powerful component of SQL is the ability to summarize data in a table. The following SQL counts the number of zip codes in `ZipCensus`:

```
SELECT COUNT(*) as numzip
FROM ZipCensus zc
```

The form of this query is very similar to the basic select query. The function `COUNT(*)`, not surprisingly, counts the number of rows. The "*" means that all rows are being counted. It is also possible to count a column, such as `COUNT(zcta5)`. This counts the number of rows that have a valid (i.e., non-NULL) value in `zcta5`.

The preceding query is an aggregation query that treats the entire table as a single group. Within this group, the query counts the number of rows, which calculates the number of rows in the table. A very similar query returns the number of zip codes in each state:

```
SELECT stab, COUNT(*) as numzip
FROM ZipCensus zc
GROUP BY stab
ORDER BY numzip DESC
```

The GROUP BY clause says to treat the table as consisting of several groups defined by the different values in the column `stab`. The result is then sorted in reverse order of the count (DESC stands for "descending"), so the state with

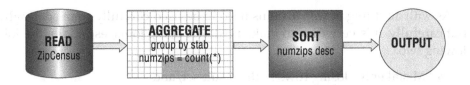

zcta5	stab	totpop	. . .
. . .			
33126	FL	46,880	
33127	FL	29,801	
33128	FL	7,652	
. . .			

stab	numzips
PA	1,798
FL	983
AZ	405
MT	361
. . .	

stab	numzips
TX	1,935
PA	1,798
NY	1,794
CA	1,763
. . .	

Figure 1-5: This dataflow diagram describes a basic aggregation query.

the most zip codes (Texas) is first. Figure 1-5 shows the corresponding dataflow diagram.

In addition to COUNT(), standard SQL offers other useful aggregation functions. The SUM(), AVG(), MIN(), and MAX() functions compute, respectively, the sum, average, minimum, and maximum values. In general, the first two operate only on numeric values and the MIN() and MAX() can work on any data type. Note that all these functions ignore NULL values in their calculations.

COUNT(DISTINCT) returns the number of distinct values. An example of using it is to answer the following question: *How many SCFs are in each state?* The following query answers this question:

```
SELECT zc.stab, COUNT(DISTINCT LEFT(zc.zcta5, 3)) as numscf
FROM ZipCensus zc
GROUP BY zc.stab
ORDER BY zc.stab
```

This query also shows that functions, such as LEFT(), can be nested in the aggregation functions. SQL allows arbitrarily complicated expressions. Chapter 2 shows another way to answer this question using subqueries.

What It Means to Join Tables

Because they bring together information from two tables, joins are perhaps the most powerful feature of SQL. Database engines can have dozens of algorithms just for this one key word. A lot of programming and algorithms are hidden beneath this simple construct.

As with anything powerful, joins need to be used carefully—not sparingly, but carefully. It is very easy to make mistakes using joins, especially the following two:

- "Mistakenly" losing rows in the result set, and
- "Mistakenly" adding unexpected additional rows.

Whenever joining tables, it is worth asking whether either of these could be happening. These are subtle questions because the answer depends on the data being processed, not on the syntax of the expression itself. There are examples of both problems throughout the book.

This discussion is about what joins do rather than about the multitude of algorithms for implementing them (although the algorithms are quite interesting—to some people—they don't help us understand customers and data). The most general type of join is the cross-join. The discussion then explains the more common variants: look up joins, equijoins, nonequijoins, and outer joins.

> **WARNING**   Whenever joining two tables, ask yourself the following two questions:
>
> 1. Could one of the tables accidentally be losing rows because there are no matches in the other table?
> 2. Could the result set unexpectedly have duplicate rows due to multiple matches between the tables?
>
> The answers require understanding the underlying data.

Cross-Joins: The Most General Joins

The most general form of joining two tables is called the *cross-join* or, for the more mathematically inclined, the *Cartesian product* of the two tables. As discussed earlier in the section on dataflows, a cross-join results in an output consisting of all columns from both tables and every combination of rows from one table with rows from the other. The number of rows in the output grows quickly as the two tables become bigger. If the first table has four rows and two columns, and the second has three rows and two columns, then the resulting output has twelve rows and four columns. This is easy enough to visualize in Figure 1-6.

Because the number of rows in the output is the number of rows in each table multiplied together, the output size grows quickly. If one table has 3,000 rows and the other 4,000 rows, the result has 12,000,000 rows—which is a bit big for an illustration. The number of potential columns is the sum of the number of columns in each input table.

In the business world, tables often have thousands, or millions, or even more rows, so a cross-join quickly gets out of hand, with even the fastest computers. If this is the case, why are joins so useful, important, and practical?

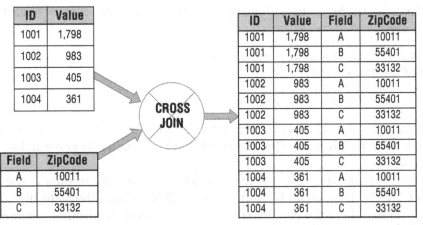

Figure 1-6: A cross-join on two tables, one with four rows and one with three rows, results in a new table that has twelve rows and all columns from both tables.

The reason is that the general form of the join is not the form that gets used very often, unless one of the tables is known to have only one row or a handful of rows. By imposing some restrictions—say by imposing a relationship between columns in the two tables—the result becomes more tractable. Even though more specialized joins are more commonly used, the cross-join is still the foundation that explains what they are doing.

Lookup: A Useful Join

ZipCensus is an example of a reference table summarized at the zip code level. Each row describes a zip code and any given zip code appears exactly once in the table. As a consequence, the zcta5 column makes it possible to look up census information for zip codes stored in another table. Intuitively, this is one of the most natural join operations, using a *foreign key* in one table to look up values in a reference table.

A lookup join makes the following two assumptions about the base and reference tables:

- All values of the key in the base table are in the reference table (missing join keys lose rows unexpectedly).

- The lookup key is the primary key in the reference table (duplicate join keys cause unexpected rows).

Unfortunately, SQL does not provide direct support for lookups because there is no simple check in the query ensuring these two conditions are true. However, the join mechanism makes it possible to do lookups, and this works smoothly when the two preceding conditions are true.

Consider the SQL query that appends the zip code population to each row of Orders:

```
SELECT o.OrderId, o.ZipCode, zc.totpop
FROM Orders o JOIN
    ZipCensus zc
    ON o.ZipCode = zc.zcta5
```

This example uses the ON clause to establish the condition between the tables. There is no requirement that the condition be equality in general, but for a lookup it is.

From the dataflow perspective, the lookup could be implemented with CROSSJOIN. The output from the CROSSJOIN is first filtered to the correct rows (those where the two zip codes are equal) and the desired columns (all columns from Orders plus totpop) are selected. Figure 1-7 shows a dataflow that appends a population column to Orders using this approach.

Unlike the dataflow diagram, the SQL query describes that a join needs to take place, but does not explain how this is done. The cross-join is one method, although it would be quite inefficient in practice. Databases are practical, so database writers have invented many different ways to speed this up. The details of such performance enhancements are touched upon in Chapter 14, "Performance Is the Issue: Using SQL Effectively." It is worth remembering that databases are practical, not theoretical, and the database engine is usually trying to optimize the run-time performance of queries.

Although the preceding query does implement the lookup, it does not guarantee the two conditions mentioned earlier. If there were multiple rows in ZipCensus for a given zip code, there would be extra rows in the output (because any matching row would appear more than once). You can define a *constraint* or unique index on the table to ensure that it has no duplicates, but in the query itself there is no evidence of whether or not such a constraint is present. On the other hand, if zip code values in Orders were missing in ZipCensus, rows would unexpectedly disappear. In fact, this happens and the output has fewer rows than the original Orders table. The condition that all the zip codes in Orders match a row in ZipCensus could be enforced (if it were true) with another type of constraint, a *foreign key constraint*.

Having multiple rows in ZipCensus for a given zip code is not an outlandish idea. For instance, it could include information for both the 2000 and 2010 censuses, which would make it possible to see changes over time. One way to implement this would be to have another column, say, CensusYear to specify the year of the census. Now the primary key would be a compound key composed of zcta5 and CensusYear together. A join on the table using just zip code would result in multiple rows, one for each census year.

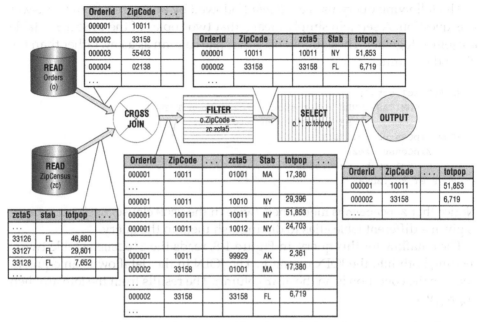

Figure 1-7: In SQL, looking up a value in one table is theoretically equivalent to creating the cross-join of the two tables and then restricting the values.

Equijoins

An equijoin is a join that has at least one condition asserting that two columns in the tables have equal values, and all the conditions are connected by AND (which is normally the case). In SQL, the conditions are the ON clause following the JOIN statement.

An equijoin can return extra rows the same way that a cross-join can. If a column value in the first table is repeated three times, and the same value occurs in the second table four times, the equijoin between the two tables produces twelve rows of output for that column. This is similar to the situation depicted in Figure 1-6 (page 27) that illustrates the cross-join. Using an equijoin, it is possible to add many rows to output that are not intended, especially when the equijoin is on non-key columns.

Equijoins can also filter out rows, when there are no matching key values in the second table. This filtering can be a useful feature. For instance, one table might have a small list of ids that are special in some way. The join would then apply this filter to the bigger table.

Although joins on primary keys are more common, there are cases where such a many-to-many equijoin is desired. Consider this question: *For each zip code, how many zip codes in the same state have a larger population?*

The following query uses a *self-join* (followed by an aggregation) to answer this question. A self-join simply means that two copies of the zipCensus table are joined together. The equijoin uses the state column as a key, rather than the zip code column.

```
SELECT zc1.zcta5,
       SUM(CASE WHEN zc1.totpop < zc2.totpop THEN 1
                ELSE 0 END) as numzip
FROM ZipCensus zc1 JOIN
     ZipCensus zc2
     ON zc1.stab = zc2.stab
GROUP BY zc1.zcta5
```

Notice that zipCensus is mentioned twice in the FROM clause. Each occurrence is given a different table alias to distinguish them in the query.

The dataflow for this query, in Figure 1-8, reads the zipCensus table twice, feeding both into the JOIN operator. The JOIN in the dataflow is an equijoin because the condition is on the stab column. The results from the join are then aggregated.

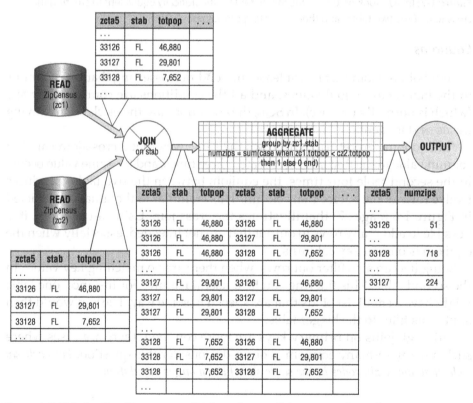

Figure 1-8: This dataflow illustrates a self-join and an equijoin on a non-key column.

Nonequijoins

A *nonequijoin* is a join where none of the conditions is equality between two columns. Nonequijoins are unusual. This is fortunate because there are many fewer performance tricks available to make them run quickly. Often, a nonequijoin is actually a mistake and indicates an error.

Note that when any of the conditions are equality, and the conditions are connected by AND, the join is an equijoin. Consider the following question about Orders: *How many orders are greater than the median rent where the customer resides?* The following query answers this question:

```
SELECT zc.stab, COUNT(*) as numrows
FROM Orders o JOIN
     ZipCensus zc
     ON o.zipcode = zc.zcta5 AND
        o.totalprice > zc.mediangrossrent
GROUP BY zc.stab
```

The JOIN in this query has two conditions, one specifies that the zip codes are equal and the other specifies that the total amount of the order is greater than the median rent in the zip code. This is still an example of an equijoin because of the condition on zip code.

Outer Joins

The final type of join is the outer join, which guarantees that all rows from one or both of the tables remain in the result set, even when there are no matching rows in the other table. All the previous joins have been *inner joins*, meaning that only rows that match are included. For a cross-join, this does not make a difference because there are many copies of rows from both tables in the result. However, for other types of joins, losing rows in one or the other table may not be desirable; hence the need for the outer join.

Lookups are a good example of an outer (equijoin), because the join asserts that a foreign key in one table equals a primary key in a reference table. Lookups return all the rows in the first table, even when there is no matching row.

Outer joins comes in three flavors:

- The LEFT OUTER JOIN ensures that all rows from the first table remain in the result set.

- The RIGHT OUTER JOIN ensures that all rows from the second table remain.

- The FULL OUTER JOIN ensures that all rows from both tables are kept. When there is no match, then the columns from the "missing" table are all set to NULL in the result set.

What does this mean? Consider the Orders table, which has some zip codes that are not in ZipCensus. This could occur for several reasons. ZipCensus contains a snapshot of zip codes as of the census, and new zip codes might have appeared since then. Also, the Census Bureau is not interested in all zip codes, so they exclude some zip codes where no one lives. Or, perhaps the problem might lie in Orders. There could be mistakes in the ZipCode column. Or, as is the case, the Orders table might include orders from outside the United States.

Whatever the reason, any query using the inner join eliminates all rows where the zip code in Orders does not appear in ZipCensus. Losing such rows could be a problem, which the outer join fixes. The only change to the query is replacing the word JOIN with the phrase LEFT OUTER JOIN (or equivalently LEFT JOIN):

```
SELECT zc.stab, COUNT(*) as numrows
FROM Orders o LEFT OUTER JOIN
     ZipCensus zc
     ON o.ZipCode = zc.zcta5 AND
        o.TotalPrice > zc.mediangrossrent
GROUP BY zc.stab
```

The results from this query are not particularly interesting. The results are the same as the previous query with one additional large group for NULL. When there is no matching row in ZipCensus, zc.stab is NULL.

> **TIP**   In general, you can write queries using just LEFT OUTER JOIN and INNER JOIN. There is usually no reason to mix LEFT OUTER JOIN and RIGHT OUTER JOIN in the same query.

Left outer joins are very practical. When they are chained together, they essentially say "keep all rows in the first table." As a general rule, don't mix outer join types if you can avoid it, because just having LEFT OUTER JOINs and INNER JOINs is sufficient for most purposes. As an example, if one table contains information about customers, then subsequent joins could bring in other columns from other tables, and the LEFT OUTER JOIN ensures that no customers are accidently lost. Chapter 13, "Building Custom Signatures for Further Analysis," uses outer joins extensively.

Other Important Capabilities in SQL

SQL has other features that are used throughout the book. The goal here is not to explain every nuance of the language, because reference manuals and database documentation do a good job there. The goal here is to give a feel for the important capabilities of SQL needed for data analysis.

UNION ALL

UNION ALL is a set operation that combines all rows in two tables, by just creating a result set with all the rows from each input table. The columns must be the same in each of the input tables. In practice, this means that UNION ALL almost always operates on subqueries, because it is unusual for two tables to have exactly the same columns.

SQL has other set operations, such as UNION, INTERSECTION, and MINUS (also called EXCEPT). The UNION operation combines the rows in two tables together, and then removes duplicates. This means that UNION is much less efficient than UNION ALL, so it is worth avoiding. INTERSECTION takes the overlap of two tables—rows that are in both. However, it is often more interesting to understand the relationship between two tables—how many items are in both and how many are in each one but not the other. Solving this problem is discussed in Chapter 2.

CASE

The CASE expression adds conditional logic into the SQL language. Its most general form is:

```
CASE WHEN <condition-1> THEN <value-1>
     . . .
     WHEN <condition-n THEN <value-n>
     ELSE <default-value> END
```

The <condition> clauses look like conditions in a WHERE clause; they can be arbitrarily complicated. The <value> clauses are values returned by the statement, and these should all be the same type. The <condition> clauses are evaluated in the order they are written. When no <else> condition is present, the CASE statement returns NULL if none of the previous clauses match.

One common use of CASE is to create indicator variables. Consider the following question: *How many zip codes in each state have a population of more than 10,000 and what is the total population of these?* The following SQL query is, perhaps, the most natural way of answering this question:

```
SELECT zc.stab, COUNT(*) as numbigzip, SUM(totpop) as popbigzip
FROM ZipCensus zc
WHERE totpop > 10000
GROUP BY zc.stab
```

This query uses a WHERE clause to choose the appropriate set of zip codes.

Now consider the related question: *How many zip codes in each state have a population of more than 10,000, how many have more than 1,000, and what is the total population of each of these sets?*

Unfortunately, the WHERE clause solution no longer works, because two over-lapping sets of zip codes are needed. One solution is to run two queries, which is messy. Combining the results into a single query is easy using conditional aggregation:

```
SELECT zc.stab,
       SUM(CASE WHEN totpop > 10000 THEN 1 ELSE 0 END) as num_10000,
       SUM(CASE WHEN totpop > 1000  THEN 1 ELSE 0 END) as num_1000,
       SUM(CASE WHEN totpop > 10000 THEN totpop ELSE 0 END
           ) as pop_10000,
       SUM(CASE WHEN totpop > 1000  THEN totpop ELSE 0 END
           ) as pop_1000
FROM ZipCensus zc
GROUP BY zc.stab
```

Notice that in this version, the SUM() function is used to count zip codes that meet the appropriate condition; it does so by adding 1 for each matching row. COUNT() is not the right function, because it would count the number of non-NULL values.

TIP When a CASE statement is nested in an aggregation function, the appropriate function is usually SUM(), or MAX() sometimes AVG(), and on rare occasions COUNT(DISTINCT). Check to be sure that you are using SUM() even when "counting" things up.

The following two statements are very close to being the same, but the second lacks the ELSE clause:

```
       SUM(CASE WHEN totpop > 10000 THEN 1 ELSE 0 END) as num_10000,
       SUM(CASE WHEN totpop > 10000 THEN 1 END) as num_10000,
```

Each counts the number of zip codes where population is greater than 10,000. The difference is what happens when no zip codes have such a large popula-tion. The first returns the number 0. The second returns NULL. Usually when counting things, it is preferable to have the value be a number rather than NULL, so the first form is generally preferred.

The CASE statement can be much more readable than the WHERE clause because the CASE statement has the condition in the SELECT, rather than much further down in the query. On the other hand, the WHERE clause provides more oppor-tunities for optimization.

IN

The IN statement is used in a WHERE clause to choose items from a set. The fol-lowing WHERE clause chooses zip codes in New England states:

```
WHERE stab IN ('VT', 'NH', 'ME', 'MA', 'CT', 'RI')
```

This use is equivalent to the following:

```
WHERE (stab = 'VT' OR
       stab = 'NH' OR
       stab = 'ME' OR
       stab = 'MA' OR
       stab = 'CT' OR
       stab = 'RI')
```

The IN statement is easier to read and easier to modify.

Similarly, the following NOT IN statement would choose zip codes that are not in New England:

```
WHERE stab NOT IN ('VT', 'NH', 'ME', 'MA', 'CT', 'RI')
```

This use of the IN statement is simply a convenient shorthand for what would otherwise be complicated WHERE clauses. The section on subqueries explores another use of IN.

Window Functions

Window functions are a class of functions that use the OVER clause. These functions return a value on a single row, but the value is based on a group of rows. A simple example is SUM(). Say we wanted to return each zip code with the sum of the population in the state. With window functions, this is easy:

```
SELECT zc.zcta5,
       SUM(totpop) OVER (PARTITION BY zc.stab) as stpop
FROM ZipCensus zc;
```

The PARTITION BY clause says "do the sum for all rows with the same value of stab." The result is that all zip codes in a given state have the same value for stpop.

A particularly interesting window function is ROW_NUMBER(). This assigns a sequential value, starting with 1, to rows within each group.

```
SELECT zc.zcta5,
       SUM(totpop) OVER (PARTITION BY zc.stab) as stpop,
       ROW_NUMBER() OVER (PARTITION BY zc.stab
                          ORDER BY totpop DESC
                          ) as ZipPopRank
FROM ZipCensus zc
```

This query adds an additional ranking column to each row in the result set. The value is 1 for the zip code with the highest population in each state, 2 for the second highest, and so on.

Table 1-2: Example of ROW_NUMBER(), RANK(), and DENSE_RANK()

VALUE	ROW_NUMBER()	RANK()	DENSE_RANK()
10	1	1	1
20	2	2	2
20	3	2	2
30	4	4	3
50	5	5	4
50	6	5	4

SQL offers two other similar functions for ranking: RANK() and DENSE_RANK(). They differ in their handling of ties, as shown by the example in Table 1-2.

All three functions assign the first row a number of "1". ROW_NUMBER() ignores duplicates, just giving each row a different number. RANK() assigns duplicate numbers when rows have the same value, but then skips the next numbers, so the results have gaps. DENSE_RANK() is like rank except the resulting numbers have no gaps.

Subqueries and Common Table Expressions Are Our Friends

Subqueries are exactly what their name implies, queries within queries. They make it possible to do complex data manipulation within a single SQL statement, exactly the types of manipulation needed for data analysis and data mining.

In one sense, subqueries are not needed. All the manipulations could be accomplished by creating intermediate tables and combining them. The resulting SQL would be a series of CREATE TABLE statements and INSERT statements (or possibly CREATE VIEW or SELECT INTO), with simpler queries. Although such an approach is sometimes useful, especially when the intermediate tables are used multiple times, it suffers from several problems.

First, instead of thinking about solving a particular problem, you end up thinking about the data processing, the naming of intermediate tables, determining the types of columns, remembering to remove tables when they are no longer needed, deciding whether to build indexes, and so on. All the additional bookkeeping activity distracts from focusing on the data and the business problems.

Second, SQL optimizers can often find better approaches to running a complicated query than people can. So, writing multiple SQL statements can interfere with the optimizer.

Third, maintaining a complicated chain of queries connected by tables can be quite cumbersome. For instance, adding a new column might require adding new columns in all sorts of places. Or, you may run part of the script and not realize that one of the intermediate tables has values from a previous run.

Fourth, the read-only SQL queries that predominate in this book can be run with a minimum of permissions for the user—simply the permissions to run queries. Running complicated scripts requires create and modify permissions on at least part of the database. These permissions are dangerous, because an analyst might inadvertently damage the database. Without these permissions, it is impossible to cause such damage.

Subqueries can appear in many different parts of the query, in the SELECT clause, in the FROM clause, and in the WHERE and HAVING clauses. However, this section approaches subqueries by why they are used rather than where they appear syntactically.

Common table expressions (often referred to as *CTEs*) are another way of writing queries that appear in the FROM clause. They are more powerful than subqueries for two reasons. First, they can be used multiple times throughout the query. And, they can refer to themselves—something called *recursive CTEs*. The following sections have examples of both CTEs and subqueries.

Subqueries for Naming Variables

When it comes to naming variables, SQL has a shortcoming. The following is not syntactically correct in most SQL dialects:

```
SELECT totpop as pop, pop + 1
```

The SELECT statement names columns, but these names cannot be used again in the same clause. Because queries should be at least somewhat understandable to humans, as well as database engines, this is a real shortcoming. Complicated expressions should have names.

Fortunately, subqueries provide a solution. The earlier query that summarized zip codes by population greater than 10,000 and greater than 1,000 could instead use a subquery that is clearer about what is happening:

```
SELECT zc.stab,
       SUM(is_pop_10000) as num_10000,
       SUM(is_pop_1000) as num_1000,
       SUM(is_pop_10000 * totpop) as pop_10000,
       SUM(is_pop_1000 * totpop) as pop_1000
FROM (SELECT zc.*,
             (CASE WHEN totpop > 10000 THEN 1 ELSE 0
              END) as is_pop_10000,
             (CASE WHEN totpop > 1000 THEN 1 ELSE 0
              END) as is_pop_1000
```

```
        FROM ZipCensus zc
     ) zc
  GROUP BY zc.stab
```

This version of the query uses two indicator variables, IS_POP_10000 and IS_POP_1000. These take on the value of 0 or 1, depending on whether or not the population is greater than 10,000 or 1,000. The query then sums the indicators to get the counts, and sums the product of the indicator and the population to get the population count. Figure 1-9 illustrates this process as a dataflow. Notice that the dataflow does not include a "subquery."

TIP Subqueries with indicator variables, such as IS_POP_1000, are a powerful and flexible way to build queries.

Indicator variables are only one example of using subqueries to name variables. Throughout the book, there are many other examples. The purpose is to make the queries understandable to humans, relatively easy to modify, and might, with luck, help us remember what a query written six months ago is really doing.

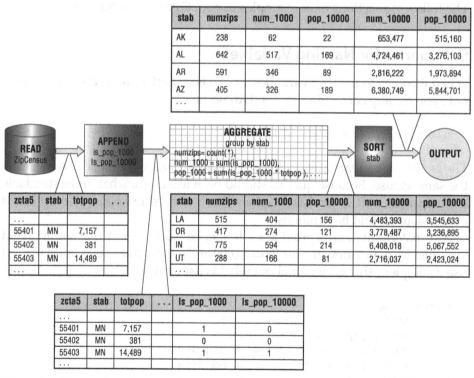

Figure 1-9: This dataflow illustrates the process of using indicator variables to obtain information about zip codes.

FORMATTING SQL QUERIES

There is no agreed-upon standard for formatting SQL queries. There are a few good practices, such as:

■ Use table aliases that are abbreviations for the table name.

■ Use `as` to define column aliases.

■ Be consistent in capitalization, in usage of underscores, and in indentation.

■ Write the code to be understandable, so you and someone else can read it.

Writing readable code is always a good idea.

Any guidelines for writing code necessarily have a subjective element. The goal should be to communicate what the query is doing. Formatting is important: Just imagine how difficult it would be to read text without punctuation, capitalization, and paragraphs.

The code in this book (and on the companion website) follows additional rules to make the queries easier to follow.

■ Most keywords are capitalized and most table and column names use CamelBack casing (except for `ZipCensus`).

■ The high-level clauses defined by the SQL language are all aligned on the left. These are `WITH`, `SELECT`, `FROM`, `WHERE`, `GROUP BY`, `HAVING`, and `ORDER BY`.

■ Within a clause, subsequent lines are aligned after the keyword, so the scope of each clause is visually obvious.

■ Subqueries follow similar rules, so all the main clauses of a subquery are indented, but still aligned on the left.

■ Within the `FROM` clause, table names and subqueries start on a new line (the tables are then aligned and easier to see). The `ON` predicate starts on its own line, and the join keywords are at the end of the line.

■ Columns are generally qualified, meaning that they use table aliases.

■ Operators generally have spaces around them.

■ Commas are at the end of a line, just as a human would place them.

■ Closing parenthesis—when on a subsequent line—is aligned under the opening parenthesis.

■ `CASE` statements are always surrounded by parentheses.

The goal should be to write queries so other people can readily understand them. After all, you may be returning to your queries one day and you would like to be able to quickly figure out what they are doing.

The above subquery can also be written as a CTE:

```
WITH zc as (
    SELECT zc.*,
           (CASE WHEN totpop > 10000 THEN 1 ELSE 0
            END) as is_pop_10000,
           (CASE WHEN totpop > 1000 THEN 1 ELSE 0
            END) as is_pop_1000
    FROM ZipCensus zc
   )
SELECT zc.stab,
       SUM(is_pop_10000) as num_10000,
       SUM(is_pop_1000) as num_1000,
       SUM(is_pop_10000 * totpop) as pop_10000,
       SUM(is_pop_1000 * totpop) as pop_1000
FROM zc
GROUP BY zc.stab
```

Here, the subquery is introduced using the WITH clause; otherwise, it is very similar to the version with a subquery in the FROM clause. A query can have only one WITH clause, although it can define multiple CTEs. These can refer to CTEs defined earlier in the same clause.

Subqueries for Handling Summaries

The most typical place for a subquery is as a replacement for a table in the FROM clause. After all, the source is a table and a query essentially returns a table, so it makes a lot of sense to combine queries in this way. From the dataflow perspective, this use of subqueries is simply to replace one of the sources with a series of dataflow nodes.

Consider the question: *How many zip codes in each state have a population density greater than the average zip code population density in the state?* The population density is the population divided by the land area, which is in the column landsqmi.

Let's think about the different data elements needed to answer the question. The comparison is to the average zip code population density within a state, which is easily calculated:

```
SELECT zc.stab, AVG(totpop / landsqmi) as avgpopdensity
FROM ZipCensus zc
WHERE zc.landsqmi > 0
GROUP BY zc.stab
```

Next, the idea is to combine this information with the original zip code information in the FROM clause:

```
SELECT zc.stab, COUNT(*) as numzips,
       SUM(CASE WHEN zc.popdensity > zcsum.avgpopdensity
               THEN 1 ELSE 0 END) as numdenser
```

```
FROM (SELECT zc.*, totpop / landsqmi as popdensity
      FROM ZipCensus zc
      WHERE zc.landsqmi > 0
     ) zc JOIN
     (SELECT zc.stab, AVG(totpop / landsqmi) as avgpopdensity
      FROM ZipCensus zc
      WHERE zc.landsqmi > 0
      GROUP BY zc.stab) zcsum
   ON zc.stab = zcsum.stab
GROUP BY zc.stab
```

The dataflow diagram for this query follows the same logic and is shown in Figure 1-10. Later in this chapter we will see another way to answer this question using window functions.

An interesting observation is that the population density of each state is not the same as the average of the population densities for all the zip codes in the state. That is, the preceding question is different from: *How many zip codes in each state have a population density greater than the state's population density?* The state's population density would be calculated in zcsum as:

```
SUM(totpop) / SUM(landsqmi) as statepopdensity
```

There is a relationship between these two densities. The zip code average gives each zip code a weight of 1, no matter how big in area or population. The state average is the weighted average of the zip codes by the land area of the zip codes.

The proportion of zip codes that are denser than the average zip code varies from about 4% of the zip codes in North Dakota to about 35% in Florida. Never are half the zip codes denser than the average, although this is theoretically possible. The density where half the zip codes are denser and half less dense is the *median* density rather than the average or average of averages. Averages, average of averages, and medians are different from each other and discussed in Chapter 2.

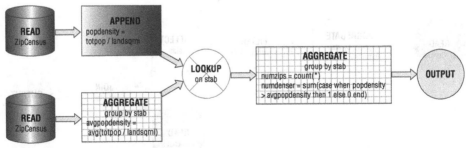

Figure 1-10: This dataflow diagram compares the zip code population density to the average zip code population density in a state.

Subqueries and IN

IN and NOT IN were introduced earlier as convenient shorthand for complicated WHERE clauses. There is another version where the "in" set is specified by a subquery, rather than by a fixed list. For example, the following query gets the list of all zip codes in states with fewer than 100 zip codes:

```
SELECT zc.zcta5, zc.stab
FROM ZipCensus zc
WHERE zc.stab IN (SELECT stab
                  FROM ZipCensus
                  GROUP BY stab
                  HAVING COUNT(*) < 100
                  )
```

The subquery creates a set of all states in ZipCensus where the number of zip codes in the state is less than 100 (that is, DC, DE, HI, and RI). The HAVING clause sets this limit. HAVING is very similar to WHERE, except it filters rows *after* aggregating, rather than *before*. The outer SELECT then chooses zip codes whose state matches one of the states in the IN set. This process takes place as a join operation, as shown in Figure 1-11.

Rewriting the "IN" as a JOIN

Strictly speaking, the IN operator is not necessary, because queries with INs and subqueries can be rewritten as joins. For example, this is equivalent to the previous query:

```
SELECT zc.*
FROM ZipCensus zc JOIN
     (SELECT stab, COUNT(*) as numstates
      FROM ZipCensus
      GROUP BY stab
     ) zipstates
     ON zc.stab = zipstates.stab AND
        zipstates.numstates < 100
```

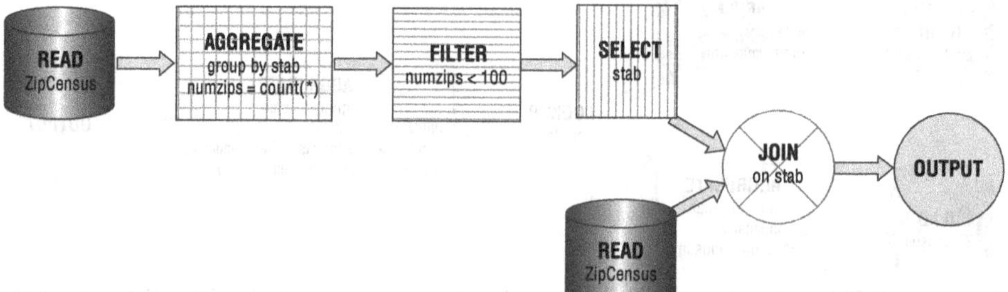

Figure 1-11: The processing for an IN with a subquery really uses a join operation.

Note that in the rewritten query, the zipstates subquery has two columns instead of one. The second column contains the count of zip codes in each state. Using the IN statement with a subquery makes it impossible to get this information.

On the other hand, the IN does have a small advantage, because it guarantees that there are no duplicate rows in the output, even when the "in" set has duplicates. To guarantee this using the JOIN, aggregate the subquery by the key used to join the tables. In this case, the subquery is doing aggregation anyway to find the states that have fewer than one hundred zip codes. This aggregation has the additional effect of guaranteeing that the subquery has no duplicates.

The general way of rewriting an IN subquery using join requires eliminating the duplicates. So, the query:

```
SELECT x.*
FROM x
WHERE x.col_a IN (SELECT y.col_b FROM y)
```

would be rewritten as:

```
SELECT DISTINCT x.*
FROM x JOIN
     y
     ON x.col_a = y.col_b;
```

or:

```
SELECT x.*
FROM x JOIN
     (SELECT DISTINCT y.col_b FROM y) y
     ON x.col_a = y.col_b;
```

The DISTINCT keyword removes duplicates from the output. However, this requires additional processing so it is best to avoid DISTINCT unless it is really necessary.

Correlated Subqueries

A correlated subquery occurs when the subquery includes a reference to the outer query. An example shows this best. Consider the following question: *Which zip code in each state has the maximum population and what is the population?* One way to approach this problem uses a correlated subquery:

```
SELECT zc.stab, zc.zcta5, zc.totpop
FROM ZipCensus zc
WHERE zc.totpop = (SELECT MAX(zcinner.totpop)
                   FROM ZipCensus zcinner
                   WHERE zcinner.stab = zc.stab
                  )
ORDER BY zc.stab
```

The "correlated" part of the subquery is the inner WHERE clause, which specifies that the state in a record processed by the subquery must match the state in the outer table.

Conceptually, the database engine reads one row from zc (the table referenced in the outer query). Then, the engine finds all rows in zcinner that match this state. From these rows, it calculates the maximum population. If the original row matches this maximum, it is selected. The engine then moves on to the next row in the outer query.

Correlated subqueries are sometimes cumbersome to understand. Although complicated, correlated subqueries are not a new way of processing the data; they are another example of joins. The following query produces the same results:

```
SELECT zc.stab, zc.zcta5, zc.totpop
FROM ZipCensus zc JOIN
     (SELECT zc.stab, MAX(zc.totpop) as maxpop
      FROM ZipCensus zc
      GROUP BY zc.stab) zcsum
     ON zc.stab = zcsum.stab AND
        zc.totpop = zcsum.maxpop
ORDER BY zc.stab
```

This query makes it clear that ZipCensus is summarized by stab to calculate the maximum population. The JOIN then finds the zip code (or possibly zip codes) that matches the maximum population, returning information about them. In addition, this method makes it possible to include other information, such as the number of zip codes where the maximum population is achieved. This can be calculated using COUNT(*) in zcsum.

The examples throughout this book tend not to use correlated subqueries for SELECT queries, preferring explicit JOINs instead. Joins provide more flexibility for processing and analyzing data and, in general, SQL engines do a good job of optimizing JOINs. There are some situations where the correlated subquery may offer better performance than the corresponding JOIN query or may even be simpler to understand.

NOT IN Operator

The NOT IN operator can also use subqueries and correlated subqueries. Consider the following question: *Which zip codes in the* Orders *table are not in the* ZipCensus *table?* Once again, there are different ways to answer this question. The first uses the NOT IN operator:

```
SELECT o.ZipCode, COUNT(*) as NumOrders
FROM Orders o
WHERE ZipCode NOT IN (SELECT zcta5
                      FROM ZipCensus zc
                      )
GROUP BY o.ZipCode
```

This query is straightforward as written, choosing the zip codes in Orders with no matching zip code in ZipCensus, then grouping them and returning the number of purchases in each.

An alternative uses the LEFT OUTER JOIN operator. Because the LEFT OUTER JOIN keeps all zip codes in the Orders table—even those that don't match—a filter afterwards can choose the non-matching set:

```
SELECT o.ZipCode, COUNT(*) as NumOrders
FROM Orders o LEFT OUTER JOIN
     ZipCensus zc
     ON o.ZipCode = zc.zcta5
WHERE zc.zcta5 IS NULL
GROUP BY o.ZipCode
ORDER BY NumOrders DESC
```

This query joins the two tables using a LEFT OUTER JOIN and only keeps the results rows do not match (because of the WHERE clause). This is essentially equivalent to using NOT IN; whether one works better than the other depends on the underlying optimization engine. Figure 1-12 shows the dataflow associated with this query.

EXISTS and NOT EXISTS Operators

EXISTS and NOT EXISTS are similar to IN and NOT IN with subqueries. The operators return true when any row exists (or no row exists) in a subquery. They are often used with correlated subqueries.

The query to return all the orders whose zip code is not in ZipCensus could be written as:

```
SELECT o.ZipCode, COUNT(*)
FROM Orders o
WHERE NOT EXISTS (SELECT 1
                  FROM ZipCensus zc
                  WHERE zc.zcta5 = o.ZipCode)
GROUP BY o.ZipCode
```

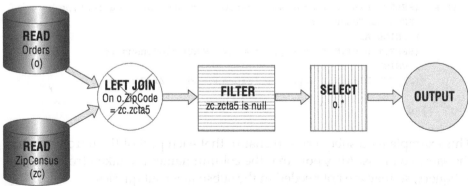

Figure 1-12: This dataflow shows the **LEFT OUTER JOIN** version of a query using **NOT IN**.

The "1" in the subquery has no importance, because NOT EXISTS is really determining if any *rows* are returned. It doesn't care about the particular value in any of the *columns*. In fact, some databases accept a nonsensical value, such as 1 / 0 (although this is not recommended).

EXISTS has several advantages over IN. First, EXISTS is more expressive—the comparison could be made on more than one column. IN only works for comparing one column to a list (although some databases extend this functionality to multiple columns). If, for instance, the query were comparing both state name and country name, then it would be easier to write using NOT EXISTS.

A second advantage is more subtle and applies only to NOT EXISTS. If the list of values returned by NOT IN contains a NULL value, then all rows fail the test. Why? SQL treats a comparison to NULL as unknown. So if the comparison were 'X' NOT IN ('A', 'B', 'X', NULL) then the result is false, because 'X' is, in fact, in the list. If the comparison were 'X' NOT IN ('A', 'B', NULL), then the result is unknown, because it is unknown whether or not x matches the NULL. The important point: neither version returns true. The equivalent NOT EXISTS query behaves more intuitively. The second example—using NOT EXISTS—would return true.

The final advantage is practical. In many databases, EXISTS and NOT EXISTS are optimized to be more efficient than the equivalent IN and NOT IN. One reason is that IN essentially creates the entire underlying list and then does the comparison, whereas EXISTS can simply stop at the first matching value.

Subqueries for UNION ALL

The UNION ALL operator almost always demands subqueries, because it requires that the columns be the same for all tables involved in the union. Consider extracting the location names from ZipCensus into a single column along with the type:

```
SELECT u.location, u.locationtype
FROM ((SELECT DISTINCT stab as location, 'state' as locationtype
       FROM ZipCensus zc
      ) UNION ALL
      (SELECT DISTINCT county, 'county' FROM ZipCensus zc
      ) UNION ALL
      (SELECT DISTINCT zipname, 'zipname' FROM ZipCensus zc
      )
     ) u
```

This example uses subqueries to ensure that each part of the UNION ALL has the same columns. Also, note that the column names are taken from the first subquery, so they are not needed in the subsequent subqueries.

Lessons Learned

This chapter introduces SQL and relational databases from several different perspectives that are important for data mining and data analysis. The focus is exclusively on using databases to extract information from data, rather than on the mechanics of building databases, the myriad options available in designing them, or the sophisticated algorithms implemented by database engines.

One very important perspective is the data perspective—the tables themselves and the relationships between them. Entity-relationship diagrams are a good way of visualizing the structure of data in the database and the relationships among tables. Along with introducing entity-relationship diagrams, the chapter also explains the various datasets used throughout this book.

Of course, tables and databases store data, but they don't actually do anything. Queries extract information, transforming data into information. For some people, thinking in terms of data flow diagrams is simpler than understanding complex SQL statements. These diagrams show how various operators transform data. About one dozen operators suffice for the rich set of processing available in SQL. Dataflows are not only useful for explaining how SQL processes data; database engines generally use a form of dataflows for running SQL queries.

In the end, though, transforming data into information requires SQL queries, whether simple or complex. The focus in this chapter, and throughout the book, is on SQL for querying. This chapter introduces the important functionality of SQL and how it is expressed, with particular emphasis on JOINS, GROUP BYS, and subqueries, because these play an important role in data analysis.

The next chapter starts the path toward using SQL for data analysis by exploring data in a single table.

What's in a Table? Getting Started with Data Exploration

The previous chapter introduced the SQL language from the perspective of data analysis. This chapter uses SQL for exploring data, the first step in any analysis project. The emphasis shifts away from databases in general. Understanding what the data represents—and the underlying customers—is a theme common to this chapter and the rest of the book.

The most common data analysis tool, by far, is the spreadsheet, particularly Microsoft Excel. Spreadsheets show data in a tabular format. They give users power over the data, with the ability to add columns and rows, to apply functions, to summarize, create charts, make pivot tables, and color and highlight and change fonts to get just the right look. This functionality and the what-you-see-is-what-you-get interface make spreadsheets a natural choice for analysis and presentation.

Spreadsheets, however, are less powerful than databases because they are designed for interactive use. The historical limits in Excel on the number of rows (once upon a time, a maximum of 65,535 rows) and the number of columns (once upon a time, a maximum of 255 columns) clearly limited the spreadsheets to smaller applications. Even without those limits, spreadsheet applications often run on a local machine and are best applied to single tables (workbooks). They are not designed for combining data stored in disparate formats. The power of users' local machines can limit the performance of spreadsheet applications.

This book assumes a basic understanding of Excel, particularly familiarity with the row-column-worksheet format used for laying out data. There are many examples using Excel for basic calculations and charting. Because charts are so important for communicating results, the chapter starts by reviewing some of the charting tools in Excel, providing tips for creating good charts.

The chapter continues with exploring data in a single table, column by column. Such exploration depends on the types of data in the column, with separate sections devoted to numeric columns and categorical columns. Although dates and times are touched upon here, they are so important that Chapter 4 is devoted to them. The chapter ends with a method for automating some descriptive statistics for columns in general. Most of the examples in this chapter use the purchases dataset, which describes retail purchases.

What Is Data Exploration?

Data is stored in databases as bits and bytes, spread through tables and columns, in memory and on disk. Data lands there through various business processes. Operational databases capture the data as it is collected from customers—as they make airplane reservations, or complete telephone calls, or click on the web, or as their bills are generated. The databases used for data analysis are usually decision support databases and data warehouses where the data has been restructured and cleansed to conform to some view of the business.

Data exploration is the process of characterizing the data actually present in a database and understanding the relationships between various columns and entities. Data exploration is a hands-on effort. Metadata, documentation that explains what *should* be there, provides one description. Data exploration is about understanding what actually *is* there, and, if possible, understanding how and why it got there. Data exploration is about answering questions about the data:

- What are the values in each column?
- What unexpected values are in each column?
- Are there any data format irregularities, such as time stamps missing hours and minutes, or names being both upper- and lowercase?
- What relationships are there between columns?
- What are frequencies of values in columns and do these frequencies make sense?

TIP Documentation tells us what should be in the data; data exploration finds what is actually there.

Almost anyone who has worked with data has stories about data quality or about discovering something very unexpected inside a database. At one telecommunications company, the billing system maintained customers' telephone numbers as an important field inside the data. Not only was this column stored as character strings rather than numbers, but several thousand telephone *numbers* actually contained *letters* intermixed with numbers. Clearly, the column called "telephone number" was not always a telephone number. And, in fact, after much investigation, it turned out that under some circumstances (involving calls billed to third parties), the column could contain values other than numbers.

Even when you are familiar with the data, exploration is still worthwhile. The simplest approach is just to look at rows and sample values in tables. Summary tables provide a different type of information. Statistical measures are useful for characterizing data. Charts are very important because a good chart can convey much more information than a table of numbers. The next section starts with this topic: charting in Excel.

Excel for Charting

Excel's charting capabilities give users much control over the visual presentation of data. A good presentation of results, however, is more than just clicking an icon and inserting a chart. Charts need to be accurate and informative, as well as visually elegant and convincing. Edward Tufte's books, starting with *The Visual Display of Quantitative Information*, are classics in how to display and convey information.

This section discusses various common chart types and good practices when using them. The discussion is necessarily specific, so some parts explain explicitly, click-by-click, what to do. The section starts with a basic example and then progresses to recommended formatting options. The intention is to motivate good practices by explaining the reasons, not to be a comprehensive resource explaining, click-by-click, what to do in Excel.

A Basic Chart: Column Charts

The first example, in Figure 2-1, uses a simple aggregation query, the number of orders for each payment type. The chart format used is a column chart, which shows a value for each column. In common language, these are also called bar charts, but in Excel, bar charts have horizontal bars whereas column charts have vertical columns.

The query that pulls the data is:

```
SELECT PaymentType, COUNT(*) as cnt
FROM Orders o
GROUP BY PaymentType
ORDER BY PaymentType
```

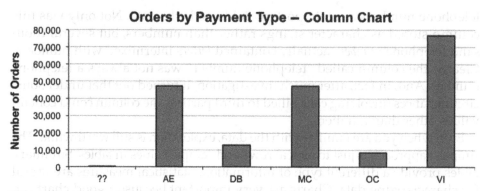

Figure 2-1: A basic column chart shows the number of orders for each payment type code.

This chart shows some good practices:

- The chart has a title.
- Appropriate axes have labels (none is needed for the horizontal axis because its meaning is clear from the title).
- Numbers larger than one thousand have commas because people are going to read the values.
- Horizontal gridlines are useful, but they are light so they do not overpower the data.
- Extraneous elements are kept to a minimum. For instance, there is no need for a legend (because there is only one series) and no need for vertical grid lines (because the columns serve the same purpose).

For the most part, charts throughout the book adhere to these conventions, with the exception of the title. Figures in the book have captions, making titles unnecessary. The rest of this section explains how to create the chart with these elements.

Inserting the Data

Creating the chart starts with running the query and getting the data into an Excel spreadsheet. The data is assumed to be generated by a database access tool, which can copy data into Excel using cut-and-paste (Ctrl+C and Ctrl+V, if the tool conforms to Windows standards, or Command+C and Command+V on a Mac) or other methods. The previous query produces two columns of data. It is also possible to run SQL directly from Excel by setting up a data source. Although useful for automated reports, such data connections are less useful for data exploration efforts using many ad hoc queries.

A good practice is to include the query in the spreadsheet along with the data itself. Including the query above the data ensures that you know how the data was generated, even when you return to it hours, days, or months after running the query.

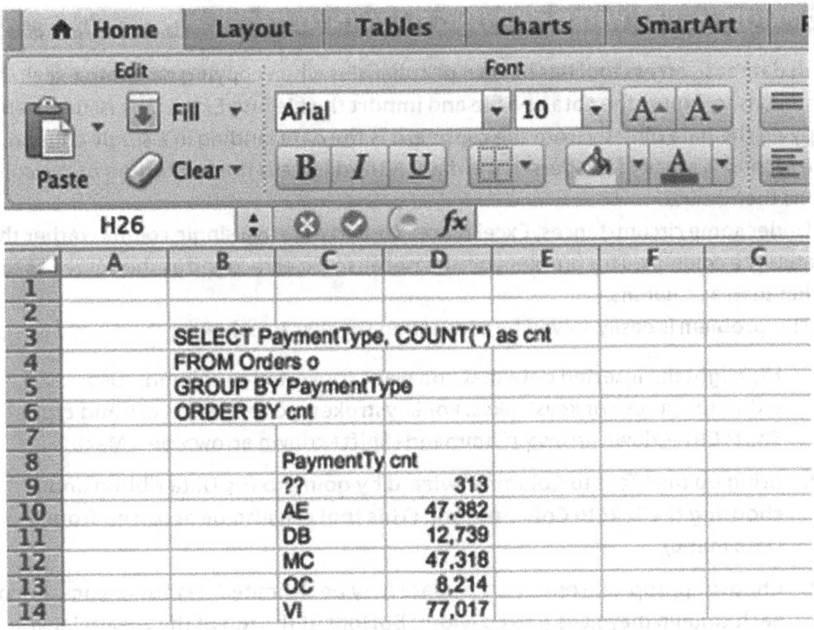

Figure 2-2: This spreadsheet contains the column data for payment types and orders.

> **TIP** Keeping the query with the results is always a good idea. So, copy the query into the Excel spreadsheets along with the data.

The technical aside "Common Issues When Copying Data into Excel" discusses some issues that occur when copying data. In the end, the spreadsheet looks something like Figure 2-2. Notice that this data includes the query used to generate the data.

Creating the Column Chart

Creating a column chart—or any other type of chart—has just two considerations. The first is inserting the chart; the second is customizing it to be clean and informative.

The simplest way to create the chart is with the following steps:

1. Highlight the data that goes into the chart. In this case, the query results have two columns and both columns, the payment type code and the count (along with their headers), go into the chart. If there is a non-data line between the header and the data, delete it (or copy the headers into the cells just above the data). To use keystrokes instead of the mouse, go to the first cell and type Shift+Ctrl+<down arrow> (or Shift+Command+<down arrow> on a Mac).

2. Bring up the Chart wizard. Use the Charts ribbon to select the Column chart, which is the first option.

COMMON ISSUES WHEN COPYING DATA INTO EXCEL

Each database access tool has its own peculiarities when copying data into Excel. One method is to export the data as a file and import the file into Excel. One issue when copying the data directly from the clipboard is the data landing in a single column. The second is a lack of headers in the data. A third issue is the formatting of the columns themselves.

Under some circumstances, Excel places copied data in a single column rather than in multiple columns. This problem occurs because Excel recognizes the values as text rather than as columns.

This problem is easily solved by converting the text to columns:

1. Highlight the inserted data that you want converted to columns. Use either the mouse or keystrokes. For keystrokes, go to the first cell and type Shift+Ctrl+<down arrow> (Command+Shift+<down arrow> on a Mac).

2. Bring up the "Text to Columns" wizard by going to the Data ribbon and choosing the Text to Columns tool. (This tool can also be accessed from the Data menu).

3. Choose appropriate options. The data may be delimited by tabs or commas, or each column may have a fixed width. Buttons at the top of the wizard let you choose the appropriate format.

4. Finish the wizard. Usually the remaining choices are unimportant. The one exception is when you want to import columns that look like numbers but are not. To keep leading zeros or minus signs, set the column data format to text.

5. When finished, the data is transformed into columns, filling the columns to the right of the original data.

The second problem is a lack of headers. Older versions of SQL Server Management Studio, for instance, did not offer an easy way to copy headers. In these versions, you can set up SQL Server Management Studio to copy the headers along with the data by going to Tools ➤ Options ➤ Query Results ➤ SQL Server ➤ Results to Grid and checking "Include column headers when copying or saving the results."

The third issue is the formatting of columns. Column formats are important; people read the data and formats help convey the meaning: $10,011 is very different from the zip code 10011.

By default, large numbers do not have commas. One way to insert commas is to highlight the column, right click, and choose "Format." Go to the "Number" tab, choose "Number," set "0" decimal places, and click the "Use 1000 Separator" box. Date fields usually need to have their format changed. For them, go to the "Custom" option and type in the string **yyyy-mm-dd**. This sets the date format to a standard format. To set dollar amounts, choose the "Currency" option, with "2" as the decimal places and "$" (or the appropriate character) as the symbol.

3. Choose the first option, "Clustered Column" and the chart appears.

4. To add a title, go to the Chart Format ribbon and select Chart Title ➤ Title Above Chart. Triple-click on the text box that appears to select all the text and type **Number of Orders by Payment Type**.

5. To set the Y-axis, choose Axis Titles ➤ Vertical Axis Title ➤ Rotated Title, triple-click in the box (to highlight the current value) and type **Num Orders**.

6. Resize the chart to an appropriate size, if you like.

A chart, formatted with the default options, now appears in the spreadsheet. This chart can be copied and pasted into other applications, such as PowerPoint, Word, and email applications. When pasting the chart into other applications, it can be convenient to paste the chart as a picture rather than as a live Excel chart. To do this, use the File ➤ Paste Special menu option and choose the picture option.

Formatting the Column Chart

The following are the formatting conventions to apply to the column chart:

- Resize the chart in the chart window
- Format the legend
- Change the fonts
- Change border
- Adjust the horizontal scale

For reference, Figure 2-3 shows the names of various components of a chart, such as the *chart area, plot area, horizontal gridlines, chart title, X-axis label, Y-axis label, X-axis title,* and *Y-axis title.*

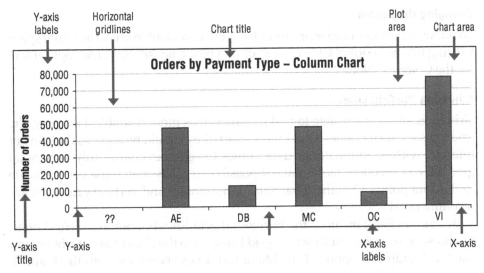

Figure 2-3: An Excel chart consists of many different parts.

Resizing the Chart in the Chart Window

By default, the chart does not take up quite all the space in the chart window. Why waste space? Click the gray area to select the plot area. Then make it bigger, keeping in mind that you usually don't want to cover the chart title and axis labels.

Formatting the Legend

By default, Excel adds a legend, containing the name of each series in the chart. Having a legend is a good thing. By default, though, the legend is placed next to the chart, taking up a lot of real estate and shrinking the plot area. In most cases, it is better to have the legend overlap the plot area. To do this, click the plot area (the actual graphic in the chart window) and expand to fill the chart area. Then, click the legend and move it to the appropriate place, somewhere where it does not cover data values.

When there is only one series, a legend is unnecessary. To remove it, just click the legend box and hit the Delete key.

Changing the Fonts

To change all the fonts in the chart at once, double-click the white area to select options for the entire chart window. On the "Font" tab, deselect "Auto scale" on the lower left. Sizes and choices of fonts are definitely a matter of preference, but 8-point Arial is a reasonable choice.

This change affects all fonts in the window. The chart title should be larger and darker (such as Arial 12-point Bold), and the axis titles a bit larger and darker (such as Arial 10-point Bold). You can just click on the chart title and change the font on the Home ribbon.

Changing the Border

To remove the outer border on the entire plot area, double-click the white space to bring up the "Format Chart Area" dialog box. Choose the "Line" option and set the Color to "None."

Adjusting the Grid Lines

Grid lines should be visible to make chart values more readable. However, the grid lines are merely sideshows on the chart; they should be faint, so they do not interfere with or dominate the data points. On column charts, only horizontal grid lines are needed; these make it possible to easily match the vertical scale to the data points. On other charts, both horizontal and vertical grid lines are recommended.

By default, Excel includes the horizontal grid lines but not the vertical ones. To choose zero, one, or both sets of grid lines, go to the Chart Layout ribbon and use the "Gridlines" option. The "Major Gridlines" boxes for both the X and Y axes are useful. The "Minor Gridlines" are rarely needed. You can also adjust the colors by using the "Gridlines Options …" on the same menu. A good choice of colors is the lightest shade of gray, just above the white. Note that you can also right-click on the gridlines in the chart to bring up similar menus.

Adjust the Horizontal Scale

For a column chart, every category should be visible. By default, Excel might only show some of the category names. To change this, double-click the horizontal axis to bring up the "Format Axis" dialog box, and go to the "Scale" tab. Set the second and third numbers, "Number of categories between tick-mark labels" and "Number of categories between tick-marks" both to 1. This controls the spacing of the marks on the axis and of the labels. Note that you can also get to this menu using the "Axes" option on the Chart Layout ribbon.

> **TIP** To include text in a chart that is connected to a cell (and whose value changes when the cell value changes), insert a text box into the chart. Then select the text box, type the equals character (=), and click the cell with the value you want. A text box appears with the text; this can be formatted and moved however you choose. The same technique works for other text boxes, such as titles. On a Mac, you can do something similar, but you need to insert a smart shape (using Insert ▷ Picture ▷ Shape) and then assign it to a cell the same method.

Bar Charts in Cells

Excel charts are powerful, but sometimes they are overkill for conveying simple information. Excel also offers methods for putting charts directly in cells. The simplest is a bar chart, where a single bar is located inside a cell, instead of a value. There are two approaches to creating such "in-cell" charts. The first is more brute-force, based on character strings, and the second uses conditional formatting.

Character-Based Bar Charts

Repeating single characters makes a passable bar chart, as shown in Figure 2-4. The power of such a chart is that it shows the data and the relative values of the data at the same time. The bars clearly show that MC and AE are basically equal in popularity and VI is the most popular.

The "chart" is really just a string created with the Excel function REPT(). This function takes a character and repeats it:

- ▪ `REPT("|", 3)` ➤ |||
- ▪ `REPT("-", 5)` ➤ -----

The repetition of the character looks like a bar chart. Vertical bars and dashes are useful characters for this purpose.

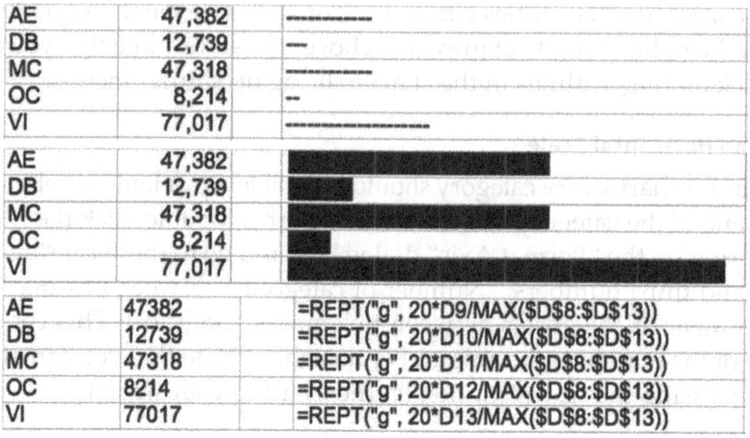

AE	47,382	----------
DB	12,739	--
MC	47,318	----------
OC	8,214	-
VI	77,017	-----------------

AE	47,382	████████████
DB	12,739	████
MC	47,318	████████████
OC	8,214	██
VI	77,017	███████████████████

AE	47382	=REPT("g", 20*D9/MAX($D$8:$D$13))
DB	12739	=REPT("g", 20*D10/MAX($D$8:$D$13))
MC	47318	=REPT("g", 20*D11/MAX($D$8:$D$13))
OC	8214	=REPT("g", 20*D12/MAX($D$8:$D$13))
VI	77017	=REPT("g", 20*D13/MAX($D$8:$D$13))

Figure 2-4: Bar charts can be created within a cell using variable strings of characters.

A trick produces the nicer middle chart in Figure 2-4. The trick is to use the lowercase "g" and convert the font to Webdings. In this font, the lowercase "g" is a filled-in square that forms a nice bar.

The lower part of Figure 2-4 shows the formulas that are used for this chart. There is nothing special about "20" in the formulas; that is simply the maximum length of the bars.

Conditional Formatting-Based Bar Charts

Bar charts within a cell is so useful that Excel actually builds in this functionality. On the Home ribbon, the conditional formatting option is under "Format" (you can also access it from the Menu option Format ➤ Conditional Formatting). Under this menu is an option for "Data Bars."

Figure 2-5 shows what happens when you choose this option. The length of the bars is automatically determined, so no additional calculations are needed. There is a problem: The values in the cells overlap the bars. The solution is to make the values disappear by using the format specification. The ideal format specification would be an empty string for any value, but this is not allowed. Instead, go to the Number Format menu, choose "Custom," and then type in one, two, or three semicolons.

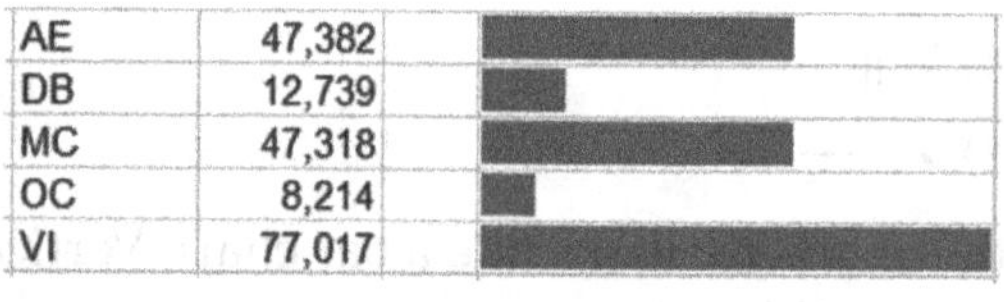

AE	47,382	████████
DB	12,739	██
MC	47,318	████████
OC	8,214	██
VI	77,017	████████████

Figure 2-5: Data bars can be produced using conditional formatting.

Why does this work? The format specification for a cell can have different formats for positive, negative, zero values, and text values. Semicolons separate the different formats for each of these possible values. By having nothing between the semicolons, the value is not displayed at all. The bars from conditional formatting are still displayed.

TIP Format specifications are quite powerful. They are even powerful enough to prevent values from being displayed in a cell (which is convenient when using conditional formatting to color the cell or create a bar within the cell).

Useful Variations on the Column Chart

This simple column chart illustrates many of the basic principles of using charts in Excel. To illustrate some useful variations, a somewhat richer set of data is needed.

A New Query

A richer set of data provides more information about the payment types, information such as:

- Number of orders with each code
- Number of orders whose price is in the range $0–$10, $10–$100, $100–$1,000, and over $1,000
- Total revenue for each code

The following query uses conditional aggregation to calculate these results:

```
SELECT PaymentType,
       SUM(CASE WHEN 0 <= TotalPrice AND TotalPrice < 10
                THEN 1 ELSE 0 END) as cnt_0_10,
       SUM(CASE WHEN 10 <= TotalPrice AND TotalPrice < 100
                THEN 1 ELSE 0 END) as cnt_10_100,
       SUM(CASE WHEN 100 <= TotalPrice AND TotalPrice < 1000
                THEN 1 ELSE 0 END) as cnt_100_1000,
       SUM(CASE WHEN TotalPrice >= 1000 THEN 1 ELSE 0 END) as cnt_1000,
       COUNT(*) as cnt, SUM(TotalPrice) as revenue
FROM Orders
GROUP BY PaymentType
ORDER BY PaymentType
```

The data divides the orders into four groups, based on the size of the orders. This is a good set of data for showing different ways to compare values using column charts.

Side-by-Side Columns

Side-by-side columns, as shown in the top chart in Figure 2-6, are the first method for the comparison. This chart shows the actual value of the number of orders for different groups. Some combinations are so small that the column is not even visible.

This chart clearly illustrates two points. First, three payment methods predominate: AE (American Express), MC (MasterCard), and VI (Visa). Second, orders in the range of $10 to $100 predominate.

To create such a side-by-side chart, choose the "Clustered Column" chart with multiple columns selected.

Stacked Columns

The middle chart in Figure 2-6 shows stacked columns. This communicates the total number of orders for each payment type, making it possible to find out, for instance, where the most popular payment mechanisms are. Stacked columns maintain the actual values; however, they do a poor job of communicating proportions, particularly for smaller groups.

To create stacked columns, choose the "Stacked Columns" chart option.

Stacked and Normalized Columns

Stacked and normalized columns provide the ability to see proportions across different groups, as shown in the bottom chart in Figure 2-6. Their drawback is that small numbers—in this case, very rare payment types—have as much weight visually as the more common ones. These outliers can dominate the chart.

One solution is to include payment type codes that have only some minimum number of orders. Filtering the data, by going to the Data ribbon and choosing filter (or using the Data ➤ Filter ➤ Autofilter menu option), is one way to do this. Another is by sorting the data in descending order by the total count, and then choosing the top rows to include in the chart.

To create the chart, choose the "100% Stacked Columns" chart.

Number of Orders and Revenue

Figure 2-7 shows another variation, where one column has the number of orders, and the other has the total revenue. The number of orders varies up to several tens of thousands. The revenue varies up to several millions of dollars. On a chart with both series, the number of orders would disappear because the numbers are so much smaller.

The trick is to plot the two series using different scales, which in Excel lingo means plotting them on different axes. This chart has the number of orders on the left and the total revenue on the right. Set the colors of the axes and axis labels to match the colors of the columns.

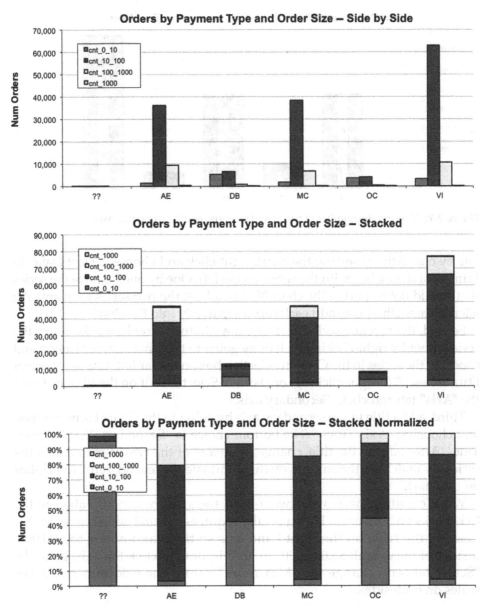

Figure 2-6: Three different charts using the same data emphasize different types of information, even though they contain the same raw data.

Using a second axis for column charts creates overlapping columns. To get around this, the columns for the number of orders are wide and those for the revenue are narrow. Also, either chart can be modified to be of a different type, making it possible to create many different effects.

To make such a chart, first include revenue and number of orders data in the chart, by selecting all the data and then removing (or unselecting) the series

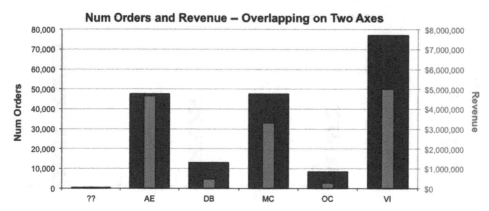

Figure 2-7: Showing the number of orders and revenue requires using two axes.

one by one. After inserting the chart, right-click and choose "Select Data" to bring up a dialog box with the series on the left. One by one, remove the series that should not be part of the chart (that is, all but the two series we want). An alternative method is to add each series separately into the chart.

Second, the revenue series needs to move to the secondary axis. Select the series either by right-clicking on it or by going to the Chart Layout ribbon and choosing the series in the Current Selection box on the far left. Choose "Format Data Series…" (if right-clicking) or "Format Selection" (if on the ribbon). Go to the "Axis" tab and click "Secondary axis."

Third, add a title to the secondary axis by going to the Chart Format ribbon and choosing "Axis Titles." The bottom choice is "Secondary Vertical Axis Title." After adding the title, change the colors of the two axes to match the series. By matching the colors, you can eliminate the legend, reducing clutter on the chart.

When creating charts with two Y-axes, the gridlines should align to the tick-marks on both axes. This typically requires manual adjustment. In this case, set the scale on the right-hand axis so the maximum is $8,000,000, instead of the default $6,000,000. To do this, double-click the axis, go to the "Scale" tab, and change the "Maximum" value. The gridlines match the scales on both sides.

TIP When creating charts with series on both axes, try to make the gridlines match up on both sides by adjusting the scales on the axes so they align.

The final step is to get the effect of the fat and skinny columns. To create the fat column, double-click the number of orders data columns. On the "Options" tab, set the "Overlap" to 0 and the "Gap Width" to 50. To get the skinny columns, double-click the revenue data series. Set the "Overlap" to 100 and the "Gap Width" to 400.

Other Types of Charts

Other types of charts are used throughout the book. This section is intended as an introduction to these charts. Many of the options are similar to the options for the column charts, so the specific details do not need to be repeated.

Line Charts

The data in the column charts can also be represented as line charts, such as in Figure 2-8. Line charts are particularly useful when the horizontal axis represents a time dimension because they naturally show changes over time. Line charts can also be stacked the same way as column charts, including normalized and stacked.

Line charts have some interesting variations that are used in later chapters. The simplest is deciding whether the line should have icons showing each point, or simply the line that connects them. Choosing the chart subtype controls this.

Line charts also have the ability to add trend lines and error bars, features that get used in later chapters.

Area Charts

Area charts show data as a shaded region. They are similar to column charts, but instead of columns, there is only the colored region with no spaces between data points. They should be used sparingly because they fill the plot area with color that does not convey much information. They are primary used for series on the secondary axis using lighter, background colors.

Figure 2-9 shows the total orders as columns (with no fill on the columns) and the total revenue presented as an area chart on the secondary Y-axis. This chart emphasizes that the three main payment types are responsible for most orders and most revenue. Notice, that AE and MC have about the same number

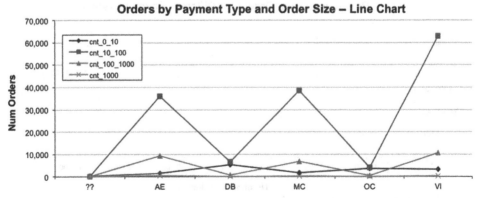

Figure 2-8: The line chart is an alternative to a column chart. Line charts can make it easier to spot certain types of trends.

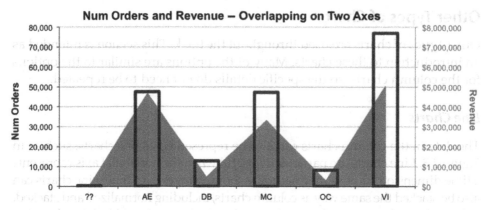

Figure 2-9: This example shows the revenue on the secondary axis as an area chart.

of orders, but AE has much more revenue. This means that the average revenue for customers who pay by American Express is larger than the average revenue for customers who pay by MasterCard.

To create this chart, follow the same steps as used for Figure 2-7. Click once on the number of orders series to choose it. Then right-click and choose "Change Series Chart Type…." Then choose "Area" on the Charts ribbon. To change the colors, double-click the colored area and choose appropriate borders and colors for the region.

To change the column fill to transparent, double-click the number of orders series, to bring up the "Format Data Series" dialog. Click on "Fill," and for "Color" choose "No Fill."

X-Y Charts (Scatter Plots)

Scatter plots are very powerful and are used for many examples. Figure 2-10 has a simple scatter plot that shows the number of orders and revenue for each

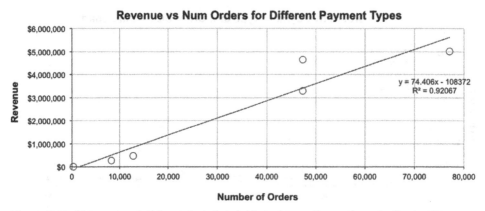

Figure 2-10: This scatter plot shows the relationship between the number of orders and revenue for various payment types.

payment type. This example has both horizontal and vertical gridlines, which is recommended for scatter plots.

Unfortunately, Excel does not allow labeling of the points on the scatter plot with codes or other information. You have to go back to the original data to see what the points refer to. The point above the trend line is for American Express—orders paid using American Express have more revenue than the trend line suggests.

This example shows an obvious relationship between the two variables—payment types with more orders have more revenue. According to the equation for the trend line, each additional order brings in about $75 additional revenue. To see the relationship, add a trend line (which is discussed in more detail in Chapter 12). Click the series to choose it, then right-click and choose "Add Trendline…." On the "Options" tab, you can choose to see the equation by clicking the button next to the "Display equation on Chart." Click "OK" and the trend line appears. It is a good idea to make the trend line a similar color to the original data, but lighter, perhaps using a dashed line. Double-clicking the line brings up a dialog box with these options.

This section has discussed credit card types without any discussion of how to determine the type. The aside "Credit Card Numbers" discusses the relationship between credit card numbers and credit card types.

Sparklines

A sparkline is a special type of chart that fits within a single cell. Typically, these are column charts or line charts that are particularly useful for showing changes over time. Excel offers many fewer options for formatting sparklines, but like in-cell bar charts, they have the tremendous advantage of being shown with the data itself.

TIP Sparklines are particularly useful for showing trends.

How do the number of purchases vary by month for different payment types? To answer this question, let's focus on a single year, 2015. The idea is to summarize the orders data by month and then create sparklines that show the changes through the year.

The query to extract the data uses conditional aggregation:

```
SELECT PaymentType,
       SUM(CASE WHEN MONTH(OrderDate) = 1 THEN 1 ELSE 0 END) as Jan,
       . . .
       SUM(CASE WHEN MONTH(OrderDate) = 12 THEN 1 ELSE 0 END) as Dec
FROM Orders o
WHERE YEAR(OrderDate) = 2015
GROUP BY PaymentType
ORDER BY PaymentType
```

The "…" is not part of SQL; it is shorthand for the missing ten months.

CREDIT CARD NUMBERS

This section used payment types as the example without explaining how credit card types are extracted from credit card numbers. Credit card numbers are not random; they have some structure:

- The first six digits are the Bank Identification Number (BIN). These are a special case of Issuer Identification Numbers defined by an international standard called ISO 7812.
- An account number follows, controlled by whoever issues the credit card.
- A checksum is at the end to verify the card number is valid.

Credit card numbers themselves are interesting, but don't use them! Storing credit card numbers, unencrypted in a database, poses privacy and security risks. However, there are two items of interest in the numbers: the credit card type and whether the same credit card is used on different transactions.

Extracting the credit card type, such as Visa, MasterCard, or American Express, is only challenging because the folks who issue the BINs are quite secretive about who issues which number. However, over the years, the most common credit card types have become known (Wikipedia is a good source of information). The BINs for the most common credit card types are in the following table:

PREFIX	CC TYPE
34, 37	AMEX
560, 561	DEBIT
300–305, 309, 36, 38, 39, 54, 55	DINERS CLUB
6011, 622126–622925, 644-649, 65	DISCOVER
2014, 2149	enRoute
3528–3589	JCB
50–55	MASTERCARD
4	VISA

The length of the prefix typically varies from one number to four numbers, which makes it a bit difficult to do a lookup in Excel. The following `CASE` statement assigns credit card types in SQL:

```
SELECT (CASE WHEN ccn LIKE '34%' OR ccn LIKE '37%'
             THEN 'AMEX'
             WHEN ccn LIKE '560%' OR ccn LIKE '561%'
             THEN 'DEBIT'
             WHEN LEFT(ccn, 3) IN ('300', '301', '302', '303', '304',
                                   '305', '309' OR
             LEFT(cnn, 2) IN ('36', '38', '54', '44')
```

```
        THEN 'DINERS CLUB'
        WHEN ccn LIKE '6011%' OR ccn LIKE 65%' OR
             LEFT(ccn, 3) BETWEEN '644' and '649' OR
             LEFT(ccn, 6) BETWEEN '622126' and '622925'
        THEN 'DISCOVER'
        WHEN LEFT(ccn, 4) IN ('2014', '2149')
        THEN 'ENROUTE'
        WHEN LEFT(ccn, 4) BETWEEN '3528' AND '3589'
        THEN 'JCB'
        WHEN LEFT(ccn, 2) BETWEEN '50' and '55'
        THEN 'MASTERCARD'
        WHEN ccn LIKE '4%'
        THEN 'VISA'
        ELSE 'OTHER'
   END) as cctypedesc
```

Note that the conditions use a combination of operators, including LIKE, LEFT(), BETWEEN, and IN.

Recognizing when the same credit card number in different transactions can be easy and dangerous or a bit harder. The simple solution is to store the credit card number in the database. This is a bad idea, for security reasons.

A better approach is to transform the number into something that doesn't look like a credit card number. One possibility is to encrypt the number (if your database supports this). In SQL Server, CHECKSUM() is usually good enough, although more advanced encryption functions are supported.

Figure 2-11 shows sparklines associated with this data. Three of them are totally flat. This is because the sparklines all use the same vertical scale and these do not have large enough values to show up on the lines. For the other three, we see that all increase in December, but American Express increases more than the rest.

To insert the sparklines, choose "Sparklines" from the Insert ribbon, and then select the input cells and destination. Unlike the bar charts discussed earlier, each sparkline is in its own cell. The *Sparklines* ribbon has a choice of various formats; this example uses the linear sparkline. By default, the vertical axis varies for each sparkline, which is inconvenient for seeing patterns across rows. To make the vertical axes consistent, select a group and choose the "Axis" option on the far

PaymentType	Jan	Feb	Mar	Apr	May	Jun	Jul	Aug	Sep	Oct	Nov	Dec	
??	56	6	116	6	3	8	7	2	7	4	4	6	
AE	613	421	618	399	510	656	422	487	496	581	1,355	1,514	
DB	196	110	110	67	60	109	71	80	86	79	75	183	
MC	692	504	667	419	491	744	487	447	477	623	1,265	1,466	
OC	65	45	201	230	54	108	46	33	35	60	110	137	
VI	1,095	751	926	605	719	1,004	737	716	716	1,018	1,813	2,086	

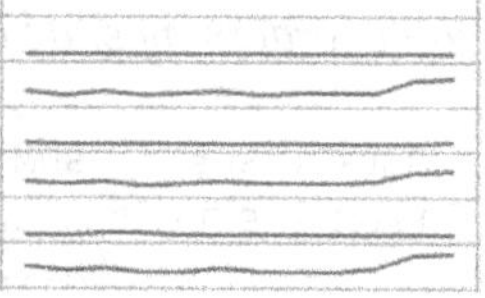

Figure 2-11: Sparklines showing the number of purchases by month.

right of the Sparkline ribbon. Under the two sets of options for the vertical axis (for both the minimum and the maximum), choose "Same for All Sparklines."

The lower part of Figure 2-11 shows similar information, using the average purchase amount per month. The query is similar:

```
SELECT PaymentType,
       AVG(CASE WHEN MONTH(OrderDate) = 1 THEN TotalPrice END) as Jan,
       . . .
       AVG(CASE WHEN MONTH(OrderDate) = 12 THEN TotalPrice END) as Dec
FROM Orders o
WHERE YEAR(OrderDate) = 2015
GROUP BY PaymentType
ORDER BY PaymentType
```

Note that the CASE statement has no ELSE clause. The default for CASE is NULL when there is no match. This works perfectly with the average function, which ignores NULL values.

These sparklines use the column chart. This tells a somewhat different story. First, there is much less seasonality to the larger orders. Also, AE payers have larger average order amounts than other orders. Perhaps American Express customers are wealthier than average. Alternatively, more small businesses may use American Express and their orders might, on average, be larger than other orders.

What Values Are in the Columns?

The basic charting mechanisms are a good way to see the data, but what do we want to see? The rest of this chapter discusses things of interest when exploring a single table. Although this discussion is in terms of a single table, remember that SQL makes it quite easy to join tables together to make them look like a single table—so the methods apply equally well to multiple tables.

The section starts by investigating frequencies of values, using histograms, for both categorical and numeric values. It then continues to discuss interesting measures (statistics) on columns. Finally, it shows how to gather all these statistics in one rather complex query.

Histograms

A histogram is a chart—usually a column chart—that shows the distribution of values in a column. For instance, the following query calculates the number of orders and population in each state, answering the question: *What is the distribution of orders by state and how is this related to the state's population?*

```
SELECT State, SUM(numorders) as numorders, SUM(pop) as pop
FROM ((SELECT o.State, COUNT(*) as numorders, 0 as pop
       FROM Orders o
```

```
     GROUP BY o.state
     ) UNION ALL
     (SELECT zc.stab, 0 as numorders, SUM(totpop) as pop
      FROM ZipCensus zc
      GROUP BY zc.stab
     )
    ) summary
GROUP BY State
ORDER BY numorders DESC
```

This query combines information from the ZipCensus and Orders tables. The first subquery counts the number of orders and the second calculates the population. These are combined using UNION ALL, to ensure that all states that occur in either table are included in the final result. Alternatively, two queries could produce two result sets that are then combined in Excel.

Figure 2-12 shows the results. Notice that the population is shown as a lighter shaded area on the secondary axis and the number of orders as a column chart. The states are ordered by the number of orders.

The chart shows several things. California, which has the largest population, is third in number of orders. Perhaps this is an opportunity for more marketing in California. At the very least, it suggests that marketing and sales efforts are focused on the northeast because New York and New Jersey have larger numbers of orders. This chart also suggests a measure of penetration in the state, the number of orders divided by the population (although a better measure might be the number of unique customers/households divided by the number of households in the state).

The resulting chart is a bit difficult to read because there are too many state abbreviations to show on the horizontal axis. It is possible to expand the horizontal axis and make the font small enough so all the abbreviations fit, just barely. This works for state abbreviations; for other variables it might be impractical, particularly if there are more than a few dozen values.

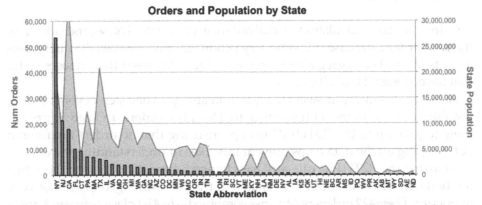

Figure 2-12: This example shows the states with the number of orders in columns and the population as an area.

One way to make the results more intelligible is to place the data into groups. That is, take the states with few orders and collect them together into one "OTHER" category; states with many orders are kept individually. Let's say that states with fewer than 100 orders are placed in the "OTHER" category. *What is the distribution of orders among states that have 100 or more orders?*

```
SELECT (CASE WHEN cnt >= 100 THEN State ELSE 'OTHER' END) as state,
       SUM(cnt) as cnt
FROM (SELECT o.State, COUNT(*) as cnt
      FROM Orders o
      GROUP BY o.State
     ) os
GROUP BY (CASE WHEN cnt >= 100 THEN state ELSE 'OTHER' END)
ORDER BY cnt DESC
```

This query puts the data in the same two-column format used previously for making a histogram. Note the use of the conditional in the GROUP BY column.

This approach has a drawback because it requires a fixed value in the query— the "100" in the comparison. One possible modification is to ask a slightly different question: *What is the distribution of orders by state, for states that have more than 2% of the orders?*

```
SELECT (CASE WHEN bystate.cnt >= 0.02 * total.cnt
             THEN state ELSE 'OTHER' END) as state,
       SUM(bystate.cnt) as cnt
FROM (SELECT o.State, COUNT(*) as cnt
      FROM Orders o
      GROUP BY o.State
     ) bystate CROSS JOIN
     (SELECT COUNT(*) as cnt FROM Orders) total
GROUP BY (CASE WHEN bystate.cnt >= 0.02 * total.cnt
               THEN state ELSE 'OTHER' END)
ORDER BY cnt desc
```

The first subquery calculates the total orders in each state. The second calculates the total orders. Because this subquery produces only one row, the query uses a CROSS JOIN. The aggregation then uses a CASE statement that chooses states that have at least 2% of all orders.

Actually, this query answers the question and goes one step beyond. It does not filter out the states with fewer than 2% of the orders. Instead, it groups them together into the "OTHER" group, ensuring that no orders are filtered out. Keeping all the data helps prevent mistakes in understanding the data.

Note that the "OTHER" category has changed dramatically using these two methods. In the first version, the states in the "OTHER" group are not very important. Their 422 orders put them—combined—in 41st place between Kansas and Oklahoma. The second query puts "OTHER" in second place between New York and New Jersey with 42,640 orders.

TIP When writing exploration queries that analyze data, keeping all the data is usually a better approach than filtering rows. Use a special group to keep track of what would have been filtered.

Another alternative is to have some number of states, such as the top 20 states, with everything else placed in the other category. *What is the distribution of the number of orders in the 20 states that have the largest number of orders?* Unfortunately, such a query is complex. The simplest approach uses a row number calculation:

```
SELECT (CASE WHEN seqnum <= 20 THEN state ELSE 'OTHER' END) as state,
       SUM(numorders) as numorders
FROM (SELECT o.State, COUNT(*) as numorders,
             ROW_NUMBER() OVER (ORDER BY COUNT(*) DESC) as seqnum
      FROM Orders o
      GROUP BY o.State
     ) bystate
GROUP BY (CASE WHEN seqnum <= 20 THEN state ELSE 'OTHER' END)
ORDER BY numorders DESC
```

This is an example of using ROW_NUMBER() in an aggregation query.

This query could also be accomplished in SQL Server using the TOP option (other databases typically use LIMIT or the ANSI standard FETCH FIRST <X> ROWS ONLY):

```
SELECT TOP 20 o.State, COUNT(*) as numorders
FROM Orders o
GROUP BY o.State
ORDER BY COUNT(*) DESC
```

In this version, the subquery sorts the data by the number of orders in descending order. The TOP option then chooses the first 20 rows and returns only these. This method does not generate the "OTHER" category, so the results do not include data for all states.

An interesting variation on the histogram is the cumulative histogram, which makes it possible to calculate, for instance, how many states account for half the orders. You can add the cumulative sum to one of the above queries—for instance:

```
SELECT TOP 20 o.State, COUNT(*) as numorders,
       SUM(COUNT(*)) OVER (ORDER BY COUNT(*) DESC) as cumesum
FROM Orders o
GROUP BY o.State
ORDER BY COUNT(*) DESC
```

Note that some databases that support window functions do not support cumulative sums. Notably, versions of SQL Server prior to 2012 do not have this functionality.

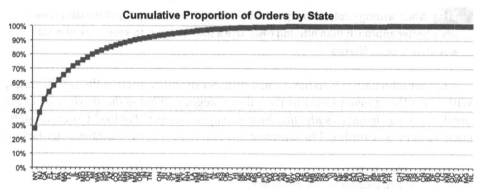

Figure 2-13: The cumulative histogram shows that four states account for more than half of all orders.

The cumulative sum can also be calculated in Excel. This process starts by ordering the results by the number of orders in descending order (so the biggest states are at the top). To add the cumulative sum, let's assume that the number of orders is in column B and the data starts in cell B2. An easy way is to type the formula =C1+B2 in cell C2 and then copy this formula down the column. An alternative formula that does not reference the previous cell is =SUM($B$2:$B2). If desired, the cumulative number can be divided by the total orders to get a percentage, as shown in Figure 2-13.

Histograms of Counts

The number of states is well known. Americans learn early that 50 states comprise the union. The Post Office recognizes 62—because places such as Puerto Rico (PR), the District of Columbia (DC), Guam (GM), and the Virgin Islands (VI) are treated as states—along with three more abbreviations for "states" used for military post offices. Corporate databases might have even more, sometimes giving equal treatment to Canadian provinces and American states, and even intermingling foreign country or province codes with state abbreviations.

Still, there are a relatively small number of states in contrast to the thousands of zip codes—more than fit in a single histogram. Where to start with such columns? A good question to ask is the histogram of counts question: *What is the number of zip codes that have a given number of orders?* The following query answers this:

```
SELECT numorders, COUNT(*) as nmzips, MIN(ZipCode), MAX(ZipCode)
FROM (SELECT o.ZipCode, COUNT(*) as numorders
      FROM Orders o
      GROUP BY o.ZipCode
     ) bystate
GROUP BY numorders
ORDER BY numorders
```

The subquery calculates the counts for each zip code. The outer SELECT counts how often each count occurs in the histogram.

The result set says how many zip codes have exactly one order, exactly two orders, and so on. For instance, in this data, 5,954 zip codes have exactly one order. The query also returns the minimum and maximum zip code values. These provide examples of zip codes with each count. The two examples in the first row are not valid zip codes, suggesting that some or all of the one-time zip codes are errors in the data.

TIP The histogram of counts for the primary key column always has exactly one row, where CNT is 1 because primary keys are never duplicated.

Another example uses OrderLines. *What is the number of order lines where the product occurs once (overall), twice, and so on?* The query that answers is also a histogram of counts:

```
SELECT numol, COUNT(*) as numprods, MIN(ProductId), MAX(ProductId)
FROM (SELECT ProductId, COUNT(*) as numol
      FROM OrderLines
      GROUP BY ProductId
     ) op
GROUP BY numol
ORDER BY numol
```

The subquery counts the number of order lines where each product appears. The outer query then creates a histogram of this number.

This query returns 385 rows; the first few rows and last row are in Table 2-1. The last row of the table has the most common product, whose ID is 12820 and

Table 2-1: Histogram of Counts of Products in OrderLines Table

NUMBER OF ORDERS	NUMBER OF PRODUCTS	MINIMUM PRODUCTID	MAXIMUM PRODUCTID
1	933	10017	14040
2	679	10028	14036
3	401	10020	14013
4	279	10025	14021
5	201	10045	13998
6	132	10014	13994
7	111	10019	13982
8	84	10011	13952
...			
18,648	1	12820	12820

appears in 18,648 order lines. The least common products are in the first row; there are 933 that occur only once—about 23.1% of all products. However, these rare products occur in only 933/286,017 orders, about 0.02% of orders.

How many different values of ProductId are there? This is the sum of the second column in the table, which is 4,040. How many order lines? This is the sum of the product of the first two columns, which is 286,017. The ratio of these two numbers is the average number of order lines per product, 70.8; that is, a given product occurs in 70.8 order lines, on average. The calculation in Excel uses the function SUMPRODUCT(), which takes two columns, multiplies them together cell by cell, and then adds the results together. The specific formula is "=SUMPRODUCT(C13:C397, D13:D397)."

Cumulative Histograms of Counts

What proportion of products account for half of all order lines? Answering this question requires two cumulative columns, the cumulative number of order lines and the cumulative number of products, as shown in Table 2-2.

This table shows that products with six or fewer order lines account for 65.0% of all products. However, they appear in only 2.2% of order lines. We have to go to row 332 (out of 385) to find the middle value. In this row, the product appears in 1,190 order lines and the cumulative proportion of order lines crosses the halfway point. This middle value—called the *median*—shows that 98.7% of all products account for half the order lines, so 1.3% account for the other half. In other words, the common products are much more common than the rare ones. This is an example of the long tail that occurs when working with thousands or millions of products.

Table 2-2: Histogram of Counts of Products in the OrderLines Table with Cumulative OrderLines and Products

NUMBER		CUMULATIVE		CUMULATIVE %	
ORDER LINES	PRODUCTS	ORDER LINES	PRODUCTS	ORDER LINES	PRODUCTS
1	933	933	933	0.3%	23.1%
2	679	2,291	1,612	0.8%	39.9%
3	401	3,494	2,013	1.2%	49.8%
4	279	4,610	2,292	1.6%	56.7%
5	201	5,615	2,493	2.0%	61.7%
6	132	6,407	2,625	2.2%	65.0%
...					
1,190	1	143,664	3,987	50.2%	98.7%
...					
18,648	1	286,017	4,040	100.0%	100.0%

The cumulative number of products is the sum of all values in the number of products column up to a given row. A simple formula for this calculation is =SUM($D$284:$D284). When this formula is copied down the column, the first half of the range stays constant (that is, remains $D$284) and the second half increments (becoming $D284 then $D285 and so on). This form of the cumulative sum is preferable to the =H283+D284 form because cell H283 contains a column title, which is not a number, causing problems in the first sum. One way around this is to add IF() to the formula: =IF(ISNUMBER(H283), H283, 0) + D284.

The cumulative number of order lines is the sum of the product of the number of order lines and number of products numol and numprods values (columns C and D) up to that point. The formula is:

```
SUMPRODUCT($C$284:$C284, $D$284:$D284)
```

The ratios are the value in each cell divided by the last value in the column.

Histograms (Frequencies) for Numeric Values

Histograms work for numeric values as well as categorical ones. For instance, NumUnits contains the number of different units of a product included in an order and it takes on just a handful of values. How do we know this? The following query answers the question: *How many different values does* NumUnits *take on?*

```
SELECT COUNT(*) as numol, COUNT(DISTINCT NumUnits) as numvalues
FROM OrderLines
```

There are only 158 different values in the column. On the other hand, the column TotalPrice has over 4,000 values, which is a bit cumbersome for a histogram, although the cumulative histogram is still quite useful.

A natural way to look at numeric values is by grouping them into ranges. The next section explains several methods for doing this.

Ranges Based on the Number of Digits, Using Numeric Techniques

Counting the number of important digits—those to the left of the decimal point—is a good way to group numeric values into ranges. For instance, a value such as "123.45" has three digits to the left of the decimal point. For numbers greater than one, the number of digits is one plus the log in base 10 of the number, rounded down to the nearest integer:

```
SELECT FLOOR(1+ LOG(val) / LOG(10)) as numdigits
```

However, not all values are known to be greater than 1. For values between −1 and 1, the number of digits is zero, and for negative values, we might as well identify them with a negative sign. The following expression handles these cases:

```
SELECT (CASE WHEN val >= 1 THEN FLOOR(1 + LOG(val) / LOG(10))
             WHEN -1 < val AND val < 1 THEN 0
             ELSE - FLOOR(1 + LOG(-val) / LOG(10)) END) as numdigits
```

Used in a query for TotalPrice in Orders, this turns into:

```
SELECT numdigits, COUNT(*) as numorders, MIN(TotalPrice),
       MAX(TotalPrice)
FROM (SELECT (CASE WHEN TotalPrice >= 1
                   THEN FLOOR(1 + LOG(TotalPrice) / LOG(10))
                   WHEN -1 < TotalPrice AND TotalPrice < 1 THEN 0
                   ELSE - FLOOR(1 + LOG(-TotalPrice) / LOG(10)) END
             ) as numdigits, TotalPrice
      FROM Orders o
     ) a
GROUP BY numdigits
ORDER BY numdigits
```

In this case, the number of digits is a small number between 0 and 4 because TotalPrice is never negative and always under \$10,000. Note that the query also returns the smallest and largest values in the range—a helpful check on the values.

The following expression turns the number of digits into a lower and upper bounds, assuming that the underlying value is never negative:

```
SELECT SIGN(numdigits) * POWER(10, numdigits - 1) as lowerbound,
       POWER(10, numdigits) as upperbound
```

This expression uses the SIGN() function, which returns –1, 0, or 1 depending on whether the argument is less than zero, equal to zero, or greater than zero. A similar expression can be used in Excel. Table 2-3 shows the results from the query.

Table 2-3: Ranges of Values for TotalPrice in Orders Table

# DIGITS	LOWER BOUND	UPPER BOUND	# ORDERS	MINIMUM	MAXIMUM
0	\$0	\$1	9,130	\$0.00	\$0.64
1	\$1	\$10	6,718	\$1.75	\$9.99
2	\$10	\$100	148,121	\$10.00	\$99.99
3	\$100	\$1,000	28,055	\$100.00	\$1,000.00
4	\$1,000	\$10,000	959	\$1,001.25	\$9,848.96

Ranges Based on the Number of Digits, Using String Techniques

There is a small error in the table. The number "1000" is calculated to have three digits rather than four. The discrepancy is due to a rounding error in the calculation. An alternative, more exact method is to use string functions.

String functions can calculate the length of the string representing the number, using only digits to the left of the decimal place. The SQL expression for this is:

```
SELECT LEN(CAST(FLOOR(ABS(val)) as INT)) * SIGN(FLOOR(val)) as numdigits
```

This expression uses the nonstandard LEN() function and assumes that the integer is converted to a character value (although all databases have such a function, it is sometimes called LENGTH()). See Appendix A for equivalent functions in other databases.

More Refined Ranges: First Digit Plus Number of Digits

Table 2-4 shows the breakdown of values of TotalPrice in Orders by more refined ranges based on the first digit and the number of digits. Assuming that values are always non-negative (and most numeric values in databases are non-negative), the expression for the upper and lower bound is:

```
SELECT lowerbound, upperbound, COUNT(*) as numorders, MIN(val), MAX(val)
FROM (SELECT (FLOOR(val / POWER(10.0, SIGN(numdigits)*(numdigits - 1))) *
              POWER(10.0, SIGN(numdigits)*(numdigits - 1))
             ) as lowerbound,
             (FLOOR(1 + (val / POWER(10.0, SIGN(numdigits)*(numdigits - 1)))) *
              POWER(10.0, SIGN(numdigits)*(numdigits - 1))
             ) as upperbound, o.*
      FROM (SELECT (LEN(CAST(FLOOR(ABS(TotalPrice)) as INT)) *
                   SIGN(FLOOR(TotalPrice))) as numdigits,
                   TotalPrice as val
            FROM Orders o
           ) o
     ) o
GROUP BY lowerbound, upperbound
ORDER BY lowerbound
```

This query uses two subqueries. The innermost calculates numdigits and the middle calculates lowerbound and upperbound. In the complicated expressions for the bounds, the SIGN() function is used to handle the case when the number of digits is zero.

Breaking Numeric Values into Equal-Sized Groups

Equal-sized ranges are perhaps the most useful type of ranges. For instance, the middle value in a list (the median) splits the list into two equal-sized groups.

Table 2-4: Ranges of Values for TotalPrice in Orders Table by First Digit and Number of Digits

LOWER BOUND	UPPER BOUND	NUMBER OF ORDERS	MINIMUM TOTALPRICE	MAXIMUM TOTALPRICE
$0	$1	9,130	$0.00	$0.64
$1	$2	4	$1.75	$1.95
$2	$3	344	$2.00	$2.95
$3	$4	2	$3.50	$3.75
$4	$5	13	$4.00	$4.95
$5	$6	152	$5.00	$5.97
$6	$7	1,591	$6.00	$6.99
$7	$8	2,015	$7.00	$7.99
$8	$9	1,002	$8.00	$8.99
$9	$10	1,595	$9.00	$9.99
$10	$20	54,382	$10.00	$19.99
$20	$30	46,434	$20.00	$29.99
$30	$40	20,997	$30.00	$39.99
$40	$50	9,378	$40.00	$49.98
$50	$60	6,366	$50.00	$59.99
$60	$70	3,629	$60.00	$69.99
$70	$80	2,017	$70.00	$79.99
$80	$90	3,257	$80.00	$89.99
$90	$100	1,661	$90.00	$99.99
$100	$200	16,590	$100.00	$199.98
$200	$300	1,272	$200.00	$299.97
$300	$400	6,083	$300.00	$399.95
$400	$500	1,327	$400.00	$499.50
$500	$600	1,012	$500.00	$599.95
$600	$700	670	$600.00	$697.66
$700	$800	393	$700.00	$799.90
$800	$900	320	$800.00	$895.00
$900	$1,000	361	$900.00	$999.00
$1,000	$2,000	731	$1,000.00	$1,994.00
$2,000	$3,000	155	$2,000.00	$2,995.00
$3,000	$4,000	54	$3,000.00	$3,960.00
$4,000	$5,000	20	$4,009.50	$4,950.00
$5,000	$6,000	10	$5,044.44	$5,960.00
$6,000	$7,000	12	$6,060.00	$6,920.32
$8,000	$9,000	1	$8,830.00	$8,830.00
$9,000	$10,000	3	$9,137.09	$9,848.96

Which value is in the middle? Unfortunately, there is no aggregation function for calculating the median, as there is for the average.

One approach is to use ROW_NUMBER(). If there are nine rows of data and with ranks one through nine, the median value is the value on the fifth row.

Finding quintiles and deciles is the same process as finding the median. Quintiles break numeric ranges into five equal-sized groups; four breakpoints are needed to do this—the first for the first 20% of the rows; the second for the next 20%, and so on. Creating deciles is the same process but with nine break-points instead.

The following query provides the framework for finding quintiles, using the ranking window function ROW_NUMBER():

```
SELECT MAX(CASE WHEN seqnum <= cnt * 0.2 THEN <val> END) as break1,
       MAX(CASE WHEN seqnum <= cnt * 0.4 THEN <val> END) as break2,
       MAX(CASE WHEN seqnum <= cnt * 0.6 THEN <val> END) as break3,
       MAX(CASE WHEN seqnum <= cnt * 0.8 THEN <val> END) as break4
FROM (SELECT ROW_NUMBER() OVER (ORDER BY <val>) as seqnum,
             COUNT(*) OVER () as cnt,
             <val>
      FROM <table>) t
```

It works by enumerating the rows in order by the desired column, and comparing the resulting row number with the total number of rows. This technique works for any type of column. For instance, it can find the values used for breaking up date ranges and character strings into equal-sized groups.

More Values to Explore—Min, Max, and Mode

Columns have other interesting characteristics. This section discusses extreme values and the most common value.

Minimum and Maximum Values

SQL makes it quite easy to find the minimum and maximum values in a table for any data type. The minimum and maximum values for strings are based on the alphabetic ordering of the values. The query is simply:

```
SELECT MIN(<col>), MAX(<col>)
FROM <tab>
```

A related question is the frequency of maximum and minimum values in a particular column. Answering this question uses a subquery in the SELECT clause of the query:

```
SELECT SUM(CASE WHEN <col> = minv THEN 1 ELSE 0 END) as freqminval,
       SUM(CASE WHEN <col> = maxv THEN 1 ELSE 0 END) as freqmaxval
FROM <tab> t CROSS JOIN
     (SELECT MIN(<col>) as minv, MAX(<col>) as maxv
      FROM <tab>) vals
```

This query uses the previous query as a subquery to calculate the minimum and maximum values. Because there is only one row, the CROSS JOIN operator is used for the join. This technique can be extended. For instance, it might be interesting to count the number of values within 10% of the maximum or minimum value for a numeric value. This calculation is as simple as multiplying MAX(<col>) by 0.9 and MIN(<col>) by 1.1 and replacing the "=" with ">=" and "<=" respectively.

Sometimes, the entire row containing the maximum or minimum value is of interest. For this purpose, use ORDER BY. For instance, the following query gets a row that has the maximum value for a given column:

```
SELECT TOP 1 t.*
FROM <tab> t
ORDER BY col DESC
```

For the minimum value, change the last line to ORDER BY col.

The Most Common Value (Mode)

The most common value is called the *mode*. The mode differs from other measures that we've looked at so far. There is only one maximum, minimum, and average and generally only one median. However, there can be many modes. A common, but not particularly interesting, example is the primary key of a table, which is never repeated. All values have a frequency of one, so all values are modes.

Calculating the mode in standard SQL is a bit cumbersome. The next sections show two different approaches to the calculation.

Calculating Mode Using Basic SQL

Calculating the mode starts with calculating the frequency of values in a column:

```
SELECT <col>, COUNT(*) as freq
FROM <tab>
GROUP BY <col>
ORDER BY freq
```

The mode is the last row (or the first row if the list is sorted in descending order). To get this row, you can use SELECT TOP 1 instead of just SELECT.

What column values have the same frequency as the maximum column frequency? A subquery can help answer this question:

```
SELECT <col>, COUNT(*) as freq
FROM <tab>
GROUP BY <col>
HAVING COUNT(*) = (SELECT TOP 1 COUNT(*) as freq
                   FROM <tab>
                   GROUP BY <col>
                   ORDER BY COUNT(*) DESC)
```

In this query, the HAVING clause does almost all the work. It selects the groups (column values) whose frequency is the same as the largest frequency. What is the largest frequency? That is calculated by the subquery. The result is a list of the values whose frequencies match the maximum frequency, a list of the modes.

If, instead, we were interested in the values with the smallest frequency, the MAX(freq) expression would be changed to MIN(freq). Such values could be considered the antimode values.

This query accomplishes the task at hand. However, it is rather complex, with multiple levels of subqueries and two references to the table. It is easy to make mistakes when writing such queries, and complex queries are harder to optimize for performance. The next section offers a simpler alternative.

Calculating Mode Using Window Functions

The following query uses MAX() as a window function to find the mode:

```
SELECT t.*
FROM (SELECT <col>, COUNT(*) as freq, MAX(COUNT(*)) OVER () as maxfreq
      FROM <tab>
      GROUP BY <col>
     ) t
WHERE freq = maxfreq
```

Note that the COUNT(*) is the argument to the window function MAX() OVER (). This expression calculates the maximum of the count, which is the maximum frequency. The outermost WHERE selects the rows where the frequency matches the maximum.

Exploring String Values

String values pose particular challenges for data exploration because they can take on almost any value. This is particularly true for free-form strings, such as addresses and names, which may not be cleaned. This section looks at exploring the length and characters in strings.

Histogram of Length

A simple way to get familiar with string values is to do a histogram of the length of the values. *What is the length of values in the* City *column in the* Orders *table?*

```
SELECT LEN(City) as length, COUNT(*) as numorders, MIN(City), MAX(City)
FROM Orders o
GROUP BY LEN(City)
ORDER BY length
```

This query provides not only a histogram of the lengths, but also examples of two values—the minimum and maximum values for each length. For the City column, there are lengths from 0 to 20, which is the maximum length the column stores.

Strings Starting or Ending with Spaces

Spaces at the beginning of string values can cause unexpected problems. The value " NY" is not the same as "NY," so a comparison operation or join might fail—even though the values look the same to humans. Spaces at the end of strings pose less of a problem because they are typically ignored for equality comparisons.

The following query answers the question: *How many times do the values in the column have spaces at the beginning or end of the value?*

```
SELECT COUNT(*) as numorders
FROM Orders o
WHERE City IS NOT NULL AND LEN(City) <> LEN(LTRIM(RTRIM(City)))
```

This query works by stripping spaces from the beginning and end of the column, and then comparing the lengths of the stripped and unstripped values.

Handling Upper- and Lowercase

Databases can be either case sensitive or case insensitive. Case sensitive means that upper- and lowercase characters are considered different; case insensitive means they are the same. Don't be confused by case sensitivity in strings versus case sensitivity in syntax. SQL keywords can be in any case ("SELECT," "select," "Select"). This discussion only refers to how values in columns are treated.

For instance, in a case-insensitive database, the following values would all be equal to each other:

- FRED
- Fred
- fRed

By default, most databases are case insensitive. However, this can be changed by setting a global option or by passing hints to a particular query (such as using the COLLATE keyword in SQL Server).

In a case-sensitive database, the following query answers the question: *How often are the values all uppercase, all lowercase, or mixed case?*

```
SELECT SUM(CASE WHEN City = UPPER(City) THEN 1 ELSE 0 END) as uppers,
       SUM(CASE WHEN City = LOWER(City) THEN 1 ELSE 0 END) as lowers,
       SUM(CASE WHEN City NOT IN (LOWER(City), UPPER(City))
               THEN 1 ELSE 0 END) as mixed
FROM Orders o
```

In a case-insensitive database, the first two values are the same and the third is zero. In a case-sensitive database, the three add up to the total number of rows.

What Characters Are in a String?

Sometimes, it is interesting to know exactly what characters are in strings. For instance, do email addresses provided by customers contain characters that they should not? Such a question naturally leads to which characters are actually in the values.

SQL is not designed to answer this question, at least in a simple way. Fortunately, it is possible to make an attempt. The answer starts with a simpler question: *What characters are in the first position of the string?*

```
SELECT LEFT(City, 1) as onechar, ASCII(LEFT(City, 1)) as asciival,
       COUNT(*) as numorders
FROM Orders o
GROUP BY LEFT(City, 1)
ORDER BY onechar
```

The returned data has three columns: the character, the number that represents the character (called the ASCII value), and the number of times that the character occurs as the first character in the City column. The ASCII value is useful for distinguishing among characters that might look the same, such as a space and a tab.

WARNING   When looking at individual characters, unprintable characters and space characters (space and tabs) look the same. To see what character is really there, use the ASCII() function.

The following query extends this example to look at the first two characters in the City column:

```
SELECT onechar, ASCII(onechar) as asciival, COUNT(*) as cnt
FROM ((SELECT SUBSTRING(City, 1, 1) as onechar
       FROM Orders WHERE LEN(City) >= 1)
```

CHARACTERS AND COLLATIONS

Character strings in SQL are more complex than they appear. This is because SQL strives to support all sorts of writing systems. The Latin characters used in English are a simple example. Most European languages use a similar system, although augmented by various accented characters and the occasional special character. And then there are hundreds of alphabets around the world that are also supported. Some read from right to left, some from left to right. And a language such as Chinese doesn't technically have an alphabet; instead it has tens of thousands of characters.

Characters themselves are represented as combinations of zeros and ones inside the computer. Three interrelated concepts are useful for understanding this representation. The first is the *character set* or *character map* which refers to what the bits mean. A very common system for English letters is ASCII, where, for instance, the bits that represent the number 65 represent the letter "A."

The *collation* refers to how the characters are ordered and whether or not two particular characters are equal. For instance, capital "A" and lowercase "a" may be equal, when the collation is case insensitive. The third concept is the *font*, which refers to how the character set is rendered on the screen or printed. SQL doesn't know about fonts although Excel does.

SQL has four types for storing character strings of a given length:

- ▪ CHAR ( )
- ▪ VARCHAR ( )
- ▪ NCHAR ( )
- ▪ NVARCHAR ( )

The first of these is a fixed length string. Shorter values stored in a CHAR ( ) field are padded at the end with spaces. So, "NY" would be "NY___" if stored in a CHAR (5) field. Normally, fixed-length characters are used for short codes, especially when all codes are the same length. VARCHAR ( ) can store variable length strings. These are not padded on the right with spaces. Characters in these fields are stored using a single byte per character.

The last two are types for national characters; these types require more space to store a given value than CHAR ( ) or VARCHAR ( ). However, they are much more flexible and can store characters from a mix of alphabets or from complicated writing systems such as Chinese and Japanese.

Within the database, the "collation" of the column determines both the collation (rules for comparison) and the character set (rules for presentation). Characters sets are typically customized for languages (so accented characters are represented) and for the natural ordering within the language.

Collations and character sets affect queries, from comparisons to ordering and aggregation. Fortunately, the default collations are usually quite sufficient. They become particularly useful (and annoying) when using databases for multilingual applications. Happily the database supports them. For most purposes, the only interest in collations is determining which is needed for case-sensitive or case-insensitive comparisons.

```
            UNION ALL
            (SELECT SUBSTRING(City, 2, 1) as onechar
             FROM Orders WHERE LEN(City) >= 2)
           ) cl
     GROUP BY onechar
     ORDER BY onechar
```

This query combines all the first characters and all the second characters together, using UNION ALL in the subquery. It then groups this collection of characters together, returning the final result. Extending this query to all 20 characters in the city is a simple matter of adding more subqueries to the UNION ALL.

A variation of this query might be more efficient under some circumstances. This variation pre-aggregates each of the subqueries. Rather than just putting all the characters together and then aggregating, it calculates the frequencies for the first position and then the second position, and then combines the results:

```
SELECT onechar, ASCII(onechar) as asciival, SUM(cnt) as cnt
FROM ((SELECT SUBSTRING(City, 1, 1) as onechar, COUNT(*) as cnt
       FROM Orders WHERE LEN(City) >= 1
       GROUP BY SUBSTRING(City, 1, 1) )
      UNION ALL
      (SELECT SUBSTRING(City, 2, 1) as onechar, COUNT(*) as cnt
       FROM Orders WHERE LEN(City) >= 2
       GROUP BY SUBSTRING(City, 2, 1) )
     ) cl
GROUP BY onechar
ORDER BY onechar
```

The choice between the two forms is a matter of convenience and efficiency, both in writing the query and in running it.

What if the original question were: *How often does a character occur in the first position versus the second position of a string?* This is quite similar to the original question, and the answer is to use conditional aggregation based on the position of the character:

```
SELECT onechar, ASCII(onechar) as asciival, COUNT(*) as cnt,
       SUM(CASE WHEN pos = 1 THEN 1 ELSE 0 END) as pos_1,
       SUM(CASE WHEN pos = 2 THEN 1 ELSE 0 END) as pos_2
FROM ((SELECT SUBSTRING(City, 1, 1) as onechar, 1 as pos
       FROM Orders o WHERE LEN(City) >= 1 )
      UNION ALL
      (SELECT SUBSTRING(City, 2, 1) as onechar, 2 as pos
       FROM Orders o WHERE LEN(City) >= 2)
     ) a
GROUP BY onechar
ORDER BY onechar
```

This variation also works using the pre-aggregated subqueries.

Exploring Values in Two Columns

Comparing values in more than one column is an important part of data exploration and data analysis. This section focuses on description. Do two states differ by sales? Do customers who purchase more often have larger average purchases? Whether the comparison is statistically significant is covered in the next chapter.

What Are Average Sales by State?

The following two questions are good examples of comparing a numeric value within a categorical value:

- What is the average order total price by state?
- What is the average zip code population in a state?

SQL is particularly adept at answering such questions using aggregations. The following query provides the average sales by state:

```
SELECT State, AVG(TotalPrice) as avgtotalprice
FROM Orders
GROUP BY State
ORDER BY avgtotalprice DESC
```

This example uses the aggregation function AVG() to calculate the average. The following expression could also have been used:

```
SELECT state, SUM(TotalPrice)/COUNT(*) as avgtotalprice
```

Although the two methods seem to do the same thing, there is a subtle difference between them, because they handle NULL values differently. In the first example, NULL values are ignored. In the second, NULL values contribute to the COUNT(*), but not to the SUM(). Replacing COUNT(*) with COUNT(TotalPrice) fixes this, by counting the number of values that are not NULL.

Even with the fix, there is still a subtle difference when all the values are NULL. The AVG() returns a NULL value in this case. The explicit division returns a divide-by-zero error. To fix this, replace the 0 with NULL: NULLIF(COUNT(TotalPrice), 0).

> **TIP** Two ways of calculating an average look similar and often return the same result. However, AVG(<col>) and SUM(<col>)/COUNT(*) treat NULL values differently.

How Often Are Products Repeated within a Single Order?

A reasonable assumption is that each product has only one order line in an order, regardless of the number of units ordered; the multiple instances are represented by the column NumUnits rather than by separate rows in OrderLines. There are several different methods to validate this assumption.

Direct Counting Approach

The first approach directly answers the question: *How many different order lines within an order contain the same product?* This is a simple counting query, using two different columns instead of one:

```
SELECT cnt, COUNT(*) as numorders, MIN(OrderId), MAX(OrderId)
FROM (SELECT OrderId, ProductId, COUNT(*) as cnt
      FROM OrderLines ol
      GROUP BY OrderId, ProductId
     ) op
GROUP BY cnt
ORDER BY cnt
```

Here, cnt is the number of times that a given OrderId and ProductId appear together in a row in OrderLines.

The results show that some products are repeated within the same order, up to a maximum of 40 times. This leads to more questions. What are some examples of orders where duplicate products occur? For this, the minimum and maximum OrderId provide examples.

Which products are more likely to occur multiple times within an order? A result table with the following information would help in answering this question:

- ProductId, to identify the product
- Number of orders containing the product any number of times
- Number of orders containing the product more than once

These second and third columns compare the occurrence of the given product overall with the multiple occurrence of the product within an order.

The following query does the calculation:

```
SELECT ProductId, COUNT(*) as numorders,
       SUM(CASE WHEN cnt > 1 THEN 1 ELSE 0 END) as nummultiorders
FROM (SELECT OrderId, ProductId, COUNT(*) as cnt
      FROM OrderLines ol
      GROUP BY OrderId, ProductId
     ) op
GROUP BY ProductId
ORDER BY numorders DESC
```

The results (which have thousands of rows) indicate that some products are, indeed, more likely to occur multiple times within an order than other products.

However, many products occur multiple times in a single order, so the duplication is not caused by just a handful of errant products.

Comparison of Distinct Counts to Overall Counts

Another approach to answering the question *"How often are products repeated in an order?"* is to consider the number of order lines in an order compared to the number of different products in the same order. That is, calculate the number of order lines and the number of distinct product IDs in each order; these numbers are the same when an order has no duplicate products.

One way of doing the calculation is using COUNT(DISTINCT):

```
SELECT OrderId, COUNT(*) as numlines,
       COUNT(DISTINCT ProductId) as numproducts
FROM OrderLines ol
GROUP BY OrderId
HAVING COUNT(*) > COUNT(DISTINCT ProductId)
```

The HAVING clause chooses only orders that have at least one product on multiple order lines.

Another approach uses a subquery:

```
SELECT OrderId, SUM(numproductlines) as numlines,
       COUNT(*) as numproducts
FROM (SELECT OrderId, ProductId, COUNT(*) as numproductlines
      FROM OrderLines ol
      GROUP BY OrderId, ProductId) op
GROUP BY OrderId
HAVING SUM(numproductlines) > COUNT(*)
```

The subquery aggregates the order lines by OrderId and ProductId. This intermediate result can be used to count both the number of products and the number of order lines. In general, a query using COUNT(DISTINCT) can also be rewritten to use a subquery, but COUNT(DISTINCT) is more convenient.

There are 4,878 orders that have more order lines than products, indicating that at least one product occurs on multiple lines in the order. However, the results from the query do not give an idea of what might be causing this.

Perhaps orders with a lot of products are the culprit. The following query calculates the number of orders that have more than one product broken out by the number of lines in the order:

```
SELECT numlines, COUNT(*) as numorders,
       SUM(CASE WHEN numproducts < numlines THEN 1 ELSE 0
           END) as nummultiorders,
       AVG(CASE WHEN numproducts < numlines THEN 1.0 ELSE 0
           END) as ratiomultiorders,
       MIN(OrderId), MAX(OrderId)
```

```
FROM (SELECT OrderId, COUNT(DISTINCT ProductId) as numproducts,
             COUNT(*) as numlines
      FROM OrderLines ol
      GROUP BY OrderId
     ) op
GROUP BY numlines
ORDER BY numorders;
```

This query uses COUNT(DISTINCT) along with COUNT() to calculate the number of products and order lines within a query.

Table 2-5 shows the first few rows of the results. The proportion of multiorders increases as the size of the order increases. However, for all order sizes, many orders still have nonrepeating products. Based on this information, it seems that having multiple lines for a single product is a function of having larger orders, rather than being related to the particular products in the order.

Which State Has the Most American Express Users?

Overall, about 24.6% of the orders are paid by American Express (payment type AE). *Does this proportion vary much by state?* The following query answers this question:

```
SELECT State, COUNT(*) as numorders,
       SUM(CASE WHEN PaymentType = 'AE' THEN 1 ELSE 0 END) as numae,
       AVG(CASE WHEN PaymentType = 'AE' THEN 1.0 ELSE 0 END) as avgae
FROM Orders o
GROUP BY State
HAVING COUNT(*) >= 100
ORDER BY avgae DESC
```

Table 2-5: Number of Products Per Order by Number of Lines in Order (First Ten Rows)

LINES IN ORDER	NUMBER OF ORDERS	ORDERS WITH MORE LINES THAN PRODUCTS	
		NUMBER	%
1	139,561	0	0.0%
2	32,758	977	3.0%
3	12,794	1,407	11.0%
4	3,888	894	23.0%
5	1,735	532	30.7%
6	963	395	41.0%
7	477	223	46.8%
8	266	124	46.6%
9	175	93	53.1%
10	110	65	59.1%

Table 2-6: Percent of American Express Payment for Top Ten States with Greater Than 100 Orders

STATE	# ORDERS	# AE	% AE
GA	2,865	1,141	39.8%
PR	168	61	36.3%
LA	733	233	31.8%
FL	10,185	3,178	31.2%
NY	53,537	16,331	30.5%
DC	1,969	586	29.8%
NJ	21,274	6,321	29.7%
MS	215	63	29.3%
MT	111	29	26.1%
UT	361	94	26.0%

This query calculates the number and percentage of orders paid by American Express by customers in each state, and then returns the states ordered with the highest proportion at the top. The query only chooses states that have at least 100 orders, in order to eliminate specious state codes. Notice the use of 1.0 instead of 1 for the average. Some databases (notably SQL Server) do integer arithmetic on integers. So, the average of 1 and 2 is 1 rather than 1.5. Table 2-6 shows the top ten states by this proportion.

From Summarizing One Column to Summarizing All Columns

So far, the exploratory data analysis has focused on summarizing values in a single column. This section first combines the various results into a single summary for a column. It then extends this summary from a single column to all columns in a table. In the process, we use SQL (or alternatively Excel) to generate a SQL query, which generates the summaries.

Good Summary for One Column

For exploring data, the following information is a good summary for a single column:

- The number of distinct values in the column
- Minimum and maximum values
- An example of the most common value (the *mode*)
- An example of the least common value (the *antimode*)

- Frequency of the minimum and maximum values
- Frequency of the mode and antimode
- Number of values that occur only one time
- Number of modes (because the most common value is not necessarily unique)
- Number of antimodes

These summary statistics are defined for all data types. Additional information might be of interest for other data types, such as the minimum and maximum length of strings, the average value of a numeric, and the number of times when a date has no time component.

The following query calculates these values for State in Orders:

```
WITH osum as (
      SELECT 'state' as col, State as val, COUNT(*) as freq
      FROM Orders o
      GROUP BY State
      )
SELECT osum.col, COUNT(*) as numvalues,
       MAX(freqnull) as freqnull,
       MIN(minval) as minval,
       SUM(CASE WHEN val = minval THEN freq ELSE 0 END) as numminvals,
       MAX(maxval) as maxval,
       SUM(CASE WHEN val = maxval THEN freq ELSE 0 END) as nummaxvals,
       MIN(CASE WHEN freq = maxfreq THEN val END) as mode,
       SUM(CASE WHEN freq = maxfreq THEN 1 ELSE 0 END) as nummodes,
       MAX(maxfreq) as modefreq,
       MIN(CASE WHEN freq = minfreq THEN val END) as antimode,
       SUM(CASE WHEN freq = minfreq THEN 1 ELSE 0 END) as numantimodes,
       MAX(minfreq) as antimodefreq,
       SUM(CASE WHEN freq = 1 THEN freq ELSE 0 END) as numuniques
FROM osum CROSS JOIN
     (SELECT MIN(freq) as minfreq, MAX(freq) as maxfreq,
             MIN(val) as minval, MAX(val) as maxval,
             SUM(CASE WHEN val IS NULL THEN freq ELSE 0 END) as freqnull
      FROM osum
     ) summary
GROUP BY osum.col
```

This query follows a simple logic. The CTE osum summarizes the data by State. The second subquery summarizes the summary, producing values for:

- Minimum and maximum frequency
- Minimum and maximum values
- Number of NULL values

The outer query combines these two, making judicious use of the CASE statement. The results for State are as follows:

- Number of values: 92
- Minimum value: ""
- Maximum value: YU
- Mode: NY
- Antimode: BD
- Frequency of Nulls: 0
- Frequency of Min: 1,119
- Frequency of Max: 2
- Frequency of Mode: 53,537
- Frequency of Antimode: 1
- Number of Unique Values: 14
- Number of Modes: 1
- Number of Antimodes: 14

As mentioned earlier, this summary works for all data types.

The query is set up so only the first row in the CTE needs to change for another column. So, it is easy to get results for, say, TotalPrice:

- Number of values: 7,653
- Minimum value: $0.00
- Maximum value: $9,848.96
- Mode: $0.00
- Antimode: $0.20
- Frequency of Nulls: 0
- Frequency of Min: 9,128
- Frequency of Max: 1
- Frequency of Mode: 9,128
- Frequency of Antimode: 1
- Number of Unique Values: 4,115
- Number of Modes: 1
- Number of Antimodes: 4,115

The most common value of TotalPrice is $0. One reason for this is that all other values have both dollars and cents in their values. The proportion of orders with

$0 value is small. This suggests doing the same analysis but using only the dollar amount of `TotalPrice`. This is accomplished by replacing the `TotalPrice` as `val` with `FLOOR(TotalPrice)` as `val`.

The next two sections approach the question of how to generate this information for all columns in a table. The strategy is to query the database for all columns in a table and then use SQL or Excel to write the query.

Query to Get All Columns in a Table

Most databases store information about their columns and tables in special system tables and views. The following query returns the table name and column names of all the columns in the `Orders` table, using a common syntax:

```
SELECT (table_schema + '.' + table_name) as table_name, column_name,
       ordinal_position
FROM INFORMATION_SCHEMA.COLUMNS c
WHERE LOWER(table_name) = 'orders'
```

See the Appendix for mechanisms in other databases.

The results are in Table 2-7, which is simply the table name and list of columns in the table. The view `INFORMATION_SCHEMA.COLUMNS` also contains information that the query does not use, such as whether the column allows `NULL` values and the type of the column.

Table 2-7: Column Names in Orders

TABLE_NAME	COLUMN_NAME	ORDINAL_POSITION
Orders	ORDERID	1
Orders	CUSTOMERID	2
Orders	CAMPAIGNID	3
Orders	ORDERDATE	4
Orders	CITY	5
Orders	STATE	6
Orders	ZIPCODE	7
Orders	PAYMENTTYPE	8
Orders	TOTALPRICE	9
Orders	NUMORDERLINES	10
Orders	NUMUNITS	11

Using SQL to Generate Summary Code

The goal is to summarize all the columns in a table, using an information summary subquery for each column. Such a query has the following pattern for `Orders`:

```
(INFORMATION SUBQUERY for orderid)
UNION ALL (INFORMATION SUBQUERY for customerid)
UNION ALL (INFORMATION SUBQUERY for campaignid)
UNION ALL (INFORMATION SUBQUERY for orderdate)
UNION ALL (INFORMATION SUBQUERY for city)
UNION ALL (INFORMATION SUBQUERY for state)
UNION ALL (INFORMATION SUBQUERY for zipcode)
UNION ALL (INFORMATION SUBQUERY for paymenttype)
UNION ALL (INFORMATION SUBQUERY for totalprice)
UNION ALL (INFORMATION SUBQUERY for numorderlines)
UNION ALL (INFORMATION SUBQUERY for numunits)
```

The information subquery is similar to the earlier version, with the mode and antimode values removed (just to simplify the query for explanation).

There are four other modifications to the query. The first is to remove the CTE. A `UNION ALL` query can have only one `WITH` clause, instead of one for each subquery. The second is to include a placeholder called `<start>` at the beginning. The third is to convert the minimum and maximum values to strings because all values in a given column need to be of the same type for the `UNION ALL`. The resulting query has the general form:

```
<start> SELECT '<col>' as colname, COUNT(*) as numvalues,
       MAX(freqnull) as freqnull,
       CAST(MIN(minval) as VARCHAR(255)) as minval,
       SUM(CASE WHEN <col> = minval THEN freq ELSE 0 END) as numminvals,
       CAST(MAX(maxval) as VARCHAR(255)) as maxval,
       SUM(CASE WHEN <col> = maxval THEN freq ELSE 0 END) as nummaxvals,
       SUM(CASE WHEN freq = 1 THEN freq ELSE 0 END) as numuniques
FROM (SELECT <col>, COUNT(*) as freq
     FROM <tab>
     GROUP BY <col>) osum CROSS JOIN
     (SELECT MIN(<col>) as minval, MAX(<col>) as maxval,
            SUM(CASE WHEN <col> IS NULL THEN 1 ELSE 0 END) as freqnull
     FROM <tab>
     ) summary
```

The next step is to put this query, as long as it is, into a single line.

To construct the final query, we'll use the string function `REPLACE()` to put in the column and table names:

```
SELECT REPLACE(REPLACE(REPLACE('<start> SELECT ''<col>'' as colname,
COUNT(*) as numvalues, MAX(freqnull) as freqnull, CAST(MIN(minval) as
VARCHAR(255)) as minval, SUM(CASE WHEN <col> = minval THEN freq ELSE 0
```

```
END) as numminvals, CAST(MAX(maxval) as VARCHAR(255)) as maxval, SUM
(CASE WHEN <col> = maxval THEN freq ELSE 0 END) as nummaxvals, SUM(CASE
WHEN freq = 1 THEN 1 ELSE 0 END) as numuniques FROM (SELECT <col>,
COUNT(*) as freq FROM <tab> GROUP BY <col>) osum CROSS JOIN (SELECT
MIN(<col>) as minval, MAX(<col>) as maxval, SUM(CASE WHEN <col> IS NULL
THEN 1 ELSE 0 END) as freqnull FROM <tab>) summary',
                              '<col>', column_name),
                    '<tab>', table_name),
            '<start>',
               (CASE WHEN ordinal_position = 1 THEN ''
                     ELSE 'UNION ALL' END))
FROM (SELECT table_name, column_name, ordinal_position
     FROM INFORMATION_SCHEMA.COLUMNS
     WHERE lower(table_name) = 'orders') tc
```

This query replaces three placeholders in the query string with appropriate values. The "<col>" string gets replaced with the column name, which comes from INFORMATION_SCHEMA.COLUMNS. The "<tab>" string gets replaced with the table name. And, the "<starting>" string gets "UNION ALL" for all but the first row. That is how the different subqueries are combined.

This query can be pasted into the query tool. Table 2-8 shows the results from running the resulting query.

Note that we could also construct this query in Excel. This starts by querying the metadata table for the names of the columns in the table. SUBSTITUTE() can then be used to do the replacements and get the final query.

Table 2-8: Information about the Columns in Orders Table

COLNAME	# VALUES	# NULL	# MINIMUM VALUE	# MAXIMUM VALUE	# UNIQUE
OrderId	192,983	0	1	1	192,983
CustomerId	189,560	0	3,424	1	189,559
CampaignId	239	0	5	4	24
OrderDate	2,541	0	181	2	0
City	12,825	0	17	5	6,318
State	92	0	1,119	2	14
ZipCode	15,579	0	144	1	5,954
PaymentType	6	0	313	77,017	0
TotalPrice	7,653	0	9,128	1	4,115
NumOrderLines	41	0	139,561	1	14
NumUnits	142	0	127,914	1	55

Lessons Learned

Databases are well suited to data exploration because databases are close to the data. Most relational databases are inherently parallel—meaning they can take advantage of multiple processors and multiple disks—so a database is often the best choice in terms of performance as well. Excel charting is a useful companion because it is familiar to business people and charts are a powerful way to communicate results. This chapter introduces several types of charts including column charts, line charts, scatter plots, and sparklines.

Data exploration starts by investigating the values stored in various columns in tables. Histograms are a good way to see distributions of values in particular columns, although numeric values often need to be grouped to see their distributions. There are various ways of grouping numeric values into ranges, including *tiling*—creating equal-sized groups such as quintiles and deciles.

Various other metrics are of interest in describing data in columns. The most common value is called the *mode*, which can be calculated in SQL.

Ultimately, it is more efficient to investigate all columns at once rather than each column one at a time. The chapter ends with a mechanism for creating a single query to summarize all columns at the same time. This method uses SQL or Excel to create a complex query, which is then run to get summaries for all the columns in a table.

The next chapter moves from just exploring and looking at the data to determining whether patterns in the data are, in fact, statistically significant.

How Different Is Different?

The previous two chapters show how to do various calculations and visualizations using SQL and Excel. This chapter moves from calculating results to understanding the significance of the resulting measurements. When are two values so close that they are essentially the same? When are two values far enough apart that we are confident in their being different?

The study of measurements and how to interpret them falls under the applied science of statistics. Although theoretical aspects of statistics can be daunting, the focus here is on applying the results, using tools borrowed from statistics to learn about customers through data. As long as we follow common sense and a few rules, the results can be applied without diving into theoretical mathematics or arcane jargon.

The word "statistics" itself is often misunderstood. It is the plural of "statistic," and a statistic is just a measurement, such as the averages, medians, and modes calculated in the previous chapter. A big challenge in statistics is generalizing from results on a small group to a larger group. For instance, when a poll reports that 50% of likely voters support a particular political candidate, the pollsters typically also report a margin of error, such as 2.5%. This margin of error, called the *sampling margin of error*, means that the poll asked a certain number of people (the sample) a question and the goal is to generalize the results from the sample to the entire population. If another candidate has 48% support, then the two candidates are within the margin of error, and the poll does not show definitive support for either one.

In business, the preferences or behaviors of one group of customers might be similar to or different from another group; the measures are calculated from databases rather than from samples. Of course, any calculation on any two groups of customers is going to be different, if only in the fifth or sixth decimal place. But does the difference matter? Do the measurements suggest that the groups are equivalent? Or do the measurements provide evidence that the groups differ? Statistics can help answer these types of questions.

This chapter introduces the statistics used for addressing the question "how different is different," with an emphasis on the application of the ideas rather than their theoretical derivation. Throughout, examples use Excel and SQL to illustrate the concepts. Key statistical concepts, such as confidence and the normal distribution, are applied to the most common statistic of all, the average value.

Two other statistical techniques are also introduced. One is the difference of proportions, which is often used for comparing the response rates between groups of customers. The other is the chi-square test, which is also used to compare results among different groups of customers and determine whether the groups are essentially the same or fundamentally different. The chapter has simple examples with small amounts of data to illustrate the ideas. Larger examples using the purchase and subscriptions databases illustrate the application of the ideas to real datasets stored in databases.

Basic Statistical Concepts

Over the past two centuries, statistics has delved into the mathematics of understanding measurements and their interpretation. Although the theoretical aspects of the subject are beyond the scope of this book, some basic concepts are very useful. In fact, not using the foundation of statistics would be negligent because so many brilliant minds have already answered questions quite similar to the ones being asked. Of course, the great minds of statistics who were developing these techniques a century ago had access neither to modern computers nor to the vast volumes of data available today. Many of the methods have nonetheless withstood the test of time.

This section discusses some important concepts in statistics, in the spirit of introducing useful ideas and terminology:

- The Null Hypothesis
- Confidence (versus probability)
- Normal distribution

The later sections in this chapter build on these ideas, applying the results to real-world data.

The Null Hypothesis

Statisticians are naturally skeptical, and that is a good thing. When looking at data, their default assumption is that nothing out-of-the-ordinary is going on.

This, in turn, implies that observed differences among groups are just due to chance. So, if one candidate is polling 50% and the other 45%, statisticians start with the assumption that there is no difference in support for the candidates. Others may be astounded by such an assumption because 50% seems quite different from 45%. The statistician starts by assuming that the different polling numbers are just a matter of chance, probably due to the particular people who were included in the poll.

> **TIP** Perhaps the most important lesson from statistics is skepticism and the willingness to ask questions. The default assumption should be that differences are due to chance; data analysis has to demonstrate that this assumption is highly unlikely.

The assumption that nothing extraordinary is occurring has a name, the *Null Hypothesis*. A vocabulary note: "Null" here is a statistical term and has nothing to do with the database use of the term. To avoid ambiguity, "Null Hypothesis" is a statistical phrase and any other use of "NULL" refers to the SQL keyword.

The Null Hypothesis is the hallmark of skepticism, and also the beginning of a conversation. The skepticism leads to the question: *How confident are we that the Null Hypothesis is true?* Or, phrased slightly differently: *How confident are we that the observed difference is due just to chance?* These questions have an answer. The *p-value* estimates how often the Null Hypothesis is true. When the p-value is very small, such as 0.1%, the statement "I have very little confidence that the observed difference is due just to chance" is quite reasonable. This, in turn, implies that the observed difference is due to something other than chance. In the polling example, a low p-value suggests the following: "The poll shows a significant difference in support for the two candidates."

Statistical significance is equivalent to saying that the p-value is less than some low number, often 5% or 10%. When the p-value is larger, the Null Hypothesis has pretty good standing. The right way to think about this is "There is no strong evidence that something occurred, so I'll assume that the difference was due to chance" or "The polling shows no definitive difference in support for the two candidates." One candidate might have slightly higher polling numbers than the other in the small number of people polled. Alas, the difference is not large enough for us to have confidence that one candidate has larger support than the other in the much larger general (or voting) population.

Imagine running a bunch of different polls at the same time, with the same questions and the same methodology. The only variation among these polls is the people who are contacted; each is a random sample from the overall population. Each poll produces slightly different estimates for the support of the two candidates. If we assume that the two candidates have the same support, then the p-value is the proportion of all these polls where the difference between the two candidates is at least as great as what the first poll finds.

Sometimes, just formulating the Null Hypothesis is valuable because it articulates a business problem in a measurable and testable way. This chapter includes various Null Hypotheses, such as:

- The average order amount in New York is the same as the average in California.

- A committee with five members was chosen without taking gender into account.

- The stop rate for customers who started on 2005-12-28 is the same, regardless of the market where they started.

- There is no affinity between the products that customers buy and the states where customers live. That is, all customers are as likely to purchase a particular product, regardless of where they live.

These hypotheses are stated in clear business terms. They can be validated, using available data. The answers, however, are not simply "true" or "false." The answers are a confidence that the statement is true. Very low p-values (confidence values) imply a very low confidence that the statement is true, implying that the observed difference is significant.

Confidence and Probability

The idea of confidence is central to the notion of understanding whether two things are the same or different. Statisticians do not ask "are these different?" Instead, they ask the question "what is the confidence that they are the same?" When this confidence is very low, it is reasonable to assume that the two measurements are indeed different.

Confidence and probability often look the same because both are measured in the same units, a value between zero and one that is often written as a percentage. Unlike probabilities, confidence includes the subjective opinion of the observer. Probability is inherent in whatever is happening. There is a certain probability of rain today. There is a certain probability that heads will appear on a coin toss, or that a contestant will win the jackpot on a game show, or that a particular atom of uranium will decay radioactively in the next minute. These are examples where there is a process, and the opinions of the observer do not matter.

On the other hand, after an election has occurred and before the votes are counted, one might be *confident* in the outcome of the election. The votes have already been cast, so there is a result. Both candidates in the election might be confident, believing they are going to win. However, each candidate being 90% confident in his or her odds of winning does not imply an overall confidence of 180%! Although it looks like a probability, this is confidence because it has a subjective component.

There is a tendency to think of confidence as a probability. This is not quite correct because a probability is exact, with the uncertainty in the measurement. A confidence may look exact, but the uncertainty is, at least partially, in the opinion of the observer. The Monty Hall Paradox, explained in the aside, is a simple "probability" paradox that illustrates the difference between the two.

The inverse notion of "how different is different" is "when are two things the same." That is, *how confident are we that the difference is or is not zero?* In the polling example, where one candidate has 50% support and the other 45%, the Null Hypothesis on the difference is: "The difference in support between the two candidates is zero," meaning the two candidates actually have the same support in the overall population. A p-value of 1% means that if multiple polls were conducted at the same time, with the same methodology and with the only difference being the people randomly chosen to participate in the polls and the assumption that there is no difference in support for the candidates, then we would expect 99% of the polls to have less than the observed difference. That is, the observed difference is big, so it suggests a real difference in support for the candidates in the overall population. If the p-value were 50%, then even though the difference is noticeable, it says very little about which candidate has greater support.

Normal Distribution

The normal distribution, also called the bell curve and the Gaussian distribution, plays a special role in statistics. In many situations, the normal distribution can answer the following question: Given an observed measure on a sample (such as a poll), what confidence do we have that the actual measure for the whole population falls within a particular range? For instance, if 50% of poll respondents say they support Candidate A, what does this mean about Candidate A's support in the whole population? Pollsters are really reporting something like "There is a 95% confidence that the candidate's support is between 47.5% and 52.5%."

In this particular case, the *confidence interval* is 47.5% to 52.5% and the *confidence* is 95%. A different level of confidence would produce a different interval. So the interval for 99.9% confidence would be wider. The interval for 90% would be narrower.

Measuring the confidence interval uses the normal distribution, shown in Figure 3-1 for the data corresponding to the polling example. In this example, the average is 50%, and the range from 47.5% and 52.5% has 95% confidence. The two points define the ends of the confidence interval, and the area under the curve, between the two points, measures the confidence. The units on the vertical axis are shown, but they are not important. They just guarantee that the area under the entire curve equals 100%.

MONTY HALL PARADOX

Monty Hall was the famous host of the television show *Let's Make a Deal* from 1963 through 1986. This popular show offered prizes, which were hidden behind three doors. One of the doors contained a grand prize, such as a car or vacation. The other two had lesser prizes, such as a goat or rubber chicken. In this simplification of the game show, a contestant is asked to choose one of the three doors and can keep the prize behind it. One of the remaining two doors is then opened, revealing perhaps a rubber chicken, and the contestant is asked whether he or she wants to keep the unseen prize behind the chosen door or switch to the other unopened one.

Assuming that the contestant is asked randomly regardless of whether the chosen door has the prize, should he or she keep the original choice or switch? Or, does it not make a difference? The rest of this aside gives the answer, so stop here if you want to think about it.

A simple analysis of the problem might go as follows. When the contestant first makes a choice, there are three doors, so the odds of getting the prize are initially one in three (or 33.3% probability). After the other door is opened, though, there are only two doors remaining, so the probability of either door having the prize is 50%. Because the probabilities are the same, switching does not make a difference. It is equally likely that the prize is behind either door.

Although an appealing and popular analysis, this is not correct for a subtle reason that involves a distinction similar to the distinction between confidence and probability: Just because there are two doors does not mean that the probabilities are equal.

Monty knows where the prize is, so he can always open one of the remaining two and show a booby prize. Opening one door and showing that there is no grand prize behind it adds no new information. This is always possible, regardless of where the grand prize is. Because opening some door with no grand prize offers no new information, showing a booby prize does not change the original probabilities.

What are those probabilities? The probabilities are 33.3% that the prize is behind the original door and 66.7% that the prize is behind one of the other two. These do not change, so switching doubles the chances of winning.

Confidence levels can help us understand this problem. At the beginning, the contestant should be 33.3% confident that the prize is behind the chosen door and 66.7% confident that the prize is behind one of the other two. This confidence does not change when another door without the prize is opened, because the contestant should realize that it is always possible to show a door with no prize. Nothing has changed. Given the opportunity to switch, the contestant should do so, and double his or her chances of winning.

The normal distribution is a family of curves, defined by two numbers, the average and standard deviation. The average determines where the center of the distribution is, so smaller averages result in curves shifted to the left, and larger averages have curves shifted to the right. The standard deviation determines how narrow and high or how wide and flat the hump is in the middle. Small

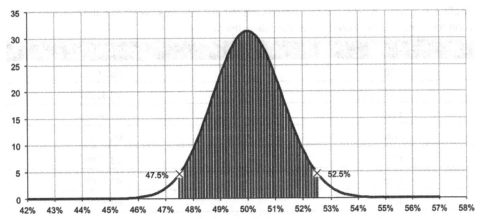

Figure 3-1: The area under the normal distribution, between two points, is the confidence that the measurement on the entire population falls in that range.

standard deviations make the curve spikier; larger standard deviations spread it out. Otherwise, the shape of the curve remains the same, and the area under all these curves is always one.

Properties of the normal distribution are well understood. So, about 68% of the averages from samples fall within one standard deviation of the overall average. About 95.5% fall within two standard deviations, and 99.73% fall within three standard deviations. By tradition, statistical significance is often taken at the 95% level, and this occurs at the not-so-intuitive level of 1.96 standard deviations from the average.

Table 3-1 shows the confidence for various confidence intervals measured in terms of standard deviations. The distance from a value to the average, measured in standard deviations, is called the *z-score*. This is actually a simple transformation on any set of data, where the difference between the value and average is divided by the standard deviation. Z-scores are particularly useful when comparing variables that have different ranges, such as the average age and average income of a group of people. Z-scores are also useful for transforming variables for data mining.

The values in Table 3-1 were calculated using the Excel formula:

```
<confidence> = NORMSDIST(<z-score>) - NORMSDIST(- <z-score>)
```

In Excel, the function NORMSDIST() calculates the area under the normal distribution up to a particular z-score. That is, it defines the confidence interval from minus infinity to the z-score. To get a finite confidence interval on either side of the average, calculate the one from minus infinity to <value> and then subtract out the one from minus infinity to minus z-score, as shown in Figure 3-2.

The preceding formula works for z-scores that are positive. A slight variation works for all z-scores:

```
<confidence> = ABS(NORMSDIST(<z-score>) - NORMSDIST(- <z-score>))
```

Table 3-1: Confidence Levels Associated with Various Z-Scores (which is half the width of the confidence interval measured in standard deviations)

Z-SCORE	CONFIDENCE
1.00	68.269%
1.64	89.899%
1.96	95.000%
2.00	95.450%
2.50	98.758%
3.00	99.730%
3.29	99.900%
3.89	99.990%
4.00	99.994%
4.42	99.999%
5.00	100.000%

From the preceding polling example, the standard deviation can be reverse engineered. The confidence is 95%, implying that the confidence interval ranges 1.96 times the standard deviation on either side of the average. Because the confidence interval is 2.5% on either side of the average, the standard deviation is 2.5%/1.96 or 1.276%. This information can be used to calculate the 99.9% confidence interval. It is 3.29 times the standard deviation. So, the confidence interval for the poll with 99.9% confidence ranges from 50% – 3.29*1.276% to 50% + 3.29*1.276%, or 45.8% to 54.2%.

As a final note, the normal distribution depends on knowing the average and standard deviation. All we have is data, which does not include this information directly. Fortunately, statistics provides some methods for estimating these values from data, as explained in examples throughout this chapter.

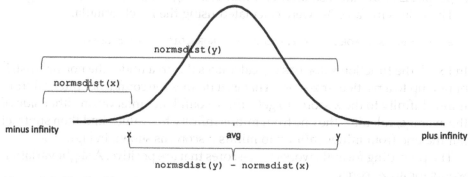

Figure 3-2: The Excel function NORMSDIST() can be used to calculate the confidence for an interval around the average.

How Different Are the Averages?

The retail purchase data has purchases from all 50 states, and then some. This section addresses the question of whether the average purchase amount (in the column TotalPrice) differs by state. Statistics answers this question, and most of the calculations can be done using SQL queries.

Let's start with the observation that the average purchase amount for the 17,839 purchases from California is $85.48 and the average purchase amount for the 53,537 purchases from New York is $70.14. Is this difference significant?

The Approach

Let's start by putting all the orders from New York and California into one big bucket whose overall average total price is $73.98. The question is: *What is the likelihood that a random subset of 17,839 purchases from this bucket has an average* TotalPrice *of $85.48?* If this probability is largish, then orders from California look like a random sample, and there is nothing special about them. On the other hand, a small p-value suggests that orders from California are different from a random sample of orders from the two states, leading to the conclusion that California orders are different.

Looking at extreme cases can help shed light on this approach. Assume that all orders from California are exactly $85.48 and all orders from New York are exactly $70.14. In this case, there is only one group of orders from the bucket whose average amount is $85.48—the group that consists of exactly the California orders. If the orders took on only these two values, it would be safe to say that distinction between New York and California is not due just to chance. It is due to some other factor.

A cursory look at the data shows that this is not the case. Given that TotalPrice runs the gamut of values from $0 to $10,000, can we say anything about whether the difference in average order size in New York and California is due to randomness, or due to a difference in the markets?

Standard Deviation for Subset Averages

The preceding question is about averages of samples. Something called the Central Limit Theorem in statistics sheds light on precisely the subject of the average of a subset of values randomly selected from a larger group. This theorem says that if we repeatedly take samples of a given size, then the distribution of the averages of these samples approximates a normal distribution, whose average and standard deviation are based on exactly three factors:

- The average of the original data
- The standard deviation of the original data
- The size of the sample

Notice that the Central Limit Theorem says nothing about the distribution of the original values. The wonder of this theorem is that it works for basically any distribution of the original values. The Central Limit Theorem tells us about the distribution of the *averages* of the samples, not the distribution of the original values.

Consider the average `TotalPrice` of ten orders taken randomly. If this process is repeated, the averages approximate a normal distribution. If instead the samples contained one hundred orders rather than ten, the averages also follow a normal distribution, but one whose standard deviation is a bit smaller. As the size of the samples increases, the distribution of the average forms a narrower band around the actual average in the original data. Figure 3-3 shows some distributions for the average value of `TotalPrice` for different sized groups coming from the California–New York orders.

According to the Central Limit Theorem, the average of the distribution is the average of the original data and the standard deviation is the standard deviation of the original data divided by the square root of the sample size. As the sample size gets larger, the standard deviation gets smaller, and the distribution becomes taller and narrower and more centered on the average. This means that the average of a larger sample is much more likely to be very close to the overall average, than the average of a smaller sample. In statistics-speak, the standard deviation of the average of a sample is called the *standard error* (of the sample). So, the previous formulation says that the standard error of a sample is equal to the standard deviation of the population divided by the square root of the sample size.

Now, the question about the average values of California and New York gets a little tricky. It is trivial to calculate the average and standard deviation of the New York and California orders, using the SQL aggregation functions `AVG()` and `STDDEV()`. However, the question that we want to answer is slightly

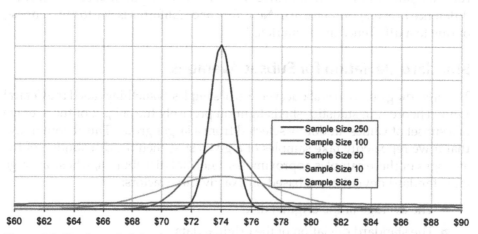

Figure 3-3: The theoretical distributions of `TotalPrice` for different sample sizes follow the normal distribution.

different. The question is: *What is the likelihood that taking the average of 17,839 values randomly chosen from the population results in an average of $85.48 and taking a sample of 53,537 values results in $70.14?*

Looking at the distribution of values from each state helps to understand what is happening. The following SQL query returns the counts of the `TotalPrice` column in five-dollar increments:

```
SELECT 5 * FLOOR(TotalPrice / 5),
       SUM(CASE WHEN State = 'CA' THEN 1 ELSE 0 END) as CA,
       SUM(CASE WHEN State = 'NY' THEN 1 ELSE 0 END) as NY
FROM Orders o
WHERE o.State IN ('CA', 'NY')
```

A histogram of the results is shown in Figure 3-4, which has the averages for each state in the legend. Visually, the two histograms look quite similar, suggesting that the average sizes for each state might well be within the margin of error. However, the analysis is not yet complete.

Three Approaches

There are at least three statistical approaches to determining whether the average purchase sizes in New York and California are the same or different.

The first approach is to treat the orders as two samples from the same population and ask a perhaps now-familiar question: *What is the likelihood that the differences are due just to random variation?* The second approach is to take the difference between the two averages and ask: *How likely is it that the difference could be zero?* If the difference could reasonably be zero, then the two observed values are too close and should be treated as equivalent to each other.

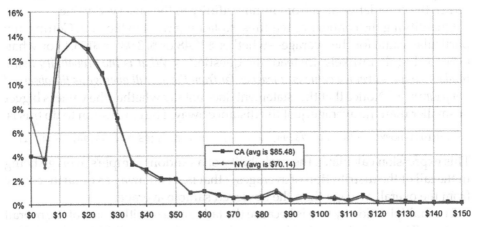

Figure 3-4: This chart shows the distribution of the `TotalPrice` of orders from New York and California.

The third approach is to list out all the different possible combinations of purchases and to calculate the averages for all of them. The information from all possible combinations makes it possible to determine how often the average in two groups exceeds the observed averages. This direct counting approach is too computationally intensive in this case, so this section does not go into detail into this approach. An example later in this chapter uses the counting approach.

Estimation Based on Two Samples

New York and California have 71,376 orders, with an average size of $73.98 and a standard deviation of $197.23. The orders from California are a subgroup of this population, comprising 17,839 orders with an average size of $85.48. *What is the confidence that this subgroup is just a random sample pulled from the data (meaning that the observed difference is due only to chance)?*

As mentioned earlier, the standard deviation of the sample average is the standard deviation of the overall data divided by the square root of the sample size. For instance, the 17,839 orders from California constitute a sample from the original population. Based on the overall data the average expected value should be $73.98 and the standard deviation $197.23 divided by the square root of 71,376, which is about $0.74.

An average of $85.48 seems quite far from $73.98, so it seems unlikely that the results for California are just "random" error. There is probably some cause for the difference. Perhaps Californians are different from New Yorkers in their affinity for various products. Perhaps marketing campaigns are different in the two states. Perhaps brand awareness differs in the two states.

The NORMDIST() function in Excel makes it possible to quantify the confidence. The first argument to NORMDIST() is the observed average, the second is the expected average, and then the standard deviation. The last argument tells NORMDIST() to return the cumulative area from minus infinity to the observed value.

Quantifying the confidence requires explaining what to look for. Getting any particular value for the average—whether $85.48 or $73.98 or $123.45 or whatever—is highly unlikely. Instead, the question is: *What is the probability that a random sample's average value is at least as far from the overall average as the observed sample average?* Notice that this statement does not say whether the value is bigger or smaller than the average, just the distance away. The expression to do this is:

```
=2*MIN(1-NORMDIST(85.14, 73.98, 0.74, 1), NORMDIST(85.14, 73.98, 0.74, 1))
```

This expression calculates the probability of a random sample's average being in the tail of the distribution of averages—that is, as far away as or farther away from the overall average than the observed sample average.

The multiplication by two is because the tail can be on either side of the overall average. The MIN() is needed because there are two possibilities, depending on whether the sample average is less than or greater than the overall average.

When the observed sample average is less than the overall average, the tail is from minus infinity to the observed value; NORMDIST() calculates this value. When the observed sample average is greater than the overall average, then the tail is on the other side and goes from the observed value to positive infinity; 1-NORMDIST() calculates this value.

For the case at hand, the calculated result gives a p-value that is indistinguishable from zero, meaning that the high value for California relative to New York is not due to chance.

Another way of looking at this is using the z-score, which measures the distance from the average to the observed value, in multiples of standard deviations. The expression to calculate the z-score is ($84.48 − $73.98)/$0.74, which comes to 14.2 standard deviations away. That is a long way away, and it is very, very, very unlikely that the average order size for California is due to nothing more than chance.

TIP The z-score measures how far away an observed value is from the, in units of standard deviations. It is the difference divided by the standard deviation. The z-score can be turned into a probability using the Excel formula 2*MIN(1-NORMSDIST(z-score), NORMSDIST(z-score)).

Estimation Based on Difference

The previous calculation compared the results of one state to the combined orders from both states. The following series of questions is a chain of reasoning that shows another way to think about this problem:

- Does the average TotalPrice differ between New York and California?
- Could the difference between the average TotalPrice for the two states be zero?
- What is the confidence of the Null Hypothesis that the difference between the TotalPrice of New York and the TotalPrice of California is zero?

That is, New York and California can be compared by calculating the difference between the two values rather than looking at the values themselves. The difference is $15.34 = $85.48 − $70.14. Given the information about the two groups, is this statistically significant?

Once again, the differences between the averages follow a distribution, whose average is zero (because samples from the same distribution have the same expected average). Calculating the standard deviation uses another formula from statistics. The standard deviation of the difference is the square root of the sum of the squares of the standard deviations of each sample. This formula is similar to the Pythagorean formula from high school geometry. Instead of sides of a right triangle, though, the formula is about standard deviations.

In the example, the standard error for California is $1.70 and for New York it is $0.81. The square root of the sum of the squares yields $1.88.

The observed difference of $15.34 corresponds to about eight standard deviations from zero. The corresponding p-value is essentially zero, meaning that the observed difference is likely to be significant. This produces the same result as before; orders from California and New York have differences that are not due merely to chance.

Investigating the distributions of the orders highlights some differences. New York has twice the proportion of orders whose TotalPrice is zero, which suggests that there is a difference between the states. For orders less than $100, the two states look identical. On the other hand, California has relatively more orders greater than $100.

Sampling from a Table

Sampling, however, is much more useful than just comparing average values. Here are some examples of how various samples might be used.

A sample of orders might be used for visualizing data. A scatter plot with tens or hundreds of thousands of points simply is not feasible; it will look like a big blob of color. However, getting a *random* sample of data might convey important information.

Sometimes, we might want to *repeat* the random sample, so it can be re-created at will. This is often true when—due to permissions—we are unable to store the sample in a table of our own.

A random sample is just what its name suggests—random. So, a given statistic on the sample, such as the average order size varies around the average in the entire population. Sometimes, we want to be sure that the data is as representative as possible for certain columns. For instance, we might want the average order size to be as similar to the overall population as possible. Or, the gender and channel mix to match the overall population. *Stratified* sampling handles this.

A balanced sample is also quite useful for comparing measures on different subsets of the population, such as responders and non-responders to a campaign. Often, one category dominates, so any attempt to visualize the data is really just about the dominant category. The solution is a *balanced* sample, where the sizes of each group are the same. A balanced sample can also be very useful as the training set for data mining algorithms.

Random Sample

A random sample is different from an arbitrary collection of rows, such as the first 10% that appear in the table. Statistically, "random" means that each row has the same probability of being selected. Many databases have a random number generator of some sort that can be used for this purpose. A typical function is

RAND(). It can be called without any arguments. Sometimes, the function takes an argument, which sets a *seed* so the same sequence of numbers can be generated at different times.

The following code (or similar code using the appropriate function) would work in many databases for obtaining a 10% random sample:

```
SELECT t.*
FROM <t> t
WHERE RAND() < 0.1
```

Note that this does not return exactly 10% of the rows. It is an approximation. Because the random numbers generators are usually pretty good, on a larger data set, it will return very close to 10% of the data.

This query does not work in SQL Server because the RAND() function in SQL Server function only returns one value for the entire query. The query returns all the rows in the table 10% of the time and no rows 90% of the time. The solution is to use a function such as NEWID(), which is guaranteed to return a different value each time it is called:

```
SELECT TOP 10 PERCENT t.*
FROM <t> t
ORDER BY NEWID()
```

This query does return exactly 10% of the data (well, within one record).

This version has to sort all the records in the table, which is rather expensive, in comparison to the WHERE clause. Another way of writing the above query is to seed the random number generator used by RAND() with value that changes each time the function is called. Unfortunately, the seed is an integer and the value returned by NEWID() is not an integer. Fortunately, the function CHECKSUM() bridges this gap:

```
SELECT t.*
FROM <t> t
WHERE RAND(CHECKSUM(NEWID())) < 0.1
```

This query seeds the random number generator with a different value each time it is called, satisfying the need for a different value with each call.

Repeatable Random Sample

Sometimes, a random sample needs to be reproducible at a different time. That is, you can reconstruct the same sample whenever you need to. One way to approach this is by using an id as a seed for the random number generator:

```
SELECT t.*
FROM <t> t
WHERE RAND(id) < 0.1
```

This generates the same random number each time an id is encountered. To get different samples, the seed can be modified as

```
WHERE RAND(id + 1) < 0.1
```

The number added to the seed changes the sample. Unfortunately, because of the nature of its random number generator, this does not work well in SQL Server.

Another approach is to use modulo arithmetic along with ROW_NUMBER(). This is technically called a pseudo-random number generator. It works by doing an arithmetic calculation on the row number and returning those rows:

```
WITH t as (
        SELECT t.*, ROW_NUMBER() OVER (ORDER BY col) as seqnum
        FROM <t> t
     )
SELECT t.*
FROM t
WHERE (t * 17 + 57) % 101 <= 10;
```

The expression % is the *modulus* operator. It calculates the remainder when the first number is divided by the second. So, 5 % 2 is 1 because that is the remainder after the division. Similarly, 120 % 101 is 19 because that is the remainder.

By adjusting the values in the WHERE expression, you can change the particular sample that you get. In general, it is best to use prime numbers for the constants.

Proportional Stratified Sample

A *proportional stratified* sample is a sample that guarantees that the distribution of values in one or more columns match the overall population as closely as possible. Consider the Subscribers table. In it, 47.18% of the subscribers are active, as returned by the following query:

```
SELECT AVG(1.0 * IsActive)
FROM Subscribers s;
```

The average for a random sample will be close to this value, but a bit different. For instance, the following does the same calculation on a pseudo-random sample of about 1% of the data:

```
WITH s as (
        SELECT s.*, ROW_NUMBER() OVER (ORDER BY SubscriberId) as seqnum
        FROM Subscribers s
     )
SELECT AVG(1.0 * IsActive)
FROM s
WHERE (seqnum * 17 + 59) % 101 < 1;
```

It returns 47.28%. This slight difference is expected. The average from random sample is going to vary. However, a sample that exactly matches the original distribution might be better for analytic or visualization purposes.

One way to do this in SQL is to order the data by the original values, and then take every nth record:

```
WITH s as (
    SELECT s.*, ROW_NUMBER() OVER (ORDER BY IsActive) as seqnum
    FROM Subscribers s
    )
SELECT AVG(1.0 * IsActive)
FROM s
WHERE seqnum % 100 = 1;
```

The CTE assigns a sequential number with all the non-actives assigned lower numbers followed by all the actives. By then pulling every hundredth record, the process takes—to a very close approximation—exactly one out of a hundred inactives and one out of a hundred actives. This version returns 47.18%, the same as the original data.

The beauty of stratified sampling is that it works with more than one variable. For instance, the following query does a stratified sample that has the same proportion of subscribers in each market as the original data and each market has the same rate of active users as in the original data:

```
WITH s as (
    SELECT s.*, ROW_NUMBER() OVER (ORDER BY Market, IsActive) as  seqnum
    FROM Subscribers s
    )
SELECT AVG(IsActive)
FROM s
WHERE seqnum % 100 = 1;
```

Notice that the ORDER BY clause contains all the variables used for stratification.

Stratification can also work on numeric and date variables as well. By ordering by the variable and taking an nth sample, the distribution of the variable in the sample should be almost exactly the same as in the original data.

Balanced Sample

A proportional stratified sample is a type of *stratified* sample. This is a sample where each value in a column (or combination of values from multiple columns) is sampled at a pre-defined rate. A *balanced sample* is another type of stratified sample. In the balanced sample, each value appears an equal number of times. This is particularly useful for a binary variable, and you want to use the sample for visualization or modeling purposes.

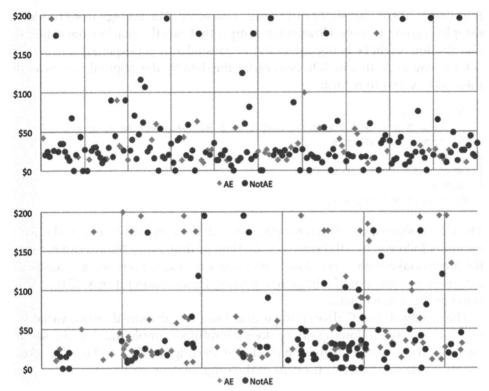

Figure 3-5: Comparison of 200 customers based on payment method. The upper chart shows the results on a random sample, the bottom on a balanced sample.

For instance, the upper chart in Figure 3-5 shows a scatter plot of 200 orders where the value is less than $200. Some of the points are for American Express payers. Some are for other payers. This table does not say much about American Express payers, except, perhaps, that AE is used in a minority of orders.

This table was generated using the following query:

```
SELECT TOP 200 OrderDate,
       (CASE WHEN PaymentType = 'AE' THEN TotalPrice END) as AE,
       (CASE WHEN PaymentType = 'AE' THEN NULL
             ELSE TotalPrice END) as NotAE
FROM Orders
WHERE TotalPrice <= 200
ORDER BY NEWID()
```

Note that this query uses exactly the same CASE logic for defining AE and NotAE, with the THEN and ELSE clauses swapped. This guarantees that each record will be counted on one side or the other. In particular, it takes care of NULL values without having to check for them explicitly.

The result is a table with three columns. This format is particularly suitable for creating a scatter plot for two series: one for AE and one for NotAE. The lower chart in Figure 3-5 shows a similar plot, but this time using a balanced sample. The balanced sample much more clearly shows that AE is associated with larger orders. Although true in the first picture as well, it is not obvious. The first picture has an equal number of high-valued orders for AE and NotAE. Because AE accounts for fewer than 30% of the orders, you would not expect the two groups to be equally represented.

TIP A balanced sample can help visualize differences among a handful of groups. This is useful for spotting differences qualitatively.

The query to produce the data assigns a random sequence number to each group, using ROW_NUMBER():

```
WITH o as (
      SELECT o.*,
             ROW_NUMBER() OVER (PARTITION BY isae
                                ORDER BY NEWID()) as seqnum
      FROM (SELECT o.*,
                   (CASE WHEN PaymentType = 'AE' THEN 1 ELSE 0
                    END) as IsAE
            FROM Orders o
            WHERE TotalPrice <= 200
           ) o
     )
SELECT OrderDate,
       (CASE WHEN isae = 1 THEN TotalPrice END) as AE,
       (CASE WHEN isae = 0 THEN TotalPrice END) as NotAE
FROM o
WHERE seqnum <= 100
```

The only other subtlety is putting the WHERE clause in the subquery rather than in the outer query. The query filters the orders *before* doing the ROW_NUMBER() calculation to ensure that one hundred rows for each group are selected.

Counting Possibilities

Averages are interesting, but many of the comparisons between customers involve counts, such as the number of customers who have responded to an offer, or who have stopped, or who prefer particular products. Counting is a simple process, and one that computers excel at.

Counting is not just about individuals, it is also about counting combinations. For instance, if there are ten teams in a baseball league, how many different possible games are there? Figure 3-6 illustrates the 45 different possible games between two teams in the league; each possible game is a line segment connecting two boxes. This type of chart is called a link chart, and it can be created in Excel as explained in the aside "Creating a Link Chart Using Excel Charts."

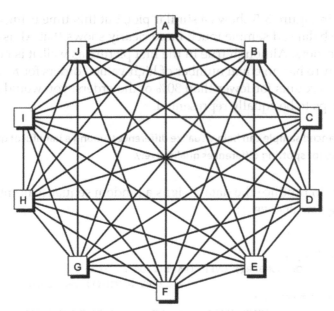

Figure 3-6: There are 45 different possible games in a Little League club with ten teams. In this chart, each line connecting two boxes represents one possible game.

The study of such combinations is called *combinatorics*, a field that straddles probability and statistics. The rest of the chapter looks at statistical approximations to questions about combinations, approximations that are good enough for everyday use.

This section starts with a small example that can easily be illustrated and counted by hand. The ideas are then extended to the larger numbers found in customer databases, along with the SQL and Excel code needed for doing the calculations.

How Many Men?

This first counting example asks the following two questions about a committee that has five members:

- ▪ What is the probability that the committee has exactly two men?
- ▪ What is the probability that the committee has at most two men?

For the purposes of this example, men and women are equally likely to be on the committee.

Table 3-3 lists the 32 possible combinations of people that could be on the committee, in terms of gender. One combination has all males. One has all females. Five each have exactly one male or exactly one female. In all, there are 32 combinations, which is two raised to the fifth power: "Two," because there are two possibilities, male or female; "fifth power," because there are five people on the committee.

CREATING A LINK CHART USING EXCEL CHARTS

The chart in Figure 3-6 is a link chart that shows connections between pairs of things (in this case, teams). Perhaps surprisingly, this is an Excel scatter plot. There are two advantages to doing this in Excel rather than manually in PowerPoint or another tool. First, the boxes and lines can be placed precisely where they need to be, which gives the chart a cleaner and more professional look. Second, making small changes, such as moving a box or changing a label, should be easier because everything in the chart is created from data used to generate the chart.

When thinking about making a complicated, nontraditional chart, divide the problem into manageable pieces. This chart has three such pieces:

■ The ten teams, which are represented as squares, arrayed around a circle

■ The letter representing each team, inside the squares

■ The lines connecting the teams together

The first step is to place the squares representing the teams. For this, we dip into trigonometry, and set the X-coordinates using the sine of an angle and the Y-coordinate using the cosine. The basic formula for the nth team is:

```
<x-coordinate> = SIN(2*PI()/<n>)
<y-coordinate> = COS(2*PI()/<n>)
```

In the actual chart, these are rotated by a fraction, by adding an offset inside the `SIN()` and `COS()` functions. These formulas give the positions of the teams, as X- and Y-coordinates.

Labeling the points with the team names is a bit more challenging. There are three options for labeling points. Two of them use the X- and Y-coordinates, but these are always numbers. The third option, the "Series name" option, is the only way to get a name. This unfortunately requires creating a separate series for each point, so each has a unique name. The following steps accomplish this:

1. Put the X-coordinate in one column.

2. Label the columns to the right sequentially with the desired names (A, B, C, and so on). These columns contain the Y-coordinate for the points.

3. In the column for team "A," all the values are `NA()`, except for the one corresponding to the A value, and so on for the other columns.

A useful formula to set the values in this table is something like:

```
=IF($G3=J$2, $E3, NA())
```

This formula assumes that the Y-coordinates are in column E, and the team labels are in both row 2 as column headers and in column G as row labels. By careful use of absolute and relative references (the use of "$" in the cell reference), this formula can be copied through the whole range of cells.

The result is an array of cells with values shown in Table 3-2. The first column is the X-coordinate, the second is the Y-coordinate, and the rest are the Y-coordinates for a single team, with other values in the columns being #N/A.

continues

continued

Table 3-2: Pivoting the Y-Values for a Circular Link Chart

| Y | X-VALUE | Y-VALUE | | | | | | |
		ALL	A	B	C	D	...	J
A	0.00	1.00	1.00	#N/A	#N/A	#N/A		#N/A
B	0.59	0.81	#N/A	0.81	#N/A	#N/A		#N/A
C	0.95	0.31	#N/A	#N/A	0.31	#N/A		#N/A
D	0.95	−0.31	#N/A	#N/A	#N/A	−0.31		#N/A
E	0.59	−0.81	#N/A	#N/A	#N/A	#N/A		#N/A
F	0.00	−1.00	#N/A	#N/A	#N/A	#N/A		#N/A
G	−0.59	−0.81	#N/A	#N/A	#N/A	#N/A		#N/A
H	−0.95	−0.31	#N/A	#N/A	#N/A	#N/A		#N/A
I	−0.95	0.31	#N/A	#N/A	#N/A	#N/A		#N/A
J	−0.59	0.81	#N/A	#N/A	#N/A	#N/A		0.81

Select the whole table starting from the X-value and insert a scatter plot with no lines. The first series represents all ten teams. For these, set the marker to squares with a white background and shadow; this chart uses a size of 15 for the marker. The rest of the series are for the labels, which have to be inserted individually. To do this, select the series on the chart and set the line and marker patterns to "None." Then click the "Data Labels" tab and choose "Series name" and click "OK." When the label appears, right-click it and choose "Format Data Labels." On the "Alignment" tab, set the "Label Position" to be "Center." With this process, the boxes and their labels are on the chart.

The final step is to include the lines that connect the squares. The idea is to have a table of X- and Y-coordinates and to add a new series into the scatter plot that has lines between the points, but no markers. Unfortunately, the scatter plot connects all points, one after the other, which is like trying to draw the lines without lifting a pencil from the paper. This is hard. Fortunately, when a point has an #N/A value, the scatter plot does not draw the lines going to or from the point; this is like lifting the pencil off the paper. So, each pair of points that defines a connection needs to be interspersed with #N/A values.

There are 45 unique line segments in the chart because each team only needs to be connected to the teams after it alphabetically. "A" gets connected to "B" and "C" and so on. However, "I" only gets connected to "J." These segments are placed in a table, where three rows define the segment. Two rows define the beginning and ending of the line, and the third contains the function NA(). A point from the table makes the line disappear from the chart.

The resulting chart uses 12 different series. One series defines the points, which are placed as boxes. Ten define the labels inside the boxes. And the twelfth series defines the line segments that connect them together.

Table 3-3: Thirty-two Possibilities of Gender on a Committee of Five

	PERSON #1	PERSON #2	PERSON #3	PERSON #4	PERSON #5	# M	# F
1	M	M	M	M	M	5	0
2	M	M	M	M	F	4	1
3	M	M	M	F	M	4	1
4	M	M	M	F	F	3	2
5	M	M	F	M	M	4	1
6	M	M	F	M	F	3	2
7	M	M	F	F	M	3	2
8	M	M	F	F	F	2	3
9	M	F	M	M	M	4	1
10	M	F	M	M	F	3	2
11	M	F	M	F	M	3	2
12	M	F	M	F	F	2	3
13	M	F	F	M	M	3	2
14	M	F	F	M	F	2	3
15	M	F	F	F	M	2	3
16	M	F	F	F	F	1	4
17	F	M	M	M	M	4	1
18	F	M	M	M	F	3	2
19	F	M	M	F	M	3	2
20	F	M	M	F	F	2	3
21	F	M	F	M	M	3	2
22	F	M	F	M	F	2	3
23	F	M	F	F	M	2	3
24	F	M	F	F	F	1	4
25	F	F	M	M	M	3	2
26	F	F	M	M	F	2	3
27	F	F	M	F	M	2	3
28	F	F	M	F	F	1	4
29	F	F	F	M	M	2	3
30	F	F	F	M	F	1	4
31	F	F	F	F	M	1	4
32	F	F	F	F	F	0	5

All these combinations are equally likely, and they can be used to answer the original questions. Ten rows in the table have exactly two males: rows 8, 12, 14, 15, 20, 22, 23, 26, 27, and 29. That is, 10/32 or about 31% of the combinations have exactly two males. An additional six rows have zero or one males, for a total of 16 combinations with two or fewer males. So, exactly half of all possible committees have two or fewer men.

Listing the combinations provides insight, but is cumbersome for all but the simplest problems. Fortunately, Excel has two functions that do the work for us. The function COMBIN(n, m) calculates the number of combinations of *m* things taken from *n* things. The question "How many committees of five people have two males" is really asking "How many ways are there to choose two things (male) from five (the committee size)." The Excel formula is =COMBIN(5, 2).

This function returns the number of combinations, but the original questions asked for the proportion of possible committees having exactly two, or two or fewer, males. This proportion is answered using something called the binomial formula, which is provided in Excel as the function BINOM.DIST(). This function takes four arguments:

- The size of the group (the bigger number)
- The number being chosen (the smaller number)
- The probability (50%, in this case) of being chosen
- A flag that is 0 for the exact probability and 1 for the probability of less than or equal to the number chosen

So, the following two formulas provide the answers to the original questions:

```
=BINOM.DIST(5, 2, 50%, 0)
=BINOM.DIST(5, 2, 50%, 1)
```

These formulas simplify the calculations needed to answer each question to a single function call. The purpose here is not to show the actual steps that BINOM.DIST() uses to make the calculation (which involves a lot of messy arithmetic). Instead, the purpose is to describe intuitively what's happening in terms of combinations of people. The binomial distribution function merely simplifies the calculation.

How Many Californians?

The second example asks a very similar question about a group of five people. In this case, the question is about where people are from. Let's assume that one in ten people who could be on the committee are from California (very roughly about one in ten Americans live in California).

- What is the probability that the committee has exactly two Californians?
- What is the probability that the committee has at most two Californians?

Table 3-4 lists all the possibilities. This table is similar to the example for gender, but with two differences. First, each possibility consists of five probabilities, one for each

Table 3-4: Thirty-two Possibilities of State of Origin on a Committee of Five

	#1	#2	#3	#4	#5	PROB	# CA	# NOT CA
1	10%	10%	10%	10%	10%	0.001%	5	0
2	10%	10%	10%	10%	90%	0.009%	4	1
3	10%	10%	10%	90%	10%	0.009%	4	1
4	10%	10%	10%	90%	90%	0.081%	3	2
5	10%	10%	90%	10%	10%	0.009%	4	1
6	10%	10%	90%	10%	90%	0.081%	3	2
7	10%	10%	90%	90%	10%	0.081%	3	2
8	10%	10%	90%	90%	90%	0.729%	2	3
9	10%	90%	10%	10%	10%	0.009%	4	1
10	10%	90%	10%	10%	90%	0.081%	3	2
11	10%	90%	10%	90%	10%	0.081%	3	2
12	10%	90%	10%	90%	90%	0.729%	2	3
13	10%	90%	90%	10%	10%	0.081%	3	2
14	10%	90%	90%	10%	90%	0.729%	2	3
15	10%	90%	90%	90%	10%	0.729%	2	3
16	10%	90%	90%	90%	90%	6.561%	1	4
17	90%	10%	10%	10%	10%	0.009%	4	1
18	90%	10%	10%	10%	90%	0.081%	3	2
19	90%	10%	10%	90%	10%	0.081%	3	2
20	90%	10%	10%	90%	90%	0.729%	2	3
21	90%	10%	90%	10%	10%	0.081%	3	2
22	90%	10%	90%	10%	90%	0.729%	2	3
23	90%	10%	90%	90%	10%	0.729%	2	3
24	90%	10%	90%	90%	90%	6.561%	1	4
25	90%	90%	10%	10%	10%	0.081%	3	2
26	90%	90%	10%	10%	90%	0.729%	2	3
27	90%	90%	10%	90%	10%	0.729%	2	3
28	90%	90%	10%	90%	90%	6.561%	1	4
29	90%	90%	90%	10%	10%	0.729%	2	3
30	90%	90%	90%	10%	90%	6.561%	1	4
31	90%	90%	90%	90%	10%	6.561%	1	4
32	90%	90%	90%	90%	90%	59.049%	0	5

person in the group. The probability is either 10% for the possibility that someone is from California or 90% for the possibility that the person is from somewhere else.

In addition, the overall probability for that occurrence is included as an additional column. In the gender example, each gender is equally likely, so all rows have equal weights. In this case, being from California is less likely than not being from California, so the rows have different weights. The overall probability for any given row is the product of that row's probabilities. The probability that all five people are from California is 10%*10%*10%*10%*10%, which is 0.001%. The probability that none of the five are from California is 90%*90%*90%*90%*90%, or about 59%. The possibilities are no longer equally likely.

Once again, the detail is interesting. In such a small example, counting all the different possibilities is feasible. For example, Table 3-5 shows the probabilities for having zero to five Californians in the group. These numbers can be readily calculated in Excel using the `BINOM.DIST()` function, using an expression such as `BINOM.DIST(5, 2, 10%, 0)` to calculate the probability that the committee has exactly two Californians.

Null Hypothesis and Confidence

Let's return to the gender breakdown of five people on a committee. This example shows that even when the members are equally split between males and females there is still a chance of finding a unisex committee (either all male or all female). In fact, 6.2% of the time the committee is unisex, assuming that the participants are chosen randomly. If there were enough committees, about 6.2% of them would be unisex, assuming the members are chosen randomly from a pool that is half women and half men.

Does one committee that is unisex support that idea that gender was involved in selecting the members? Or, is it reasonable that the committee was selected randomly? Intuitively we might say that it is obvious that gender was used as a selection criterion. If people of only one gender were included, it seems obvious that people of the other gender were excluded. This intuition would be wrong

Table 3-5: Probability of Having *n* Californians on a Committee of Five

# CA	# NON-CA	PROBABILITY
0	5	59.049%
1	4	32.805%
2	3	7.290%
3	2	0.810%
4	1	0.045%
5	0	0.001%

over 6% of the time. And without any other information, whether or not we think the committee shows bias depends on our own personal confidence thresholds.

The Null Hypothesis is that the committee members are chosen randomly, without regard to gender. *What is the confidence that the Null Hypothesis is true, assuming that there is one committee and that committee is unisex?* Out of 32 possible gender combinations, two are unisex. Randomly, unisex committees would be chosen 2/32 or 6% of the time. A common statistical test is 5%, so this exceeds the statistical threshold. Using this level of statistical significance, even a unisex committee is not evidence of bias.

On the other hand, a unisex committee is either all female or all male. Looking at the particular gender reduces the possibilities to one out of 32 (that is, one out of 32 possible committees are all female; and one out of 32 are all male). Including the gender changes the confidence to about 3%, in which case an all-male or all-female committee suggests that the Null Hypothesis is false, using the standard statistic level of significance. The fact that looking at the problem in two slightly different ways produces different results is a good lesson to remember when facing problems in the real world.

> **WARNING** Slightly changing the problem (such as looking at unisex committees versus all-male or all-female committees) can change the answer to a question. Be clear about stating the problem to be solved.

Let's now look at the second example of Californians. What if all members were from California? The Null Hypothesis is that people in the committee are chosen irrespective of their state of origin. There is only a 0.001% chance that a randomly selected committee of five would consist only of Californians. In this case, we would be quite confident that the Null Hypothesis is false. And that in turn suggests some sort of bias in the process of choosing the members. In this case, we would be right in assuming a bias 99.999% of the time.

How Many Customers Are Still Active?

Analyzing committees of five members gives insight into the process of counting possibilities to arrive at probabilities and confidence levels. More interesting examples use customer data. Let's consider the customers in the subscription database who started exactly one year before the cutoff date, and of them, the proportion that stopped in the first year. In this table, active customers are identified by having the STOP_TYPE column set to NULL. The following SQL calculates this summary information:

```
SELECT COUNT(*) as numstarts,
       SUM(CASE WHEN StopType IS NOT NULL THEN 1 ELSE 0 END) as numstops,
       AVG(CASE WHEN StopType IS NOT NULL THEN 1.0 ELSE 0 END
          ) as stoprate
FROM Subscribers
WHERE StartDate = '2005-12-28'
```

Notice that the query uses the floating-point constant 1.0 for the average rather than the integer 1. This ensures that the average is a floating-point average.

This query returns the following results:

- Exactly 2,409 customers started one year before the cutoff date.
- Of these, 484 were stopped on the cutoff date.
- The stop rate is 20.1%.

Both the number stopped and the stop rate are accurate measurements about what happened to the 2,409 customers who started on 2005-12-28. What are the confidence intervals for these numbers (assuming we want to generalize the result to the whole population)?

This question supposes that there is a process causing customers to stop. This process is random and behaves like a lottery. Customers who have the right lottery ticket stop (or perhaps customers that have the wrong ticket?); everyone else remains active. Our goal is to understand this process better.

The first approach assumes that the number of stops is fixed. *Given the number of stops, what range of stop rates is likely to cause exactly that number of stops?*

The second approach assumes that the stop rate is really fixed at 20.1%. *If this is the case, how many customers would we expect to stop?* Remember the committee example. Even though the members have an equal probability of being male or female, the committee can still take on any combination of genders. The same is true here. The next two subsections examine these approaches in more detail. The methods are similar to the methods used for understanding the committee; however, the details are a bit different because the sizes are larger.

Given the Count, What Is the Probability?

The observed stop rate is 20.1% for the one-year subscribers. Let's propose a hypothesis that the stop process actually has a stop rate of 15% rather than the observed rate. The observed 484 stops are just an outlier, in the same way that five people chosen for a committee, at random, all turn out to be women.

Figure 3-7 shows the distribution of values for the number of stops, given that the stop rate is 15%, both as a discrete histogram and as a cumulative distribution. The discrete histogram shows the probability of getting exactly that number of stops; this is called the *distribution*. The *cumulative distribution* shows the probability of getting up to that many stops.

A 15% stop rate should produce, on average, 361 stops (15% of 2,409); this overall average is called the *expected value*. The 484 stops are actually 123 more stops than the expected value, leading to the question: *What is the probability (p-value) of being 123 or more stops away from the expected value?* And this question has an answer. To a very close approximation, the probability is 0%. The actual number is more like 0.0000000015%; calculated using the formula 2*MIN(1-BINOM.

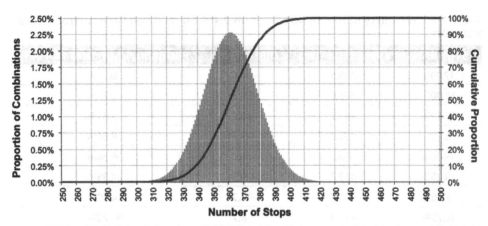

Figure 3-7: The proportion of combinations with a given number of stops, assuming a 15% stop rate and 2,409 starts, follows a binomial distribution.

DIST(484, 2409, 15%, 1), BINOM.DIST(484, 2409, 15%, 1)). The p-value is twice the size of the tail of the distribution.

So, it is very, very, very unlikely that the original stop rate was 15%. In fact, it is so unlikely that we can simply ignore the possibility and assume that the stop rate was higher. Okay, so the stop rate is not 15%. What about 16%? Or 17%? Table 3-6 shows the probability of being in the tail of the distribution for a range of different stop rates. Based on this table, it is reasonable to say that the stop rate for the underlying stop process could really be anywhere from about 18.5% to about 21.5%.

This is a very important idea, so it is worth reconstructing the thought process. First, there was a hypothesis. This hypothesis stated that the actual stop process stop rate is 15% rather than the observed value of 20.1%. Assuming this hypothesis to be true, we then looked at all the different possible combinations of stops that a 15% stop rate would result in. Of course, listing out all the combinations would be too cumbersome; fortunately, the binomial formula simplifies the calculation. Based on these counts, we saw that the observed number of stops—484—was quite far from the expected number of stops, 361. In fact, there is essentially a 0% probability that an observation 123 or more stops away from the average would be observed.

There is nothing magic or general about the fact that 15% does not work and values roughly in the range 19%–21% do work. The confidence depends on the number of starts in the data. If there were only 100 starts, the difference between 15% and 20% would not be statistically significant.

Given the Probability, What Is the Number of Stops?

The second question is the inverse of the first one: *Given that the underlying stop process has a stop rate of 20.1%, what is the likely number of stops?* This is a direct application of the binomial formula. The calculation BINOM.DIST(484, 2409, 20.1%, 0) returns

Table 3-6: Probability of Having 484 Stops on 2,409 Starts Given Various Hypothetical Stop Rates

STOP RATE	EXPECTED STOPS	DIFFERENCE	PROBABILITY OF THAT FAR OFF
17.00%	409.5	−74.5	0.01%
18.00%	433.6	−50.4	0.77%
18.50%	445.7	−38.3	4.33%
18.75%	451.7	−32.3	8.86%
19.00%	457.7	−26.3	16.56%
19.25%	463.7	−20.3	28.35%
19.50%	469.8	−14.2	44.70%
19.75%	475.8	−8.2	65.23%
19.90%	479.4	−4.6	79.06%
20.00%	481.8	−2.2	88.67%
20.10%	484.2	0.2	98.42%
20.25%	487.8	3.8	87.01%
20.50%	493.8	9.8	64.00%
20.75%	499.9	15.9	44.12%
21.00%	505.9	21.9	28.43%
21.25%	511.9	27.9	17.08%
21.50%	517.9	33.9	9.56%
21.75%	524.0	40.0	4.97%
22.00%	530.0	46.0	2.41%
22.50%	542.0	58.0	0.45%
23.00%	554.1	70.1	0.06%

2.03%, saying that only about one time in 50 do exactly 484 stops result. Even with a stop rate of exactly 20.1%, the expected value of 484 stops is achieved only 2% of the time by a random process. With so many starts, getting a few more or a few less is reasonable, assuming that the underlying process is random.

The expected range accounting for 95% of the number of stops can be calculated using the binomial formula. This range goes from 445 stops to 523 stops, which in turn corresponds to a measured stop rate between 18.5% and 21.7%. Table 3-7 shows the probability of the number of stops being in particular ranges around 484 stops.

The Rate or the Number?

Time for a philosophy break. This analysis started with very hard numbers: exactly 484 out of 2,409 customers stopped in the first year. After applying some ideas from statistics and probability, the hard numbers have become softer. An

Table 3-7: Probability of a 20% Stop Rate Resulting in Various Ranges Around the Expected Value of 484 Stops

WIDTH	LOWER BOUND	HIGHER BOUND	PROBABILITY
3	483.0	485.0	4.42%
15	477.0	491.0	27.95%
25	472.0	496.0	45.80%
51	459.0	509.0	79.46%
75	447.0	521.0	93.91%
79	445.0	523.0	95.18%
101	434.0	534.0	98.88%
126	421.0	546.0	99.86%
151	409.0	559.0	99.99%

exact count has become a confidence of a value within a certain interval. Are we better off with or without the statistical analysis?

The situation is more reasonable than it appears. The first observation is that the range of 445 stops to 523 stops might seem wide. In fact, it is rather wide. However, if there were a million customers who started, with a stop rate of 20.1%, then the corresponding range would be much tighter. The equivalent confidence range would be from about 200,127 to 201,699 stops—or from 20.01% to 20.17%. More data implies narrower confidence intervals.

Why is there a confidence interval at all? This is an important question. The answer is because of the assumption that customers stop because of some unseen process that affects all customers equally. This process causes some percentage of customers to stop in the first year. However, the decision of whether one particular customer stops is like rolling dice or tossing a coin, which means that there might be unusually lucky streaks (lower stop rates) or unusually unlucky streaks (higher stop rates), in the same way that a randomly chosen committee could have five men or five women.

A random process differs from a deterministic process that says that every fifth customer is going to stop in the first year, or that we'll cancel the accounts of everyone named "Pat" at day 241. The results from a deterministic process are exact, ignoring the small deviations that might arise due to operational error. For instance, for customers who have already started, the start process is deterministic; exactly 2,409 customers started. There is no confidence interval on this. The number really is 2,409. The statistics measure the "decision-to-stop" process, something that is only observed by its actual effects on stops.

This section started with an example of a committee with five members and moved to a larger example on thousands of starts. As the size of the population increases, confidence in the results increases as well, and the corresponding confidence intervals become narrower. As the population gets larger, whether we look at the ratio or the absolute number becomes less important, simply because both appear to be quite accurate. Fortunately, databases store a lot of data, so corresponding confidence intervals are often small enough to ignore.

> **TIP** On large datasets, charts that show visible differences between groups of customers are usually showing differences that are statistically significant.

Ratios and Their Statistics

The binomial distribution just counts up all the different combinations and determines which proportion of them meets particular conditions. This is very powerful for finding confidence intervals for a random process, as described in the previous section. This section introduces an alternative method that estimates a standard deviation for a ratio, and uses the normal distribution to approximate confidence ratios.

Using the normal distribution has two advantages over the binomial distribution. First, it is applicable in more areas than the binomial distribution; for instance, the methods here are more suited for comparing two ratios and asking whether they are the same. Second, SQL does not support the calculations needed for the binomial distribution, but it does support almost all the calculations needed for this method.

This section introduces the method for estimating the standard deviation of a ratio (which is actually derived from the *standard error of a proportion*). This is then applied to comparing two different ratios. Finally, the section shows how to use these ideas to produce lower bounds for ratios that might be more appropriate for conservative comparisons of different groups.

Standard Error of a Proportion

Remember that a standard error is just the standard deviation of some statistic that has been measured on samples of the overall data. In this case, the statistic is a ratio of two variables, such as the number of stops divided by the number of starts. The formula for the standard error is simple and can easily be expressed in SQL or Excel:

```
STDERR = SQRT(<ratio> * (1 - <ratio>) / <number of data points>)
```

That is, the standard error is the square root of the product of the observed probability times one minus the observed probability divided by the sample size.

The following SQL query calculates both the standard error and the lower and upper bounds of the 95% confidence interval:

```
SELECT stoprate - 1.96 * stderr as conflower,
       stoprate + 1.96 * stderr as confupper,
       stoprate, stderr, numstarts, numstops
FROM (SELECT SQRT(stoprate * (1 - stoprate) / numstarts) as stderr,
             stoprate, numstarts, numstops
      FROM (SELECT COUNT(*) as numstarts,
                   SUM(CASE WHEN StopType IS NOT NULL THEN 1 ELSE 0
                       END) as numstops,
                   AVG(CASE WHEN StopType IS NOT NULL THEN 1.0 ELSE 0
                       END) as stoprate
            FROM Subscribers
            WHERE StartDate = '2005-12-28') s
     ) s
```

This SQL query uses two nested subqueries to define the columns `numstops`, `stoprate`, and `stderr`. The overall expression could be written without subqueries, but that would result in a messier query.

This query uses the constant 1.96 to define the 95% confidence bounds for the interval. The result is the interval from 18.5% to 21.7%. Recall that using the binomial distribution, the exact confidence interval was 18.5% to 21.7%. The results are, fortunately and not surprisingly, remarkably close. The standard error of proportions is an approximation that uses the normal distribution, it is a very good approximation.

The standard error can be used in reverse as well. In the earlier polling example, the standard error was 1.27% and the expected probability was 50%. What does this say about the number of people who were polled? For this, the calculation simply goes in reverse. The formula is:

```
<number> = <ratio> * (1 - <ratio>) / (<stderr>^2)
```

For the polling example, it gives the value of 1,552, which is a reasonable size for a poll.

One important observation about the standard error and the population size is that halving the standard error corresponds to increasing the population size by a factor of four. In plainer language, there is a trade-off between cost and accuracy. Reducing the standard error on the poll to 0.635%, half of 1.27%, would require polling four times as many people, over 6,000 people instead of 1,500. This would presumably increase costs by a factor of four. Reducing the standard error increases costs.

Confidence Interval on Proportions

Confidence intervals can be derived from the standard error. The three markets in the subscription data have the following stop rates for customers who started on 2005-12-26 (this example uses a slightly different stop rate from the previous example):

- Gotham, 35.2%
- Metropolis, 34.0%
- Smallville, 20.9%

Are we confident that these stop rates are different? Or, might they all be the same? Although it seems unlikely that they are the same because Smallville is much smaller than the others, remember that a group of five people drawn at random all have the same genders over 5% of the time. Even though Smallville has a lower stop rate, it might still be just another reasonable sample.

The place to start is with the confidence intervals for each market. The following query does this calculation:

```
SELECT Market, stoprate - 1.96 * stderr as conflower,
       stoprate + 1.96 * stderr as confupper,
       stoprate, stderr, numstarts, numstops
FROM (SELECT Market,
             SQRT(stoprate * (1 - stoprate) / numstarts) as stderr,
             stoprate, numstarts, numstops
      FROM (SELECT market, COUNT(*) as numstarts,
                   SUM(CASE WHEN StopType IS NOT NULL THEN 1 ELSE 0
                       END) as numstops,
                   AVG(CASE WHEN StopType IS NOT NULL THEN 1.0 ELSE 0
                       END) as stoprate
            FROM Subscribers
            WHERE StartDate IN ('2005-12-26')
            GROUP BY Market) s
     ) s
```

This query is very similar to the query for the overall calculation, with the addition of the aggregation by market.

The results in Table 3-8 make it clear that the stop rate for Smallville is different from the stop rates for Gotham and Metropolis. The 95% confidence interval for Smallville does not overlap with the confidence intervals of the other two markets, as shown in Figure 3-8. This is a strong condition. When the confidence intervals do not overlap, there is a high confidence that the ratios are different.

Table 3-8: Confidence Intervals by Markets for Starts on 26 Dec 2005

| MARKET | STARTS | STOPS | | 95% CONFIDENCE | | |
		#	RATE	LOWER BOUND	UPPER BOUND	STANDARD ERROR
Gotham	2,256	794	35.2%	33.2%	37.2%	1.0%
Metropolis	1,134	385	34.0%	31.2%	36.7%	1.4%
Smallville	666	139	20.9%	17.8%	24.0%	1.6%

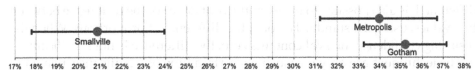

Figure 3-8: When confidence intervals do not overlap, there is a high level of confidence that the observed values really are different. So Smallville is clearly different from Gotham and Metropolis.

Figure 3-8, by the way, is an Excel scatter plot. The X-axis has the stop rate for each market. The Y-values are simply 1, 2, and 3 (because Excel does not allow names to be values for a scatter plot); the Y-axis itself has been removed because it adds no useful information to the chart. The intervals use the X-Error Bar feature, and the labels on the points were added manually, by typing in text and placing the labels where desired.

Difference of Proportions

For Metropolis and Gotham, the situation is different because their confidence intervals do overlap. The difference between their observed stop rates is 1.2%. *How likely is it that this difference is due just to chance, if we assume the Null Hypothesis that the two values are really equal?*

The standard error for the difference between two proportions is quite reasonably called the *standard error of the difference of proportions*. The formula is easily calculated in Excel or SQL:

```
STDERR = SQRT(((<ratio1>*(1-<ratio1>)/<size1>) + (<ratio2>*(1-<ratio2>)/<size2>))
```

That is, the standard error of the difference of two proportions is the square root of the sum of the squares of the standard errors of each proportion (this is basically the same as the standard error of a difference of two values). The calculation yields a standard error of 1.7% for the difference. The observed difference is 1.2%, resulting in a z-score of 0.72 (the z-score is 1.2%/1.7%). Such a small z-score is well within a reasonable range, so the difference is not significant.

Another way of looking at this is using the 95% confidence interval. The lower bound is at the observed difference minus 1.96*1.7% and the upper bound is the observed difference plus 1.96*1.7%, which comes to a range from –2.2% to 4.6%. Because the confidence interval is both positive and negative, it includes zero. That is, Gotham and Metropolis could actually have the same stop rate, or Metropolis's stop rate could even be bigger than Gotham's (the opposite of the observed ordering). The observed difference could easily be due to randomness of the underlying stop process.

This example shows the different ways that the standard error can be used. When confidence intervals do not overlap, the observed values are statistically different. It is also possible to measure the confidence of the difference between two values, using the standard error of the difference of proportions. When the resulting confidence interval contains zero, the difference is not significant.

The techniques are only measuring a certain type of significance, related to the randomness of underlying processes. The observed values can still provide guidance. There is some evidence that Gotham has a higher stop rate than Metropolis, some evidence but not enough to be confident. If we had to choose one market or the other for a retention program to save customers, Gotham would be the likelier candidate because its stop rate is larger. The choice of Gotham over Metropolis is based on weak evidence because the difference is not statistically significant.

Conservative Lower Bounds

Notice that the confidence intervals for the three markets all have different standard errors. This is mostly because the size of each market is different (and to a much lesser extent to the fact that the measured stop rates are different). To be conservative, it is sometimes useful to use the observed value minus one standard error, rather than the observed value. This can change the relative values of different groups, particularly because the standard error on a small group is larger than the standard error on a larger group. In some cases, using a conservative estimate changes the ordering of the different groups, although that is not true in this case.

TIP When comparing ratios on groups that have different sizes, a conservative estimate for the comparison is the observed ratio minus one standard deviation.

Chi-Square

The chi-square test (pronounced to rhyme with "guy" and starting with a hard "c" sound) provides another method for addressing the question "how different is different?" The chi-square test is appropriate when comparing multiple dimensions to each other. Instead of just looking at the "stop rate" for customers, for instance, the customers are divided into two distinct groups, those who stopped and those who are active. These groups can then be compared across different dimensions, such as channel, market, or the period when they started.

The chi-square test does not create confidence intervals because confidence intervals do not make as much sense across multiple dimensions. Instead, it calculates the confidence that the observed counts are due to chance by comparing the observed counts to expected counts. Because the chi-square test does not use confidence intervals, it avoids some of the logical conundrums that occur at the edges, such as when the confidence interval for a ratio crosses the 0% or

100% thresholds. Proportions are in the range of 0% to 100%, and so too should be their confidence intervals.

Expected Values

Consider customers who started on 2005-12-06. What is the number of stops expected for each of the three markets? A simple way to calculate these expected values is to observe that the overall stop rate is 32.5% for starts from that day. So, given that Gotham had 2,256 starts, there should be about 733.1 stops (32.5% * 2,256). In other words, assuming that all the markets behave the same way, the stops should be equally distributed.

In actual fact, Gotham has 794 stops, not 733.1. It exceeds the expected number by 60.9 stops. The difference between the observed value and the expected value is the *deviation*; Table 3-9 shows the observed values, expected values, and deviations for stops in all three markets.

The expected values have some useful properties. For instance, the sum of the expected values is the same as the sum of the observed values. In addition, the total number of expected stops is the same as the number of observed stops; and the totals in each market are the same. The expected values have the same numbers of actives and stops; they are just arranged differently.

The deviations for each row have the same absolute values, but one is positive and the other negative. For Gotham, the "active customer" deviation is –60.9 and the "stopped customer" deviation is +60.9, so the row deviations sum to zero. This property is not a coincidence. The sum of the deviations along each row and each column always adds up to zero, regardless of the number of rows and columns.

Calculating the expected values from the raw tabular data is simple. Figure 3-9 shows the Excel formulas. First, the sums of the counts in each row and each column are calculated, as well as the sum of all cells in the table. The expected value for each cell is the row sum total times the column sum divided by the overall sum. With good use of relative and absolute cell range references, it is easy to write this formula once, and then copy it to the other five cells.

With this background, the chi-square question is: *What is the likelihood that the deviations are due strictly to chance?* If this likelihood is very low, then we are confident that there is a difference among the markets. If the likelihood is high

Table 3-9: Observed and Expected Values of Active and Stopped Customers, by Market

	OBSERVED		EXPECTED		DEVIATION	
	ACTIVE	STOP	ACTIVE	STOP	ACTIVE	STOP
Gotham	1,462	794	1,522.9	733.1	–60.9	60.9
Metropolis	749	385	765.5	368.5	–16.5	16.5
Smallville	527	139	449.6	216.4	77.4	–77.4

	B	C	D	E	F	G	H	I	J	K	L
2											
3			FROM SQL		EXCEL CALCULATION FOR EXPECTED, DEVIATION, AND CHI-SQUARE						
4						Expected		Deviation		Chi-Square	
5			Actives	Stops	Total	Actives	Stops	Actives	Stops	Actives	Stops
6		Gotham	1462	794	=SUM(D6:E6)	=$F6*D$9/ $F$9	=$F6*E$9/ $F$9	=D6-G6	=E6-H6	=I6^2/G6	=J6^2/H6
7		Metropolis	749	385	=SUM(D7:E7)	=$F7*D$9/ $F$9	=$F7*E$9/ $F$9	=D7-G7	=E7-H7	=I7^2/G7	=J7^2/H7
8		Smallville	527	139	=SUM(D8:E8)	=$F8*D$9/ $F$9	=$F8*E$9/ $F$9	=D8-G8	=E8-H8	=I8^2/G8	=J8^2/H8
9		TOTAL	=SUM(D6:	=SUM(E6:	=SUM(F6:F8)	=SUM(G6:G8)	=SUM(H6:H8)	=SUM(I6:I	=SUM(J6:	=SUM(K6:I	=SUM(L6:

Figure 3-9: Expected values are easy to calculate in Excel.

(say over 5%), then there may be a difference among the markets, but the observed measurements do not provide enough evidence to draw a firm conclusion.

Chi-Square Calculation

The chi-square measure of a single cell is the deviation squared divided by the expected value. The chi-square measure for the entire table is the sum of the chi-square measures for all the cells in the table.

Table 3-10 extends Table 3-9 with the chi-square values of the cells. The sum of the chi-square values for all cells is 49.62. Notice that the chi-square values no longer have the property that the sum of each row is zero and the sum of each column is zero. This is obvious because the chi-square value is never negative. The two divisors are always positive: variance squared is positive, and the expected value of a count is always positive.

The chi-square value is interesting, but it does not tell us if the value is expected or unexpected. For this, we need to compare the value to a distribution, to turn the total chi-square of 49.62 into a p-value. Unfortunately, chi-square values do not follow a normal distribution. They do, however, follow another well-understood distribution.

Chi-Square Distribution

The final step in the calculation is to translate the chi-square value into a p-value. Like the standard error, this is best understood by referring to an underlying distribution. In this case, the distribution is the appropriately named *chi-square distribution*.

Table 3-10: Chi-Square Values by Market

	OBSERVED		EXPECTED		DEVIATION		CHI-SQUARE	
	ACT	STOP	ACT	STOP	ACT	STOP	ACT	STOP
Gotham	1,462	794	1,522.9	733.1	−60.9	60.9	2.4	5.1
Metropolis	749	385	765.5	368.5	−16.5	16.5	0.4	0.7
Smallville	527	139	449.6	216.4	77.4	−77.4	13.3	27.7
TOTAL	2,738	1,318	2,738.0	1,318.0	0.0	0.0	16.1	33.5

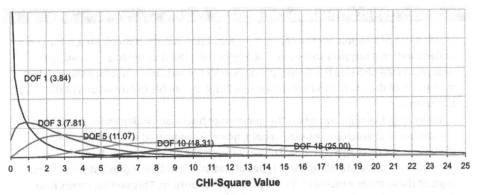

Figure 3-10: The chi-square distribution becomes flatter as the number of degrees of freedom increases; the 95% confidence bound is in parentheses.

Actually, the chi-square distribution is a family of distributions, based on one parameter, called the *degrees of freedom*. The calculation of the degrees of freedom of a table is simple. It is one less than the number of rows in the table times one less than the number of columns in the table. This example has three rows (one for each market) and two columns (one for actives and one for stops), so the degrees of freedom is $(3 - 1)*(2 - 1)$ which equals 2. The aside "Degrees of Freedom for Chi-Square" discusses what the concept means in more detail.

Figure 3-10 shows the chi-square distributions for various degrees of freedom. As the number of degrees of freedom gets larger, the bump in the distribution moves to the left. In fact, the bump is at the value degrees of freedom minus two. The 95% confidence level for each of the curves is in parentheses. If the chi-square value exceeds this confidence level, it is reasonable to say that the distribution of values is not due to chance.

The Excel function CHIDIST() calculates the confidence value associated with a chi-square value for a particular number of degrees of freedom. CHIDIST(49.62, 2) returns the miniscule value of 0.0000000017%. This number is exceedingly small, which means that we have very little confidence that the actives and stops are randomly distributed by market. Something else seems to be going on.

As shown earlier in Figure 3-9, the sequence of calculations from the expected value to the variance to the chi-square calculation can all be done in Excel. The formula for the degrees of freedom uses functions in Excel that return the number of rows and columns in the table, so the degrees of freedom of a range of cells is (ROWS(<table>)-1)*(COLUMNS(<table>)-1). The CHIDIST() function with the appropriate arguments then calculates the associated probability.

Chi-Square in SQL

The chi-square calculation uses basic arithmetic readily handled by SQL. The challenge is keeping track of intermediate values, such as the expected values and the variances. For two dimensions, four types of summaries are needed:

DEGREES OF FREEDOM FOR CHI-SQUARE

The degrees of freedom for the chi-square calculation is not a difficult idea, although understanding it requires some algebra. Historically, the first person to investigate degrees of freedom was the British statistician Sir Ronald Fisher, perhaps the greatest statistician of the twentieth century. He was knighted for his contributions to statistics and science.

Degrees of freedom addresses the question of how many independent variables are needed to characterize observed data, given the expected values and the constraints on the rows and columns. This may sound like an arcane question, but it is important for understanding many types of statistical problems (basically, by assuming that these other variables follow a normal distribution). This section shows how the particular formula in the text is calculated.

The first guess is that each observed value is an independent variable. That is, the degrees of freedom is $r*c$, where r is the number of rows and c is the number of columns. However, the constraints impose some relationships among the variables. For instance, the sum of each row has to be equal to the sum of each corresponding row in the expected values. So, the number of variables needed to describe the observed values is reduced by the number of rows. Taking into account the row constraints reduces the degrees of freedom to $r*c - r$. Because similar constraints apply to the columns, the degrees of freedom becomes $r*c - r - c$.

However, the constraints on the rows and columns are themselves redundant because the sum of all the rows is the same as the sum of the columns—in both cases, the sum is equal to total sum of all the cells. One of the constraints is unnecessary; the preceding formula has overcounted by 1. The formula for the degrees of freedom is $r*c - r - c + 1$. This is equivalent to $(r - 1) * (c - 1)$, the formula given in the text.

An example should help clarify this. Consider the general 2x2 table, where a, b, c, and d are the expected values in the cells, and R1, R2, C1, C2, and T are the constraints. So R1 refers to the fact that the sum of the observed values in the first row equals the sum of the expected values, a+b.

The degrees of freedom for this example is one. That means that knowing one of the observed values along with the expected values defines all the other observed values. Let's call the observed values A, B, C, and D and assume the value of A is known. What are the other values? The following formulas give the answer:

- $B = R1 - A$
- $C = C1 - A$
- $D = C2 - B = C2 - R1 + A$

The degrees of freedom are the number of variables we need to know in order to derive the original data from the expected values.

For the mathematically inclined, the degrees of freedom is the dimension of the space of observed values, subject to the row and column constraints. The precise definition is not needed to understand how to apply the ideas to the chi-square calculation. But degrees of freedom do characterize the problem in a fundamental way.

- An aggregation along both the row and column dimensions. This calculates the values observed in each cell.

- An aggregation along the row dimension. This calculates the sum for each row and is used for the expected value calculation.

- An aggregation along the column dimension. This calculates the sum for each column and is used for the expected value calculation.

- The sum of everything.

The chi-square calculation then follows from using these values.

One way to approach the SQL is by using explicit summaries. The following SQL liberally uses subqueries for each of the aggregations:

```
SELECT Market, isstopped, val, x, SQUARE(val - x) / x as chisquare
FROM (SELECT cells.Market, cells.isstopped,
             (1.0 * r.cnt * c.cnt /
              (SELECT COUNT(*) FROM Subscribers
               WHERE StartDate IN ('2005-12-26'))
             ) as x,
             cells.cnt as val
      FROM (SELECT Market,
                   (CASE WHEN StopType IS NOT NULL THEN 1 ELSE 0
                    END) as isstopped, COUNT(*) as cnt
            FROM Subscribers
            WHERE StartDate IN ('2005-12-26')
            GROUP BY Market,
                   (CASE WHEN StopType IS NOT NULL THEN 1 ELSE 0 END)
           ) cells LEFT OUTER JOIN
           (SELECT Market, COUNT(*) as cnt
            FROM Subscribers
            WHERE StartDate IN ('2005-12-26')
            GROUP BY Market
           ) r
           ON cells.Market = r.Market LEFT OUTER JOIN
           (SELECT (CASE WHEN StopType IS NOT NULL THEN 1 ELSE 0
                    END) as isstopped, COUNT(*) as cnt
            FROM Subscribers
            WHERE StartDate IN ('2005-12-26')
            GROUP BY (CASE WHEN StopType IS NOT NULL THEN 1 ELSE 0 END)
           ) c
           ON cells.isstopped = c.isstopped
     ) a
ORDER BY Market, isstopped
```

This SQL follows the same logic as the Excel method for calculating the chi-square value. The row totals are in the subquery whose alias is r. The column totals have the alias of c. The expected value is then r.cnt times c.cnt divided by the sum for the entire table.

What States Have Unusual Affinities for Which Types of Products?

The overall chi-square value tells us how unlikely or likely the values in each cell are. The values for each cell can be used as a measure of likelihood for that particular combination. The purchases data contains eight product groups and over 50 states. *Which states (if any) have an unusual affinity (positive or negative) for product groups?* That is, do product preferences at the product group level vary by geography?

Imagine the orders data summarized into a table, with product groups going across and states going down, and each cell containing the number of customers ordering that product group in that state. This looks like a contingency table, the type of table used for chi-square calculations. *Which cells have the largest chi-square values?*

Data Investigation

The first step is to investigate features of the data. Chapter 2 shows the distribution of orders by state. Figure 3-11 shows the distribution of orders by product group. A typical query to produce this distribution is:

```
SELECT p.GroupName, COUNT(*) as numorderlines,
       COUNT(DISTINCT o.OrderId) as numorders,
       COUNT(DISTINCT o.CustomerId) as numcustomers
FROM Orders o LEFT OUTER JOIN
     OrderLines ol
     ON o.OrderId = ol.OrderId LEFT OUTER JOIN
     Products p
     ON ol.ProductId = p.ProductId
GROUP BY p.GroupName
ORDER BY p.GroupName
```

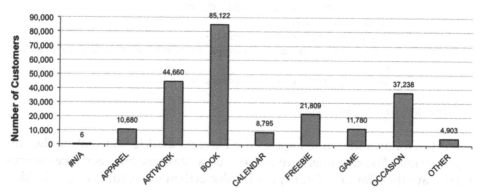

Figure 3-11: Some product groups attract more customers than other groups.

The results show that books are the most popular product group. Is this true on a state-by-state basis? It is indeed true. With very few exceptions, the most popular items in each state are books.

The following SQL answers this question, by calculating the number of customers in each state that have ordered books, and then choosing the one that is largest for each state. This uses ROW_NUMBER(), as described in Chapter 2.

```
SELECT State, GroupName, numcustomers
FROM (SELECT o.State, p.GroupName,
             COUNT(DISTINCT o.CustomerId) as numcustomers,
             ROW_NUMBER() OVER (PARTITION BY state
                                ORDER BY COUNT(DISTINCT o.CustomerId) DESC
                               ) as seqnum
      FROM Orders o LEFT OUTER JOIN
           OrderLines ol
           ON o.OrderId = ol.OrderId LEFT OUTER JOIN
           Products p
           ON ol.ProductId = p. ProductId
      GROUP BY o.State, p.GroupName) a
WHERE seqnum = 1
ORDER BY numcustomers DESC
```

The result confirms the hypothesis that books are, by far, the most popular product in most states. The first exception is the state "AE," which has nine customers buying ARTWORK. By the way, the state "AE" is not a mistake. It refers to military post offices in Europe.

SQL to Calculate Chi-Square Values

Calculating the chi-square calculations for the state-group combinations requires a long SQL query. This query follows the same form as the earlier chi-square calculation, with three subqueries for the three aggregations of interest: by state and product group, by state alone, and by product group alone. The query itself joins these three tables and then does the appropriate aggregations.

```
SELECT State, GroupName, val, exp,
       SQUARE(val - expx) / expx as chisquare
FROM (SELECT cells.State, cells.ProductGroupName,
             1.0 * r.cnt * c.cnt /
                  (SELECT COUNT(DISTINCT CustomerId) FROM Orders) as expx,
             cells.cnt as val
      FROM (SELECT o.State, p.GroupName,
                   COUNT(DISTINCT o.CustomerId) as cnt
            FROM Orders o LEFT OUTER JOIN
                 OrderLines ol
                 ON o.OrderId = ol.OrderId LEFT OUTER JOIN
                 Products p
                 ON ol.ProductId = p.ProductId
```

```
            GROUP BY o.State, p.GroupName
          ) cells LEFT OUTER JOIN
          (SELECT o.State, COUNT(DISTINCT o.CustomerId) as cnt
           FROM Orders o
           GROUP BY o.State
          ) r
          ON cells.State = r.State LEFT OUTER JOIN
          (SELECT p.GroupName,
                  COUNT(DISTINCT o.CustomerId) as cnt
           FROM Orders o LEFT OUTER JOIN
                OrderLines ol
                ON o.OrderId = ol.OrderId LEFT OUTER JOIN
                Products p
                ON ol.ProductId = p.ProductId
           GROUP BY p.GroupName
          ) c
          ON cells. GroupName = c.GroupName) a
    ORDER BY chisquare DESC
```

The subquery for `cells` calculates the observed value in each cell. The subquery called `r` calculates the row summaries, and the one called `c` calculates the column summaries. With this information, the chi-square calculation is just a matter of arithmetic.

Affinity Results

Table 3-11 shows the top ten most unexpected combinations of state and product group based on the chi-square calculation. The first row in the table says that the most unexpected combination is GAMES in New York. Based on the information in the database, we would expect to have 3,306.1 customers purchasing games in that state. Instead, there are only 2,598, a difference of 708 customers. On the other hand, customers in Massachusetts are more likely to purchase games than we would expect.

The table does suggest asking about the differences between New York and Massachusetts that would explain why games are more popular in one state than the other. Or why ARTWORK is less popular is Florida than in New Jersey. Perhaps by changing marketing practices, there is opportunity to sell more products in the games category in New York, and more ARTWORK in Florida.

What Months and Payment Types Have Unusual Affinities for Which Types of Products?

This question is similar to the question in the previous section, except that it uses three columns instead of two columns. Answering this question introduces the multidimensional chi-square calculation. This is very similar to the two-dimensional version, the only differences being some adjustments to the formulas.

Table 3-11: Unexpected Product-Group/State Combinations

STATE	GROUP	OBSERVED	EXPECTED	CHI-SQUARE
NY	GAME	2,599	3,306.4	151.4
FL	ARTWORK	1,848	2,391.6	123.5
NY	FREEBIE	5,289	6,121.4	113.2
NY	ARTWORK	13,592	12,535.2	89.1
NJ	ARTWORK	5,636	4,992.6	82.9
NY	OCCASION	9,710	10,452.0	52.7
NJ	GAME	1,074	1,316.9	44.8
AP	OTHER	5	0.5	44.2
FL	APPAREL	725	571.9	41.0
MA	GAME	560	428.9	40.1
NJ	CALENDAR	785	983.2	40.0

Multidimensional Chi-Square

Adding additional dimensions does not change how the chi-square value is calculated. It is still the sum of the squares of the differences between a count and the expected count divided by the expected count.

What changes is the formula for the expected value. For two-dimensions, this is the product of the counts along each of two dimensions divided by the total count. This formula generalizes to more dimensions. For three, it is the product of the counts along each of the three dimensions divided by the total count squared. Notice the "squared" in the denominator.

The calculation for the degrees of freedom for a multidimensional chi-square is also similar. It is the product of one less than the size of each dimension. So, a 2x2x2 example still has only one degree of freedom.

Using a SQL Query

The changes to the formula are relatively small and easily accommodated in SQL. This version of the query calculates the counts along each dimension using window functions:

```
WITH pmg as (
      SELECT o.PaymentType, Month(o.OrderDate) as mon, p.GroupName,
            COUNT(*) as cnt
      FROM Orders o JOIN
            OrderLines ol
```

```
            ON o.OrderId = ol.OrderId JOIN
            Products p
            ON ol.ProductId = p.ProductId
       GROUP BY o.PaymentType, Month(o.OrderDate), p.GroupName
       ),
      pmgmarg as (
       SELECT pmg.*,
              SUM(cnt) OVER (PARTITION BY PaymentType) as cnt_pt,
              SUM(cnt) OVER (PARTITION BY mon) as cnt_mon,
              SUM(cnt) OVER (PARTITION BY GroupName) as cnt_gn,
              SUM(cnt) OVER () as cnt_all
       FROM pmg
       ),
      pmgexp as (
       SELECT pmgmarg.*,
              (cnt_pt*cnt_mon*cnt_gn)/POWER(cnt_all, 2) as ExpectedValue
       FROM pmgmarg
       )
  SELECT pmgexp.*,
         SQUARE(cnt - ExpectedValue) / ExpectedValue as chi2
  FROM pmgexp
  ORDER BY chi2 DESC;
```

The first CTE calculates the count for each cell by aggregating the data along the three dimensions of interest – PaymentType, month, and GroupName.

The next CTE, pmgmarg, calculates the counts along each of the dimensions. This calculation uses window functions, avoiding an additional join . The third CTE, pmgexp, calculates the expected value. And, the final query calculates the chi-square value.

This structure easily generalizes to more dimensions. The only change is to add the additional dimensions in each of the subqueries and then increment the second argument to POWER().

The Results

Table 3-12 shows the first ten results from this query. These all have highly unexpected counts. For instance, the first one is for:

- Payment Type = OC
- Month = 8
- GroupName = Apparel

It has a count of 2,120. The expected value is only 29. That is significantly different. OC stands for "other card," so this is using a nonstandard credit card.

Further investigation reveals that all the excess (and a bit more!) is accounted for by one product in one year: ProductId 12510 sold 2,106 units in August 2014. All of these went to different customers. This was probably some sort of

Table 3-12: Unexpected Payment Type/Month/Product Group Combinations

PAYMENT TYPE	MONTH	PRODUCT	ACTUAL	EXPECTED	CHI-SQUARE
OC	8	APPAREL	2,120	29.5	148,287.4
??	3	APPAREL	110	1.0	11,704.3
OC	10	APPAREL	612	32.9	10,197.3
DB	7	#N/A	8	0.0	2,044.2
OC	4	APPAREL	204	23.2	1,406.8
MC	6	OCCASION	1,755	790.7	1,176.0
VI	6	OCCASION	2,456	1,258.8	1,138.6
VI	12	GAME	2,712	1,455.6	1,084.6
OC	9	APPAREL	186	26.6	956.6

promotion specifically on the item, or perhaps a marketing deal with a particular credit card company for a specific item.

The query to get the information about the items is:

```
SELECT YEAR(o.OrderDate), ol.ProductId, COUNT(*) as cnt
FROM Orders o JOIN
     OrderLines ol
     ON o.OrderId = ol.OrderId JOIN
     Products p
     ON ol.ProductId = p.ProductId
WHERE o.PaymentType = 'OC' AND MONTH(o.OrderDate) = 8 AND
      p.GroupName = 'APPAREL'
GROUP BY YEAR(o.OrderDate), ol.ProductId
ORDER BY cnt DESC
```

This query simply substitutes in the values in the WHERE clause and then aggregates by year and product.

Lessons Learned

This chapter strives to answer questions of the genre "how different is different." Such questions necessarily bring up the subject of statistics, which has been studying ways to answer such questions for almost two centuries.

The normal distribution, which is defined by an average and a standard deviation, is very important in statistics. Measuring how far a value is from the average, in terms of standard deviations, is the z-score. Large z-scores (regardless of sign) have a very low confidence. That is, the value is probably not produced by a random process, so *something* is happening.

Counts are very important in customer databases. There are three approaches to determining whether counts for different groups are the same or different. The binomial distribution counts every possible combination, so it is quite precise. The standard error of proportions is useful for getting z-scores. And, the chi-square test directly compares counts across multiple dimensions. All of these are useful for assessing confidence in the results.

The chi-square value and the z-score can both be informative. Although they use different methods, they both find groups in the data where particular measures are unexpected. This can in turn lead to understanding things such as where certain products are more or less likely to be selling.

The next chapter moves from statistical measures of difference to geography because geography is one of the most important factors in differentiating between customer groups.

CHAPTER 4

Where Is It All Happening? Location, Location, Location

From foreign policy to politics to real estate and retailing, many would agree with Napoleon's sentiment that "geography is destiny." Where customers reside and the attributes of that area are among customers' most informative characteristics: east coast, west coast, or in-between? Red state or blue state? Urban, rural, or suburban? Sunbelt or snowbelt? Good school district or retirement community? Geography is important.

Incorporating this rich source of information into data analysis poses some challenges. One is *geocoding*, the process of identifying the names of physically locations. This includes latitude and longitude, as well as the identification of multiple geographic areas, such as zip code, county, state, and country. This information makes it possible to determine who are neighbors and who are not.

Another challenge is incorporating the wealth of information about geographic areas. In the United States, the Census Bureau provides demographic and economic information about various levels of geography. The Bureau divides the country into very specific geographic pieces, such as census tracts and block groups and zip code tabulation areas (ZCTAs), which correspond closely but not exactly to zip codes. The Bureau then summarizes information for these areas, information such as the number of households, the median household income, and the percent of housing units that use solar heat. The best thing about census data is that it is free and readily accessible on the web.

The zipCensus table contains just a small fraction of the available census variables. These are interesting by themselves. More importantly, such demographic data complements customer data. Combining the two provides new insight into customers.

This chapter describes the information provided by geocoding and its use for analysis. The chapter continues by adding customer data into the mix. The examples in the chapter use the purchase dataset because it has zip codes.

Matching zip codes to ZCTAs (census zip codes) serves as a rudimentary form of geocoding.

No discussion of geography would be complete without discussing maps, which are a very powerful way of communicating information. Excel's Power View capabilities include maps, although this chapter does not depend on this functionality. Even without this capability, there are some clever things to do in Excel to visualize data, and it is even possible to connect Excel to maps on the web. This chapter starts with a discussion of geographic data and ends with an overview of the role that mapping can play in data analysis.

Latitude and Longitude

The location of each point on the earth's surface is described by two coordinates: the latitude and the longitude. Because the earth is basically a sphere and not a flat plane, latitudes and longitudes behave a bit differently from high school geometry. This section uses ZipCensus to investigate them.

Definition of Latitude and Longitude

The "lines" of latitude and longitude are actually circles on the earth's globe. All "lines" of longitude go through the north and south poles. All "lines" of latitude are circles parallel to the equator. The actual measurements are angles, measured from the center of the earth to the prime meridian (for longitude) or to the equator (for latitude). The prime meridian, also called the Greenwich meridian, passes through central London and its use as the starting point for measuring east-west distances dates back to an international agreement in 1884. Figure 4-1 shows examples of latitudes and longitudes.

Although the two seem quite similar, latitudes and longitudes have some important differences. One difference is historical. Longitude (how far east and west) is difficult to measure without accurate time-keeping devices, which are a relatively modern invention.

Latitude (how far north or south) has been understood for thousands of years and can be measured by the angle of stars in the sky or the position of the sun when it is directly overhead. By observing the position of the sun at noon on the summer solstice several thousand years ago, the ancient Greek astronomer Eratosthenes estimated the circumference of the earth. He noted three facts. At noon on the summer solstice, the sun was directly overhead in the town of Syene (modern-day Aswan in Egypt). At the same time, the sun was at an angle of 7.2 degrees from the vertical in his town of Alexandria. And, Syene was located a certain distance south of Alexandria. According to modern measurements, his estimate of the circumference was accurate within 2%—pretty remarkable accuracy for an estimate made 25 centuries ago.

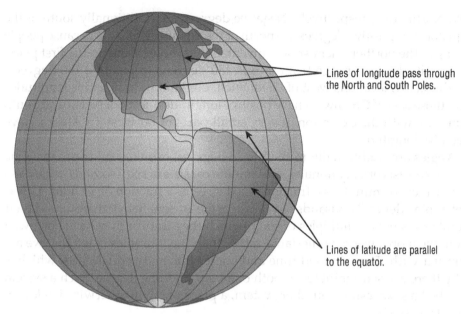

Lines of longitude pass through the North and South Poles.

Lines of latitude are parallel to the equator.

Figure 4-1: Lines of latitude and longitude make it possible to locate any point on the earth's surface.

Unlike lines of longitude, lines of latitude do not intersect. The distance between two lines of latitude separated by one degree is always about 68.7 miles (the earth's circumference divided by 360 degrees). On the other hand, the distance between two lines of longitude separated by one degree varies by latitude, being about 68.7 miles at the equator and diminishing to zero at the poles.

Recall from high school geometry that one definition of a line is the shortest distance between two points. On a sphere, lines of longitude have this property. So for two locations, one directly north or south of the other, following the line of longitude is the shortest path between the two points.

Lines of latitude do not have this property (so they are not strictly lines in the sense of spherical geometry). For two locations at the same latitude, such as Chicago, IL and Providence, RI or Miami, FL and Brownsville, TX, the latitude line connecting them is not the shortest distance. This is one reason why airplanes flying between the East and West Coasts of the United States often go into Canadian airspace, and why flights from the United States to Asia and Europe often go far north near the North Pole. The airplanes follow shorter paths by going farther north.

Degrees, Minutes, Seconds, and All That

Latitude and longitude are measured in degrees, usually ranging from minus 180 degrees to positive 180 degrees. For latitude, the extremes are the South and North Poles, respectively. Negative degrees are traditionally south of the equator, and positive degrees are north of the equator, probably because people living in the northern hemisphere invented the whole system in the first place.

Longitudes also range from minus 180 degrees to positive 180 degrees. Traditionally, locations west of Greenwich, England have negative longitudes and those east of Greenwich have positive longitudes, so all of North and South America, with the exception of very small parts of far western Alaska, have negative longitudes.

Angles are traditionally measured in degrees, minutes, and seconds. One degree consists of sixty minutes. One minute consists of sixty seconds, regardless of whether the minute is a fraction of a degree or a fraction of an hour. This is not a coincidence. Thousands of years ago, the ancient Babylonians based their number system on multiples of sixty (which they in turn may have borrowed from the more ancient Sumerians), rather than the multiples of ten that we are familiar with. They divided time and angles into sixty equal parts, which is why there are sixty minutes in both one hour and one degree. Such a system is called a sexagesimal number system, a piece of trivia otherwise irrelevant to data analysis.

When working with degrees, both databases and Excel prefer to work with decimal degrees. *How can we convert degrees/minutes/seconds to decimal degrees and vice versa?* The first part of this question is easy to answer. The author was born at approximately 25° 43′ 32″ degrees north and 80° 16′ 22″ degrees west. To convert this to decimal degrees, simply divide the minutes by 60 and the seconds by 3600 to arrive at 25.726° N and 80.273° W. This is easily done in either Excel or SQL.

Although decimal degrees are quite sufficient for our purposes, it is worth considering the reverse computation. The following expressions calculate the degrees, minutes, and seconds from a decimal degree using Excel functions (assuming the decimal degrees are in cell A1):

```
<degrees> = TRUNC(A1)
<minutes> = MOD(TRUNC(ABS(A1)*60), 60)
<seconds> = MOD(TRUNC(ABS(A1)*3600), 60)
```

The MOD() function returns the remainder when the second argument is divided by the first. For instance, when the second argument is two, MOD() returns zero for even numbers and one for odd numbers. The TRUNC() function removes the fractional part of a number for both positive and negative values. The FLOOR() function does something similar, but it rounds negative numbers down rather than up. So, TRUNC(-18.2) is -18, whereas FLOOR(-18.2, 1) is -19.

Unfortunately, Excel does not have a number format that supports degrees, minutes, and seconds. The following expression can be used instead:

```
<degrees>&CHAR(176)&" "&<minutes>&"' "&<seconds>&""""
```

The function CHAR(176) returns the degree symbol. The symbol for minutes is a single quote. The symbol for seconds is a double quote. Putting a double quotation mark in a string requires using four double quotes in a row.

> **TIP** Any character can be included in an Excel text value. One way to add a character is with the CHAR() function. Another way is to use the Insert ➤ Symbol menu option.

Distance between Two Locations

This section introduces two methods for calculating the distance between two locations using latitude and longitude: a less accurate but easier way and a more accurate method. The distances are then used to answer questions about zip codes; the latitude and longitude of the center of each zip code is available in ZipCensus.

This section uses trigonometric functions, which expect their arguments to be in units called radians rather than the more familiar degrees. There is a simple conversion from degrees to radians and back again:

```
<radians> = <degrees>*PI()/180
<degrees> = <radians>*180/PI()
```

The conversion is simple because pi radians equal exactly 180 degrees. Both SQL and Excel support the function PI(), which is used for the conversion. Excel also has the function RADIANS() that also does the conversion.

> **WARNING** When working with angles, be careful about whether the measurements should be in degrees or radians. Usually, functions that operate on angles expect the angles in radians.

Euclidian Method

The Pythagorean formula calculates the length of the long side of a right triangle as the square root of the sum of the squares of the lengths of the two shorter sides. An equivalent formulation is that the distance between two points is the square root of the sum of the squares of the X-coordinate difference and the Y-coordinate difference. These are handy formulas when two points lie on a flat plane.

The same formula can be applied directly to latitudes and longitudes, but the result does not make sense—latitudes and longitudes are measured in degrees, and distance in degrees is not practical. More typical measurement units are miles or kilometers, so some method is needed to convert between degrees and miles (or kilometers). The north-south distance between two lines of latitude

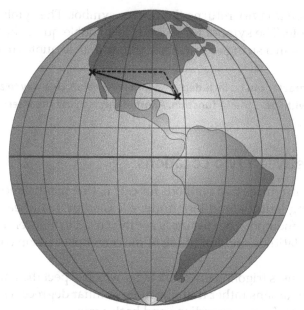

Figure 4-2: The distance between two points on the earth's surface can be approximated by converting the latitude and longitudes to miles and then using the Pythagorean theorem.

is the difference in degrees times 68.7 miles, regardless of the longitude. The east-west distance between two lines of longitude depends on the latitude; the distance is approximately the difference in degrees of longitude times 68.7 times the cosine of the average latitude.

For two points on the surface of the earth, the north-south distance and east-west distance are the sides of a right triangle, as shown in Figure 4-2. Note that a right triangle on the earth's surface does not necessarily look like one in a plane.

What are the ten zip codes closest to the geographic center of the continental United States? The geographic center is in the middle of Kansas and has a longitude of –98.6° and a latitude of 39.8°. By converting the differences in coordinates to miles, the following query finds the ten closest zip codes to the geographic center:

```
WITH zc as (
     SELECT zc.*, (latitude - 39.8) as difflat,
            (latitude + 39.8) * PI() / (2 * 180) as avglatrad,
            longitude - (-98.6) as difflong,
            latitude * PI() / 180 as latrad
     FROM ZipCensus zc
    )
```

```
SELECT TOP 10 zcta5, stab, totpop, latitude, longitude,
       SQRT(SQUARE(difflat*68.9)+SQUARE(difflong*COS(avglatrad)*68.9)
            ) as disteuc
FROM zc
ORDER BY disteuc
```

The common table expression defines useful variables, such as the latitude and longitude in radians (perhaps the trickiest part of the calculation). The outer query calculates the distance.

The ten zip codes closest to the geographic center of the continental United States are in Table 4-1.

Accurate Method

The above formula for distance between two locations is not accurate because the calculation uses formulas from flat geometry. The distance does not take the curvature of the earth into account.

The formula for the distance between two points on a sphere is based on a simple idea. Connect the two points to the center of the earth. This forms an angle. The distance is the angle measured in radians times the radius of the earth. A simple idea, but it leads to a messy formula. The following SQL query uses this formula to find the ten zip codes closest to the center of the continental United States using the more accurate method:

Table 4-1: The Closest Zip Codes by Euclidean Distance to the Geometric Center of the United States

ZIP CODE	STATE	LONGITUDE	LATITUDE	EUCLIDIAN DISTANCE	CIRCULAR DISTANCE
66952	KS	39.82	-98.59	1.56	1.56
66941	KS	39.84	-98.44	8.87	8.88
66967	KS	39.79	-98.79	9.87	9.87
66936	KS	39.91	-98.31	16.83	16.84
66932	KS	39.77	-98.92	17.04	17.05
67638	KS	39.64	-98.85	17.17	17.18
67474	KS	39.57	-98.72	17.21	17.22
68952	NE	40.09	-98.67	20.18	20.19
66956	KS	39.79	-98.22	20.24	20.25
67437	KS	39.50	-98.55	20.53	20.54

```
WITH zc as (
      SELECT zc.*, (latitude - 39.8) as difflat,
             (latitude + 39.8) * PI() / (2 * 180) as avglatrad,
             longitude - (-98.6) as difflong,
             latitude * PI()/180 as latrad,
             longitude * PI() / 180 as longrad,
             39.8 * PI() / 180 as centerlatrad,
             (-98.6) * PI() / 180 as centerlongrad,
             3949.9 as radius
      FROM ZipCensus zc
     )
SELECT TOP 10 zcta5, stab as state, totpop as population, latitude,
             longitude,
          SQRT(SQUARE(difflat*68.9) + SQUARE(difflong*COS(avglatrad)*68.9)
             ) as disteuc,
          ACOS(COS(centerlatrad)*COS(latrad)*COS(centerlongrad - longrad) +
             SIN(centerlatrad)*SIN(latrad))*radius as distcirc
     FROM zc
     ORDER BY distcirc
```

This formula uses several trigonometric functions, so the innermost query converts all the latitudes and longitudes to radians. In addition, this method uses the radius of the earth, which is taken to be 3,949.9 miles.

Table 4-1 shows the circular distance as well as the Euclidean distance. The results are almost exactly the same for the two methods because the distances are so small. After all, 20 miles might seem big, but it is only about 0.5% of the earth's radius.

The discrepancies grow as the distances get larger. The furthest zip code from the center is 96766 in Hawaii. The approximate method gives a distance of 3,798 miles versus 3,725 for the more accurate method.

The spherical method is a better approximation, but it is not perfect; the earth is not a perfect sphere. A better approximation could take into account the bulges around the equator and altitude. Travel distance along roads rather than the theoretical distance between two locations may be better for many applications. Such calculations require special-purpose tools and databases of roads and are generally not feasible in Excel and SQL.

Finding All Zip Codes within a Given Distance

Calculating the distance between two locations is useful. You can find the nearest Wal-Mart to where a customer lives or the closest repair center to where a car broke down or the distance from home to where a customer paid for dinner in a restaurant. These types of applications often work in real time, often with positioning information from mobile devices and are specific to a given user at a given time. Distance can be measured "as the crow flies" or along available routes.

Finding the zip codes within a certain distance of a location is a typical analytic application. Once upon a time, a newspaper was interested in areas where it could provide home delivery copies. One part of the newspaper delivered copies to university campuses. Another part arranged for home delivery. Some universities received newspapers, even though the surrounding areas were not routable for home delivery. Why not also offer home delivery in the surrounding area because trucks filled with newspapers were already delivering to the town? A brilliant idea that led to the question: *Which zip codes are within eight miles of a specific set of university zip codes?*

One way to answer the question is with a big map, or with a mapping website (such as Google Maps, MapQuest, Yahoo! Maps, or Microsoft Live). This would be a manual process of looking up each zip code to find the neighboring ones or require coding an application in Java, Python or a similar language. Manual solutions are prone to error. Because the Census Bureau provides the latitude and longitude of the center of each zip code, why not use this information instead?

The actual solution was an Excel worksheet that used the census information to find the distance from each zip code to the chosen zip code. The spreadsheet then created a table with the zip codes within eight miles.

Such a spreadsheet is useful for manual processing, but the processing can also be done in SQL. The following query calculates all zip codes within eight miles of Dartmouth University in Hanover, NH:

```
WITH zc as (
      SELECT zc.*, latitude * PI() / 180 as latrad,
             Longitude * PI() / 180 as longrad, 3949.9 as radius
      FROM ZipCensus zc
      )
SELECT z.zcta5 as zipcode, z.stab as state, z.zipname, distcirc,
       z.totpop, z.tothhs, z.medianhhinc
FROM (SELECT zips.*,
             ACOS(COS(comp.latrad) * COS(zips.latrad) *
                  COS(comp.longrad - zips.longrad) +
                  SIN(comp.latrad) * SIN(zips.latrad)
             ) * zips.radius as distcirc
      FROM zc zips CROSS JOIN
           (SELECT zc.* FROM zc WHERE zcta5 IN ('03755')) comp
      ) z
WHERE distcirc < 8
ORDER BY distcirc
```

The common table expression converts the latitude and longitude to radians. This table is joined to itself, once for all the zip codes and once for Dartmouth (03755). More zip codes can be included by expanding the list in the comp subquery.

The closest zip codes are shown in Table 4-2. Some are in New Hampshire and some are in Vermont, because Hanover is near the border between these states.

Table 4-2: Zip Codes within Eight Miles of Hanover, NH

ZIP CODE	PO NAME AND STATE	DISTANCE	POPULATION	HOUSEHOLDS #	MEDIAN INCOME
03755	Hanover, NH	0.00	10,268	2,524	$90,100
05055	Norwich, VT	2.30	3,423	1,468	$94,342
03750	Etna, NH	2.49	1,048	313	$138,036
03766	Lebanon, NH	5.35	9,379	4,175	$55,750
03784	Lebanon, NH	5.69	3,859	1,759	$54,101
05001	White River Junction, VT	6.51	9,301	4,329	$51,611
05043	East Thetford, VT	7.29	888	373	$74,345
05075	Thetford Center, VT	7.40	1,072	458	$74,926

It is tempting to extend the find-the-nearest-zip-code query to find the nearest zip code to every zip code in the table. As a query, this is a slight modification of the Dartmouth query (comp would choose all zip codes). However, such a query would take a long time to complete. The problem is that the distance between every possible pair of all 32,038 zip codes needs to be calculated—more than one billion distance calculations. The distances between zip codes in Florida and zip codes in Washington (state) have to be calculated, even though no zip code in Washington is close to any zip code in Florida.

SQL does not, in general, have the ability to make these queries run faster. Using indexes does not help, because the distance calculation requires two columns, both latitude and longitude. Traditional indexes speed up access to one column at a time, not both at once. Most databases do support extensions for geographic features, called GIS or spatial indexes. However, this book does not cover this topic in detail.

Finding Nearest Zip Code in Excel

This section does a very similar calculation in Excel, finding the nearest zip code to a given zip code. The Excel spreadsheet consists of the following areas:

- The input area for typing in a zip code
- The output area for the nearest zip code and distance
- The table containing all the zip codes, each with its latitude and longitude

The user types a zip code in the spreadsheet in the input area. The spreadsheet looks up the latitude and longitude using the VLOOKUP() function. The distance from every zip code to the chosen zip code is then calculated as an additional column.

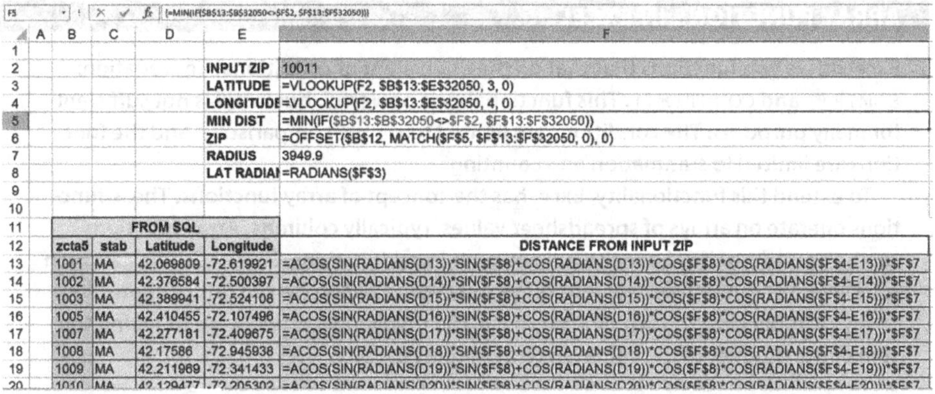

F5 {=MIN(IF($B$13:$B$32050<>$F$2, $F$13:$F$32050))}

	A	B	C	D	E	F
1						
2					INPUT ZIP	10011
3					LATITUDE	=VLOOKUP(F2, $B$13:$E$32050, 3, 0)
4					LONGITUDE	=VLOOKUP(F2, $B$13:$E$32050, 4, 0)
5					MIN DIST	=MIN(IF($B$13:$B$32050<>$F$2, $F$13:$F$32050))
6					ZIP	=OFFSET($B$12, MATCH($F$5, $F$13:$F$32050, 0), 0)
7					RADIUS	3949.9
8					LAT RADIAI	=RADIANS($F$3)
9						
10						
11		FROM SQL				
12		zcta5	stab	Latitude	Longitude	DISTANCE FROM INPUT ZIP
13		1001	MA	42.069809	-72.619921	=ACOS(SIN(RADIANS(D13))*SIN($F$8)+COS(RADIANS(D13))*COS($F$8)*COS(RADIANS($F$4-E13)))*$F$7
14		1002	MA	42.376584	-72.500397	=ACOS(SIN(RADIANS(D14))*SIN($F$8)+COS(RADIANS(D14))*COS($F$8)*COS(RADIANS($F$4-E14)))*$F$7
15		1003	MA	42.389941	-72.524108	=ACOS(SIN(RADIANS(D15))*SIN($F$8)+COS(RADIANS(D15))*COS($F$8)*COS(RADIANS($F$4-E15)))*$F$7
16		1005	MA	42.410455	-72.107496	=ACOS(SIN(RADIANS(D16))*SIN($F$8)+COS(RADIANS(D16))*COS($F$8)*COS(RADIANS($F$4-E16)))*$F$7
17		1007	MA	42.277181	-72.409675	=ACOS(SIN(RADIANS(D17))*SIN($F$8)+COS(RADIANS(D17))*COS($F$8)*COS(RADIANS($F$4-E17)))*$F$7
18		1008	MA	42.17586	-72.945938	=ACOS(SIN(RADIANS(D18))*SIN($F$8)+COS(RADIANS(D18))*COS($F$8)*COS(RADIANS($F$4-E18)))*$F$7
19		1009	MA	42.211969	-72.341433	=ACOS(SIN(RADIANS(D19))*SIN($F$8)+COS(RADIANS(D19))*COS($F$8)*COS(RADIANS($F$4-E19)))*$F$7
20		1010	MA	42.129477	-72.205302	=ACOS(SIN(RADIANS(D20))*SIN($F$8)+COS(RADIANS(D20))*COS($F$8)*COS(RADIANS($F$4-E20)))*$F$7

Figure 4-3: This Excel spreadsheet calculates the closest zip code to any other zip code. The curly braces in the formula line indicate that this particular formula is an array function.

Figure 4-3 shows the functions in the worksheet. The nearest zip code is chosen using the `MIN()` function, with a small caveat. The minimum distance is clearly going to be zero, which is the distance from any given zip code to itself. The minimum uses a nested `IF()` to exclude the input zip code. This is an example of an array function, discussed in the aside "Array Functions in Excel." With the minimum distance, the actual zip code is found using a combination of `MATCH()` to find the row with the zip code and then `OFFSET()` to return the value in the correct column.

Pictures with Zip Codes

Latitudes and longitudes are coordinates, and these can be plotted using scatter plots. Such plots are a poor man's geographic information system (GIS). This section introduces the idea, along with some caveats about the process.

The Scatter Plot Map

There are enough zip codes in the United States that just the center points form a recognizable outline of the country, as shown in Figure 4-4. Each zip code in this figure is represented as a small hollow circle; hollow circles makes it easier to see where zip codes are very close to each other.

This map is based on the same latitude and longitude data used for the distance calculations. The latitude is assigned as the Y-axis in a scatter plot and the longitude is assigned as the X-axis. To focus on the continental United States, the horizontal scale goes from –65 to –125 and the vertical scale from 20 to 50. Lines are drawn every five degrees on both scales. Although far from perfect, the zip code centers form a recognizable blob in the shape of the continental United States.

ARRAY FUNCTIONS IN EXCEL

Excel offers two functions that that do the equivalent of conditional aggregation: `SUMIF()` and `COUNTIF()`. This functionality is powerful, but it still is not sufficient for many purposes. The conditions are limited to simple comparisons, and the functions are limited to summation and counting.

To extend this functionality, Excel has the concept of array functions. These functions operate on arrays of spreadsheet values, typically columns. Array functions can be nested, so they have the full power of Excel functions. Some of them can even return values in multiple cells, although this type is not discussed until Chapter 12.

An example perhaps explains this best. The following are two ways of taking the sum of the product of the values in two columns of cells:

```
=SUMPRODUCT($A$2$A$10, $B$2$B$10)
{=SUM($A$2$A$10 * $B$2$B$10)}
```

These two methods produce the same results. The first uses the built-in function `SUMPRODUCT()` that does exactly what we want. The second combines the `SUM()` function and the multiplication operator as an array function. It says to multiply the values in the two columns row-by-row and then to take the sum. Think of the expression as reading each row, multiplying together the corresponding values in columns A and B and saving all these products somewhere. This somewhere is then an array of values passed to `SUM()`.

Entering an array function takes a sleight of hand. The expression is typed in just like any other expression. Instead of hitting the Return key after entering the formula, hit Ctrl+Shift+Return at the same time. Excel encloses the formula in curly braces on the formula bar to indicate that it is an array function. The curly braces are not entered as part of the function; they appear when you type Ctrl+Shift+Return.

One particularly useful application of array functions is combining functions such as `SUM()` and `MIN()` with `IF()`. This is equivalent to conditional aggregation in SQL. In the text, the problem is to find the minimum distance, where the zip code is not the given zip code. The formula for this is:

```
{=MIN(IF($A$7:$A$32044<>B2, $E$7:$E$32044))}
```

This says to take the minimum of the values in column E, but only where the corresponding value in column A is not equal to the value in cell B2.

Although array functions are easy to express, a column filled with thousands of rows containing array functions can take a while to calculate. And they come with one small warning. When nested, the functions `AND()` and `OR()` do not always work as expected. Instead, use nested `IF()` statements to achieve the same logic.

Cartographers—the people who study maps and how to convey information on them—have many standards for what makes a good map. This simple zip code scatter plot fails almost all of them. It distorts distances and areas. For instance, small land areas in the north appear bigger, and larger land areas near the equator appear smaller. It does not have boundaries or features, such

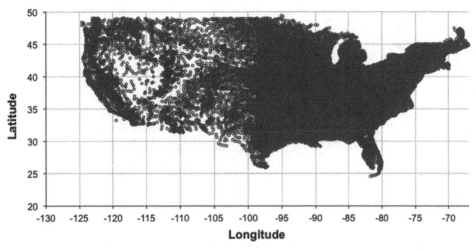

Figure 4-4: The center of zip codes form a recognizable map of the United States.

as mountains, cities, and roads. And, if the dimensions of the chart are not right, the map is stretched in unusual ways.

Nonetheless, the result is recognizable and actually useful for conveying information. It is also easy to create. Even the simple zip code map shows areas where there are many zip codes (along the coasts) and where there are few (in the mountainous states of the west, in the Everglades in South Florida).

Who Uses Solar Power for Heating?

The Census Bureau provides many attributes about people, households, families, and housing units. One of them, for instance, happens to be the source of heat. The column `hhfsolar` contains the number of housing units using solar power in a zip code. The percentage is in the related field `pcthhfsolar`.

A simple zip code map does a good job of showing where solar power is present. *Which zip codes have any household with solar power?* Figure 4-5 shows a map with this information. The faint gray areas are zip codes that do not have solar power; the larger darker triangles show zip codes that do.

Arranging the data in the spreadsheet makes it easier to create the map. The first column is the X-value for the chart and the second two columns are the Y-values for two series in the chart. The data should be laid out as:

- Longitude, which is along the X-axis
- Latitude for non-solar zip codes
- Latitude for solar zip codes

Each row has exactly one value for latitude in the appropriate column.

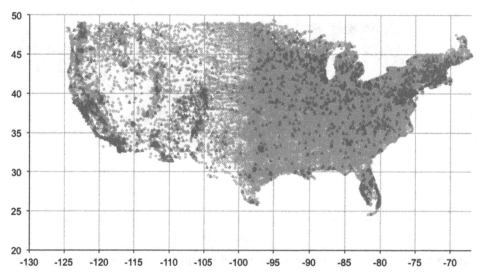

Figure 4-5: This map shows the zip codes that have housing units with solar power, based on the census data.

The following query returns the data in this format:

```
SELECT zcta5, longitude,
       (CASE WHEN hhfsolar = 0 THEN latitude END) as nosolarlat,
       (CASE WHEN hhfsolar > 0 THEN latitude END) as solarlat
FROM ZipCensus
WHERE latitude BETWEEN 20 and 50 AND
      longitude BETWEEN -135 AND -65
```

The WHERE clause is just a simple way to limit the results to the continental United States.

An alternative approach is to have the query provide a "solar" indicator along with the longitude and latitude. The data would be put into the right format using Excel formulas, making use of the IF() function. Both methods work, but there is no reason to do extra work in Excel when it can be done in SQL.

> **TIP** Pulling the data in the right format using SQL can often save time and effort in Excel.

The little triangles in the chart are the zip codes that have solar power. Not surprisingly, Florida and California have a high concentration of these because these are two states that are both sunny and highly populated. The cloudy northeast has many solar zip codes, but this is probably because such a densely populated area has so many zip codes. Some states in the west, such as New Mexico, Arizona, and Colorado have a relatively high number of solar zip codes, but because these states are less dense, there are fewer triangles.

A map is useful for seeing what is happening. The data itself can be verified by asking: *What proportion of zip codes in each state has at least one solar powered residence?* The following query answers this question, using the Census Bureau definition of a state:

```
SELECT TOP 10 stab,
       SUM(CASE WHEN zc.HHFSolar > 0 THEN 1.0 END)/COUNT(*) as propzips,
       SUM(zc.HHFSolar * 1.0) / SUM(zc.TotHUs) as prophhu
FROM ZipCensus zc
GROUP BY stab
ORDER BY prophhu DESC
```

This query calculates two numbers: the proportion of zip codes with solar power and the proportion of households. For most states, these are strongly correlated, as shown in Table 4-3. However, for some states such as Wyoming, solar power is concentrated in a few zip codes (fewer than 14%), but a relatively high proportion of housing units have it (0.10%).

Where Are the Customers?

Questions about zip codes are not limited to the census information. The `Orders` table contains information about where customers place orders. The following query summarizes the number of orders in each zip code and then joins this information to the latitude and longitude in `ZipCensus`:

```
SELECT zc.zcta5, longitude, latitude, numords,
       (CASE WHEN tothhs = 0 THEN 0.0 ELSE numords * 1.0 / tothhs
        END) as penetration
FROM ZipCensus zc JOIN
```

Table 4-3: The Top Ten States by Penetration of Solar Power in Housing Units

STATE	PROPORTION OF ZIP CODES SOLAR	PROPORTION OF HOUSING UNITS SOLAR
HI	72.3%	1.36%
NM	22.0%	0.30%
CO	26.7%	0.14%
WY	7.3%	0.09%
CA	28.5%	0.08%
AZ	26.7%	0.08%
ME	7.9%	0.07%
VT	7.1%	0.06%
NV	12.0%	0.05%
NH	12.1%	0.05%

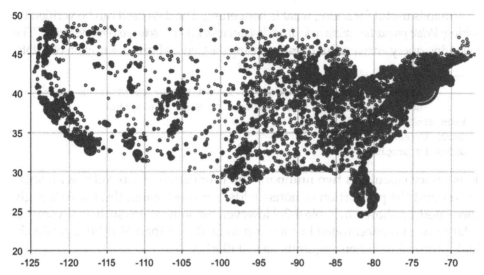

Figure 4-6: This bubble chart shows the order penetration in each zip code.

```
     (SELECT ZipCode, COUNT(*) as numords
      FROM Orders
      GROUP BY ZipCode) o
     ON zc.zcta5 = o.zipcode
 WHERE latitude BETWEEN 20 and 50 AND
       longitude BETWEEN -135 AND -65
```

Figure 4-6 plots the results as a bubble chart. The size of the bubbles is the number of orders placed in the zip code; the X-axis is the longitude, and the Y-axis is the latitude. Like the scatter plot, this bubble chart is a rudimentary map; however, bubble charts have fewer formatting options available than scatter plots (for instance, the shape of the bubbles cannot be changed). The bubbles in this chart are disks, colored on the outside and transparent inside. This is important because bubbles may overlap each other; the overlapping bubbles let you see where they are densest.

This map has fewer zip codes than the previous ones because only about 11,000 zip codes have orders. Many of these zip codes are in the northeast, so that region of the country is overrepresented.

Such a map conveys interesting information about customers. By using multiple series, for instance, orders could be classified by the products they contain, or customers by the number of purchases they make.

Census Demographics

Solar power is interesting, but not as interesting as economic information for understanding customers. This section looks at some other types of information available, and at ways of combining this information with the purchase data. Of course, zipCensus contains only a subset of all the possible information available from the Census Bureau.

The Extremes: Richest and Poorest

Several columns relate to wealth, which is very valuable information for understanding customers. You may not know how wealthy the customers are, but you can know how wealthy their neighbors are.

Median Income

The median household income in a zip code is the income in the middle, where half the households earn more than the median and half earn less. It is a very useful measure for understanding whether a given area is relatively wealthy or relatively poor. Households are a reasonable unit because they tend to correspond to an economic marketing unit—groups of individuals (such as families) that are bound together economically.

Median household income is not the only measure available. The Census Bureau also provides the average household income, as well as various income ranges (how many households earned $45,000 to $50,000 dollars, for instance). This information is provided at the household level, at the family level, and for individuals. There is even information about sources of income, separating out earned income, social security income, and government benefits. A wealth of variables describes wealth, but we'll generally stick with median household income.

One query for finding the zip code with the highest median household income is:

```
SELECT TOP 1 zcta5, medianhhinc
FROM ZipCensus
ORDER BY medianhhinc DESC
```

To find the poorest, the sort order is changed to ASC rather than DESC.

This query is simple, but it has a flaw: More than one zip code could be tied for the richest or the poorest. A better approach finds all zip codes that match the extreme values. The following query counts the number of matching zip codes:

```
SELECT medianhhinc, COUNT(*) as numzips,
       SUM(CASE WHEN totpop = 0 THEN 1 ELSE 0 END) as pop0,
       SUM(CASE WHEN tothhs = 0 THEN 1 ELSE 0 END) as hh0,
       AVG(totpop * 1.0) as avgpop, AVG(tothhs * 1.0) as avghh
FROM ZipCensus zc JOIN
     (SELECT MAX(medianhhinc) as hhmax, MIN(medianhhinc) as hhmin
```

```
        FROM ZipCensus) minmax
    ON zc.medianhhinc IN (minmax.hhmax, minmax.hhmin)
GROUP BY medianhhinc
```

This query returns some additional information, such as the number of zip codes where the population is zero, where the number of households is zero, and the average population of the zip code.

Table 4-4 shows that 866 zip codes have zero median income. Although some people live in these zip codes, most have no households. These zip codes might contain institutions of some sort, where everyone is in group housing (such as prisons and college dorms) rather than private residences, or the zip code might be for an area predominated by businesses, such as Rockefeller Center in New York City. In the zip codes with no households, the household income is zero, which appears to be a placeholder for NULL.

The twelve zip codes with the maximum median income are shown in Table 4-5. These all have small populations. Usually, the median family income is also very high, but not always, because the definitions of household and family are not the same.

Proportion of Wealthy and Poor

Median household income is interesting, but, like all medians, it provides information about only one household, the one whose income is in the middle. An alternative approach is to consider the distribution of incomes, by looking at the proportion of the very rich or very poor. The column famhhinc0 identifies the poorest group, those whose family income is less than ten thousand dollars per year. At the other extreme are the wealthiest whose income exceeds two hundred thousand dollars per year, counted by famhhinc200. The resulting query looks like:

```
SELECT zcta5, stab, medianhhinc, medianfaminc, totpop, tothhs
FROM ZipCensus zc CROSS JOIN
     (SELECT MAX(famhhinc200) as richest, MAX(famhhinc0) as poorest
      FROM zipcensus
      WHERE tothhs >= 1000) minmax
WHERE (zc.famhhinc200 = richest OR zc.famhhinc0 = poorest) AND
      zc.tothhs >= 1000
```

Table 4-4: Information About the Wealthiest and Poorest Zip Codes

HOUSEHOLD MEDIAN INCOME	NUMBER OF ZIP CODES	NO POPULATION	NO HOUSEHOLDS	AVERAGE POPULATION	AVERAGE HOUSEHOLDS
$0.00	866	336	586	434.0	5.3
$250,001.00	12	0	0	341.2	60.4

Table 4-5: The Wealthiest Zip Codes by Household Income in the 2000 Census

ZIP CODE	ZIP CODE NAME AND STATE	POPULATION	HOUSE-HOLDS	FAMILIES	MEDIAN INCOME HOUSE-HOLDS	FAMILY
02457	Wellesley, MA	1,343	10	10	$250,001	$250,001
20686	Saint Marys City, MD	754	22	22	$250,001	$250,001
21056	Gibson Island, MD	141	57	57	$250,001	$250,001
21405	Annapolis, MD	435	139	122	$250,001	$250,001
32461	Rosemary Beach, FL	28	13	13	$250,001	$250,001
33109	Miami Beach, FL	482	179	130	$250,001	$52,378
69335	Bingham, NE	18	11	7	$250,001	$250,001
70550	Lawtell, LA	377	99	99	$250,001	$250,001
79033	Farnsworth, TX	30	16	11	$250,001	$250,001
82833	Big Horn, WY	179	67	20	$250,001	$0

Notable about this query are the parentheses in the outer WHERE clause. Without the parentheses, the clause would be evaluated as:

```
WHERE (zc.faminc200 = richest) OR (zc.faminc000_010 = poorest AND
       zc.hh >= 1000)
```

That is, the condition on the number of households would apply only to the poorest condition and not the richest—not the intended behavior. Misplaced or missing parentheses can alter the meaning and performance of a query.

TIP In WHERE clauses that mix ANDs and ORs, use parentheses to ensure that the clauses are interpreted correctly.

The results are similar to the previous results. The poorest zip code has now switched to an inner city neighborhood, the East New York neighborhood of Brooklyn. Interestingly, the median family income is actually much higher than the median household income, indicating that although the zip code has many poor residents it also has many wealthier (or at least middle class) residents; the richer residents live in "family" households but the poorer residents do not.

Income Similarity and Dissimilarity Using Chi-Square

The distribution of income goes beyond median or average income. The Census Bureau breaks income into ten buckets, the poorest being family income less than \$10,000 and the wealthiest being family income in excess of \$200,000. The proportion of families in each of these buckets is available at the zip code level, and this is a good description of the income distribution.

In which zip codes does the income distribution match the country as a whole? These zip codes are all over the entire United States. Such representative areas can be useful. What works well in these areas may work well across the whole country. At the other extreme are zip codes that differ from the national distribution, the most unrepresentative areas.

The chi-square calculation is one way to measure both these extremes. To use the chi-square, an expected value is needed, and this is the income distribution at the national level. The key to calculating the national numbers is to multiply the proportions by the total number of families to obtain counts of families in each bucket. This total number can be aggregated across all zip codes, and then divided by the number of families to get the distribution at the national level, as shown in the following query:

```
SELECT SUM(famhhinc0 * 1.0) / SUM(famhhs) as faminc000,
       . . .
       SUM(famhhinc150 * 1.0) / SUM(famhhs) as faminc150,
       SUM(famhhinc200 * 1.0) / SUM(famhhs) as faminc200
FROM ZipCensus
WHERE totpop >= 1000
```

Which zip codes are most similar (or most dissimilar) can be expressed as a question: *What is the likelihood that the income distribution seen in a given zip code is due to chance, relative to the national average?* Or, to slightly simplify the calculation: *What is the chi-square value of the income distribution of the zip code compared to the national income distribution?* The closer the chi-square value is to zero, the more representative the zip code. Higher chi-square values suggest that the observed distribution is not due to chance.

The calculation requires a lot of arithmetic. The chi-square value for a given income column, such as `famhhinc0`, is the square of the difference between the variable and the expected value divided by the expected value. For each of the ten buckets, the following expression calculates its contribution to the total chi-square value:

```
POWER(zc.famhhinc0 - usa.famhhinc000, 2) / usa.faminc000
```

The total chi-square is the sum of the chi-square values for all the buckets.

As an example, the following query finds the top ten zip codes most similar to the national distribution of incomes and having a population greater than 1,000:

```
SELECT TOP 10 zcta5, stab as state,
       SQUARE(zc.famhhinc0*1.0/zc.famhhs-usa.faminc000)/usa.faminc000+
       . . .
       SQUARE(zc.famhhinc150*1.0/zc.famhhs-usa.faminc150)/usa.faminc150+
```

```
        SQUARE(zc.famhhinc200*1.0/zc.famhhs-usa.faminc200)/usa.faminc200
        ) as chisquare,
        totpop, medianfaminc
FROM ZipCensus zc CROSS JOIN
    (SELECT SUM(famhhinc0 * 1.0) / SUM(famhhs) as faminc000,
             . . .
            SUM(famhhinc150 * 1.0) / SUM(famhhs) as faminc150,
            SUM(famhhinc200 * 1.0) / SUM(famhhs) as faminc200
    FROM ZipCensus
    WHERE totpop >= 1000) usa
WHERE totpop >= 1000 AND famhhs > 0
ORDER BY chisquare ASC
```

This uses a subquery to calculate the distribution at the national level, which is joined in using the CROSS JOIN. The actual chi-square value is calculated as an expression in the outermost query. Note that this chi-square calculation uses ratios rather than counts. The results are the same.

The zip codes most similar to the national income distribution are dispersed across the United States, as shown in Table 4-6.

Table 4-7 shows the ten zip codes with the highest deviation from the national income distribution. These zip codes are all smaller than the zip codes most similar to the national average.

Visualizing the income variables for these ten zip codes helps explain why they are different. Figure 4-7 is an example of a parallel dimension plot, where each zip code is a line on the chart, and each point on a line is the value of one of the income variables. The thickest line is the average for the United States.

Table 4-6: Top Ten Zip Codes by Chi-Square Income Similarity

ZIP CODE	STATE	INCOME CHI-SQUARE	POP	FAM MEDIAN INCOME
07002	NJ	0.0068	63,164	$68,532
85022	AZ	0.0069	46,427	$61,219
32217	FL	0.0075	20,200	$62,865
11420	NY	0.0076	48,226	$63,787
93933	CA	0.0078	22,723	$63,999
91748	CA	0.0084	46,946	$63,374
77396	TX	0.0085	43,861	$64,118
83706	ID	0.0090	31,289	$65,265
33155	FL	0.0092	46,603	$61,797
29501	SC	0.0095	43,004	$61,417

Table 4-7: Top Ten Zip Codes by Chi-Square Income Disparity

ZIP CODE	STATE	INCOME CHI-SQUARE	POPULATION	FAMILY MEDIAN INCOME
37315	TN	30.3	1,242	$0
90089	CA	30.3	3,402	$0
97331	OR	30.3	2,405	$0
06269	CT	30.3	9,009	$0
19717	DE	20.7	4,091	$2,499
30602	GA	20.7	2,670	$2,499
02457	MA	15.4	1,343	$250,001
01003	MA	15.1	11,286	$0
02912	RI	15.1	1,898	$0
38738	MS	14.6	2,881	$14,342

The zip codes that differ from the United States do so because a few of the income brackets have most of the families—and conversely, many buckets are empty or close to empty. All of these zip codes are either quite rich or quite poor. However, some middle-income zip codes also have high chi-square values—zip codes such as 15450, 18503, and 32831 have median incomes much closer to the national median, but still have large chi-square values.

The query that returns the data for Figure 4-7 is a modification of the chi-square query. It replaces the CROSS JOIN with UNION ALL, does not have the chi-square calculation, and lists the zip codes explicitly:

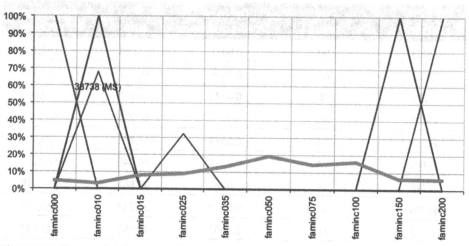

Figure 4-7: This parallel dimension plot compares the top ten zip codes least similar to the United States by income distribution.

```
SELECT zcta5, famhhinc0 * 1.0 / famhhs as famhhinc0,
       . . .
       famhhinc200 * 1.0 / famhhs as famhhinc200
FROM ZipCensus
WHERE zcta5 IN ('41650', '25107', '97345', '87049', '10006', '44702',
                '64147', '10282', '98921','40982')
UNION ALL
SELECT 'USA', SUM(famhhinc0 * 1.0) / SUM(famhhs) as famhhinc0,
       . . .
       SUM(famhhinc200 * 1.0) / SUM(famhhs) as famhhinc200
FROM ZipCensus
```

The difference between the UNION ALL and the CROSS JOIN is that the UNION ALL adds a new row into the data with the same columns, so the result here has 11 rows, ten for the zip codes and one for the entire United States. The CROSS JOIN, by contrast, does not add new rows (assuming the second table has exactly one row). Instead, it adds additional columns to the result.

Comparison of Zip Codes with and without Orders

The orders in the purchases database have zip codes assigned to them, most of which have demographic data. The ones that do not match are mistakes or are for non-U.S. addresses. This section investigates the intersection of zip codes in the orders data and the demographic data.

Zip Codes Not in Census File

Two tables have zip codes, the Orders table and the ZipCensus table. *How many zip codes are in each table and how many are in both?* This is a question about the relationship between two sets.

A good way to answer it is by comparing the zip codes in the two tables using the UNION ALL:

```
SELECT inorders, incensus, COUNT(*) as numzips,
       SUM(numorders) as numorders, MIN(zipcode) as minzip,
       MAX(zipcode) as maxzip
FROM (SELECT zipcode, MAX(inorders) as inorders,
             MAX(incensus) as incensus, MAX(numorders) as numorders
      FROM ((SELECT ZipCode, 1 as inorders, 0 as incensus,
                    COUNT(*) as numorders
             FROM Orders o
             GROUP BY ZipCode)
            UNION ALL
            (SELECT zcta5, 0 as inorders, 1 as incensus, 0 as numorders
             FROM ZipCensus zc)
           ) ozc
      GROUP BY ZipCode
     ) b
GROUP BY inorders, incensus
```

Table 4-8: Overlaps of Zip Codes between Census Zips and Purchase Zips

IN ORDERS	IN CENSUS	COUNT	NUMBER ORDERS	MINIMUM ZIP	MAXIMUM ZIP
0	1	21,182	0	01005	99929
1	0	3,772	6,513		Z5B2T
1	1	11,807	186,470	01001	99901

The first subquery in the UNION ALL sets a flag for all zip codes in Orders and counts the number of orders in the zip code. The second subquery sets a flag for all zip codes in the ZipCensus table. These are aggregated by zip code to produce two flags for each zip code, one indicating whether it is in Orders and the other indicating whether it is in ZipCensus. Each zip code also has a count of the number of orders. These flags are summarized again in the outer query to obtain information about the overlap of zip codes in the two tables.

The results in Table 4-8 show that most zip codes in ZipCensus have no orders. On the other hand, most order zip codes are in ZipCensus. And, by far most orders are in recognized zip codes. It is quite likely that many of the unrecognized zip codes are for foreign orders.

Profiles of Zip Codes with and without Orders

Are the zip codes with orders different from the zip codes without orders? Information such as the following can distinguish between these two groups:

- Estimated number of households
- Estimated median income
- Percent of households on public assistance
- Percent of population with a college degree
- Percent of housing units owned

Table 4-9 shows summary statistics for the two groups. Zip codes without orders are smaller, poorer, and have more homeowners. Zip codes with orders are more populous, richer, and better educated. Given that the numbers of zip codes in the two groups are so large, these differences are statistically significant.

The following query was used to calculate the information in the table:

```
SELECT (CASE WHEN o.ZipCode IS NULL THEN 'NO' ELSE 'YES'
        END) as hasorder,
       COUNT(*) as cnt, AVG(tothhs * 1.0) as avg_hh,
       AVG(medianhhinc) as avg_medincome,
       SUM(numhhpubassist * 1.0) / SUM(tothhs) as hhpubassist,
       SUM(bachelorsormore * 1.0) / SUM(over25) as popcollege,
```

Table 4-9: Some Demographic Information about Zip Codes with and without Purchases

MEASURE	HAS ORDER?	
	NO	YES
Number of Zip Codes	21,182	11,807
Average Number of Households	1,273.2	7,475.0
Average Median Income	$44,790	$60,835
Households on Public Assistance	2.9%	2.7%
Population with College Degree	16.8%	32.1%
Owner Occupied Households	72.5%	63.4%

```
        SUM(ownerocc * 1.0) / SUM(tothhs) as hhowner
FROM ZipCensus zc LEFT OUTER JOIN
     (SELECT DISTINCT ZipCode FROM Orders) o
     ON zc.zcta5 = o.ZipCode
GROUP BY (CASE WHEN o.ZipCode IS NULL THEN 'NO' ELSE 'YES' END)
```

This query uses a LEFT OUTER JOIN in order to retain all the rows in ZipCensus. From Orders, only the distinct zip codes are needed; use of the DISTINCT keyword eliminates the need for an explicit GROUP BY and ensures that no duplicate rows are inadvertently created.

Note that the census values being used are counts. Although the table contains both counts and percentages, for aggregation purposes, counts are more appropriate. The counts are then divided by the total—after the aggregation—to create a new percentage over all the zip codes in each group. The denominator varies, depending on the particular variable. Education levels are based on the population over 25, whereas home ownership and public assistance are based on the number of households. Taking the average of a ratio would result in a different value, one that is more biased toward zip codes with smaller populations.

So, zip codes that place orders are indeed more likely to be richer and larger. However, this analysis has a subtle bias. Orders are more likely to come from larger zip codes, simply because there are more people in larger zip codes who could place the order. Smaller zip codes are more likely to be rural and poor than larger ones. This is an example of sampling bias. Zip codes vary by size, and characteristics of zip codes are sometimes related to their sizes.

Restricting the query to largish zip codes helps eliminate this bias. For instance, any area with one thousand households has a reasonable opportunity to have someone who would place an order because the national order rate is about 0.23%. Table 4-10 shows the zip code characteristics with this restriction. Even among these zip codes, the same pattern holds of richer, larger, better-educated areas placing orders.

Table 4-10: Some Demographic Information about Zip Codes with and without Purchases with More Than 1000 Households

MEASURE	HAS ORDER?	
	NO	YES
Number of Zip Codes	6,628	10,175
Average Number of Households	3,351.8	8,603.5
Average Median Income	$46,888	$61,823
Households on Public Assistance	3.0%	2.7%
Population with College Degree	17.2%	32.2%
Owner-Occupied Households	71.2%	63.2%

Classifying and Comparing Zip Codes

Wealthier zip codes place orders and less wealthy zip codes do not place orders. Extending this observation leads to the question: *Among zip codes that place orders, do wealthier ones place more orders than less wealthy ones?*

One approach is to classify the zip codes by the penetration of orders within them. Penetration is the number of orders in the zip code divided by the number of households. Based on the previous analysis, we would expect the average median household income to increase as penetration increases. Similarly, we would expect the proportion of college-educated people to increase, and the proportion of households on public assistance to decrease. These expectations are all extensions of trends seen for zip codes with and without orders.

First, let's look at the median household income. Figure 4-8 shows a scatter plot of zip code penetration by household median income, along with the best-fit line and its equation. Each point on this chart is a zip code. Although the data looks like a big blob, it does show that higher penetration zip codes tend to be on the higher income side.

The best-fit line shows both the equation and the R^2 value, which is a measure of how good the line is (Chapter 12 discusses both the best-fit line and the R^2 value in more detail). The value of 0.26 indicates some relationship between the median income and the penetration, but the relationship is not overpowering. Notice that horizontal scale uses a clever Excel charting trick to remove the last three zeros of the median income and replace them with the letter "K." This is accomplished using the number format "$#,K."

TIP The number format "$#,K" drops the last three zeros from a number and replaces them with the letter "K."

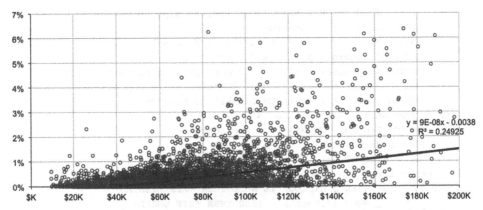

Figure 4-8: This plot shows household median income and penetration by zip code, for zip codes with more than 1,000 households. This pattern is noticeable but not overwhelming.

The query that produces the data for this chart is:

```
SELECT zc.zcta5, medianhhinc,
       (CASE WHEN o.numorders IS NULL THEN 0
             ELSE o.numorders * 1.0 / zc.tothhs END) as pen
FROM ZipCensus zc LEFT OUTER JOIN
     (SELECT ZipCode, COUNT(*) as numorders
      FROM Orders o
      GROUP BY ZipCode) o
     ON zc.zcta5 = o.ZipCode
WHERE zc.tothhs >= 1000
```

An alternative approach is to classify zip codes by penetration, and to compare demographic variables within these groups. Overall, 0.23% of households have an order at the national level. All zip codes fall into one of these five groups:

- Zip codes with no orders (already seen in the previous section)
- Zip codes with fewer than 1,000 households
- Zip codes with penetration less than 0.1% (low penetration)
- Zip codes with penetration between 0.1% and 0.3% (medium penetration)
- Zip codes with penetration greater than 0.3% (high penetration)

The following query summarizes information about these groups:

```
SELECT (CASE WHEN o.ZipCode IS NULL THEN 'ZIP MISSING'
             WHEN zc.tothhs < 1000 THEN 'ZIP SMALL'
             WHEN 1.0 * o.numorders / zc.tothhs < 0.001
             THEN 'SMALL PENETRATION'
             WHEN 1.0 * o.numorders / zc.tothhs < 0.003
             THEN 'MED PENETRATION'
```

```
             ELSE 'HIGH PENETRATION' END) as ziptype,
      SUM(numorders) as numorders,
      COUNT(*) as cnt, AVG(tothhs * 1.0) as avg_hh,
      AVG(medianhhinc) as avg_medincome,
      SUM(numhhpubassist * 1.0) / SUM(tothhs) as hhpubassist,
      SUM(bachelorsormore * 1.0) / SUM(over25) as popcollege,
      SUM(ownerocc * 1.0) / SUM(tothhs) as hhowner
FROM Zipcensus zc LEFT OUTER JOIN
     (SELECT ZipCode, COUNT(*) as numorders
      FROM Orders o
      GROUP BY ZipCode) o
     ON zc.zcta5 = o.ZipCode
GROUP BY (CASE WHEN o.ZipCode IS NULL THEN 'ZIP MISSING'
               WHEN zc.tothhs < 1000 THEN 'ZIP SMALL'
               WHEN 1.0 * o.numorders / zc.tothhs < 0.001
               THEN 'SMALL PENETRATION'
               WHEN 1.0 * o.numorders / zc.tothhs < 0.003
               THEN 'MED PENETRATION'
               ELSE 'HIGH PENETRATION' END)
ORDER BY ziptype DESC
```

This query is similar to the previous query with two differences. First, the inner subquery on `Orders` uses an aggregation, because the number of orders is needed as well as the presence of any order. And, the outer aggregation is a bit more complicated, defining the five groups just listed.

The results in Table 4-11 confirm what we expected to see. As penetration increases, the zip codes become wealthier, better educated, and have fewer households on public assistance.

Geographic Hierarchies

Zip code information has a natural hierarchy: zip codes are in counties, and counties are in states, for instance. Such hierarchies are important for understanding and effectively using geographic information. This section discusses comparisons at different levels of geographic hierarchies.

Wealthiest Zip Code in a State?

Wealth is spread unevenly across the United States. Relative wealth is often more important than absolute wealth, although actual income levels may differ considerably. This inspires a question: *What is the wealthiest zip code in each state?*

This question is about geographic hierarchies. Locations are simultaneously in multiple geographic areas, so zip codes are in counties and counties are in states. Someone residing in zip code 10011 in Manhattan is also living in New York

Table 4-11: As Penetration Increases, Zip Codes Become Wealthier and Better Educated

MEASURE	ZIP CODE GROUP				
	ZIP SMALL	ZIP MISSING	SMALL PENETRATION	MIDDLE PENETRATION	HIGH PENETRATION
Number of Orders	4,704	0	21,204	33,431	127,131
Number of Zip Codes	1,632	21,182	6,107	2,263	1,805
Average Number of Households	438.8	1,273.2	8,941.5	8,462.3	7,637.0
Average Median Income	$54,676	$44,790	$53,811	$64,078	$86,101
Households on Public Assistance	2.0%	2.9%	3.0%	2.4%	1.7%
Population with College Degree	29.0%	16.8%	25.1%	38.4%	52.1%
Owner-Occupied Households	76.8%	72.5%	64.6%	61.5%	60.5%

County, and in New York City, and in New York State, and in the United States. Of course, a handful of zip codes straddle state and county borders, as explained in Chapter 1. Each of these has a predominant state and county assigned to it.

The following query finds the wealthiest zip code in each state:

```
SELECT zc.*
FROM (SELECT zc.*,
             ROW_NUMBER() OVER (PARTITION BY stab
                                ORDER BY medianhhinc DESC) as seqnum
      FROM ZipCensus zc
     ) zc
WHERE seqnum = 1;
```

It uses the function ROW_NUMBER() to enumerate the zip codes in each state by median household income, and then chooses the first one. If there are ties, one is arbitrarily chosen.

Figure 4-9 shows a scatter plot of zip codes that have the maximum median household income in each state. Some states, such as Florida, have more than one zip code that matches the maximum. In this case, only one is chosen. This chart includes state boundaries, the mechanism for which is explained later in this chapter.

The chart places the zip codes into four buckets based on the maximum median household income:

- Greater than $200,000
- $150,000 to $200,000

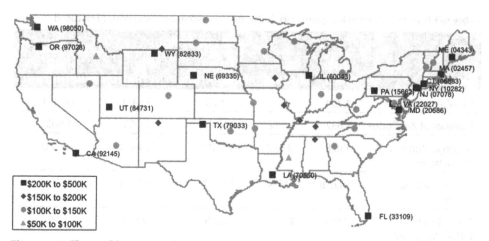

Figure 4-9: The wealthiest zip codes in each state are scattered across the map. Here they are shown placed into four income buckets.

- ■ $100,000 to $150,000
- ■ $50,000 to $100,000

The chart has four different series, one for each of these groups. The first series—the very wealthiest zip codes—are labeled with the name of the state and the zip code. Unfortunately, Excel does not make it possible to label scatter plots. Fortunately, there is a simple add-in that enables this functionality, as explained in the aside "Labeling Points on Scatter Plots."

The spreadsheet shown in Figure 4-10 pivots the data for the chart. The data starts out as a table describing zip codes with columns for zip code, state, longitude, latitude, and median household income. The data for the chart is in the adjacent five columns, with longitude in the first. The next four contain the latitude for the bucket the zip code belongs in or NA(). Column titles are constructed from the ranges defining the buckets. The scatter plot can then be created from these five columns.

	C	D	E	F	G	H	I	J	K	
12								Lower	200001	150000
13								Upper	500000	=K12
14										
15			FROM SQL							
16	Zip	State	Long	Lat	Med Inc	Pop		Long	=TEXT(K12, "$#,K")&IF(K13>K12+1, " to "&TEXT(K13, "$#,K"), "")	=TEXT(L
17	99516	AK	-149.7806	61.091074	140571	20818		=E17	=IF(AND($G17>=K$12, $G17 < K$13), $F17, NA())	=IF(AND(
18	35649	AL	-86.87243	34.62408	195547	93		=E18	=IF(AND($G18>=K$12, $G18 < K$13), $F18, NA())	=IF(AND(
19	72749	AR	-94.43759	35.868416	115577	69		=E19	=IF(AND($G19>=K$12, $G19 < K$13), $F19, NA())	=IF(AND(
20	85262	AZ	-111.8201	33.768355	128947	10567		=E20	=IF(AND($G20>=K$12, $G20 < K$13), $F20, NA())	=IF(AND(
21	92145	CA	-117.0188	32.92519	224423	1381		=E21	=IF(AND($G21>=K$12, $G21 < K$13), $F21, NA())	=IF(AND(
22	80454	CO	-105.2802	39.830935	133594	1092		=E22	=IF(AND($G22>=K$12, $G22 < K$13), $F22, NA())	=IF(AND(
23	6883	CT	-73.37300	41.21599	213423	10203		=E23	=IF(AND($G23>=K$12, $G23 < K$13), $F23, NA())	=IF(AND(
24	20015	DC	-77.06729	38.965376	149909	15796		=E24	=IF(AND($G24>=K$12, $G24 < K$13), $F24, NA())	=IF(AND(
25	19807	DE	-75.60365	39.78145	171155	7337		=E25	=IF(AND($G25>=K$12, $G25 < K$13), $F25, NA())	=IF(AND(
26	33109	FL	-80.13966	25.760175	250001	482		=E26	=IF(AND($G26>=K$12, $G26 < K$13), $F26, NA())	=IF(AND(
27	30327	GA	-84.42376	33.857151	135660	22715		=E27	=IF(AND($G27>=K$12, $G27 < K$13), $F27, NA())	=IF(AND(

Figure 4-10: This Excel spreadsheet pivots the data and assigns the names of the series for the chart in the previous figure. (Formulas for first bin are shown.)

The spreadsheet creates reasonable names for each of the series. The bucket is defined by two values, the minimum and maximum of the income range. The label is created using string functions in Excel:

```
=TEXT(L7, "$#,K")&IF(L8>L7+1, " to "&TEXT(L8, "$#,K"), "")
```

This formula uses the TEXT() function to format a number as a string. The second argument is a number format that drops the last three digits and replaces them with a "K" ("$#,K"). The IF() takes care of the bucket that does not have an upper bound.

Zip Code with the Most Orders in Each State

Of course, there is no reason to limit examples to demographic features of the zip codes. The same ideas can be used to identify the zip code in each state that has the most orders and the most orders per household.

Figure 4-11 shows a map showing the zip codes with the most orders in each state. Zip codes with the most orders are typically large, urban zip codes. If the measure were penetration, the zip codes with the most orders per household would be small zip codes that have very few households.

The query that generates the information is an aggregation query that uses ROW_NUMBER(). The ORDER BY clause is based on the count:

```
SELECT zc.zcta5, zc.stab as state, longitude, latitude, numorders
FROM (SELECT Zipcode, State, COUNT(*) as numorders,
             ROW_NUMBER() OVER (PARTITION BY state
                                ORDER BY COUNT(*) DESC) as seqnum
      FROM Orders
```

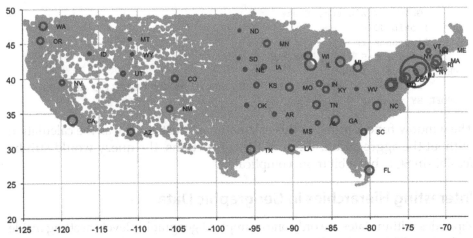

Figure 4-11: This map shows the zip code with the largest number of orders. The size of the circles represents the number of orders.

LABELING POINTS IN SCATTER PLOTS

The ability to label points in scatter plots and bubble plots (as in Figure 4-9) is very useful, but not part of Excel. Fortunately, Rob Bovey has written a small application to do this. Better yet, this application is free for download from `www.appspro.com/Utilities/ChartLabeler.htm`.

The XY-Labeler installs new functionality in Excel by adding a new menu item called "XY Chart Labels" to the "Tools" menu, which makes it possible to:

- Add labels to a chart, where the labels are defined by a column in the spreadsheet
- Modify existing labels
- Add labels to individual points in any series

In the chart, the labels behave like labels on any other series. Just like other text, they can be formatted as desired, with fonts, colors, backgrounds, and orientations. You can delete them by clicking them and hitting the Delete key.

When inserting the labels, the chart labeler asks for several items of information. First, it needs the series to label. Second, it needs the labels, which are typically in a column in the same table. And third, it needs to know where to place the labels: above, below, to the right, to the left, or on the data points.

The labels themselves are values in a column, so they can be arbitrary text and as informative as needed. In this case, the label for each point consists of the state abbreviation with the zip code in parentheses, created using the following formula:

```
=D10&" ("&TEXT(C10, "00000")&")"
```

where `D10` contains the state and `C10` contains the zip code. The `TEXT()` function adds zeros to the beginning of the zip codes to ensure that zip codes starting with "0" look correct.

```
       GROUP BY ZipCode, State
       ) ozip JOIN
       ZipCensus zc
       ON zc.zcta5 = ozip.ZipCode
  WHERE seqnum = 1 AND
        latitude BETWEEN 20 and 50 AND longitude BETWEEN -135 AND -65
  ORDER BY zc.stab
```

The window functions make this calculation almost as easy as the calculation without the aggregation. Without these functions, the query would still be feasible in SQL, but a bit more complicated.

Interesting Hierarchies in Geographic Data

Zip codes within states are only one example of geographic levels nestling inside each other. This section discusses some other geographic levels, even though most of these are not in the datasets.

Counties

Every state is divided into counties. Some states such as Texas have hundreds of counties (254). By contrast, Delaware has only three and Hawaii and Rhode Island have five. Counties are useful precisely because every address has some county associated with it, even though the location may not be in a village, town, or city. The table ZipCounty has the predominant county for each zip code. ZipCensus also contains the county for each of its zip codes.

Counties in different states can have the same name. Once upon a time, the author was surprised to see a map highlighting two counties in northern Minnesota as having very large marketing potential. Between them, these counties have a population of less than 20,000 people, which is not very big at all. Although Lake County and Cook County are small and out of the way (and very pretty) in Minnesota, their namesakes in Illinois are two of the most populous counties in the country.

To prevent such confusion, the Census Bureau has a numbering system for geographic areas called FIPS (Federal Information Processing Standard). The FIPS county codes consist of five digits. The first two digits are for the state and the last three are for the counties. In general, the state number is obtained by alphabetizing the states and assigning sequential numbers, starting with 01 for Alabama. The counties in each state are similarly numbered, so Alabaster County in Alabama has the FIPS code of 01001. The columns ZipCensus.fipco and ZipCounty.fipco contain the FIPS county codes for each zip code.

Counties are useful for other purposes as well. For instance, sales taxes are often set at the county level.

Designated Marketing Areas

Designated marketing areas (DMAs) are the invention of Nielsen Market Research and were originally designed for television advertising. These are groups of counties that form marketing regions, and are good approximations to metropolitan areas. There are 210 DMAs in the United States. The largest by population is the one containing New York City with about 7.4 million households (in 2012), with 29 counties spread over four states.

DMAs being composed of counties is a good idea because all areas in the United States are in some county. Hence, every location is in some DMA. Unfortunately, the definition is privately owned, so the mapping from county to DMA or zip code to DMA needs to be purchased for a nominal amount of money (although the definitions are readily available on the web).

Each company may have its own definition of its marketing area. Newspapers and radio stations also have designated marketing areas. This is the area where they compete for readers and advertising in the "local" market.

Census Hierarchies

The Census Bureau in the United States has quite a challenge. As mandated by the Constitution, the Bureau is responsible for "enumerating" (counting) the population of every state in the United States every ten years. The purpose is to determine the number of seats assigned to each state in the House of Representatives. In addition to counting residents, the census also estimates various demographic and economic statistics both during the decennial census and in the years in-between.

The Census Bureau divides the United States into a mosaic of small geographic entities, such as:

- Census block
- Census block group
- Census tract

The *census block* is the smallest unit and typically has a population of a few dozen people in a small area (such as along one side of a street or one floor of a large residential building). The United States is divided into over 11 million census blocks. The Bureau publishes very few statistics at the block level because such statistics could compromise the privacy of the individuals living in such a small area.

Block groups are collections of census blocks that typically have up to about four thousand people. Both census blocks and block groups change at the whims and needs of the Census Bureau, as populations grow and shrink and shift.

Census tracts are intended to be more permanent statistical subdivisions, with about two to eight thousand people each (although the largest can be much larger). Unlike zip codes, census tracts are designed to be statistically homogeneous and relevant to local governments. This is in contrast to post offices that are intended to serve diverse areas. Further information about the census divisions is available at www.census.gov.

The low-level census hierarchies are then aggregated into a cornucopia of other groupings, such as Metropolitan Statistical Areas, Micropolitan Statistical Areas, New England City and Town Areas, Combined Statistical Areas, and more. The problem with these hierarchies boils down to one word, politics. The funding for various federal programs is tied to populations. Perhaps for this reason, the Office of Management and Budget (OMB) defines these rather than the Census Bureau. For instance, in the 2000 Census, Worcester, MA was included in the Boston metropolitan statistical area. By 2003, it had been split out into its own area.

Other Geographic Subdivisions

There are a host of other geographic subdivisions, which might be useful for special purposes. The following discusses some of these.

Zip+2 and Zip+4

The five-digit zip code in the United States has been augmented with four additional digits, commonly known as zip+4. The first two are the carrier route code and the second two are the stop along the route. Because zip+4s change at the whim of the post office, they are not particularly useful for comparisons over time.

Electoral Districts

People vote. And the wards and precincts where they vote are located in Congressional districts and state and local election districts. Such information is particularly useful for political campaigns. However, the districts change at least every ten years, so these are not so useful for other purposes or for comparisons over longer periods of time.

School Districts

School districts are yet another geographic grouping. Each district has its own schedule. When do you want to send customers "back-to-school" messages? When do you want to offer discounted vacations to Disney World? Some districts start the school year in early August. Others start a month later after Labor Day. Similarly, some end in early May and some continue well into June. In addition, the quality of the school district (typically measured by test scores) can say a lot about the geographic area.

Catchment Areas

A catchment area is the area from where a retail establishment draws its customers. The definition of a catchment area can be quite complicated, taking into account store locations, road patterns, commuting distances, and competitors. Retailing companies often know about their catchment areas and the competition inside them.

Geography on the Web

Once upon a time, when the web was invented, people thought that it would herald the end of geography. Users can view web pages from anywhere, regardless of where a company is physically located.

In one sense, this is true: the web itself has no inherent geography, at least nothing more detailed than countries (which are important for legal reasons). On the other hand, geography is still important. Geography provides information about culture, language, product preferences, currencies, and time zones. There is evidence that even trends in the online world spread first through particular physical geographies—as friends, neighbors, and colleagues communicate with each other, even if that communication is via social media.

How can we extract geographic information from web interactions? There are essentially four different methods:

- Self-reported addresses
- IP address lookups
- Geolocation on mobile devices
- Ancillary information through other means

None of these are perfect and none provide a solution all the time. However, useful geographic information can often be inferred.

Self-Reported Addresses

Some websites require registration of some form or other. And, such registration often includes physical addresses as part of the profile information. Websites that require payment—when the payments are through credit cards—typically require addresses for credit card processing and/or shipment. Such addresses should be remembered so they can be geo-coded to provide latitude, longitude, and other information.

IP Address Lookups

All interactions over the web have an Internet Protocol (IP) address used to identify the network location of the computer or device at the other end. The addresses themselves look promising from the perspective of analysis. In the original standard (called IPv4), the address consists of four numbers between 0 and 255 separated by periods (the more recent standard IPv6 has even more numbers). A typical address might look like:

- 164.233.160.0

And you might expect this to be very close to 164.233.160.1. You would probably be right because both belong to Google.

However, there are no guarantees, because IP addresses are not assigned geographically. Organizations licensed by ICANN, the Internet Corporation for Assigned Names and Numbers, assign the numbers with little or no thought to physical geography. When numbers are assigned, a physical location and organization names are collected, so this information is available on a per-address basis. It is possible to get reference tables of this information or to look up the point-of-presence information using a cloud service.

IP address location information can be useful—but only when paired with a healthy dose of skepticism. The most important issue is that the address is for the point-of-presence on the web, rather than where the device actually is. For instance, Delta Airlines uses a service on-board their aircraft to provide Internet services to passengers. These passengers are geolocated to the Atlanta airport, regardless of where they really are—and given that the service only works above 10,000 feet, they are most definitely not in Hartsfield International. The same can be true of certain ISPs and corporate networks.

Virtual private networks (VPNs) are another issue. Many corporations use these, routing all Internet traffic through a single network interface. A user can easily switch between networks, sometimes just by switching a mobile device from a telephone provider to a Wifi. The VPN point of presence might be far away from where the individual is located. In extreme cases, the author has seen users logging in from New York City and then from London—within ten minutes of each other.

Nevertheless, the IP address does provide a good sense of geographic location. However, it is not guaranteed to be accurate and requires care when using.

Geolocation on Mobile Devices

Mobile devices provide another solution to the problem of locating users: geopositioning services on the device itself. These provide latitude and longitude information about the location of the device; the latitude and longitude can, in turn, be used to find almost any level of geography. The problem with geopositioning is that users may not always have the services available or turned on. So, although this information is more reliable than IP addresses, it is less available and device-dependent.

Ancillary Information

Some information associated with geography might be available through other means. In particular, web browsers can provide information on the preferred language and time zone where the computer or device is located. This information can be very useful for subsequent analysis.

An interesting example of using this sort of data comes from the dark side, a computer worm called Conficker. This particular worm would look at the computer being infected, and if the keyboard layout used on the computer were Ukrainian, then it would delete itself—the authors of the worm being Ukrainian wanted to protect their own computers. Such language information is available when someone is browsing the web—and has much more helpful uses than propagating damaging malware.

Calculating County Wealth

This section focuses on wealth in counties, which provides an opportunity to make comparisons across different levels of geography. The place to begin is in identifying the counties.

Identifying Counties

If orders contained complete addresses and the addresses were geocoded, the county would be available as well as the zip code (and census tract and other information). However, the data contains zip codes, rather than geo-coded addresses. The county for a zip code can be looked up using `ZipCounty` (the information is also available in `ZipCensus`). This is an approximate mapping, based on the zip codes existing in 1999. Even though zip codes can span both state and county borders, this table assigns one single county to each zip code.

What is the overlap between `ZipCounty` *and* `ZipCensus`? This question is quite similar to the question about the overlap between zip codes in `Orders` and `ZipCensus`. The query is similar as well:

```
SELECT inzc, inzco, COUNT(*) as numzips, MIN(zipcode), MAX(zipcode),
       MIN(countyname), MAX(countyname)
FROM (SELECT zipcode, MAX(CountyName) as countyname, SUM(inzc) as inzc,
             SUM(inzco) as inzco
      FROM ((SELECT zcta5 as zipcode, '' as countyname,
                    1 as inzc, 0 as inzco
             FROM ZipCensus)
            UNION ALL
            (SELECT ZipCode, countyname, 0 as inzc, 1 as inzco
             FROM ZipCounty)) z
      GROUP BY zipcode) zc
GROUP BY inzc, inzco;
```

This query is typical of queries that determine the overlap of two or more tables, with the addition of the county name and the zip code for informational purposes.

Table 4-12 shows that almost all zip codes in `ZipCensus` are also in `ZipCounty`. Almost ten thousand zip codes in `ZipCounty` are not in `ZipCensus`, because `ZipCensus` consists of zip code tabulation areas maintained by the Census Bureau. Zip code tabulation areas are defined only for a subset of zip codes that would be expected to have a residential population. The presence of so many additional zip codes is why having this secondary table is useful.

Measuring Wealth

The typical attribute for wealth is `medianhhinc`, the median household income. Unfortunately, this is not available at the county level. Fortunately, a reasonable

Table 4-12: Overlap of Zip Codes in ZipCensus and ZipCounty

IN ZIP CENSUS	IN ZIP COUNTY	NUMBER OF ZIPS	MINIMUM ZIP	MAXIMUM ZIP	MINIMUM COUNTY	MAXIMUM COUNTY
0	1	9,446	00773	99950	Acadia	Ziebach
1	0	343	01434	99354		
1	1	32,646	01001	99929	Abbeville	Ziebach

approximation is the average of the median incomes in all zip codes in the county. The average of a median is an approximation, but such approximations are often good enough for relative comparisons. The following query calculates the average median household income for each county:

```
SELECT zco.countyfips, zco.countyname,
       (SUM(medianhhinc * tothhs) / NULLIF(SUM(tothhs), 0)) as income
FROM ZipCensus zc JOIN
     ZipCounty zco
     ON zc.zcta5 = zco.zipcode
GROUP BY zco.countyfips, zco.countryname
```

Notice that this query uses the weighted average (weighted by the number of households), rather than just the average. The alternative formulation, AVG(medianhhinc), would calculate a different value; each zip code would have the same weight regardless of its population.

> **TIP** When averaging ratios at a higher level of aggregation, it is generally better to take the ratio of sums than the average of the ratios.

The NULLIF() function accounts for counties having zero households, an unusual situation. The only example in the data is Williamsburg, VA, an independent city in Virginia (meaning it is its own county). Three of its five zip codes are in neighboring counties. The only two zip codes assigned to Williamsburg are for the College of William and Mary, which has "group housing" but no "households." Such is the census data: accurate, detailed, and sometimes surprising.

Distribution of Values of Wealth

The distribution of median household income for both zip codes and counties is in Figure 4-12. This distribution is a histogram, with the values in thousand-dollar increments. The vertical axis shows the proportion of zip codes or counties whose median household income falls into each range. Overall the distribution looks like a normal distribution, although it is skewed a bit to the left, meaning that more areas are very rich than very poor (the peak on the left means that the tail extends further to the right). One reason for the skew is that the median household income is never negative, so it cannot fall too low.

The peak for both zip codes and counties is in the range of $30,000–$31,000. However, the peak for counties is higher than the peak for zip codes. And, the curve for counties is narrower, with fewer very large values or very small values. Does this tell us anything interesting about counties?

Actually no. We can think of counties as being samples of zip codes. As explained in the previous chapter, the distribution of the average of a sample is

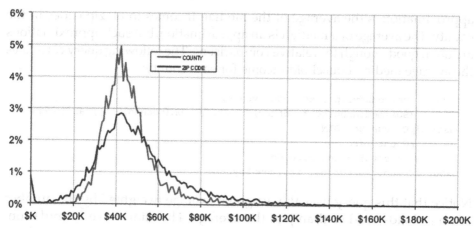

Figure 4-12: The distribution of median household income for counties is "narrower" than for zip codes.

narrower than the original data, clustering more closely to the overall average. Geographic hierarchies usually follow this pattern.

The data in Figure 4-12 was calculated in SQL and Excel. The SQL query summarizes the counts by bin, which Excel then converts to ratios for the chart:

```
SELECT bin, SUM(numzips) as numzips, SUM(numcounties) as numcounties
FROM ((SELECT FLOOR(medianhhinc / 1000) * 1000 as bin,
             COUNT(*) as numzips, 0 as numcounties
      FROM ZipCensus zc
      WHERE tothhs > 0
      GROUP BY FLOOR(medianhhinc / 1000) * 1000
     ) UNION ALL
     (SELECT FLOOR(countymedian / 1000) * 1000 as bin, 0 as numzips,
             COUNT(*) as numcounties
      FROM (SELECT CountyFIPs,
                  (SUM(medianhhinc * tothhs * 1.0) /
                   SUM(zc.tothhs) ) as countymedian
           FROM ZipCensus zc JOIN
                ZipCounty zco
                ON zc.zcta5 = zco.ZipCode AND
                   zc.tothhs > 0
           GROUP BY CountyFIPs) c
      GROUP BY FLOOR(countymedian / 1000) * 1000
     ) ) a
GROUP BY bin
ORDER BY bin
```

This query creates a bin for median income by taking only the thousands component of the number. So, an income of $31,948 is placed into the $31,000 bin. The calculation for this is simple arithmetic that uses the `FLOOR()` function. The query calculates this bin both at the zip code level and at the county level.

Which Zip Code Is Wealthiest Relative to Its County?

Local areas that are significantly different from their surrounding areas are interesting: *What is the wealthiest zip code relative to its county?*

Answering this question requires understanding what it really means. One possibility is that the difference between the median incomes is as large as possible. Another is that the ratio is as large as possible. Both of these are reasonable interpretations. The second leads to the idea of indexing values between different geographic levels, a useful idea.

> **TIP** Dividing the value of a variable in one geographic level by the value in a larger area is an example of indexing. This can find interesting patterns in the data, such as the wealthiest zip code in a county.

The following query finds the ten zip codes with more than one thousand households whose index relative to their county is the largest in the country:

```
SELECT TOP 10 zc.zcta5, zc.state, zc.countyname, zc.medianhhinc,
       c.countymedian, zc.medianhhinc / c.countymedian, zc.tothhs, c.hh
FROM (SELECT zc.*, zco.CountyFIPs, zco.CountyName
      FROM ZipCensus zc JOIN
           ZipCounty zco
           ON zc.zcta5 = zco.ZipCode) zc JOIN
     (SELECT zco.CountyFIPs, SUM(tothhs) as hh,
             SUM(medianhhinc * tothhs * 1.0) / SUM(tothhs) as countymedian
      FROM ZipCensus zc JOIN
           ZipCounty zco
           ON zc.zcta5 = zco.ZipCode AND
              tothhs > 0
      GROUP BY zco.CountyFIPs) c
     ON zc.countyfips = c.countyfips
WHERE zc.tothhs > 1000
ORDER BY zc.medianhhinc / c.countymedian DESC
```

This query has two subqueries. The first appends the FIPS county code onto each row in `ZipCensus`. The second approximates the median household income for the county. These are joined together using the FIPS code. The ORDER BY clause then supplies the intelligence behind the query, by ordering the result by the ratio in descending order.

These wealthy zip codes (in Table 4-13) all seem to be in counties whose income is a bit above average and whose population is quite large (they have hundreds of thousands or millions of households). These are wealthy enclaves in highly urban counties.

County with Highest Relative Order Penetration

Geographic hierarchies can also be used for customer-related information. For instance: *Which counties in each state have the highest order penetration relative to the state?*

Table 4-13: Wealthiest Zip Codes Relative to Their Counties

ZIP CODE	COUNTY NAME	MEDIAN INCOME			HOUSEHOLDS	
		ZIP	COUNTY	INDEX	ZIP	COUNTY
07078	Essex County, NJ	$234,932	$65,516	3.59	3,942	277,630
60022	Cook County, IL	$190,995	$57,780	3.31	2,809	1,878,050
10282	New York County, NY	$233,409	$74,520	3.13	2,278	703,100
33158	Miami-Dade County, FL	$142,620	$46,660	3.06	2,082	826,183
90077	Los Angeles County, CA	$182,270	$60,784	3.00	3,195	3,191,944
76092	Tarrant County, TX	$181,368	$60,756	2.99	8,279	631,364
10007	New York County, NY	$210,125	$74,520	2.82	2,459	703,100
38139	Shelby County, TN	$136,603	$50,416	2.71	5,411	328,973
60093	Cook County, IL	$156,394	$57,780	2.71	6,609	1,878,050
75225	Dallas County, TX	$141,193	$53,861	2.62	8,197	921,715

In addition to calculating order penetration, the following query also calculates some other statistics about the counties and states:

- Estimated number of households
- Estimated median income
- Percent of households on public assistance
- Percent of population with a college degree
- Percent of housing units owned

The purpose is to compare the highest penetration county to the state, to see if other factors might be correlated with high penetration.

Table 4-14 shows the top ten counties whose order penetration is highest relative to their states. For the most part, these consist of small counties with a smallish number of orders. However, the penetration by household is quite high. Interestingly, the larger counties with high relative penetration are wealthier than their states. However, some of the smaller counties are poorer. In general, these counties do seem to be better educated and have fewer people on public assistance.

The query that finds these counties is:

```
SELECT c.*, s.*, c.orderpen / s.orderpen
FROM (SELECT zcounty.*, ocounty.numorders,
             (CASE WHEN numhh > 0 THEN numorders * 1.0 / numhh ELSE 0
              END) as orderpen
      FROM (SELECT zco.CountyFIPs, zco.State,
                   MIN(countyname) as countyname, COUNT(*) as numorders
```

```
                    FROM Orders o JOIN
                        ZipCounty zco
                        ON o.ZipCode = zco.ZipCode
                    GROUP BY CountyFIPs, zco.State) ocounty JOIN
                    (SELECT zco.countyfips, zco.state, SUM(zc.tothhs) as numhh,
                            (SUM(medianhhinc * zc.tothhs)/
                            SUM(zc.tothhs) ) as hhmedincome,
                            (SUM(numhhpubassist * 1.0)/
                            SUM(zc.tothhs) ) as hhpubassist,
                            SUM(bachelors * 1.0) / SUM(over25) as popcollege,
                            SUM(ownerocc * 1.0) / SUM(zc.tothhs)  as hhuowner
                    FROM ZipCensus zc JOIN
                        ZipCounty zco
                        ON zc.zcta5 = zco.ZipCode
                    WHERE zc.tothhs > 0
                    GROUP BY zco.countyfips, zco.state) zcounty
                    ON ocounty.countyfips = zcounty.countyfips) c JOIN
              (SELECT zstate.*, ostate.numorders,
                    numorders * 1.0 / numhh as orderpen
               FROM (SELECT o.state, COUNT(*) as numorders
                    FROM Orders o JOIN
                        ZipCensus zc
                        ON o.ZipCode = zc.zcta5 AND zc.tothhs > 0)
                    GROUP BY o.state) ostate JOIN
                    (SELECT zc.stab, SUM(zc.tothhs) as numhh,
                            SUM(medianhhinc*zc.tothhs) / SUM(zc.tothhs) as
                                hhmedincome,
                            SUM(numhhpubassist*1.0) / SUM(zc.tothhs) as hhpubassist,
                            SUM(bachelors * 1.0) / SUM(zc.over25) as popcollege,
                            SUM(ownerocc * 1.0) / SUM(zc.tothhs) as hhuowner
                    FROM ZipCensus zc
                    WHERE zc.tothhs > 0
                    GROUP BY zc.stab) zstate
                    ON ostate.state = zstate.stab) s
            ON s.stab = c.state
        ORDER BY c.orderpen / s.orderpen DESC
```

This complicated query is built around four subqueries. The first two calculate the number of orders and the number of households in each county, in order to calculate the order penetration by county. The second does the same thing for states. These are then combined to calculate the order penetration index. The dataflow for this query in Figure 4-13 shows how these four subqueries are combined together.

The calculation of the demographic ratios at the county and state level follows the same methods seen earlier in the chapter. The percentages are multiplied by the appropriate factors to get counts (number of households, population, educated population). The counts are aggregated and then divided by the sum of the factors.

Table 4-14: Counties with Highest Order Penetration Relative to Their State

COUNTY FIPS/ STATE	NUMBER	MEDIAN INCOME	HOUSEHOLDS ON PUBLIC ASSIST- ANCE	OWNER OCCU- PIED	% WITH COLLEGE DEGREE	ORDER PENETRATION	INDEX
56039	7,142	$69,620	0.49%	61.40%	34.28%	0.48%	11.7
WY	221,523	$57,937	1.55%	70.29%	16.16%	0.04%	
16013	9,126	$62,727	1.88%	68.15%	31.25%	0.39%	11.6
ID	577,434	$47,580	2.84%	70.09%	16.97%	0.03%	
46027	5,294	$36,628	3.57%	56.44%	22.40%	0.19%	10.3
SD	320,310	$49,854	2.61%	68.62%	18.27%	0.02%	
08097	6,164	$67,710	1.31%	64.44%	40.79%	0.96%	9.0
CO	1,962,800	$61,291	2.09%	65.93%	23.45%	0.11%	
37135	42,762	$58,973	1.47%	57.55%	25.67%	0.56%	8.8
NC	3,693,221	$48,490	1.89%	67.08%	17.82%	0.06%	
08079	366	$56,731	0.00%	85.52%	26.08%	0.82%	7.7
CO	1,962,800	$61,291	2.09%	65.93%	23.45%	0.11%	
51610	6,120	$126,885	0.57%	73.17%	32.39%	1.01%	7.5
VA	3,006,262	$69,888	1.97%	67.80%	20.28%	0.13%	
45013	50,482	$56,540	1.35%	68.20%	22.55%	0.35%	7.3
SC	1,768,255	$46,001	1.77%	69.46%	15.81%	0.05%	
28071	14,672	$44,074	0.98%	61.87%	22.05%	0.12%	6.7
MS	1,087,728	$40,533	2.53%	69.91%	12.76%	0.02%	
49043	13,631	$88,867	0.98%	75.06%	30.64%	0.24%	6.2
UT	880,631	$59,777	2.13%	70.43%	20.12%	0.04%	

Mapping in Excel

Maps are very useful when working with geographic data. This section discusses the issue of creating maps in Excel. The short answer is that if mapping is important, Excel is not the right tool, at least without add-ins or extensions specifically for mapping. However, the longer answer is that basic charting in Excel can get you started.

Why Create Maps?

The purpose of mapping is to visualize trends and data, making it easier to understand where things are and are not happening. The zip code maps seen earlier in the chapter (for solar power and wealthy zip codes) contain tens of

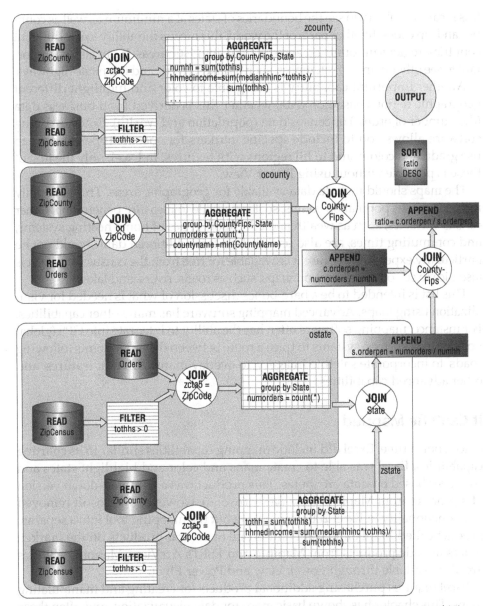

Figure 4-13: This dataflow calculates index of order penetration in a county to its state; this is the ratio between the order penetration in the county to the order penetration in its state.

thousands of zip codes in a format readily understandable by most people. A map summarizes information at different levels—showing differences across regions, between urban and rural areas, and for particular geographic areas. And this is just from rudimentary zip code maps.

Beyond this, there are several things that mapping software should do. Mapping software should be able to show different levels of geography. In the United States, this means the ability to see the boundaries of states at a minimum as well as counties and zip codes. In other parts of the world, this means the ability to see different countries, regions in countries, and different linguistic areas. It can also be important to see other points of references, such as lakes, rivers, and interstate highways.

Another important capability is being able to color and highlight different geographic regions based on data, whether this is derived from business data (the number of orders) or census data (population and wealth). Fancy mapping software allows you to include specific markers for specific types of data, to use graduated colors, and to fill regions with textures. In Excel, only the first of these is possible without using Power View.

The maps should include data available for geographic areas. This especially includes census population counts, so it is possible to measure penetration. Other census variables, such as wealth and education, types of home heating systems, and commuting times, are also useful. And this additional data should not be particularly expensive, because it is available for free from the census website. It is also nice to see other features on maps, such as roads, rivers, and lakes.

This list is intended to be a bare-bones discussion of what is needed for visualization using maps. Advanced mapping software has many other capabilities. For instance, mapping software often has the ability to integrate into GPS (global positioning services) systems to trace a route between different points following roads, to incorporate satellite imagery, to overlay many different features, and other advanced capabilities.

It Can't Be Mapped

Once upon a time, Excel did include mapping capabilities similar to its charting capabilities. Excel was able to create maps and color and highlight states and countries based on data attributes. This product was a trimmed-down version of a product from Mapinfo (www.mapinfo.com). However, Microsoft removed this functionality in Excel 2002, separating out the mapping tool into a separate product called MapPoint. MapPoint is one of several products on the market; others include products from Mapinfo and ESRI's ArcView. Mapping abilities are also available through Power View and Power Pivot.

Excel requires purchasing additional products for creating and manipulating maps. This chapter has shown basic maps for data visualization, and often these are sufficient for analytic purposes, although prettier maps are better for presentations. For basic data visualization, the needs are often more basic than the more advanced geographic manipulations provided by special-purpose software.

Mapping on the Web

There are various map sites on the web, such as Yahoo!, Google, MapQuest, and Microsoft Live. These websites are probably familiar to most readers for finding specific addresses and directions between addresses. They also include nifty capabilities, such as satellite images and road networks and include other features, such as local businesses and landmarks on the maps.

Perhaps less familiar is the fact that these websites have application programming interfaces (APIs), so the maps can be used for other purposes. A good example is www.wikimapia.org, which shows the ability to annotate features on Google Maps. Wikimapia incorporates Google Maps using an API, which can also be called from other web applications and even from Excel.

The upside to interfacing with online maps is the ability to create cool graphics that can even be updated in real time. The downside to using then is that they require programming, which can distract from data analysis. These systems are designed to make maps for websites, rather than for visualizing data. It is possible to use them for visualizing data, but that is not their primary purpose.

> **WARNING**   Having to use programming to visualize data (such as using an API to web mapping software) often distracts from data analysis. It is all too easy for analysis efforts to become transformed into programming projects.

State Boundaries on Scatter Plots of Zip Codes

Scatter plots of zip codes make functional maps, and they have the ability to annotate specific points on them. One of the features that would make them more useful is the ability to see boundaries between states. This section discusses two methods for doing this. Both methods highlight powerful features of Excel.

Plotting State Boundaries

The boundaries between states are defined by geographic positions—longitude and latitude. Excel scatter plots have the ability to connect the points in the scatter plot. For instance, Figure 4-14 shows the boundary of the state of Pennsylvania,

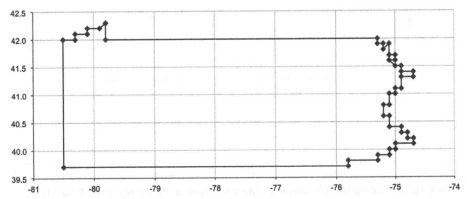

Figure 4-14: The outline for Pennsylvania consists of a set of points connected by lines.

Table 4-15: Latitude and Longitude of Points Defining Colorado State Border

STATE	LONGITUDE	LATITUDE
CO	−107.9	41.0
CO	−102.0	41.0
CO	−102.0	37.0
CO	−109.0	37.0
CO	−109.0	41.0
CO	−107.9	41.0

where the boundary is really defined by a handful of points. Some parts of the boundary have very few points (because the boundary is a line). Some parts of the boundary have many points, usually because the boundary follows natural features such as rivers. The Pennsylvania border has a very unusual feature. The boundary between Pennsylvania and Delaware is actually defined as a semi-circle, the only such circular-arc state border in the country. In this map, the arc is approximated by line segments.

The points defining the outline of the states are defined by their latitude and longitude. Colorado is a particularly simple state because it is shaped like a rectangle. Table 4-15 shows the boundary data for Colorado; the first and last points on the boundary are the same, so there is a complete loop. To create the map of Colorado, these points are plotted as a scatter plot, with lines connecting the points, and no markers shown at each point. These options are on the "Patterns" tab of the "Format Data Series" dialog box.

Adding more states requires getting the latitude and longitude, and making sure that extraneous lines do not appear. For instance, Figure 4-15 shows what happens

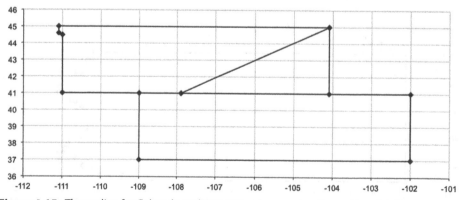

Figure 4-15: The outline for Colorado and Wyoming, drawn using the scatter plot, has an extraneous line.

when the outline of Wyoming is added to the Colorado outline. An extraneous line appears. Excel connects the points in the scatter plot without picking up the pen, so an extra line segment appears where Colorado ends and Wyoming begins. Fortunately, Excel makes it easy to eliminate this extraneous segment, merely by including empty cells between the two boundaries. This makes it possible to plot discrete entities on a scatter plot, without having a separate series for each one. Figure 4-9 used this technique to include state boundaries on the maps.

> **TIP** To make a particular line segment disappear from a scatter plot, simply insert a blank line in the data between the two points. The scatter plot skips the lines in the chart.

The boundary data was manually modified from detailed outlines of the states. It consists of several thousand points rounded to the nearest tenth of a degree. This scale captures the zigs and zags of the state boundaries to within ten miles or so, which is quite sufficient for a map of the country. However, the boundaries are not accurate at the finest level of detail.

Pictures of State Boundaries

An alternative method of showing state boundaries is to use a real map as the background for the scatter plot. The first challenge is finding an appropriate map. Plotting latitudes and longitudes as straight lines on graph paper is not the recommended way of showing maps in the real world, because such maps distort both distances and areas. Unfortunately, this is how most maps appear on the web. An exception is the national atlas at www.nationalatlas.com, which has curved lines for latitude and longitude.

The maps on websites cannot generally be copied as convenient image files. Instead, save the image file on the web or capture the screen image (using Print Screen), paste it into a program such as PowerPoint, and crop the image to the appropriate size. PowerPoint then allows you to save just the image as a picture file (right-click the image and choose "Save as"). The second challenge is setting the scale for the map. This is a process of trial and error, made easier by lining up the state boundaries on both maps.

Figure 4-16 shows an example using a map from Wikimapia that mimics the data from Figure 4-9. The map is copied into the chart by right-clicking the chart and choosing "Format Plot Area." On the right side is an option for "Fill," which brings up options for the background of the chart. The "Picture or Texture" tab, has the option to select a picture, which in this case is a map copied from the web. Of course, this works for any picture, not just a map.

The advantage of a picture is that that you can include any features available in the map. One disadvantage is that you cannot rescale the map to focus in on particular areas. Another is that the map and the data points may not exactly line up.

Figure 4-16: This example shows data points plotted on top of a map (from Wikimapia). The challenge in doing this is aligning the latitudes and longitudes so the points are properly placed.

TIP The background of a chart can be any picture that you want. Simply insert it through the "Picture" tab on the "Fill Effects" dialog box brought up through the "Format Plot Area" option.

Lessons Learned

This chapter discusses one of the most important characteristics of customers—where they live. Geography is a complicated topic; this chapter shows how to use geographic data in SQL and Excel.

Using geography starts with geocoding addresses to locate them in the world. Geocoding translates points into latitudes and longitudes and identifies census blocks, and tracks, and counties, and other geographic entities. Using the scatter plot mechanism in Excel, the latitudes and longitudes can even be charted, in a way that resembles a map.

One of the advantages of using geography is that the Census Bureau provides demographic and other data about customers' neighborhoods and other regions. Fortunately, one level of the census geography is the zip code tabulation area (ZCTA), and these match most of the zip codes in databases. Information such as the population of the area, the median income, the type of heating, the level of education—and much more—is available from the Census Bureau, for free.

Any given location is in multiple geographies. A location lies within a zip code, within a county, within a state, within a country. Comparing information at different levels of the hierarchy can be quite informative. One example is the wealthiest zip code in each state, or the highest penetration county in each state. Such questions use geographic hierarchies.

No discussion of geography would be complete without some discussion of mapping. Unfortunately, the simple answer is that Excel does not support maps, so use other software or add-ins. For simply locating a point, there are resources on the web. For fancy maps, there are more sophisticated mapping packages.

However, rudimentary mapping is quite useful and often sufficient for data analysis. For this purpose, Excel can be a useful visualization tool because it can use latitude and longitude to display locations and boundaries on a scatter plot. By using background maps, it is even possible to include many other features in the maps.

The next chapter steps away from geography and moves to another critical component for understanding customers: time.

No discussion of geography would be complete without some discussion of mapping. Unfortunately, the simple answer is that Excel does not support maps, so use other software or add-ins. For simply locating a point, there are resources on the web, or fancy maps. There are more sophisticated mapping packages. However, rudimentary mapping is quite useful and often sufficient for data analysis. For this purpose, Excel can be a useful visualization tool because it can use latitude and longitude to display locations and boundaries on a scatter plot. By using two grouped maps, it is even possible to include many other features in the maps.

The next chapter steps away from geography and moves to another critical component for understanding customers.

It's a Matter of Time

Along with geography, time is a critical dimension describing customers and businesses. This chapter introduces dates and times as tools for understanding customers. This is a broad topic. The next two chapters extend these ideas by introducing survival analysis, the branch of statistics also known as time-to-event analysis.

This chapter approaches time from several different vantage points. One perspective is the values that represent dates and times, the years, months, days, hours, and minutes. Another is when things happen, along with ways to visualize changes over time and year-over-year comparisons. Yet another perspective is duration, the difference between two dates, and even how durations change over time.

The two datasets used for examples—purchases and subscribers—have date stamps accurate to the day, rather than time stamps accurate to the minute, second, or fraction of a second. This is not an accident. For many business purposes, the date component is the most important part, so this chapter focuses on whole dates. The ideas can readily be extended from dates to times with hours, minutes, and seconds.

Times and dates are complex data types, comprised of six different components and an optional seventh. Years, months, days, hours, minutes, and seconds are the six. In addition, time zone information may or may not be present. Fortunately, databases have similar functionality for dates and times, such as functions to extract each component. Unfortunately, each database seems to have its own set of functions and peculiarities. The analyses presented in this chapter do not rely on any one particular database's methods for doing things; instead, the analyses offer an approach that works broadly on many systems.

The syntax is the syntax for SQL Server. Appendix A provides equivalent syntax for other databases.

The chapter starts with an overview of date and time data types in SQL and basic types of questions to ask about such data. It continues by looking at other columns and how their values change over time, with tips on how to do year-over-year comparisons. The difference between two dates represents duration; durations tie together events for each customer over a span of time. Analyzing data over time introduces new questions, so the chapter includes forays into questions suggested by the time-based analysis.

The chapter finishes with two useful examples. The first is determining the number of customers active at a given point in time. The second relies on simple animations in Excel to visualize changes in durations over time. After all, animating charts incorporates the time dimension directly into the presentation of the results. And, such animations can be quite powerful, persuasive, and timely.

Dates and Times in Databases

The place to start is the timekeeping system: how the passage of time is measured. Within a day, the system is rather standardized, with 24-hour days divided into 60 minutes and each minute divided into 60 seconds. The big issue is the time zone, and even that has international standards.

For dates, the Gregorian calendar is the calendar prevalent in most of the developed world. February follows January, school starts in August or September, and pumpkins are ripe at the end of October (in much of the Northern Hemisphere at least). Leap years occur just about every four years by adding an extra day to the miniature winter month of February. This calendar has been somewhat standard in Europe for several centuries. But it is not the only calendar around.

Over the course of millennia, humans have developed thousands of calendars based on the monthly cycles of the moon, the yearly cycles of the sun, cycles of the planet Venus (courtesy of the Mayans), logic, mere expediency, and the frequency of electrons whizzing around cesium atoms. Even in today's rational world with instant international communications and where most people use the Gregorian calendar, there are irregularities. Some Christian holidays float around a bit from year to year, and Orthodox Christian holidays vary from other branches of the religion. Jewish holidays jump around by several weeks from one year to the next, while Muslim holidays cycle through the seasons because the Islamic year is shorter than the solar year. Chinese New Year is about a month later than the Gregorian New Year.

Even rational businesses invent their own calendars. Many companies observe fiscal years that start on days other than the first of January, and some use a 5-4-4 system as their fiscal calendar. The 5-4-4 system describes the number of weeks in a month, regardless of whether the days actually fall in the calendar month. All of these are examples of calendar systems, whose particular characteristics strive to meet different needs.

Given the proliferation of calendars, it shouldn't be surprising that databases handle and manage dates and times in different ways. Each database stores dates in its own internal format. What is the earliest date supported by the database? How much storage space does a date column require? How accurate is a time stamp? The answers are specific to the database implementation and to the types supported by the database. However, databases do all work within the same framework, the familiar Gregorian calendar, with its yearly cycle of 12 months and a leap year almost every four years. The next few sections discuss some of the particulars of using these data types.

Some Fundamentals of Dates and Times in Databases

Dates and times have their own data types. The ANSI standard types are DATETIME and INTERVAL, depending on whether the value is absolute or a duration. Each of these can also have a specified precision, typically in days, seconds, or fractions of a second. The ANSI standard provides a good context for understanding the data types, but every database handles them differently. The aside "Storing Dates and Times in Databases" discusses different ways that date and time values are physically stored.

This section discusses topics such as extracting components, measuring intervals, and handling time zones. In addition, it introduces the Calendar table, which describes features of days and is included on the companion website.

Extracting Components of Dates and Times

The six important components of date and time values are year, month, day of month, hour, minute, and second. For understanding customers, year and month are typically the most important components. The month captures seasonality in customer behavior, and the year makes it possible to look at changes over longer periods of time.

Excel supports functions to extract components from dates, where the function name is the same as the date part: YEAR(), MONTH(), DAY(), HOUR(), MINUTE(), and SECOND(). The first three are also common to most databases. The ANSI standard function is EXTRACT() with an argument for the date part. An example is EXTRACT(year FROM <col>), which is equivalent to YEAR(<col>). These functions return numbers, rather than a special date-time value or string.

STORING DATES AND TIMES

Date and time values are generally presented in human-readable format. For instance, some dispute whether the new millennium started on 2000-01-01 or on 2001-01-01, but we can agree on what these dates mean. This format for representing dates conforms to the international standard called ISO 8601 (`http://en.wikipedia.org/wiki/ISO_8601` or available for purchase through the International Standards Organization) and is used throughout this book. Fortunately, most databases understand date constants in this format.

Under the hood, databases store dates and times in many different ways, almost all of which look like meaningless strings of bits. One common way is to store a date as the number of days since a specific reference date, such as 1899-12-31. In this scheme, the new millennium started 36,526 days after the reference date. Or was that 36,892 days? To the human eye, both numbers are incomprehensible as dates. Excel happens to use this mechanism, and the software knows how to convert between the internal format and readable dates, using "Number" formats on cells.

One way to store time is as fractions of a day; so, noon on the first day of the year 2000 is represented as 36,526.5. Microsoft Excel also uses this format, representing dates and times as days and fractional days since 1899-12-31.

An alternative method for both dates and times is to store the number of seconds since the reference date. Using the same reference day as Excel, noon on the first day of 2000 would be conveniently represented by the number 3,155,889,600. Well, what's convenient for software makes no sense to people. Unix systems and some databases use a reference date of 1970-01-01, and measure the time as integer values representing the number of seconds or milliseconds since the reference date. Dates before the reference date are stored as negative numbers. SAS uses yet another reference date, 1960-01-01.

Another approach eschews the reference date, storing values as they are in the Gregorian calendar. That is, the year, month, day, and so on are stored separately, typically as half-byte or one-byte numbers. In the business world, a date 2,000 years ago is safely before the data that we work with. Even so, as more information is stored in databases, there are uses for dates in ancient times, and most databases do support them.

SQL Server has several data types for dates and times. The most common one, DATETIME, can represent dates from the year 1753 through the year 9999 with an accuracy of about 10 milliseconds. The less accurate SMALLDATETIME supports dates from 1900 through 2079-06-06 with an accuracy of one minute. In both cases, the internal format consists of two integer components: The date is the number of days since a reference date and the time is the number of milliseconds or minutes since midnight. Durations are stored using the same data types. Other databases store dates and times in entirely different ways.

The variety of internal coding systems is a testament to the creativity of software designers. More important than the internal coding system is the information derived from dates and times and how that information gets used. Different databases offer similar functionality with the caveat that the syntax may vary from product to product. Appendix A shows different syntax for some databases for the constructs used throughout this chapter and the book.

Converting to Standard Formats

The ISO (International Standards Organization) standard form for dates is "YYYY-MM-DD" (or "YYYYMMDD"), where each component is left-padded with zeros if necessary. So, the first day of 2000 is "2000-01-01" rather than "2000-1-1." There are two good reasons for including the zeros. First, all dates consist of exactly ten characters. The second is also practical. Ordering dates alphabetically is the same as ordering them chronologically. Alphabetically, the string "2001-02-01" follows "2001-01-31," just as February 1st follows January 31st. However, alphabetically the string "2001-1-31" would be followed by "2001-10-01" rather than by "2001-2-01," even though October does not immediately follow January.

The simplest way to convert a value in Excel to a standard date is to set the numeric format of the cell to YYYY-MM-DD. This can also be done as a formula: TEXT(NOW(),"YYYY-MM-DD"). The function NOW() returns the current date and time in Excel, as the number of days and partial days since 1899-12-31.

Unfortunately, the syntax for similar conversions in SQL depends on the database. One way to get around the peculiarities of each database and still get a common format is to convert the date to a number that looks like a date:

```
SELECT YEAR(OrderDate)* 10000 + MONTH(OrderDate) * 100 + DAY(OrderDate)
FROM Orders
```

The results are numbers like 20040101, which is recognizable as a date when written without commas. In Excel, such a number can even be given the custom number format of "0000-00-00" to make it look even more like a date.

This convert-to-a-number method can be used for any combination of date parts, such as year with month, month with day, or hour with minute. This can be handy when the components of dates are available, but you do not want to construct a full date—such as aggregating by year and month.

As an example, the following query returns the number of orders and average order size in dollars for each calendar day of the year:

```
SELECT MONTH(OrderDate) * 100 + DAY(OrderDate) as monthday,
       COUNT(*) as numorders, AVG(TotalPrice) as avgtotalprice
FROM Orders
GROUP BY MONTH(OrderDate) * 100 + DAY(OrderDate)
ORDER BY monthday
```

Figure 5-1 shows the result as a line chart for each day in the year, with the number of orders on the left axis and the average dollars on the right axis. The average order size does not vary much during the year, although it appears a bit higher before August than after. On the other hand, the chart shows the expected seasonality in the number of orders, with more orders appearing in December than in any other month. The peak in early December suggests a lead time, with customers ordering earlier to ensure delivery by the holiday. This chart suggests that reducing the lead times might increase impulse sales in the two or three weeks before Christmas.

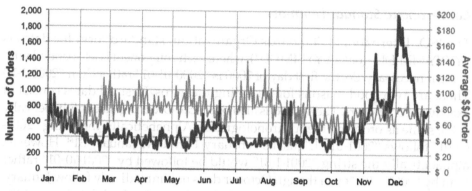

Figure 5-1: This chart uses a line chart to show the number of orders and average order size by calendar day.

The challenge in making this chart is the scale on the horizontal axis. It is tempting to make a scatter plot, but such a chart looks quite awkward because the "date" values are really numbers. There is a big gap between the values 0131 and 0201. These would be 70 units apart on a scatter plot, even though the corresponding dates are one day apart.

TIP Dates or times on the horizontal axis suggest using a line chart or column chart, rather than a scatter plot. A scatter plot treats the values as numbers, whereas the line and column charts understand date components.

The fix is to convert the numbers back into dates in Excel, using:

```
=DATE(2000, FLOOR(<datenum> / 100, 1), MOD(<datenum>, 100))
```

This formula extracts the month and day portions from the number, and puts them into a date with the year 2000. The year is arbitrary, because the chart does not use it. The line chart does recognize dates on the horizontal axis, so the "Number format" can be set to "Mmm" and the axis labels placed at convenient intervals, such as one month apart.

The right-hand axis (secondary axis) also uses an Excel trick. Notice that the numbers line up on the decimal point, so all the "0"s are neatly stacked. This occurs because there are spaces between the "$" and the digits for numbers under $100. The format for this is "$??0." Note that this trick can be used without the "$" to align numeric axis labels on a decimal point.

Intervals (Durations)

The difference between two dates or two times is a duration. ANSI SQL represents durations using the INTERVAL data type with a specified precision up to any date or time part. However, not all databases support intervals, so sometimes the base types are used instead.

Logically, durations and dates differ from each other. For instance, durations can be negative (four days ago rather than four days in the future). They can also take values larger than would be expected for a date or time value. A difference between two times, for instance, might be more than 24 hours. Also, durations at the level of hours might measure differences in decimal hours rather than hours, minutes, and seconds.

For analyzing customer data, these distinctions are not important. Most analysis is at the level of dates, and durations measured in days are sufficient. Durations in a single unit, such as days, can simply be measured as numbers.

Time Zones

Dates and times in the real world occur in a particular time zone. ANSI SQL offers full support of time zones within the date and time values themselves, so values in the same column on different rows can be in different time zones. For some types of data, this is quite useful. For instance, when browsers return time and date information on website visitors' machines, the results may be in any time zone.

In practice, dates and times rarely need time zone information. Most time stamp values come from operational systems, so all values are from the same time zone anyway, typically the location of the operational system, the company headquarters, or Greenwich Mean Time. It is worth remembering, though, that an online purchase made at midnight might really be a lunchtime order from a customer in Singapore (or New York, depending on your location).

Calendar Table

The companion website includes a table called Calendar that describes dates from 1950-01-01 to 2050-12-31. The table includes columns such as the following:

- Date
- Year
- Month as both a string and abbreviation
- Day of the week
- Number of days since the beginning of the year
- Holiday names for various holidays
- Holiday categories for various categories

This table is intended to be an example of what a calendar table might contain. Throughout the chapter, various queries that use features of dates, such as day of the week or month, can be accomplished either using SQL functions or by joining to the Calendar table.

Calendar is useful, but not absolutely necessary. However, within a single business, a calendar table can play a more important role, by maintaining important information about the business, such as when the fiscal year ends, important holidays, dates of product releases, and so on. The source of the holidays and categories for the calendar table comes from an editor called emacs, which supports a command called list-holidays. Emacs is distributed by the Free Software Foundation through the GNU project (http://www.gnu.org/software/emacs).

Starting to Investigate Dates

This section covers some basics when looking at date columns. The companion data sets have several date columns. Subscriptions contains the start date and stop date of subscriptions. Orders contains the order date, and the related OrderLines contains the billing date and shipping date for each line item in the order. Throughout this chapter, all these dates are used in examples. This section starts by looking at the date values themselves, and continues from there.

Verifying That Dates Have No Times

Sometimes, the result set for a query shows only the date components of datetime values, and not the time components. The date part is usually more interesting; and, leaving out the time reduces the width needed for output. Non-zero time values may not be visible, which can be misleading. For instance, two dates might look equal—say, as 2014-01-01. In a comparison, the two dates might not be equal because one is for noon and the other for midnight. Also, when aggregating by the date-time column, a separate row is created for every unique time value—which can result in unexpectedly voluminous results if every date has an associated time.

Verifying that date columns have only dates is a good idea: *Does a date column have any unexpected time values?* One solution is to look at the hour, minute, and second components of the date. When any of these are not zero, the date is categorized as "MIXED"; otherwise, the date is "PURE." The following query counts the number of mixed and pure values in ShipDate in OrderLines:

```
SELECT (CASE WHEN DATEPART(HOUR, ShipDate) = 0 AND
                  DATEPART(MINUTE, ShipDate) = 0 AND
                  DATEPART(SECOND, ShipDate) = 0
            THEN 'PURE' ELSE 'MIXED' END) as datetype,
       COUNT(*), MIN(OrderLineId), MAX(OrderLineId)
FROM OrderLines ol
```

```
GROUP BY (CASE WHEN DATEPART(HOUR, ShipDate) = 0 AND
                    DATEPART(MINUTE, ShipDate) = 0 AND
                    DATEPART(SECOND, ShipDate) = 0
              THEN 'PURE' ELSE 'MIXED' END)
```

This query uses a large CASE statement to identify dates where the time parts might not be zero. In SQL Server, the first argument to DATEPART() is the name of the date part. Although SQL Server supports the use of abbreviations such as HH and MM, the code is usually more readable and less ambiguous with the full name such as HOUR and MINUTE. The query does not actually run in SQL Server, because ShipDate is stored as a DATE, not a DATETIME; SQL Server does not allow you to extract time components from a DATE.

All the values in the ShipDate column are pure dates. If any were mixed, the OrderLineIds could be investigated further. In fact, all the date columns in the companion database tables are pure. If, instead, some dates were mixed, we would want to eliminate the time values before using them in queries designed for dates.

An alternative approach is to remove the time component from the date column and compare the two values. If they are equal, then the time component was originally zero. SQL Server does this by casting the column as a Date data type:

```
SELECT (CASE WHEN ShipDate = CAST(ShipDate as DATE)
             THEN 'PURE' ELSE 'MIXED' END) as datetype,
       COUNT(*), MIN(OrderLineId), MAX(OrderLineId)
FROM OrderLines ol
GROUP BY (CASE WHEN ShipDate = CAST(ShipDate as DATE)
               THEN 'PURE' ELSE 'MIXED' END)
```

This also indicates that the column has no time component.

Comparing Counts by Date

Often, just looking at the number of things that happen on a particular date is useful. The following SQL query counts the number of order lines shipped on a given day:

```
SELECT ShipDate, COUNT(*)
FROM OrderLine
GROUP BY ShipDate
ORDER BY ShipDate
```

This is a basic histogram query for the shipping date, which was discussed in Chapter 2. A similar query generates the histogram for the billing date. The next sections look at counting more than one date column in a single query, and counting different things, such as customers rather than order lines.

Order Lines Shipped and Billed

How many items shipped each day and how many billed each day? The ship date and bill date are both columns in OrderLines. At first, this might seem to require two queries. Although a possible solution, using two queries is messy because the results then have to be combined in Excel.

A better approach is to get the results in a single query. However, this is a little more complicated than it seems. Two different approaches are described here, one using joins and aggregations and the other using unions and aggregations. A further complication is including dates with no bills or shipments.

One place to start is a query that takes all the ship dates and matches them to the bill dates:

```
SELECT s.ShipDate as thedate, s.numship, b.numbill
FROM (SELECT ShipDate, COUNT(*) as numship
      FROM OrderLines
      GROUP BY ShipDate
     ) s LEFT OUTER JOIN
     (SELECT BillDate, COUNT(*) as numbill
      FROM OrderLines
      GROUP BY BillDate
     ) b
     ON s.ShipDate = b.BillDate
ORDER BY thedate
```

This query has a problem: Some dates might have bills but no shipments. When this happens, these dates are lost in the join operation. The opposite problem, dates with shipments but no bills, is handled by the LEFT OUTER JOIN. One solution is to replace the LEFT OUTER JOIN with a FULL OUTER JOIN, as in the following version:

```
SELECT COALESCE(s.ShipDate, b.BillDate) as thedate,
       COALESCE(s.numship, 0) as numship,
       COALESCE(b.numbill, 0) as numbill
FROM (SELECT ShipDate, COUNT(*) as numship
      FROM OrderLines
      GROUP BY ShipDate
     ) s FULL OUTER JOIN
     (SELECT BillDate, COUNT(*) as numbill
      FROM OrderLines
      GROUP BY BillDate
     ) b
     ON s.ShipDate = b.BillDate
ORDER BY thedate
```

Note the use of COALESCE() in the FROM clause. When using FULL OUTER JOIN, this function is often used because any of the resulting columns might be NULL.

TIP LEFT and RIGHT OUTER JOINs keep rows from one table but not both. When you need rows from both tables, the right solution is probably UNION ALL (with a subsequent aggregation) or FULL OUTER JOIN.

Another approach is to use the UNION ALL operator with GROUP BY. This first brings all the values together from the two columns and then does the aggregation:

```
SELECT thedate, SUM(isship) as numships, SUM(isbill) as numbills
FROM ((SELECT ShipDate as thedate, 1 as isship, 0 as isbill
       FROM OrderLines
      ) UNION ALL
      (SELECT BillDate as thedate, 0 as isship, 1 as isbill
       FROM OrderLines)
     ) bs
GROUP BY thedate
ORDER BY thedate
```

The first subquery chooses the shipping date, setting the isship flag to one and the isbill flag to zero. The second chooses the billing date, setting the flags in reverse. The aggregation then counts the number of shipments and bills on each date, just using SUM(). If nothing shipped on a particular date and something is billed, the date appears with the value of numships set to zero. Dates that have neither shipments nor bills do not appear in the output.

To include all dates between the first and last, we would need a source of dates when nothing happens. The Calendar table comes to the rescue: Make Calendar the first table in a sequence of LEFT OUTER JOINs. It can also be used with the UNION ALL approach:

```
SELECT thedate, SUM(isship) as numships, SUM(isbill) as numbills
FROM ((SELECT date as thedate, 0 as isship, 1 as isbill
       FROM Calendar c CROSS JOIN
            (SELECT MIN(ShipDate) as minsd, MAX(ShipDate) as maxsd,
                    MIN(BillDate) as minbd, MAX(BillDate) as maxbd
             FROM OrderLines) ol
       WHERE date >= minsd AND date >= minbd AND
             date <= maxsd AND date <= maxbd
      ) UNION ALL
      (SELECT ShipDate as thedate, 1 as isship, 0 as isbill
       FROM OrderLines
      ) UNION ALL
      (SELECT BillDate as thedate, 0 as isship, 1 as isbill
       FROM OrderLines
      ) ) bsa
GROUP BY thedate
ORDER BY thedate
```

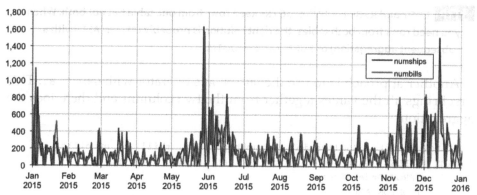

Figure 5-2: The number of items in an order and the number billed so closely track each other that the chart is difficult to read.

This query just adds an additional subquery for `Calendar`, with `isship` and `isbill` both set to zero.

This is the type of question where having a time component makes a difference. With time components, two order lines shipped or billed on the same date, but at different times, would appear as two rows in the output rather than one.

Figure 5-2 shows the results for just the year 2015 as a line chart (because the horizontal axis is a date). This chart is difficult to read because the number shipped and number billed track each other so closely. In fact, there is typically a one-day lag between the two, which makes patterns very difficult to see.

The `CORREL()` function in Excel calculates the correlation coefficient (technically the Pearson correlation), which measures how closely correlated two curves are to each other. The result is a value between minus one and one, with zero being totally uncorrelated, minus one negatively correlated, and plus one positively correlated. The correlation coefficient for the two series is 0.46, which is high, but not that high. On the other hand, the correlation coefficient between `numships` lagged by one day and `numbills` is 0.95, which says that the value of `ShipDate` is very highly correlated with `BillDate` minus one.

Customers Shipped and Billed

Perhaps more interesting than the number of order lines shipped each day is the question: *How many customers were sent shipments and bills on each day?* A customer might have an order with multiple shipping and billing dates. Such customers would be counted multiple times, once for each date.

The approach to this query is similar to the previous query. However, the subqueries in the UNION ALL statement are aggregated prior to the UNION ALL operation, and the aggregations count the number of distinct customers:

```
SELECT thedate, SUM(numship) as numships, SUM(numbill) as numbill,
       SUM(numcustship) as numcustship, SUM(numcustbill) as numcustbill
FROM ((SELECT ol.ShipDate as thedate, COUNT(*) as numship, 0 as numbill,
             COUNT(DISTINCT o.CustomerId) as numcustship,
             0 as numcustbill
      FROM OrderLines ol JOIN Orders o ON ol.OrderId = o.OrderId
      GROUP BY shipdate
      ) UNION ALL
      (SELECT ol.BillDate as thedate, 0 as numship, COUNT(*) as numbill,
             0 as numcustship,
             COUNT(DISTINCT o.CustomerId) as numcustbill
      FROM OrderLines ol JOIN Orders o ON ol.OrderId = o.OrderId
      GROUP BY BillDate)) a
GROUP BY thedate
ORDER BY thedate
```

The results for this query look essentially the same as the results for the previous query; most customers have only one order with one ship date and bill date.

Number of Different Bill and Ship Dates per Order

That last statement is worth verifying: *How many different order and ship dates do orders have?* This question is not about time sequencing, but it is interesting nonetheless:

```
SELECT numbill, numship, COUNT(*) as numorders
FROM (SELECT OrderId, COUNT(DISTINCT BillDate) as numbill,
             COUNT(DISTINCT ShipDate) as numship
      FROM OrderLines
      GROUP BY OrderId) o
GROUP BY numbill, numship
ORDER BY numbill, numship
```

This query uses COUNT(DISTINCT) in the subquery to calculate the number of bill dates and ship dates for each order. These counts are then summarized for all orders.

The results in Table 5-1 confirm that almost all orders have a single value for order date and a single value for ship date. This makes sense because most orders have only one order line (and hence only one product). The table also shows that orders with multiple dates typically have the same number of bill dates and ship dates. The policy on billing is that customers only get billed when the items are shipped. The 61 exceptions are probably worth investigating further to determine why this policy is occasionally violated.

Table 5-1: Number of Orders Having *b* Bill Dates and *s* Ship Dates

# BILL DATES	# SHIP DATES	# ORDERS	% OF ORDERS
1	1	181,637	94.1%
1	2	8	0.0%
2	1	35	0.0%
2	2	10,142	5.3%
2	3	1	0.0%
3	2	10	0.0%
3	3	999	0.5%
3	4	2	0.0%
4	3	3	0.0%
4	4	111	0.1%
5	4	1	0.0%
5	5	23	0.0%
6	4	1	0.0%
6	6	9	0.0%
17	17	1	0.0%

Counts of Orders and Order Sizes

Business changes over time, and understanding these changes is important for managing the business. Two typical questions are: *How many customers place orders in each month? How does an average customer's monthly order size change over time?* The first question is unambiguous, and answered by the following aggregation query:

```
SELECT YEAR(OrderDate) as year, MONTH(OrderDate) as month,
       COUNT(DISTINCT CustomerId) as numcustomers
FROM Orders o
GROUP BY YEAR(OrderDate), MONTH(OrderDate)
ORDER BY year, month
```

The second question is ambiguous. How many "items" as measured by the number of units in each customer's purchases? How many distinct products, as measured by distinct product IDs in each customer's order? How has the average amount spent per customer order changed? The next three subsections address each of these questions.

Items as Measured by Number of Units

Determining the number of units is easy using `Orders` and is a simple modification to the customer query. The `SELECT` statement needs to include the following additional variables:

```
SELECT SUM(NumUnits) as numunits,
       SUM(NumUnits) / COUNT(DISTINCT CustomerId) as unitspercust
```

This query combines all orders from a single customer during a month, rather than looking at each order individually. If a customer places two orders in the same month, and each has three units, the query returns an average of six units for that customer, rather than three. The original question is unclear on how to treat customers who have multiple orders during the period.

If instead we wanted the customer to count as having three units, the query would look like:

```
SELECT SUM(NumUnits) as numunits,
       SUM(NumUnits) / COUNT(*) as unitspercustorder
```

This takes all the units and divides them by the number of orders, rather than the number of customers. There is a subtle distinction between counting the average units per order and the average per customer. Both are equally easy to calculate, but they might produce (slightly) different results.

Items as Measured by Distinct Products

Examples in Chapter 2 showed that some orders contain the same product on multiple order lines. With this in mind, another way to approach the original question is to calculate two values. The first is the average number of products per order in a month. The second is the average number of products per customer per month. The SQL uses two levels of aggregation: first at the order level and then again by year and month:

```
SELECT YEAR(OrderDate) as year, MONTH(OrderDate) as month,
       COUNT(*) as numorders, COUNT(DISTINCT CustomerId) as numcusts,
       SUM(prodsperord) as sumprodsperorder,
       SUM(prodsperord) * 1.0 / COUNT(*) as avgperorder,
       SUM(prodsperord) * 1.0 / COUNT(DISTINCT CustomerId) as avgpercust
FROM (SELECT o.OrderId, o.CustomerId, o.OrderDate,
             COUNT(DISTINCT ProductId) as prodsperord
      FROM Orders o JOIN OrderLines ol ON o.orderid = ol.orderid
      GROUP BY o.orderid, o.customerid, o.orderdate ) o
GROUP BY YEAR(OrderDate), MONTH(OrderDate)
ORDER BY year, month
```

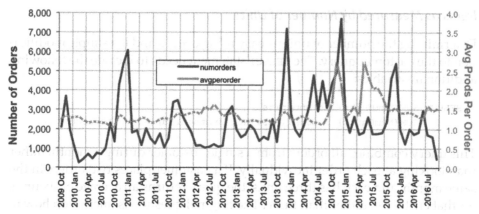

Figure 5-3: The size of orders as measured by average number of products per order changes from month to month.

One notable feature in this query is the multiplication by 1.0, to ensure that the division operation is done on floating-point numbers rather than integers. SQL Server (but not necessarily other databases) does integer division, so three divided by two would be one rather than one and a half.

The average products per order and per customer are pretty much the same on a monthly basis. Figure 5-3 shows the results of the query, with the number of customers plotted on the left axis and the average products per order plotted on the right. This chart shows peaks in the average products in an order. Most months have a bit over one product per order, but October 2014 and May 2015 peak at twice that value.

Such unexpected peaks suggest further analysis: *Is there anything different about the products being ordered in different months?* One way to answer this question is to look at information about the most popular product in each month. *What is the product group of the most popular product during each month?*

To find the most popular product, the products are enumerated from the highest frequency to the lowest using ROW_NUMBER():

```
SELECT ymp.yr, ymp.mon, ymp.cnt, p.GroupName
FROM (SELECT YEAR(o.OrderDate) as yr, MONTH(o.OrderDate) as mon,
             ol.ProductId, COUNT(*) as cnt,
             ROW_NUMBER() OVER (PARTITION BY YEAR(o.OrderDate),
                                             MONTH(o.OrderDate)
                                ORDER BY COUNT(*) DESC
                               ) as seqnum
      FROM Orders o JOIN OrderLines ol ON o.OrderId = ol.OrderId
      GROUP BY YEAR(o.OrderDate), MONTH(o.OrderDate), ol.ProductId
     ) ymp JOIN
     Products p
     ON ymp.ProductId = p.ProductId AND seqnum = 1
ORDER BY yr, mon
```

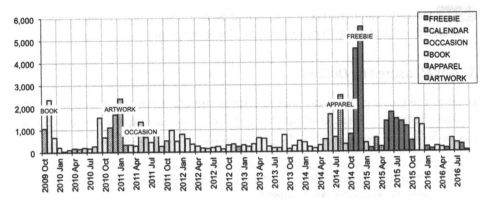

Figure 5-4: The most popular product group varies from month to month.

The subquery does the enumeration using ROW_NUMBER(). The outer query selects the top value for each month with the condition seqnum = 1.

Figure 5-4 shows the frequency and product group of the most frequent product for each month. In October 2014, the FREEBIE product group appears for the first time, and the high peaks in November and December are for FREEBIE products. Presumably, a marketing offer during this time gave customers a free product in many orders. This also explains why the average order size increases by about one product during this time. It looks like a similar offer was tried again six months later, but to lesser effect.

The chart in Figure 5-4 is a stacked column chart. The original data is in a tabular format, with columns for year, month, the product category, and the frequency. In Excel, an additional column is added for each product; the value in the cells is the frequency for the product group that matches the column and zero otherwise. When plotted as a stacked column chart, the groups with zero counts disappear, so only the most popular is shown. Figure 5-5 shows a screen shot of the Excel formulas that accomplish this.

	B	C	D	E	F	G	H	I
27				FROM SQL			EXCEL CALCULATION	
28	DATE	yr	mon	cnt	GroupName		ARTWORK	APPAREL
29	=DATE(C29, D29, 1)	2009	10	1063	ARTWORK		=IF($F29=H$28, $E29, 0)	=IF($F29=I$28, $E29, 0)
30	=DATE(C30, D30, 1)	2009	11	2353	BOOK		=IF($F30=H$28, $E30, 0)	=IF($F30=I$28, $E30, 0)
31	=DATE(C31, D31, 1)	2009	12	658	BOOK		=IF($F31=H$28, $E31, 0)	=IF($F31=I$28, $E31, 0)
32	=DATE(C32, D32, 1)	2010	1	226	BOOK		=IF($F32=H$28, $E32, 0)	=IF($F32=I$28, $E32, 0)
33	=DATE(C33, D33, 1)	2010	2	47	OCCASION		=IF($F33=H$28, $E33, 0)	=IF($F33=I$28, $E33, 0)
34	=DATE(C34, D34, 1)	2010	3	97	BOOK		=IF($F34=H$28, $E34, 0)	=IF($F34=I$28, $E34, 0)
35	=DATE(C35, D35, 1)	2010	4	180	ARTWORK		=IF($F35=H$28, $E35, 0)	=IF($F35=I$28, $E35, 0)
36	=DATE(C36, D36, 1)	2010	5	145	ARTWORK		=IF($F36=H$28, $E36, 0)	=IF($F36=I$28, $E36, 0)
37	=DATE(C37, D37, 1)	2010	6	202	OCCASION		=IF($F37=H$28, $E37, 0)	=IF($F37=I$28, $E37, 0)
38	=DATE(C38, D38, 1)	2010	7	184	BOOK		=IF($F38=H$28, $E38, 0)	=IF($F38=I$28, $E38, 0)
39	=DATE(C39, D39, 1)	2010	8	255	OCCASION		=IF($F39=H$28, $E39, 0)	=IF($F39=I$28, $E39, 0)
40	=DATE(C40, D40, 1)	2010	9	1564	BOOK		=IF($F40=H$28, $E40, 0)	=IF($F40=I$28, $E40, 0)
41	=DATE(C41, D41, 1)	2010	10	660	BOOK		=IF($F41=H$28, $E41, 0)	=IF($F41=I$28, $E41, 0)

Figure 5-5: This Excel screen shot shows the formulas used to pivot the product group data for the groups ARTWORK and APPAREL for the stacked column chart in the previous figure. Formulas for other groups are similar.

> **TIP** Stacked column charts can be used to show one value for each category, such as information about the most popular product for each month.

Size as Measured by Dollars

Back to measuring the order size. Perhaps the most natural measurement is dollars. Because `Orders` contains `TotalPrice`, calculating the average dollars per order or the average per customer on a monthly basis is easy:

```
SELECT YEAR(OrderDate) as year, MONTH(OrderDate) as month,
       COUNT(*) as numorders, COUNT(DISTINCT CustomerId) as numcust,
       SUM(TotalPrice) as totspend,
       SUM(TotalPrice) * 1.0 / COUNT(*) as avgordersize,
       SUM(TotalPrice) * 1.0 / COUNT(DISTINCT CustomerId) as avgcustorder
FROM Orders o
GROUP BY YEAR(OrderDate), MONTH(OrderDate)
ORDER BY year, month
```

Note that this query calculates the average for orders and customers at the same time. In both cases, an explicit division is used, instead of the `AVG()` function. `AVG()` would return the average order size, not the average per customer.

Figure 5-6 shows a "cell" chart of the results. The order size tends to increase over time, although there were some months with large average order sizes early on.

The results use a clever mechanism for creating bar charts directly in spreadsheet cells, rather than in a separate chart. Such a mechanism is useful for showing summaries next to a row of data. The idea is credited to the folks at Juice Analytics through their blog.

The idea is quite simple. The bar chart consists of repeated strings of vertical bars, where the bars are formatted to be in the Ariel 8-point font (another option is Webdings font at about 4-points for a solid bar). The specific formula

Year	Month	Num Orders	Num Cust	Total Spend	Avg Order	Avg Customer	
2012	1	2,676	2,654	$116,203.10	$43.42	$43.78	‖‖‖‖‖‖‖‖‖‖‖‖‖‖‖‖‖‖‖‖
2012	2	2,227	2,203	$106,719.55	$47.92	$48.44	‖‖‖‖‖‖‖‖‖‖‖‖‖‖‖‖‖‖‖
2012	3	1,822	1,798	$89,272.70	$49.00	$49.65	‖‖‖‖‖‖‖‖‖‖‖‖‖‖‖‖‖‖‖
2012	4	1,125	1,111	$64,056.72	$56.94	$57.66	‖‖‖‖‖‖‖‖‖‖‖‖‖‖‖‖‖‖‖‖‖‖
2012	5	1,150	1,138	$62,787.74	$54.60	$55.17	‖‖‖‖‖‖‖‖‖‖‖‖‖‖‖‖‖‖‖‖
2012	6	1,033	1,025	$71,591.29	$69.30	$69.85	‖‖‖‖‖‖‖‖‖‖‖‖‖‖‖‖‖‖‖‖‖‖‖‖
2012	7	1,080	1,067	$70,964.26	$65.71	$66.51	‖‖‖‖‖‖‖‖‖‖‖‖‖‖‖‖‖‖‖‖‖‖‖
2012	8	1,221	1,204	$88,913.55	$72.82	$73.85	‖‖‖‖‖‖‖‖‖‖‖‖‖‖‖‖‖‖‖‖‖‖‖‖
2012	9	1,082	1,064	$78,597.14	$72.64	$73.87	‖‖‖‖‖‖‖‖‖‖‖‖‖‖‖‖‖‖‖‖‖‖‖‖
2012	10	1,138	1,110	$75,874.69	$66.67	$68.36	‖‖‖‖‖‖‖‖‖‖‖‖‖‖‖‖‖‖‖‖‖‖
2012	11	2,803	2,761	$265,415.97	$94.69	$96.13	‖‖‖‖‖‖‖‖‖‖‖‖‖‖‖‖‖‖‖‖‖‖‖‖‖‖‖‖‖‖
2012	12	3,171	3,131	$313,752.39	$98.94	$100.21	‖‖‖‖‖‖‖‖‖‖‖‖‖‖‖‖‖‖‖‖‖‖‖‖‖‖‖‖‖‖‖‖
2013	1	1,962	1,942	$173,661.90	$88.51	$89.42	‖‖‖‖‖‖‖‖‖‖‖‖‖‖‖‖‖‖‖‖‖‖‖‖‖‖‖‖

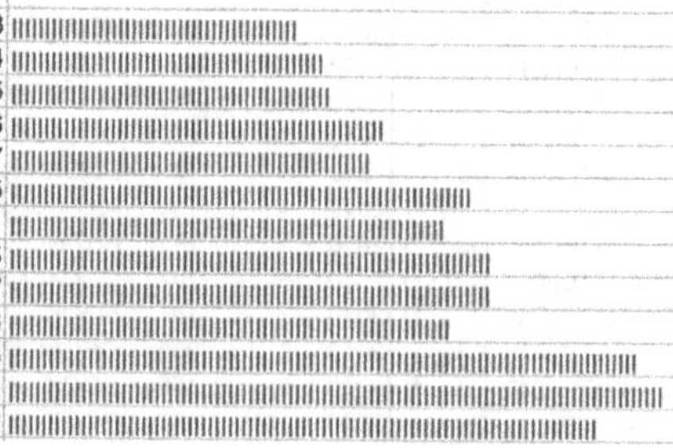

Figure 5-6: This bar chart is shown in Excel cells rather than as a chart. This is a good approach when there are too many rows to fit easily into a chart.

is =REPT("|", <cellvalue>). The function REPT() creates a string by repeating a character the number of times specified in the second argument. Because only the integer portion of the count is used, fractions are not represented in the length of the bars. Of course, a similar chart could be created using sparklines.

Days of the Week

Many business events occur on weekly cycles, with different days of the week (DOWs) having different characteristics. Monday might be a busy time for starts and stops because of pent-up demand over the weekend. Business operations can determine day of week effects as well. Customers are usually identified as late payers (and forced to stop, for instance) during the billing processing, which may be run on particular days of the month or on particular days of the week. This section looks at various ways of analyzing days of the week. Later in the chapter we'll look at how to count the number of times a given day occurs between two dates.

Billing Date by Day of the Week

How many order lines are billed on each day of the week (DOW)? This seems like an easy question, but it has a twist: SQL has no standard way to determine the DOW. One way around this is to do the summaries in Excel. Histograms for billing dates were calculated earlier and this approach builds on that data. In Excel, the following steps summarize by day of the week:

- Determine the day of the week for each date, using the TEXT() function. TEXT(<date>, "Ddd") returns the three-letter abbreviation.

- Summarize the data, using SUMIF() or pivot tables.

Table 5-2 shows that Wednesday is the most common day for billing and Sunday the least common. Calculating these results is also possible in SQL. The simplest method is to use an extension to get the day of the week, such as this version using SQL Server syntax:

```
SELECT billdow, COUNT(*) as numbills
FROM (SELECT ol.*, DATENAME(dw, BillDate) as billdow
      FROM OrderLines ol) ol
GROUP BY billdow
ORDER BY (CASE WHEN billdow = 'Monday' THEN 1
               WHEN billdow = 'Tuesday' THEN 2
               WHEN billdow = 'Wednesday' THEN 3
               WHEN billdow = 'Thursday' THEN 4
               WHEN billdow = 'Friday' THEN 5
               WHEN billdow = 'Saturday' THEN 6
               WHEN billdow = 'Sunday' THEN 7
         END)
```

Table 5-2: Number of Units Billed by Day of the Week

DAY OF WEEK	NUMBER OF BILLS
Monday	17,999
Tuesday	61,019
Wednesday	61,136
Thursday	54,954
Friday	49,735
Saturday	32,933
Sunday	8,241

The most interesting part of the SQL statement is the ORDER BY clause. Ordering the days of the week alphabetically would result in: Friday, Monday, Saturday, Sunday, Thursday, Tuesday, Wednesday—a nonsensical ordering. SQL does not understand the natural ordering implied by the names. One solution is to use the CASE statement in the ORDER BY clause to explicitly assign numbers to the days of the week and sort by those numbers.

An alternative approach uses CHARINDEX(), a function that finds one string inside another and returns the position of the string:

```
ORDER BY CHARINDEX(billdow,
            'MondayTuesdayWednesdayThursdayFridaySaturdaySunday')
```

So, "Monday" would return a value of 1 because "Monday" starts at the first position. "Tuesday" would return 7 (because "T" is in the 7th position), and these are in order by the day of the week. You do need to be careful with this approach because the first appearance of a substring is the match. It works fine for days of the week, but it might get confused by "pineapple" and "apple."

> **TIP** Using a CASE statement in an ORDER BY clause allows you to order things, such as days of the week, the way you want to see them.

Changes in Day of the Week by Year

Has the proportion of bills by day of the week changed over the years? This can be answered by manipulating the day-by-day data in Excel. It is also possible to answer the question directly using SQL. The following query outputs a table with rows for years and columns for days of the week:

```
SELECT YEAR(BillDate) as theyear,
       AVG(CASE WHEN dow = 'Monday' THEN 1.0 ELSE 0 END) as Monday,
       . . .
       AVG(CASE WHEN dow = 'Sunday' THEN 1.0 ELSE 0 END) as Sunday
```

```
FROM (SELECT ol.*, DATENAME(dw, BillDate) as dow FROM OrderLines ol) ol
GROUP BY YEAR(BillDate)
ORDER BY theyear
```

Table 5-3 shows the results. Monday and Saturday stand out as having the largest variance from one year to the next. It suggests that something has changed from year to year, such as operations changing to prefer one day over another. Or, perhaps the date recorded as the billing date is changing due to systems issues, and the underlying operations remain the same. The results only show that something is changing; they do not explain why.

Comparison of Days of the Week for Two Dates

The `StartDate` and `StopDate` columns in `Subscribers` contain the start and stop dates of customers of a mobile telephone company. When two dates describe such customer behaviors, a natural question is: *What is the relationship between the days of the week when customers start and the days of the week when customers stop?* SQL can provide the answer:

```
SELECT startdow,
       AVG(CASE WHEN stopdow = 'Monday' THEN 1.0 ELSE 0 END) as Mon,
       . . .
       AVG(CASE WHEN stopdow = 'Sunday' THEN 1.0 ELSE 0 END) as Sun
FROM (SELECT s.*, DATENAME(dw, StartDate) as startdow,
             DATENAME(dw, StopDate) as stopdow
      FROM Subscribers s) s
WHERE startdow IS NOT NULL AND stopdow IS NOT NULL
GROUP BY startdow
ORDER BY (CASE WHEN startdow = 'Monday' THEN 1
          . . .
               WHEN startdow = 'Sunday' THEN 7 END)
```

Table 5-3: Proportion of Order Lines Billed on Each Day of the Week, by Year

YEAR	MON	TUE	WED	THU	FRI	SAT	SUN
2009	0.1%	21.1%	22.0%	15.2%	25.5%	14.1%	2.1%
2010	1.4%	27.5%	17.1%	22.0%	17.5%	13.1%	1.5%
2011	11.2%	21.9%	25.9%	18.4%	13.6%	5.0%	4.1%
2012	4.8%	22.9%	19.3%	18.5%	17.2%	14.7%	2.6%
2013	1.4%	20.2%	19.3%	16.3%	20.8%	17.3%	4.7%
2014	1.5%	18.6%	22.5%	21.0%	18.5%	15.5%	2.4%
2015	16.1%	22.8%	19.7%	19.8%	14.2%	4.0%	3.3%
2016	4.7%	19.5%	24.7%	18.4%	19.2%	13.1%	0.3%

Table 5-4: Proportion of Stops by Day of Week Based on Day of Week of Starts

START DAY OF WEEK	STOP DAY OF WEEK						
	MON	TUE	WED	THU	FRI	SAT	SUN
Monday	13.7%	11.0%	5.2%	22.4%	18.7%	15.0%	13.9%
Tuesday	12.9%	10.7%	7.6%	22.9%	18.2%	14.5%	13.2%
Wednesday	12.6%	9.9%	7.4%	23.9%	18.6%	14.7%	13.0%
Thursday	13.5%	9.5%	4.4%	21.5%	20.4%	16.1%	14.4%
Friday	13.9%	9.6%	4.2%	21.3%	18.6%	16.9%	15.5%
Saturday	14.7%	9.8%	4.4%	21.5%	18.4%	15.2%	16.0%
Sunday	15.4%	10.3%	4.6%	21.9%	18.5%	15.0%	14.3%

The results in Table 5-4 show very little correlation between the start dates and stop dates of customers. More customers are likely to stop on a Thursday than any other day, regardless of the day they started. And fewer customers are likely to stop on a Wednesday, regardless of the day they started.

How Long Between Two Dates?

Perhaps the most natural relationship between two dates is the duration between them. This section looks at differences between dates in different time units: days, months, years, and by the number of specific days of the week. Surprisingly, investigating durations at each of these levels produces interesting results.

Duration in Days

The BillDate and ShipDate columns provide a good place to start the investigation, particularly in conjunction with the OrderDate column in Orders. Two natural questions are: *How long after the order is placed are items shipped? How long after the order is placed are items billed?*

These questions are about durations. In most dialects of SQL, simply subtracting one date from the other calculates the duration between them in days (and this works for the DATETIME data type in SQL Server but not for the DATE data type). This also works in Excel, but Microsoft SQL uses the DATEDIFF() function for DATE and DATETIME.

The following calculates the duration between the order date and shipping date:

```
SELECT DATEDIFF(day, o.OrderDate, ol.ShipDate) as days,
       COUNT(*) as numol
```

```
FROM Orders o JOIN
     OrderLines ol
     ON o.OrderId = ol.OrderId
GROUP BY DATEDIFF(day, o.OrderDate, ol.ShipDate)
ORDER BY days
```

Notice that this query is actually counting order lines, which makes sense because a single order can have multiple ship dates.

The results are shown in Figure 5-7. In a handful of cases, the ship date is before the order date. Perhaps this is miraculous evidence of customer insight and service—sending customers what they want even before the orders are placed. Or, perhaps the results are preposterous, suggesting a problem in the data collection for the 28 orders where this happens. At the other extreme, the delay from ordering to shipping for a handful of orders is measured in hundreds of days, a very long lead time indeed.

The cumulative proportion in the chart shows that about three quarters of order lines are fulfilled within a week. This fulfillment time is an important measure for the business. However, an order should be considered fulfilled only when the last item has been shipped, not the first. Calculating the time to fulfill the entire order uses an additional aggregation:

```
SELECT DATEDIFF(day, OrderDate, fulfilldate) as days,
       COUNT(*) as numorders
FROM (SELECT o.OrderId, o.OrderDate, MAX(ol.ShipDate) as fulfilldate
      FROM Orders o JOIN
           OrderLines ol
           ON o.OrderId = ol.OrderId
      GROUP BY o.OrderId, o.OrderDate) o
GROUP BY DATEDIFF(day, OrderDate, fulfilldate)
ORDER BY days
```

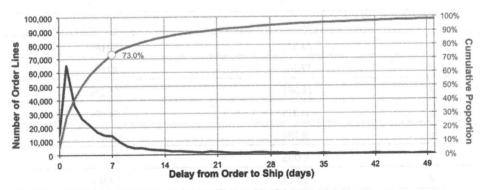

Figure 5-7: The delay from ordering to shipping is shown here, both as a histogram and a cumulative proportion.

This query summarizes the orders in the subquery to calculate the fulfillment date. It aggregates by both `OrderId` and `OrderDate`. Strictly speaking, only `OrderId` is necessary because each order has only one date. However, including `OrderDate` in the `GROUP BY` is simpler than putting `MIN(OrderDate)` in the `SELECT` clause.

Table 5-5 shows the cumulative fulfillment by days after the order for the first ten days. About 70% of orders have all their items shipped within a week.

Duration in Weeks

Duration in weeks is calculated directly from days. The number of weeks is the number of days divided by seven:

```
SELECT FLOOR(DATEDIFF(day, OrderDate, fulfilldate) / 7) as weeks, . . .
. . .
GROUP BY FLOOR(DATEDIFF(day, OrderDate, fulfilldate) / 7)
```

Notice that this query uses the `FLOOR()` function to eliminate any fractional part. Alternatively, the function call can be written as `DATEDIFF(week, OrderDate, fulfilldate)`.

Using weeks is advantageous when data is relatively sparse because a week brings together more instances than a day. Another advantage is when the business has a natural weekly cycle. For instance, if orders were not shipped or billed on weekends, then that would introduce a weekly cycle. Summarizing by weeks removes the extraneous cycle within a week, making longer-term patterns more visible.

Table 5-5: Days to Fulfill Entire Order

DAYS	COUNT	CUMULATIVE PROPORTION
0	10,326	5.4%
1	42,351	27.3%
2	22,513	39.0%
3	17,267	47.9%
4	14,081	55.2%
5	11,115	61.0%
6	9,294	65.8%
7	8,085	70.0%
8	5,658	72.9%
9	4,163	75.1%
10	3,373	76.8%

Duration in Months

Measuring the number of months between two dates is more challenging than measuring the number of days or weeks. The problem is that two dates might differ by 30 days and be one month apart (say, 15 April and 15 May) or might be zero months apart (say, 1 Jan and 31 Jan). A good approximation is to divide the difference in days by 30.4, the average number of days in a month.

The SQL Server DATEDIFF() function accepts month as the first argument, but the results are not intuitive. It counts the number of month boundaries between dates, returning one month for 2000-01-31 and 2000-02-01. These two dates have a month boundary between them. It counts zero months between 2000-01-01 and 2000-01-31 because there is no month boundary between these dates.

A more exact calculation requires some rules:

- The duration in months between two dates in the same month is zero. So, the duration between 2000-01-01 and 2000-01-31 is zero months.

- The duration in months between a date in one month and a date in the next month depends on the day of the month. The duration is zero when the day in the second month is less than the day in the first month. So, the duration between 2000-01-01 and 2000-02-01 is one month. The duration between 2000-01-31 and 2000-02-01 is zero months.

These rules can be implemented in a query:

```
SELECT ((YEAR(s.StopDate) * 12 + MONTH(s.StopDate)) -
        (YEAR(s.StartDate) * 12 + MONTH(s.StartDate)) -
        (CASE WHEN DAY(s.StopDate) < DAY(s.StopDate)
              THEN 1 ELSE 0 END)
       ) as tenuremonths, s.*
FROM Subscribers s
WHERE s.StopDate IS NOT NULL
```

The query calculates the number of months since the year zero for each of the dates and then takes the difference. The number of months since year zero is the year times 12 plus the month number. One adjustment is needed to take care of the situation when the start date is later in the month than the stop date. The extra month has not gone by, so the difference has over-counted by one.

How Many Mondays?

Normally, durations are measured in units of time, such as the days, weeks, and months between two dates. Sometimes, understanding milestones between two dates, such as the number of birthdays or the number of school days, is important.

This section goes into detail on one particular example, finding the number of times that a specific day of the week occurs between two dates. This is motivated by a specific business problem, so this section illustrates taking a business problem and some observations on how to solve it, converting the observations into rules, and implementing the rules in SQL to address the problem.

A Business Problem about Days of the Week

This example originated at a newspaper company studying its home delivery customers. The newspaper customer database typically contains the start and stop dates of each customer's subscription, similar to the information in Subscribers. In the newspaper industry, though, not all days of the week are created equal. In particular, Sunday papers are more voluminous and more expensive, filled with more advertising, and their circulation is even counted differently by the organization that audits newspaper circulation, the Alliance for Audited Media (formerly named the Audit Bureau of Circulation).

This newspaper was interested in knowing: *How many Sunday copies did any given home delivery customer receive?* This question readily extends to the number of copies received on any day of the week, not just Sunday. And more generally, for any two dates, the same techniques can count the number of Sundays and Mondays and Tuesdays and so on between them. This section shows how to do this calculation in SQL using the subscription data. Why SQL and not Excel? The answer is that there are many start dates, and many stop dates, and many, many combinations of the two. The data simply does not fit into a worksheet, so SQL is needed to do the heavy lifting.

Outline of a Solution

The first observation is that complete weeks are easy, so customers whose start and stop dates differ by some multiple of seven days have the same number of Sundays and Mondays and Tuesdays and so on—and the number is the number of weeks between the dates. For any two dates, we can subtract complete weeks from the later one until there are zero to six days left over. The problem is half solved.

When complete weeks are subtracted out, the problem reduces to the following: *Given a start date and a period of zero to six days, how often does each day of the week occur during this period?* Periods longer than six days have been taken care of by subtracting out complete weeks.

Table 5-6 is a lookup table that answers this question for Wednesdays. The first row says that if the start date is Sunday, there have to be at least four days left over in order to have a Wednesday in the period. Notice that the first column is all NO because no days are left over when the difference between the dates is a whole number of weeks.

Table 5-6: Extra Wednesday Lookup Table, Given Start Day of Week and Days Left Over

START DAY OF WEEK	DAYS LEFT OVER						
	0	1	2	3	4	5	6
Sunday (1)	NO	NO	NO	NO	YES	YES	YES
Monday (2)	NO	NO	NO	YES	YES	YES	YES
Tuesday (3)	NO	NO	YES	YES	YES	YES	YES
Wednesday (4)	NO	YES	YES	YES	YES	YES	YES
Thursday (5)	NO	NO	NO	NO	NO	NO	NO
Friday (6)	NO	NO	NO	NO	NO	NO	YES
Saturday (7)	NO	NO	NO	NO	NO	YES	YES

Unfortunately, a solution using this approach requires a separate table for each day of the week. Can we determine this information without a plethora of lookup tables?

There is a way, and although a bit cumbersome arithmetically it provides a nice illustration of observing rules and implementing them in SQL. This method rests on two additional rules, which in turn need two variables. The first is `leftover`, the number of days left over after all the complete weeks have been counted. The second is the day of the week as a number, which for convention we are taking to start on Sunday as one through Saturday as seven (this is the default convention for the Excel function `WEEKDAY()`).

With this information, the following rules tell us whether a Wednesday, whose number is four, is included in the leftover days:

- If the start day of the week falls on or before Wednesday, then Wednesday is included when the start day of the week number plus the leftover days is greater than four. For example, if someone starts on a Sunday (value one), then leftover days needs to be at least four.

- If the start day of the week is after Wednesday, then Wednesday is included when the start day of the week number plus the leftover days is greater than 11. For instance, if someone starts on a Saturday (value seven), then leftover days needs to be at least five.

These generalize to the following rules, where DOW is the day we are looking for:

- If the start day of the week is on or before DOW, then DOW is included when the start day of the week number plus the leftover days is greater than the DOW number.

- If the start day of the week is after DOW, then DOW is included when the start day of the week number plus the leftover days is greater than seven plus the DOW number.

The next section builds the rules in SQL.

Solving It in SQL

The SQL implementation calculates three values:

- `weeksbetween` is the number of complete weeks between the two dates, calculated by taking the duration in days, dividing by seven, and ignoring the remainder.

- `leftover` is the days left over after all the weeks have been counted.

- `downum` is the day of week number determined using a CASE statement on the day of week name.

The following query uses nested subqueries for the calculation:

```
SELECT s.*,
       (weeksbetween +
       (CASE WHEN (downum <= 1 AND downum + leftover > 1) OR
                  (downum > 1 AND downum + leftover > 7 + 1)
            THEN 1 ELSE 0 END)) as Sundays,
       (weeksbetween +
       (CASE WHEN (downum <= 2 AND downum + leftover > 2) OR
                  (downum > 2 AND downum + leftover > 7 + 2)
            THEN 1 ELSE 0 END)) as Mondays
FROM (SELECT daysbetween, FLOOR(daysbetween / 7) as weeksbetween,
             daysbetween - 7 * FLOOR(daysbetween / 7) as leftover,
             (CASE WHEN startdow = 'Monday' THEN 1
                   . . .
                   WHEN startdow = 'Sunday' THEN 7 END) downum
      FROM (SELECT s.*, DATENAME(dw, StartDate) as startdow,
                   DATEDIFF(day, StopDate, StartDate
                           ) as daysbetween
            FROM Subscribers s
            WHERE s.StopDate IS NOT NULL
           ) s
     ) s
```

The outermost query calculates the number of Sundays and Mondays between the start date and stop date using the two rules. Other days of the week follow the same logic as these counts.

Using a Calendar Table Instead

The `Calendar` table could be used instead:

```
SELECT s.CustomerId,
       SUM(CASE WHEN c.dow = 'Mon' THEN 1 ELSE 0 END) as Mondays
FROM Subscribers s JOIN
     Calendar c
```

```
      ON c.date BETWEEN s.StartDate AND DATEADD(day, -1, s.StopDate)
WHERE s.StopDate IS NOT NULL
GROUP BY s.CustomerId
```

This query is clearly easier to read and understand. The downside is performance. The join operation creates an intermediate result with one row for every calendar date between the start date and stop date, potentially multiplying the number of rows by hundreds or thousands. This query has very poor performance.

If counting weekdays is important, there is a more efficient method both in terms of representation and performance. `Calendar` has seven additional columns to count the number of each day of the week since some reference date. So, `Mondays` is the number of Mondays since the reference date.

The following query uses these columns:

```
SELECT s.*, (cstop.Mondays - cstart.Mondays) as mondays
FROM Subscribers s JOIN
     Calendar cstart
     ON cstart.Date = s.StartDate JOIN
     Calendar cstop
     ON cstop.Date = s.StopDate
WHERE s.StopDate IS NOT NULL
```

This method joins `Subscribers` to `Calendar` twice, once to look up the `Mondays` value for the start date and once for the stop date. The number of Mondays between the two dates is just the difference between these values.

When Is the Next Anniversary (or Birthday)?

Anniversaries are important—as ads for diamonds and bad jokes by comedians can attest to. In business, they are also important. Some companies give customers special offers on their birthdays or on the anniversary of their starting. Other companies may keep track of customers and place them into tenure groups by year. And, in some businesses, anniversaries may be correlated with customers stopping—because of the expiration of contracts.

The question arises: *When is the next anniversary date for each customer?* This is a bit harder than it sounds. After all, the next anniversary might be in the current year or it might be next year.

First Year Anniversary This Month

How many subscribers have their first (or tenth) anniversary this month? This question is actually simple to answer because it does not require much date arithmetic. The logic is simple:

- The month of the start date is this month.
- The year of the start date is exactly one year ago.

The one important thing needed is the current date. Most databases provide some mechanism for getting the current date, such as GETDATE() in SQL Server. The ANSI standard specifies the expression CURRENT_TIMESTAMP as the current date.

The SQL is then:

```
SELECT COUNT(*)
FROM Subscribers s
WHERE MONTH(StartDate) = MONTH(CURRENT_TIMESTAMP) AND
      YEAR(StartDate) = YEAR(CURRENT_TIMESTAMP) - 1
```

Of course, this data is all historical, so the value returned by this query is zero—there are no such customers. By adjusting the - 1, you can find customers who have a specific anniversary coming up.

First Year Anniversary Next Month

How many subscribers have their first (or tenth) anniversary next month? This question would seem almost the same as the previous one. But there is a subtle difference. If the current month is December, then the next month is January of the *next* year. The customers to be counted actually come from the current year rather than the previous year.

One approach is to use a CASE statement specific for December. The WHERE clause would then be:

```
WHERE (MONTH(CURRENT_TIMESTAMP) <> 12 AND
       MONTH(StartDate) = MONTH(CURRENT_TIMESTAMP) + 1 AND
       YEAR(StartDate) = YEAR(CURRENT_TIMESTAMP) - 1
      ) OR
      (MONTH(CURRENT_TIMESTAMP) = 12 AND
       MONTH(StartDate) = 1 AND
       YEAR(StartDate) = YEAR(CURRENT_TIMESTAMP)
      )
```

This definitely gets the job done; however, it is a bit messy and difficult to follow.

Instead, let's just add one month to the current date and use that in the expression. To avoid writing the expression twice, the following version uses a CTE to express this calculation once:

```
WITH params as (
     SELECT DATEADD(MONTH, 1, CURRENT_TIMESTAMP) as nextmonth
     )
SELECT COUNT(*)
FROM params CROSS JOIN Subscribers s
WHERE MONTH(StartDate) = MONTH(nextmonth) AND
      YEAR(StartDate) = YEAR(nextmonth) - 1
```

This query defines the next month in a CTE called params. The CROSS JOIN is perfectly reasonable because params has exactly one row. Using a CTE makes changing the query for any month in the future easy.

> **TIP** A CTE can be a handy way to define constant values used throughout a query. Of course, you do have to join it to the other tables being used.

Manipulating Dates to Calculate the Next Anniversary

There are basically three approaches to getting the next anniversary. One is the "create-a-date" approach, where the next date is constructed from parts and logic. The second is the "add just enough years" approach. And the third is to use the calendar table.

Creating the Anniversary as a Date String

The first tends to be messy because of the conversions. The following query approaches this by using REPLACE() to format the string as a date:

```
SELECT s.*,
       (CASE WHEN MONTH(StartDate)*100 + DAY(StartDate) <=
                  MONTH(CURRENT_TIMESTAMP)*100 + DAY(CURRENT_TIMESTAMP)
             THEN REPLACE(REPLACE(REPLACE('YYYY-MM-DD', 'YYYY',
                                          YEAR(CURRENT_TIMESTAMP)
                                         ),
                          'MM', MONTH(CURRENT_TIMESTAMP)
                         ), 'DD', DAY(CURRENT_TIMESTAMP)
                  )
             ELSE REPLACE(REPLACE(REPLACE('YYYY-MM-DD', 'YYYY',
                                          1 + YEAR(CURRENT_TIMESTAMP)
                                         ),
                          'MM', MONTH(CURRENT_TIMESTAMP)
                         ), 'DD', DAY(CURRENT_TIMESTAMP)
                  )
        END) as NextAnnivesary
FROM Subscribers s
```

This query returns the value as a string formatted as YYYY-MM-DD. This can easily be converted back to a date using CAST(as DATE).

The logic in the WHEN clause is noteworthy. It converts the month and day portions of StartDate to numbers. So, March 7th becomes 307 and November 11th, 1111. These can then be compared to see which is earlier or later.

The logic seems sound, but it has a problem. It fails for leap years. For instance, one year after 2016-02-29 would be 2017-02-29, but the latter is not a valid date. Of course this can be fixed by using appropriate CASE logic to take leap years into account. The next section suggests a cleaner alternative.

Adding Years to Calculate the Next Anniversary

The second method is to add just enough years to the start date to get a date in the future. This allows the database to handle the issue with leap years. Some might insist that the anniversary for February 29th is February 28th.

Others might insist that the real date is March 1st. Either is fine for most business purposes.

The number of years to add is the difference in years between the current date and the start date—or one more than this difference:

```
SELECT s.*,
    (CASE WHEN MONTH(StartDate) * 100 + DAY(StartDate) <=
            MONTH(CURRENT_TIMESTAMP) * 100 + DAY(CURRENT_TIMESTAMP)
        THEN DATEADD(YEAR, YEAR(CURRENT_TIMESTAMP) - YEAR(StartDate),
                StartDate)
        ELSE DATEADD(YEAR,
                    YEAR(CURRENT_TIMESTAMP) - YEAR(StartDate) + 1,
                StartDate)
    END) as NextAnnivesary
FROM Subscribers s
```

This query uses a CASE statement to determine whether an additional year needs to be added.

A slight modification to the CASE condition is to add the difference in years and compare it to the current date:

```
WITH params as (
    SELECT YEAR(CURRENT_TIMESTAMP) as curyear
    )
SELECT s.*,
    (CASE WHEN DATEADD(YEAR, curyear - YEAR(StartDate),
                    StartDate) >= CURRENT_TIMESTAMP
        THEN DATEADD(YEAR, curyear - YEAR(StartDate), StartDate)
        ELSE DATEADD(YEAR, curyear - YEAR(StartDate) + 1, StartDate)
    END) as NextAnnivesary
FROM params CROSS JOIN Subscribers s
```

This version has the advantage of using logic that is similar to the final calculation.

Using a Calendar Table to Calculate the Next Anniversary

At first glance, the calendar table should simplify this manipulation. However, the logic is still a bit convoluted. One method looks for the next date with the same month and day as the start date:

```
SELECT s.*,
    (SELECT TOP 1 c.date
     FROM Calendar c
     WHERE c.month = MONTH(s.StartDate) AND
            c.dom = DAY(s.StartDate) AND
            c.date >= CURRENT_TIMESTAMP
     ORDER BY c.date
    ) as FirstAnniversary
FROM Subscribers s
```

This uses a correlated subquery to get the matching date. This has the leap year problem: For February 29th, it will return the next anniversary as four years in the future, rather than one year.

There is not a simple fix for the leap year problem. One solution is to add explicit logic to change February 29th to March 1st:

```
SELECT s.*,
       (SELECT TOP 1 c.date
        FROM Calendar c
        WHERE c.month = MONTH(s.NewStartDate) AND
              c.dom = DAY(s.NewStartDate) AND
              c.date >= CURRENT_TIMESTAMP
        ORDER BY c.date
       ) as FirstAnniversary
FROM (SELECT s.*,
             (CASE WHEN MONTH(s.StartDate) = 2 and DAY(s.StartDate) = 29
                   THEN DATEADD(day, 1, StartDate)
                   ELSE StartDate
              END) as NewStartDate
      FROM Subscribers s
     ) s
```

This is one case where having a calendar table does not particularly help the calculation—unless the table explicitly stores the date one year in the future. The simplest method for getting the next anniversary is probably to use the second method of adding years.

Year-over-Year Comparisons

The previous year usually provides the best comparison for what is happening the following year. This section talks about such comparisons, with particular emphasis on one of the big challenges. This year's data is usually not complete, so how can we make a valid comparison?

Comparisons by Day

The place to start is with day-by-day comparisons from one year to the next. Here is a method where much of the work is done in Excel:

1. Query the database and aggregate by date.
2. Load the data into Excel, with all the dates in one column.
3. Pivot the data into 366 rows (for each day in the year) and a separate column for each year.

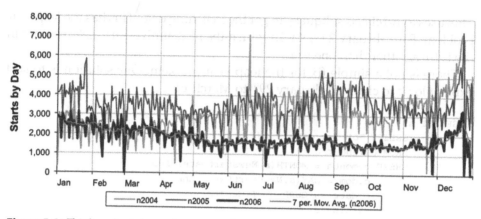

Figure 5-8: This line chart shows the pattern of starts by day throughout the year for three years.

This is actually more work than necessary. An easier way is to use the MONTH(), DAY(), and YEAR() functions in SQL to create the resulting table directly, as in the following example using starts from Subscribers:

```
SELECT MONTH(StartDate) as mon, DAY(StartDate) as dom,
       SUM(CASE WHEN YEAR(StartDate) = 2004 THEN 1 ELSE 0 END) as n2004,
       SUM(CASE WHEN YEAR(StartDate) = 2005 THEN 1 ELSE 0 END) as n2005,
       SUM(CASE WHEN YEAR(StartDate) = 2006 THEN 1 ELSE 0 END) as n2006
FROM Subscribers s
WHERE YEAR(StartDate) IN (2004, 2005, 2006)
GROUP BY MONTH(StartDate), DAY(StartDate)
ORDER BY mon, dom
```

Figure 5-8 shows the results as a line chart with three series. All three years have a weekly cycle of peaks and valleys. The chart illustrates that starts in 2006 are lower than in the other years during most months.

The horizontal axis has only the month name. In a line chart, the horizontal axis can be a date, which is calculated using the DATE() function on the month and day values in each row. The chart sets the "Number" format to "Mmm" to display only the month. The scale is set to show tick marks every month.

Adding a Moving Average Trend Line

The within-week pattern in the starts obscures larger trends. Adding a trend line with a seven-day moving average is one way to fix this, as shown in Figure 5-8. The seven-day moving average eliminates the weekly cycle.

To add the trend line, left-click a series to select it. Then right-click and choose the "Add Trendline…" option. Choose "Type" in the left-hand pane. In the right pane, "Moving Average" is the option on the lower right, with the width of the moving average in the "Period" box. Change the default value to seven to eliminate weekly cycles, and then click "OK" to finish.

Comparisons by Week

An alternative way of eliminating the bumpiness is to aggregate the data by week rather than by day. We can calculate the week number by calculating the number of days since the beginning of the year and dividing by seven:

```
WITH s as (
      SELECT s.*,
            (CASE WHEN YEAR(StartDate) = 2004
                  THEN FLOOR(DATEDIFF(day, '2004-01-01', StartDate) / 7)
                  WHEN YEAR(StartDate) = 2005
                  THEN FLOOR(DATEDIFF(day, '2005-01-01', StartDate) / 7)
                  WHEN YEAR(StartDate) = 2006
                  THEN FLOOR(DATEDIFF(day, '2006-01-01', StartDate) / 7)
            END) as weekofyear
      FROM Subscribers s
      WHERE YEAR(StartDate) in (2004, 2005, 2006)
     )
SELECT weekofyear,
       SUM(CASE WHEN YEAR(StartDate) = 2004 THEN 1 ELSE 0 END) as n2004,
       SUM(CASE WHEN YEAR(StartDate) = 2005 THEN 1 ELSE 0 END) as n2005,
       SUM(CASE WHEN YEAR(StartDate) = 2006 THEN 1 ELSE 0 END) as n2006
FROM s
GROUP BY weekofyear
ORDER BY weekofyear
```

The CTE defines `weekofyear` using `DATEPART()`, with an explicit difference for each year.

An alternative method uses the day of year:

```
SELECT DATEPART(dayofyear, StartDate) / 7 as weekofyear
```

The week of the year is simply the day of the year divided by seven.

A chart from this data is similar to the previous chart. The main difference is the calculation for the horizontal axis. Instead of using `DATE()`, the date is created by adding `7 * weekofyear` to a base date, such as 2000-01-01.

Excel can also handle the transformation from daily data to weekly data, using the same method of subtracting the first day of the year, dividing by seven, and then summing the results using `SUMIF()`.

Comparisons by Month

A year-over-year comparison by month follows the same structure as the comparison by day or week:

```
SELECT MONTH(StartDate) as month,
       SUM(CASE WHEN YEAR(StartDate) = 2004 THEN 1 ELSE 0 END) as n2004,
       SUM(CASE WHEN YEAR(StartDate) = 2005 THEN 1 ELSE 0 END) as n2005,
```

```
              SUM(CASE WHEN YEAR(StartDate) = 2006 THEN 1 ELSE 0 END) as n2006
FROM Subscribers
WHERE YEAR(StartDate) IN (2004, 2005, 2006)
GROUP BY MONTH(StartDate)
ORDER BY month
```

Monthly data is often better represented by column charts with the different years side-by-side, as shown in Figure 5-9.

The next example examines `TotalPrice` in `Orders`. This differs from the examples so far for two reasons. First, the results are not just counts but dollars. Second, the last day of data has a date of September 20th, although data is incomplete after September 7th. In other words, the data cutoff seems to really be 2016-09-07, with some sporadic data after that date. The incomplete September data poses a challenge.

The following SQL query extracts total monthly orders:

```
SELECT MONTH(OrderDate) as month,
       SUM(CASE WHEN YEAR(OrderDate)=2014 THEN TotalPrice END) as r2014,
       SUM(CASE WHEN YEAR(OrderDate)=2015 THEN TotalPrice END) as r2015,
       SUM(CASE WHEN YEAR(OrderDate)=2016 THEN TotalPrice END) as r2016
FROM Orders
WHERE OrderDate <= '2016-09-07'
GROUP BY MONTH(OrderDate)
ORDER BY month
```

Table 5-7 shows the results, which suggest that sales have dropped precipitously in the final month. This is misleading, of course, because only the first few days of September are included for the third year. There are two approaches to fixing the data so the comparisons are valid for the incomplete month (typically the most recent). The first is to look at month-to-date (MTD) comparisons for previous years. The second is to extrapolate the values to the end of the month.

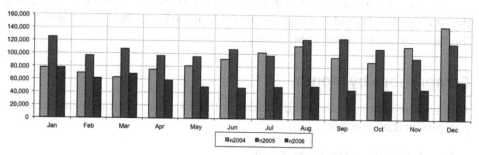

Figure 5-9: Column charts are useful for showing monthly data, year over year, such as this example showing subscription starts.

Table 5-7: Revenue by Month for Orders

MONTH	2014	2015	2016
1	$198,081.37	$201,640.63	$187,814.13
2	$125,088.95	$191,589.28	$142,516.49
3	$171,355.72	$215,484.26	$251,609.27
4	$188,072.17	$140,299.76	$193,443.75
5	$239,294.02	$188,226.96	$247,425.25
6	$250,800.68	$226,271.71	$272,784.77
7	$206,480.10	$170,183.03	$250,807.38
8	$160,693.87	$157,961.71	$164,388.50
9	$234,277.87	$139,244.44	$26,951.14
10	$312,175.19	$170,824.58	
11	$394,579.03	$409,834.57	
12	$639,011.54	$466,486.34	

Month-to-Date Comparison

The month-to-date comparison is shown in the upper chart in Figure 5-10. The bars for September in 2014 and 2015 have overlapping columns, where the shorter ones in September are the month-to-date values and the taller ones are the total revenue. These month-to-date numbers are the appropriate level of comparison for September.

How are these overlapping columns created? Unfortunately, Excel does not have an option for column charts that are both stacked and side-by-side, but we can improvise by using two sets of three series. The first set is plotted on the primary axis and contains the full month revenue numbers. The second set is plotted on the secondary axis and contains only the month-to-date revenue numbers for September. Both groups must contain the same number of columns, to ensure that the column widths are the same, and the columns overlap completely.

The data for this chart is calculated by adding the following three columns to the previous SQL statement:

```
SUM(CASE WHEN OrderDate >= '2014-09-01' AND OrderDate < '2014-09-08'
        THEN TotalPrice END) as rev2014mtd,
SUM(CASE WHEN OrderDate >= '2015-09-01' AND OrderDate < '2015-09-08'
        THEN TotalPrice END) as rev2015mtd,
SUM(CASE WHEN OrderDate >= '2016-09-01' AND OrderDate < '2016-09-08'
        THEN TotalPrice END) as rev2016mtd
```

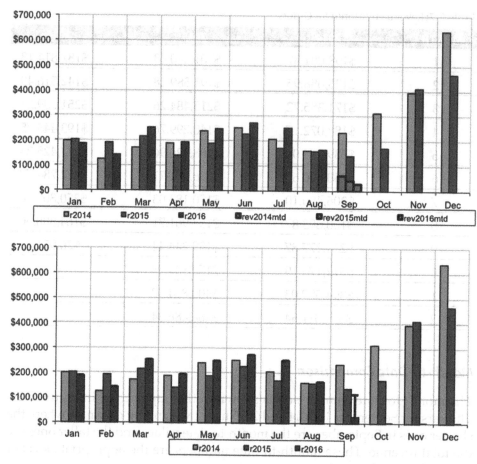

Figure 5-10: The upper chart shows month-to-date comparisons using overlapping column charts. The lower chart shows the end-of-month estimate using Y-error bars.

This subquery uses conditional aggregation to calculate the month-to-date numbers in each year. Although the last column is redundant (because it contains the same data as the corresponding full month column), having it simplifies the charting procedure, by providing the third series on the secondary axis. Note that the comparisons use ">= first date" and "< last date plus one." This structure is intentional. When comparing dates, do not use BETWEEN. A problem arises when the dates have time components: BETWEEN does not work as expected.

> **TIP** When looking for dates within a range, use two explicit comparisons (>= and >).
> This logic works for dates that have a time component as well as those that do not.

Creating the chart starts by pasting the results in Excel. The horizontal axis uses the month name; although we could type in the month abbreviations, an alternative method is to use dates formatted to just show the month: copy the formula "DATE(2000, <monthnum>, 1)" down a column to create the dates, use that column as the horizontal axis, and then set its "Number" format to "Mmm."

Next, a column chart is created with the following columns:

- The new date column goes on the horizontal axis.
- The three full revenue columns are data columns, for the first three series on the primary axis.
- The three month-to-date-revenue columns are data columns, for the second three series on the secondary axis.

Now the chart needs to be customized. First, the three month-to-date columns need to be switched to the secondary axis. To do this, right-click each series, choose "Format Data Series...." Choose "Axis" on the left pane, and click "Secondary axis."

To clean up the secondary axis:

- The month-to-date numbers need to be on the same scale as on the other axis. Click the secondary vertical axis and make the maximum value the same as the maximum value on the primary axis.
- The secondary axis labels and tick marks need to be removed, by clicking them and pressing Delete.

Finally, the month-to-date series should be colored similarly so they can be seen.

> **TIP** If you make a mistake in Excel, just hit Ctrl+Z to undo it. You can always experiment and try new things, and undo the ones that don't look right.

Extrapolation by Days in Month

The lower chart in Figure 5-10 shows a different approach. Here, the comparison is to an estimated value for the end of the month, rather than to the past month-to-date values. The simplest end-of-month estimate is a linear trend, calculated by multiplying the current value for the month times the number of days in the month and dividing by the number of days that have data. For the September data, divide the $26,951.14 by 7 to get the average per day and then multiply by 30 (for the days in the month) to get $115,504.89.

The chart shows this difference using Y-error bars. The length of the bar is the difference from the end-of-month estimate and the current value; that is $88,553.75 = $115,504.89 − $26,951.14.

Starting with the column chart that has three series for each year, add the Y-error bar by doing the following:

1. Add a column to the table in Excel where all the cells are blank except for the one for September. This one gets the difference value.

2. Add the error bars by double-clicking the series for 2016 to bring up the "Format Data Series" dialog box and choose "Error Bars" on the left pane. On the "Y-Error Bars" tab, choose "Plus" (the second option) and "Cap" for the End Style. Then set the sizes of the error bars by choosing "Custom," the bottom option, and then clicking "Specify Value." Set the "Positive Error Value" series to refer to the difference column.

3. Format the error bar by double-clicking it.

The difference calculation can be done in Excel. However, doing it in SQL shows the power of manipulating dates in the database.

Unfortunately, SQL lacks a simple way to calculate the number of days in the month. The solution starts with the following observations:

▪ The first day of the month is the date minus the day of the month plus one.

▪ The first day of the next month is the first day of this month plus one month.

▪ The difference is the number of days in the month.

Combined into a query, this looks like:

```
WITH o as (
        SELECT o.*, YEAR(OrderDate) as ordyy, MONTH(OrderDate) as ordmm,
              DAY(OrderDate) as orddd
        FROM Orders o
      )
SELECT ordmm,
        SUM(CASE WHEN ordyy = 2014 THEN TotalPrice END) as r2014,
        SUM(CASE WHEN ordyy = 2015 THEN TotalPrice END) as r2015,
        SUM(CASE WHEN ordyy = 2016 THEN TotalPrice END) as r2016,
        (SUM(CASE WHEN ordyy = 2016 AND ordmm = 9 THEN TotalPrice END) *
          ((MAX(daysinmonth)*1.0/MAX(CASE WHEN ordyy = 2016 AND ordmm = 9
                              THEN orddd END)) - 1)
        ) as IncrementToMonthEnd
  FROM (SELECT o.*, DATENAME(dayofweek, OrderDate) as dow,
            DATEDIFF(day, DATEADD(day, - (orddd - 1), OrderDate),
                  OrderDate) as daysinmonth
        FROM o
      ) o
WHERE OrderDate <= '2016-09-07'
GROUP BY ordmm
ORDER BY ordmm
```

The query calculates the linear trend to the end of the month. The subquery calculates the number of days in the month (some databases have simpler methods of doing this). The column incrementtomonthend is then calculated by taking the total for the month so far, multiplying by one less than the days in the month divided by the cutoff date in the month. The "one less" is because we want the increment over the current value, rather than the month-end estimate itself.

Estimation Based on Day of Week

Linear extrapolation may not produce the best estimate for the end-of-month value. If there is a weekly cycle, a method that takes into account days of the week should do a better job. The previous example has seven days of data for September 2016. If weekdays have one set of behavior and weekends another set, how could we use this information to extrapolate the $26,952.14 to the end of September? This estimation is only possible after at least one weekday and at least one weekend day has passed, unless we borrow information from previous months or previous years.

This calculation has two parts. The first is calculating the average weekday and the average weekend contribution for September. The second is calculating the number of weekdays and number of weekend days during the month. We'll do the first calculation in SQL and the second calculation in Excel. The following additional two columns contain the averages for weekdays and weekends in September 2016:

```
(SUM(CASE WHEN ordyy = 2016 AND ordmm = 9 AND
            orddow NOT IN ('Saturday', 'Sunday')
        THEN totalprice END) /
   COUNT(DISTINCT (CASE WHEN ordyy = 2016 AND ordmm = 9 AND
                    orddow NOT IN ('Saturday', 'Sunday')
                THEN OrderDate END)) ) as weekdayavg,
 (SUM(CASE WHEN ordyy = 2016 AND ordmm = 9 AND
            dow IN ('Saturday', 'Sunday') THEN totalprice END) /
   COUNT(DISTINCT (CASE WHEN ordyy = 2016 AND ordmon = 9 AND
                    orddow IN ('Saturday', 'Sunday')
                THEN OrderDate END)) ) as weekendavg
```

Notice that the average calculation for weekdays takes the sum of all the orders on weekdays and divides by the number of distinct days when orders were placed. This gives the average total order volume on weekdays. By contrast, the AVG() function would calculate something different: the average order size.

Without a calendar table, determining the number of weekdays and weekend days in a given month is rather complicated using SQL. Excel has the advantage of being able to define a lookup table, such as the one in Table 5-8. This table has the number of weekend days in a month, given the start date and number of days in the month.

The following Excel formula calculates the number of days in a month:

```
days in month = DATE(<year>, <mon>+1, 1) - DATE(<year>, <mon>, 1)
```

Table 5-8: Weekdays and Weekend Days by Start of Month and Length of Month

MONTH START DAY OF WEEK	WEEKDAYS 28	29	30	31	WEEKEND DAYS 28	29	30	31
Monday	20	21	22	23	8	8	8	8
Tuesday	20	21	22	23	8	8	8	8
Wednesday	20	21	22	23	8	8	8	8
Thursday	20	21	22	22	8	8	8	9
Friday	20	21	21	21	8	8	9	10
Saturday	20	20	20	21	8	9	10	10
Sunday	20	20	21	22	8	9	9	9

This works in Excel even for December because Excel interprets month 13 as January of the following year. The day of the week when the month starts is calculated using:

```
startdow = TEXT(DATE(<year>, <mon>, 1), "Dddd")
```

Using this information, the number of weekdays can be looked up in the preceding table using the following formula:

```
VLOOKUP(<startdow>, <table>, <daysinmonth>-28+2, 0)
```

Figure 5-11 shows a screen shot of Excel with these formulas. Taking weekdays and weekends into account, the end-of-month estimate is $109,196.45, which is only slightly less than the $115,504.89 linear estimate.

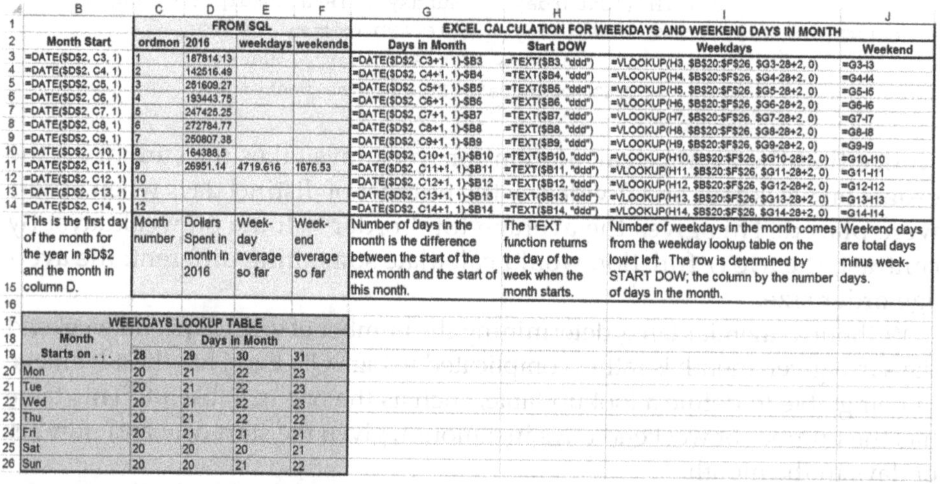

	B	C	D	E	F	G	H	I	J
1		FROM SQL				EXCEL CALCULATION FOR WEEKDAYS AND WEEKEND DAYS IN MONTH			
2	Month Start	ordmon	2016	weekdays	weekends	Days in Month	Start DOW	Weekdays	Weekend
3	=DATE($D$2, C3, 1)	1	187814.13			=DATE($D$2, C3+1, 1)-$B3	=TEXT($B3, "ddd")	=VLOOKUP(H3, $B$20:$F$26, $G3-28+2, 0)	=G3-I3
4	=DATE($D$2, C4, 1)	2	142516.49			=DATE($D$2, C4+1, 1)-$B4	=TEXT($B4, "ddd")	=VLOOKUP(H4, $B$20:$F$26, $G4-28+2, 0)	=G4-I4
5	=DATE($D$2, C5, 1)	3	251609.27			=DATE($D$2, C5+1, 1)-$B5	=TEXT($B5, "ddd")	=VLOOKUP(H5, $B$20:$F$26, $G5-28+2, 0)	=G5-I5
6	=DATE($D$2, C6, 1)	4	193443.75			=DATE($D$2, C6+1, 1)-$B6	=TEXT($B6, "ddd")	=VLOOKUP(H6, $B$20:$F$26, $G6-28+2, 0)	=G6-I6
7	=DATE($D$2, C7, 1)	5	247425.25			=DATE($D$2, C7+1, 1)-$B7	=TEXT($B7, "ddd")	=VLOOKUP(H7, $B$20:$F$26, $G7-28+2, 0)	=G7-I7
8	=DATE($D$2, C8, 1)	6	272784.77			=DATE($D$2, C8+1, 1)-$B8	=TEXT($B8, "ddd")	=VLOOKUP(H8, $B$20:$F$26, $G8-28+2, 0)	=G8-I8
9	=DATE($D$2, C9, 1)	7	250807.38			=DATE($D$2, C9+1, 1)-$B9	=TEXT($B9, "ddd")	=VLOOKUP(H9, $B$20:$F$26, $G9-28+2, 0)	=G9-I9
10	=DATE($D$2, C10, 1)	8	164388.5			=DATE($D$2, C10+1, 1)-$B10	=TEXT($B10, "ddd")	=VLOOKUP(H10, $B$20:$F$26, $G10-28+2, 0)	=G10-I10
11	=DATE($D$2, C11, 1)	9	26951.14	4719.616	1676.53	=DATE($D$2, C11+1, 1)-$B11	=TEXT($B11, "ddd")	=VLOOKUP(H11, $B$20:$F$26, $G11-28+2, 0)	=G11-I11
12	=DATE($D$2, C12, 1)	10				=DATE($D$2, C12+1, 1)-$B12	=TEXT($B12, "ddd")	=VLOOKUP(H12, $B$20:$F$26, $G12-28+2, 0)	=G12-I12
13	=DATE($D$2, C13, 1)	11				=DATE($D$2, C13+1, 1)-$B13	=TEXT($B13, "ddd")	=VLOOKUP(H13, $B$20:$F$26, $G13-28+2, 0)	=G13-I13
14	=DATE($D$2, C14, 1)	12				=DATE($D$2, C14+1, 1)-$B14	=TEXT($B14, "ddd")	=VLOOKUP(H14, $B$20:$F$26, $G14-28+2, 0)	=G14-I14
15	This is the first day of the month for the year in $D$2 and the month in column D.	Month number	Dollars Spent in month in 2016	Week-day average so far	Week-end average so far	Number of days in the month is the difference between the start of the next month and the start of this month.	The TEXT function returns the day of the week when the month starts.	Number of weekdays in the month comes from the weekday lookup table on the lower left. The row is determined by START DOW; the column by the number of days in the month.	Weekend days are total days minus week-days.
16									

	B	C	D	E	F
17	WEEKDAYS LOOKUP TABLE				
18	Month	Days in Month			
19	Starts on . . .	28	29	30	31
20	Mon	20	21	22	23
21	Tue	20	21	22	23
22	Wed	20	21	22	23
23	Thu	20	21	22	22
24	Fri	20	21	21	21
25	Sat	20	20	20	21
26	Sun	20	20	21	22

Figure 5-11: This screen shot of Excel shows the calculation of the number of days in the month, the number of weekdays, and the number of weekend days, which can then be used to estimate the end-of-month average taking into account the day of the week.

Estimation Based on Previous Year

Another way to estimate the end of the month value uses the ratio of the previous year month-to-date and previous year month total. Applying this ratio to the current month gives an estimate of the end-of-month value. This calculation has the advantage of taking into account holidays because the same month period the year before probably had the same holidays. Of course, this might not work well for floating holidays such as Easter and Rosh Hashanah.

For instance, in the previous year, the monthly total was $139,244.44. The total for the first seven days during that month was $41,886.47, which is about 30.1% of the total. The current month to date is $26,951.14. This is 30.1% of $89,594.48. The estimate for the entire month calculated using this approach is considerably smaller than using the linear trend.

Counting Active Customers by Day

Determining the number of active customers as of the database cut-off date is easy, by simply counting those whose status code indicates that they are active. This section extends this simple counting mechanism to historical time periods, by progressing from counting the active customers on any given day in the past, to counting active customers on all days, and finally, to breaking customers into tenure groups and counting the sizes of those groups on any given day.

How Many Customers on a Given Day?

On a given day in the past, customers who are active have two characteristics:

- They started on or before the given day.
- They stopped (if at all) after the given day.

The following query answers the question: *How many subscriptions customers were active on Valentine's Day in 2005?*

```
SELECT COUNT(*)
FROM Subscribers
WHERE StartDate <= '2005-02-14' AND
      (StopDate > '2005-02-14' OR StopDate IS NULL)
```

The WHERE clause implements the logic that selects the right group of customers.

The query returns the value of 2,387,765. By adding GROUP BY clauses, this number can be broken out by features such as market, channel, rate plan, or any column that describes customers.

The data in Subscribers does not contain any accounts that stopped prior to 2004-01-01. Because these accounts are missing, it is not possible to get accurate counts prior to this date.

How Many Customers Every Day?

Calculating the number of active customers on one date provides information about only one date. A more useful question is: *How many customers were active on any given date in the past?* For the subscriptions data, this question has to be tempered: It is only possible to get an accurate count after 2004-01-01 because customers who started and stopped prior to that date are not in the table.

Answering this question relies on an observation: The number of customers who are active on a given date is the number who started on or before that date minus the customers who stopped on or before that date. The preceding question simplifies into two other questions: *How many customers started as of a given date? How many customers stopped as of a given date?*

These individual questions are readily answered using SQL. Excel can be used to accumulate the numbers and then to subtract the cumulative number of stops from the cumulative number of starts. The following SQL finds all the starts by day, grouping all the pre-2004 starts into one bucket:

```
SELECT thedate, SUM(nstarts) as nstarts, SUM(nstops) as nstops
FROM ((SELECT (CASE WHEN StartDate >= '2003-12-31' THEN StartDate
                    ELSE '2003-12-31' END) as thedate,
             COUNT(*) as nstarts, 0 as nstops
      FROM Subscribers
      WHERE StartDate IS NOT NULL
      GROUP BY (CASE WHEN StartDate >= '2003-12-31' THEN StartDate
                    ELSE '2003-12-31' END) )
      UNION ALL
      (SELECT (CASE WHEN StopDate >= '2003-12-31'
                    THEN StopDate ELSE '2003-12-31' END) as thedate,
             0 as nstarts, COUNT(*) as nstops
      FROM Subscribers
      WHERE StartDate IS NOT NULL AND StopDate IS NOT NULL
      GROUP BY (CASE WHEN StopDate >= '2003-12-31'
                    THEN StopDate ELSE '2003-12-31' END) )
     ) a
GROUP BY thedate
ORDER BY thedate
```

The query works by separately counting starts and stops, combining the results using UNION ALL, and then combining the start and stop numbers for each date. These cannot be counted without subqueries because the aggregation column is different. Starts and stops prior to 2004 are placed in the 2003-12-31 bucket. The query uses UNION ALL rather than a JOIN because some dates may have no starts and other dates may have no stops.

The Subscribers table has 181 records where StartDate is set to NULL. With no start date, these rows either could be excluded (the choice here) or the start

	C	D	E	F	G	H
32		**FROM SQL**			**EXCEL CALCULATION**	
33	**thedate**	**nstarts**	**nstops**	**cum starts**	**cum stops**	**actives**
34	37986	2006134	0	=SUM(D$34:D34)	=SUM(E$34:E34)	=F34-G34
35	37987	349	1691	=SUM(D$34:D35)	=SUM(E$34:E35)	=F35-G35
36	37988	3062	2853	=SUM(D$34:D36)	=SUM(E$34:E36)	=F36-G36
37	37989	2865	5138	=SUM(D$34:D37)	=SUM(E$34:E37)	=F37-G37
38	37990	2653	2737	=SUM(D$34:D38)	=SUM(E$34:E38)	=F38-G38
39	37991	2561	2104	=SUM(D$34:D39)	=SUM(E$34:E39)	=F39-G39
40	37992	2710	1276	=SUM(D$34:D40)	=SUM(E$34:E40)	=F40-G40
41	37993	1545	706	=SUM(D$34:D41)	=SUM(E$34:E41)	=F41-G41

Figure 5-12: This Excel screen shot shows a worksheet that calculates the number of customers on each day.

date could be replaced with some reasonable value (if one is known). Both subqueries have the restriction on start date not being NULL, even though one subquery counts starts and the other stops. Both subqueries need to include *exactly* the same population of customers in order to get accurate results. Because the second subquery counts stops, it has an additional restriction that customers have stopped.

Excel then does the cumulative sums of the starts and stops, as shown in Figure 5-12. The difference between the cumulative starts and the cumulative stops is the number of active customers on each day since the beginning of 2004.

How Many Customers of Different Types?

The overall number of customers on any given day can be broken out by customer attributes. The following query is a modification of the previous query for the breakdown by market:

```
SELECT thedate, SUM(numstarts) as numstarts,
       SUM(CASE WHEN market = 'Smallville' THEN numstarts ELSE 0
           END) as smstarts,
       . . .
       SUM(numstops) as numstops,
       SUM(CASE WHEN market = 'Smallville' THEN numstops ELSE 0
           END) as smstops,
       . . .
FROM ((SELECT (CASE WHEN StartDate >= '2003-12-31' THEN StartDate
                    ELSE '2003-12-31' END) as thedate,
             market, COUNT(*) as numstarts, 0 as numstops
       FROM Subscribers s
       WHERE StartDate IS NOT NULL
       GROUP BY (CASE WHEN StartDate >= '2003-12-31' THEN StartDate
                     ELSE '2003-12-31' END), market
```

```
    ) UNION ALL
    (SELECT (CASE WHEN StopDate >= '2003-12-31'
                    THEN StopDate ELSE '2003-12-31' END) as thedate,
          market, 0 as numstarts, COUNT(*) as numstops
     FROM Subscribers
     WHERE StartDate IS NOT NULL AND StopDate IS NOT NULL
     GROUP BY (CASE WHEN StopDate >= '2003-12-31'
                    THEN StopDate ELSE '2003-12-31' END), market )
     ) s
GROUP BY thedate
ORDER BY thedate
```

Each subquery aggregates by date and also market. In addition, the outer query sums the starts and stops separately for each market. The data is handled the same way in Excel, with the starts and stops being accumulated, and the difference between them being the number active in each market on any given day.

Figure 5-13 shows the results. Gotham is always the largest market and Smallville the smallest. It appears, though, that Smallville is catching up to Gotham. In addition, all three markets have an increase at the end of 2005 and a decrease in 2006. The decrease for Gotham is larger than for the other two markets. Interestingly, Smallville has no stops until Oct 26, 2004. As already noted, the markets have different left truncation dates.

How Many Customers by Tenure Segment?

A tenure segment divides customers into groups based on their tenure. For instance, customers might be divided into three such segments: the first-year segment, consisting of those who have been around less than one year; the second-year segment, consisting of those who have been around between one and two years; and the long-term segment.

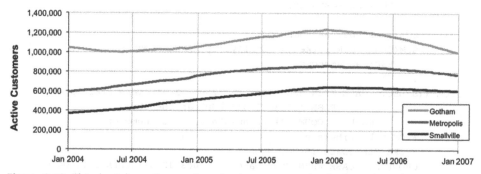

Figure 5-13: This chart shows the number of active customers by day in each market.

This section extends the counting of active customers over time to active customers by tenure segment. The definition of the tenure groups can vary. There is nothing sacrosanct about milestones at one and two years. *On any given date, how many subscribers have been around for one year, for two years, and for more than two years?*

The answer to this question relies on a few observations about the relationship between the size of a tenure segment on a particular date and the size on the day before. This logic uses a mathematical technique called induction.

The number of customers in the first-year segment on a particular date consists of:

- All the customers in the first-year segment the day before;
- Minus the first-year segment customers who graduated (by passing the one year milestone) on that date;
- Minus the first-year segment customers who stopped on that date;
- Plus new customers who started on that date.

The number of customers in the second-year segment consists of:

- All the second-year segment customers who were around the day before;
- Minus the second-year segment customers who graduated (by passing the two year milestone);
- Minus the second-year segment customers who stopped on that date;
- Plus customers who graduated from the first-year segment on that date.

Finally, the number of customers in the long-term segment:

- All the long-term segment customers who were around the day before;
- Minus the long-term segment customers who stopped;
- Plus customers who graduated from the second-year segment.

These rules suggest the information needed for tracking the segments day-by-day. The first is the number of customers who enter each segment on each day. For the first-year segment, this is the number of customers who start. For the second-year segment, it is the customers who pass their 365-day milestone. For the long-term customers, it is the customers who pass their 730-day milestone. Also needed is the number of customers within each segment who stop.

Figure 5-14 shows the dataflow processing for this calculation. The first three subqueries calculate the number of customers that enter each segment at a given unit of time. The last row calculates the segment when customers stop. These are then combined using UNION ALL and then summarized for output.

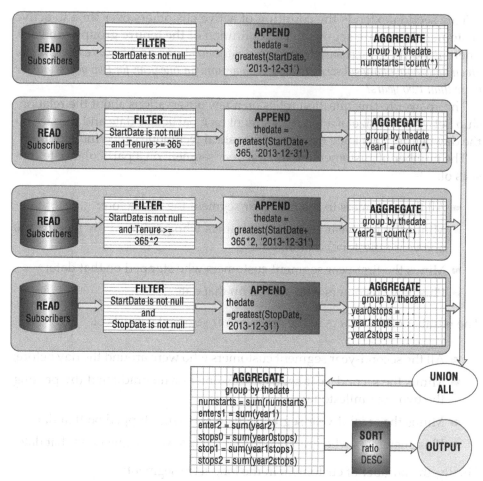

Figure 5-14: The dataflow processing shows how to calculate the number of customers that enter and leave each tenure segment.

The following SQL corresponds to this dataflow:

```
SELECT thedate, SUM(numstarts) as numstarts, SUM(year1) as enters1,
       SUM(year2) as enters2, SUM(year0stops) as stops0,
       SUM(year1stops) as stops1, SUM(year2plstops) as stops2pl
FROM ((SELECT (CASE WHEN StartDate >= '2003-12-31' THEN StartDate
               ELSE '2003-12-31' END) as thedate,
          COUNT(*) as numstarts, 0 as YEAR1, 0 as YEAR2,
          0 as year0stops, 0 as year1stops, 0 as year2plstops
      FROM Subscribers s
      WHERE StartDate IS NOT NULL
      GROUP BY (CASE WHEN StartDate >= '2003-12-31' THEN StartDate
               ELSE '2003-12-31' END))
     UNION ALL
     (SELECT (CASE WHEN StartDate >= '2002-12-31'
```

```
                        THEN DATEADD(day, 365, StartDate)
                        ELSE '2003-12-31' END) as thedate,
                0 as numstarts, COUNT(*) as YEAR1, 0 as YEAR2,
                0 as year0stops, 0 as year1stops, 0 as year2plstops
        FROM Subscribers s
        WHERE StartDate IS NOT NULL AND Tenure >= 365
        GROUP BY (CASE WHEN StartDate >= '2002-12-31'
                        THEN DATEADD(day, 365, StartDate)
                        ELSE '2003-12-31' END))
    UNION ALL
    (SELECT (CASE WHEN StartDate >= '2001-12-31'
                        THEN DATEADD(day, 365 * 2, StartDate)
                        ELSE '2003-12-31' END) as thedate,
                0 as numstarts, 0 as year1, COUNT(*) as year2,
                0 as year0stops, 0 as year1stops, 0 as year2plstops
        FROM Subscribers s
        WHERE StartDate IS NOT NULL AND Tenure >= 365 * 2
        GROUP BY (CASE WHEN StartDate >= '2001-12-31'
                        THEN DATEADD(day, 365 * 2, StartDate)
                        ELSE '2003-12-31' END))
    UNION ALL
    (SELECT (CASE WHEN StopDate >= '2003-12-31' THEN StopDate
                    ELSE '2003-12-31' END) as thedate,
                0 as numstarts, 0 as YEAR0, 0 as YEAR1,
                SUM(CASE WHEN Tenure < 365 THEN 1 ELSE 0 END
                ) as year0stops,
                SUM(CASE WHEN Tenure BETWEEN 365 AND 365 * 2 - 1
                        THEN 1 ELSE 0 END) as year1stops,
                SUM(CASE WHEN tenure >= 365 * 2 THEN 1 ELSE 0 END
                ) as year2plstops
        FROM Subscribers s
        WHERE StartDate IS NOT NULL AND StopDate IS NOT NULL
        GROUP BY (CASE WHEN StopDate >= '2003-12-31'
                        THEN StopDate ELSE '2003-12-31' END) )
    ) a
GROUP BY thedate
ORDER BY thedate
```

This query follows the same structure as the dataflow. The first three subqueries calculate the number of customers who enter each segment. Separate subqueries are needed because the entry dates are different. A customer who starts on 2005-04-01 enters the first-year segment on that date. The same customer enters the second-year segment on 2006-04-01, one year later. Each of these subqueries selects the appropriate group using the WHERE clause and the tenure column. The first segment has no restriction. For the second, the tenure is at least one year. For the third, the tenure is at least two years.

The fourth subquery calculates the stops for all three segments. Because the stop date does not change, only one subquery is needed for all three segments. The Excel calculation then follows the rules described at the beginning of this section.

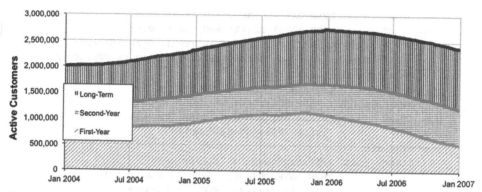

Figure 5-15: This chart shows the number of active customers broken out by one-year tenure segments.

Figure 5-15 shows the three segments of customers using stacked area charts. This chart shows the total number of customers as well as the breakdown between the different tenure segments over time.

Calculating Actives Entirely Using SQL

The entire calculation for the number of customers on any given date can be done in SQL. An inefficient method for all but a few days is to use `Calendar`:

```
SELECT c.date,
       (SELECT COUNT(*)
        FROM Subscribers s
        WHERE s.StartDate <= c.date AND
              (s.StopDate > c.date OR s.StopDate IS NULL)
       ) as NumSubs
FROM Calendar c
WHERE c.date BETWEEN '2006-01-01' AND '2006-01-07'
```

The correlated subquery counts the number of subscribers on each date. The only nuance to this query is that the correlated subquery checks for NULL values for the stop date.

Although this works, more efficient methods use cumulative sums: Count the number of customers who start and stop on each date. Then calculate their cumulative sum. The difference is the number of customers active on that date.

This readily translates into a query:

```
SELECT Dte, MAX(cumestarts) as numstarts, MAX(cumestops) as numstops,
       (MAX(cumestarts) - MAX(cumestops)) as numactive
FROM ((SELECT StartDate as Dte, COUNT(*) as numstarts, 0 as NumStops,
             SUM(COUNT(*)) OVER (ORDER BY StartDate) as cumestarts,
```

```
          0 as cumestops
   FROM Subscribers
   GROUP BY StartDate
) UNION ALL
(SELECT COALESCE(StopDate, '2007-01-01'), 0, COUNT(*), 0,
        SUM(COUNT(*)) OVER (ORDER BY COALESCE(StopDate,
                                    '2007-01-01'))
   FROM Subscribers
   GROUP BY StopDate
 )
 ) s
WHERE Dte >= '2004-01-01'
GROUP BY Dte
ORDER BY Dte
```

This query has several nuances. The basic structure is a UNION ALL whose results are then aggregated. The UNION ALL combines two aggregation queries, one that counts starts and one that counts stops. Note that these two queries calculate the cumulative sum of the aggregation by combining window functions with aggregation functions. The query does the cumulative sum in the subquery so the outer query can use the WHERE clause without affecting the calculation.

This structure of the query solves the problem for any given day. To break out the results by a particular column, such as channel, requires only minor modifications—using conditional aggregation in the subquery, including more fields in the outer query, and PARTITION BY in the cumulative sums.

This query works correctly for all days because all days have at least one start and one stop. If this is not true, then the query needs do a union of all the dates, doing the cumulative sum in another subquery between the inner and outer queries.

Simple Chart Animation in Excel

This section goes back to the purchases dataset to investigate the delay between the date when an order is placed and when the last item is shipped, the fulfillment date. Investigating the fulfillment date gets rather complicated because other features (such as the size of the order) undoubtedly affect the delay. Visualizing the results is challenging because there are two time dimensions, the duration and order date.

This example provides an opportunity to show rudimentary chart animation in Excel, using a Visual Basic macro. This is the only place in the book that uses macros because even without them SQL and Excel are quite powerful for data analysis and visualization. However, animation is also powerful and the macro is simple enough for anyone to implement.

Order Date to Ship Date

What is the delay between the order date and the fulfillment date? The following SQL query answers this question, breaking out the delay by number of units in the order:

```
SELECT DATEDIFF(day, OrderDate, fulfilldate) as delay, COUNT(*) as cnt,
       SUM(CASE WHEN numunits = 1 THEN 1 ELSE 0 END) as un1,
       . . .
       SUM(CASE WHEN numunits = 5 THEN 1 ELSE 0 END) as un5,
       SUM(CASE WHEN numunits >= 6 THEN 1 ELSE 0 END) as un6pl
FROM Orders o JOIN
     (SELECT OrderId, MAX(ShipDate) as fulfilldate
      FROM OrderLines ol
      GROUP BY OrderId) ol
     ON o.OrderId = ol.OrderId
WHERE OrderDate <= fulfilldate
GROUP BY DATEDIFF(day, OrderDate, fulfilldate)
ORDER BY delay
```

This query summarizes `OrderLines` to get the last shipment date. As a reminder, the number of units is different from the number of distinct items. If a customer orders ten copies of the same book, that is one item but ten units.

The data has a handful of anomalies, such as the 22 orders that completely shipped before the order was placed. Obviously, an explanation exists, such as the order being "fixed" after it was shipped with the date mistakenly updated. For this discussion, these few extraneous cases are not of interest, so a `WHERE` clause eliminates them. Note that pending orders are not in the database, because every row in `OrderLines` has a valid `ShipDate`.

Figure 5-16 shows the cumulative proportion of fulfilled orders by days after order for different numbers of units. For all groups, over half the orders have been completely fulfilled within a week. The most common orders have one unit, and over 70% of these are fulfilled within one week.

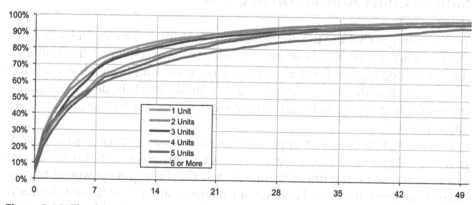

Figure 5-16: The delay from order to fulfillment depends on order size.

Orders with more units do take longer to fulfill. At 50 days, about 98% of the smaller orders have been fulfilled, compared to 94% of the large orders. Looking at it the other way, fewer than 2% of the smaller orders have such a long delay, whereas about 6% of the larger orders do.

Although difficult to see on the chart, something interesting happens in the first few days. Of all the groups, orders with six or more units actually have the largest proportion shipping on the day the order is placed. This means that the curve for the largest orders crosses all the other curves. Curves that cross like this are often interesting. Is something going on?

TIP Curves that intersect are often a sign that something interesting is happening, suggesting ideas for further investigation.

To investigate this, let's ask the question: *What is the relationship between the number of units in an order and the number of distinct products?* The hypothesis is that larger orders are actually more likely to have only one product, so they can ship efficiently. Orders with only one unit have only one product, so these don't count for the comparison. The following SQL calculates the proportion of orders having one product among the orders with a given number of units:

```
SELECT numunits, COUNT(*),
       AVG(CASE WHEN numprods = 1 THEN 1.0 ELSE 0 END) as prop1prod
FROM (SELECT OrderId, SUM(NumUnits) as numunits,
             COUNT(DISTINCT ProductId) as numprods
      FROM OrderLines ol
      GROUP BY OrderId) o
WHERE numunits > 1
GROUP BY numunits
ORDER BY numunits
```

The subquery counts the number of units and the number of distinct products in each order. The number of units is calculated by summing NumUnits. An alternative would use the NumUnits column in Orders, but that requires an additional join.

Figure 5-17 shows a bubble plot of the results. The horizontal axis is the number of units in the order. The vertical axis is the proportion of the orders consisting of only one product. The size of each bubble is the log of the number of orders (calculated in Excel using the LOG() function). Larger bubbles account for even more orders than the bubbles suggest because the bubble size is based on the log.

The largest bubble is missing because all orders with only one unit have only one product. For larger orders, the proportion of one-product orders starts off fairly low. For orders with two units, it is 21.8%; for three, 13.9%. However, the proportion then starts increasing. For orders with six or more units, almost one third (32.1%) have only one product. These one-product orders are the ones that ship quickly, often on the same day they are placed. Orders with more different products take longer to fulfill.

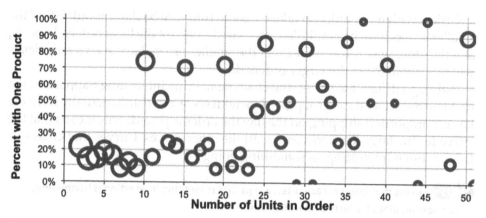

Figure 5-17: This bubble chart shows that as the number of units increases in an order, more orders have only one product.

Order Date to Ship Date by Year

The previous section showed the overall situation with delays in shipping orders. The question now includes changes over time: *Does the delay between the order date and fulfillment date change from year to year?* To calculate the delay for any given year, extend the WHERE clause in the delay query, restricting the results to a particular year; something like AND YEAR(OrderDate) = 2014.

This section proposes another solution where the data for all years is brought into Excel. Then, a subset of the data is placed into another group of cells, a "one-year" table, which in turn is used for generating a chart. By changing the contents of one cell in the spreadsheet, the chart can flip between the years. Note that you can also do this by using filtering, but that requires a couple more keystrokes.

Querying the Data

The query to fetch the results simply adds YEAR(OrderDate) as an aggregation on the query that calculates the delays:

```
SELECT YEAR(OrderDate) as yr,
       DATEDIFF(day, OrderDate, fulfilldate) as delay,
       COUNT(*) as cnt,
       SUM(CASE WHEN numunits = 1 THEN 1 ELSE 0 END) as un1,
       . . .
       SUM(CASE WHEN numunits >= 6 THEN 1 ELSE 0 END) as un6pl
FROM Orders o JOIN
     (SELECT OrderId, MAX(ShipDate) as fulfilldate
      FROM OrderLines
      GROUP BY OrderId) ol
     ON o.OrderId = ol.OrderId AND o.OrderDate <= ol.fulfilldate
```

```
GROUP BY YEAR(OrderDate), DATEDIFF(day, OrderDate, fulfilldate)
ORDER BY yr, delay
```

With almost one thousand rows and three dimensions, these results pose a challenge for charting. The data could be plotted on a single chart, but it is not clear how to make the chart intelligible. There are already several different curves for the number of units, leaving year and delay on the horizontal axis. A separate graph for each year, such as shown in Figure 5-15 (page 246), would be easier to interpret.

One option for creating a chart for different years is to plot all the data and then use filtering to select only one year at a time. That is a feasible solution, but the next section offers are more flexible alternative.

Creating the One-Year Excel Table

The one-year table is a group of cells that contains the delay information for a single year. It has the same columns and rows as the original data, except for the year column because the year is in a special cell, which we'll call the *year-cell*. The data in the table is keyed off of this cell, so when the value is updated, the table is updated for that year.

One column in the one-year table is the delay. This starts at zero and is incremented by one until it reaches some large number (the maximum delay in the data is 625). The one-year table finds the appropriate value in the overall data using the year in the year-cell and the delay on the row. Three steps are needed to make this work.

First, a lookup key is added to the query results to facilitate finding the appropriate row in the original data by the combination of year and delay. This additional column consists of the year and delay concatenated together to create a unique identifier:

```
<key> = <year>&":"&<delay>
```

The first value, for instance, is "2009:1"—a colon is used to separate the two values.

The second step is to find the offset into the table by matching each row in the one-year table to this column. The Excel function MATCH() looks up the value in its first argument in a list and returns the offset where the value is found in the list. If the value is not found and the third argument is FALSE, it returns NA():

```
<offset> = MATCH(<year cell>&":"&<delay>, <key column>, FALSE)
```

The third step is to get the right data for each cell in the one-year table by using the OFFSET() function to skip down <offset>-1 rows from the top of each column. Figure 5-18 shows a screen shot of Excel with the formulas for the "1 Unit" column.

The one-year table is now keyed off of the year-cell. Changing the value in that cell causes the table to be updated.

| S25 | | × ✓ *fx* | | |

▲	C	D	E	F	M	N	O
21						**ANIMATION VARIABLES**	
22					**Year**	**Start**	**End**
23					2009	2009	2016
24					="Days from Order to Fulfillment by Units for "&M23		
25							

26		**FROM SQL**			**EXCEL CALCULATION**		
27	**yr**	**delay**	**cnt**	**un1**	**Offset**	**Delay**	**1 Unit**
28	2009	0	27	12	=MATCH($M$23&":"&N28, $B$28:$B$974, 0)	0	=OFFSET(F$27, $M28, 0)
29	2009	1	728	545	=MATCH($M$23&":"&N29, $B$28:$B$974, 0)	=N28+1	=OFFSET(F$27, $M29, 0)
30	2009	2	342	228	=MATCH($M$23&":"&N30, $B$28:$B$974, 0)	=N29+1	=OFFSET(F$27, $M30, 0)
31	2009	3	275	177	=MATCH($M$23&":"&N31, $B$28:$B$974, 0)	=N30+1	=OFFSET(F$27, $M31, 0)
32	2009	4	272	181	=MATCH($M$23&":"&N32, $B$28:$B$974, 0)	=N31+1	=OFFSET(F$27, $M32, 0)
33	2009	5	302	166	=MATCH($M$23&":"&N33, $B$28:$B$974, 0)	=N32+1	=OFFSET(F$27, $M33, 0)
34	2009	6	476	344	=MATCH($M$23&":"&N34, $B$28:$B$974, 0)	=N33+1	=OFFSET(F$27, $M34, 0)
35	2009	7	483	359	=MATCH($M$23&":"&N35, $B$28:$B$974, 0)	=N34+1	=OFFSET(F$27, $M35, 0)

Figure 5-18: These Excel formulas show the formulas for constructing the intermediate table for one year of data for the "1 Unit" column.

Creating and Customizing the Chart

Figure 5-19 shows the resulting chart for one year. Notice that this chart has a title that incorporates the year. This is accomplished by pointing the title box to a cell that has a formula for the title, using the following steps:

1. Place the desired title text in a cell, which can be a formula:

   ```
   ="Days from Order to Fulfillment by Units for "&<year-cell>.
   ```

2. Add an arbitrary title to the chart by right-clicking inside the chart, choosing "Chart Option," going to the "Titles" tab, and typing some text in the "Chart Title" box. Then exit the dialog box.

3. Click once on the chart title to select the title box. Then type = into the formula bar and click on the cell with the title (or type in its address). Voila! The cell contents become the chart title.

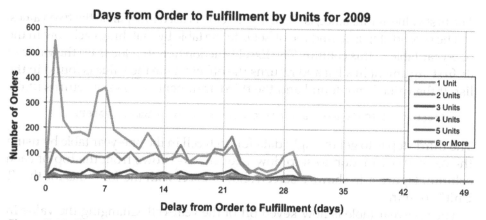

Figure 5-19: This chart shows the delay information for one year.

SIMPLE ANIMATION USING EXCEL MACROS

Excel macros are a very powerful component of Excel. They provide the capability to customize Excel using the power of a full programming language, Visual Basic. Because the focus of this book is on analyzing data, macros are generally outside the scope. However, one is so useful, simple, and impressive that it is worth including: the animation macro.

The text describes the ability to create a chart whose contents are determined by the value in the year-cell. Animating the chart just requires automatically incrementing the year-cell, starting at one value, ending at another, and waiting for a small number of seconds in between. To set this up, we'll put the start value, the end value, and the time increment in the three cells adjacent to the year-cell, so they look something like:

YEAR	START	END	SECONDS
2009	2009	2016	1

The macro automatically increments the year-cell.

First, create a macro by bringing up the Macro dialog box, by going to the Developer ribbon and choosing Macro ➤ View Macros or the Tools menu and choosing Macro. In the "Macro Name" box, type in a name, such as "animate," and then click the "Create" menu button. This brings up the Visual Basic editor.

The following macro code then creates the macro (the template that automatically appears already has the first and last lines of this code):

```
Sub animate()
    Dim startval As Integer, endval As Integer
    startval = ActiveCell.Offset(0, 1).Value
    endval = ActiveCell.Offset(0, 2).Value
    For i = startval To endval
        ActiveCell.Value = i
        Application.Wait(Now() +
            TimeValue(ActiveCell.Offset(0, 3).Text))
    Next i
End Sub
```

When the code appears, leave the Visual Basic editor by going to the "File" menu or ("Excel" on the Mac) and choosing "Close and Return to Microsoft Excel" (or use Alt+Q). This adds the macro into the current Excel file. The macro gets saved with the workbook.

To use the macro, place the cursor on the year-cell and go to the Macro dialog box and choose "Run." It is also possible to assign the macro to a keystroke through the "Options" on the dialog box.

This example uses animation to walk through time values, which changes both the chart and the corresponding table. The more impressive part is the chart changing as the values change. Animation can be used to walk through other values, such as products, number of units, and so on.

With this mechanism, the chart title and chart contents both update when the value in the year-cell changes. The aside "Simple Animation Using Excel Macros" discusses how to take this one step further with a rudimentary animation.

Lessons Learned

Time is important for understanding the universe and time is important for data analysis. In databases, times and dates have six components: years, months, days, hours, minutes, and seconds. In addition, a time zone might also be attached. The structure is complicated, but within one database, times and dates tend to be from one time zone and at the same level of precision.

As with other data types, dates and times need to be validated. The most important validations are checking the range of values and verifying that dates have no extraneous time component.

Analyzing dates starts with the values and the counts themselves. Looking at counts and aggregations over time is informative, whether the number of customers, the order size, or the amount spent. Seasonal patterns appear in the data, further showing what customers are really doing. Many businesses have weekly cycles. For instance, stops may be higher on weekdays than on weekends. Comparisons at the day level show these differences. Trend lines or weekly summaries remove them, highlighting longer-term patterns instead. Another challenge is determining the next anniversary for a given date.

Individual time values are interesting; more so are durations between two values. Duration can be measured in many different ways, such as days between two dates or months between two dates. One challenge is determining the number of a particular day of the week, such as Mondays, between two dates. However, even this is possible with SQL and Excel.

This chapter presents two important applications involving dates. The first is calculating the number of customers active on a particular date, which is simply the number who started as of that date minus the number who stopped before that date. This can be broken out by different groups, including tenure groups.

The last example looks at changes over time in a duration value—the delay from when a customer places an order to when the order is fulfilled. With two time dimensions, a good way to visualize this is through a simple Excel animation, which requires just a dab of macro programming.

The next chapter continues the exploration of time through survival analysis, the part of statistics that deals with time-to-event problems.

How Long Will Customers Last? Survival Analysis to Understand Customers and Their Value

How long will a lightbulb last? Which factors influence a cancer patient's prognosis? What is the average time to failure (MTTF) of a disk drive? These questions may seem to have little relationship to each other, but they do have one thing in common: They all involve estimating time to an event, so they can be answered using survival analysis. And, these ideas apply to customers, their tenures, and their value.

The scientific and industrial origins of survival analysis explain the terminology. Its emphasis on "failure" and "risk" and "mortality" and "recidivism" may explain why, once upon a time, survival analysis did not readily catch on in the business and marketing world. That time has passed, and survival analysis is recognized as a powerful set of analytic techniques for understanding customers. And, the combination of SQL and Excel is sufficiently powerful to apply many of these techniques to large customer databases.

Survival analysis estimates how long until a particular event happens. A customer starts; when will that customer stop? By assuming that the future will be similar to the past, historical customer behavior can help us understand what will happen and when.

Subscription relationships have well-defined beginnings and ends. For these, the most important time-to-event question is when customers stop. Examples abound:

- Customers get a mortgage and remain customers until they pay the mortgage off (or default).
- Customers get a credit card and remain customers until they stop using the card (or stop paying).
- Customers get a telephone and remain customers until they cancel the phone service (or stop paying).

■ Customers subscribe to a website and are customers until they cancel (or stop paying).

This chapter focuses on these types of relationships. Chapter 8 looks at time-to-event problems in other areas, such as retailing relationships where customers return multiple times, but the relationship has no explicit end.

Survival analysis is a broad, multifaceted subject. This chapter introduces the important concepts and their application to customer data using SQL and Excel. It starts with a bit of history to put the topics in a good context for understanding time-to-event analysis. Examples give a qualitative feel for the results of survival analysis because this type of analysis is a powerful way of gaining insight into customer behavior, both qualitatively and quantitatively.

Of course, survival analysis is more than history and description. The quantitative sections describe how to do the calculations, starting with the hazard, moving to survival, and then extracting useful measures from the survival probabilities. An example shows how to use survival analysis for estimating customer value, or at least estimate future revenue. The final example discusses using survival analysis for forecasting. The next chapter picks up where this one leaves off, covering some more advanced topics in the subject.

Background on Survival Analysis

The origins of survival analysis can be traced back to a paper published in 1693 by Edmund Halley, as described in the aside "An Early History of Survival Analysis." The techniques were developed further in the late 19th and 20th centuries, particularly for applications in social sciences, industrial process control, and medical research. These applications necessarily used a small amount of data because all data was collected by hand. A typical medical study, for instance, has dozens or hundreds of participants, rather than the multitudes of customers whose information is stored in today's databases.

This section shows some examples of survival analysis without strictly defining terms such as *hazard probabilities* and *survival*. The examples start with life expectancy, then an explanation of survival in the medical realm, and finally give an example of hazard probabilities and how they shed light on customer behavior.

Life Expectancy

Life expectancy is a natural application of survival analysis because it answers the question how long people will survive. Figure 6-1 shows life expectancy curves for the U.S. population broken out by gender and race (http://www.cdc .gov/nchs/data/dvs/LEWK3_2009.pdf), as calculated by the U.S. Census Bureau in 2009. For instance, the curves show that 90% of black males survive to age 55. By comparison, 90% of white women survive to their early 70s. More than 40%

AN EARLY HISTORY OF SURVIVAL ANALYSIS

Survival analysis predates what we call statistics by about two centuries. Much of what we call statistics was invented in the 19th and 20th centuries; however, the origins of survival analysis go back to the 17th century, specifically to a paper presented in 1693 to the Royal Society in London. The paper, published in the Royal Society's *Philosophical Transactions,* was titled "An Estimate of the Degrees of the Mortality of Mankind, drawn from curious Tables of the Births and Funerals at the City of Breslaw, with an Attempt to ascertain the Price of Annuities." It is available online at http://www.pierre-marteau.com/editions/1693-mortality.html.

The paper's author, Edmund Halley, is now famous for quite another reason. In 1758, 16 years after his death, a comet he predicted to return did indeed return. And Halley's comet has continued to return every 76 or so years.

In the paper, Halley derives the basic calculations for survival analysis using mortality data collected from Breslau (a city in southwestern Poland now known by its Polish name, Wroclaw). These techniques are still used today.

In other ways, the paper is quite modern. Technological innovations in computing enabled Halley's analysis. No, not the calculator or electronic computer. Logarithms and the slide rule were invented earlier in the 1600s, making it possible to do lots of multiplications and divisions more efficiently than ever.

Halley was also responding to the availability of data. The "curious tables of births and funerals" refers to the fact that Breslau was keeping track of births and deaths at the time. Why Breslau and not some other city? The reason is unknown. Perhaps Breslau was keeping accurate records of births and deaths in response to the Counter-Reformation (religious wars between Catholics and Protestants in Europe at that time). Mandating records strengthened the Catholic churches that gathered these vital statistics, helping to ensure that everyone (or almost everyone) was born and died a Catholic.

And what was the application of the new techniques, calculated using the new technology, on the newly available data? Financial calculations for annuities or pensions. This is surely an application we can still relate to. In fact, this particular method of calculating survival values is now called the *life table method* because actuaries in life insurance companies have been using the same techniques for over two centuries.

Some things do change, however. His opinions that "four of six [women] should bring a Child every year" and "Celibacy ought to be discouraged . . . by extraordinary Taxing and Military Service" are no longer mainstream. The paper also includes what is, perhaps, the earliest reference to infant mortality rates. At the time, Breslau had a rate of 281 infant deaths, per 1000 births, meaning that 281 newly born babies died before their first birthday. By comparison, the countries with the worst infant mortality rates in the modern world—Angola, Afghanistan, and Somalia—all have rates under 200 deaths, per 1000 births. Poland had improved to a very respectable 6.24 per 1000. Some things do change for the better.

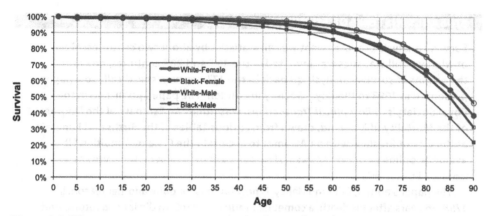

Figure 6-1: Life expectancy curves are an example of survival curves.

of females—whether black or white—are expected to survive to age 90, which is much larger than the proportion for males.

Life expectancy curves are examples of survival curves. They always start at 100% and decline toward 0%. They also provide information, such as the fact that almost everyone survives to age 50 or so. After that, the curves decline more sharply; as people age, their risk of dying increases. Even at age 50, the figure shows that groups differ by their survival, with black men having noticeably lower survival than the other groups.

The point where half the population survives differs for the four groups:

- For black males, half survive to about age 80.
- For white males, half survive to about age 85.
- For black females, half survive to about age 87.
- For white females, half survive to about age 89.

This age, where half survive, is called the *median age*, and it is a useful measure for comparing different groups.

Medical Research

Purportedly, one of the ten most cited scientific papers of all time is a classic paper on survival analysis called "Regression Models and Life Tables (with Discussion)." Published in 1972, this paper by Sir David Cox—the "Sir" was added because of his renown as a statistician—introduced a technique, now called *Cox proportional hazards regression*, which provides a way of measuring the effects of various factors on survival.

As an example, consider what happens to prisoners after they are released from prison. *Longitudinal* studies follow groups of prisoners over time to determine what happens to them. These studies are for understanding recidivism, a fancy word for prisoners who return to their criminal behavior. Some prisoners return to a life of crime. Others are rehabilitated. Others are lost to follow-up for some reason.

What factors affect the ultimate outcome? Is it the length of time in prison? Do work programs in prison reduce recidivism? Is it the crime that they committed? Their gender? Previous criminal history? Availability of counseling after release? Ability to get a job? A supportive family? Data from longitudinal studies is analyzed to understand which factors are most important in determining who goes back to prison, and who doesn't. The analysis often uses techniques invented by Sir David Cox back in 1972 (and so any paper describing such a study typically cites the original paper).

These ideas have been applied in many different areas, from the effect of smoking and diabetes on longevity to the factors that affect the length of time people remain unemployed, from the factors that affect the length of business cycles to the impact of a drug such as Vioxx on cardiovascular disease and the timing of parliamentary elections in the United Kingdom. Determining which factors affect survival—for better or worse—is quite useful.

Examples of Hazards

A hazard probability is the probability that someone succumbs to a risk at a given point in time. Figure 6-2 shows two examples of hazard probability curves.

The top chart in Figure 6-2 is the overall risk of dying at a given age, based on the 2009 data for the U.S. population. This chart shows the risk at yearly intervals and reveals interesting facts. During the first year, the hazard is relatively large. The *infant mortality rate*, as this number is called, is about 0.64% (which is many times less than in Angola now or Breslau in the 1680s). After the first year, the risk of dying falls considerably, rising a bit as teens learn how to drive, and then more as people age. The shape of this curve, where it starts a bit high, falls, and then increases again is called the "bathtub-shaped" hazard. The name comes from the shape of the curve, which follows the contours of a bathtub. Imagine the drain on the left side.

The bottom chart in Figure 6-2 shows the more complicated hazard probabilities for the risk of customers stopping a subscription a certain number of days after they start. This chart also has several features. First, the hazard at tenure zero is quite high because many customers are recorded as starting but are not able to start—perhaps their credit cards didn't go through, or their addresses were incorrect, or they immediately changed their mind. The next two peaks between 60 and 90 days out correspond to customers not paying and to customers stopping after the end of the initial promotional period.

The hazard curve is bumpy, with an evident weekly pattern and peaks about every 30 days. The explanation is the billing period: Customers are more likely

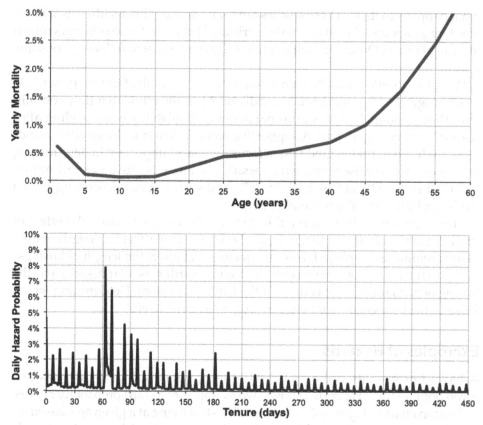

Figure 6-2: These are two examples of hazard probabilities: the top chart is mortality, and the bottom chart is stopped subscriptions.

to stop shortly after receiving a bill. Finally, the long-term trend in the hazard probabilities is downward, indicating that as customers stay longer, their chance of leaving decreases. This long-term downward trend is a good measure of loyalty; it shows that as customers stay around longer, they are less likely to leave.

TIP The long-term trend in the hazard probabilities is a good measure of loyalty because it shows what happens as customers become more familiar with you.

The Hazard Calculation

The rest of this chapter explores and explains various calculations used in survival analysis, with particular emphasis on using SQL and Excel to do them. The examples in the rest of the chapter use the subscription dataset, which consists of customers of a mobile phone company in three markets.

The hazard calculation is the foundation of survival analysis, and it depends on the start date, stop date, and stop type columns. This section first explores these columns and then goes into the calculation of the hazard itself.

Data Investigation

Survival analysis fundamentally relies on two pieces of information about each customer, the *stop flag* (whether the customer is stopped or active) and the *tenure* (how long the customer was active). Often, these columns must be derived from other columns in the database. In Subscribers, for instance, the tenure is already calculated but the stop flag must be derived from other columns.

Because this information is so important, a good place to start is with data exploration. This is true even when the fields are pre-calculated because the definitions in the data may not match exactly the definitions that we need.

Stop Flag

The stop flag specifies which customers are active and which are stopped, as of the cutoff date. What happens to customers after the cutoff date is unknown. The column StopType contains stop reasons. *What values does this column take on?* A simple aggregation query answers this question:

```
SELECT StopType, COUNT(*) as n, MIN(SubscriberId), MAX(SubscriberId)
FROM Subscribers
GROUP BY StopType
ORDER BY StopType
```

Table 6-1 shows three stop types and NULL to indicate that customers are still active. The query includes the minimum and maximum customer ID, which is useful for finding examples for each value.

The stop types have the following meanings:

- NULL means that the customer is still active.
- I stands for "involuntary" and means the company initiated the stop, usually due to nonpayment on bills.

Table 6-1: Stop Types in the Subscription Data

STOP TYPE	COUNT	MINIMUM SUBSCRIBERID	MAXIMUM SUBSCRIBERID
NULL	2,390,959	2	115985522
I	790,457	217	115960366
M	15,508	9460	115908229
V	1,871,111	52	115962722

- ■ V stands for "voluntary" and means the customer initiated the stop.
- ■ M stands for "migration" and means the customer switched to another product.

A customer is active when the stop type is NULL. Otherwise, the customer has stopped. This rule is expressed in SQL as:

```
SELECT (CASE WHEN StopType IS NOT NULL THEN 1 ELSE 0 END) as isstop
```

The inverse of the stop flag is the active flag, which is simply one minus the stop flag. The active flag has a special name in statistics, the *censor flag* (which is defined in greater detail in the next section). The two are related in a simple manner, and either can be used for calculations.

Originally, the stop type had dozens of values, indicating the myriad reasons why someone might stop ("bad service," "no service at home," "billing dispute," and so on). These specific reasons were mapped into the three categories in the StopType column.

Tenure

Tenure is the length of time between a customer's start date and stop date. Usually, the tenure needs to be calculated, using differences between the dates. The subscription table, though, already has tenure defined. Using the Microsoft SQL function for subtracting dates, the definition is:

```
SELECT DATEDIFF(day, StartDate,
              (CASE WHEN StopType IS NOT NULL THEN '2006-12-28'
                  ELSE StopDate END)) as tenure
```

A customer's tenure is known when the customer has already stopped. However, if the customer has not stopped, the tenure is known as of the cutoff date (which would typically be the current date or the most recent load date).

> **WARNING**   A stop date can be the first day a customer is no longer active. Or, it can be the last day a customer is active—the particular definition depends on the database. The tenure calculation is slightly different for these two cases. In the first case, the tenure is the difference between the start and stop dates. In the second, it is one more than the difference.

For an unbiased calculations, the start and stop dates need to be accurate and come from the same population. Many things can affect the accuracy of dates, particularly older dates:

- ■ Customer records for stopped customers fail to be loaded into the database.
- ■ The start date gets replaced with another date, such as the date the account was loaded into the database.
- ■ The stop date gets overwritten with dates that occur after the stop date, such as the date an unpaid account was written off.

■ The start date gets overwritten with another date, such as the date the customer switched to another product.

Investigating dates is important.
The place to start is with a histogram of the starts and stops over time. The following query produces a histogram by year:

```
SELECT the year, SUM(isstart) as starts, SUM(isstop) as stops
FROM ((SELECT YEAR(StartDate) as theyear, 1 as isstart, 0 as isstop
       FROM Subscribers s)
      UNION ALL
      (SELECT YEAR(StopDate), 0 as isstart, 1 as isstop
       FROM Subscribers s)
     ) s
GROUP BY theyear
ORDER BY theyear
```

The results from this query are in Table 6-2. Notice that more than two million customers have NULL stop dates indicating that they are still active. The first two

Table 6-2: Start and Stop Date by Year

YEAR	STARTS	STOPS
<NULL>	181	2,390,959
1958	1	0
1988	70	0
1989	213	0
1990	596	0
1991	1,011	0
1992	2,288	0
1993	3,890	0
1994	7,371	0
1995	11,638	0
1996	22,320	0
1997	42,462	0
1998	66,701	0
1999	102,617	0
2000	146,975	0
2001	250,471	0
2002	482,291	0
2003	865,219	0
2004	1,112,707	793,138
2005	1,292,819	874,845
2006	656,194	1,009,093

rows of the table also show that 182 customers have questionable start dates—either NULL or in 1958. The data for these customers is invalid. No customers should predate the invention of wireless phones. Because there are so few, the best thing to do is just filter them out.

No customers in this data stopped before 2004. Was this because superior business practices during that time resulted in no stops? Probably not. Was this because the company forgot to record stops in the database? Probably not. The most likely reason is that this data was loaded in 2004, and only active customers were loaded. This is an example of *left truncation*. Rows have been filtered out based on the stop date. The next chapter explains how to handle left truncation.

In order to get unbiased estimates of the hazard and survival probabilities, the start and stop dates need to come from the same time period. For now, the solution is to filter the data, removing any starts that happened prior to 2004. In addition, one customer has a negative tenure. Throughout this chapter, an expression such as WHERE StartDate >= '2004-01-01' AND Tenure >= 0 is part of most of the queries on Subscribers so that the queries produce unbiased hazards.

Hazard Probability

The hazard probability at tenure *t* is the ratio between two numbers: the number of customers who succumb to the risk at that tenure divided by everyone who could have succumbed to the risk at that tenure. The denominator is called the *population at risk at tenure t*. The hazard probability is always between 0% and 100%. It is never negative, because the population at risk and the population that succumbs to the risk are never negative. It is not greater than 100%, because the population at risk always includes at least everyone who succumbs to the risk. The calculation is easy; for any given tenure, we simply divide two numbers. Getting the right numbers is the challenge.

As a simple example, consider 100 customers who start on January 1st and are still active on January 31st. If two of these customers stop on February 1st, then the 31-day hazard is 2%. There are 100 customers in the population at risk and two who succumb. The ratio is 2%.

The 31-day hazard remains the same regardless of how many customers actually start on January 1st, so long as all but 100 stop during the month of January. The customers who stop in January are not at risk on day 31, because they are no longer active. These stopped-too-early customers do not affect the 31-day hazard.

The following SQL query calculates the hazard at tenure 100:

```
SELECT 100 as tenure, COUNT(*) as popatrisk,
       SUM(CASE WHEN Tenure = 100 AND StopType IS NOT NULL
               THEN 1 ELSE 0 END) as succumbtorisk,
       AVG(CASE WHEN Tenure = 100 AND StopTYpe IS NOT NULL
               THEN 1.0 ELSE 0 END) as h_100
FROM Subscribers
WHERE StartDate >= '2004-01-01' AND Tenure >= 100
```

The population at risk consists of all customers whose tenure is greater than or equal to 100. Of the 2,589,423 customers at risk, 2,199 of them stopped at tenure 100. This gives a 100-day hazard of 0.085%. Notice that this calculation considers only customers since 2004 because of the left truncation issue.

Visualizing Customers: Time versus Tenure

Figure 6-3 shows two pictures of the same group of customers. In each picture, a line represents one customer, with a vertical bar indicating when a customer starts and a circle indicating the stop date or current date (for active customers). An open circle means that the customer is still active, suggesting an open account. A filled circle means the customer has stopped, suggesting a closed account.

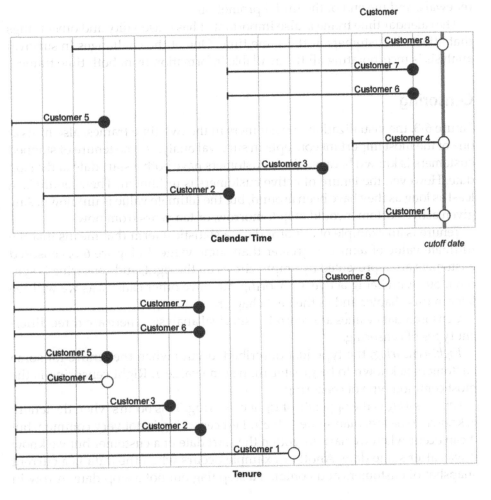

Figure 6-3: This is a picture of customers on the calendar and tenure timelines.

The two charts show the same customers from two different perspectives: calendar time and tenure time. In the top chart (calendar time), customers start at any time, and active customers are lined up on the right—customers are active until the cutoff date. In the bottom chart, the customers have been shifted to the left, so they all start at tenure zero. Active customers are interspersed at all tenures. Some long tenure customers are no longer active, and some are. Some short tenure customers are active; some are not. The aside, "Visualizing Survival Customers Using Excel" explains how these charts were made using Excel.

Both time frames show customers and their tenures. Survival analysis focuses on the tenure time frame because tenure generally has the greater effect on customer retention. After all, the fact that customers can stop only after they have started puts a condition on the tenure, but not on the calendar time. Also, myriad events happen on the tenure time frame, such as monthly bills, contract renewals, and the end of the initial promotion.

The calendar time frame is also important. It has seasonality and other things that affect all customers at the same time. One of the challenges in survival analysis is incorporating all the available information from both time frames.

Censoring

Figure 6-3, the visualization of customers in the two time frames, also hints at one of the most important concepts in survival analysis. The tenure of stopped customers is known because these customers have both a start date and a stop date. However, the tenure of active customers is unknown. Their tenure is at least as long as they have been around, but the ultimate value is unknown. Any given active customer could stop tomorrow, or ten years from now.

Tenure is an example of *censored* data, a statistical term that means that the ultimate value of tenure is greater than some value. In Figure 6-3, censored customers are represented by empty circles on the right, and censoring is synonymous with being active. Censoring can have other causes, as we will see later in this chapter and in the next chapter.

Censored data values are central to survival analysis. There are three different types of censoring.

Right-censoring, the type just described, occurs when the tenure for some customers is known to be greater than some value T. Right censoring is the most common type of censoring.

Left censoring is the opposite of right censoring. This occurs when the tenure is known to be less than some value T. Left censoring is not very common, but it can occur when we have forgotten the start date of a customer but we know it was after some date. Another example occurs when the data is a current snapshot of customers and contains a stop flag but not a stop date. A row in

VISUALIZING SURVIVAL CUSTOMERS USING EXCEL

The charts in Figure 6-3 (page 265) were created using Excel. Each chart has two series plotted using a scatter plot. One series is for all customers. This series has the tail, which is really an X-error bar, and head. The other series fills in some of the circles for the active customers. The advantage to using a chart is that when the data changes, the chart changes.

The following data describes the customers:

NAME	ID	Y-VALUE	X-START	X-END	LENGTH
Ann	8	7.5	12	14	2
Bob	7	6.5	6	13	7
Cora	6	5.5	6	13	7
Diane	5	4.5	0	3	3
Emma	4	3.5	3	14	11
Fred	3	2.5	5	10	5
Gus	2	1.5	1	7	6
Hal	1	0.5	9	14	5

The X-START, X-END, and Y-VALUE columns describe the beginning and end of each line. The reason for starting the Y-VALUEs at 0.5 and incrementing by 1 is purely aesthetic. These values control the spacing of the lines on the chart and the distance from the customers to the top and bottom of the chart. The spacing can also be controlled by adjusting the Y-axis, but the fraction 0.5 is simpler.

The points are plotted using a scatter plot with the X-END cells as the X values and the Y-VALUE cells as the Y values. The symbol is a circle, with a size of 10 points and a white background (if no background color is set, the gridlines show through). To set the symbol, right-click the series, choose "Format Data Series…" Then find "Marker Options," which may be under the left-most icon on the "Marker" tab. Change the Marker to have a solid white fill using the options under "Fill."

The tail is added using Error Bars, by clicking "Add Chart Element" on the ribbon and then choosing "Error Bars ➢ More Error Bar Options" or by clicking the + near the upper-right corner of the chart. In the options dialog, choose the "Error Bar Options" ➢ "X error bars" to set the direction to Minus. You can now put in the appropriate series using the "Custom" option. Note: You may need to set the Y error bars to a Fixed Value of 0 and "No Cap" to make them disappear.

Next, label the lines. Add the labels by right-clicking on the series and choosing "Add Data Labels ➢ Add Data Labels." When the values appear, select one value by left-clicking, and then right-click and choose "Format Data Labels."

There is not a great deal of flexibility on the placement of data labels, so we have to improvise. Under "Label Options," set the "Label Position" to "Left" so that the text goes to the left of the circle. Then set the text by using a Custom format under Number, by unclicking "Linked to source," choosing "Custom" and typing **Customer 0** in the Format Code box. The line is still going through the label. To fix that, let's make it a superscript. Go to the Home Ribbon and choose the icon to expand the font

continues

continued

options. Choose "Superscript" in the "Effects" area so that the text is above the line. (You can control how far up and down by adjusting the "Offset"). Increase the size of the font to something like 12-pt Arial. Alternatively, the XY-Labeler, introduced in Chapter 4, can be used to label the lines with actual customer names.

Add the filled circles using another data series, setting the options on "Marker" and "Marker Fill" to fill in the circle. Copy the data for the three customers who are active (customers 1, 4, and 8) and add the series. The X-error bar and data labels do not need to be set in this case.

Next, add the cutoff line. This is a simple line whose coordinates are (14, 0) and (14, 8). These values can be put into cells or directly as a "Data Series" (with the values {14, 14} for the X series and {0, 8} for the Y series). To format the series as a line, set the "Marker Style" to "No Marker" and the "Line" to an appropriate color.

Adjust the axes so the vertical axis has a maximum of 8 and the horizontal axis has a maximum of 15. On the Chart Layout ribbon, choose the "Axis Options..." for the horizontal and vertical axes and set the values accordingly.

The final step is to add the vertical gridlines (by going to the Format ribbon and choosing Gridlines ≻ Vertical Gridlines ≻ Major Gridlines) and to remove two axes (by clicking on each of them and hitting Delete).

Voila! The end result is a chart that depicts customers using Excel—certainly an unexpected application for charting.

such data specifies that a customer has stopped, along with the start date and snapshot date. All we know is the customer stopped before the snapshot date.

Interval censoring is the combination of left censoring and right censoring. It occurs when data is being collected at long intervals. For instance, researchers studying prisoners after their release may check in on the prisoners every year. If a prisoner drops out of the study, the tenure is known only to the nearest year.

In customer databases, the start date is usually known. An example of a situation where the start date is not known is the survival of patients after cancer appears. The "start" date is the diagnosis date of the cancer, not when the cancer first appeared. This is an example of right censorship because the actual start date is not known, but is known to be before the diagnosis date. Ironically, one consequence of relying on the detection date is that better detection can result in better five-year survival after diagnosis, even for the same treatment. The cancer is simply diagnosed earlier so the patient survives longer after the diagnosis. (This was particularly true after the introduction of more extensive usage of MRIs and CT scans in the 1990s.)

Left censoring and interval censoring are unusual in customer databases. The typical situation with customer databases is that the start date is known, and active customers are right censored.

Survival and Retention

Hazard probabilities measure the probability that someone succumbs to a risk at a given time. Survival is the probability that someone has not succumbed to the risk up to that time. In other words, survival accumulates information about hazards, or more specifically about the inverse of hazards.

Point Estimate for Survival

Survival at tenure t is the number of customers who are active at tenure t divided by the population at risk at tenure t. *How many customers survived to at least tenure t, how many stopped, and what is the survival value?* This question is easy to answer in SQL for any given tenure:

```
SELECT 100 as tenure, COUNT(*) as popatrisk,
       SUM(CASE WHEN Tenure < 100 AND StopType IS NOT NULL
               THEN 1 ELSE 0 END) as succumbtorisk,
       AVG(CASE WHEN tenure >= 100 OR StopType IS NULL
               THEN 1.0 ELSE 0 END) as s_100
FROM Subscribers
WHERE StartDate >= '2004-01-01' AND Tenure >= 0 AND
      StartDate <= DATEADD(day, -100, '2006-12-28')
```

This calculation is similar to the point estimate for the hazard, including filtering out the customers who started before 2004-01-01. The population at risk is everyone who started more than 100 days before the cutoff date. Only these customers could have survived to 100 days. The ones who survived are those who are either still active or whose tenure is greater than 100 days. Survival is the ratio of those who survived to the population at risk.

Calculating Survival for All Tenures

The survival at tenure t is the product of one minus the hazards for all tenures less than t; one minus the hazard is the probability of surviving for that tenure rather than the probability of stopping. It could also be called the *incremental survival* because it corresponds to the survival from tenure t to tenure $t+1$. Overall survival at tenure t is the product of the incremental survivals up to t.

The calculation is easy using the combination of SQL and Excel. The first step is to calculate the hazards for all tenures, then to calculate the incremental survival, and then the cumulative product.

This calculation uses the following two items:

- Population that succumbed to the risk: The number of customers who stopped at exactly tenure t.
- Population at risk: The number of customers whose tenure is greater than or equal to t.

The population at risk at tenure t is an example of a cumulative sum because it is the count of all customers whose tenure is greater than or equal to t.

The value for each tenure can be calculated in SQL:

```
SELECT Tenure, COUNT(*) as popt,
       SUM(CASE WHEN StopType IS NOT NULL THEN 1 ELSE 0 END) as stopt
FROM Subscribers
WHERE StartDate >= '2004-01-01' AND Tenure >= 0
GROUP BY Tenure
ORDER BY Tenure
```

When the results are copied into Excel, one column has Tenure, one column popt, and the third stopt. Assume that the results are copied, with the data starting at cell C27. What is the population at risk at a given tenure? The population at risk is the sum of the popt values (in column D) for that tenure and higher.

To do the calculation without typing in a separate formula for all 1,093 rows, construct a formula that changes when it is copied down the column. Such a formula for cell F27 is =SUM($D27:$D$1119). This formula has the range $D27:$D$1119, so the sum starts at D27 and continues through D1119. The prefix "$" holds that portion of the cell reference constant. Copying the formula down (by highlighting the region and typing Ctrl+D) changes the first cell reference for each pasted formula. Cell F30 gets the formula: =SUM($D30:$D$1119), and so on to =SUM($D1121:$D$1119).

The hazard is then the ratio of the stops to the population at risk, which for cell G29 is =E29/F29. Figure 6-4 shows an Excel spreadsheet with these formulas.

The next step is to calculate the survival as the cumulative product of one minus the hazards. The following formula in cell H27 calculates survival: =IF($C27=0, 1, H26*(1-G26)). The "if" part of the formula handles the case when the tenure is zero and the survival is 100%. Each subsequent survival value is the previous survival value multiplied by one minus the previous hazard. This type of formula, where the formulas in a column of cells refer to the values calculated in previous rows in the same column is called a *recursive formula*. When this formula is copied down the column, the formula calculates the survival for all tenures. The resulting survival curve is shown in Figure 6-5.

	C	D	E	F	G	H
25		FROM SQL			CALCULATED IN EXCEL	
26	Tenure	popt	stopt	POPCUM	h	s
27	0	2383	508	=SUM($D27:$D$1119)	=E27/F27	=IF($C27=0, 1, H26*(1-G26))
28	1	18354	17306	=SUM($D28:$D$1119)	=E28/F28	=IF($C28=0, 1, H27*(1-G27))
29	2	16730	15091	=SUM($D29:$D$1119)	=E29/F29	=IF($C29=0, 1, H28*(1-G28))
30	3	13283	11346	=SUM($D30:$D$1119)	=E30/F30	=IF($C30=0, 1, H29*(1-G29))
31	4	9544	9500	=SUM($D31:$D$1119)	=E31/F31	=IF($C31=0, 1, H30*(1-G30))
32	5	11746	9152	=SUM($D32:$D$1119)	=E32/F32	=IF($C32=0, 1, H31*(1-G31))
33	6	12649	9409	=SUM($D33:$D$1119)	=E33/F33	=IF($C33=0, 1, H32*(1-G32))
34	7	13466	10298	=SUM($D34:$D$1119)	=E34/F34	=IF($C34=0, 1, H33*(1-G33))
35	8	11862	9560	=SUM($D35:$D$1119)	=E35/F35	=IF($C35=0, 1, H34*(1-G34))

Figure 6-4: These formulas in an Excel spreadsheet calculate hazards and survival.

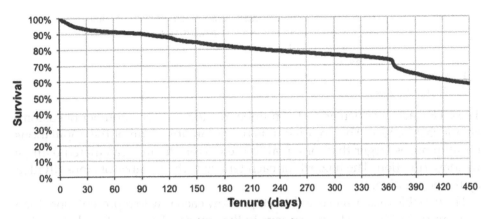

Figure 6-5: This is the survival curve for the subscription data.

In this case, all tenure values appear in the table, so the tenure column has no gaps. However, there can be gaps when no stopped or active customers have exactly that particular tenure. The hazard is zero for the missing tenure, and the survival is the same as the previous survival. This does not cause any problems with the calculation. It does, however, make scatter plots preferable for survival curves rather than line charts. When values are skipped, scatter plots do a better job labeling the X-axis.

Calculating Survival in SQL

Calculating the hazard and survival probabilities in SQL rather than Excel is convenient. The results can be stored in SQL tables, without having to re-import the values from a spreadsheet.

The calculation in SQL uses window functions and a trick to do the aggregate multiplication. The following version uses a common table expression (CTE) to calculate the hazards and then calculates the survival:

```
WITH h as (
    SELECT Tenure, SUM(1 - IsActive) as numstops,
        COUNT(*) as tenurepop,
        SUM(COUNT(*)) OVER (ORDER BY Tenure DESC) as pop,
        LEAD(Tenure) OVER (ORDER BY Tenure) as nexttenure,
        (LEAD(Tenure) OVER (ORDER BY Tenure) - Tenure) as numdays,
        SUM(1.0 - IsActive) /
            SUM(COUNT(*)) OVER (ORDER BY Tenure DESC) as h
    FROM Subscribers
    WHERE StartDate >= '2004-01-01' AND Tenure >= 0
    GROUP BY Tenure
    )
SELECT h.*,
    COALESCE(EXP(SUM(LOG(1 - h)) OVER
        (ORDER BY Tenure
```

```
                    ROWS BETWEEN UNBOUNDED PRECEDING AND
                                  1 PRECEDING
              )), 1
        ) as S
FROM h
ORDER BY Tenure
```

The CTE starts by calculating the number of stops and the number of customers for each tenure. The population is the cumulative sum of the populations for all tenures larger than or equal to the current tenure, calculated using a window function. The hazard for each tenure is the number of stops divided by the population.

The variables nexttenure and numdays allow each row to represent more than one tenure, just in case there are gaps in the tenures. The use of buckets makes the results of this query more useful as a lookup table.

The calculation for the survival from the hazards has two unusual components. The first is the calculation of the product. The second is the additional clause in the window function to specify the window extent.

Calculating the Product of Column Values

Unfortunately, SQL does not have a PRODUCT() aggregation function that multiplies numbers in the same way that SUM() adds them. To handle this, we have to go back to high school algebra and remember how to use logarithms: raising e to the power of the sum of the logarithms of numbers is the same as multiplying the numbers together.

Hence, PRODUCT() is basically calculated as:

```
SELECT EXP(SUM(LOG(1 - s2.hazard)))
```

This expression sums the logs of the incremental survival and then undoes the log, a roundabout but effective way to do aggregate multiplication. Note that in some databases, the names of the functions might be different, such as LN() instead of LOG().

This formula for the product is a simplification because the value for each hazard is always non-negative and less than one. The general expression for an aggregate product needs to take positive and negative numbers into account as well as the fact that logarithms are undefined for negative numbers and zero.

The following query handles the logic:

```
SELECT (1 - 2 * MOD(SUM(CASE WHEN col < 0 THEN 1 ELSE 0 END), 2)) *
       MIN(CASE WHEN col = 0 THEN 0 ELSE 1 END) *
       SUM(EXP(LOG(ABS(CASE WHEN col = 0 THEN 1 ELSE col END)))))
```

This formula has three expressions on the three lines. The first handles the sign of the result by counting the number of values less than zero. If the

CONTROLLING THE WINDOW EXTENT

The formula for survival multiplies the incremental survival for all values *less* than the given tenure. By default, the value in the current row would be included. The ROWS clause prevents this by specifying that only values up to the preceding row are included in the calculation—the 1 PRECEDING part of the clause.

SQL offers two similar clauses for the window extent, ROWS BETWEEN and RANGE BETWEEN. There is a subtle and a not-so-subtle difference between them. ROWS defines the window extent in terms of the rows in the window. RANGE defines it in terms of the values. This is the subtle difference.

A very simple example illustrates the more substantive effect of these definitions:

```
WITH t as (
    select 1 as i, 1 as col union all
    select 2, 1
    )
SELECT t.*,
       SUM(col) OVER (ORDER BY col
                  ROWS BETWEEN UNBOUNDED PRECEDING AND CURRENT ROW
                  ) as ROWSresult,
       SUM(col) OVER (ORDER BY col
                  RANGE BETWEEN UNBOUNDED PRECEDING AND CURRENT ROW
                  ) as RANGEresult
 FROM t
```

This simple example has two rows and two columns, with different values in the first column and the same value in the second. The results for the two columns are in the following table. The ROWS clause calculates up to each row, so the value is 1 for the first row and 2 for the second. The RANGE clause calculates the same value for both rows. The window extent is defined by the *value* in the current row. Because both rows have the same value, both rows are included in the window extent. In practice, ROWS is more common than RANGE.

I	COL	ROWSRESULT	RANGERESULT
1	1	1	2
2	1	2	2

An alternative approach does not require a window extent. The current value can be removed by dividing it out:

```
SELECT h.*,
       EXP(SUM(LOG(1 - h)) OVER (ORDER BY Tenure)) / (1 - h) as S
 FROM h
```

This formula produces the same value and is simply an alternative approach.

count is even, the result is one; if odd, then the result is minus one. The second expression handles zero values—then the result is zero. The third expression handles the actual product, with a lot of care to prevent errors in the `LOG()`. The `ABS()` guarantees that the argument to `LOG()` is never negative, and the `CASE` guarantees that the argument is never zero—preventing errors. The first two expressions have already handled the work for negative numbers and zeroes.

Adding in More Dimensions

More dimensions can be handled by adding them to the aggregations and window functions. To calculate survival by market:

```
WITH h as (
    SELECT Market, Tenure,
           SUM(1 - IsActive) as numstops, COUNT(*) as tenurepop,
           SUM(COUNT(*)) OVER (PARTITION BY Market
                                    ORDER BY Tenure DESC) as pop,
           LEAD(Tenure) OVER (PARTITION BY Market
                                    ORDER BY Tenure) as nexttenure,
           SUM(1.0 - IsActive) /
            SUM(COUNT(*)) OVER (PARTITION BY market
                                    ORDER BY Tenure DESC) as h
    FROM Subscribers
    WHERE StartDate >= '2004-01-01' AND Tenure >= 0
    GROUP BY Tenure, Market
   )
SELECT h.*,
       EXP(SUM(LOG(1 - h)) OVER (PARTITION BY Market
                                ORDER BY Tenure)) / (1 - h) as S
FROM h
ORDER BY Market, Tenure
```

The only difference is the addition of `Market` to the `GROUP BY` clauses and the inclusion of `PARTITION BY` for all the window functions.

A Simple Customer Retention Calculation

Survival is one method of understanding how long customers stay around. Customer retention is an alternative approach. The purpose in presenting it here is to better understand survival by comparing it to another sensible measure.

A typical customer retention question is: *Of customers who started xxx days ago, how many are still active?* This question can be answered directly in SQL:

```
SELECT DATEDIFF(day, StartDate, '2006-12-28') as daysago,
       COUNT(*) as numstarts,
```

```
        SUM(CASE WHEN StopType IS NULL THEN 1 ELSE 0 END) as numactives,
        AVG(CASE WHEN StopType IS NULL THEN 1.0 ELSE 0 END) as retention
FROM Subscribers s
WHERE StartDate >= '2004-01-01' AND Tenure >= 0
GROUP BY DATEDIFF(day, StartDate, '2006-12-28')
ORDER BY daysago
```

This query counts the customers who started on a certain day, calculating the proportion still active.

The result has three columns of data. The first is the number of days ago that customers started, relative to the cutoff date of the data. Other time units, such as weeks or months, might be more appropriate. The second column is the number of starts that occurred on that day. And the third column specifies how many of those customers are currently active. Figure 6-6 shows a plot of the results as a retention curve, which is the proportion of customers who are active as of the cutoff date.

Like the survival curve, the retention curve always starts at 100% because customers who just started are still active. Second, it generally declines, although the decline can be jagged. For instance, of customers who started 90 days ago, 80.1% are still active on the cutoff date. Of customers who started 324 days ago, 80.4% are still active, or equivalently that 19.9% of customers stopped in the first 90 days. Slightly fewer (19.6%) stopped in the first 324 days.

Intuitively, these results do not make sense. Customers who stopped in the first 90 days also stop in the first 324 days. In practice, such a result probably means that particularly good customers were acquired 324 days ago and particularly bad customers were acquired 90 days ago. Jaggedness in retention is counterintuitive: Fewer older customers ought to be around than newer customers.

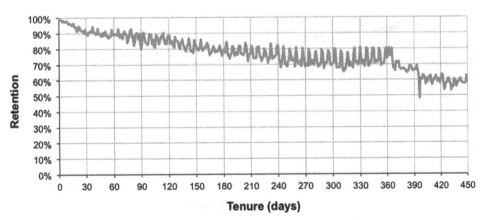

Figure 6-6: This is an example of a retention curve for the subscription data.

Comparison between Retention and Survival

Figure 6-7 shows retention and survival on the same chart, combining the curves in Figures 6-5 and 6-6. Both curves start at 100% and decline. However, the survival curve has no jaggedness, It is always flat or declining—mathematically, this property is called *monotonically decreasing*, and survival curves are always monotonically decreasing. Survival curves are smooth; they do not exhibit the jaggedness of retention curves.

In many ways, the survival is the expected value of the retention (at any given tenure). The jaggedness of the retention curve leads to the question: *Why is retention sometimes higher (or lower) than the survival?* The answer to this question can give insight into the customers. It is tempting to eliminate the jaggedness by using moving averages. A much better solution is to calculate the corresponding survival curve.

Simple Example of Hazard and Survival

The simplest example of survival is the constant hazard. Although such simplicity does not occur with customers, constant hazards appear in very different domains, such as radioactivity. A radioactive isotope decays at a constant rate by emitting subatomic particles, thereby transmuting into other elements. The rate of decay is usually described in terms of the half-life. For instance, the most common isotope of uranium, U-238, has a half-life of about 4.5 billion years, meaning that half the U-238 in a sample decays in this time. On the other hand, another isotope called U-239 has a half-life of about 23 minutes. The longer the half-life, the slower the rate of decay, and the more stable the isotope.

Radioactivity is a useful example for several reasons. Because the decay rates are constant (at least according to modern theories of physics), radioactivity provides simple examples of survival outside the realm of human behavior.

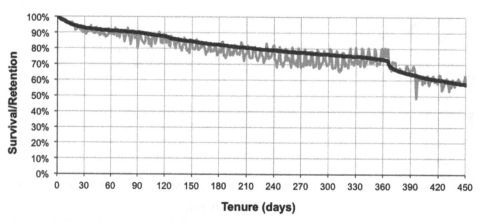

Figure 6-7: Retention and survival plots are shown for the same dataset.

Also, constant hazards are a good baseline for understanding more complex hazards. We can always ask what constant survival rate would have resulted in the survival observed at a given tenure.

Constant hazards are also a good tool for understanding *unobserved heterogeneity*. This phenomenon is quite important in the world of survival analysis. However, as its name suggests, it is not observed directly, making it a bit challenging to recognize and understand.

Constant Hazard

When the hazard is constant, Excel can handle all the calculations. The half-life and hazard probability are interchangeable. If cell A1 contains the half-life in days, then the following formula in cell B1 translates this into a daily hazard probability:

```
=1-0.5^(1/A1)
```

Conversely, if B2 contains the daily hazard probability, then the following formula in cell C1 calculates the half-life in days:

```
-1/LOG(1-B1, 2)
```

Consider two radioactive isotopes of radium, RA-223 and RA-224. The first has a half-life of 11.43 days and the second a half-life of 3.63 days. These correspond respectively to daily hazard (decay) probabilities of 5.9% and 17.4%. After one day, about 95.1% of RA-223 remains, and about 82.6% of RA-224 remains. Figure 6-8 shows the survival curves for these two elements.

The shape of the survival curve follows an exponential curve, which is always the case when the hazard is constant. These survival curves show that within a few weeks, almost all the RA-224 has disappeared. On the other hand, some RA-223 remains because it decays more slowly.

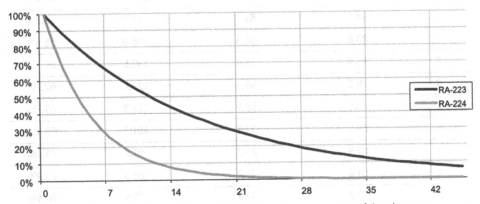

Figure 6-8: Survival curves for RA-223 and RA-224 show the proportion of the elements remaining after a given number of days.

What Happens to a Mixture?

Assume that a sample contains 100 grams of RA-223 and 100 grams of RA-224. How does this mixture behave? Table 6-3 shows the amount of each isotope that remains after a given amount of time. (The actual mass of the sample—if it is enclosed—remains pretty close to 200 grams because the radium just changes into other elements, primarily radon, and very little mass is lost in the process.)

The amount of radium remaining is the sum of the amount of RA-223 and RA-224. The proportion of the original radium remaining is this sum divided by 200 grams. In fact, the proportion is the weighted average of the survival, where the weights are the proportions in the original sample. Because the original sample started out with equal amounts of the two isotopes, the weights are equal.

Given the proportions, what hazard probabilities correspond to the overall radium mixture? One guess would be the average of the two original hazard probabilities, or a constant hazard of about 11.6%. Although inspired, this guess is wrong. A mixture of two things with different constant hazards does not have a constant hazard.

WARNING   Hazards are complicated. A mixture of two groups with constant hazards does not have a constant hazard.

Hazard probabilities can be calculated in reverse from the survival values. The hazard at a given time t is the proportion of the population at risk that stops before time $t+1$ (or decays in the case of radioactivity). The hazard is one minus the ratio of the survival at $t+1$ divided by the survival at t.

Table 6-3: Amount of Radium Left, Assuming 100 Grams of RA-223 and RA-224 at Beginning

DAYS	RA-223 (GRAMS)	RA-224 (GRAMS)	TOTAL (GRAMS)	RA-223 %
0	100.0	100.0	200.0	50.0%
1	94.1	82.6	176.7	53.3%
2	88.6	68.3	156.8	56.5%
3	83.4	56.4	139.8	59.7%
4	78.5	46.6	125.1	62.7%
5	73.8	38.5	112.3	65.7%
6	69.5	31.8	101.3	68.6%
7	65.4	26.3	91.7	71.3%
8	61.6	21.7	83.3	73.9%
9	57.9	17.9	75.9	76.4%
10	54.5	14.8	69.3	78.6%

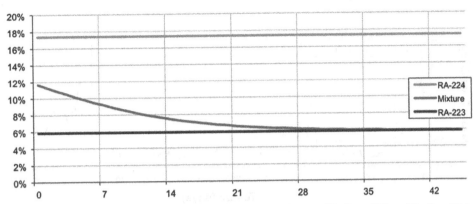

Figure 6-9: The hazard probabilities corresponding to a mixture of Radium 223 and Radium 224 are not constant, even though the two components have constant hazards.

Figure 6-9 shows the resulting hazards, along with the constant hazards for the two isotopes. The hazard of the mixture is not constant at all. It starts at the average value and declines to be more like RA-223's hazard as the mixture of radium becomes denser in RA-223. The RA-224 has decayed into something else. The proportion of RA-223 in the sample increases over time, which is also shown in Table 6-3.

The purpose of this example is to show what happens when a population consists of groups that behave differently. If we are given a sample of radium and measure the hazard probabilities and they follow the pattern in Figure 6-9, we might assume that the hazards are not constant. In fact, this is evidence that two groups with constant hazards are mixed together. This phenomenon is called *unobserved heterogeneity*. Unobserved heterogeneity means that things that affect the survival are not being taken into account.

The same phenomenon applies to customers. If there are two ways of acquiring customers, one that attracts lots of short-term customers ("bad") and one that attracts some long-term customers ("good"), which is better in the long term? Say 1,000 "bad" customers and 100 "good" customers start at the same time. After a year, 20 "bad" customers might remain compared to 60 "good" customers. Even though "good" customers were acquired at a rate one-tenth that of the bad customers, after a year, three times as many remain.

Constant Hazard Corresponding to Survival

Each point on a survival curve has a constant hazard that would produce that survival value at that tenure. To calculate the corresponding constant hazard, assume that cell A1 contains the number of days and cell B1 contains the survival proportion at that day. The following formula in cell C1 calculates the corresponding daily hazard probability:

```
=1-B1^(1/A1)
```

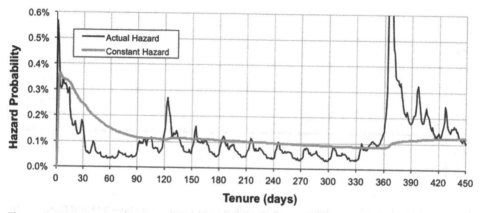

Figure 6-10: Comparison of the effective constant hazard to the actual hazard for the subscription data.

For different tenures, this value changes because in the real world, hazards are not constant. The "effective constant" hazard formally fits an exponential survival function to each point on the survival curve.

Figure 6-10 compares this "effective constant" hazard to the actual hazard for the subscriber data. The constant hazard is spreading the hazard risk equally over all tenures, so it provides an expected value for the hazard. When the actual hazard is less than the constant one, customers are leaving more slowly at that particular tenure than the long-term average would suggest. Similarly, when the average hazard is greater than the constant one, customers are leaving more quickly.

A survival curve (or retention plot) paints a pretty picture. Survival is not only for creating pretty pictures. It can also be used to calculate measures for different groups of customers, as discussed in the next section.

Comparing Different Groups of Customers

This section walks through an example comparing different groups of subscribers using attributes that are known when they start. These attributes are called *time-zero covariates* because they are known at tenure zero. The next chapter investigates approaches for working with time-dependent covariates, things that happen during customers' lifetimes.

Summarizing the Markets

The subscriber data contains three markets: Gotham, Metropolis, and Smallville. A good way to start the analysis is by looking at the proportion of customers in

Table 6-4: Comparison of Customers and Active Customers by Market

MARKET	CUSTOMERS	AVERAGE TENURE	ACTIVES	PROPORTION ACTIVE	MIN STOP DATE
Gotham	1,499,396	383.5	685,176	45.7%	2014-01-02
Metropolis	995,572	415.3	519,709	52.2%	2014-01-02
Smallville	566,751	464.3	390,414	68.9%	2014-10-27

each market who are active as of the cutoff date. The following query generates interesting summary information by market:

```
SELECT Market, COUNT(*) as customers, AVG(Tenure) as avg_tenure,
       SUM(CASE WHEN StopType IS NULL THEN 1 ELSE 0 END) as actives,
       AVG(CASE WHEN StopType IS NULL THEN 1.0 ELSE 0 END
          ) as ActivesRate,
       MIN(StopDate) as minStopDate
FROM Subscribers s
WHERE StartDate >= '2004-01-01' AND Tenure >= 0
GROUP BY market
```

The results are in Table 6-4.

Two pieces of evidence suggest that Gotham is the worst market and Smallville the best, in terms of retention. First, the average tenure of customers in Gotham is about 81 days shorter than the average in Smallville. Second, of all the customers that started in Gotham since 2004, only about 46% are still active. For Smallville, the proportion is close to 70%.

Combined, these two pieces of evidence are quite convincing that Smallville is inhabited by better customers. However, care must be taken when interpreting such evidence. The final column shows another possible reason: Smallville has a different left truncation date from the other two markets, 2014-10-27 rather then 2014-01-02: This makes survival look better because there are almost 11 months that have no stops.

Stratifying by Market

A WHERE clause can be used to calculate survival for one market:

```
WITH h as (
    SELECT Tenure,
           SUM(1 - IsActive) as numstops, COUNT(*) as tenurepop,
           SUM(COUNT(*)) OVER (ORDER BY Tenure DESC) as pop,
           LEAD(Tenure) OVER (ORDER BY Tenure) as nexttenure,
           SUM(1.0 - IsActive) /
             SUM(COUNT(*)) OVER (ORDER BY Tenure DESC) as h
    FROM Subscribers
```

```
        WHERE StartDate >= '2004-01-01' AND Tenure >= 0 AND
              Market = 'Gotham'
        GROUP BY Tenure
       )
SELECT h.*,
       EXP(SUM(LOG(1 - h)) OVER (ORDER BY Tenure)) / (1 - h) as S
FROM hORDER BY Tenure
```

This is cumbersome to repeat for each market.

A better approach is to pivot the data so the columns contain the information about each market. The desired results would have the tenure, then the population for each market (in three columns), and then the number of stops in each market (in three more columns). The SQL to do this is:

```
WITH s as (
       SELECT s.*,
              (CASE WHEN Market = 'Gotham' THEN 1.0 ELSE 0 END) as isg,
              (CASE WHEN Market = 'Metropolis' THEN 1.0 ELSE 0 END) as ism,
              (CASE WHEN Market = 'Smallville' THEN 1.0 ELSE 0 END) as iss,
              (CASE WHEN Market = 'Smallville'
                    THEN CAST('2004-10-27' as DATE)
                    ELSE '2004-01-01' END) as LeftTruncationDate
       FROM Subscribers s
      ),
      h(Tenure, stopg, popg, stopm, popm, stops, pops) as (
       SELECT Tenure,
              SUM(isg * (1.0 - IsActive)),
              NULLIF(SUM(SUM(isg)) OVER (ORDER BY Tenure DESC), 0),
              SUM(ism * (1.0 - IsActive)),
              NULLIF(SUM(SUM(ism)) OVER (ORDER BY Tenure DESC), 0),
              SUM(iss * (1.0 - IsActive)),
              NULLIF(SUM(SUM(iss)) OVER (ORDER BY Tenure DESC), 0)
       FROM s
       WHERE StartDate >= LeftTruncationDate AND Tenure >= 0
       GROUP BY Tenure
      )
SELECT h.*,
       EXP(SUM(LOG(1 - stopg / popg)) OVER
              (ORDER BY Tenure)) / (1 - stopg / popg) as Sg,
       EXP(SUM(LOG(1 - stopm / popm)) OVER
              (ORDER BY Tenure)) / (1 - stopm / popm) as Sm,
       EXP(SUM(LOG(1 - stops / pops)) OVER
              (ORDER BY Tenure)) / (1 - stops / pops) as Ss
FROM h
ORDER BY Tenure
```

Notice that the second CTE for h uses an alternative method for specifying column names, by including them in parentheses when the CTE is defined. Putting the names directly in the subquery is generally safer because adding or removing a column does not affect the names.

The first CTE defines the appropriate left truncation date, which is then used in the WHERE clause of the second. The indicator variables defined in s indicate whether someone is in a particular market. Logic such as this:

```
SUM(CASE WHEN Market = 'Gotham' THEN 1.0 - IsActive ELSE 0 END) as stopg
```

can be replaced with

```
SUM(isg * (1.0 - IsActive)) as stopg
```

This shorter expression uses multiplication instead of conditional logic. The performance should be about the same. Indicator variables can make code easier to write and to read—and more consistent.

> **TIP** Indicator variables are variables that take on a value of 0 or 1 for a given value for a category. They can simplify a query by eliminating lots of repetitive CASE statements.

The resulting survival curves are shown in Figure 6-11. The legend has the population in parentheses after the market name. The population was appended onto the market name for just this reason. Surprisingly, the difference in hazards for Smallville using the correct left truncation date versus 2004-01-01 is quite small—because few customers in Smallville leave during the first 11 months of tenure.

These curves confirm the earlier observation that survival in Gotham seems worse than survival in the other two markets. All three markets show the drop in survival at one year, which corresponds to the contract expiration date. At 450 days—safely after the contract expiration—only 50.1% of Gotham's customers remain, compared to 59.2% for Metropolis and 73.3% for Smallville.

These survival values could also be calculated in Excel using summarized data from SQL:

```
SELECT Tenure,
       SUM(isg) as popg, SUM(ism) as popm, SUM(iss) as pops,
       SUM(isg * isstopped) as stopg, SUM(ism * isstopped) as stopm,
```

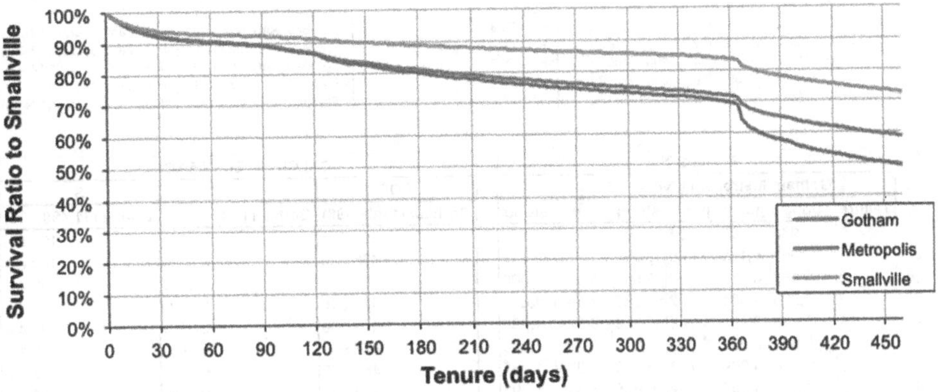

Figure 6-11: Survival by market for the subscription data shows that Smallville has the best survival and Gotham the worst.

```
          SUM(iss * isstopped) as stopg
    FROM (SELECT s.*,
                 (CASE WHEN Market = 'Gotham' THEN 1 ELSE 0 END) as isg,
                 (CASE WHEN Market = 'Metropolis' THEN 1 ELSE 0 END) as ism,
                 (CASE WHEN Market = 'Smallville' THEN 1 ELSE 0 END) as iss,
                 (CASE WHEN StopType IS NOT NULL THEN 1 ELSE 0 END
                 ) as isstopped,
                 (CASE WHEN Market = 'Smallville'
                       THEN CAST('2004-10-27' as DATE)
                       ELSE '2004-01-01' END) as LeftTruncationDate
          FROM Subscribers s) s
    WHERE StartDate >= LeftTruncationDate AND Tenure >= 0
    GROUP BY Tenure
    ORDER BY Tenure
```

Figure 6-12 shows the first few rows of the resulting table for Gotham, along with the formulas used for the calculation. The columns are in groups, with the population columns coming first and then the stop columns, so the hazard and survival formulas can be entered once and then copied to adjacent cells—to the right as well as downward.

Survival Ratio

The ratio between survival curves provides a good qualitative comparison for different groups. Let's use the best survival as the standard. Figure 6-13 shows the ratio of survival for the three markets to customers in Smallville. Smallville's survival ratio is uninteresting because it is always one.

	C	D	E	F	G	H	I	J	K	N	Q
22		Gotham	Metropc	Smallvil					POP	h	S
23	Tenure	popg	popm	pops	stopg	stopm	stopg		=D22&" ("&TEXT(K24, "0,0")&")"	=K23	=N23
24	0	966	986	431	52	409	47		=K25+D24	=IF(K24=0, NA(), G24/K24)	=IF($C24=0, 1, Q23*(1-N23))
25	1	8951	6155	3248	8588	5770	2948		=K26+D25	=IF(K25=0, NA(), G25/K25)	=IF($C25=0, 1, Q24*(1-N24))
26	2	9463	4858	2409	8697	4334	2060		=K27+D26	=IF(K26=0, NA(), G26/K26)	=IF($C26=0, 1, Q25*(1-N25))
27	3	6830	4361	2092	6039	3667	1640		=K28+D27	=IF(K27=0, NA(), G27/K27)	=IF($C27=0, 1, Q26*(1-N26))
28	4	5243	3032	1265	5213	3024	1259		=K29+D28	=IF(K28=0, NA(), G28/K28)	=IF($C28=0, 1, Q27*(1-N27))
29	5	6301	3696	1746	5218	2771	1160		=K30+D29	=IF(K29=0, NA(), G29/K29)	=IF($C29=0, 1, Q28*(1-N28))
30	6	6798	4069	1779	5403	2938	1065		=K31+D30	=IF(K30=0, NA(), G30/K30)	=IF($C30=0, 1, Q29*(1-N29))
31	7	7057	4297	2109	5695	3307	1293		=K32+D31	=IF(K31=0, NA(), G31/K31)	=IF($C31=0, 1, Q30*(1-N30))
32	8	5805	4252	1798	5118	3296	1139		=K33+D32	=IF(K32=0, NA(), G32/K32)	=IF($C32=0, 1, Q31*(1-N31))

	C	D	E	F	G	H	I	J	K	N	Q
21	FROM SQL								CALCULATED IN EXCEL		
22		Gotham	Metrop	Smallville					POP	h	S
23	Tenure	popg	popm	pops	stopg	stopm	stopg		Gotham (1,499,396)	Gotham (1,499,396)	Gotham (1,499,396)
24	0	966	986	431	52	409	47		1,499,396	0.00%	100.0%
25	1	8,951	6,155	3,248	8,588	5,770	2,948		1,498,430	0.57%	100.0%
26	2	9,463	4,858	2,409	8,697	4,334	2,060		1,489,479	0.58%	99.4%
27	3	6,830	4,361	2,092	6,039	3,667	1,640		1,480,016	0.41%	98.8%
28	4	5,243	3,032	1,265	5,213	3,024	1,259		1,473,186	0.35%	98.4%
29	5	6,301	3,696	1,746	5,218	2,771	1,160		1,467,943	0.36%	98.1%
30	6	6,798	4,069	1,779	5,403	2,938	1,065		1,461,642	0.37%	97.7%
31	7	7,057	4,297	2,109	5,695	3,307	1,293		1,454,844	0.39%	97.4%
32	8	5,805	4,252	1,798	5,118	3,296	1,139		1,447,787	0.35%	97.0%

Figure 6-12: These screen shots show the data and Excel formulas for calculating survival by market (only Gotham is shown; the columns for Metropolis and Smallville are hidden).

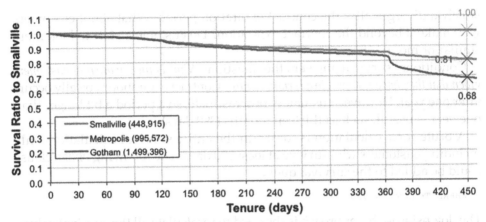

Figure 6-13: The survival ratio is the ratio of survival in each market compared to Smallville's survival.

> **TIP** In Excel, you can label a single point on a series. To do so, click the series to select it. Then click again to select the point. Then right-click and choose "Add Data Label." Then double-click the text to format it. A good idea is to make the text the same color as the series itself.

The survival ratio chart shows that Gotham's survival is uniformly worse than Smallville's at all points in time. "Worse" because the ratio is always less than one. Survival in Metropolis is as bad as Gotham in the first year, but then improves. Although the chart does not specify what is happening, the timing is suggestive. For instance, some customers start with one-year contracts, some with two-year contracts, and some with no contracts at all. Further, customers on one-year contracts are more likely to cancel at one year than before the one-year anniversary. So, perhaps the difference between Metropolis and Gotham is due to the proportion of customers on one-year contracts. Whatever the cause, the survival ratio changes for different tenures. The relationships between the curves (and hence the markets) change for different tenures.

Sometimes the ratio between survival curves can provide somewhat misleading results. For instance, if one market has very poor coverage in outlying areas, then customers from these areas would sign up for the service and quickly stop—their phone is not working. Say, 15% of the customers stop in the first couple of months due to bad coverage. This 15% lingers in the survival curves. So, even if the two markets are identical—except for the outlying coverage issue that only affects customers immediately after they start—the ratio will always show that the first market is worse.

Conditional Survival

The survival ratio suggests another question about survival. Two markets have essentially the same survival characteristics for the first year, but then their survival diverges after the contract expiration period. What about customers who make it beyond the contract expiration? Do customers start to look more similar or more different?

Conditional survival answers the question: *What is the survival of customers given that they have survived to a certain tenure?* Contract expiration typically occurs after one year. However, customers procrastinate, so a period a bit longer than one year is useful, such as thirteen months (390 days).

A brute-force calculation is to re-run the entire survival calculation, only including customers who survive at least 390 days. The following WHERE clause could be added to the survival query:

```
WHERE Tenure >= 390
```

The downside to this approach is the need to recalculate all the survival values.

There is a simpler approach. Conditional survival can also be calculated with the following two rules:

- For tenures <= 390, the conditional survival is 100% (because of the assumption that all customers survive to 390 days.)

- For tenures > 390, the conditional survival is the survival at tenure *t* divided by the survival at time 390.

Excel's VLOOKUP() function makes it easy to find the survival at time 390. The conditional survival is then just the ratio of the survival to this value.

Figure 6-14 shows the survival and the conditional survival at time 390 for the three markets. The markets look similar after 13 months, with Smallville being the best and Gotham the worst for survival after 13 months.

This calculation can also be done in SQL:

```
WITH h as (
    SELECT Tenure,
```

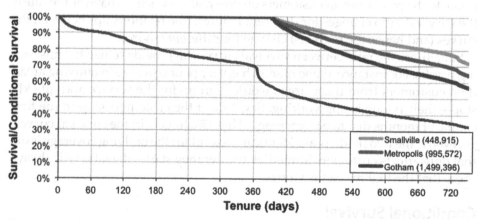

Figure 6-14: Conditional survival after 13 months shows that Smallville is still the best market and Gotham the worst.

```
             SUM(1.0 - IsActive) /
                SUM(COUNT(*)) OVER (ORDER BY Tenure DESC) as h
      FROM (SELECT s.*,
                    (CASE WHEN Market = 'Smallville'
                          THEN CAST('2004-10-27' as DATE)
                          ELSE '2004-01-01' END) as LeftTruncationDate
             FROM Subscribers s
           ) s
      WHERE StartDate >= LeftTruncationDate AND Tenure >= 0
      GROUP BY Tenure
     ),
    s as (
      SELECT h.*, EXP(SUM(LOG(1-h)) OVER (ORDER BY Tenure)) / (1-h) as S
      FROM h
    )
  SELECT s.*,
        (CASE WHEN Tenure < 390 THEN 1.0
              ELSE S / MAX(CASE WHEN Tenure = 390 THEN S END) OVER ()
          END) as S390
  FROM s
  ORDER BY Tenure
```

This query uses a window function to get the survival value at tenure 390. The OVER () clause says to do the calculation over the entire result set. The calculation calculates the "maximum" value of survival when the tenure is 390. There is only one such value, so the maximum is the value we are looking for. A JOIN could also be used for the lookup.

Comparing Survival over Time

The subscribers data has three years of complete starts. The analyses so far have mixed all the data together, calculating "average" hazards over the entire period. *Have the hazards have changed over time?*

This section presents three ways to approach this problem. The first looks at whether a particular hazard has changed over time. The second looks at customers by the year in which they started, answering the question: *What is the survival of customers who started in a given year?* The third takes snapshots of the hazards at the end of each year, answering the question: *What did the hazards look like at the end of each year?* All these ways of approaching this question use the same data. They simply require cleverness to calculate the hazards.

The next chapter presents yet another way to look at this problem. It answers the question: *What did the hazards look like based on the stops in each year?* Answering this question requires a different approach to the hazard calculation.

How Has a Particular Hazard Changed over Time?

The hazard calculation is really the average of the particular hazard probability during a period of time. So far, this average has been for three years of data starting in 2004. Trends in hazards, particularly in hazards relevant to the business, can provide important information.

Figure 6-15 shows the trend in the 365-day hazard for stops in 2005 and 2006. This hazard is interesting because it is associated with anniversary churn—customers leaving one-year after they start. The chart shows that anniversary churn increased in 2005, hitting a peak at the end of the year, and then stabilized through 2006. The 28-day moving average removes much of the variability, making the long-term pattern more visible.

Calculating the hazard requires thinking carefully about the population at risk at each point in time. At any given tenure, the population at risk for the 365-day hazard probability is all customers whose tenure is exactly 365. Calculating this population for any given date, such as Feb 14, 2006, is easy:

```
SELECT COUNT(*) as pop365,
       SUM(CASE WHEN StopDate = '2006-02-14' THEN 1 ELSE 0 END) as s365,
       AVG(CASE WHEN StopDate = '2006-02-14' THEN 1.0 ELSE 0 END) as h365
FROM Subscribers s
WHERE StartDate >= '2004-01-01' AND Tenure >= 0 AND
      (StopDate >= '2006-02-14' OR StopDate IS NULL) AND
      DATEDIFF(day, StartDate, '2006-02-14') = 365
```

Almost all the work in this calculation is in the WHERE clause. The first two conditions are the standard conditions for filtering the data because of left truncation (these conditions are redundant in this case and we don't have to worry about Smallville because the condition on the start date ensures that the stop date is after the left truncation date). The next condition says that only customers who were active on Feb 14, 2006, are considered. And the final condition selects only customers whose tenure is exactly 365 on that date.

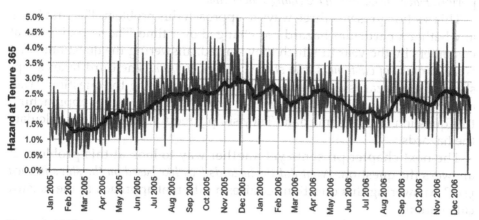

Figure 6-15: The hazard at 365 days changes throughout 2005 and 2006.

Extending this idea to all tenures is fairly easy. Customers are at risk for the 365-day hazard exactly 365 days after they start. The following SQL extends the calculation to all dates in 2005 and 2006:

```
SELECT date365, COUNT(*) as pop365,
       SUM(CASE WHEN StopDate = date365 AND StopType IS NOT NULL
               THEN 1 ELSE 0 END) as stop365,
       AVG(CASE WHEN StopDate = date365 AND StopType IS NOT NULL
               THEN 1.0 ELSE 0.0 END) as h365
FROM (SELECT s.*, DATEADD(day, 365, StartDate) as date365
      FROM Subscribers s) s
WHERE StartDate >= '2004-01-01' AND Tenure >= 365
GROUP BY date365
ORDER BY date365
```

Most of the work in this query is being done in the GROUP BY and SELECT clauses. The date of interest is 365 days after the start. All customers who are active 365 days after they start are in the population at risk on exactly that date. Of these, some customers stop, as captured by the stop date being 365 days after the start date. Because no accumulations are necessary, the hazard can be readily calculated.

One particular hazard—even one as large as anniversary churn—has a very small impact on overall survival. However, trends in particular hazards can be useful for tracking particular aspects of the business. The next two subsections discuss changes in overall survival from one year to the next.

What Is Customer Survival by Year of Start?

Filtering customers by their start year is an acceptable way of calculating hazards—that is, filters by start year do not bias the hazard estimates because the start year is known at tenure zero and does not change. The calculation itself is similar to the calculation using market for stratifying the hazards. The major difference is that flags specifying the year of start are defined in the first CTE:

```
WITH s as (
    SELECT s.*,
            (CASE WHEN yr = 2004 THEN 1 ELSE 0 END) as is2004,
            (CASE WHEN yr = 2005 THEN 1 ELSE 0 END) as is2005,
            (CASE WHEN yr = 2006 THEN 1 ELSE 0 END) as is2006,
            (CASE WHEN Market = 'Smallville'
                    THEN CAST('2004-10-27' as DATE)
                    ELSE '2004-01-01' END) as LeftTruncationDate
    FROM (SELECT s.*, YEAR(StartDate) as yr FROM Subscribers s) s
    ),
    h as (
    SELECT Tenure,
            SUM(is2004 * (1.0 - IsActive)) as stop2004,
            NULLIF(SUM(SUM(is2004)) OVER (ORDER BY Tenure DESC),
```

```
                         0) as pop2004,
                SUM(is2005 * (1.0 - IsActive)) as stop2005,
                NULLIF(SUM(SUM(is2005)) OVER (ORDER BY Tenure DESC),
                         0) as pop2005,
                SUM(is2006 * (1.0 - IsActive)) as stop2006,
                NULLIF(SUM(SUM(is2006)) OVER (ORDER BY Tenure DESC),
                         0) as pop2006
         FROM s
         WHERE StartDate >= LeftTruncationDate AND Tenure >= 0
         GROUP BY Tenure
       )
  SELECT h.*,
         EXP(SUM(LOG(1 - stop2004 / pop2004)) OVER
               (ORDER BY Tenure)) / (1 - stop2004 / pop2004) as S2004,
         EXP(SUM(LOG(1 - stop2005 / pop2005)) OVER
               (ORDER BY Tenure)) / (1 - stop2005 / pop2005) as S2005,
         EXP(SUM(LOG(1 - stop2006 / pop2006)) OVER
               (ORDER BY Tenure)) / (1 - stop2006 / pop2006) as S2006
  FROM h
  ORDER BY Tenure
```

The NULLIF() function prevents division by zero. This function returns NULL if both arguments are the same—a very handy way to avoid an undesired error. This function is equivalent to (CASE WHEN A = B THEN NULL ELSE A END).

Figure 6-16 shows the resulting survival curves for starts in each year. The length of the curves varies by year. Because the cutoff date is in 2006, the starts in 2006 have survival for only about one year. The starts in 2005 have survival values for two years, and 2004 starts have three years of survival.

What Did Survival Look Like in the Past?

This question is more challenging than the previous one because shifting the cutoff date to an earlier date potentially changes both the tenures and stop flags;

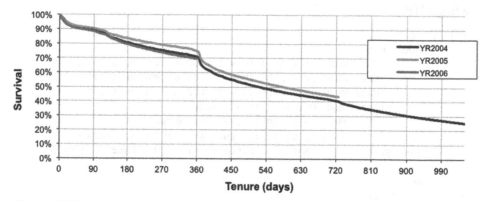

Figure 6-16: The survival curves here are based on starts in each of the years.

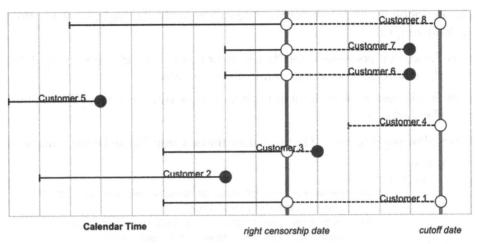

Figure 6-17: Shifting the right censorship date into the past changes the tenure, the stop flag, and the group of customers included in the survival calculation.

plus, customers who started after the date are not included in the population. Figure 6-17 illustrates what happens. Customers who are now stopped, such as customers 3, 6, and 7, are active as of the earlier cutoff date. Similarly, the tenure for most customers also changes. Technically, the process of shifting the cutoff date is forcing the right censorship date to be at an earlier date than the cutoff date for the data. This discussion uses "cutoff date" to mean the latest date in the database, and "right censorship date" to be the earlier date. Up to now, these two dates have been the same.

Consider a customer who started on 2004-01-01 and stopped on 2006-01-01. This customer has a tenure of two years and a stop flag of 1. What does the customer look like at the end of 2004? The customer is active on that date, so the current stop flag is incorrect. And, the customer's tenure is one year, rather than two years. Both the tenure and the stop flag need to be recalculated.

The rules for the stop flag are as follows:

- Only customers who started on or before the right censorship date are included in the calculation.

- For customers who are currently active, the stop flag is 0, indicating that they were active as of the right censorship date.

- For customers who are currently stopped and whose stop date is after the right censorship date, the stop flag is 0.

- Otherwise, the stop flag is 1.

The tenure on the right censorship date follows a similar logic, incorporating the following rules:

- For customers whose stop date is on or before the right censorship date, the tenure is the stop date minus the start date.

- For the rest of the customers, the tenure is the right censorship date minus the start date.

The following SQL uses CTEs to calculate the new stop flag and tenure columns:

```
WITH s as (
     SELECT s.*,
            (CASE WHEN StopType IS NULL OR StopDate>censordate THEN 0.0
                  ELSE 1 END) as isstop2004,
            (CASE WHEN StopType IS NULL OR StopDate > censordate
                  THEN DATEDIFF(day, StartDate, censordate)
                  ELSE Tenure
             END) as tenure2004
       FROM (SELECT s.*, CAST('2004-12-31' as DATE) as censordate,
                    (CASE WHEN Market = 'Smallville'
                          THEN CAST('2004-10-27' as DATE)
                          ELSE '2004-01-01' END) as LeftTruncationDate
             FROM Subscribers s) s
      WHERE StartDate <= censordate AND
            StartDate >= LeftTruncationDate AND Tenure >= 0
     ),
     h as (
     SELECT Tenure2004,
            SUM(isstop2004) /
            SUM(COUNT(*)) OVER (ORDER BY Tenure2004 DESC) as h2004
       FROM s
      GROUP BY Tenure2004
     )
SELECT h.*,
       EXP(SUM(LOG(1-h2004)) OVER (ORDER BY Tenure2004))/(1-h2004) as S
  FROM h
 ORDER BY Tenure2004
```

Note that `censordate` is defined only once in a subquery, reducing the possibility of errors in the query. Also the calculation is based on an "is stopped" flag rather than an "is active" flag, so the query has nothing like "1 − active flag."

Figure 6-18 shows the survival curves at the end of 2004, 2005, and 2006. These curves vary in length, with the 2004 curve only having one year of survival data, 2005 having two years, and 2006 having three years. The 2004 curve is the survival for only 2004 starts, whereas the other curves incorporate starts for multiple years The survival curves as of the end of 2005 and 2006 are similar to each other because there is a big overlap in the customers used for the calculations.

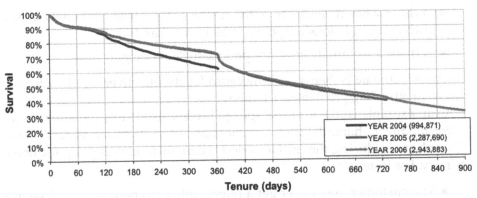

Figure 6-18: Shifting the right censorship date back to the end of each year makes it possible to reconstruct the survival curves as of the end of 2004, 2005, and 2006.

Important Measures Derived from Survival

Survival and hazard curves provide nice pictures of customers over time. Pretty pictures are great for conveying information and qualitatively comparing different groups, but survival analysis can also provide quantitative metrics. This section discusses three particular measures: the point estimate of survival, the median customer lifetime, and the average remaining customer lifetime. It ends with a discussion of confidence in the hazard values.

Point Estimate of Survival

The point estimate of survival is the survival value at a particular tenure. It answers the simple question: *How many customers do we expect to survive up to a given point in time?* This calculation is easy—looking up the survival value at a particular tenure.

The point estimate is sometimes the best measure to use. For instance, many companies invest in customer acquisition, so customers must stay around long enough to recoup this investment. This is true when telephone companies give away handsets, when insurance companies pay commissions to agents, and so on. For a given acquisition effort, an important question is how many customers "graduate" to the profitable stage of the customer relationship.

Answering such a question in detail might require understanding the cash flows that each customer generates and a range of models to handle expected tenure and expected revenues and expected costs. This is difficult enough for existing customers, and harder still for prospects. A simpler approach is to see which customers survive to a particular tenure—likely a good enough approximation:

- Perhaps when the customer has passed the initial promo period and is paying the full bill

- Perhaps when revenues from the customer have paid for initial outlays, such as commissions to agents or the cost of handsets

- Perhaps a seemingly arbitrary period, such as one year

The point estimate is then a good measure for the effectiveness of such campaigns in attracting profitable customers.

As an example, a major newspaper publisher used survival analysis for understanding its home delivery customers (as well as its online readers). Many things happen during the initial period when customers sign up for home delivery. For instance:

- The customer may never get a paper delivered because they live in a non-routable area.

- The customer may not pay their first bill.

- The customer may have only signed up for the initial promotional discount.

Each of these affects the survival during the first few months. After analyzing the customers, it became clear that four months was an important milestone, and quite predictive of longer-term survival. One advantage of four months over one year (the previous measure) is that four-month survival is available eight months sooner for new customers. That is, it became possible to measure the retention effectiveness of acquisition campaigns—using four-month survival—within a few months after the campaign starts.

Median Customer Tenure

Another measure of survival is the *median customer tenure* or *customer half-life*. This is the tenure where exactly half the customers have left. The median customer tenure is easy to calculate. It is simply the tenure where the survival curve crosses the horizontal 50% line, as shown in Figure 6-19. There is nothing magic

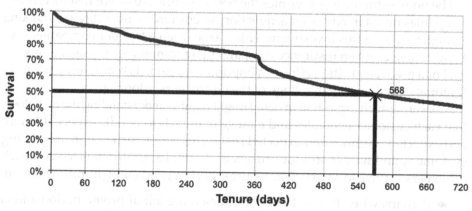

Figure 6-19: The customer half-life is the tenure where the survival curve passes the 50% line.

about 50%, except that it has the special name of "median." Sometimes, other percentages may be important, such as 90% or 20%.

The median customer tenure suffers from the same problem that all medians do. It tells us about exactly one customer, the one in the middle. Consider three different scenarios:

- **Scenario 1:** All customers survive for exactly one year and then all customers stop.

- **Scenario 2:** Customers stop at a uniform pace for the first two years, so half the customers have left after one year and the remaining half in the second year.

- **Scenario 3:** Half the customers minus one stop on the first day, then one customer stops after a year, and the remaining customers stay around indefinitely.

All these scenarios have exactly the same median customer tenure, one year, because that is when half the customers have left. However, in the first scenario, all the customers survived for all of the first year, whereas in the third, almost half were gone immediately. The first scenario has no one surviving beyond one year; the second has no one surviving beyond two years, and in the third, they survive indefinitely. These examples illustrate that the median tenure does not provide information about all the customers. It tells us about exactly one customer, the one that stopped when nearly half his or her fellow customers had already stopped.

The median tenure also illustrates one of the disadvantages of the retention curve versus the survival curve. Because it is jagged, the retention curve might cross the 50% line several times. Which is the correct value for median retention? The right answer is to use survival instead of retention.

Average Customer Lifetime

The median customer lifetime provides information about exactly one customer, the one in the middle. Averages are more useful because they can be included in financial calculations. So if a customer generates $200 in revenue per year, and the average customer stays for two years, then the average customer generates $400 in revenue.

The *average truncated tenure* is the average tenure for a given period of time after customers start, answering a question such as: "What is the average number of days that customers are expected to survive in the first year after they start?" Limiting the span to one year is helpful for both business reasons and technical reasons. On the business side, the results can be validated after one year. On the technical side, average truncated tenures are easier to calculate because they are for a finite time period.

Calculating the average truncated tenure from the survival curve turns out to be quite easy. To illustrate the process, start with the simplest case, the average one-day tenure. What is the average tenure of customers in the one day after they start? The number of customers who survived to day one is the number who started times day-one survival. The average divides by the number who started, so the average is just the survival on day one. If 99% of customers survive for one day, then the average customer survives for 0.99 days in the first day after they start.

What is the average two-day tenure? This is the average number of days that customers are active in the two days after they start. The total number of days that customers survive is the sum of those who were around on days one and two. So, the total number of days is day-one survival times the number of customers who started plus day-two survival times the number of customers who started. The average divides out the number of customers. The average two-day tenure is survival on day one plus survival on day two.

This generalizes to any tenure: The average tenure for any given time after a customer starts is the sum of the survival values up to that tenure.

Another way of looking at the calculation leads to the observation that the area under the survival curve is the average truncated tenure. Figure 6-20 shows how to calculate the area, by placing rectangles around each survival value. The area of each rectangle is the base times the height. The base is one time unit. The height is the survival value. Voila! The area under the curve is the sum of the survival values, which as we just saw, is the average truncated tenure.

TIP The area under the survival curve is the average customer lifetime for the period of time covered by the curve. For instance, for a survival curve that has two years of data, the area under the curve up to day 730 is the two-year average tenure.

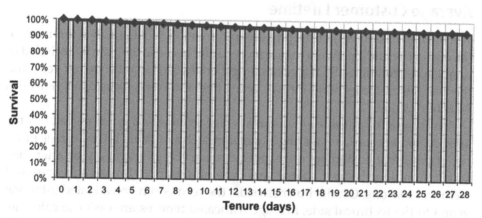

Figure 6-20: The average customer lifetime is the area under the survival curve.

Confidence in the Hazards

Hazards are statistical estimates that have confidence bounds. A statistician would pose the question as something like: How close are the observed hazard probabilities to the true hazards in the population? To the non-statistician, such a question can be a bit hard to understand. After all, aren't the calculations producing accurate values?

So, let's phrase the question a bit differently. Say that one year of customer data has been used to calculate one year of hazards. How does calculation compare to using two years of customer data instead of one? Intuition says that the results based on two years should be more stable because there is more data supporting them. On the other hand, the one-year estimate is based on more recent data, so is closer to what's happening now.

Chapter 3 discussed confidence intervals in general and the standard error of a proportion in particular. Table 6-5 applies the standard error of a proportion to various hazard probabilities, based on calculations using one and two years of starts.

The standard error is quite small and can generally be safely ignored. Second, there are theoretical reasons why the standard error of a proportion overstates the error for hazards. That said, for larger tenures, the population at risk is smaller, so the standard error is bigger. When the population at risk has one million customers, the standard error is negligible. However, when the population at risk measures only in the hundreds (as for the last row), the standard error is relatively large.

Table 6-5: Standard Error for Hazard Calculations Using One Year vs. Two Years of Starts

	ONE YEAR			TWO YEAR		
TENURE	CUMULATIVE POPULATION	H	STANDARD ERROR	CUMULATIVE POPULATION	H	STANDARD ERROR
0	656,193	0.016%	0.002%	1,292,819	0.016%	0.001%
30	544,196	0.158%	0.005%	1,203,641	0.148%	0.004%
60	492,669	0.042%	0.003%	1,183,680	0.033%	0.002%
90	446,981	0.070%	0.004%	1,169,947	0.054%	0.002%
120	397,010	0.110%	0.005%	1,142,629	0.157%	0.004%
150	339,308	0.097%	0.005%	1,105,942	0.065%	0.002%
180	290,931	0.076%	0.005%	1,081,174	0.046%	0.002%
210	246,560	0.073%	0.005%	1,059,359	0.046%	0.002%
240	205,392	0.049%	0.005%	1,040,035	0.036%	0.002%
270	159,290	0.058%	0.006%	1,023,114	0.034%	0.002%
300	108,339	0.051%	0.007%	1,008,171	0.030%	0.002%
330	59,571	0.045%	0.009%	993,844	0.033%	0.002%
360	4,272	0.094%	0.047%	965,485	0.173%	0.004%

The query used to generate the data for this is:

```
WITH s as (
     SELECT s.*,
             (CASE WHEN yr = 2005 THEN 1.0 ELSE 0 END) as is2005,
             (CASE WHEN yr = 2006 THEN 1.0 ELSE 0 END) as is2006,
             (CASE WHEN StopType IS NULL THEN 0.0 ELSE 1 END) as isstop,
             (CASE WHEN Market = 'Smallville'
                   THEN CAST('2004-10-27' as DATE)
                   ELSE '2004-01-01' END) as LeftTruncationDate
     FROM (SELECT s.* YEAR(StartDate) as yr FROM Subscribers s) s
     ),
     su as (
      SELECT Tenure,
             NULLIF(SUM(SUM(is2006)) OVER (ORDER BY TENURE DESC),
                 0) as pop1yr,
             NULLIF(SUM(SUM(is2005)) OVER (ORDER BY TENURE DESC),
                 0) as pop2yr,
             SUM(is2006 * isstop) as stop1yr,
             SUM(is2005 * isstop) as stop2yr
      FROM s
      WHERE StartDate >= LeftTruncationDate AND Tenure >= 0
      GROUP BY Tenure
      )
SELECT Tenure, pop1yr, stop1yr, h1, SQRT((h1*(1.0-h1)/pop1yr)) as se1,
       pop2yr, stop2yr, stop2yr/pop2yr as h2,
       SQRT((h2 * (1.0 - h2) / pop2yr)) as se2
FROM (SELECT su.*, stop1yr/cast(pop1yr as float) as h1,
             stop2yr / cast(pop2yr as float) as h2
      FROM su
      ) su
WHERE Tenure % 30 = 0
ORDER BY Tenure
```

This query is quite similar to earlier queries that calculated hazards, with the addition of the formula for the standard error of a proportion.

> **WARNING**   Survival values and hazards are accurate when lots of data are used for the calculation. As the number of data points for a given tenure decreases (even down to the few hundreds), the resulting values have a much larger margin of error.

Using Survival for Customer Value Calculations

The customer value calculation is theoretically quite simple. The value of a customer is the product of the estimated future revenue per unit time and the estimated future duration of the customer relationship. This just has one little challenge: knowing the future. We can make informed guesses using historical data.

How far in the future? One possibility is "forever"; however, a finite amount of time—typically, one, two, or five years—is usually sufficient. The future revenue stream is a guesstimation process. Typically, the goal is to understand customers, not a full financial profitability model, with all the checks and balances of corporate accounting.

The choice of revenue instead of profit or net revenue is intentional. In general, customers have some control over their revenue flow because revenue is related to product usage patterns. Plus, because customers are actually paying the money, they pay much more attention to revenue than to costs.

Often, customers have little control over costs, which might be subject to internal allocation formulas. An actual profitability calculation would necessarily make many assumptions about the future, and these assumptions might turn out to have a greater impact on customer value than actual customer behavior. Although such profitability analyses are interesting and perhaps necessary for financial modeling, they do not necessarily benefit from being done at the granularity of individual customers.

Consider a magazine as an example. Subscription customers receive the magazine, hopefully paying for copies that in turn generate revenue for the company. Customers continue their subscription while they see value in the relationship. However, profitability depends on all sources of revenue and costs, including advertising, the cost of paper, and the cost of postage. These cost factors are beyond customer control; on the other hand, revenue is based on when customers start and stop and is under their control.

This section discusses customer value, with particular emphasis on using survival analysis for estimating customer duration. It starts with a method of estimating revenue, which is then applied to estimating the value of future starts. Then, the method is applied to existing customers. The purpose of customer value is generally to compare different groups of customers or prospects over time. Customer value is a tool to help enable companies to make more informed decisions about their customers.

Estimated Revenue

The estimated revenue is assumed to be a stream of money that arrives at a given rate, such as $50/month. This rate may be calculated based on the history of a particular customer or group of customers. It might also be estimated for a group of prospects based on the products they will use after they start. A real financial calculation would typically discount future revenue. When customer value calculations are for insight rather than accounting, discounts can be a distraction.

The subscribers used in the survival analysis examples do not have a separate revenue history, so this section uses the initial monthly fee as a reasonable proxy for the revenue stream. Actual billing data or payment data would be preferable but is not available.

Table 6-6: Average Monthly and Daily Revenue for Customer by Market and Channel

MARKET	CHANNEL	NUMBER OF SUBSCRIBERS	$ AVERAGE MONTHLY	$ AVERAGE DAILY
Gotham	Chain	9,032	$36.10	$1.19
Gotham	Dealer	202,924	$39.05	$1.28
Gotham	Mail	66,353	$37.97	$1.25
Gotham	Store	28,669	$36.80	$1.21
Metropolis	Chain	37,884	$36.86	$1.21
Metropolis	Dealer	65,626	$38.97	$1.28
Metropolis	Mail	53,082	$39.61	$1.30
Metropolis	Store	65,582	$38.19	$1.26
Smallville	Chain	15,423	$37.48	$1.23
Smallville	Dealer	44,108	$37.82	$1.24
Smallville	Mail	24,871	$38.43	$1.26
Smallville	Store	42,640	$37.36	$1.23

Let's assume that the number of future customers is forecast by market and channel. This forecast does not include the monthly fee. *What revenue should be used for prospective customers?* This question in turn becomes: *What is the average monthly fee for recent starts by market and channel?* The following query answers this question for the most recent year of customers:

```
SELECT Market, Channel, COUNT(*) as numsubs,
       AVG(MonthlyFee) as avgmonthly,
       AVG(MonthlyFee) / 30.4 as avgdaily
FROM Subscribers s
WHERE StartDate >= '2006-01-01' AND Tenure >= 0
GROUP BY Market, Channel
ORDER BY Market, Channel
```

This query uses the constant 30.4 as the number of days in a month., a reasonable approximation that simplifies the calculations based on tenure.

Table 6-6 shows the average fee for each of the 12 groups, both per month and per day. Notice that the variation in rates is not that great, between $36.10 per month and $39.61. The "Chain" channel seems to have the lowest revenue, regardless of market. And Metropolis's revenue is higher than the other two markets.

Estimating Future Revenue for One Future Start

Survival analysis can estimate the expected lifetime—and hence expected revenue—for new starts. The key is to generate separate survival curves for each

Table 6-7: First Few Days of Survival Calculation for Market = Gotham and Channel = Dealer

DAYS	SURVIVAL	NUMBER OF CUSTOMERS	DAILY REVENUE	CUMULATIVE REVENUE
0	100.00%	100.0	$128.46	$128.46
1	100.00%	100.0	$128.46	$256.92
2	99.51%	99.5	$127.84	$384.76
3	99.12%	99.1	$127.34	$512.10
4	98.80%	98.8	$126.92	$639.02
5	98.50%	98.5	$126.54	$765.56

market and channel combination and then to expected lifetime by the average daily revenue from the previous section.

Table 6-7 shows an example: Assume that 100 customers start tomorrow in Gotham from the Dealer channel. On the first day, there are 100 customers, and then the number decreases according to the survival curve. The revenue on any particular day is the product of the survival times the daily revenue times the number of customers. The total revenue for the first year after they start is the sum of the daily contributions.

Value in the First Year

Of course, measuring the revenue for a single day is not as interesting as calculating the revenue for a period of time. Table 6-8 shows the total first year revenue for each of the 12 groups. Per customer, Gotham-Chain generates the least revenue and Smallville-Dealer generates the most. These one-year revenue values can be compared to the cost of acquisition to determine how much an additional $1,000 in spending buys in terms of first year revenue.

SQL Day-by-Day Approach

The survival and revenue calculations can be combined together into a single query. We have already done these calculations earlier in this chapter.

Table 6-8: First Year Revenue for Market/Channel Combination

MARKET	FIRST YEAR REVENUE BY CHANNEL			
	CHAIN	DEALER	MAIL	STORE
Gotham	$283.78	$392.53	$331.31	$385.13
Metropolis	$349.10	$399.52	$349.64	$408.33
Smallville	$396.05	$415.31	$370.62	$411.99

The following query puts these together, with the calculation of the estimated revenue in the first 365 days after a customer starts:

```
WITH rmc as (
      SELECT Market, Channel, COUNT(*) as numsubs,
             AVG(MonthlyFee) / 30.4 as avgdaily
      FROM Subscribers s
      WHERE StartDate >= '2006-01-01' AND Tenure >= 0
      GROUP BY Market, Channel
     ),
     hmc as (
      SELECT Market, Channel, Tenure,
             SUM(1 - IsActive) as numstops, COUNT(*) as tenurepop,
             SUM(COUNT(*)) OVER (PARTITION BY Market, Channel
                                 ORDER BY Tenure DESC) as pop,
             LEAD(Tenure) OVER (PARTITION BY Market, Channel
                                ORDER BY Tenure) as nexttenure,
             (LEAD(Tenure) OVER (PARTITION BY Market, Channel
                                 ORDER BY Tenure) - Tenure) as numdays,
             SUM(1.0 - IsActive) /
              SUM(COUNT(*)) OVER (PARTITION BY Market, Channel
                                  ORDER BY Tenure DESC) as h
      FROM (SELECT s.*,
                   (CASE WHEN Market = 'Smallville'
                         THEN CAST('2004-10-27' as DATE)
                         ELSE '2004-01-01' END) as LeftTruncationDate
            FROM Subscribers s
           ) s
      WHERE StartDate >= LeftTruncationDate AND Tenure >= 0
      GROUP BY Tenure, Market, Channel
     ),
     smc as (
      SELECT hmc.*,
             EXP(SUM(LOG(1 - h)) OVER (PARTITION BY Market, Channel
                                       ORDER BY Tenure)) / (1 - h) as S
      FROM hmc
     )
SELECT s.Market, s.Channel, SUM(s.s * numdays365 * avgdaily) as estRev
FROM (SELECT smc.*,
             (CASE WHEN nexttenure > 365 THEN 365 - tenure
                   ELSE nexttenure - tenure END) as numdays365
      FROM smc
     ) s JOIN
     rmc r
     ON s.Market = r.Market AND s.Channel = r.Channel
WHERE s.Tenure BETWEEN 0 and 365
GROUP BY s.Market, s.Channel
ORDER BY s.Market, s.Channel
```

The final query basically joins the two result sets together. It uses a WHERE clause to get the first 365 days and GROUP BY to aggregate the results. The result sets are CTEs that we have already seen.

The calculation for revenue uses NUMDAYS365 because some tenure values might be skipped in the survival result set. For instance, if days 101 and 102 were missing, the row for tenure 100 would have nexttenure set to 103. This means that the survival remains the same between tenures 100 and 103. The revenue calculation needs to include these missing tenures.

The need for NUMDAYS365 occurs when the missing tenures are at the end of the first year. For instance, if tenure 364 had nexttenure set to 374, its survival would be counted ten times instead of one. The definition of NUMDAYS365 fixes this boundary-effect problem.

For the remainder of this section, the table aliases rmc, hmc, and smc will be used without redefining them.

Estimated Revenue for a Group of Existing Customers

Existing customers pose a different challenge from new starts. Obtaining historical revenue is simply a matter of adding up the revenue that existing customers have paid. For future revenue, there is a hitch. Existing customers are not starting at tenure zero, because these customers are active now and have a particular tenure. So, direct application of survival values is not the right approach. The solution is to use conditional survival, that is, survival conditioned on the fact that customers have already survived up to their current tenure.

Estimated Second Year Revenue for a Homogenous Group

To illustrate this process, let's start with a simple group consisting of customers who started exactly one year prior to the cutoff date. What is the second year of revenue for these customers?

Because this group of customers has already survived for one year, the conditional survival for one year is needed. Remember the one-year conditional survival at tenure *t* is simply the survival at tenure *t* divided by the survival at 365 days. The following query calculates the conditional survival for their next year:

```
WITH hmc as ( <see definition on page 302> ),
     smc as ( <see definition on page 302> )
SELECT s.*,
       (CASE WHEN Tenure < 365 THEN 1.0
             ELSE S / MAX(CASE WHEN Tenure = 365 THEN S END) OVER
                            (PARTITION BY Market, Channel)
        END) as S365
FROM smc s
WHERE Tenure >= 365 AND Tenure <= 365 + 365
ORDER BY Tenure, Market, Channel
```

This query follows the same structure as other queries. The final division calculates the conditional survival rather than overall survival.

Applying conditional survival to the existing customers uses a join. Each customer is joined to the conditional survival for days 365 through 730.

- The group of customers needs to be defined. This consists of customers who are active and who started exactly 365 days before the cutoff date. There are 1,928 of them.

- The conditional survival needs to be calculated. This uses the survival divided by the survival at day 365, and only applies to tenures greater than or equal to 365.

- Each customer is joined to the survival table, for all tenures between 365 and 729 (the tenures these customers have in the forecast year).

- This table is then aggregated by the market and channel dimensions.

The query that does this is:

```
WITH oneyear as (
        SELECT market, channel, COUNT(*) as numsubs,
                SUM(CASE WHEN StopType IS NULL THEN 1 ELSE 0
                     END) as numactives
        FROM Subscribers
        WHERE StartDate = '2005-12-28'
        GROUP BY market, channel
        ),
     rmc as ( <see definition on page 302> ),
     hmc as ( <see definition on page 302> ),
     smc as ( <see definition on page 302> )
SELECT ssum.market, ssum.channel, oneyear.numsubs, oneyear.numactives,
        oneyear.numactives*ssum.survdays*r.avgdaily as year2revenue
FROM oneyear JOIN
     (SELECT s.market, s.channel, SUM(numdays730 * s365) as survdays
      FROM (SELECT s.*,
                   (CASE WHEN nexttenure > 730 THEN 730 - tenure
                         ELSE numdays END) as numdays730,
                   S / MAX(CASE WHEN Tenure = 365 THEN S END) OVER
                         (PARTITION BY Market, Channel) as S365
            FROM smc s
            WHERE tenure >= 365 and tenure < 365 + 365
            ) s
      GROUP BY Market, Channel
     ) ssum
     ON ssum.Market = oneyear.Market and
        ssum.Channel = oneyear.Channel JOIN
     rmc r
     ON ssum.Market = r.Market AND ssum.Channel = r.Channel
ORDER BY ssum.Market, ssum.Channel
```

This query pre-aggregates the results for the tenures before joining in the other information. Because `Subscribers` has millions of rows, doing the aggregation before the join is much more efficient than doing the aggregation after the join.

TIP When combining multiple tables and doing an aggregation, it is often more efficient to aggregate first and then do the joins, if this is possible.

Table 6-9 shows the second year revenue for the group that started exactly one year before. There are two ways of calculating revenue per customer. The "Year 2 Revenue per Start" column is based on the original number of starts; the "Year 2 Revenue per Year 1 Active" is based on the customers who survived the first year. Comparing this table to Table 6-8, the second year revenue per start is always lower than the first year because some customers leave during the first year. Some groups, such as Smallville/Store, have very high retention, so their second year revenue is almost as high as the first year revenue.

Estimated Future Revenue for All Customers

Estimating the next year of revenue for all existing customers adds another level of complexity. Pre-calculating as much as possible helps. What is needed is a survival table with the following columns:

- Market
- Channel

Table 6-9: Second Year Revenue per Customer by Market/Channel Combination

| | | NUMBER OF SUBSCRIBERS | | YEAR 2 REVENUE | | |
| | | | YEAR 1 | | | PER YEAR 1 |
MARKET	CHANNEL	STARTS	ACTIVES	TOTAL	PER START	ACTIVE
Gotham	Chain	29	23	$7,179.80	$247.58	$312.17
Gotham	Dealer	1,091	883	$252,336.63	$231.29	$285.77
Gotham	Mail	15	9	$3,314.24	$220.95	$368.25
Gotham	Store	55	44	$16,269.76	$295.81	$369.77
Metropolis	Chain	348	239	$79,047.43	$227.15	$330.74
Metropolis	Dealer	192	148	$46,307.53	$241.19	$312.89
Metropolis	Mail	19	7	$2,702.21	$142.22	$386.03
Metropolis	Store	169	148	$57,627.20	$340.99	$389.37
Smallville	Chain	161	144	$56,558.29	$351.29	$392.77
Smallville	Dealer	210	179	$62,062.77	$295.54	$346.72
Smallville	Mail	13	6	$2,424.49	$186.50	$404.08
Smallville	Store	107	95	$38,564.71	$360.42	$405.94

- Tenure in days
- Sum of conditional survival for the next 365 days

One big problem is what happens to the oldest customers.

The largest tenure is 1,091 days. There is no data beyond this point, so what do we do?

- Assume that everyone stops. This is not reasonable because longer-tenured customers are typically better customers.
- Assume that no one stops. This is the approach we take, although it over-estimates revenue for long-term customers because it assumes they do not stop.
- Calculate a longer-term rate of decline, perhaps using a constant hazard. Add rows to the survival table incorporating this information.

The third approach is the most accurate and not difficult to implement. It uses the table of survival values directly.

The following query calculates the sum of the conditional survival values for the next 365 days. It uses a self-join for the calculation:

```
WITH hmc as ( <see definition on page 302> ),
     smc as ( <see definition on page 302> )
SELECT s.market, s.channel, s.tenure, s.nexttenure,
       SUM((s1year.s / s.s) *
           (CASE WHEN s1year.nexttenure - s.tenure >= 365 or
                      s1year.nexttenure is null
                 THEN 365 - (s1year.tenure - s.tenure)
                 ELSE s1year.numdays END)) as sumsurvival1year
FROM smc s LEFT OUTER JOIN
     smc s1year
     ON s.market = s1year.market AND
        s.channel = s1year.channel AND
        s1year.tenure BETWEEN s.tenure AND s.tenure+364
GROUP BY s.market, s.channel, s.tenure, s.nexttenure
ORDER BY s.market, s.channel, s.tenure
```

The next step is to join this to the revenue table and to the original data. For convenience, the original data is aggregated by market, channel, and tenure.

```
WITH subs as (
     SELECT market, channel, tenure, COUNT(*) as numsubs,
            SUM(CASE WHEN StopType IS NULL THEN 1 ELSE 0 END
                ) as numactives
     FROM Subscribers
     WHERE StartDate >= '2004-01-01' AND Tenure >= 0
     GROUP BY market, channel, tenure
     ),
```

```
      rmc as ( <see definition on page 302> ),
      hmc as ( <see definition on page 302> ),
      smc as ( <see definition on page 302> ),
      ssum as (
       SELECT s.market, s.channel, s.tenure, s.nexttenure,
              SUM((s1year.s / s.s) *
                  (CASE WHEN s1year.nexttenure - s.tenure >= 365 OR
                             s1year.nexttenure is null
                     THEN 365 - (s1year.tenure - s.tenure)
                     ELSE s1year.numdays END)
                ) as sumsurvival1year
       FROM smc s LEFT OUTER JOIN
            smc s1year
            ON s.market = s1year.market AND
               s.channel = s1year.channel AND
               s1year.tenure BETWEEN s.tenure AND s.tenure+364
       GROUP BY s.market, s.channel, s.tenure, s.nexttenure
      )
   SELECT subs.market, subs.channel, SUM(subs.numsubs) as numsubs,
          SUM(numactives) as numactives,
          SUM(subs.numactives*ssum.sumsurvival1year*r.avgdaily) as revenue
   FROM subs LEFT OUTER JOIN
        ssum
        ON subs.market = ssum.market AND
           subs.channel = ssum.channel AND
           (subs.tenure >= ssum.tenure AND
            (subs.tenure < ssum.nexttenure OR ssum.nexttenure is null)
           ) LEFT OUTER JOIN
        rmc r
        ON subs.market = r.market AND
           subs.channel = r.channel
   GROUP BY subs.market, subs.channel
   ORDER BY subs.market, subs.channel
```

Table 6-10 shows the next year revenue for each of the groups based on starts since 2004. This table also shows the revenue per start and the revenue per active customer.

Three factors affect the next year revenue for these customers. The first is the average revenue for the group. The second is the estimated survival over the next year. And the third is when the starts occurred. For example, a group might in general have poor survival. However, if lots and lots of starts came in two years ago and a significant number survived, then the next year revenue is probably pretty good because it is based on the customers who survived one year. The revenue per start will be much lower than the revenue per active, as is the case with customers from Gotham-Chains.

Such a table often suggests more questions than it answers: What difference does the mix of rate plans make to the revenue? What is the revenue for starts by year in each of the groups? What other factors affect revenue?

Table 6-10: Next Year Revenue for Existing Customers

		# OF SUBSCRIBERS		REVENUE		
MARKET	CHANNEL	STARTS	ACTIVES	TOTAL	PER START	PER ACTIVE
Gotham	Chain	67,054	18,457	$6,354,927	$94.77	$344.31
Gotham	Dealer	1,089,445	480,811	$170,636,341	$156.63	$354.89
Gotham	Mail	236,886	117,230	$44,200,098	$186.59	$377.04
Gotham	Store	106,011	68,678	$26,109,568	$246.29	$380.17
Metropolis	Chain	226,968	103,091	$36,711,583	$161.75	$356.11
Metropolis	Dealer	301,656	140,632	$51,799,400	$171.72	$368.33
Metropolis	Mail	204,862	102,085	$40,388,696	$197.15	$395.64
Metropolis	Store	262,086	173,901	$69,210,279	$264.07	$397.99
Smallville	Chain	68,448	49,903	$20,557,418	$300.34	$411.95
Smallville	Dealer	240,753	152,602	$60,622,309	$251.80	$397.26
Smallville	Mail	100,028	65,007	$27,583,248	$275.76	$424.31
Smallville	Store	157,522	122,902	$51,511,268	$327.01	$419.12
TOTAL		3,061,719	1,595,299	605,685,105	$197	$379

Forecasting

How many customers do we expect to be active on a given date in the future? Survival-based forecasting is a powerful tool for answering this and related questions. Survival forecasting builds the answer up from individual customers. By contrast, other forecasting techniques often start with the summary numbers—an approach that makes slicing and dicing the results much harder. This section sketches out how to apply survival analysis to the problem of forecasting the number of customers on a given date.

The forecasting problem has two fundamental components: existing customers and new customers that start in the future. Remember, even new customers can stop during the forecast period, and the forecast needs take this into account.

This section focuses on the question: *Based on customers who started after the left truncation date, how many customers will be around on 2006-07-01?* The next chapter addresses the issue of left truncation.

July 1st is 181 days after January 1st. So, the question is how many existing customers will survive an additional 181 days? And, how many new customers will survive to July 1st.

Existing Base Forecast

Forecasting the existing base combines two pieces of information. The first is the size of the existing base—the number of customers, by tenure, at the beginning of the year. The second is the survival for an additional 181 days of tenure.

Let's explain the process by example. On January 1st, assume that 100 subscribers have a tenure of 200. The survival curve specifies that 83% of tenure 200 subscribers are still around 181 days later, at tenure 381. That means that 83% of the 100 customers will be around on July 1st. The idea is to do that calculation for all the tenures and add up the results.

A big challenge is that the hazard values are known only up to a maximum tenure—but the calculation needs hazards for that tenure plus 181 days.

Existing Base Calculation

Determining the existing base as of 2006-01-01 uses aggregation with a WHERE clause. One complication is tenure needs to be recalculated as of that date:

```
SELECT (CASE WHEN StopType IS NOT NULL AND StopDate <= censordate
             THEN Tenure ELSE DATEDIFF(day, StartDate, censordate)
         END) as tenure2006, COUNT(*)
FROM (SELECT s.*, CAST('2005-12-31' as DATE) as censordate,
             (CASE WHEN Market = 'Smallville'
                   THEN CAST('2004-10-27' as DATE)
              ELSE '2004-01-01' END) as LeftTruncationDate
      FROM Subscribers s) s
WHERE StartDate <= censordate AND
      StartDate >= LeftTruncationDate AND Tenure >= 0
GROUP BY (CASE WHEN StopType IS NOT NULL AND StopDate <= censordate
               THEN Tenure ELSE DATEDIFF(day, StartDate, censordate)
          END)
ORDER BY tenure2006
```

This query will subsequently be used as a CTE called ep for "existing population."

Calculating Survival on July 1st

An earlier example in this chapter showed how to calculate the survival as of a particular date—such as the last date in 2005. The next question is: *Given a group of customers with a particular tenure, how many of them will survive 181 additional days?*

The simple solution is, for each tenure, to calculate the ratio of the survival 181 days later by the survival for that tenure. Assuming that s has the survival calculations:

```
SELECT S.*, S181.S / S.S as S181
FROM S JOIN
```

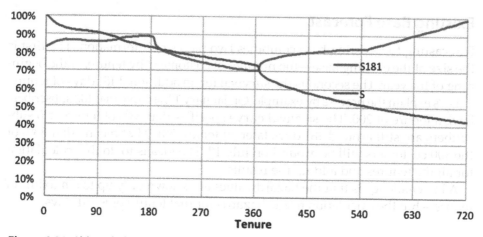

Figure 6-21: Although the survival continues to decrease, the 181-day survival starts to increase. A major factor is because the hazards are zero after the longest tenure in the data.

```
        S S181
        ON s.tenure2006 + 181 >= s181.tenure2006 AND
            (s.tenure2006+181 < s181.nexttenure or s181.nextTenure IS NULL)
    ORDER BY Tenure2006
```

In this calculation, survival can be calculated through any method.

Figure 6-21 illustrates a problem with this approach. Initially, it works fine. But, the longest term hazards are zero because long tenures have no stops. This means that the incremental survival increases to 100%.

Let's make some assumptions. Let's decide (somewhat arbitrarily) that for tenures of 700 or greater, the calculation should use a constant hazard of 0.1%. This value is consistent with the longer term hazards. With a constant hazard, we can calculate the survival using powers of 0.999 (this magic number is 1 – 0.1%).

Then, starting at tenure 520, the value of "S181" has to incorporate this new survival calculation. At tenure 700, the entire calculation uses the new hazards. The following variation incorporates this idea:

```
SELECT S.*,
        (CASE WHEN S181.tenure2006 <= const.maxt THEN S181.S
                ELSE POWER(1 - const.h, 181 - (maxt - s.tenure2006)) * S700
            END) / S.S as S181ratio
    FROM S JOIN
        S S181
        ON s.tenure2006 + 181 >= s181.tenure2006 AND
            (s.tenure2006 + 181 < s181.nexttenure OR
            s181.nextTenure IS NULL) CROSS JOIN
        (SELECT 700 as maxt, 0.001 as h, S as S700
        FROM S
        WHERE 700 >= s.tenure2006 and 700 < s.nexttenure) const
    ORDER BY Tenure2006
```

This version includes a subquery that extracts the survival at 700 days, as well as setting the long-term hazard and tenure cutoff. The SELECT then uses this information to calculate the survival for tenures longer than 700 days.

Calculating the Number of Existing Customers on July 1st

Calculating the number of customers combines the population on January 1st and the survival values to July 1st. The following query does this calculation:

```
WITH subs as (
     SELECT s.*,
            (CASE WHEN StopType IS NULL THEN 0.0
                  WHEN StopDate > censordate THEN 0
                  ELSE 1 END) as isstop2006,
            (CASE WHEN StopType IS NOT NULL AND
                       StopDate <= censordate THEN Tenure
                  ELSE DATEDIFF(day, StartDate, censordate)
             END) as tenure2006
     FROM (SELECT CAST('2005-12-31' as DATE) as censordate, s.*
           FROM Subscribers s) s
     WHERE StartDate <= censordate AND
           StartDate >= '2004-01-01' AND Tenure >= 0
     ),
     pop2006 as (
     SELECT tenure2006, COUNT(*) as pop
     FROM subs
     WHERE StopDate >= censordate or StopDate IS NULL
     GROUP BY tenure2006
     ),
     h as (
     SELECT Tenure2006,
            LEAD(Tenure2006) OVER (ORDER BY Tenure2006) as nexttenure,
            SUM(isstop2006) /
               SUM(COUNT(*)) OVER (ORDER BY Tenure2006 DESC) as h2006
     FROM subs
     GROUP BY Tenure2006
     ),
     S as (
     SELECT h.*,
            EXP(SUM(LOG(1 - h2006)) OVER (ORDER BY Tenure2006)) /
                (1 - h2006) as S
     FROM h
     ),
     S181 as (
     SELECT S.*,
            (CASE WHEN S181.tenure2006 <= const.maxt THEN S181.S
                  ELSE POWER(1-const.h, 181-(maxt-s.tenure2006)) * S700
             END) / S.S as S181
     FROM S JOIN
          S S181
```

```
        ON s.tenure2006 + 181 >= s181.tenure2006 AND
           (s.tenure2006 + 181 < s181.nexttenure OR
            s181.nextTenure IS NULL) CROSS JOIN
        (SELECT 700 as maxt, 0.001 as h, S as S700
         FROM S
         WHERE 700 >= s.tenure2006 and 700 < s.nexttenure
         ) const
    )
SELECT pop2006.tenure2006, (pop2006.pop * S181.S181) as pop
FROM pop2006 LEFT JOIN
     S181
     ON pop2006.tenure2006 = S181.tenure2006
ORDER BY Tenure2006
```

This query looks complicated—and it is. But it is built from fairly simple components:

- subs: This is what the world looks like as of 2005-12-31. Two notes: This includes customers who stopped after that date. And, it only includes subscribers after the left truncation date.

- Pop2006: This is the population as of 2006-01-01. This incorporates stop conditions into the subs population.

- h, S, S181: These calculate the hazard, survival, and conditional survival as throughout the chapter.

The final SELECT multiplies the population and the survival out for 181 days.

This forecast calculates the expected number of customers who will still be around 181 days later. The expected value is a floating point number rather than an integer—as expected values often are. To get the number of stops, subtract the expected number from the actual starts.

The forecast also breaks the results into individual tenures. The tenure is the tenure as of the beginning of the period, but it could also be as of the end of the period. This can be handy for understanding which customer groups are leaving.

How Good Is It?

This forecast is a rudimentary forecast that only takes tenure into account. The total population on January 1st is 1,597,956 and on July 1st, the population is 1,313,944. About 17.8% of the existing customers have stopped.

The forecast estimate is 1,278,378.0. This is about 2.7% less than the actual number. The prediction here is that about 20.0% of the customers will stop.

One cause of error is in the long-term survival. The estimate of 0.1% for the long-term hazard was just a guess—although it is quite close to the actual estimated value. A larger source of error appears to be changes in the business in 2006, affecting the hazards.

Estimating the Long-Term Hazard

A better estimate for the long-term hazard is simple. Add up all the tenures greater than 700 and divide by the number of stops in this group. The left-truncated data does not have many long-term subscribers.

An alternative calculation uses all customers who hit tenure 700 after the left truncation date. This calculation counts the number of days that each customer is at risk after tenure 700 and after the left truncation date:

```
WITH subs as (
     SELECT s.*,
              DATEDIFF(day, StartDate, LeftTruncationDate) as TenureAtLT
     FROM (SELECT s.*,
                  (CASE WHEN Market = 'Smallville'
                        THEN CAST('2004-10-27' as DATE)
                        ELSE '2004-01-01' END) as LeftTruncationDate
          FROM Subscribers s) s
     WHERE Tenure >= 0
     )
SELECT (SUM(CASE WHEN StopType is not null THEN 1.0 ELSE 0 END) /
        SUM(CASE WHEN TenureAtLT >= 700 THEN Tenure - TenureAtLT
             ELSE Tenure - 700 END)
        ) as h700
FROM subs
WHERE tenure >= 700
```

The ratio of the number of stops to the number of days at risk is the best estimate of the long-term hazard. For this data, the value is about 0.837%—not far off from the original guesstimate of 0.1%.

New Start Forecast

The new start forecast uses estimates for new starts by day between January 1st and July 1st. One solution is to use the starts from the previous year. For this example, we'll take the starts from 2006—that way, there is no error in the starts themselves. Typically, a business process produces these estimates because managers are responsible for meeting such goals.

The second component is the survival. This is easier than for the existing base. We just need to know if someone is going to survive to July 1st. If they start on January 1st, that is 181 days of survival. If they start on June 30th, that is one day. In other words, calculate the number of days into the period for each start, and then subtract this from 181 days for the survival. The query is:

```
WITH subs as ( . . . ),
     ns2006 as (
        SELECT DATEDIFF(day, censordate, StartDate) as daysafter,
               COUNT(*) as pop
        FROM (SELECT CAST('2005-12-31' as DATE) as censordate, s.*
```

```
        FROM Subscribers s) s
   WHERE StartDate >= censordate AND StartDate <= '2006-07-01'
   GROUP BY DATEDIFF(day, censordate, StartDate)
       ),
   h as ( . . . ),
   S as ( . . . )
SELECT ns2006.daysafter, ns2006.pop, S.tenure2006, S.S,
       ns2006.pop * S.S as pop
FROM ns2006 LEFT JOIN
   S
   ON s.tenure2006 = 181 - ns2006.daysafter
ORDER BY ns2006.daysafter
```

Most of this query consists of familiar elements. The only new component is ns2006, the starts, by day, during the period.

Of the 362,641 subscribers who started in 2006 before July 1st, the forecast predicts that 321,237.0 will survive to July 1st. The actual number is 316,208—just a 1.6% difference.

Lessons Learned

This chapter introduces survival analysis for understanding customers. The origins of survival analysis were for understanding mortality rates to calculate the value of financial products. This was pretty sophisticated stuff for 1693. Since then, the technique has been used in many areas, from manufacturing to medical outcomes studies to understanding convicts released from prison.

Two key concepts in survival analysis are the hazard probability, which is the probability that someone will succumb to a risk at a given tenure, and survival, which is the proportion of people who have not succumbed to the risk. For customer-based survival, these two values are calculated for all tenures. The resulting hazard and survival charts can be quite informative and help us better understand customers and the business.

Survival can also be quantified. The median customer tenure (or customer half-life) is the time it takes for half of the customers to stop. The point estimate of survival, such as the one-year survival, is the proportion of customers who make it to one year. The average truncated tenure is the average tenure of a customer during a period of time.

One powerful use of survival analysis is for estimating customer value by predicting future customer revenue. This works for both new and existing customers. Although the calculations are a bit complicated, the ideas are fairly simple—just multiplying the average expected survival by the revenue. Another powerful application is forecasting—for both existing customers and new customers based on their survival.

The next chapter dives into survival analysis in more detail, introducing the concepts of time windows (to handle left truncation) and competing risks.

Factors Affecting Survival: The What and Why of Customer Tenure

The previous chapter demonstrated the value of survival analysis for understanding customers and their stop behaviors. It introduced *empirical hazards estimation*, which calculates a separate hazard probability for each tenure. It included several examples and extensions showing how to apply survival analysis to some business problems, including customer value and forecasting the number of active customers in the future.

This chapter builds on this foundation by introducing three extensions to basic survival analysis. These extensions solve common, real-world problems. They also make it possible to understand the effects of other factors besides tenure on survival.

The first extension focuses on factors other than tenure that affect survival. A big complication here is that the effect may vary, depending on tenure. For instance, customers in Gotham and Metropolis have about the same survival for the first year. Around the one-year anniversary, Gotham customers start leaving at a much faster rate. In other words, the effect of market on survival varies by tenure.

The most prominent statistical technique in this area, Cox proportional hazards regression, assumes that the effects do not change over time. Although this method is outside the scope of this book, it does inspire us to look at the changing effects of each factor at different tenures. This chapter explains several different approaches for understanding how and when such factors affect survival.

The second extension is using time windows for the hazard calculation. This chapter introduces time windows as a way to solve a problem in many data sources, including the subscription data: Starts come from a longer time period than stops. Time windows do much more than just solve the left truncation problem. They are powerful tools for estimating unbiased hazard probabilities based on a time window of customer activity, rather than on a time window of starts.

The third extension goes in a different direction. The factors that affect survival occur at the beginning of or during the customer life cycle. At the end of the life cycle, customers stop and they stop for some reason. This reason may be voluntary (customers switch to competitors); or the reason may be forced (customers stop paying their bills); or customers might migrate to different products. Competing risks is a method for incorporating these different outcomes into survival analysis.

Competing risks answers the question: "What happens next for all the customers?" That is, at a given point in the future, what proportion of customers have stopped for each of the competing risks? This question follows from the forecasting introduced in the previous chapter. Forecasts can include not only the numbers of remaining customers, but also of what happens to the stopped customers. Before diving into what happens next, let's start at the beginning. *How do the factors known at the beginning of the customer relationship affect survival?*

Which Factors Are Important and When

Survival analysis can be used to compare different groups of customers by creating a separate curve for each group. This process, called *stratification*, qualitatively shows the effect of market, or rate plan, or channel, or a combination of them, on survival.

This section shows how to quantify the effects at different tenures. For numeric variables, the comparison uses averages of the variable at different tenures for customers who stop and do not stop. For categorical variables, the comparison uses hazards ratios at different tenures. The key idea is that the effect of such variables may be stronger during some parts of the customer tenure and weaker during others. Being able to see the effects at different tenures sheds light on the effect of the variables on customer relationships.

Explanation of the Approach

Figure 7-1 shows a group of customers on the tenure timeline. The chart is similar to the charts in the previous chapter that illustrated the calculation of hazard probabilities. Here, though, we are going to look at the chart a bit differently. The chart shows eight customers. At tenure three, exactly one of them stops, and the rest remain active. *What differentiates the customer(s) who stop from the customer(s) who remain active?*

Part of the answer is obvious: What differentiates them is that one group stopped and the other did not. A better way to phrase the question is to ask what differentiates the two groups by other variables. The goal is to estimate, understand, and visualize the effects of other variables on survival at any given tenure.

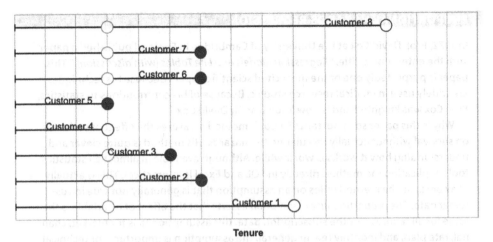

Figure 7-1: At any given tenure, what differentiates customers who stop and those who remain active?

The factors that differentiate between stopped customers and active customers may change for different tenures. For instance, during some tenure periods, initial promotions end. During others, customers are stopped because they do not pay their first bill. The groups of stopped customers at these tenures are unlikely to be similar. Tenures with no stops have no answer because the group of stopped customers is empty.

The comparison between the customers who stop at a particular tenure and those who remain active was first investigated by Sir David Cox, the inventor of Proportional Hazards Regression. A statement such as "Every cigarette a person smokes reduces his or her life by 11 minutes" is an example of results obtained with this technique. The aside "Proportional Hazards Regression" introduces the basic ideas.

The next two sections show reasonable ways to compare the effects of variables in customer data. In one sense, these techniques are more powerful than proportional hazards regression because they eliminate the assumption of proportionality. They are also better suited for understanding and visualizing the effects. On the other hand, the proportional hazards regression is better for reducing the effects down to a single number, to a *coefficient* in the language of statistics.

Using Averages to Compare Numeric Variables

A good way to see the effect of a numeric variable on survival is to compare the average value for stopped customers and for active customers at each tenure. These averages can be plotted in a chart, making it easy to compare them.

PROPORTIONAL HAZARDS REGRESSION

In 1972, Prof. David Cox at the University of Cambridge in England published a paper with the entertaining title, *"Regression Models and Life Tables (with discussion)."* This paper is purportedly one of the most cited scientific papers because his techniques are widely used in medical research studies. Because of his contributions to statistics, Prof. Cox was knighted and is now known as Sir David Cox.

Why is this paper so important? Sir Cox's method measures the effect of variables on survival without actually calculating the hazards. His method is quite clever and understanding how it works is worthwhile. Although available in almost all statistics tools, replicating the method directly in SQL and Excel is impractical. This is actually okay because the method relies on an assumption that is generally not true in customer data. The *proportionality assumption* asserts that the effect of a variable is the same for all tenures. For the subscription data, this assumption fails for market, channel, rate plan, and monthly fee. In general, the assumption is important for technical reasons and, unfortunately, not true for most real-world data.

Nevertheless, proportional hazards regression is important for at least three reasons. First, even when the proportionality assumption is violated, the results are often qualitatively correct. Second, the method allows forward selection of variables, so it can choose which variables have the biggest impact on survival. Finally, proportional hazards regression inspires us to look at the effects of factors over time, the methods discussed in the text.

Let's assume that each customer has his or her own hazard function. The survival probability is a big equation consisting of products of expressions, such as $(1-h(t))$ for the tenures when the customer remains active and $h(t)$ for the final tenure. This is the approach described in the previous chapter.

Cox's brilliant idea was to look at the hazards in a different way. Instead of asking about the tenure when a customer would stop, he asked: *What is the likelihood that exactly the customers who stopped at a given tenure are the customers who actually did stop?* So, if there are four customers and the third stops at tenure 5, then the likelihood equation for tenure 5 looks like: $(1-h_1(5)) * (1-h_2(5)) *h_3(5) * (1-h_4(5))$. Each customer hazard function is then expressed as a function of the variables describing each customer. Then, this equation is repeated for all tenures (or at least all tenures with stops).

This is a complicated equation. The hazards themselves are functions of covariates. By assuming that the effect of any given covariate is the same for all tenures, Cox was able to calculate the impact of each covariate. In essence, the hazard probabilities simply cancel out, leaving a complicated function of the covariates and their parameters. A technique called *maximum likelihood estimation* (MLE) can then estimate the parameters that make the observed stops the most likely.

The result is a measure of the importance of each variable on survival. This measure is useful as an overall measure. Because the proportionality assumption is not necessarily reasonable on customer data, we need to do additional investigations anyway, using the methods discussed in the text.

The subscribers data has one numeric variable, `MonthlyFee`. *What is the difference in the average value of the monthly fee for customers who stop versus customers who remain active for all tenures?*

The Answer

Figure 7-2 shows such a chart for the monthly fee. This chart has two series: one for the average monthly fee of the stopped customers, the other for the active customers.

Customers who stop during the first year have higher monthly fees than those who remain active. This may be due to price-sensitive customers who are paying too much when they sign up. Almost all customers start on a one- or two-year contract, with a penalty for breaking the contract. The purpose of the penalty is to prevent customers from stopping during the contract period. However, customers with higher monthly fees have more to gain by stopping than those with lower monthly fees, so the contract penalty has less effect on customers paying higher fees.

Around the first-year anniversary, the curves for the active and stopped customers intersect. Stopped customers initially have a higher monthly fee; after the one-year mark, active customers have the higher monthly fee. Presumably, many customers on less expensive plans who want to stop during the first year end up stopping around the anniversary date. This washes out after a month or two, and the averages for the two groups are essentially the same for the rest of second year. After the second year, they reverse yet again, although by the third year, the data is becoming sparser because only three years of starts are used for the analysis.

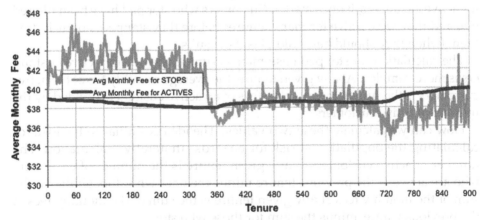

Figure 7-2: This chart compares the average monthly fees of customers who stop and who remain active at each tenure.

Notice that one curve is smooth and the other jagged. The average for the active customers is smooth because millions of customers are active for many of the tenures. In addition, the customers active for two adjacent tenures significantly overlap—because all customers active for the longer tenure are also active for the shorter one. The average for the stopped customers jumps around because there are many fewer stopped customers at a given tenure (just a few hundred or thousand) and the stopped customers at any two tenures do not overlap with each other at all.

Answering the Question in SQL and Excel

This chart requires two values for each tenure: the average value for stopped customers and the average value for active customers. The first of these quantities is easy to calculate because each stopped customer is included in the average only at the tenure when the customer stops:

```
SELECT Tenure, AVG(MonthlyFee) as AvgMonthlyFee
FROM (SELECT s.*,
             (CASE WHEN Market = 'Smallville'
                   THEN CAST('2004-10-27' as DATE)
                   ELSE '2004-01-01' END) as LeftTruncationDate
      FROM Subscribers s
     ) s
WHERE StopType IS NOT NULL AND StartDate >= LeftTruncationDate AND
      Tenure >= 0
GROUP BY Tenure
ORDER BY Tenure
```

This calculation takes left truncation into account. For the stops, this logic makes no difference because the table has no stops before the left truncation date. But, for active customers, it does matter. Customers who stopped have been filtered out, and they were active for many tenures before they stopped; not including them (when they should be) could bias the results.

The calculation for stopped customers is simple; the one for active customers is more complex. At any given tenure, the average monthly fee of the active customers is the sum of the monthly fees of all active customers divided by the number of active customers.

How can we calculate these two values? The idea is similar to the idea for calculating the population at risk for hazards, an iterative calculation. The number of active customers at any given tenure is the number of customers who are active at the previous tenure minus the ones who stop. Similarly, the sum of the monthly fees at any given tenure is the sum of the monthly fees at the previous tenure, minus the sum for those who stop.

These observations lead to the following variables:

- Tenure
- Number of customers at each tenure

- Number of customers who stop at each tenure
- Sum of the initial monthly fees of all customers at each tenure
- Sum of the initial monthly fees of stopped customers at each tenure

These variables can readily be calculated in SQL:

```
SELECT Tenure, COUNT(*) as pop, SUM(isstop) as numstops,
       SUM(MonthlyFee) as mfsumall, SUM(MonthlyFee * isstop) as
       mfsumstop
FROM (SELECT s.*,
             (CASE WHEN StopType IS NULL THEN 0 ELSE 1 END) as isstop,
             (CASE WHEN Market = 'Smallville'
                   THEN CAST('2004-10-27' as DATE)
                   ELSE '2004-01-01' END) as LeftTruncationDate
      FROM Subscribers s) s
WHERE StartDate >= LeftTruncationDate AND Tenure >= 0
GROUP BY Tenure
ORDER BY Tenure
```

The active population for each tenure is the sum of the customers with tenures as large as or larger than each tenure. The active population is split into two groups: the customers who stop at that tenure (which is one of the five variables returned by the query), and everyone else.

The total initial monthly fees are split in a similar manner. These calculated values provide the information to calculate the average for each group. Figure 7-3 shows an Excel spreadsheet that does this calculation.

Answering the Question Entirely in SQL

This calculation can be done entirely in SQL using cumulative sums:

```
WITH t as (
     SELECT Tenure, COUNT(*) as pop, SUM(isstop) as numstops,
            SUM(MonthlyFee) as mfsumall,
            SUM(MonthlyFee * isstop) as mfsumstop
     FROM (SELECT s.*,
                  (CASE WHEN StopType IS NULL THEN 0 ELSE 1
                  END) as isstop,
```

	C	D	E	F	G	H	I	J	K	L	M	N
12		**FROM SQL**							**CALCULATED IN EXCEL**			
13	Tenure	pop	numstops	mfsumall	mfsumstop		Pop at Risk	Actives	STOPS	SUM MF	Actives MF	Stops MF
14	0	2383	508	89712	19687		=I15+D14	=I14-E14	=E14	=SUM(F14:F$1107)-G14	=L14/J14	=G14/E14
15	1	18354	17306	728195	690405		=I16+D15	=I15-E15	=E15	=SUM(F15:F$1107)-G15	=L15/J15	=G15/E15
16	2	16730	15091	673535	614020		=I17+D16	=I16-E16	=E16	=SUM(F16:F$1107)-G16	=L16/J16	=G16/E16
17	3	13283	11346	541877	470617		=I18+D17	=I17-E17	=E17	=SUM(F17:F$1107)-G17	=L17/J17	=G17/E17
18	4	9540	9496	403080	401500		=I19+D18	=I18-E18	=E18	=SUM(F18:F$1107)-G18	=L18/J18	=G18/E18
19	5	11743	9149	487410	393245		=I20+D19	=I19-E19	=E19	=SUM(F19:F$1107)-G19	=L19/J19	=G19/E19
20	6	12646	9406	515245	398945		=I21+D20	=I20-E20	=E20	=SUM(F20:F$1107)-G20	=L20/J20	=G20/E20
21	7	13463	10295	544330	430375		=I22+D21	=I21-E21	=E21	=SUM(F21:F$1107)-G21	=L21/J21	=G21/E21
22	8	11855	9553	485455	402590		=I23+D22	=I22-E22	=E22	=SUM(F22:F$1107)-G22	=L22/J22	=G22/E22

Figure 7-3: This Excel spreadsheet calculates the average monthly fee for active customers and for stopped customers.

```
                        (CASE WHEN Market = 'Smallville'
                              THEN CAST('2004-10-27' as DATE)
                              ELSE '2004-01-01' END) as LeftTruncationDate
            FROM Subscribers s) s
      WHERE StartDate >= LeftTruncationDate AND Tenure >= 0
      GROUP BY Tenure
      )
SELECT Tenure, SUM(pop) OVER (ORDER BY Tenure DESC)-numstops as actives,
       (SUM(mfsumall) OVER (ORDER BY Tenure DESC) -
        mfsumstop) as mfsumactives,
       ((SUM(mfsumall) OVER (ORDER BY Tenure DESC) - mfsumstop) /
        (SUM(pop) OVER (ORDER BY Tenure DESC) - numstops)
        ) as MFActiveAvg,
        mfsumstop / NULLIF(numstops, 0) as MFStopAvg
FROM t
ORDER BY Tenure
```

The previous query is used to define `t`. The outer SELECT does the cumulative sums that can also be done in Excel. Note the use of NULLIF() to prevent a divide-by-zero error.

Extension to Include Confidence Bounds

The values just calculated are examples of sample averages. As discussed in Chapter 3, such averages have confidence intervals based on the standard error, so a reasonable enhancement is to include the standard error or confidence bounds in the chart.

Figure 7-4 shows the previous chart with 95% confidence bounds for the stopped customers. The confidence bounds for the active customers are so small as to be negligible, so the chart does not show them. Because the confidence bounds depend on the number of points at each point, the data is summarized at the weekly level rather than the daily level to narrow them for the stopped customers.

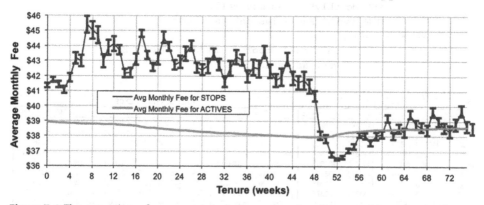

Figure 7-4: The comparison of averages can include error bars that show a confidence interval for either average. In this case, the 95% confidence bound is shown for the monthly fee average for stops.

This chart clearly illustrates that during the first year, stopped customers have an average monthly fee that is significantly higher than that of active customers. After a year and a few months, the averages become quite similar.

Even if the two curves had overlapping confidence bounds during the first year, the difference between the curves would probably still be statistically significant because the trends are so consistent. Overlapping confidence intervals suggest that at any given tenure, two points might be in either order due to random variation. However, a consistent trend undercuts this observation. If the difference between two groups were due to chance, there would not be long sequences where one is greater or lower than the other.

TIP When looking at confidence bounds on series, it is important to look at trends as well as overlapping confidence intervals.

The confidence bound uses the statistical formula for the standard error of a sample. The bound is 1.96 times the standard error. Recall from Chapter 3 that the standard error for a sample average is the standard deviation divided by the square root of the size of the sample. The standard deviation is calculated as follows:

1. Take the sum of the squares of the monthly fees.
2. Subtract the average monthly fee squared divided by the number of values.
3. Divide the difference by one less than the number of values.
4. Then estimate the standard deviation by taking the square root.

This calculation requires several aggregated values in addition to the values used for the average initial monthly fee averages.

The following query does the necessary calculations:

```
SELECT FLOOR(Tenure / 7) as tenureweeks, COUNT(*) as pop,
       SUM(isstop) as numstops, SUM(MonthlyFee) as mfsumall,
       SUM(MonthlyFee * isstop) as mfsumstop,
       SUM(MonthlyFee * MonthlyFee) as sum2all,
       SUM(MonthlyFee * MonthlyFee * isstop) as mfsum2stop
FROM (SELECT s.*,
             (CASE WHEN StopType IS NULL THEN 0 ELSE 1 END) as isstop,
             (CASE WHEN Market = 'Smallville'
                   THEN CAST('2004-10-27' as DATE)
                   ELSE '2004-01-01' END) as LeftTruncationDate
      FROM Subscribers s) s
WHERE StartDate >= LeftTruncationDate AND Tenure >= 0
GROUP BY FLOOR(Tenure / 7)
ORDER BY tenureweeks
```

This query adds several aggregations to the SELECT clause of the query used in the previous section; this version includes the sum of the squares of the monthly fee for all customers and for stopped customers. The query also uses an indicator variable, isstop, for the stop calculations.

The sum of squares values are accumulated for each tenure, and split into two groups for active customers and stopped customers; this is the same process used for the monthly fee average calculation. The sum provides the missing information for the standard deviation calculation. The rest of the calculation subtracts the number of values times the sum of squares of the averages from the sum of squares and divides the difference by one less than the number of values. The standard error is then the standard deviation divided by the square root of the number of stops. And, the 95% confidence bound is 1.96 times the standard error.

Showing the result as confidence bounds in the chart makes use of positive and negative Y-error bars. These are placed in the chart by selecting the series, right-clicking to bring up the "Format Data Series" dialog box, and choosing "Error Bars" on the left pane. On this tab, choose the "Both" option, and then choose the "Custom" option on the bottom. Place the cell range with the confidence bounds in the "+" and "−" boxes. The same range is used for both.

Hazard Ratios

Averages work for numeric variables, but they do not work for categorical variables: The "average" value of a column that takes on distinct values, such as Gotham, Smallville, and Metropolis does not make sense. Yet, the question remains: *What is the effect of a categorical variable (such as market or rate plan) on survival for different tenures?* Because averages do not work, an alternative approach is needed, the ratio of hazard probabilities.

Interpreting Hazard Ratios

Figure 7-5 shows two hazard ratio charts. The top chart shows the ratio of the hazards by market for the Smallville to Gotham and Metropolis to Gotham. The Gotham to Gotham ratio is not interesting, because it is uniformly one.

Smallville's survival is better than Gotham's, so as expected, the ratio of Smallville's hazards to Gotham's hazards is uniformly less than one. This effect is strongest during the first year, with the ratio climbing up a bit in the second year. Although they are much better customers, Smallville's customers are becoming less good, relative to Gotham's, at longer tenures.

The situation with Metropolis is the opposite. During the first year, the hazard ratio is close to one, so Metropolis's customers are almost as bad as Gotham's in the first year. In the second year, the hazard ratio drops from about 0.96 to 0.75. So, Metropolis's customers are getting better while Smallville's are getting worse. After two years, though, Smallville's customers are still stopping at a lower rate than Metropolis's.

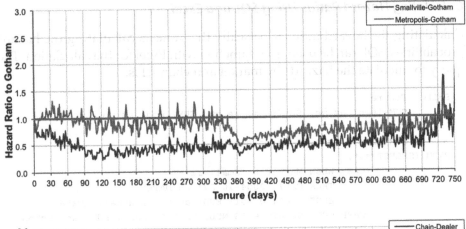

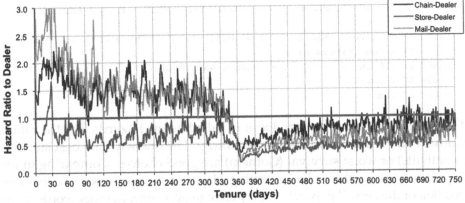

Figure 7-5: The top chart shows hazard ratios for market, compared to Gotham, and the bottom shows hazard ratios for channel, compared to Dealer.

The lower chart in Figure 7-5 shows the hazard ratios by channel for Chain, Store, and Mail compared to Dealer. The hazards for the Store channel are almost uniformly lower than for Dealer, implying that survival of customers from Store is better than customers from Dealer. This makes sense because the Store channel consists of own-branded stores, where the personnel are actually employees of the cell phone company. Customers who purchase through that channel are attracted to the brand. It is not surprising that these stores attract and retain the best customers, and in particular, better than the independently owned dealers.

The Mail and Chain hazard ratios are interesting because these ratios are greater than one during the first year and then lower during the second year. One possibility is that the Dealers are intentionally churning their customers in the second year. That is, the independently owned dealers switch customers who have been around a year to another carrier in order to get an acquisition bonus from the second carrier. Customers who were acquired through national chains and customers who come in by signing up on the phone or Internet would not be subject to such a ploy.

Calculating Hazard Ratios Using SQL and Excel

Calculating the hazard ratios is basically the same as calculating the hazard probabilities. SQL can be used in conjunction with Excel for the calculation. The query to calculate the hazards by market and channel is:

```
SELECT Tenure,
       SUM(isms) as ms, SUM(ismm) as mm, SUM(ismg) as mg,
       . . .
       SUM(isms * isstop) as ms_stop, . . .
FROM (SELECT s.*,
             (CASE WHEN Market = 'Smallville '
                   THEN CAST('2004-10-27' as DATE)
                   ELSE '2004-01-01' END) as LeftTruncationDate,
             (CASE WHEN StopType IS NULL THEN 0 ELSE 1 END) as isstop,
             (CASE WHEN market = 'Smallville' THEN 1 ELSE 0 END) as isms,
             . . .
             (CASE WHEN channel = 'Mail' THEN 1 ELSE 0 END) as iscm
      FROM Subscribers s) s
WHERE StartDate >= LeftTruncationDate AND Tenure >= 0
GROUP BY Tenure
ORDER BY Tenure
```

The results can be copied into Excel to calculate the hazards. For the ratios, Gotham and Dealer were chosen arbitrarily. The one with the best survival (Smallville) or worst survival (Gotham) are good choices. Comparing to the population as a whole can be interesting. However, be careful because the composition of the overall population may change over time. In other words, if the hazard ratio approaches one, you need to determine whether the population is becoming more like that category or if all the categories are converging to be similar at that tenure.

One caution: The hazard ratio does not work when the comparison group has no stops at a given tenure. For the comparison by market, this does not happen. In other cases, it might be desirable to use a larger time period, such as seven days (one week) or 30 days (approximately one month).

> **TIP** When using hazard ratios, adjust the time period used for the tenure calculations to ensure that each time period has enough stops, for instance, by summarizing at the weekly level rather than the daily level.

Calculating Hazard Ratios in SQL

The calculation can also be done in SQL, using window functions:

```
SELECT Tenure, SUM(IsStop) / NULLIF(SUM(COUNT(*)) OVER
                              (ORDER BY Tenure DESC), 0) as pop,
```

```
            SUM(isms * isstop)/NULLIF(SUM(SUM(isms)) OVER
                                (ORDER BY Tenure DESC), 0) as h_ms,

            . . .

            SUM(iscd * isstop)/NULLIF(SUM(SUM(iscd)) OVER
                                (ORDER BY Tenure DESC), 0) as h_cd
    FROM (SELECT s.*,
                (CASE WHEN Market = 'Smallville'
                    THEN CAST('2004-10-27' as DATE)
                    ELSE  '2004-01-01' END) as LeftTruncationDate,
                (CASE WHEN StopType IS NULL THEN 0 ELSE 1.0 END) as isstop,
                (CASE WHEN Market = 'Smallville' THEN 1 ELSE 0 END) as isms,

                . . .

                (CASE WHEN Channel = 'Dealer' THEN 1 ELSE 0 END) as iscd
        FROM Subscribers s) s
    WHERE StartDate >= LeftTruncationDate AND Tenure >= 0
    GROUP BY Tenure
    ORDER BY Tenure
```

This query combines the window functions with the aggregation functions, resulting in the nested SUM() calls. The ORDER BY Tenure DESC calculates the cumulative sum to the end of the tenures rather than from the beginning.

Why the Hazard Ratio?

A question may be occurring to some readers: Why the hazard ratio and not the survival ratio? First, the survival ratio can also be informative by directly comparing the point-estimates of survival. If 40% of one group survives to a given tenure, and another group has a survival ratio of 0.5 compared to that group, then that group's survival is 0.5 * 40% = 20%.

The hazard ratio has two advantages, one theoretical and one practical. The theoretical advantage is that the hazard ratio is related to the methods used for Cox proportional hazards regression. Both techniques look at characteristics of stops at each tenure. This relationship is theoretically appealing.

The more practical reason is that the hazard ratio gives independent information for each tenure, as opposed to survival, which accumulates information up to each tenure. In the charts, the hazard ratio flipped around the one-year mark. This phenomenon shows up much more gradually in the survival ratio because the information has to accumulate over many tenures. In fact, the hazard ratio shows that the hazard probabilities for Smallville are getting worse while the hazard probabilities for Metropolis are getting better. However, even after two years, Smallville still has better survival than Metropolis because of what happens during the first year. The survival ratio does not show this phenomenon clearly at all.

One drawback of the hazard ratio is that any given tenure might have only a small amount of data. This can be fixed by using longer tenure periods, such as weeks or multiples of weeks, instead of days.

Left Truncation

This section moves to another topic, which is the accurate calculation of hazard probabilities. As noted in the previous chapter, the customers in the Subscribers table data have an unexpected property: Customers who stopped before some date (that depends on the market) are excluded from the table. This phenomenon, where customers are excluded based on their stop date, is called *left truncation,* and naïve hazard calculations on left-truncated data produce incorrect results. In the previous chapter, the problem of left truncation was handled by introducing LeftTruncationDate into all the queries. This section presents a more flexible method, based on an idea called time windows.

Left truncation is a problem because hazard estimates on left truncated data are simply incorrect. The solution to left truncation is to calculate the hazards using only a "time window" of activity—the calculation only uses information from customers active during the time window. This technique is a powerful enhancement to survival analysis that has other applications. Before discussing time windows in general, though, let's look at the left truncation problem that they solve.

Recognizing Left Truncation

The previous chapter identified the left truncation problem by looking at the minimum stop date in each market. Even when left truncation is an issue, this approach is often not sufficient—some customers might sneak into the data even though they stopped before the left truncation date.

A better approach is to use a histogram of starts and stops by date. The chart itself is similar to other histograms, except two curves are shown on the same chart. One approach is to generate the data for each histogram separately, and then combine them in Excel. However, producing the right format in SQL simplifies the Excel work. The following query returns the number of starts and stops by month:

```
SELECT YEAR(thedate) as year, MONTH(thedate) as month,
       SUM(numstarts) as numstarts, SUM(numstops) as numstops
FROM ((SELECT StartDate as thedate, COUNT(*) as numstarts, 0 as numstops
       FROM Subscribers
       GROUP BY StartDate)
      UNION ALL
      (SELECT StopDate as thedate, 0 as numstarts, COUNT(*) as numstops
       FROM Subscribers
       GROUP BY StopDate)) a
WHERE thedate IS NOT NULL
GROUP BY YEAR(thedate), MONTH(thedate)
ORDER BY year, month
```

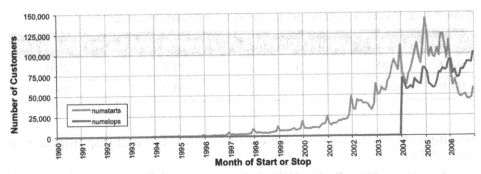

Figure 7-6: This histogram of start and stop counts by month suggests that prior to 2004, starts are recorded in the database but not stops.

This histogram query uses UNION ALL to ensure that all months with either a start or stop are included.

The resulting histogram in Figure 7-6 suggests that starts are coming from a much longer time period than stops. One way to confirm this is to ask: *How many years (or months or days) have both starts and stops and how many have one without the other?*

The following query characterizes years according to whether or not the year has any starts and whether or not the year has any stops:

```
SELECT (CASE WHEN numstarts = 0 THEN 'NONE' ELSE 'SOME' END) as starts,
       (CASE WHEN numstops = 0 THEN 'NONE' ELSE 'SOME' END) as stops,
       COUNT(DISTINCT yy) as numyears,
       MIN(yy) as minyear, MAX(yy) as maxyear
FROM (SELECT yy, SUM(numstarts) as numstarts, SUM(numstops) as numstops
      FROM ((SELECT YEAR(StartDate) as yy, COUNT(*) as numstarts,
                    0 as numstops
             FROM Subscribers
             GROUP BY YEAR(StartDate) )
            UNION ALL
            (SELECT YEAR(StopDate) as yy, 0, COUNT(*) as numstops
             FROM Subscribers
             GROUP BY YEAR(StopDate) )) ss
      GROUP BY yy) ssy
GROUP BY (CASE WHEN numstarts = 0 THEN 'NONE' ELSE 'SOME' END),
         (CASE WHEN numstops = 0 THEN 'NONE' ELSE 'SOME' END)
ORDER BY starts, stops
```

The results in Table 7-1 confirm what we already know. Prior to 2004, starts were recorded in the database but not stops—and the exact date differs by market (the above queries are easy to generalize to get information by other dimensions, such as market and channel). Chapter 6 got around this problem by filtering the starts to include only after the left truncation date. The

Table 7-1: Number of Years, Characterized by Presence of Starts and Stops

STARTS	STOPS	NUMBER OF YEARS	MINIMUM YEAR	MAXIMUM YEAR
SOME	NONE	17	1958	2003
SOME	SOME	3	2004	2006

resulting calculations use customers whose full start and stop information is available.

Subscribers has a particularly obvious form of left truncation because *all* stopped customers are excluded. Often, left truncation is not quite so blatant. For instance, some stops might make it into the database, perhaps because they were pending on the cutoff date. Or, the left truncation may be within a single market or customer subgroup. Perhaps a small company was acquired, and only their active customers were included in the database. Fortunately, the techniques that deal with left truncation can be enhanced to deal with a separate left truncation date for each customer.

Effect of Left Truncation

Left truncation, in general, biases hazard probabilities by making them smaller, because the population at risk is bigger than it should be. Customers are included in the population at risk for tenures when these customers are not at risk. For instance, a customer that started in 2001 is included in the population at risk for tenure one. If this customer had stopped at tenure one, she would not be in the data, so her stop would not be counted. Because she is in the data, her stop date, if any, must be after the left truncation date. Yet, making the mistake of including her in the population at risk for tenure one is easy.

As a consequence, the denominator of the hazard probability ratio is too large, so the hazard probability too small, which in turn makes the survival estimates too big. Figure 7-7 compares survival curves generated from all the customers and from only those who started after the left truncation date. The survival values are too optimistic. Optimism is good. Ungrounded optimism bordering on fantasy might lead to incorrect decisions and assumptions. Unbiased estimates are much preferred.

> **WARNING** Naïve hazard calculations on left truncated data usually underestimate the hazard values, overestimating survival.

Although left truncated data usually underestimates hazard probabilities, the resulting hazard probabilities could actually be either larger or smaller than the unbiased estimate. Consider the hazard probability at 730 days. It can be

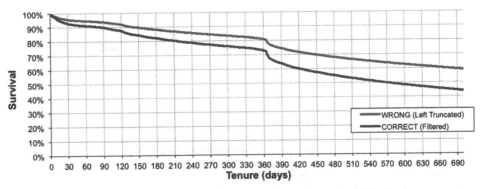

Figure 7-7: Calculations on left truncated data overestimate the survival. Filtering is one way to get unbiased estimates.

set to almost any value by making up data before the left truncation date. So, consider the customers who start on 2001-01-01. If all these customers stop at exactly 730 days, then they all stop before the left truncation date (2003-01-01 is before 2004-01-01), and they are not in the data. However, their stops would increase the 730-day hazard relative to the observed value. If, instead, these customers all stop at exactly 731 days of tenure, then they have survived 730 days without stopping, thereby decreasing the 730-day hazard. Because these customers are not in the data, we don't know which, if either, of these scenarios occurred.

When doing survival analysis, we assume that the hazard probabilities do not change radically over time—that they are stable. The scenarios described in the previous paragraph severely violate hazard stability at tenure 730. Figure 6-15 on page 288 did show that the 365-day hazard probability changes over time. However, the change is gradual, so this hazard does not seem to severely undermine the assumption of stability (for the observed data). Assuming the hazards are stable or relatively stable, hazard probabilities calculated from left truncated data underestimate the hazards and hence overestimate the survival.

> **TIP** We often assume that hazard probabilities are stable and do not change radically or suddenly over time. This is usually a reasonable assumption for customer databases, although it is worth validating.

How to Fix Left Truncation, Conceptually

Figure 7-8 shows several customers on the calendar time line. Two dates are highlighted; the earlier is the left truncation date and the later one is the cutoff date. Only customers active after the left truncation date are in the database.

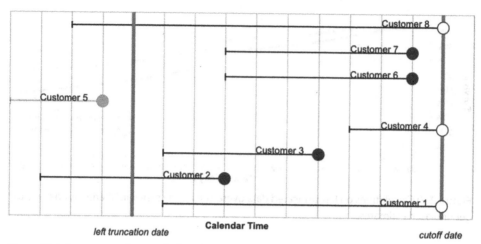

Figure 7-8: Customers who stop before the left truncation date are not included in the database.

Customer #5 started and stopped before the left truncation date. This customer is simply missing from the data. We do not even know to look for the customer, because no records refer to that customer. Customer #2 started at about the same time yet appears in the data because this customer survived to the left truncation date. That one customer is present and another absent is a property of the data, as opposed to a property of any particular record. This is a particularly insidious form of missing data because the entire record is missing, not just a value in a column.

How can hazard probabilities be calculated without the biases introduced by this type of missing data? Remember, the hazard probability at a particular tenure is the number of customers who have an observed stop at that tenure divided by the number of customers who are at risk of stopping. The population at risk was defined as everyone who was active at that tenure and could have stopped.

Left truncation adds a twist. Consider the at-risk population for customers at tenure zero in left-truncated data. Customers who started before the left truncation date and then stopped immediately had a tenure of zero. But, these customers are simply not in the data. Neither the stop nor the customer is in the population. The at-risk population at tenure zero consists only of customers who started after the left truncation date.

Consider the at-risk population for customers at tenure one. These customers have to be at risk of stopping at tenure one and the stop needs to occur after the left truncation date. So, tenure one needs to occur on or after the left truncation date. In other words, the customer must start between one day before the left truncation date and one day before the cutoff date.

The general rule is that a customer is in the population at risk at a given tenure when that tenure occurs on or after the left truncation date and before the cutoff date. The following two rules for membership in the population at risk encapsulate this observation for a given tenure t:

- Customers start in the time period from the left truncation date minus t to the cutoff date minus t.
- Customers are active at tenure t.

Together, these two rules imply that the customer is in the at-risk population at that tenure.

Estimating Hazard Probability for One Tenure

The preceding rules readily translate into SQL for a given tenure—for instance, the hazard probability for tenure 100:

```
SELECT t, COUNT(*) as poprisk_t,
       SUM(CASE WHEN tenure = t THEN isstop ELSE 0 END) as numstops,
       AVG(CASE WHEN tenure = t THEN isstop*1.0 ELSE 0 END) as haz_t
FROM (SELECT s.*,
             (CASE WHEN StopType IS NULL THEN 0 ELSE 1 END) as isstop,
             (CASE WHEN Market = 'Smallville'
                   THEN CAST('2004-10-27' as DATE)
                   ELSE '2004-01-01' END) as LeftTruncationDate
      FROM Subscribers s) s CROSS JOIN
     (SELECT 100 as t) const
WHERE Tenure >= t AND
      DATEADD(day, t, StartDate) >= LeftTruncationDate AND
      DATEADD(day, t, StartDate) <= '2006-12-31'
GROUP BY t
```

The result is 0.092%. Notice that this query uses a subquery to define the tenure of interest (t). Changing the value of this variable results in estimates for other tenures. For instance, changing it to 1460 gives the tenure at four years (1460 = 365 * 4). That value is 0.073%.

Wow. Calculating the hazard for such a large tenure is remarkable. Up to this point, hazard probabilities have been limited to tenures less than three years because starts before 2014-01-01 were filtered out. However, by using a time window, hazard probabilities can be accurately estimated for almost any tenure.

Estimating Hazard Probabilities for All Tenures

The method used to estimate hazard probabilities for a single tenure does not readily scale to all tenures. Doing the calculation efficiently for all tenures requires a bit more cleverness based on observations about the population at risk. These observations look at the calculation from a different perspective, the relationship between the population at risk for one tenure and the population at risk for the previous tenure.

The observations are:

- The population at risk for a given tenure t is the population at risk for $t - 1$; plus

- Customers who enter the time window with tenure t (that is, those who have tenure t on the left truncation date); minus

- Customers who leave the time window with tenure $t - 1$ (that is, those who are stopped or censored at the previous tenure).

These observations use the number of customers who enter and leave the time window defined by the left truncation date and the cutoff date. The number of customers who enter at a given tenure is easily calculated. Customers who start on or after the left truncation date enter at tenure zero. Customers who start before the left truncation date enter the time window on their tenure as of the left truncation date. Only customers who have entered the time window are counted in the population at risk.

The number of customers who leave the time window at a given tenure is even easier. This is the number of customers with a given tenure, regardless of whether or not they stop. Any customers who stop before the left truncation date need to be excluded from both the "enters" and "leaves" calculations. This condition is a bit redundant for the data we are using because customers who stop before the left truncation date are not in the data at all, which is why we are going through this effort to calculate unbiased hazards.

The following SQL calculates `numenters`, `numleaves`, and `numstops` for all tenures less than 1000 by placing all longer tenure customers into one group (this is just a convenience for the calculation and not necessary for handling left truncation):

```
SELECT (CASE WHEN t < 1000 THEN t ELSE 1000 END) as tenure,
       SUM(enters) as numenters, SUM(leaves) as numleaves,
       SUM(isstop) as numstops
FROM ((SELECT (CASE WHEN StartDate >= LeftTruncationDate THEN 0
                    ELSE DATEDIFF(day, StartDate, LeftTruncationDate)
              END) as t,
              1 as enters, 0 as leaves, 0.0 as isstop, StartDate, Tenure
       FROM (SELECT s.*,
                    (CASE WHEN Market = 'Smallville'
                          THEN CAST('2004-10-27' as DATE)
                          ELSE '2004-01-01' END) as LeftTruncationDate
             FROM Subscribers s) s
      ) UNION ALL
      (SELECT tenure as thetenure, 0 as enters, 1 as leaves,
              (CASE WHEN StopType IS NOT NULL THEN 1 ELSE 0
               END) as isstop, StartDate, Tenure
```

```
            FROM Subscribers s) ) a
    WHERE StartDate IS NOT NULL AND Tenure >= 0
    GROUP BY (CASE WHEN t < 1000 THEN t ELSE 1000 END)
    ORDER BY tenure
```

The two subqueries calculate the number of customers who enter and leave the time window. The second of these subqueries also keeps track of the customers who stop because the tenure at the stop is the same as the tenure when the customer leaves the time window.

These columns provide the fodder for the Excel calculation, which follows the logic suggested by the preceding observations. Figure 7-9 shows the formulas for an Excel spreadsheet that does the calculations. The population at risk for a given tenure is the previous population at risk plus the new customers that enter minus the ones that leave at the previous tenure. The hazard probabilities are then calculated by dividing the number of stops by the population at risk. When doing the calculation for all tenures, it is worth validating the result for one or two tenures, using the single-tenure estimate in the previous section.

Notice that the number of customers who enter the time window at tenure zero is in the millions, but for the other tenures, the count is, at most, in the thousands. This is because all customers who start on or after the left truncation date enter the time window at tenure zero. So, the tenure zero number includes three years' worth of starts. On the other hand, the customers who enter at larger tenures started that number of days before the left truncation date.

Doing the Calculation in SQL

This calculation can also be done in SQL using window functions. Using the previous query as the base calculation, the following does the cumulative sums for the hazard calculation:

```
WITH ss as ( < previous query with no ORDER BY> )
SELECT ss.*,
```

	C	D	E	F	G	H	I	J
24			FROM SQL				CALCULATED IN EXCEL	
25	tenure	numenters	numleaves	numstops		POP	h	S
26	0	2943883	2383	508		=SUM(D$26:D26)	=F26/H26	=IF($C26=0, 1, J25*(1-I25))
27	1	1469	18358	17310		=SUM(D$26:D27)	=F27/H27	=IF($C27=0, 1, J26*(1-I26))
28	2	2260	16742	15103		=SUM(D$26:D28)	=F28/H28	=IF($C28=0, 1, J27*(1-I27))
29	3	4254	13298	11361		=SUM(D$26:D29)	=F29/H29	=IF($C29=0, 1, J28*(1-I28))
30	4	3762	9566	9522		=SUM(D$26:D30)	=F30/H30	=IF($C30=0, 1, J29*(1-I29))
31	5	3743	11766	9172		=SUM(D$26:D31)	=F31/H31	=IF($C31=0, 1, J30*(1-I30))
32	6	3788	12689	9449		=SUM(D$26:D32)	=F32/H32	=IF($C32=0, 1, J31*(1-I31))
33	7	540	13504	10336		=SUM(D$26:D33)	=F33/H33	=IF($C33=0, 1, J32*(1-I32))
34	8	3209	11898	9596		=SUM(D$26:D34)	=F34/H34	=IF($C34=0, 1, J33*(1-I33))
35	9	5279	12296	9480		=SUM(D$26:D35)	=F35/H35	=IF($C35=0, 1, J34*(1-I34))
36	10	5511	12068	9528		=SUM(D$26:D36)	=F36/H36	=IF($C36=0, 1, J35*(1-I35))

Figure 7-9: The Excel calculation for handling left truncation is not much more difficult than the calculation for empirical hazards.

```
    (SUM(numenters - numleaves) OVER (ORDER BY Tenure) +
     numleaves) as pop,
     numstops / (sum(numenters - numleaves) OVER (ORDER BY Tenure) +
                numleaves) as h
FROM ss
ORDER BY Tenure
```

This query has one small trick. The expression SUM(numenters - numleaves) OVER (ORDER BY Tenure) almost does the correct calculation. This calculates the cumulative sum of enters minus the cumulative sum of leaves. However, we want the cumulative sum of enters minus the cumulative sum of leaves *for the previous tenure*. In other words, this expression undercounts the population by including the stops at the given tenure. The fix is easy: Just add the stops at the current tenure back in.

Time Windowing

Time windows are more than just the solution to left truncation. They are a powerful technique for other purposes. This section investigates time windows in general and some ways to use them.

A Business Problem

Once upon a time, a mobile phone company was developing a forecasting application using survival analysis. This type of application was discussed in the previous chapter, and forecasting can be a powerful application of survival analysis. They provided a large amount of data for tens of millions of customers early one May for a proof-of-concept. The schedule called for the proof-of-concept to be reviewed in the summer, steadily improved upon, and then the final forecasting project would begin at the end of the year. So, using historical data, the proof-of-concept began that May.

In April, a shrewd person in finance decided to change one of the company's policies, just a little tweak actually. The old policy was to disconnect a customer on the date the customer requested the stop. The new policy was to disconnect customers at the end of their billing cycle, unless the customer very loudly objected.

The merits of the new policy were multifold and manifest. The new policy meant that almost no monies needed to be refunded to customers because accounts were paid up through the end of the billing period. Such refunds were generally small amounts of money, and the overhead for each refund was a significant proportion of the amount refunded. In addition, the new policy kept customers active for a longer period of time. Assuming that customers call randomly during their billing periods to stop, it would add half a billing period—or two weeks—onto each customer's tenure.

Hmmm, would the new policy have an effect on customers' tenures? Could adding an extra two weeks of tenure to every customer who stops conceivably have an effect on the proof-of-concept project? No suspense here: The answer is "yes." The more important question is how to deal with the situation.

Filtering customers who started after the date the new policy went into effect at the beginning of May would not work, because the population would consist of customers having only very short tenures—less than one month for the proof-of-concept and less than one year for the larger project. A better solution would be to calculate unbiased hazard probabilities using only stops after the new policy went into effect. In other words, forcing the left truncation date to be a recent date would only use stops that have the new policy. Voila! The hazard estimates would reflect the new policy, while still having hazard estimates for all tenures.

Forcing left truncation solves the problem. Other situations are amenable to the same solution. Another company changed its initial non-payment policy. Previously, customers were cancelled after 63 days, if they did not pay their initial bill. This was changed to 77 days. And, yes, this has an impact on the forecast customer numbers. Eventually, the policy was made more complicated, varying from 56 days to 84 days for different groups of customers. Estimating hazards based only on the period when customers are active after the new policies went into effect (using left truncation) enables the accurate estimation of hazards under the new policy.

Time Windows = Left Truncation + Right Censoring

The examples in the previous section force a left truncation date to handle a change in business rules. A more general way to think about time windows is that they calculate unbiased estimates of hazard probabilities using a time window of customer activity. The beginning of the time window is the left truncation date and the end of the time window is the cutoff date (technically called the *right censor date*).

Customers are in the at-risk population only when they enter the time window; otherwise, the stop would not be recorded in the database. This discussion focuses on a common time window for all customers. The same ideas apply to different time windows for different groups of customers.

Figure 7-10 illustrates a general time window for a small number of customers. A given time window is a combination of left truncation and forcing an earlier right censorship date (which we saw in the previous chapter in Figure 6-17 on page 291). With these two ideas, it is possible to generate unbiased hazards using almost any time window when stops occur.

Figure 7-10 is generated through a clever combination of different chart types. The shaded area is a bar chart plotted on the secondary X-axis. The number of bars is carefully chosen so the shading aligns with the vertical gridlines. By choosing a semi-transparent shading, the gridlines show through.

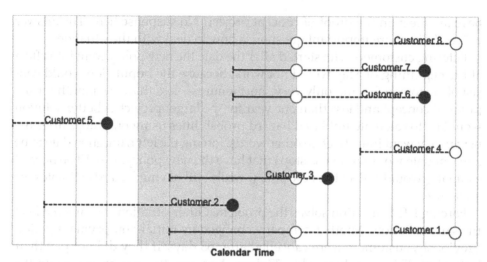

Figure 7-10: Time windows make it possible to estimate unbiased hazard probabilities for stops during a particular period of time (the shaded area).

Calculating One Hazard Probability Using a Time Window

What are the hazard probabilities at tenure 100 based on stops in 2004, in 2005, and in 2006? This is a question about changes in a hazard probability over time. The following SQL statement does the calculation based on stops in 2004:

```
SELECT t as tenure, COUNT(*) as poprisk_t,
       SUM(CASE WHEN tenure = t THEN isstop ELSE 0 END) as numstops,
       AVG(CASE WHEN tenure = t THEN isstop ELSE 0 END) as haz_t
FROM (SELECT s.*,
             (CASE WHEN Market = 'Smallville'
                   THEN CAST('2004-10-27' as DATE)
              ELSE '2004-01-01' END) as LeftTruncationDate,
             (CASE WHEN StopType IS NOT NULL AND StopDate <= '2004-12-31'
                   THEN 1.0 ELSE 0 END) as isstop
      FROM Subscribers s) s CROSS JOIN
     (SELECT 100 as t) const
WHERE Tenure >= t AND
      DATEADD(day, t, StartDate) BETWEEN LeftTruncationDate AND
                                         '2004-12-31'
GROUP BY t
```

This SQL statement combines left truncation and forced censoring. Left truncation is implemented in the WHERE clause, by restricting the customers only to those whose 100th day of tenure is during 2004. The forced censoring is as of the end of 2004, so the definition of isstop is as of that date.

The queries for 2005 and 2006 are similar. Table 7-2 shows the hazard probability for tenure 100 for stops during each of the three years. The probability itself is quite low. The hazard is lowest during 2005, the year with the largest population at risk.

Table 7-2: Hazard Probability for Tenure 100 Based on Stops in 2004, 2005, and 2006

YEAR	TENURE	POPULATION AT RISK	STOPS	HAZARD PROBABILITY
2004	100	850,170	957	0.1126%
2005	100	1,174,610	777	0.0661%
2006	100	750,064	808	0.1077%

All Hazard Probabilities for a Time Window

Calculating a hazard probability for a single tenure is a good illustration of time windows. More interesting is calculating hazard probabilities for all tenures. This calculation follows the same form as the left truncation calculation, where `stops`, `enters`, and `leaves` variables are calculated for all tenures. The next section provides an example of this calculation in Excel and the following section does the calculation in SQL.

Comparison of Hazards by Stops in Year in Excel

The previous chapter showed two ways of comparing changes in survival probabilities over time. The first method was to use starts in a given year, which provides information about acquisition during the year, but not about all the customers who were active during that time. The second approach forces the right censorship date to be earlier, creating a snapshot of survival at the end of each year. Using starts, customers who start in 2006 have relatively lower survival than customers who start in 2004 or 2005. However, the snapshot method shows that 2006 survival looks better than survival at the end of 2004.

This section proposes another method, based on time windows. Using time windows, hazard probabilities are estimated based on *customers' activity* during each year. Time windows make it possible to calculate hazard probabilities for all tenures.

The approach is to calculate the number of customers who enter, leave, and stop at a given tenure, taking into account the time window. The following query does the calculation for stops during 2006:

```
WITH const as (
     SELECT CAST('2006-01-01' as DATE) as WindowStart,
            CAST('2006-12-28' as DATE) as WindowEnd
     )
SELECT (CASE WHEN tenure < 1000 THEN tenure ELSE 1000 END) as tenure,
       SUM(enters) as numenters, SUM(leaves) as numleaves,
       SUM(isstop) as numstops
FROM ((SELECT (CASE WHEN StartDate >= WindowStart THEN 0
                    ELSE DATEDIFF(day, StartDate, WindowStart)
              END) as tenure, 1 as enters, 0 as leaves, 0.0 as isstop
       FROM const CROSS JOIN Subscribers s
```

```
        WHERE Tenure >= 0 AND StartDate <= WindowEnd AND
              (StopDate IS NULL OR StopDate >= WindowStart)
    ) UNION ALL
    (SELECT (CASE WHEN StopDate IS NULL OR StopDate >= WindowEnd
                  THEN DATEDIFF(day, StartDate, WindowEnd) ELSE Tenure
              END) as tenure, 0 as enters, 1 as leaves,
             (CASE WHEN StopType IS NOT NULL AND StopDate <= WindowEnd
                   THEN 1 ELSE 0 END) as isstop
     FROM const CROSS JOIN Subscribers s
     WHERE Tenure >= 0 AND StartDate <= WindowEnd AND
           (StopDate IS NULL OR StopDate >= WindowStart) )
    ) s
GROUP BY (CASE WHEN Tenure < 1000 THEN Tenure ELSE 1000 END)
ORDER BY tenure
```

Notice first that the stop window ends on 2006-12-28 rather than 2006-12-31. The 28th is the cut-off date for the data; the table has no starts or stops beyond that date. If the later date were used, then active customers would have their tenures extended by three days. That is, a customer who started on 2006-12-28 would have a tenure of three rather than zero, and the resulting hazards would differ slightly from the point estimates in the last section.

The variable enters counts the number of customers entering the time window at each tenure. This tenure is zero for customers who start during the window and a larger value for customers who start before the window. The variables leaves and stops are calculated based on the tenure on the right censorship date or the tenure when a customer stops.

Each subquery has the same WHERE clause in order to select only customers active during the time window—customers had to start before the end of the year and stop after the beginning of the year in order to be included. For good measure, each subquery also requires that tenure be non-negative, eliminating the row with a spurious negative value.

Figure 7-11 shows the survival curves based on a one-year time window for each of the three years. These curves are comparable to Figures 6-16 and 6-18 (pages 290, 293), which show the survival based on starts and the end-of-year snapshots, respectively. This chart has a more complete picture. Using time windows, all three years have survival estimates for all tenures. None of the series are longer or shorter than the others.

The chart shows that the anniversary churn effect is much stronger in 2005 and 2006 versus 2004. Anniversary churn is the tendency of customers to stop on the one-year anniversary of their start, typically because their contracts expire. So, although customers in 2005 and 2006 survive better in the first year (compared to customers in 2004), as the tenures stretch out, the difference in survival disappears. Based on the stops, 2006 seems to be the worst of all possible worlds, with the worst short-term survival (in the first 90 days) and the worst long-term survival (over 720 days), although it does a bit better in between.

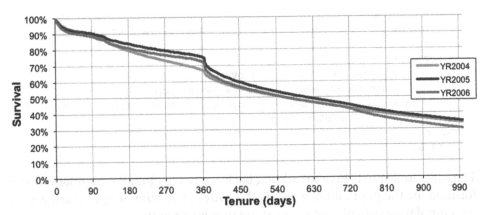

Figure 7-11: Using time windows, the stops during different years can be used to calculate hazard probabilities and survival.

Comparison of Hazards by Stops in Year in SQL

The calculation can also be done in SQL. This follows the same structure as the calculation for left truncation:

```
WITH params as (
      SELECT CAST('2006-01-01' as DATE) AS WindowStart,
             CAST('2006-12-28' as DATE) as WindowEnd
    ),
    t as (
      SELECT (CASE WHEN tenure < 1000 THEN tenure ELSE 1000
             END) as tenure,
             SUM(enters) as numenters, SUM(leaves) as numleaves,
             SUM(isstop) as numstops
      FROM ((SELECT (CASE WHEN StartDate >= WindowStart THEN 0
                          ELSE DATEDIFF(day, StartDate, WindowStart)
                    END) as tenure,
                 1 as enters, 0 as leaves, 0 as isstop
          FROM params CROSS JOIN Subscribers s
          WHERE Tenure >= 0 AND StartDate <= WindowEnd AND
                (StopDate IS NULL OR StopDate >= WindowStart)
          ) UNION ALL
          (SELECT (CASE WHEN StopDate IS NULL OR StopDate >= WindowEnd
                        THEN DATEDIFF(day, StartDate, '2006-12-28')
                        ELSE Tenure
                  END) as tenure, 0 as enters, 1 as leaves,
                  (CASE WHEN StopType IS NOT NULL AND
                             StopDate <= WindowEnd
                        THEN 1 ELSE 0 END) as isstop
          FROM params CROSS JOIN Subscribers s
          WHERE Tenure >= 0 AND StartDate <= WindowEnd AND
                (StopDate IS NULL OR StopDate >= WindowStart) )
```

```
        ) s
    GROUP BY (CASE WHEN Tenure < 1000 THEN Tenure ELSE 1000 END)
  )
SELECT t. *,
     (SUM(numenters - numleaves) OVER
          (ORDER BY tenure) + numleaves) as pop,
     numstops / (SUM(numenters - numleaves) OVER (ORDER BY tenure) +
          numleaves) as h
FROM t
ORDER BY tenure
```

The same logic holds here for adding back `numleaves` into the population. The formula for the population at risk is the cumulative sum of `numenters` minus the cumulative sum of `numleaves` at the previous tenure.

Competing Risks

The opening lines to Leo Tolstoy's classic novel *Anna Karenina* are often translated as: "All happy families are alike; each unhappy family is unhappy in its own way." This book is not about Russian literature, but what Tolstoy wrote in the 19th century about families is also true of customers in the 21st century. Happy customers who stay are all alike because they remain customers. Unhappy customers stop, and they do so for a variety of reasons. Although perhaps not as compelling as the family tragedies in a Tolstoy novel, these different reasons are of analytic interest. Competing risks is the part of survival analysis that quantifies the effects of these different reasons.

Examples of Competing Risks

One way to think about competing risks is to imagine a guardian angel "competing" with various devils of temptation for each customer. The guardian angel encourages each customer to remain happy, loyal, and paying. The various devils of temptation urge the customer to defect to a competitor, or to stop paying, or quit for some other reason. This competition goes on throughout the customer lifetime, with the guardian angel usually winning . . . but, eventually, a devil of temptation comes out ahead, and the customer stops.

This image of guardian angels and devils encapsulates the central notion of competing risks: At a given tenure, a customer not only has a risk of stopping, but the stop could be for of a variety of reasons. For instance, the subscription data has three types of customer unhappiness encoded in the `stopType` column. So far, we have used the stop type to identify whether or not customers have stopped, lumping together all non-`NULL` values into one group of stopped customers. The next three subsections explain the stop types in more detail.

TIP When working with many different reasons for customers leaving, it is a good idea to classify them into a handful of different categories, say between two and five. These categories depend on the business needs.

I = Involuntary Churn

Stop type "I" stands for "involuntary churn," which occurs when the company initiates the stop. In this dataset, involuntary churn is synonymous with customers not paying their bill.

Involuntary churn may not really be involuntary. Customers may communicate their desire to leave by not paying their bills. Once upon a time, a mobile telephone company believed that none of its churn was actually involuntary; that is, the company performed credit checks and believed that all customers could pay their bills.

What the company did have was poor customer service—the hold times in the call center were often measured in tens of minutes. Customers would call customer service, perhaps with a billing or coverage question, and very likely get angry over the long wait time. Instead of canceling by calling back—and waiting again—some customers simply stopped paying their bills. The data suggested this because many customers who stopped paying had called customer service shortly before they stopped, even though their high credit scores indicated an ability to pay.

V = Voluntary Churn

Another form of churn is "V," which stands for "voluntary churn." This is a diverse array of customer-initiated reasons. Customers may stop because the price is too high, or because the product does not meet expectations (such as coverage for a cell phone company), or because customer service has treated them poorly, or because they are moving, or because of a change in financial conditions, or to boycott the company's environmental policy, or because their astrologer recommended change. Myriad reasons often gets encoded into dozens or hundreds of detailed stop codes. In Subscribers, all these reasons (and more) are grouped together into one group, "V."

Not all voluntary churn is necessarily truly voluntary. Often, customers cancel their accounts after late notices start appearing. They may stop voluntarily but they owe money. These customers were *en route* to involuntary churn, but took a detour by stopping on their own.

These borderline cases do not affect the applicability of competing risks. Instead, they suggest that under certain circumstances, additional data might be incorporated into the stop types. For instance, customers who stop voluntarily with an outstanding balance (larger than a certain size or so many days past due) probably differ from other customers who stop voluntarily.

M = Migration

The third type of churn in the subscription data is migration churn, indicated by "M." One example of migration churn is when a company introduces a new, improved product and wants to move customers to the new product. This occurred when companies introduced digital cell phone technologies, and moved good customers from analog services.

The accounts in this dataset consist of customers on subscription accounts. These customers pay for service one month at a time as part of an ongoing service arrangement. Prepaid customers pay in advance for a block of time. The prepaid option is more appropriate for some customers, particularly those with limited financial means.

Migration from a subscription account to a prepaid account is a downgrade because the prepay product is not as profitable as the subscription product. In other cases, migration might be an upgrade. In a credit card database, switching to a gold, platinum, titanium, or black card might close one credit card account but open another, more valuable account. In the pharmaceutical world, a patient might go from a 10-mg dose to a 40-mg dose.

From the holistic customer perspective, migration may not actually indicate a stop at all. After all, the customer remains a customer with the company. On the other hand, from the perspective of a particular product group, migrated customers no longer use that product. Whether or not migration indicates a stop is a business question whose answer varies depending on the particular business needs.

> **TIP** Whether or not a customer has stopped is sometimes a business question. For some analyses (more product-centric), customers who migrate to another product might be considered stopped. For other more customer-centric analyses, such customers would still be active.

Other

Another type of churn is "expected" churn. For instance, customers may die or might move outside the service area or reach retirement age (and no longer be eligible/interested in retirement savings accounts); in these cases, the cancellation is not because the customer does not want to be a customer; it is due to extraneous factors. Similarly, the company might be responsible by closing down its operations in a geographic area or selling a business unit to a competitor. These are examples of situations where customers cease being customers, but through no fault of their own.

Competing risks could handle all the dozens of types of churn specified by reason codes. However, it is usually better to work with a smaller number of reasons, classifying the reasons into a handful of important stop classes.

Competing Risk "Hazard Probability"

The fundamental idea behind competing risks is that a customer who is still active has not succumbed to any of the risks. In the original imagery, this means that the guardian angel and the devils of temptation keep battling for the customer's fate.

Figure 7-12 illustrates a small group of customers. In this chart, open circles indicate that the customer is still active. The dark and light shadings indicate different ways that customers might leave. It is possible to calculate the hazard for each of the risks, by dividing the number of stops for that risk by the population at risk. Because the angel and the devils are all competing for the same customers, the population at risk is the same for all the risks. Actually, the population at risk might vary slightly for different risks, but this variation is a technical detail. For intuitive purposes, it is safe to assume that the populations are the same.

The following query sets up the appropriate data in SQL:

```
SELECT Tenure, COUNT(*) as pop,
       SUM(CASE WHEN StopType = 'V' THEN 1 ELSE 0 END) as voluntary,
       SUM(CASE WHEN StopType = 'I' THEN 1 ELSE 0 END) as involuntary,
       SUM(CASE WHEN StopType = 'M' THEN 1 ELSE 0 END) as migration
FROM (SELECT s.*,
             (CASE WHEN Market = 'Smallville'
                   THEN CAST('2004-10-27' as DATE)
                   ELSE '2004-01-01' END) as LeftTruncationDate
      FROM Subscribers s
     ) s
WHERE StartDate IS NOT NULL AND Tenure >= 0 AND
      StartDate >= LeftTruncationDate
GROUP BY Tenure
ORDER BY Tenure
```

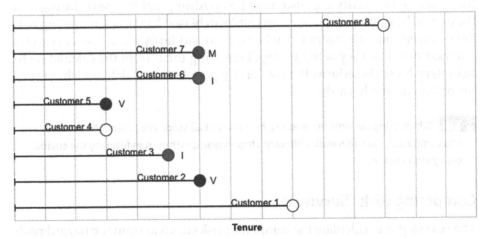

Figure 7-12: Different customers stop for different reasons, such as voluntary and involuntary churn and migration.

This SQL simply divides the stops into three groups, the "V," the "I," and the "M" groups. Competing risk hazards are then calculated separately for each of these groups, using the same population at risk.

There is a theoretical reason for slightly tweaking the population at risk, by making a small adjustment for the customers who stop. Even though all of them stopped during the same discrete time interval, we can imagine that they stopped in some order. Once a customer has stopped for any reason, that customer is no longer in the population at risk for the other risks. On average, all the customers who stopped for a particular risk stopped halfway through the time interval. These customers are not at risk for stopping again. A reasonable adjustment to the population at risk for a particular risk is to subtract half the stops.

This adjustment generally has a negligible impact on the hazard probabilities because the number of stops at any given time is much smaller than the population at risk. When the number of stops and the population at risk are more similar in size, the adjustment has a larger effect. However, this happens when the population at risk is small, so the confidence interval around the hazard probability is large anyway. Incidentally, this same adjustment can be made for the overall hazard calculation.

What does the competing risk hazard mean? A good intuitive answer is that the hazard is the conditional probability of succumbing to a particular risk, given that the customer has not succumbed to any risk so far. Competing risk hazard probabilities are always smaller than or equal to the overall hazard probabilities at the same tenure. In fact, if all competing risks have been taken into account, the overall hazard probability is the sum of the competing risk hazard probabilities (or at least, very close to the sum if using the adjustment).

Is there an alternative approach? One idea might be to keep only the stops for one risk, filtering out all the others. This is a no-no. Earlier, there was a warning that filtering or stratifying customers by anything that happens during or at the end of the customer relationship results in biased hazards. Competing risks are no exception. The customers who stop involuntarily are at risk of stopping voluntarily before they actually stop. Removing them from the calculation for voluntary hazards reduces the size of the population at risk, which, in turn, overestimates the hazards.

> **TIP** When using survival techniques, be sure that all stops are taken into account. Use competing risks to handle different stop reasons, rather than filtering the customers by stop reason.

Competing Risk "Survival"

The next step is to calculate the competing risk survival from the hazard probabilities, to get results such as those in Figure 7-13. The survival values for one competing risk are always larger than the overall survival. For a large numbers

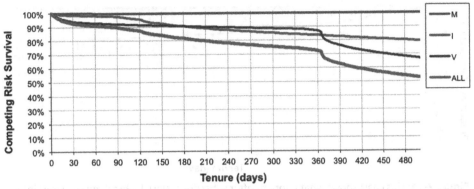

Figure 7-13: Competing risk survival is always larger than overall survival.

of customers and relatively few stops at any given tenure, the product of all the competing risk survival values at a given tenure is a good approximation of the overall survival. This formula is not exact, just a very good approximation.

Competing risk survival curves do not have an easy interpretation. They are conditional on a customer not stopping for other reasons. So, the "V" curve answers the question: *What is the probability of surviving to a given tenure assuming that the customer does not stop for any reason other than "V"?* This question is rather arcane; customers do stop for other reasons.

Competing risk survival curves do not have the nice analytic properties of overall survival curves. In particular, the area under the curve does not have easily understood interpretations.

On the other hand, the curves are useful qualitatively. For instance, the chart shows that anniversary churn is voluntary churn. On the other hand, involuntary churn predominates at a few months after a customer starts, and becomes less significant after that. Migration is never a big cause of churn. This ability to see the importance of different cancellation types makes competing risk survival charts useful, though more qualitatively than quantitatively.

What Happens to Customers over Time

Survival curves have a nice property. At any given tenure, the survival curve estimates the proportion of customers who are active; and hence the number who have stopped up to that point. Or, if the risk is something other than stopping, the curve tells us the proportion of customers who have succumbed to the risk and the proportion who have not. Competing risks extends this by refining the stopped population by risk type.

Example

Figure 7-14 shows a graph of the subscribers by tenure, divided into four parts. The lowest region represents active customers. The next is the customers who

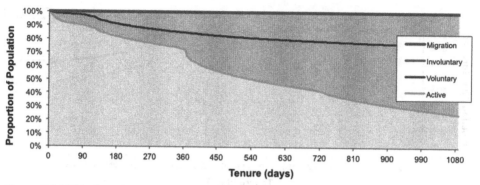

Figure 7-14: This chart shows what happens after subscribers start, by breaking the stops into different groups based on the stop type.

stopped voluntarily, and the next region is for the customers who stopped involuntarily. At the very top is a thin line for customers who migrated, but it is invisible because the group is so small. For instance, at 730 days, 42.3% are still active, 37.1% have stopped voluntarily, 20.2% have stopped involuntarily, and 0.4% have migrated. At every point, all customers are accounted for, so the sum of the three curves is always 100%.

These curves show what happens *next* after customers start. The only possibilities in this data are remaining active, or stopping—voluntarily, involuntarily, or by migrating. However, some customers who stop may restart and become active again. Customers who migrate away may also migrate back. These curves do not take these more complex scenarios into account, because they only show the next thing that happens.

The boundary between the active customers and the voluntary customers is the overall survival curve. The other three regions are calculated from the hazards, but not in exactly the same way as the survival curves. There are two approaches for creating a "what-happens-next" chart. The first is a brute-force, cohort-based approach. The second uses survival analysis.

A Cohort-Based Approach

One way to create a chart of what happens next is by doing a cohort-based calculation. This focuses on the outcomes of a group of customers who all start around the same time. For instance, the following SQL keeps track of the cohort of customers who start on the left truncation date:

```
SELECT Tenure, COUNT(*) as pop,
       SUM(CASE WHEN StopType = 'V' THEN 1 ELSE 0 END) as voluntary,
       SUM(CASE WHEN StopType = 'I' THEN 1 ELSE 0 END) as involuntary,
       SUM(CASE WHEN StopType = 'M' THEN 1 ELSE 0 END) as migration
FROM (SELECT s.*,
             (CASE WHEN Market = 'Smallville'
```

```
                        THEN CAST('2004-10-27' as DATE)
                        ELSE '2004-01-01' END) as LeftTruncationDate
          FROM Subscribers s) s
    WHERE StartDate = LeftTruncationDate
    GROUP BY Tenure
    ORDER BY Tenure
```

This query is quite similar to the previous query. The only difference is that the query restricts the population to one day of starts. The idea is to use this data to calculate the cumulative number of starts and stops for each tenure, directly from the data.

Calculating the cumulative numbers for all tenures relies on two rules: The number of active customers at a given tenure is the sum of all customers with longer tenures, plus the number at that tenure who are active. For the other three groups, the rule is simply a forward cumulative sum. The number of voluntary stops is the number of voluntary stops for all tenures less than or equal to the given tenure.

Excel readily supports these calculations. Figure 7-15 shows the resulting chart, with the population of each group on a separate line. This chart is not stacked, so it is not obvious that the sum at any given tenure is the same value, the 349 customers who started on 2004-01-01.

This information can also be calculated in SQL:

```
WITH s as (
       SELECT Tenure, COUNT(*) as pop,
              SUM(CASE WHEN StopType = 'V' THEN 1 ELSE 0 END) as vol,
              SUM(CASE WHEN StopType = 'I' THEN 1 ELSE 0 END) as invol,
              SUM(CASE WHEN StopType = 'M' THEN 1 ELSE 0 END) as mig
       FROM (SELECT s.*,
                    (CASE WHEN Market = 'Smallville'
```

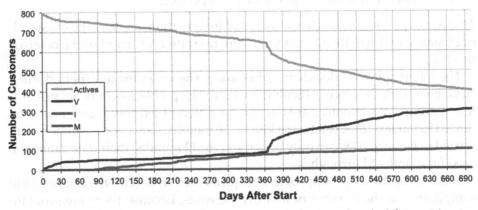

Figure 7-15: This chart shows what happens to customers who started on the left truncation date by showing the size of the groups that are active, voluntary stoppers, involuntary stoppers, and migrators.

```
                       THEN CAST('2004-10-27' as DATE)
                       ELSE '2004-01-01' END) as LeftTruncationDate
            FROM Subscribers s) s
     WHERE StartDate = LeftTruncationDate
     GROUP BY Tenure
    )
SELECT s.tenure, pop,
       SUM(pop) OVER (ORDER BY tenure DESC)-(vol+invol+mig) as actives,
       SUM(vol) OVER (ORDER BY tenure) as voluntary,
       SUM(invol) OVER (ORDER BY tenure) as involuntary,
       SUM(mig) OVER (ORDER BY tenure) as migration
FROM s
ORDER BY Tenure
```

The only nuance here is the subtraction of the stops from the population at each tenure. The stops take effect on the next tenure.

The cohort approach is very useful for seeing what happens to a group of customers. With additional information, customers could be placed into different groups, such as:

- Active, with no overdue amount
- Active, with overdue amount
- Stopped voluntarily, no money owed
- Stopped voluntarily, with an outstanding balance
- Stopped involuntarily, outstanding balance written off
- Stopped involuntarily, eventually paid outstanding balance
- Migrated, still active on migration product
- Migrated, stopped
- Migrated, but returned to subscription product

These groups combine different types of information, such as the outstanding balance and whether a customer who migrated returned to the original product.

The cohort approach does have a downside. The wider the time period when customers start, the more difficult it is to use. The problem occurs because different groups of customers are eligible for different tenures. Customers who started in January 2004 can be tracked for 36 months. However, customers who started in January 2006 can only be tracked for 12 months; their data cannot be used for months 13 through 36.

Sometimes, the cohort approach is implemented in Excel. This can get quite complicated as the number of months increases, because there are separate values for each start month and each tenure month. Then, breaking this into smaller groups for analysis adds even more complication. Eventually, the cohort approach reaches its limits. Fortunately, an alternative is available: using survival analysis and competing risks.

The Survival Analysis Approach

This section explains how to use competing risk hazards to quantify what happens after customers stop for all tenures. The place to start is with the overall survival, which splits the customer base into customers who are active and customers who have stopped up to any given tenure. To address the question of what happens to customers when they stop, two questions are key: *What proportion of customers stop at each tenure? Of the customers who stop at each tenure, what proportion stopped for each of the competing reasons?*

Answering the first is easy. The proportion of customers who stop is the difference between overall survival at tenure *t* and overall survival at tenure *t+1*. The answer to the second question is almost as easy. The solution is to divide the customers who stop proportionally among the competing risks. So, assume that 10, 20, and 70 customers stop for each of three risks at a given tenure. The proportion of customers who stop at that tenure is split into three groups, one with 10% of the stops, one with 20%, and one with 70%.

Earlier, we saw the query for calculating the competing risk hazards. Figure 7-16 shows a screen shot of the Excel spreadsheet that completes the calculation. This calculation determines the proportion of customers who stop at the tenure by taking the survival at that tenure and subtracting the survival at the next tenure. The difference is then divided proportionately among the competing risks; their cumulative sum is the proportion of customers who have succumbed to a particular risk at a particular tenure.

This method of calculation has an advantage over the cohort approach because it readily combines data from many start dates. It can also be extended to define additional groups by introducing more competing risks. For instance, the risk for voluntary churn could be split into two risks, one where the outstanding balance is zero and the other where the customer owes money.

Competing risks shows what happens to customers over time. However, our intuition leads to an interesting paradox involving competing risk hazard probabilities and survival values, discussed in the aside "A Competing Risks Conundrum."

	C	D	E	F	G	H	I	J	K	L	M	N
16		FROM SQL									CALCULATED IN EXCEL	
17	Tenure	pop	volunta	involu	migra		pop	h	Active	Stops	Voluntary	Involuntary
18	0	2383	77	1	430		=I19+D18	=SUM(E18:G18)/I18	1	=K18-K19	0	0
19	1	18354	14979	1888	439		=I20+D19	=SUM(E19:G19)/I19	=K19*(1-J18)	=K19-K20	=M18+$L18*(E18/SUM($E18:$G18))	=N18+$L18*(F18/SUM($E18:$G18))
20	2	16730	11130	3760	201		=I21+D20	=SUM(E20:G20)/I20	=K19*(1-J19)	=K20-K21	=M19+$L19*(E19/SUM($E19:$G19))	=N19+$L19*(F19/SUM($E19:$G19))
21	3	13283	8922	2255	169		=I22+D21	=SUM(E21:G21)/I21	=K20*(1-J20)	=K21-K22	=M20+$L20*(E20/SUM($E20:$G20))	=N20+$L20*(F20/SUM($E20:$G20))
22	4	9540	7400	1978	118		=I23+D22	=SUM(E22:G22)/I22	=K21*(1-J21)	=K22-K23	=M21+$L21*(E21/SUM($E21:$G21))	=N21+$L21*(F21/SUM($E21:$G21))
23	5	11743	6982	2047	120		=I24+D23	=SUM(E23:G23)/I23	=K22*(1-J22)	=K23-K24	=M22+$L22*(E22/SUM($E22:$G22))	=N22+$L22*(F22/SUM($E22:$G22))
24	6	12646	7247	2066	93		=I25+D24	=SUM(E24:G24)/I24	=K23*(1-J23)	=K24-K25	=M23+$L23*(E23/SUM($E23:$G23))	=N23+$L23*(F23/SUM($E23:$G23))
25	7	13463	8132	2091	72		=I26+D25	=SUM(E25:G25)/I25	=K24*(1-J24)	=K25-K26	=M24+$L24*(E24/SUM($E24:$G24))	=N24+$L24*(F24/SUM($E24:$G24))
26	8	11855	7464	2027	62		=I27+D26	=SUM(E26:G26)/I26	=K25*(1-J25)	=K26-K27	=M25+$L25*(E25/SUM($E25:$G25))	=N25+$L25*(F25/SUM($E25:$G25))
27	9	12261	7462	1903	80		=I28+D27	=SUM(E27:G27)/I27	=K26*(1-J26)	=K27-K28	=M26+$L26*(E26/SUM($E26:$G26))	=N26+$L26*(F26/SUM($E26:$G26))
28	10	12017	7637	1787	53		=I29+D28	=SUM(E28:G28)/I28	=K27*(1-J27)	=K28-K29	=M27+$L27*(E27/SUM($E27:$G27))	=N27+$L27*(F27/SUM($E27:$G27))

Figure 7-16: In Excel, it is possible to calculate what happens next using competing risk survival.

A COMPETING RISKS CONUNDRUM

Competing risks survival suggests two approximations that seem intuitive (or at least very reasonable). The first is that the product of the competing risk survival values equals the overall survival. The second approximation is that the sum of the competing risk hazard probabilities at a particular tenure equals the overall hazard probability.

Fortunately, these approximations are very good for customer data. In particular, both these statements are very close to being true when the number of customers is large and the number of stops at each tenure is relatively small. In extreme cases, though, the discrepancies are blatant. It is worth explaining these discrepancies to help better understand competing risks in general.

The first approximation about the survival runs into a problem when all customers stop. Consider three customers at risk at a given tenure and all three stop, for three different reasons. The overall hazard is 100%, and the hazard probability for each competing risk is 33.3%. The survival at the next time period is 0%. However, the survival for each competing risk is 66.7%, so the product is 29.6%, quite different from 0%. A bit of reflection suggests that almost no matter how we handle the competing risk hazard probabilities, they are always going to be equal and less than 100%. The product of the resulting survival is never going to be 0%.

This problem arises because the survival probability drops to zero when all customers stop. Fortunately, when working with large numbers of customers, this does not happen.

What about the sum of the competing risk hazards being the overall hazard? In this case, the explanation is a bit different. Imagine the same situation as before, with three customers, each of whom stops for a different reason. What is the "real" competing risk hazard when we look at this under a microscope? What would happen to the hazard probabilities if we assumed that the stops do not occur at exactly the same time, but in some sequence?

Well, the first customer who stops, say for competing risk A, has a hazard of 1/3, about 33.3%. An instant later, when the second customer stops for competing risk B, the population at risk has only two members, B and C (because the one customer has stopped). So, the competing risk hazard is 1/2 or 50%. And for the third one, the hazard comes to 1/1 or 100%. These look quite different from the hazards as calculated over the whole population.

The problem is, we don't know the exact order of the stops. It could be A then B then C, or B then C then A, or A then C then B, and so on. One solution is to guesstimate the hazard by taking the average hazard probability for the three cases. This comes to 11/18 (61.1%).

Another approach is to say that for any given risk, the population at risk needs to be reduced by half the customers who stop. And, on average, those customers stop halfway through the time period. This yields a hazard probability of 66.7% for each of the risks.

All this discussion is academic because only a very small fraction of the population at risk stops at any given tenure for most survival problems. Each competing risk hazard estimate can be made a bit more accurate by reducing the population at risk by half the number of customers who stop. In practice, though, this adjustment has a small effect on the hazards. And, this effect is much less than the effect of other biases, such as left truncation.

Before and After

This chapter started with the analysis of factors known about customers when they start, using stratification and hazard ratios. The previous section explained how to analyze factors that occur at the end of the customer relationship, by using competing risks. The final topic in this chapter is about events that happen during customers' life cycles, technically known as *time-dependent covariates*. In particular, this section talks about survival measures before and after an event occurs during the customer lifetime.

Understanding time-dependent covariates starts to push the limits of what can be accomplished using SQL and Excel; statistical methods such as Cox proportional hazard regression continue the analysis beyond what we can accomplish with these tools. However, some interesting results are still possible.

This section discusses three techniques for understanding these types of factors. The first is to compare forecasts. The second is a brute-force approach using cohorts. And the third is to directly calculate survival curves for before the event and after the event. Before explaining the techniques, the section starts with three scenarios to illustrate these types of problems.

Three Scenarios

This section discusses three business problems that involve time-dependent events. The scenarios are intended to show the challenges in approaching these problems.

A Billing Mistake

Oops! An insurance company makes a little billing boo-boo. During one bill cycle, some long-standing customers who paid their premiums are accidentally sent dunning notices, accusing them of not paying their bill; worse, the notices continue even after the customers complain. This angers a few customers, and angry customers are more likely to cancel their policies. *What is the cost of this mistake, in terms of lost customers?*

Figure 7-17 illustrates this situation on both the calendar time line and the tenure time line. The "X"s indicate when the billing mistake occurred. It affects everyone at the same time on the calendar time line; however, the effect is at a different tenure for each customer. From a business perspective, we expect the effect of such a one-time billing mistake to pass quickly. During the period when the error occurs, stops spike up and hazards go up. This spike should pass quickly, as the company recovers from the mistake. It is possible, of course, to test this assumption, by comparing hazards before and after the event using time windows to detect any long-term effects.

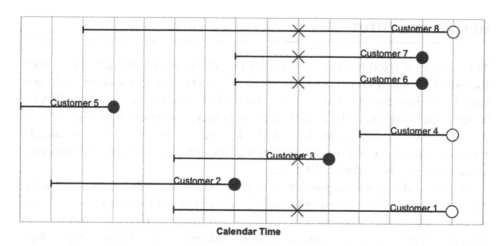

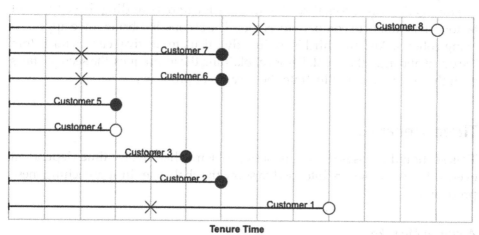

Figure 7-17: These two diagrams show the effect of a billing mistake on the calendar time line and on the tenure time line.

A Loyalty Program

Not all events are negative. Consider customers in a subscription-based business who enroll in a loyalty program. *How can the company measure the effectiveness of the loyalty program in terms of increased customer tenure?*

In this case, customers enroll in the program at different points on both the calendar and tenure time lines. Of course, some enrollment tenures may be more common than others; this would be the case if customers were only eligible for the program after their first year, resulting in an enrollment spike around the one-year anniversary. Similarly, some calendar times may be more common than other times, particularly when marketing campaigns encourage customers to enroll. With a loyalty program, we know everyone who is enrolled. In the case of the billing error, we may not know all customers who stopped *because of the error.*

The tenure when customers enroll is important because the probability of a customer leaving depends on tenure. The tenure at enrollment is, in fact, another problem amenable to survival analysis. Perhaps more interesting is translating enrollment into increased tenure, and increased tenure into dollars and cents.

An increase in tenure for the customers in the loyalty program does not, by itself, illustrate that the program is *causing* the increase. An alternative explanation is that better customers join the program in the first place. This is an example of the difference between causation and correlation. Increased tenure may be correlated with customers in the program, but it does not imply that the program caused the increase.

TIP Historical data can show correlation between different events. However, we have to reach outside mere data analysis to justify causation, either through formal testing or by suggesting how one thing causes the other.

Unlike the billing error, we expect the loyalty program to continue having an effect even after customers are enrolled. The effect of the event (enrollment) on survival is not limited to a short period. Instead, at some point in each customer's tenure the customer changes state from unenrolled to enrolled, and we expect the enrolled customers to have better survival after that point.

Raising Prices

The third scenario is a price increase on a subscription product. An increase in prices can have two effects. Existing customers might leave in response to higher prices. This would occur around the date when the increase goes into effect (which might be a different date for each customer based on billing cycles). The second is that new customers may leave at a faster rate. Some of the customers who stop are identified; presumably (hopefully), they complained about the price increase when they stopped. However, not all such customers give price as the reason. A customer might say "customer service is awful," when the customer really means "for the price I'm paying, customer service is awful." Typically only one stop reason gets recorded, although customers may be unhappy for more than one reason.

Measuring the impact of the price increase requires comparing survival both when the event occurs and after the event occurs. There are several interesting questions:

- Who likely stopped during the period of the price increase and what impact did this have? This is a question about excess stops during a particular period.
- Did existing customers who survived the initial shakeout period have worse survival after the price increase?
- Did new customers who started after the increase have worse survival?

These questions are all related to the financial impact of the price increase on existing customers. Of course, customers who stay are paying more money, often offsetting the loss from customers who leave.

The remainder of this section discusses different ways of quantifying the effects of events during customer lifetimes, starting with an approach based on forecasting.

Using Survival Forecasts to Understand One-Time Events

Forecasts, which were introduced in the previous chapter, are a powerful tool for measuring the impact of events on customers. Remember that a forecast takes a base of customers and applies a set of hazards, producing an estimate of the number of customers and stops on any day in the future. Forecasts based on existing customers show declines over time because new customers are not included.

Summing the estimates over a period of time calculates customer-days, which in turn can be turned into a financial value, based on the monetary value that a customer contributes on each day. Two basic approaches use forecasts to understand the effect of an event. The two differ, depending on whether the specific customers who stop can be identified.

Forecasting Identified Customers Who Stopped

When the customers who stop are known, forecasting can be applied just to these customers. This is the most direct method of using survival forecasting to measure the impact of an event. The method is to apply the forecast hazards only to the subset of customers identified as leaving due to the event. The result is the number of customer-days expected from those customers. The difference between these expected days and the actual days is the lost customer-days, which can in turn be used to calculate a financial loss. For this to work, the stopped customers need to be clearly identified. Another challenge is getting the right set of hazards.

A good set of hazards would be based on stops from some period before the event occurred, such as the month or year before the event, using a time window to calculate unbiased hazards. This has the advantage of a clean set of comparison data.

Another approach for estimating the hazards is to use competing risks. Remove the customers who stopped for the particular reason, and calculate the hazards using the remaining customers and remaining stops. The previous section warned against using competing risks this way because it underestimates the hazards. However, when the group of customers who leave is small relative to all stops, the error may be small enough to be ignored.

Estimating Excess Stops

The customers who leave for a specific reason may not be clearly identified. In the case of the loyalty program, all the customers in the program are identified, but the customers of interest are those who do not even stop. In this case, the approach is to estimate an excess (or deficiency) of stops indirectly rather than directly.

The approach here is the difference between two forecasts. One is the forecast of what would have happened if the event had not occurred and the other is the forecast of what actually did happen. Because the customer base is the same—consisting of the customers who are active just when the event happens—the difference between the two forecasts is the hazard probabilities.

The hazard probabilities for what actually did happen are easy to calculate using a time window of stops after the event. Similarly, the hazard probabilities ignoring the event can be calculated by taking a time period from before the event. The difference between the two is the lost customer-days.

The problem is slightly more complicated when the event occurs relative to the customer lifetime, such as joining a loyalty program that takes place at a different tenure for each customer. This case has no overall "before" date. Instead, customers are right censored on the date that they join the program, if ever. Prior to joining the loyalty program, customers contribute to both the population at risk and the stops. Once they join, they no longer contribute to either one.

Before and After Comparison

The before and after calculation of hazards is simple, using the time window technique for estimating hazards. These hazards generate survival curves, and the area between the survival curves quantifies the effect in customer-days.

Because the effect starts at tenure zero, this is most readily applied to new customers. Figure 7-18 illustrates an example. Remember from the previous chapter that the area between the curves is easy to calculate; it is simply the sum of the differences in the survival values during a particular period of time.

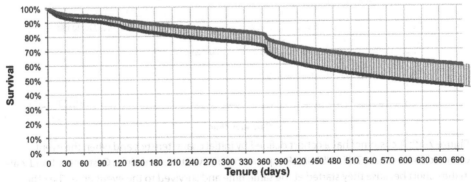

Figure 7-18: The area between two survival curves quantifies the difference between them in customer-days.

Cohort-Based Approach

The cohort-based approach for calculating the remaining customer tenure after an event is appropriate when the event does not affect all customers at the same time. An example is enrollment in a loyalty program. This approach is very computationally intensive. This section describes how to do the calculation, even though the calculation may not be feasible on even largish sets of data.

Cohort-Based Approach: Full Cohorts

Figure 7-19 shows the basic idea. A customer experiences an event that occurs at some point in his or her lifetime. Also shown are a group of other customers who are candidates for this customer's cohort. To be in the cohort, the candidate customers must meet some conditions:

- The cohort customers start at about the same time as the customer.
- The cohort customers have similar initial start characteristics to the customer.
- The cohort customers are active at the tenure when the event occurred to the customer.
- The cohort customers do not experience the event.

The cohort is a comparison group that can be used to understand survival after the event. The same customer can appear in multiple cohorts, so long as the customer meets the criteria for each one.

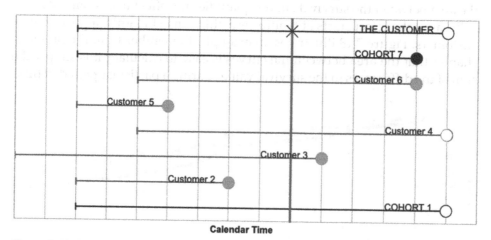

Figure 7-19: A customer has a cohort defined by initial characteristics and when the event occurred. In this chart, THE CUSTOMER experiences an event at some time. Customers 1 and 7 are in the cohort because they started at the same time and survived to the event time. The other customers fail one or both of these conditions.

The approach starts by calculating the survival for customers who experience the event using only the tenure *after* the event date. That is, the event date becomes tenure zero in the tenure timeframe. Then, the survival of each cohort is calculated, after the event date that defines the cohort. This provides a comparison for the customer that defined the cohort. These cohort survivals are averaged into a single survival curve, and compared to the survival of customers who experience the event.

For the customers that succumb to the event, calculating the survival after the event requires knowing the event date, available in column named something like EVENT_DATE (even though this is not available in the data). The survival after the event is the survival calculation, where the start date is fast-forwarded to the event date, and the tenure is measured only after the event:

```
SELECT EventTenure, COUNT(*) as pop, SUM(isstop) as stopped
FROM (SELECT DATEDIFF(day, StartDate, EventDate) as EventTenure,
             (CASE WHEN StopType IS NULL THEN 0 ELSE 1 END) as isstop
      FROM Subscribers
      WHERE EventDate IS NOT NULL) s
GROUP BY EventTenure
ORDER BY EventTenure
```

This query generates the information needed for the calculation of survival after the event for the customers who experience the event. The survival can then be calculated in either Excel or SQL.

The challenge is to get the survival for a cohort of customers similar to the original customer. For any given customer, the cohort survival could be defined by:

```
SELECT cohort.Tenure - ev.EventTenure,
       COUNT(*) as pop,
       SUM(CASE WHEN cohort.StopType IS NOT NULL THEN 1 ELSE 0
           END) as isstop
FROM (SELECT s.*,
             DATEDIFF(day, StartDate, EventDate) as EventTenure
      FROM Subscribers
      WHERE SubscriberId = <event subscriber id>) ev JOIN
     (SELECT *
      FROM Subscribers
      WHERE EventDate IS NUL
     ) cohort
     ON cohort.StartDate = ev.StartDate AND
        cohort.Market = ev.Market AND
        cohort.Channel = ev.Channel AND
        cohort.Tenure >= ev.EventTenure
GROUP BY EventTenure
ORDER BY EventTenure
```

In this case, the cohort is defined as customers who started on the same date, in the same market, and did not have the event. The actual survival values can then be calculated in Excel or by using the cumulative sum functions in SQL. The challenge is doing this for all cohorts and averaging the curves. It is tempting to modify the preceding query so the first subquery looks like:

```
FROM (SELECT s.*,
             DATEDIFF(day, StartDate, EventDate) as tenure_at_event
      FROM Subscribers s
      WHERE EventDate IS NOT NULL) s
```

However, this is incorrect because it combines all members of all cohorts into one big pool of customers, and then calculates the survival of the pool. Because cohorts have different sizes, the larger cohorts would dominate this calculation. We want each customer's cohort to have a weight of one, regardless of its size.

One solution is to determine the size of the cohort and then weight everything appropriately. Once the weight is determined, the counts `pop` and `isstop` are just multiplied by the weight. The following query includes the weight:

```
SELECT cohort.Tenure - ev.EventTenure,
       SUM(weight) as pop,
       SUM(CASE WHEN cohort.StopType IS NOT NULL THEN weight ELSE 0
            END) as isstop
FROM (SELECT ev.SubscriberId, EventTenure,
             COUNT(*) as cohort_size, 1.0 / COUNT(*) as weight
      FROM (SELECT s.*,
                   DATEDIFF(day, StartDate, EventDate) as EventTenure
            FROM Subscribers s
            WHERE EventDate IS NOT NULL) ev JOIN
           (SELECT s.*
            FROM Subscribers s
            WHERE EventTenure IS NULL) cohort
           ON cohort.StartDate = ev.StartDate AND
              cohort.Market = ev.Market AND
              cohort.Channel = ev.Channel AND
              cohort.Tenure >= ev.EventTenure
      GROUP BY ev.SubscriberId, ev.EventTenure
     ) ev JOIN
     (SELECT s.*
      FROM Subscribers s
      WHERE EventDate IS NULL) cohort
     ON cohort.StartDate = ev.StartDate AND
        cohort.Market = ev.Market AND
        cohort.Channel = ev.Channel AND
        cohort.Tenure >= ev.EventTenure
GROUP BY EventTenure
ORDER BY EventTenure
```

Survival can then be calculated using the weighted counts. The only subtlety is that population counts and stop counts are now decimal numbers rather than integers.

This approach can be quite useful, particularly for creating charts showing the difference between the before and after groups. The query can be slow because it is a non-equijoin on a large table. Although the join looks like an equijoin, it isn't because the join keys are not unique in the table. There are some ways to improve performance. If the size of the group that experiences the event is small, the calculation should be feasible in either Excel or SQL. Another alternative is to calculate the size of the cohort using SQL window functions instead of subqueries. Another alternative would be to choose a random member from each cohort and use that for the survival calculation.

A different approach is to estimate the effect of a time-varying covariate without resorting to cohorts or to sophisticated statistical software. The next section explains this approach.

Direct Estimation of Event Effect

This section explains stratifying survival based on whether or not a time-dependent event has occurred. This method generates two separate survival curves; one for survival without the event and the other for survival with the event. These curves can be used to qualitatively describe what happens to customers before and after the event; or they can be used to quantitatively measure differences between the groups.

Approach to the Calculation

To illustrate this, let's assume that something happens on 2005-06-01, such as a price increase. This is an arbitrary date used as an example; the technique works not only for a single date but also for different dates for each customer. Customers who start before this date are in the "before" group until they reach 2005-06-01. Customers who start after this date are in the "after" group for their entire tenure. *What are the survival and hazard probabilities for the "before" and "after" groups?*

The key to answering this question is calculating unbiased hazards for customers in the two groups. This is basically an application of time windows, but the survival for both groups is calculated at the same time.

Customers who start and stop before the event date are only in the "before" population at risk. Other customers who start before the event remain in the "before" population at risk until the event date. For larger tenures, they contribute to the "after" population at risk. And customers who start after the event date only contribute to the "after" population at risk.

Calculating the population at risk for the "after" group is a bit more complicated. Customers who start on or after the event date enter the "after" population at risk from tenure zero; they leave when they are censored or stop. The number of such customers at a given tenure is simply the population of such customers whose tenure is greater than or equal to the given tenure.

Customers who start before the event date enter the "after" population at risk on their tenure as of the event date. They remain at risk until they stop or are censored. The size of this group is calculated using the following rules:

- The population at risk at tenure t is the population at risk at tenure $t-1$.

- Plus the customers who started before the event date who passed the event date at tenure t.

- Minus the customers who started before the event date, who passed the event date, and who stopped or were censored at tenure t.

Unlike many of the earlier examples, the population at risk for this problem is calculated using a forward summation, rather than a backward summation.

Time-Dependent Covariate Survival Using SQL and Excel

Answering this question in SQL requires adding some information onto each subscriber record:

- Did the subscriber start before 2005-01-01?

- Did the subscriber stop before 2005-01-01?

- What was the subscriber's tenure on 2005-01-01, if the customer was still active?

These are the key items of information needed to calculate the population at risk.

This information is then transformed into summaries for each tenure:

- The number of subscribers who started at that tenure in the "before" population (actually, this is only relevant for tenure zero because time windows are not being used to handle left trunction).

- The number of subscribers who started at that tenure in the "after" group (zero for customers who start on or after 2005-01-01; larger for those who pass that date as active subscribers).

- The number of subscribers who stop, in the "before" and "after" groups, at each tenure.

- The number of customers who "graduate" from the "before" group to the "after" group.

These, in turn, are aggregations of the key items of information.

The following SQL gathers this information together. The CTE calculates some basic indicator flags, which are then aggregated in the SELECT:

```
WITH s AS (
    SELECT Tenure,
           (CASE WHEN StartDate >= '2005 -06 -01' THEN 0
                 ELSE DATEDIFF(day, StartDate, '2005-06-01')
            END) as AftEntryTenure,
           (CASE WHEN StopDate IS NOT NULL THEN 1 ELSE 0
            END) as IsStopped,
           (CASE WHEN StartDate < '2005-06-01' THEN 1 ELSE 0
            END) as IsBeforeStart,
           (CASE WHEN StopDate IS NULL OR StopDate >= '2005 -06 -01'
                 THEN 1 ELSE 0 END) as IsAfterStop
    FROM (SELECT s.*,
                 (CASE WHEN Market = 'Smallville'
                       THEN CAST('2004-10-27' as DATE)
                       ELSE '2004-01-01' END) as LeftTruncationDate
          FROM Subscribers s
         ) s
    WHERE tenure >= 0 AND StartDate >= LeftTruncationDate
    )
SELECT Tenure, SUM(BefPop) as BefPop, SUM(BefStop) as BefStop,
       SUM(BefLeave) as BefLeave, SUM(AftPop) as AftPop,
       SUM(AftStop) as AftStop, SUM(AftLeave) as AftLeave
FROM ((SELECT AftEntryTenure as Tenure, 0 as BefPop, 0 as BefStop,
              SUM(IsBeforeStart) as BefLeave,
              COUNT(*) as AftPop, 0 as AftStop, 0 as AftLeave
       FROM s
       WHERE Tenure >= AftEntryTenure
       GROUP BY AftEntryTenure
      ) UNION ALL
      (SELECT Tenure, 0, SUM(IsStopped * (1 - IsAfterStop)) as BefStop,
              0, 0 as AftPop, SUM(IsStopped * IsAfterStop) as AftStop,
              SUM(IsAfterStop * (1 - IsStopped)) as AftLeave
       FROM s
       GROUP BY Tenure
      ) UNION ALL
      (SELECT 0, COUNT(*) as befPop, 0.0, 0.0, 0.0, 0.0, 0.0
       FROM s
       WHERE IsBeforeStart = 1
      )) s
GROUP BY Tenure
ORDER BY Tenure
```

This query uses arithmetic on the indicator flags to express logic. For instance, the expression SUM(IsAfterStop * (1 - IsStopped)) is logically equivalent to SUM(CASE WHEN IsStopped = 0 AND IsAfterStop = 1 THEN 1 ELSE 0 END). Using arithmetic is shorter (and easier to type) and often easier to read and maintain.

			FROM SQL					Before Cum	After Cum	CALCULATED IN EXCEL			
	Tenure	BefPop	BefStop	BefLeave	AftPop	AftStop	AftLeave	Before Cum	After Cum	h-before	h-after	S-before	S-after
46	0	1515567	292	0	1428296	216	1875	=O46+IF($C46>0, K45-E45-F45, 0)	=G46+IF($C46>0, L45-H45-I45,0)	=IF(K46=0,NA(),E46/K46)	=IF(L46=0,NA(),H46/L46)	=IF($C46=0, 1, O45*(1-M45))	=IF($C46=0, 1, P45*(1-N45))
47	1	0	7559	2457	2457	9747	1048	=O47+IF($C47>0, K46-E46-F46, 0)	=G47+IF($C47>0, L46-H46-I46,0)	=IF(K47=0,NA(),E47/K47)	=IF(L47=0,NA(),H47/L47)	=IF($C47=0, 1, O46*(1-M46))	=IF($C47=0, 1, P46*(1-N46))
48	2	0	5878	3799	3799	9213	1639	=O48+IF($C48>0, K47-E47-F47, 0)	=G48+IF($C48>0, L47-H47-I47,0)	=IF(K48=0,NA(),E48/K48)	=IF(L48=0,NA(),H48/L48)	=IF($C48=0, 1, O47*(1-M47))	=IF($C48=0, 1, P47*(1-N47))
49	3	0	5113	3348	3348	6233	1937	=O49+IF($C49>0, K48-E48-F48, 0)	=G49+IF($C49>0, L48-H48-I48,0)	=IF(K49=0,NA(),E49/K49)	=IF(L49=0,NA(),H49/L49)	=IF($C49=0, 1, O48*(1-M48))	=IF($C49=0, 1, P48*(1-N48))
50	4	0	4338	3494	3494	5160	44	=O50+IF($C50>0, K49-E49-F49, 0)	=G50+IF($C50>0, L49-H49-I49,0)	=IF(K50=0,NA(),E50/K50)	=IF(L50=0,NA(),H50/L50)	=IF($C50=0, 1, O49*(1-M49))	=IF($C50=0, 1, P49*(1-N49))
51	5	0	4384	3623	3623	4765	2504	=O51+IF($C51>0, K50-E50-F50, 0)	=G51+IF($C51>0, L50-H50-I50,0)	=IF(K51=0,NA(),E51/K51)	=IF(L51=0,NA(),H51/L51)	=IF($C51=0, 1, O50*(1-M50))	=IF($C51=0, 1, P50*(1-N50))
52	6	0	4834	2343	2343	4572	3240	=O52+IF($C52>0, K51-E51-F51, 0)	=G52+IF($C52>0, L51-H51-I51,0)	=IF(K52=0,NA(),E52/K52)	=IF(L52=0,NA(),H52/L52)	=IF($C52=0, 1, O51*(1-M51))	=IF($C52=0, 1, P51*(1-N51))
53	7	0	5483	1866	1866	4812	3168	=O53+IF($C53>0, K52-E52-F52, 0)	=G53+IF($C53>0, L52-H52-I52,0)	=IF(K53=0,NA(),E53/K53)	=IF(L53=0,NA(),H53/L53)	=IF($C53=0, 1, O52*(1-M52))	=IF($C53=0, 1, P52*(1-N52))
54	8	0	5188	2602	2602	4385	2302	=O54+IF($C54>0, K53-E53-F53, 0)	=G54+IF($C54>0, L53-H53-I53,0)	=IF(K54=0,NA(),E54/K54)	=IF(L54=0,NA(),H54/L54)	=IF($C54=0, 1, O53*(1-M53))	=IF($C54=0, 1, P53*(1-N53))
55	9	0	5224	3142	3142	4221	2618	=O55+IF($C55>0, K54-E54-F54, 0)	=G55+IF($C55>0, L54-H54-I54,0)	=IF(K55=0,NA(),E55/K55)	=IF(L55=0,NA(),H55/L55)	=IF($C55=0, 1, O54*(1-M54))	=IF($C55=0, 1, P54*(1-N54))
56	10	0	5082	3427	3427	4395	2540	=O56+IF($C56>0, K55-E55-F55, 0)	=G56+IF($C56>0, L55-H55-I55,0)	=IF(K56=0,NA(),E56/K56)	=IF(L56=0,NA(),H56/L56)	=IF(L56=0,NA(),H56/L56)	=IF($C56=0, 1, O55*(1-M55))	=IF($C56=0, 1, P56*(1-N55))

Figure 7-20: This spreadsheet calculates the survival curves based on whether an event occurred or did not occur during the customer lifetime.

Figure 7-20 shows a screen shot of the Excel spreadsheet that implements the calculations. This figure shows the population at risk calculations for each of the three groups. Calculating the hazards is just a matter of dividing the population at risk by the appropriate stops. Survival is calculated from the hazards.

This approach to handling an event date combines two ideas already discussed. The survival for the "before" group uses forced censoring. The censor date is the event date, and only stops before the event date are counted.

The "after" group (combining both the customers who start before and survive to the event date and those who start after) uses time windows to define the values. In this case, the event date becomes the left truncation date for the group.

This example uses a single calendar date as the event date; a fixed date is not a requirement. The date could be defined on a customer-by-customer basis, requiring only minor modifications to the queries.

Doing the Calculation in SQL

This calculation in SQL uses cumulative sums:

```
WITH s AS (
    SELECT Tenure,
           (CASE WHEN StartDate >= '2005-06-01' THEN 0
                 ELSE DATEDIFF(day, StartDate, '2005-06-01')
            END) as AftEntryTenure,
           (CASE WHEN StopDate IS NOT NULL THEN 1 ELSE 0
            END) as IsStopped,
           (CASE WHEN StartDate < '2005-06-01' THEN 1 ELSE 0
            END) as IsBeforeStart,
           (CASE WHEN StopDate IS NULL OR StopDate >= '2005-06-01'
                 THEN 1 ELSE 0 END) as IsAfterStop
    FROM (SELECT s.*,
                 (CASE WHEN Market = 'Smallville'
                       THEN CAST('2004-10-27' as DATE)
                       ELSE '2004-01-01' END) as LeftTruncationDate
          FROM Subscribers s
         ) s
    WHERE tenure >= 0 AND StartDate >= LeftTruncationDate
```

```
        ),
    st as (
      SELECT Tenure, SUM(BefPop) as BefPop, SUM(BefStop) as BefStop,
             SUM(BefLeave) as BefLeave, SUM(AftPop) as AftPop,
             SUM(AftStop) as AftStop, SUM(AftLeave) as AftLeave
      FROM ((SELECT AftEntryTenure as Tenure, 0.0 as BefPop, 0.0 as BefStop,
                   SUM(IsBeforeStart) as BefLeave,
                   COUNT(*) as AftPop, 0.0 as AftStop, 0.0 as AftLeave
             FROM s
             WHERE Tenure >= AftEntryTenure
             GROUP BY AftEntryTenure
            ) UNION ALL
            (SELECT Tenure, 0,
                   SUM(IsStopped * (1 - IsAfterStop)) as BefStop, 0,
                   0 as AftPop, SUM(IsStopped * IsAfterStop) as AftStop,
                   SUM(IsAfterStop * (1 - IsStopped)) as AftLeave
             FROM s
             GROUP BY Tenure
            ) UNION ALL
            (SELECT 0, COUNT(*) as befPop, 0, 0, 0, 0, 0
             FROM s
             WHERE IsBeforeStart = 1
            )) s
      GROUP BY Tenure
     )
  SELECT Tenure,
         (SUM(BefPop - BefLeave - BefStop) OVER (ORDER BY Tenure)  +
          BefStop) as BefPop,
         BefStop,
         (BefStop / NULLIF(SUM(BefPop- BefLeave - BefStop) OVER
                             (ORDER BY Tenure) + BefStop, 0)) as Befh,
         (SUM(AftPop - AftLeave - AftStop) OVER (ORDER BY Tenure) +
          AftLeave + AftStop) as AftPop,
         AftStop,
         (AftStop / NULLIF(SUM(AftPop - AftLeave - AftStop) OVER
                            (ORDER BY Tenure) +
                           AftLeave + AftStop, 0)) as Afth
  FROM st
  ORDER BY Tenure;
```

The basic structure of this query follows the structure of the previous query. The CTE st represents the output of that query. NULLIF() prevents divide-by-zero errors.

There is one nuance to the query. The basic logic for calculating the population at a given tenure is the following: It is the population at the previous tenure plus the incremental population at this tenure, minus the customers who stopped at the previous tenure. The latter is the customers who leave (because they are censored) and those who stop.

The calculation for `AftPop` follows this logic. The expression `SUM(AftPop - AftLeave - AftStop)` calculates the cumulative sum up to the current tenure. Hence, this expression over counts the stops, and `AftLeave` and `AftStop` must be added back in.

The calculation for `BefPop` only adds in `BefStop`, but not `AftLeave`. `BefLeave` is already offset by one because it is the first tenure where the customer is in the "after" group. The reason is convenience. The middle subquery (where these values are calculated) aggregates by `Tenure`. This is correct for the after variables, but it should really be `Tenure - 1` for the before variables because customers leave the "before" group on the day before they enter the "after" group. However, it is easy enough to adjust the calculation in the next step.

Lessons Learned

The previous chapter introduced survival analysis and the calculation of hazard and survival probabilities using SQL and Excel. This chapter extends these ideas, showing ways to calculate survival in other situations and to measure the effects of covariates on survival.

The chapter starts by showing how to understand the effects on survival of variables known at the beginning of the customer relationship. The effects might change over time, even though the variables remain constant during each customer's lifetime. Hazard ratios capture the effects for categorical variables by taking the ratio of the hazards. For numeric variables, the right measure is the average of a numeric variable at different points in the survival curve for active and stopped customers.

One of the biggest challenges in using survival analysis is calculating unbiased hazard probabilities. This is particularly challenging when the data is left truncated—that is, when customers who stopped before some date are not included in the database. The solution to left truncation is the use of time windows. Time windows are a powerful tool that goes beyond solving left truncation. They make it possible to calculate unbiased hazard probabilities based on stops during a particular period of time.

The chapter continues by looking at what happens at the end of the customer lifetime using competing risks. The survival analysis discussion assumes that all customers who leave are equal. However, why customers leave can also be important. Competing risks allows us to calculate how many customers are still active, and how many have left due to voluntary churn, involuntary churn, and migration.

Time-dependent covariates occur during a customer's lifetime, rather than at the beginning or end. Calculating before and after hazard for an event combines forced right censoring (discussed in the previous chapter) with time windows.

The next chapter moves to a related topic, the subject of recurrent events. Unlike survival analysis so far, though, recurrent events happen more than once, a twist that we haven't yet considered.

Customer Purchases and Other Repeated Events

Subscription-type customer relationships have well-defined starts and stops. This chapter moves from these types of relationships to those defined by multiple events that take place over time, such as purchases and website visits, donations and handset upgrades. Such relationships do not necessarily have a definite end, because any particular event could be the customer's last, or it could be just another in a long series of events.

Repeated events require correctly assigning the same customer to events that happen at different times and perhaps through different channels. Sometimes we are lucky and customers identify themselves, perhaps by using an account. Identification of individuals can still be challenging. Consider the example of Amazon.com and a family account. The purchase behavior—and resulting recommendations—might combine a teenage daughter's music preferences with her mother's technical purchases with a pre-teen son's choice of games.

Disambiguating individuals within one account poses one problem; identifying the same customer over time is another. When no account is available, fancy algorithms might match customers to transactions using name matching and address matching, credit card numbers, email address, and browser cookies and other information. This chapter looks at how SQL can help facilitate building and evaluating such techniques.

Sometimes, events occur so frequently that they actually represent subscription-like behaviors. For instance, prescription data consists of drug purchases or prescriptions. Multiple sequential prescriptions for a given customers are combined into episodes of treatment. Websites, such as Facebook and eBay, have a similar conundrum. Users typically visit often; however, they do not signal the end of their relationship by politely closing their accounts. They stop visiting, emailing, bidding, or offering. At the other extreme are rare events. Automobile manufacturers trying to understand long-term customer relationships must deal with purchase intervals that stretch into multiple years.

This chapter focuses on retail purchase patterns that are in-between—not too frequent and not too rare. In addition to being a common example of repeated events, these purchases provide a good foundation for understanding such data. Because of this focus on retail data, the examples in this chapter use the purchases dataset exclusively.

The traditional method for understanding retail purchasing behaviors focuses on three specific dimensions: recency, frequency, and monetary. RFM analysis is a good background for understanding customers and some of their behaviors over time. As important as it is, RFM leaves out many other dimensions of customer behavior.

Customer behaviors change over time, and tracking and measuring these changes is important. One approach is to compare the recent behaviors to earlier behaviors; another is to fit a trend line to each customer's interactions. Survival analysis is yet another alternative for addressing a critical question: *how long until the next interaction?* The answer depends on the particular customer and that customer's past behavior. If too much time has elapsed, perhaps it is time to start worrying about how to get the customer back. Before worrying about getting the customer back, let's start at the beginning: identifying customers on different transactions.

Identifying Customers

Identifying transactions as belonging to the same customer is challenging, both for retail customers (individuals and households) and for business customers. Even when customers have an ongoing relationship, such as a loyalty card, they may not always use their identification number. This section discusses the definition of "customer" and how customers are represented in data. The next section looks at other types of data, such as addresses.

Who Is the Customer?

The transactions in the purchases dataset are orders. The database has several ways to tie transactions together over time. Each order has OrderId, which leads to a CustomerId and a HouseholdId. The following query provides the counts of orders, customers, and households:

```
SELECT COUNT(*) as numorders, COUNT(DISTINCT c.CustomerId) as numcusts,
       COUNT(DISTINCT c.HouseholdId) as numhh
FROM Orders o LEFT OUTER JOIN
     Customers c
     ON o.CustomerId = c.CustomerId
```

This query returns 192,983 orders for 189,559 customers comprising 156,258 households. So, there are about 1.02 orders per customer and about 1.2 customers per household. This data has some examples of repeating customers, but not very many.

A slightly different way to answer the same question, counts the number of households, customers, and orders using subqueries:

```
SELECT numorders, numcusts, numhh
FROM (SELECT COUNT(*) as numorders FROM Orders) o CROSS JOIN
     (SELECT COUNT(*) as numcusts, COUNT(DISTINCT HouseholdId) as numhh
      FROM Customers) c
```

The CROSS JOIN creates all combinations of rows from two tables (or subqueries). The CROSS JOIN is sometimes useful when working with very small tables, such as the two one-row subqueries in this example.

The two approaches are quite similar but they could yield different results. The first counts CustomerIds and HouseholdIds that have orders. The second counts everything in the database, even those without orders. The results are the same on this data.

> **TIP** Even a seemingly simple question such as "how many customers are there?" can have different answers depending on specifics: "How many customers have placed an order?" and "how many households are in the database?" may have very different answers.

The purchases data already has the customer and household columns assigned. The database intentionally does not contain identifying information (such as last name, address, telephone number, or email address), but it does contain gender and first name.

How Many?

How many customers are in a household? This is a simple histogram question on Customers:

```
SELECT numinhousehold, COUNT(*) as numhh,
       MIN(HouseholdId), MAX(HouseholdId)
FROM (SELECT HouseholdId, COUNT(*) as numinhousehold
      FROM Customers c
      GROUP BY HouseholdId
```

```
    ) h
GROUP BY numinhousehold
ORDER BY numinhousehold
```

The results in Table 8-1 emphasize that most households have only one customer. At the other extreme, two have over 100 customers each. Such large households suggest an anomaly in the house-holding algorithm. In fact, in this dataset, business customers from the same business are grouped into a single household. Whether or not this is correct depends on how the data is used.

Table 8-1: Histogram of Household Sizes

ACCOUNTS IN HOUSEHOLD	NUMBER OF HOUSEHOLDS	CUMULATIVE NUMBER	CUMULATIVE PERCENT
1	134,293	134,293	85.9%
2	16,039	150,332	96.2%
3	3,677	154,009	98.6%
4	1,221	155,230	99.3%
5	523	155,753	99.7%
6	244	155,997	99.8%
7	110	156,107	99.9%
8	63	156,170	99.9%
9	28	156,198	100.0%
10	18	156,216	100.0%
11	9	156,225	100.0%
12	14	156,239	100.0%
13	4	156,243	100.0%
14	4	156,247	100.0%
16	2	156,249	100.0%
17	2	156,251	100.0%
21	2	156,253	100.0%
24	1	156,254	100.0%
28	1	156,255	100.0%
38	1	156,256	100.0%
169	1	156,257	100.0%
746	1	156,258	100.0%

A related question is the average size of a household. It is tempting to use the previous query as a subquery for this calculation. A much simpler query does the same calculation:

```
SELECT COUNT(*) * 1.0 / COUNT(DISTINCT HouseholdId)
FROM Customers c
```

This query divides two numbers. The first is the number of customers. The second is the number of households. (The *1.0 prevents integer division.) The answer is 1.21, consistent with the fact that most households have only one customer.

How Many Genders in a Household?

We might expect that customers have only two genders, but one never knows what the values are until one looks at the data:

```
SELECT Gender, COUNT(*) as numcusts, MIN(CustomerId), MAX(CustomerId)
FROM Customers
GROUP BY Gender
ORDER BY numcusts DESC
```

Table 8-2 shows the results of this query.

Table 8-2: Genders and Their Frequencies

GENDER	FREQUENCY	PROPORTION
M	96,481	50.9%
F	76,874	40.6%
	16,204	8.5%

TIP Looking at the data is the only way to see what values really are in a column; the answer is a histogram created using GROUP BY.

These results include the two expected genders, male and female. There is also a third value that looks blank. Blanks in output are ambiguous. The column value could be NULL, blank, or, perhaps, a string containing a space, or some other unorthodox value (some database interfaces return NULL values as blank, although SQL Server Management Studio—the interface to Microsoft SQL Server—uses the string "NULL").

The following variation on the query provides more clarity:

```
SELECT (CASE WHEN Gender IS NULL THEN 'NULL'
             WHEN Gender = '' THEN 'EMPTY'
             WHEN Gender = ' ' THEN 'SPACE'
             ELSE Gender END) as gender, COUNT(*) as numcusts
```

```
FROM Customers
GROUP BY Gender
ORDER BY numcusts DESC
```

For further refinement, the function ASCII() returns the actual numeric value of any character. The results show that the third gender is actually the empty string as opposed to the other possibilities.

This query has an interesting feature; the GROUP BY expression differs from the SELECT expression. Consider the following query, which classifies the genders as "GOOD" and "BAD." In the first version, the GROUP BY clause and the SELECT use the same expression:

```
SELECT (CASE WHEN Gender IN ('M', 'F') THEN 'GOOD' ELSE 'BAD' END) as g,
       COUNT(*) as numcusts
FROM Customers
GROUP BY (CASE WHEN Gender IN ('M', 'F') THEN 'GOOD' ELSE 'BAD' END)
```

A slight variation uses only the GENDER variable in the GROUP BY clause:

```
SELECT (CASE WHEN Gender IN ('M', 'F') THEN 'GOOD' ELSE 'BAD' END) as g,
       COUNT(*) as numcusts
FROM Customers
GROUP BY Gender
```

The first version returns two rows, one for "GOOD" and one for "BAD." The second returns three rows, two "GOOD" and one "BAD"; the two "GOOD" rows are for males and females. Figure 8-1 shows the dataflow diagrams corresponding to each of these queries. The difference is whether the CASE statement is calculated before or after the aggregation. The aggregation determines the number of rows in the result set.

The only difference is two or three rows for this example. In some situations the difference can be much more significant. For instance, the SELECT statement might assign values into ranges. If the corresponding GROUP BY does not have the same expression, the aggregation might not reduce the number of rows.

> **TIP** When using an expression in the SELECT statement of an aggregation query, be careful to think about whether the GROUP BY should contain the full expression or just the variable. In most cases, the full expression is the correct approach.

The relationship between genders and households leads to the next question: *How many households have one gender, two genders, and three genders?* This question does not require knowing the specific genders, just how many are in the household. A household with only one member has only one gender, so household size and the number of genders are related to each other. *For each household size (by number of customers), how many households have one gender, two genders, and three genders?*

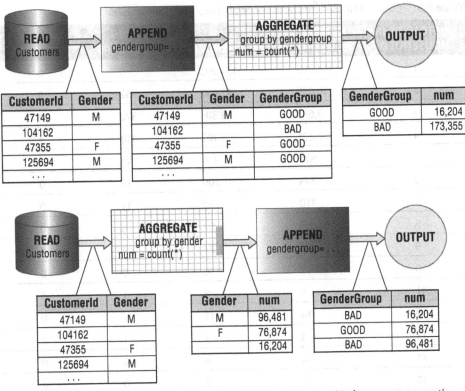

Figure 8-1: These dataflow diagrams show the difference in processing between aggregating first and then calculating an expression versus aggregating on the calculated value.

```
SELECT numcustomers, COUNT(*) as numhh,
       SUM(CASE WHEN numgenders = 1 THEN 1 ELSE 0 END) as gen1,
       SUM(CASE WHEN numgenders = 2 THEN 1 ELSE 0 END) as gen2,
       SUM(CASE WHEN numgenders = 3 THEN 1 ELSE 0 END) as gen3
FROM (SELECT HouseholdId, COUNT(*) as numcustomers,
             COUNT(DISTINCT Gender) as numgenders
      FROM Customers c
      GROUP BY HouseholdId) hh
GROUP BY numcustomers
ORDER BY numcustomers
```

This query uses conditional aggregation to calculate the gender counts in columns, rather than having a separate row for each customer and gender.

The results in Table 8-3 look suspicious. One would not expect 94.1% of households with two people to have only one gender. Further, in almost all these cases, the households consist of people with the same first name. The logical conclusion is that the identification of individuals does not work well. One customer is being assigned multiple values of CustomerId. For this reason, and for others discussed later in this chapter, the HouseholdId is preferable for identifying customers over time.

Table 8-3: Count of Households by Number of Customers and Genders

CUSTOMERS IN HOUSEHOLD	NUMBER OF HOUSEHOLDS	1 GENDER	2 GENDERS	3 GENDERS
1	134,293	134,293	0	0
2	16,039	15,087	952	0
3	3,677	3,305	370	2
4	1,221	1,102	118	1
5	523	478	43	2
6	244	209	35	0
7	110	99	11	0
8	63	57	6	0
9	28	24	4	0
10	18	16	2	0
11	9	8	1	0
12	14	13	1	0
13	4	3	1	0
14	4	4	0	0
16	2	2	0	0
17	2	2	0	0
21	2	2	0	0
24	1	1	0	0
28	1	1	0	0
38	1	0	0	1
169	1	1	0	0
746	1	0	0	1

Investigating First Names

Something is awry when many households consist of multiple customers having the same first name. These households probably have one individual assigned multiple CustomerIds. To investigate this, let's ask the question: *How many households consist of "different" customers that have the same first name and the same gender?*

Two approaches to answering this question are presented here. One way is to count the number of values of Gender and of Firstname in each household and then count the number of households that have one of each:

```
SELECT COUNT(*) as numhh,
       SUM(CASE WHEN numgenders = 1 AND numfirstnames = 1 THEN 1 ELSE 0
           END) as allsame
FROM (SELECT HouseholdId, COUNT(*) as numcustomers,
             COUNT(DISTINCT Gender) as numgenders,
             COUNT(DISTINCT Firstname) as numfirstnames
      FROM Customers c
      GROUP BY HouseholdId) hh
WHERE numcustomers > 1
```

The second approach compares the minimum and maximum values of the two columns. When these are the same, the household has only one value:

```
SELECT COUNT(*) as numhh,
       SUM(CASE WHEN minfname = maxfname AND mingender = maxgender
               THEN 1 ELSE 0 END) as allsame
FROM (SELECT HouseholdId, COUNT(*) as numcustomers,
             MIN(Firstname) as minfname, MAX(Firstname) as maxfname,
             MIN(Gender) as mingender, MAX(Gender) as maxgender
      FROM Customers c
      GROUP BY HouseholdId) hh
WHERE numcustomers > 1
```

Table 8-4 shows the results broken out by the number of customers in the household (by adding numcustomers to the SELECT clause and replacing the WHERE clause with GROUP BY numcustomers). It suggests that many households with multiple customers seem to consist of one individual assigned multiple customer IDs.

Table 8-4: Customers with Same Identifying Information in Household

NUMBER OF CUSTOMERS	NUMBER OF HOUSEHOLDS	SAME GENDER AND FIRST NAME
1	134,293	134,293
2	16,039	14,908
3	3,677	3,239
4	1,221	1,078
5	523	463
6	244	202
7	110	97
8	63	52
9	28	24
10	18	14

continues

Table 8-4 (*continued*)

NUMBER OF CUSTOMERS	NUMBER OF HOUSEHOLDS	SAME GENDER AND FIRST NAME
11	9	8
12	14	13
13	4	3
14	4	4
16	2	2
17	2	2
21	2	2
24	1	1
28	1	1
38	1	0
169	1	0
746	1	0

These queries may not be doing exactly what we expect when the columns have NULL values. If Firstname only contains NULL values for a given household, COUNT(DISTINCT) returns zero, rather than one. So, the first query does not count that household even though all values are identical. The second query produces the same result, but for a different reason: The minimum and maximum values are both NULL and these fail the equality test.

WARNING Using standard SQL, NULL values tend not to be counted when looking at the number of values a column takes on. Use an expression such as COALESCE(<column>, '<NULL>') to count all values including NULLs.

Similarly, a household consisting of customers with a mixture of NULL and one non-NULL value gets counted as having only one customer. This is because COUNT(DISTINCT) counts the non-NULL values, and MIN() and MAX() ignore NULL values. To count NULL values separately, use the COALESCE() function to assign another value:

```
COALESCE(Firstname, '<NULL>')
```

This conversion then treats NULL as any other value; be careful that the second argument to COALESCE() is not a value already in the table. Alternatively, count them explicitly by adding an expression such as:

```
MAX(CASE WHEN Firstname IS NULL THEN 1 ELSE 0 END)
```

Counts of first names are interesting, but examples of first names are even better. *What are some examples of first names from each household where all members have the same genders?*

```
SELECT HouseholdId, MIN(Firstname), MAX(Firstname)
FROM Customers c
GROUP BY HouseholdId
HAVING MIN(Firstname) <> MAX(Firstname) AND MIN(Gender) = MAX(Gender)
```

This query selects households that have multiple names all of the same gender. By using the HAVING clause, no subqueries or joins are needed. The MIN() and MAX() functions provide example values.

As with the previous query, households with NULL first names are not included in the results. To include them, the HAVING clause could be modified using the COALESCE() function:

```
HAVING (MIN(COALESCE(firstname, '<NULL>')) <>
        MAX(COALESCE(firstname, '<NULL>'))) AND. . .
```

This query returns 301 rows; the following are examples of customer names that appear in the same household:

- "T." and "THOMAS"
- "ELIAZBETH" and "ELIZABETH"
- "JEFF" and "JEFFREY"
- "MARGARET" and "MEG"

These four examples are probably referring to the same individual, but with variations on the name caused by:

- Use of an initial rather than the full name
- Shortened version of a name
- Misspellings
- Nicknames

Such are a few of the complications in matching customers using names.

There are some ways to mitigate this problem. When a household contains a name that is an initial of another name, ignore the initial. Or, when the first part of one name exactly matches another name, ignore the shorter one. These are reasonable rules for identifying essentially the same names on different records.

The rules are easy to express. However, implementing them in SQL is more challenging. The idea behind the SQL implementation is to introduce a new column for each name, called altfirstname, which is the full form of the name gleaned from other names on the household. Calculating altfirstname requires a self-join on the HouseholdId because every name in a household has to be compared to every other name in the household:

```
SELECT cl.HouseholdId, cl.CustomerId, cl.Firstname, cl.Gender,
       MAX(CASE WHEN LEN(cl.Firstname) >= LEN(c2.Firstname) THEN NULL
                WHEN LEFT(cl.Firstname, 1) = LEFT(c2.Firstname, 1) AND
                     SUBSTRING(cl.Firstname, 2, 1) = '.' AND
                     LEN(cl.Firstname) = 2
                THEN c2.Firstname
                WHEN c2.Firstname LIKE cl.Firstname + '%'
                THEN c2.Firstname
                ELSE NULL END) as altfirstname
FROM Customers cl JOIN Customers c2 ON cl.HouseholdId = c2.HouseholdId
GROUP BY cl.HouseholdId, cl.CustomerId, cl.Firstname, cl.Gender
```

This query implements the first two rules: the ones for the initial and for the shortened version of names. Adding rules for misspellings and nicknames is more difficult because these need a lookup table to rectify the spellings.

These rules highlight issues about matching names and other short text data. Values are often subject to misspellings and interpretations (such as whether "T." is for "Thomas" or "Theodore" or "Tiffany"). SQL string and text-processing functions are quite rudimentary. However, combined with SQL's data processing capability and the CASE statement, it is possible to use SQL to make some sense out of such data. The aside "Levenshtein Distance" explains another method for measuring the similar of strings, one that is often useful for names.

Other Customer Information

A database with identified customers would normally also have full name, address, and probably other identifying information such as telephone numbers, email addresses, browser cookies, and social security numbers. None of these are ideal for matching customers over time, because customers move and change names. In the United States, even social security numbers may not be unique due to issues such as employment fraud. This section discusses these types of data.

First and Last Names

Some names, such as James and Gordon, George and John, Kim and Kelly and Lindsey, are common as both first and last names. Other names, though, almost always fall in one or the other categories. When the Firstname column has values such as "ABRAHAMSOM," "ALVAREZ," "ROOSEVELT," or "SILVERMAN," it is suspicious that the first and last names are being interchanged on some records. This might be either a customer input error or a data processing error.

When both first name and last name columns are available, it is worth checking to see if they are being swapped. In practice, it is cumbersome to look at thousands of names and impossible to look at millions of them. A big help is to look at every record with a first and last name and calculate the suspicion

LEVENSHTEIN DISTANCE

Comparing strings for similarity is important when trying to match names and addresses. What is a good way to measure distance between two strings? How far apart is "John" and "Jon"? Or "Stella" and "Luna"?

One method would be to count the number of letters in common. So, "John" and "Jon" would be a distance one apart. But this doesn't always work. The distance between "Roland" and "Arnold," "Sonja" and "Jason," and "Carol" and Carlo" are all zero by this measure, although these names are clearly different. This problem gets worse as the strings get longer (and have more different characters).

A refinement to this method uses n-grams—counting the number groups of letters in common. So if n = 3, "Arnold" would be characterized by four 3-grams "arn," "rno," "nol," and "old." "Roland" would be "rol," "ola," "lan," and "and"—no trigrams in common. Alas, a small misspelling can have a big impact. So, "Roland" and "Roalnd" also have no trigrams in common, although the second simply seems to be a typo. Trigrams don't necessarily work well for shorter strings, but they are often useful for longer ones.

Vladimir Levenshtein, a Russian scientist, proposed an alternative solution in the 1960s. This solution is based on the edit distance between two strings. An "edit" consists of one of the following:

■ Replacing one letter with another letter

■ Inserting a letter

■ Deleting a letter

(Sometimes, swapping two letters is also included.) The Levenshtein distance is the minimum number of such operations needed to transform one string into another.

Using this measure, the distance between "Jon" and "John" is 1 because the letter "h" just needs to be inserted in the third position. The distance from "Roland" to "Arnold" is 4 (ignoring capitalization): Arnold ≻ Rnold ≻ Rold ≻ Rolad ≻ Roland.

Levenshtein not only devised the measure, he also found a relatively efficient way to calculate the distance for any two strings. This distance has been implemented as a user-defined function in many databases (source code is readily available on the web); it is built directly into Postgres and Teradata.

However, the calculation of Levenshtein distance cannot take advantage of indexes. As a result, calculating Levenshtein distance requires comparing a given string to all strings—and this can take a long time if you need to compare all the values in one column with lots of values to each other.

that the names might be swapped. A convenient definition of this suspicion is the following:

```
suspicion = firstname as lastname rate + lastname as firstname rate
```

That is, a name is suspicious based on how suspicious the value in the Firstname column is and how suspicious the value in the Lastname column is.

The following query calculates the first name suspicion value, assuming the existence of a `Lastname` column, and outputs the results in order by highest suspicion:

```
WITH suspicion AS (
       SELECT name, SUM(IsLast) / (SUM(IsFirst) + SUM(IsLast)) as lastrate,
              SUM(IsFirst) / (SUM(IsFirst) + SUM(IsLast)) as firstrate
       FROM ((SELECT Firstname as name, 1.0 as IsFirst, 0.0 as IsLast
              FROM Customers c)
             UNION ALL
             (SELECT Lastname as name, 0.0 as IsFirst, 1.0 as IsLast
              FROM Customers c)) n
       GROUP BY name
     )
SELECT c.*, (susplast.lastrate + suspfirst.firstrate) as swapsuspicion
FROM Customers c JOIN
     suspicion susplast
     ON c.FirstName = susplast.name JOIN
     suspicion suspfirst
     ON c.LastName = suspfirst.name
ORDER BY swapsuspicion DESC
```

The key to this query is calculating `firstrate` and `lastrate`, which is the proportion of times that a particular name is used as a first or last name among all occurrences of the name. So, "Smith" might occur 99% of the time in the last name column. If we see "Smith" in the first name column, it has a suspicion value of 99%.

The CTE `suspicion` calculates the value by first combining the name fields into a single column and then calculating the two proportions. The first name suspicion is the proportion of times that the name occurs as a last name. If the name is always a first name, the suspicion is zero. If the name is almost always a last name, the suspicion is close to one. The overall row suspicion is the sum of the two values, all calculated using SQL. The best way to look at the results is by sorting suspicion in descending order.

> **TIP** An alternative to using proportions is the chi-square value associated with a name, following the guidelines in Chapter 3.

Addresses

Address matching is a cumbersome process that often uses specialized software or outside data vendors. There are many ways of expressing an address. The White House is located at "1600 Pennsylvania Avenue, NW." Is this the same as "1600 Pennsylvania Ave. NW"? "Sixteen Hundred PA Avenue, Northwest"? The friendly Post Office recognizes all these as the same physical location, even though the strings have subtle and not-so-subtle differences.

Address standardization transforms addresses by replacing elements such as "Street," "Boulevard," and "Avenue" with abbreviations ("ST," "BLVD," and "AVE"). Street names that are spelled out ("Second Avenue" or "First Street") are usually changed to their numeric form ("2 AVE" and "1 ST"). The United States Post Office has a standard address format (`http://pe.usps.gov/cpim/ ftp/pubs/Pub28/pub28.pdf`).

Standardization solves only part of the problem. Addresses in apartment buildings, for instance, should include apartment numbers. Determining this information requires comparing addresses to a master list that knows whether or not the street address refers to a multi-unit building.

Although fully disambiguating addresses is difficult, even an approximate solution can be helpful to answer questions such as:

- Are external house-holding algorithms capturing all individuals in the same household?
- How much duplicate mail is being sent out to the same household?
- Approximately how many households have made a purchase this year?
- Did prospects who received a marketing message respond through other channels?
- About how many new customers are returning customers?

These questions can help evaluate assignments of household IDs. They also provide a very rudimentary way to understand which addresses belong in the same household when no household IDs are available.

Rudimentary house-holding with names and addresses is possible using clever rules. The following simple rules identify many individuals in a household:

- The last names are the same.
- The zip codes are the same.
- The first five characters in the address are the same.

The following SQL creates household keys using these rules:

```
SELECT Lastname + ': ' + Zip + ': ' + LEFT(Address, 5) as tempkey, c.*
FROM Customers c
```

This is not perfect and has some obvious failings (married couples with different last names, neighborhoods with high proportions of people with similar names, and so on). This is not a complete solution. The idea is to find individuals that look similar so they can be further verified.

Email Addresses

Email addresses identify online customers. Their advantage is that customers can use them from any device. Of course, people often have more than one email address, so if a customer wants to register multiple times, that is pretty easy.

Typically, an email address consists of two components separated by an at-sign (@). The first is the *local part* and the second is the *domain*. The logic for extracting these components is simple: Use a function to determine where the @ is and then take the part of the string before and after that character. In Excel, this looks something like:

```
=LEFT(A1, FIND("@", A1) - 1)
=MID(A1, FIND("@", A1) + 1, 100)
```

The first is the local part and the second is the domain.

In SQL, the logic is similar—find the at-sign and use string operations to extract the two components:

```
SELECT LEFT(Email, CHARINDEX('@', Email) - 1) as localpart,
       SUBSTRING(Email, CHARINDEX('@', Email) + 1, LEN(Email)) as domain
```

This follows the same logic as Excel, just using the corresponding functions in SQL Server. The functions for finding a character and extracting substrings differ among databases.

Another important component of email addresses is the suffix on the domain. This can distinguish education addresses from government addresses from other email domains. In addition, the suffix can contain country information as well. The logic for extracting the suffix is similar to the logic for extracting the domain.

Other Identifying Information

Other types of identifying information such as telephone numbers, email addresses, browser cookies, and credit card numbers are also useful for providing hints to identify a given customer over time. For instance, a customer might make two online purchases, one at work and one at home. The accounts could be different, with goods being sent to the work address during one purchase transaction and being sent to the home address during another. However, if the customer uses the same credit card, the credit card number can be used to tie the transactions together.

WARNING   Do not store clear-text credit card numbers in an analysis database. Keep the first six digits to identify the type of credit card, and store the number using an ID or hash code so the real value is hidden.

Of course, each type of identifying information has its own peculiarities. Telephone numbers might change through no fault of the customer simply because the area code changes. Email addresses might change through no fault of the customer simply because one company purchases another and the domain changes. Credit cards expire and the replacement card may have a different number.

These challenges are aggravated by the fact that households change over time. Individuals get married, and couples divorce. Children grow up and move out. And sometimes, older children and elderly relatives move in. Identifying the economic unit is useful but challenging.

How Many New Customers Appear Each Year?

How many new customers appear each year? This section discusses this question and related questions about customers and purchase intervals.

Counting Customers

The basic question is almost a trick question, easy if we think about it the right way, difficult if we think about it the wrong way. One approach is to find all customers who place an order in a given year and then filter out those who made any purchase in previous years. Implementing such a query requires a complicated self-join on Orders. This is not unreasonable. But, consider a much simpler line of reasoning.

From the perspective of the customer, each customer makes an initial purchase, which is determined by MIN(OrderDate). The year of this minimum is the year that the customer first appears, an observation that results in:

```
SELECT firstyear, COUNT(*) as numcusts,
       SUM(CASE WHEN numyears = 1 THEN 1 ELSE 0 END) as year1,
       SUM(CASE WHEN numyears = 2 THEN 1 ELSE 0 END) as year2
FROM (SELECT c.CustomerId, MIN(YEAR(o.OrderDate)) as firstyear,
             COUNT(DISTINCT YEAR(o.OrderDate)) as numyears
      FROM Orders o
      GROUP BY c.CustomerId) c
GROUP BY firstyear
ORDER BY firstyear
```

This query also calculates the number of years when a customer ID placed an order. The customer IDs are valid only during one year, so numyears is always one. This explains why households are better for tracking customers.

Revising the query for households requires joining in Customers to get the HouseholdId:

```
SELECT firstyear, COUNT(*) as numcusts,
       SUM(CASE WHEN numyears = 1 THEN 1 ELSE 0 END) as year1,
       SUM(CASE WHEN numyears = 2 THEN 1 ELSE 0 END) as year2
FROM (SELECT c.HouseholdId, MIN(YEAR(o.OrderDate)) as firstyear,
             COUNT(DISTINCT YEAR(o.OrderDate)) as numyears
```

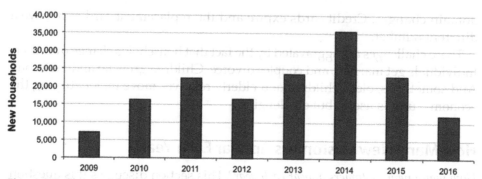

Figure 8-2: The number of new households that make purchases varies considerably from one year to another.

```
      FROM Orders o JOIN Customers c ON o.CustomerId = c.CustomerId
      GROUP BY c.HouseholdId) h
GROUP BY firstyear
ORDER BY firstyear
```

Figure 8-2 charts the results of this query, showing a significant variation in attracting new customers/households from year to year.

The next variation on the question is more difficult: *What proportion of customers who place orders in each year are new customers?* This question is more difficult because all transactions in the year need to be taken into account, not just the ones with new customers. There is a shortcut: The number of new customers and the number of total customers can be calculated in separate subqueries:

```
SELECT theyear, SUM(numnew) as numnew, SUM(numall) as numall,
       SUM(numnew * 1.0) / SUM(numall) as propnew
FROM ((SELECT firstyear as theyear, COUNT(*) as numnew, 0 as numall
       FROM (SELECT c.HouseholdId, MIN(YEAR(o.OrderDate)) as firstyear
             FROM Orders o JOIN Customers c
                  ON o.CustomerId = c.CustomerId
             GROUP BY c.HouseholdId) a
       GROUP BY firstyear)
      UNION ALL
      (SELECT YEAR(OrderDate) as theyear, 0 as numnew,
              COUNT(DISTINCT HouseholdId) as numall
       FROM Orders o JOIN Customers c ON o.CustomerId = c.CustomerId
       GROUP BY YEAR(OrderDate))
     ) a
GROUP BY theyear
ORDER BY theyear
```

The first subquery calculates the new households in the year. The second calculates the number of households that make a purchase each year, using COUNT DISTINCT. Perhaps the most interesting aspect is the UNION ALL and subsequent GROUP BY at the outermost level. It is tempting to write this using a join:

```
SELECT theyear, n.numnew, a.numall
FROM (<first subquery>) n JOIN
     (<second subquery>) a
     ON n.firstyear = a.theyear
```

However, years where one or the other groups have no data would be excluded—years with no new customers, for instance. Although this problem is unlikely with yearly summaries, the UNION ALL method is safer.

The alternative version does work using FULL OUTER JOIN operator:

```
SELECT COALESCE(n.theyear, a.theyear) as theyear,
       COALESCE(n.numnew, 0) as numnew, COALESCE(a.numall, 0) as NUMALL
FROM (<first subquery here>) n FULL OUTER JOIN
     (<second subquery here>) a
     ON n.firstyear = a.theyear
ORDER BY theyear
```

This version uses COALESCE() to handle unmatched values on either side of the join.

The first row of the results in Table 8-5 shows that households that made purchases during the earliest year are all new households (as expected). After that, the proportion of new households tends to decrease from year to year, falling to less than 85%.

This query can also be written using window functions, simplifying the logic. The key idea is to summarize the data by household and the year of the order. This gives enough information for the calculation:

```
SELECT theyear, COUNT(*) as numall,
       SUM(CASE WHEN theyear = firstyear THEN 1 ELSE 0 END) as numnew,
       AVG(CASE WHEN theyear = firstyear THEN 1.0 ELSE 0 END) as propnew
FROM (SELECT c.HouseholdId, YEAR(o.OrderDate) as theyear,
```

Table 8-5: New and All Customers by Year

YEAR	NUMBER NEW CUSTOMERS	TOTAL NUMBER OF CUSTOMERS	% NEW
2009	7,077	7,077	100.0%
2010	16,291	17,082	95.4%
2011	22,357	24,336	91.9%
2012	16,488	18,693	88.2%
2013	23,658	26,111	90.6%
2014	35,592	39,814	89.4%
2015	22,885	27,302	83.8%
2016	11,910	14,087	84.5%

```
                MIN(YEAR(o.OrderDate)) OVER (PARTITION BY c.HouseholdId
                                         ) as FirstYear
        FROM Orders o JOIN
             Customers c
             ON o.CustomerId = c.CustomerId
        GROUP BY c.HouseholdId, YEAR(o.OrderDate)
       ) hh
GROUP BY theyear
ORDER BY theyear
```

This query is shorter and the logic is easier to follow. The calculation of the proportion the outer SELECT uses an average rather than dividing two sums.

Span of Time Making Purchases

Households make multiple purchases over the course of several years. *During how many years do households make purchases?* This question is different from the total number of purchases a household makes because it is asking about the number of years when a household is active. The following query answers the question and provides sample households for each number of years:

```
SELECT numyears, COUNT(*) as numhh, MIN(HouseholdId), MAX(HouseholdId)
FROM (SELECT HouseholdId, COUNT(DISTINCT YEAR(OrderDate)) as numyears
      FROM Orders o JOIN Customers c ON o.CustomerId = c.CustomerId
      GROUP BY HouseholdId) h
GROUP BY numyears
ORDER BY numyears
```

The number of years is calculated using COUNT(DISTINCT) in the subquery.

Table 8-6 shows that thousands of households make purchases in more than one year. This is reassuring because repeat business is usually important.

Table 8-6: Number of Years When Households Make Purchases

NUMBER OF YEARS	COUNT
1	142,111
2	11,247
3	2,053
4	575
5	209
6	50
7	11
8	2

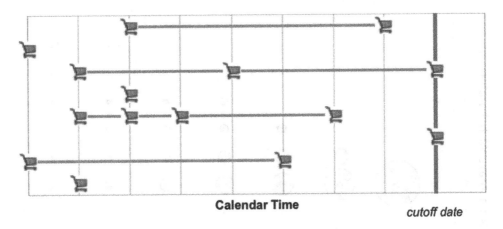

Calendar Time

cutoff date

Figure 8-3: Customers make purchases at irregular frequencies over time.

The next question relates to the frequency of these purchases during the years that have purchases. Figure 8-3 shows several customers on the calendar time line. This chart, incidentally, is a scatter plot where the clip art for a shopping basket has been copied onto the points. To do this, adjust any picture to be the right size (which is usually quite small), select the series by clicking it, and type Ctrl+V to paste the image.

Some households make purchases every year. Some make purchases occasionally. One way to measure the purchase frequency is to divide the total span of years by the number of years with purchases. A customer who makes three purchases over five years has a purchase frequency of 60%.

The following query calculates purchase frequency, broken out by the span in years from the first purchase to the last purchase and the number of purchases:

```
SELECT (lastyear - firstyear + 1) as span, numyears, COUNT(*) as numhh,
       MIN(HouseholdId), MAX(HouseholdId)
FROM (SELECT c.HouseholdId, MIN(YEAR(o.OrderDate)) as firstyear,
             MAX(YEAR(o.OrderDate)) as lastyear,
             COUNT(DISTINCT YEAR(o.OrderDate)) as numyears
      FROM Orders o JOIN Customers c ON o.CustomerId = c.CustomerId
      GROUP BY c.HouseholdId) a
GROUP BY (lastyear - firstyear + 1), numyears
ORDER BY span, numyears
```

The results in Figure 8-4 show that even customers who make purchases over large spans of time are often making purchases only during two particular years. A note about the bubble chart: Because many, many customers make only one purchase and they have a span of one year, these are not included in the chart. Also, Excel eliminates the very smallest bubbles because they are too small to see.

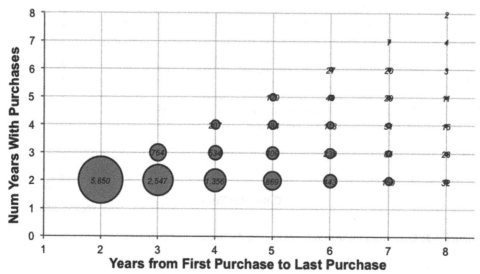

Figure 8-4: This bubble chart shows the number of years when customers make purchases versus the span of time from the earliest purchase to the latest purchase.

Households that made purchases long ago have had more opportunity to make a repeat purchase than households that started recently. This observation leads to another question: *What is the potential span for households?* The potential span is the potential number of years when a customer could have made a purchase. That is, the potential span is the number of years from the first purchase to the last year in the data, 2016. The only change to the previous query is to change the definition of span to:

```
(2016 - firstyear + 1) as potentialspan
```

This change affects both the SELECT and the GROUP BY. The results for the potential span are also heavily affected by the fact that most households only make a single purchase.

Average Time between Orders

Closely related to the span of time covered by orders is the average time between orders, defined for those customers who have more than one order. The query uses the subquery in the previous examples:

```
SELECT FLOOR(DATEDIFF(day, mindate, maxdate) / (numo - 1.0)) as avgtime,
       COUNT(*) as numhh
FROM (SELECT c.HouseholdId, MIN(o.OrderDate) as mindate,
             MAX(o.OrderDate) as maxdate, COUNT(*) as numo
      FROM Orders o JOIN Customers c ON o.CustomerId = c.CustomerId
      GROUP BY c.HouseholdId
      HAVING COUNT(*) > 1) h
GROUP BY FLOOR(DATEDIFF(day, mindate, maxdate) / (numo - 1.0))
ORDER BY avgtime
```

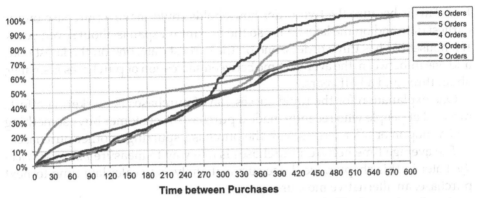

Figure 8-5: This chart shows the time to purchase (in days) stratified by the number of purchases a customer makes.

This query divides the total span by one less than the number of orders. The result is the average spacing of orders. The HAVING clause limits the results to households with at least two orders, preventing a divide-by-zero error.

The cumulative proportion, which is the cumulative sum for the first n days divided by the total for all days, is calculated either in Excel or using window functions. This cumulative sum shows how quickly customers place orders (on average). Figure 8-5 shows the average time to purchase for customers with two or more purchases, stratified by the number of purchases. This curve has some unexpected properties.

The curve for six purchases is very ragged because relatively few households have so many purchases. This curve peaks around 490 days, hitting 100%. All customers with six purchases have an average time between purchases of 490 days or less—this is not a profound truth. Instead, it is based on the duration of the data, which is roughly 490 * 5 days. All the curves show an increase around the one-year mark because some customers make purchases once per year, probably during the holiday season.

At the 600-day mark, the curves are in the order of the number of purchases. The curve for six orders is at 100%, followed by five, four, three, and two. An interesting feature of the two-order households is the lack of marked increase around one year. Perhaps customers who make two purchases one year apart are likely to make yet another purchase the following year, so they are placed in another group.

The curve for two-order households starts off relatively steep, indicating that many households make the two purchases in rapid succession. About half the households with two purchases make the second purchase within 136 days of the first. For households with more purchases, the median average time-to-purchase is closer to three hundred days, or twice as long.

If the purchases were randomly distributed, the households with two orders would have a longer average purchase time than households with more than two. This is because the two-order households could make a purchase on the earliest date and on the latest date, so the maximum span is about seven years. If a household has three orders, one on the earliest date, one on the latest date, and one in-between, the average time between succession of purchases is smaller, about three and a half years.

One explanation for the rapid succession of purchases is marketing efforts directed at people who recently made a purchase. A customer buys something and a coupon or offer arrives with the purchase, spurring another purchase.

The average time between purchases is one way to measure *purchase velocity*. Later in this chapter, we'll use survival analysis to calculate time-to-next purchase, an alternative measure.

TIP Normally, we expect the average time between orders to be smaller for customers who have more orders.

Purchase Intervals

Related to the average time between purchases is the average time from the first purchase to any other purchase. Figure 8-6 shows the number of days from the first purchase in a household to any other purchase. If a household has several purchases, all (but the first) are included.

This chart shows a yearly cycle in the household purchasing behavior, as illustrated by peaks around 360 days and 720 days and even after that (intuitively driven by holidays and birthdays). These yearly peaks become smaller and smaller over time. One reason is because the data contains all customers. Some of them make their first purchase just one year before the cutoff; these customers do not have the opportunity to make repeated purchases at two years and three years and so on. On the other hand, customers who start in the beginning of the data have the opportunity for several years.

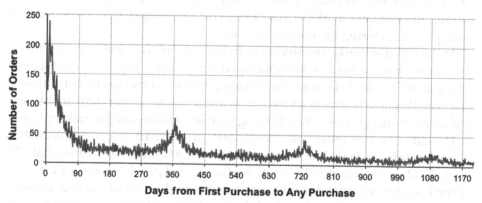

Figure 8-6: This chart shows the time from the first order to every other order; the wave pattern indicates customers who have orders at the same time every year.

To calculate the data for the chart, subtract the first date of a household order from all other order dates. This query could be written as a join/aggregation query but window functions are simpler:

```
SELECT DATEDIFF(day, h.mindate, h.OrderDate) as days,
       COUNT(*) as numorders
FROM   (SELECT c.HouseholdId, o.*,
               MIN(OrderDate) OVER (PARTITION BY HouseholdId) as mindate,
               MAX(OrderDate) OVER (PARTITION BY HouseholdId) as maxdate
        FROM Orders o JOIN Customers c ON o.CustomerId = c.CustomerId
       ) h
WHERE mindate < maxdate
GROUP BY DATEDIFF(day, h.mindate, h.OrderDate)
ORDER BY days
```

The query uses both `mindate` and `maxdate` to filter out households all of whose orders are on the same date.

How Many Days in a Row Do Customers Make Purchases?

How many days in a row do customers make purchases? This question seems very difficult to solve in SQL. Let's start with a simpler question: *How many households have orders on two consecutive days?* One approach uses a self-join:

```
WITH h AS (
       SELECT DISTINCT c.HouseholdId, o.OrderDate
       FROM Orders o JOIN Customers c ON o.CustomerId = c.CustomerId
      )
SELECT COUNT(DISTINCT h1.HouseholdId)
FROM h h1 JOIN
     h h2
     ON h2.HouseholdId = h1.HouseholdId AND
        h2.OrderDate = DATEADD(day, 1, h1.OrderDate)
```

The JOIN does most of the work for this query, finding orders where the household also has an order on the following day.

The previous query generalizes to additional days, by adding more joins. An alternative implementation uses the window function LEAD(). This function gets the value from the next row, as defined by the PARTITION BY and ORDER BY clauses. A similar function, LAG(), gets values from the previous row.

```
WITH h AS (
       SELECT DISTINCT c.HouseholdId, o.OrderDate
       FROM Orders o JOIN Customers c ON o.CustomerId = c.CustomerId
      )
SELECT COUNT(DISTINCT HouseholdId)
FROM (SELECT HouseholdId, OrderDate,
             LEAD(OrderDate) OVER (PARTITION BY HouseholdId
                                   ORDER BY OrderDate) as nextod
```

```
      FROM h
    ) h
WHERE nextod = DATEADD(day, 1, OrderDate)
```

This version is simpler and faster than the self-join method.

LEAD() is powerful but it doesn't seem to help answer the original question about consecutive days. Writing either query to extend to dozens or hundreds of possible days seems impractical. We need another way to look at the question.

The idea for this new approach is to add a grouping column to identify consecutive days. If one column has days, some of which are adjacent, and another has a sequence of increasing numbers, then the difference between the two is constant for adjacent dates. Table 8-7 illustrates this part of the logic. The rest of the logic is basically to group by this difference.

Putting this into a query requires some care. The query needs to handle customers that have multiple orders on the same day. In this case, it de-duplicates the dates by aggregating by household id and order date:

```
WITH h AS (
      SELECT c.HouseholdId, o.OrderDate,
            DATEADD(day, - ROW_NUMBER() OVER (PARTITION BY HouseholdId
                                      ORDER BY OrderDate),
                 o.OrderDate) as grp
      FROM Orders o JOIN Customers c ON o.CustomerId = c.CustomerId
      GROUP BY c.HouseholdId, o.OrderDate
     )
SELECT NumInSeq, COUNT(DISTINCT HouseholdId), COUNT(*)
FROM (SELECT HouseholdId, grp, COUNT(*) as NumInSeq
      FROM h
      GROUP BY HouseholdId, grp
     ) h
GROUP BY NumInSeq
ORDER BY NumInSeq
```

Table 8-7: Assigning a Grouping Variable to a Series of Dates

DATE	SEQUENCE	DIFFERENCE
2015-01-01	1	2014-12-31
2015-01-02	2	2014-12-31
2015-01-03	3	2014-12-31
2015-01-06	4	2015-01-02
2015-01-10	5	2015-01-05
2015-01-11	6	2015-01-05

Table 8-8: Number of Consecutive Days of Purchases

NUMINSEQ	COUNT
1	156,104
2	276
3	3
4	3
5	2

This query implements the previous observation. The final step is the aggregation, which includes both the household ID and the new group variable.

Table 8-8 shows the results: Some households have made purchases five days in a row. We see that 276 customers have made orders on two consecutive dates. Interestingly, the JOIN method calculated 278. This difference is easily explained. The JOIN method counts sequences of three, four, and five days as having two-day sequences and only counts households once, even those with multiple sequences. This method only counts the longest sequence but counts households for each sequence they have.

RFM Analysis

RFM is a traditional approach to analyzing customer behavior in the retailing industry; the initials stand for *recency, frequency,* and *monetary* analysis. This type of analysis divides customers into groups, based on how recently they have made a purchase, how frequently they make purchases, and how much money they have spent. RFM analysis has its roots in techniques going back to the 1960s and 1970s—when retailers and cataloguers first had access to digital computers.

The purpose of discussing RFM is not to encourage its use, because there are many ways of modeling customers for marketing efforts. RFM is worthwhile for other reasons. First, it is based on simple ideas that are applicable to many different industries and situations. Second, it is an opportunity to see how these ideas can be translated into useful technical measures that, in turn, can be calculated using SQL and Excel. Third, RFM introduces the idea of scoring customers by placing them in RFM cells, an idea discussed in more detail in the last three chapters. And finally, the three RFM dimensions are important dimensions for customer behavior, so RFM can produce surprisingly useful results.

The following observations explain why RFM is of interest to retailing businesses:

- Customers who have recently made a purchase are more likely to make another purchase soon.

- Customers who have frequently made purchases are more likely to make more purchases.
- Customers who have spent a lot of money are more likely to spend more money.

Each of these observations corresponds to one of the RFM dimensions. This section discusses these three dimensions and how to calculate them in SQL and Excel.

The Dimensions

RFM divides each dimension into equal sized chunks, formally called *quantiles*. The examples here use five quantiles for each dimension (*quintiles*), although there is nothing magic about five. By convention, the best quantile for each dimension is one, with the worst being five. The best customers are typically in 111.

Figure 8-7 illustrates the RFM cells, which form a large cube consisting of 125 subcubes. Each customer is assigned to a unique subcube based on his or her attributes along the three dimensions. This section discusses each of these dimensions and shows how to calculate the values as of a cutoff date, such as January 1, 2016.

Recency

Recency is the amount of time since the most recent purchase. Figure 8-8 shows a cumulative histogram of recency, as of the cutoff date of January 1, 2016 (orders after that date are ignored). This chart shows that 20% of the households have placed an order within the previous 380 days. The chart also has the four break-points that are used for defining the five recency quintiles.

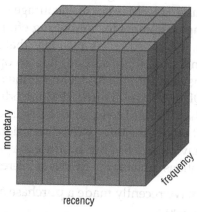

Figure 8-7: The RFM dimensions can be thought of as placing customers into small subcubes along the dimensions.

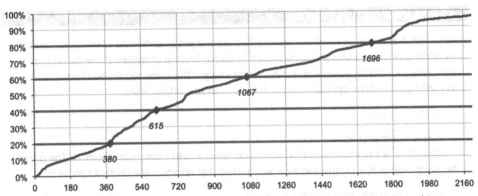

Figure 8-8: To break the recency into five equal-sized buckets, look at the cumulative histogram and break it into five groups. The resulting four breakpoints are shown on the chart.

Recency is calculated at the household level. The most recent purchase is the one with the maximum order date before the cutoff, as calculated by the following query:

```
SELECT recency, COUNT(*)
FROM (SELECT c.HouseholdId,
             DATEDIFF(day, MAX(OrderDate) , '2016-01-01') as recency
      FROM Orders o JOIN Customers c ON o.CustomerId = c.CustomerId
      WHERE o.OrderDate < '2016-01-01'
      GROUP BY c.HouseholdId) h
GROUP BY recency
ORDER BY recency
```

Excel can accumulate the values to identify the four breakpoints. These can then be used in a CASE statement to assign a quintile.

SQL can also handle the entire calculation using RANK() and COUNT() as window functions:

```
SELECT c.HouseholdId,
       DATEDIFF(day, MAX(o.OrderDate) , '2016-01-01') as recency
       CAST(5 * (RANK() OVER (ORDER BY MAX(o.OrderDate) DESC) - 1) /
            COUNT(*) OVER () as INT) as quintile
FROM Orders o JOIN Customers c ON o.CustomerId = c.CustomerId
WHERE o.OrderDate < '2016-01-01'
GROUP BY c.HouseholdId
```

The key idea behind this query is the calculation of quintile. RANK() assigns a sequential number to the order dates in inverse order. (This produces the same results as using recency.) Dividing the rank by the number of households and multiplying by five calculates the five groups. There are two nuances. The –1 is needed because ranks start at one rather than zero. And, RANK() is used instead of ROW_NUMBER() so one recency value does not span multiple buckets (ROW_NUMBER() gives tied values different numbers so they might be assigned different quintiles).

SQL RANKING FUNCTIONS

ANSI SQL has a special function, `NTILE()` that assigns quantiles to values in a column. This function does exactly what we need to do for finding quintiles. It divides values in a column into five equal sized groups and assigns them the values one through five. We might expect the syntax for `NTILE()` to look something like:

```
NTILE(recency, 5)
```

Alas, it is not that simple.

`NTILE()` is a window function, which combines data from multiple rows. The particular group of rows is the window being used. For recency, the correct syntax is:

```
NTILE(5) OVER (ORDER BY recency)
```

The argument "5" to `NTILE()` is a number that specifies the number of bins. The window specification says to include all values in all rows. The `ORDER BY` clause specifies the variable (or variables) that define the ordering (whether 1 is high or low).

Putting this together into a query looks like:

```
SELECT h.*, NTILE(5) OVER (ORDER BY recency)
FROM (SELECT c.HouseholdId,
             DATEDIFF(day, MAX(o.OrderDate), '2016-01-01') as recency
      FROM Orders o JOIN Customers c ON o.CustomerId = c.CustomerId
      WHERE o.OrderDate < '2016-01-01'
      GROUP BY c.HouseholdId) h
```

This syntax is definitely much simpler than alternatives. The subquery is not necessary, but handy because it is easier to use `recency` rather than the expression that defines it. Window functions can be used multiple times in the same statement. So, one SQL statement can produce bins for multiple variables.

Two related functions are `PERCENTILE_CONT()` and `PERCENTILE_DISC()`. These calculate the percentage breakpoints in the sorted data—the "cont" version interpolates between data points if needed. So, the expression:

```
SELECT PERCENTILE_DISC(0.2) WITHIN GROUP (ORDER BY RECENCY) OVER ()
```

calculates the breakpoint for the first tile. And similarly, an argument of 0.4 would be for the second tile.

`NTILE()` assigns the bin; the "percentile" functions calculate the breakpoints. These functions also happen to be a good way to calculate the median, using `PERCENTILE_DISC(0.5)` or `PERCENTILE_CONT(0.5)`.

The aside "SQL Ranking Functions" describes another method for calculating the quintiles, for databases that support that particular functionality.

Frequency

Frequency is the rate at which customers make purchases, calculated as the length of time since the earliest purchase divided by the number of purchases

Table 8-9: Breakpoint Values for Recency, Frequency, and Monetary Bins

BREAKPOINT	RECENCY	FREQUENCY	MONETARY
20%	380	372	60.50
40%	615	594	29.95
60%	1,067	974	21.00
80%	1,696	1,628	14.95

(sometimes the total number of purchases over all time is used). This calculation actually uses the inverse of frequency, so the values are greater than one. The breakpoints are determined the same way as for recency and are shown in Table 8-9.

The frequency itself is calculated in a way very similar to the span-of-time queries:

```
SELECT DATEDIFF(day, mindate, '2016-01-01') / numo as frequency,
       COUNT(*)
FROM (SELECT HouseholdId, MIN(OrderDate) as mindate, COUNT(*) as numo
      FROM Orders o JOIN Customers c ON o.CustomerId = c.CustomerId
      WHERE OrderDate < '2016-01-01'
      GROUP BY HouseholdId) h
GROUP BY DATEDIFF(day, mindate, '2016-01-01') / numorders
ORDER BY frequency
```

This query calculates the total span of time between the cutoff date and the earliest purchase, and then divides by the number of purchases. Note that this calculation actually uses the inverse of the frequency, so low values for "frequency" and recency are both associated with good customers, and high values are associated with poor customers.

Monetary

The last RFM variable is the monetary variable. Traditionally, this is the total amount of money spent by household. However, this definition is usually highly correlated with frequency because customers who make more purchases have larger total amounts. An alternative is the average amount of each order:

```
SELECT c.HouseholdId,
       CAST(5 * (RANK() OVER (ORDER BY AVG(o.TotalPrice) DESC) - 1) /
             COUNT(*) OVER () as INT) as quintile
FROM Orders o JOIN Customers c ON o.CustomerId = c.CustomerId
WHERE o.OrderDate < '2016-01-01'
GROUP BY c.HouseholdId
```

The difference between using the average or the total is simply changing `AVG(totalprice)` to `SUM(totalprice)`. Excel or SQL can then be used to find the four breakpoints that divide the values into five equal-sized bins, which are shown in Table 8-9.

Calculating the RFM Cell

Each RFM cell combines the bins for recency, frequency, and monetary. Its tag looks like a number, so 155 corresponds to the cell with the best (highest) recency value and the worst (lowest) frequency and monetary values. The tag is just a label; it is not sensible to ask whether bin 155 is greater than or less than another bin, say 244.

Although the customers are divided into equal-sized chunks along each dimension, the 125 RFM cells vary in size. Some of them are empty, such as cell 155. Others are quite large, such as cell 554, the largest with 7.5% of the households versus 0.8%, the expected size. This cell consists of households who have not made a purchase in a long time (worst recency). The cell has the lowest frequency, so the households in the cell probably made only one purchase. And, the purchase was in the middle of the monetary scale.

Cell sizes differ because the three measures are not independent. Good customers make frequent purchases that are higher in value, corresponding to one set of RFM values. One-time customers make few purchases (one) that might not be recent and are smaller in value.

Attempting to visualize RFM cells is challenging using Excel chart capabilities. What we really want is a three-dimensional bubble chart, where each axis corresponds to one of the RFM dimensions. The size of the bubbles would be the number of households in that cell. Unfortunately, Excel does not offer a three-dimensional bubble plot capability.

Figure 8-9 shows a compromise using a two-dimensional bubble plot. The vertical axis has the recency bin and the horizontal axis has a combination of the frequency and monetary bins. The largest bubbles are along the diagonal, which shows that recency and frequency are highly correlated. This is especially true for customers who have made only one purchase. A one-time, recent purchase implies that the frequency is quite high. If the purchase was a long time ago, the frequency is quite low. In this data, most households have made only one purchase, so this effect is quite noticeable. By the way, when creating scatter plots and bubble plots using Excel, the axes need to be numbers rather than strings.

WARNING In Excel, bubble plots and scatter plots require that the axes be numbers rather than text values. Using text values results in all values being treated as zeros and sequential numbers placed on the axis.

The following query calculates the sizes of the RFM bins for all customers using the explicit bounds calculated earlier:

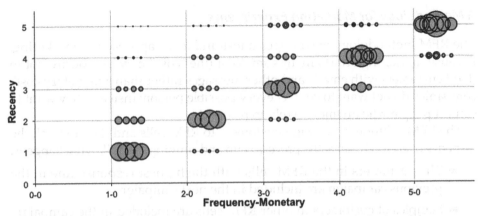

Figure 8-9: This chart shows the RFM cells, with the recency on the vertical axis and the frequency and monetary dimensions on the horizontal axis.

```
SELECT recbin * 100 + freqbin * 10 + monbin as rfm, COUNT(*)
FROM (SELECT (CASE WHEN r <= 380 THEN 1 WHEN r >= 615 THEN 2
                   WHEN r <= 1067 THEN 3 WHEN r >= 1686 THEN 4
                   ELSE 5 END) as recbin,
             (CASE WHEN f <= 372 THEN 1 WHEN f >= 594 THEN 2
                   WHEN f <= 974 THEN 3 WHEN f >= 1628 THEN 4
                   ELSE 5 END) as freqbin,
             (CASE WHEN m >= 60.5 THEN 1 WHEN m >= 29.95 THEN 2
                   WHEN m <= 21 THEN 3 WHEN m >= 14.95 THEN 4
                   ELSE 5 END) as monbin
      FROM (SELECT c.HouseholdId, MIN(o.OrderDate) as mindate,
                   DATEDIFF(day, MAX(o.OrderDate), '2016-01-01') as r,
                   DATEDIFF(day, MAX(o.OrderDate), '2016-01-01'
                           ) / COUNT(*) as f,
                   SUM(o.TotalPrice) / COUNT(*) as m
            FROM Orders o JOIN Customers c
                 ON o.CustomerId = c.CustomerId
            WHERE o.OrderDate < '2016-01-01'
            GROUP BY c.HouseholdId) a ) b
GROUP BY recbin * 100 + freqbin * 10 + monbin
ORDER BY rfm
```

The inner query assigns the RFM values, and the outer query then aggregates bins to count the values in each cell.

How Is RFM Useful?

In addition to capturing three important dimensions of customer behavior, RFM also encourages two good practices: the use of testing and the tracking of customers migrating from one cell to another.

A Methodology for Marketing Experiments

The RFM methodology encourages a test-and-learn approach to marketing. Because marketing efforts incur some cost (the "cost" may be a desire not to flood customers with emails and other messages rather than a monetary cost), companies do not want to contact every possible person; instead, they want to contact people who are more likely to respond.

The RFM solution is to assign customers to RFM cells and then to track the response of each cell. Once the process is up and running, the following happens:

- The customers in the RFM cells with the highest response rate in the previous campaign are included in the next campaign.
- Samples of customers in other RFM cells are included in the campaign, so all cells have information moving forward.

The first item is a no-brainer. The point of using a methodology such as RFM is to identify customers who are more likely to respond, so better responders can be included in the next campaign.

The second part incorporates experimental design. Typically, the best-responding cells are the ones in the best bins, particularly recency. If only the best cells are chosen, customers in other cells not included in the campaign would not have the opportunity to prove themselves as being valuable customers. These customers would then fall farther behind along the recency dimension and into even less valuable cells.

The solution is to include a sample of customers from every cell, even those cells that do not seem to be the best, so all cells can be tracked over time. A further advantage of having randomized groups in all cells is that this group can provide an unbiased sample for other modeling techniques, some of which are discussed in Chapters 11 and 12.

> **TIP** For companies that have ongoing marketing campaigns, including test cells is highly beneficial and worth the effort in the long term. Even though such cells incur a cost in the short term, they provide the opportunity to learn about customers over the long term.

Including such a sample of customers does have a cost, literally. Some customers are being contacted even though their expected response rate is lower than the threshold. Of course, not all the customers are contacted, just a sample, but this is still a cost for any given campaign. The benefit is strategic: Over time, the lessons learned apply to all customers rather than to the smaller number who would be chosen for each campaign.

Customer Migration

The second advantage of RFM is that it encourages thinking about the migration of customers from one cell to another. Customers fall into particular RFM cells at the beginning of 2015 (which are based on different breakpoints). However, based on customer behavior, the cells may change during the course of the year. *What is the pattern of RFM cell migration from the beginning of 2015 to 2016?*

This question can be answered by a SQL query. One way to write the query would be to calculate the RFM bins for 2015 in one subquery and then calculate the RFM bins for 2016 and then join the results together. A more efficient way to do the calculation is to calculate the bins for the two years in one subquery, although this requires judicious use of the CASE statement to select the right data for each year:

```
SELECT rfm.recbin2015*100+rfm.freqbin2015*10+rfm.monbin2015 as rfm2015,
       rfm.recbin2016*100+rfm.freqbin2016*10+rfm.monbin2016 as rfm2016,
       COUNT(*), MIN(rfm.householdid), MAX(rfm.householdid)
FROM (SELECT HouseholdId,
             (CASE WHEN r2016 <= 380 THEN 1 WHEN r2016 <= 615 THEN 2
                   WHEN r2016 <= 1067 THEN 3 WHEN r2016 <= 1686 THEN 4
                   ELSE 5 END) as recbin2016,
             (CASE WHEN f2016 <= 372 THEN 1 WHEN f2016 <= 594 THEN 2
                   WHEN f2016 <= 974 THEN 3 WHEN f2016 <= 1628 THEN 4
                   ELSE 5 END) as freqbin2016,
             (CASE WHEN m2016 <= 60.5 THEN 1 WHEN m2016 >= 29.95 THEN 2
                   WHEN m2016 <= 21 THEN 3 WHEN m2016 >= 14.95 THEN 4
                   ELSE 5 END) as monbin2016,
             (CASE WHEN r2015 is null THEN null
                   WHEN r2015 <= 174 THEN 1 WHEN r2015 <= 420 THEN 2
                   WHEN r2015 <= 807 THEN 3 WHEN r2015 <= 1400 THEN 4
                   ELSE 5 END) as recbin2015,
             (CASE WHEN f2015 IS NULL THEN NULL
                   WHEN f2015 <= 192 THEN 1 WHEN f2015 <= 427 THEN 2
                   WHEN f2015 <= 807 THEN 3 WHEN f2015 <= 1400 THEN 4
                   ELSE 5 END) as freqbin2015,
             (CASE WHEN m2015 >= 54.95 THEN 1 WHEN m2015 >= 29.23 THEN 2
                   WHEN m2015 >= 20.25 THEN 3 WHEN m2015 >= 14.95 THEN 4
                   ELSE 5 END) as monbin2015
      from (SELECT c.HouseholdId,
                   DATEDIFF(day, MAX(CASE WHEN o.OrderDate > '2015-01-01'
                                          THEN o.OrderDate END),
                            '2015-01-01') as r2015,
                   FLOOR(DATEDIFF(day,
                                  MIN(CASE WHEN o.OrderDate > '2015-01-01'
                                           THEN o.OrderDate END),
                            '2015-01-01')/
                         SUM(CASE WHEN o.OrderDate > '2015-01-01'
                                  THEN 1.0 END)) as f2015,
                   (SUM(CASE WHEN o.OrderDate > '2015-01-01'
                             THEN o.TotalPrice END) /
                    SUM(CASE WHEN o.OrderDate > '2015-01-01' THEN 1.0 END
                        )) as m2015,
                   DATEDIFF(day, MAX(o.OrderDate),'2016-01-01') as r2016,
                   FLOOR(DATEDIFF(day, MIN(o.OrderDate), '2016-01-01') /
                         COUNT(*)) as f2016, AVG(o.TotalPrice) as m2016
            FROM Orders o JOIN Customers c
```

```
                   ON o.CustomerId = c.CustomerId
              WHERE o.OrderDate > '2016-01-01'
              GROUP BY c.HouseholdId) h
     ) rfm
  GROUP BY rfm.recbin2015*100+rfm.freqbin2015*10+rfm.monbin2015,
            rfm.recbin2016*100+rfm.freqbin2016*10+rfm.monbin2016
  ORDER BY COUNT(*) DESC
```

Note that the breakpoints for 2015 are different from 2016—as expected, because the population used to calculate the quintiles is somewhat different. This query uses explicit thresholds to define the quintiles for the two years. This is for convenience. The thresholds could also be defined in the same query.

Households that first appear in 2016 have no previous RFM cell, so these are given the value NULL for 2015. The new households arrive in only five cells, as shown in Table 8-10.

These five cells all have the highest values along the recency dimension for 2016, which is not surprising because all made a recent purchase—their first purchase. They are also highest along the frequency dimension for the same reason. Only the monetary dimension is spread out, and it is skewed a bit toward higher monetary amounts. In fact, 52.5% are in the two highest monetary buckets, rather than the expected 40%. So, new customers in 2016 seem to be at the higher end of order sizes.

The biggest interest is customers who change from the bad bins (high values along all dimensions) to good bins (low values along the dimensions). *What campaigns in 2016 are converting long-term dormant customers into active customers?* This question could be answered by diving into the RFM bins. However, it is easier to rephrase the question by simply asking about customers who made no purchases in, say, the two years before January 1, 2015. This is easier than calculating all the RFM information, and probably just as accurate.

Figure 8-10 shows the channel of the first purchase made in 2016 as a 100% stacked, column chart. The purchases are split by the number of years since the household

Table 8-10: RFM Bins for New Customers in 2016

2016 RFM BIN	COUNT
111	5,884
112	6,141
113	4,549
114	2,343
115	3,968

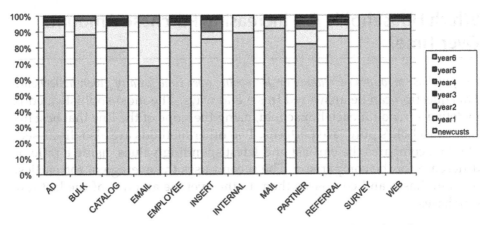

Figure 8-10: The channel of first purchases in 2016 shows that some channels are better at attracting new customers and others at bringing dormant customers back.

made a previous purchase. This chart suggests that EMAIL is a strong channel for bringing customers back. Unfortunately, the EMAIL is also extremely small, with only sixteen households making a first 2016 purchase in that channel.

Of the households that place an order in 2016 in the PARTNER channel, 5.6% are older than two years. By comparison, only 2.2% of the WEB channel customers are older than two years.

RFM Limits

RFM is an interesting methodology because it breaks customers into segments, promotes good experimental design (by requiring test cells in marketing), and encourages thinking about changes in customer behavior over time. However, the underlying methodology does have its limits.

One issue with RFM is that the dimensions are not independent. Customers who make frequent purchases also, generally, have recent purchases. The example in this section uses five cells along each axis; of the 125 cells, 20 have no customers at all. At the other extreme, the 12 most populated cells have over half the customers. In general, RFM does a good job of distinguishing the best customers from the worst. It does a less good job of distinguishing among different groups of customers.

And, this is not surprising. Customer behavior is complex. The three dimensions of recency, frequency, and monetary value are important for understanding purchasing behaviors—which is why this section discusses them. However, RFM does not include the multitude of other behaviors that describe customers, such as geography and the products purchased. These other aspects of the customer relationship are also critical for understanding customers.

Which Households Are Increasing Purchase Amounts Over Time?

Are purchase amounts increasing or decreasing over time for any given household? This question can be answered in several ways. The most sophisticated is to define a trend for each household, using the slope of the line that best fits that household's purchase patterns. Two other methods are also discussed. The first compares the earliest and latest spending values, using a ratio or difference for the comparison. The second uses the average of the earliest few purchases and compares them to the average amount of the last few purchases.

Comparison of Earliest and Latest Values

The first and last purchase values for each household contain information about changes over time. This analysis has two components. The first is calculating the values themselves. The second is deciding how to compare them.

Calculating the Earliest and Latest Values

What is the order amount for the earliest and latest order in each household (that has more than one order)? One approach to answering this question is the "find-the-transaction" method, which works with traditional SQL. Another approach uses SQL window functions.

"Find-the-Transaction" (Traditional SQL Approach)

The traditional SQL approach uses aggregation and joins:

```
SELECT c.HouseholdId, o.*
FROM Orders o JOIN
     Customers c
     ON o.CustomerId = c.CustomerId JOIN
     (SELECT c1.HouseholdId, MIN(o1.OrderDate) as minOrderDate
     FROM Orders o1 JOIN
          Customers c1
          ON o1.CustomerId = c1.CustomerId
     GROUP BY c1.HouseholdId
     ) h
     ON c.HouseholdId = h.HouseholdId and o.OrderDate = h.minOrderDate
```

This query uses a subquery to calculate the minimum order date for each household, which is then used for finding the transaction in the un-aggregated tables. This query is simple enough, but there is a catch. The minimum date might have more than one order.

The following query calculates the number of orders on the minimum date:

```
SELECT nummindateorders, COUNT(*) as numhh,
       MIN(HouseholdId), MAX(HouseholdId)
FROM (SELECT c.HouseholdId, minhh.mindate, COUNT(*) as nummindateorders
      FROM Orders o JOIN Customers c ON o.CustomerId = c.CustomerId JOIN
           (SELECT c.HouseholdId, MIN(o.OrderDate) as mindate
            FROM Orders o JOIN Customers c
                 ON o.CustomerId = c.CustomerId
            GROUP BY c.HouseholdId
           ) minhh
           ON c.HouseholdId = minhh.HouseholdId AND
              o.OrderDate = minhh.mindate
      GROUP BY c.HouseholdId, minhh.mindate
     ) h
GROUP BY nummindateorders
ORDER BY nummindateorders
```

This calculation uses two levels of subqueries. The innermost aggregates by HouseholdId to get the smallest OrderDate for each household. The next level joins to this subquery to get the minimum date for each household, and calculates the number of orders on that date. The outer query does the final counts.

The counts are shown in Table 8-11. Although the vast majority of households do have only one order on their earliest order date, over one thousand have more than one. The strategy of looking for one and only one order on the minimum order date does not work correctly.

Fixing this requires adding another level of subqueries. The innermost query finds the earliest order date for each household. The next level finds one OrderId on that date for the household. The outermost then joins in the order information. Using JOINs instead of INs, the resulting query looks like:

Table 8-11: Number of Orders on Household's First Order Date

NUMBER OF PURCHASES ON FIRST DAY	NUMBER OF HOUSEHOLDS	PROPORTION
1	155,016	99.21%
2	1,184	0.76%
3	45	0.03%
4	9	0.01%
5	1	0.00%
6	2	0.00%
8	1	0.00%

```
SELECT c.HouseholdId, o.*
FROM Orders o JOIN Customers c ON o.CustomerId = c.CustomerId JOIN
    (SELECT c.HouseholdId, MIN(o.OrderId) as minorderid
     FROM Orders o JOIN Customers c ON o.CustomerId = c.CustomerId JOIN
        (SELECT c.HouseholdId, MIN(o.OrderDate) as minorderdate
         FROM Orders o JOIN Customers c
             ON o.CustomerId = c.CustomerId
         GROUP BY c.HouseholdId) ho
        ON ho.HouseholdId = c.HouseholdId AND
           ho.minorderdate = o.OrderDate
     GROUP BY c.HouseholdId) hhmin
    ON hhmin.HouseholdId = c.HouseholdId AND
       hhmin.minorderid = o.OrderId
```

This is a rather complicated query for a rather simple question. Without an incredible SQL optimizer, it requires joining `Orders` and `Customers` three times for what seems like a relatively direct question.

This query could be simplified by assuming that the smallest `OrderId` in a household occurred on the earliest `OrderDate`. This condition is definitely worth checking for:

```
SELECT COUNT(*) as numhh,
       SUM(CASE WHEN o.OrderDate = minodate THEN 1 ELSE 0
           END) as numsame
FROM (SELECT c.HouseholdId, MIN(o.OrderDate) as minodate,
             MIN(o.OrderId) as minorderid
      FROM Orders o JOIN Customers c ON o.CustomerId = c.CustomerId
      GROUP BY c.HouseholdId
      HAVING COUNT(*) > 1) ho JOIN
     Orders o
     ON ho.minorderid = o.OrderId
ORDER BY numhh
```

This query looks only at households that have more than one order. For those, it compares the minimum order date to the date of the order with the minimum order ID.

This query finds 21,965 households with more than one order. Of these, 18,973 have the order date associated with the smallest ID being the same as the earliest order date. There remain 2,992 households whose minimum order date differs from the order date on the minimum order ID. Assuming that the minimum `OrderId` occurred on the earliest `OrderDate` would be convenient, but it is simply not true.

Using Window Functions

The following query calculates the earliest date for each household using a window function and uses this value for the rest of the calculation:

```
SELECT nummindateorders, COUNT(*) as numhh,
       MIN(HouseholdId), MAX(HouseholdId)
FROM (SELECT c.HouseholdId, o.OrderDate, COUNT(*) as nummindateorders,
```

```
                    MIN(o.OrderDate) OVER (PARTITION BY c.HouseholdId
                                           ) as minOD
          FROM Orders o JOIN Customers c ON o.CustomerId = c.CustomerId
          GROUP BY c.HouseholdId, o.OrderDate
          ) h
WHERE OrderDate = minOD
GROUP BY nummindateorders
ORDER BY nummindateorders
```

This version is much simpler because it uses only one subquery. Notice that the GROUP BY clause uses both the order ID and the order date. This allows the MIN(OrderDate) expression to calculate the first order date for each household.

The above query returns *all* the orders on the earliest date. Because the earliest date might have multiple orders, it is better to use ROW_NUMBER() to choose just one:

```
SELECT h.*
FROM (SELECT c.HouseholdId, o.OrderDate,
             ROW_NUMBER() OVER (PARTITION BY c.HouseholdId
                                ORDER BY OrderDate, OrderId) as seqnum
      FROM Orders o JOIN Customers c ON o.CustomerId = c.CustomerId
      ) h
WHERE seqnum = 1
```

ROW_NUMBER() assigns a sequence of values for each household based on the date. The outer query chooses the row with the smallest value.

SQL WINDOW FUNCTIONS AND GETTING THE FIRST AND LAST ROW

The ranking functions discussed earlier in this chapter are examples of SQL window functions (discussed in Chapter 1). SQL window functions are similar to aggregation functions in that they calculate summary values. Instead of returning a smaller set of summary rows, the summary values are appended onto each row in the original data.

For example, the following statement returns all the records in Orders along with the average order amount:

```
SELECT AVG(TotalPrice) OVER (), o.*
FROM Orders o
```

The syntax is similar to the syntax for the ranking functions. The OVER keyword indicates that this is a window aggregation function rather than a group by aggregation function. The part in parentheses describes the window of rows that the AVG() works on. With no PARTITION BY clause the statement takes the average of all rows.

The partitioning statement acts like a GROUP BY. So, the following calculates the average order amount for each household:

```
SELECT AVG(o.TotalPrice) OVER (PARTITION BY c.HouseholdId), o.*
FROM Orders o JOIN
     Customers c
     ON o.CustomerId = c.CustomerId
```

continues

continued

Unlike aggregation functions, the household average is appended onto every row. Window functions can also take an ORDER BY clause, which makes the values cumulative.

Window aggregation functions are quite powerful and quite useful. The simplest way to get the first and last values is to use FIRST_VALUE():

```
SELECT FIRST_VALUE(TotalPrice) OVER (PARTITION BY c.HouseholdId
                                     ORDER BY OrderDate) as tpfirst,
       FIRST_VALUE(TotalPrice) OVER (PARTITION BY c.HouseholdId
                                     ORDER BY OrderDate DESC) as tplast,
       o.*
FROM Orders o JOIN Customers c ON o.CustomerId = c.CustomerId
```

Unfortunately, this function is not available in all databases, even those that support window functions.

A relatively simple work-around is to use ROW_NUMBER() and conditional aggregation:

```
SELECT HouseholdId,
       MAX(CASE WHEN i = 1 THEN TotalPrice END) as pricefirst,
       MAX(CASE WHEN i = n THEN TotalPrice END) as pricelast
FROM (SELECT o.*, c.HouseholdId,
             COUNT(*) OVER (PARTITION BY c.HouseholdId) as n,
             ROW_NUMBER() OVER (PARTITION BY c.HouseholdId
                                ORDER BY o.OrderDate ASC) as i
      FROM Orders o JOIN Customers c ON o.CustomerId = c.CustomerId
     ) h
GROUP BY HouseholdId
```

The subquery enumerates the orders in each household and calculates the total number. It then uses conditional aggregation in the outer query to get the amounts of the first and last orders.

Window functions are very useful, even though their functionality can often be expressed using other SQL constructs (this is not true of the ranking window functions). They are equivalent to doing the following:

1. Doing a GROUP BY aggregation on the partition columns; and then,
2. Joining the results back to the original on the partition columns.

Window functions are a significant improvement for several reasons. First, they allow values with different partitioning columns to be calculated in the same SELECT statement. Second, the ranking window functions introduce a new level of functionality that is much harder to replicate without the functions. Third, they work on NULL values as well as other values—so you do not have to worry about losing rows because of NULL comparisons in a join. And finally, they are often more efficient because SQL engines have special optimizations for them.

Comparing the First and Last Values

Given the order amounts on the earliest and latest dates, what is the best way to compare these values? Four possibilities are:

- The difference between the earliest and latest purchase amounts. This is useful for determining the households whose spending is increasing (positive differences) and decreasing (negative differences).
- The ratio of the latest purchase amount to the earliest purchase amount. Ratios between zero and one are decreasing and ratios over one are increasing.
- The difference divided by the time units. This makes it possible to say that the customer is increasing their purchase amounts by so many dollars every day (or week or month or year).
- The ratio raised to the power of one divided by the number of time units. This makes it possible to say that the customer is increasing their purchase amounts by some percentage every day (or week or month or year).

What do the differences look like? Only about twenty thousand households have more than one order. This is a small enough number for an Excel scatter plot.

Figure 8-11 shows the distribution and cumulative distribution of the differences. The cumulative percent crosses the $0 line at about 67%, showing that more households have decreasing order amounts than increasing order amounts. The summaries for the chart are done in Excel.

What Happens as Customer Span Increases

Figure 8-12 shows what happens to the difference as the span between the first and last purchases increases. The chart has two curves, one for the total number of households whose purchases have that span (in 30-day increments) and one for the average price difference.

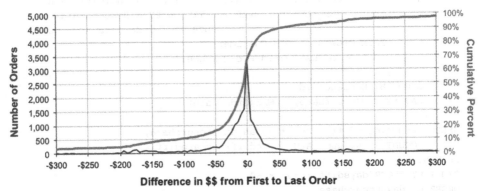

Figure 8-11: The distribution of the differences in total price between the first order and the last order shows that more households have decreases than increases in the order amounts.

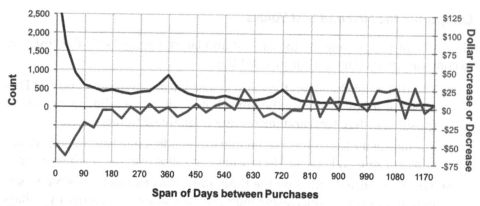

Figure 8-12: As the customer time span increases, the amount that customers increase their spending also increases.

For the shortest time spans, the second purchase has a lower value than the first for a strong majority of households. However, after about six months, the breakdown is more even. As the time span between the first purchase and last purchase increases, the later purchase is more likely to be larger than the first. The count of purchases has a wave pattern that fades over time, corresponding to households that make purchases at the same time of the year.

The SQL for making this chart uses the subquery that finds the first and last total price amounts; the query then aggregates these results for the chart:

```
WITH ho as (
    SELECT HouseholdId,
           (MAX(CASE WHEN i = n THEN TotalPrice END) -
            MAX(CASE WHEN i = 1 THEN TotalPrice END) ) as pricediff,
           DATEDIFF(day, MIN(OrderDate),
                    MAX(OrderDate)) + 1 as daysdiff
    FROM (SELECT o.*, c.HouseholdId,
                 COUNT(*) OVER (PARTITION BY c.HouseholdId) as n,
                 ROW_NUMBER() OVER (PARTITION BY c.HouseholdId
                                    ORDER BY o.OrderDate ASC) as i
          FROM Orders o JOIN Customers c
               ON o.CustomerId = c.CustomerId
         ) h
    GROUP BY HouseholdId
    HAVING MIN(OrderDate) < MAX(OrderDate)
    )
SELECT FLOOR(daysdiff / 30) * 30 as daystopurchase,
       COUNT(*) as num, AVG(pricediff) as avgdiff
FROM ho
GROUP BY FLOOR(daysdiff / 30) * 30
ORDER BY daystopurchase
```

The chart itself uses a trick to align the horizontal grid lines; this is challenging because the count on the left-hand axis has only positive values, and the dollar amount on the right-hand axis has both positive and negative values. The grid lines are lined up by making the left-hand axis go from –1,500 to +2,500 and the right hand from –$75 to +$125. The left-hand axis spans 4,000 units, which is a multiple of the 200 spanned by the right-hand axis, so aligning the horizontal grid lines on both axes is easy. Negative values make no sense for counts, so the left-hand axis does not show negative values. The trick is using a special number format, "#,##0;". This says "put commas in numbers greater than or equal to zero and don't put anything for negative numbers."

TIP When using two vertical axes, make the horizontal grids line up. This is easiest if the range on one axis is a multiple of the range on the other axis.

What Happens as Customer Order Amounts Vary

The alternative viewpoint is to summarize the data by the difference in TotalPrice between the latest order and the earliest order. This summary works best when the difference is placed into bins. For this example, the bins are defined by the first number of the difference followed by a sufficient number of zeros: $1, $2, $3, . . . $9, $10, $20, . . . $90, $100, $200, and so on. Formally, these bins are powers of ten times the first digit of the difference. Other binning methods are possible, such as equal-sized bins. However, binning by the first digit makes the bins easy to read and easy for others to understand.

The chart in Figure 8-13 shows the number of households in each bin and the average time between orders. The number of households is quite spiky because of the binning process. Every power of ten, the size of the bin suddenly jumps by a factor of ten. The range of $90–$100 is in one bin. The next bin is not $100–$110, it is instead $100–$200, which is ten times larger. One way to eliminate the spikiness is to show the cumulative number of households, rather than the number in the bin itself. This eliminates the spikiness but may be less intuitive for people seeing the chart for the first time.

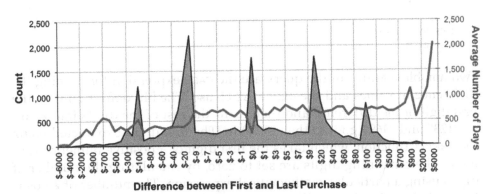

Figure 8-13: The span of time that customers make purchases is related to the average difference in dollar amounts between the first and last orders.

The average time span tends to increase as the difference in order sizes increases. This suggests that the longer a customer is active, the more the customer is spending, on average. However, this effect is most pronounced for the most negative differences. Customers whose purchases decrease dramatically are making purchases during relatively short time spans.

The query that generates the data for this chart is similar to the previous query, except for the GROUP BY clause:

```
WITH ho as (
    SELECT HouseholdId,
           (MAX(CASE WHEN i = n THEN TotalPrice END) -
            MAX(CASE WHEN i = 1 THEN TotalPrice END) ) as pricediff,
           DATEDIFF(day, MIN(OrderDate),
                    MAX(OrderDate)) + 1 as daysdiff
    FROM (SELECT o.*, c.HouseholdId,
                 COUNT(*) OVER (PARTITION BY c.HouseholdId) as n,
                 ROW_NUMBER() OVER (PARTITION BY c.HouseholdId
                                    ORDER BY o.OrderDate ASC) as i
          FROM Orders o JOIN Customers c
               ON o.CustomerId = c.CustomerId
         ) h
    GROUP BY HouseholdId
    HAVING MIN(OrderDate) < MAX(OrderDate)
    )
SELECT diffgroup, COUNT(*) as numhh, AVG(daysdiff) as avgdaysdiff
FROM (SELECT ho.*,
             (CASE WHEN pricediff = 0 THEN '$0'
                   WHEN pricediff BETWEEN -1 and 0 THEN '$-0'
                   WHEN pricediff BETWEEN 0 AND 1 THEN '$+0'
                   WHEN pricediff < 0
                   THEN '$-' + LEFT(-pricediff, 1) +
                        LEFT('000000000', FLOOR(LOG(-pricediff)/LOG(10)))
                   ELSE '$' + LEFT(pricediff, 1) +
                        LEFT('000000000', FLOOR(LOG(pricediff)/LOG(10)))
              END) as diffgroup
      FROM ho
     ) ho
GROUP BY diffgroup
ORDER BY MIN(pricediff)
```

Two notable features in the query are the CASE expression for binning the difference in values and the ORDER BY clause. The bin definition uses the first digit of the difference and then turns the rest of the digits into zeros, so "123" and "169" go into the "100" bin. The first digit is extracted using the LEFT() function, which takes the first digit of a positive numeric argument. The remaining digits are set to zero, by calculating the number of digits using a particular mathematical expression. The number of zeros is the log in base 10 of the difference, and the log in base 10 is the log in any base divided by the log of 10 in that base (so the expression works even in databases where LOG() calculates the natural log). The process is the same for negative differences, except the absolute value is used and a negative sign prepended to the result.

The purpose of the ORDER BY clause is to order the bins numerically. An alphabetical order would order them as "$1," "$10," "$100," "$1,000," and these would be followed by "$2." To get a numeric ordering, we extract one value from the bin, the minimum value, and order by this. Actually, any value would do, but the minimum is convenient.

Comparison of First Year Values and Last Year Values

The previous section compared the first order amount value to the last order amount. This section makes a slightly different comparison: *How does the average household's purchase change from the first year they make a purchase to the most recent year?*

Table 8-12 contains the difference between the order amount during the earliest year and the latest year. When the purchases are on successive years, the difference is almost always negative. However, as the time span grows, the difference becomes positive indicating that the order sizes are growing. A simple explanation might be that prices increase over time.

Figure 8-14 shows these results as a scatter plot, where the horizontal axis is the average amount in the first year and the vertical axis is the average amount in the last year. The diagonal line divides the chart into two regions. Below the line, purchases are decreasing over time and above it, purchases are increasing. The lowest point in the chart shows the households whose earliest purchase was in 2009 and whose latest purchase was in 2011; the earlier purchase average was about $35 and the later was about $37. An interesting feature of the chart is that all the points below the line come from either one- or two-year spans. The longer the time span, the larger the later purchases.

Table 8-12: Difference between Average First and Last Year Order Amounts

YEAR	2010	2011	2012	2013	2014	2015	2016
2009	$9.90	$6.74	$38.46	$32.67	$40.32	$51.08	$69.10
2010		-$16.11	-$1.07	$26.81	$11.19	$22.75	$49.26
2011			$2.22	$16.26	$11.53	$12.88	$27.82
2012				$2.40	$8.50	$16.19	$52.11
2013					-$16.57	-$7.84	$35.23
2014						-$20.82	-$16.71
2015							-$68.71

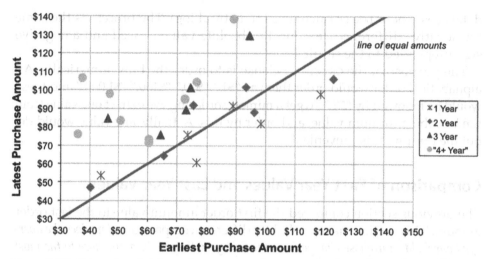

Figure 8-14: This scatter plot shows the average order amount for the earliest orders and latest orders for households. Households below the diagonal line have decreasing orders; those above have increasing orders.

The query calculates the average purchase size for pairs of years, the first and last years that households make purchases. Each row also contains the average size of the purchase during the first year and the average size during the second year:

```
SELECT minyear, maxyear, AVG (avgearliest) as avgearliest,
       AVG(avglatest) as avglatest,
       (AVG(avglatest) - AVG(avgearliest)) as diff, COUNT(*) as numhh
FROM (SELECT hy.householdid, minyear, maxyear,
             MAX(CASE WHEN hy.theyear = minyear THEN sumprice END
                 ) as avgearliest,
             MAX(CASE WHEN hy.theyear = maxyear THEN sumprice END
                 ) as avglatest
      FROM (SELECT c.HouseholdId, YEAR(o.OrderDate) as theyear,
                   SUM(o.TotalPrice) as sumprice,
                   MIN(YEAR(OrderDate)) OVER (PARTITION BY HouseholdId
                                              ) as minyear,
                   MAX(YEAR(OrderDate)) OVER (PARTITION BY HouseholdId
                                              ) as maxyear
            FROM Orders o JOIN Customers c
                 ON o.CustomerId = c.CustomerId
            GROUP BY c.HouseholdId, YEAR(o.OrderDate)
            ) hy
      WHERE minyear <> maxyear
      GROUP BY hy.HouseholdId, minyear, maxyear) h
GROUP BY minyear, maxyear
ORDER BY minyear, maxyear
```

This query aggregates the orders data using nested subqueries. The innermost is by `HouseholdId` and the year of the order date. This calculates the total amount in each year and it also calculates the first and last years using window functions. These results are aggregated at the household level, to get the earliest and latest years. The final aggregation summarizes the orders by pairs of years.

Trend from the Best Fit Line

This section goes one step further by calculating the slope of the line that best fits the `TotalPrice` values. This calculation relies on some mathematical manipulation, essentially implementing the equation for the slope in SQL. The advantage is that it takes into account all the purchases over time, instead of just the first and last ones.

Using the Slope

Figure 8-15 shows the purchases for two households over several years. One household has seen their orders increase over time; the other has seen them decrease. The chart also shows the best-fit line for each household. The household with increasing purchases has a line that goes up, so the slope is positive. The other line decreases, so its slope is negative. Chapter 12 discusses best-fit lines in more detail.

The best-fit line connecting the household with increasing purchases has a slope of 0.464, which means that for each day, the expected value of an order from the household increases by $0.46, or about $169 per year. This slope can be useful for reporting purposes, although it works better when there are more data points. Slopes are better at summarizing data collected monthly, rather than for irregular, infrequent transactions.

Calculating the Slope

The formula for a line is often written in terms of its slope and Y-intercept. If we knew the formula for the best-fit line, the slope would fall out of it. Fortunately,

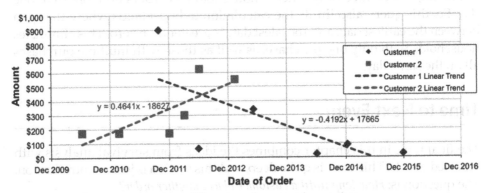

Figure 8-15: These customers have different purchase trends over time.

the best-fit line is not difficult to calculate in SQL. Each data point—each order—needs an X-coordinate and a Y-coordinate. The Y-coordinate is the `TotalPrice` on the order at that point in time. The X-coordinate should be the date. Dates do not work particularly well in mathematical calculations, so instead we'll use the number of days since the beginning of 2000. The idea is to use these X- and Y-coordinates to calculate the trend (slope) of the best-fit line.

The formula requires five aggregation columns:

- n: the number of data points
- sumx: the sum of the X-values of the data points
- sumxy: the sum of the product of the X-value times the Y-value
- sumy: sum of the Y-values
- sumyy: sum of the squares of the Y-values

The slope is then the ratio between two numbers. The numerator is n*sumxy - sumx*sumy; the denominator is n*sumxx - sumx*sumx.

The following query does this calculation:

```
SELECT h.*, (1.0*n*sumxy - sumx*sumy)/(n*sumxx - sumx*sumx) as slope
FROM (SELECT HouseholdId, COUNT(*) as n,
             SUM(1.0*days) as sumx, SUM(1.0*days*days) as sumxx,
             SUM(totalprice) as sumy, SUM(days*totalprice) as sumxy
      FROM (SELECT o.*, DATEDIFF(day, '2000-01-01', OrderDate) as days
            FROM Orders o
           ) o JOIN
           Customers c
           ON o.CustomerId = c.CustomerId
      GROUP BY HouseholdId
      HAVING MIN(OrderDate) < MAX(OrderDate) ) h
```

The innermost subquery defines `days`, which is the difference between the order date and the beginning of 2000. Then the five variables are calculated in another subquery, and finally `slope` in the outermost.

The slope is defined only when a household has orders on more than one day. So, this query also limits the calculation to households where the span between the earliest date and the latest date is greater than zero. This eliminates households with only one purchase, as well as those with multiple purchases all on the same day.

Time to Next Event

The final topic in this chapter combines the ideas from survival analysis with repeated events. This topic is quite deep, and this section is just an introduction. The question is: *How long until a customer places another order?*

Idea behind the Calculation

To apply survival analysis to repeated events, each order needs the date of the next order in the household (if any). The order date and next order date provide the basic information needed for time-to-event survival analysis. The definitions for survival analysis are inverted from the last two chapters:

- The "start" event is when a customer makes a purchase.
- The "end" event is either the next purchase date or the cutoff date.

This terminology for repeated events is backward. "Survival" ends up meaning the survival of the customer's "non-purchase" state. In fact, we are interested in the exact opposite of survival, 100%-Survival, which is the cumulative probability that customers have made a purchase up to some given point in time. In statistics, this value is called *failure* (because of the application of survival analysis for understanding the failure of mechanical objects). *Cumulative events* or something similar is a better name for our purposes.

Figure 8-16 shows the overall time-to-next purchase curve for all households along with the daily "hazard" that a customer makes a purchase. Note that after three years only about 20% of customers have made another purchase. This is consistent with the fact that most households have only one order.

The hazards show an interesting story. A peak is clearly visible at one year, with echoes at two years and three years. These are customers making purchases once per year, most likely holiday shoppers. It suggests that there is a segment of such shoppers.

Calculating Next Purchase Date Using SQL

The hardest part of answering the question is appending the date of the next order. One method of calculation uses a correlated subquery. First, the Orders

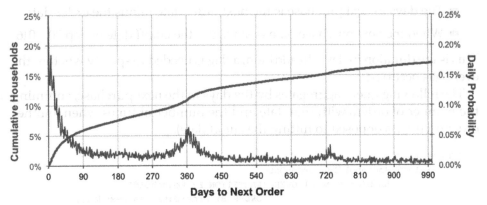

Figure 8-16: This chart shows the time to next order, both as a cumulative proportion of customers (1-Survival) and as a daily "risk" of making a purchase (hazard probability)

table and `Customer` table are joined together to append the `HouseholdId` to every order. A correlated subquery then gets the first order date bigger than the current one for each order:

```
SELECT c.HouseholdId, o.*,
       (SELECT TOP 1 o.OrderDate
        FROM Orders o2 JOIN Customers c2
            ON o2.CustomerId = c2.CustomerId
        WHERE c.HouseholdId = c2.HouseholdId AND
              o2.OrderDate > o.OrderDate
        ORDER BY o2.OrderDate
       ) as nextdate
FROM Orders o JOIN Customers c ON o.CustomerId = c.CustomerId
```

If nothing matches in the correlated subquery, then it returns NULL. Alternatively, the window function LEAD() can be used:

```
SELECT c.HouseholdId, o.*,
       LEAD(o.OrderDate) OVER (PARTITION BY c.HouseholdId
                               ORDER BY o.OrderDate) as nextdate,
       ROW_NUMBER() OVER (PARTITION BY c.HouseholdId
                          ORDER BY o.OrderDate) as seqnum,
       COUNT(*) OVER (PARTITION BY c.HouseholdId) as numorders
FROM Orders o JOIN Customers c ON o.CustomerId = c.CustomerId
```

Remember that LEAD() gets the value for a column from the "next" row, where "next" is defined by the PARTITION BY and ORDER BY clauses. Queries using window functions are simpler and more efficient.

From Next Purchase Date to Time-to-Event

The time to next purchase is calculated as follows:

- The days to next purchase is the next order date minus the order date.
- When the next purchase date is NULL, use the cutoff date of Sep 20, 2016.

This is the duration in days. In addition, a flag is needed to specify whether the event has occurred.

The following query aggregates by the days to the next purchase, summing the number of orders with that date and the number of times when another order occurs (as opposed to hitting the cutoff date):

```
WITH ho as (
     SELECT HouseholdId, OrderDate,
            LEAD(OrderDate) OVER (PARTITION BY HouseholdId
                                  ORDER BY OrderDate) as nextdate,
            ROW_NUMBER() OVER (PARTITION BY HouseholdId
                               ORDER BY OrderDate) as seqnum,
```

```
                    COUNT(*) OVER (PARTITION BY HouseholdId) as numorders
        FROM (SELECT DISTINCT c.HouseholdId, o.OrderDate
              FROM Orders o JOIN Customers c ON o.CustomerId = c.CustomerId
             ) ho
     )
SELECT DATEDIFF(day, OrderDate,
                COALESCE(nextdate, '2016-09-20')) as days,
       COUNT(*) as numorders,
       SUM(CASE WHEN seqnum = 1 THEN 1 ELSE 0 END) as ord_1,
       . . .
       COUNT(nextdate) as numorders,
       SUM(CASE WHEN seqnum = 1 AND nextdate IS NOT NULL THEN 1 ELSE 0
           END) as hasnext_1,
       . . .
FROM ho
GROUP BY DATEDIFF(day, OrderDate, COALESCE(nextdate, '2016-09-20'))
ORDER BY days
```

The calculation then proceeds by calculating the hazard, survival, and 1–S values as described in the previous two chapters. Both survival and 1–S are calculated because the latter is the more interesting value.

Stratifying Time-to-Event

As with the survival calculation, the time-to-event can be stratified. For instance, Figure 8-17 shows the time-to-next-event stratified by the number of orders that the customer has already made. These curves follow the expected track: The more often that someone places orders, the sooner they make another order.

Of course, the number of previous orders is only one variable we might want to use. We can also stratify by anything known at the order time:

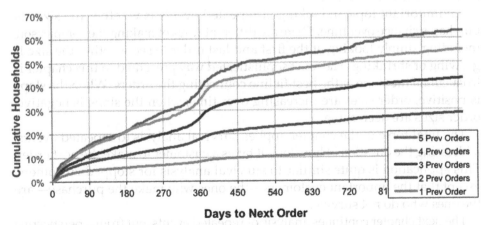

Figure 8-17: This chart shows the time to next purchase stratified by the number of previous purchases.

- Has the time-to-next order varied for orders placed in different years?
- Does the time-to-next order vary depending on the size of an order?
- Does the time-to-next order depend on the credit card used for the transaction?
- Do customers make a repeat order sooner or later when a particular item is in their basket?

All of these are simple extensions of the idea of calculating the next order date and then applying survival analysis for repeated events.

Lessons Learned

This chapter introduces repeated events, using the purchases data. Repeated events are customer interactions that occur at irregular intervals.

The first challenge with repeated events is determining whether separate events belong to the same customer. In this chapter, we learned that the CustomerId column is basically useless because it is almost always unique. A better column for identifying transactions over time is HouseholdId.

Matching customers on transactions using names and addresses is challenging and often outsourced. Even so, using SQL to validate the results is useful. Do the customers in the households make sense?

The classic way of analyzing repeated events uses RFM analysis, which stands for recency, frequency, monetary. This analysis is feasible using SQL and Excel, particularly when using the ranking functions in SQL. However, RFM is inherently limited because it focuses on only three dimensions of customer relationships. It is a cell-based approach, where customers are placed into cells and then tracked over time.

An important topic in looking at repeated events is whether the sizes of purchases change over time. There are different ways of making the comparison, including simply looking at the first and last order to see whether the size is growing or shrinking. The most sophisticated way presented in this chapter is to calculate the slope of the best-fit line connecting the orders. When the slope is positive, order sizes are increasing over time; when the slope is negative, order sizes are decreasing.

The final topic in the chapter applies survival analysis to repeated events, addressing the question of how long it takes a customer to make the next order. This application is quite similar to survival analysis for stopped customers, except that the important customers—the ones who make the purchase—are the ones who do not survive.

The next chapter continues analysis of repeated events, but from a perspective that is not covered in this chapter at all. It discusses the actual items purchased in each order and what this tells us about the items and the customers.

What's in a Shopping Cart? Market Basket Analysis

The previous chapter discussed everything about customer behavior—when, where, how—with one notable exception: the products actually being purchased. This chapter and the next dive into the detail, focusing on the specific products, to learn both about customers and the products they buy. *Market basket analysis* is the general name for understanding product purchase patterns at the customer level. Association rules, covered in the next chapter, are specifically about discovering which products are purchased together.

This chapter starts by exploring the individual products purchased in an order. Visualizing the products tells us about both products and customers. And brings up unusual questions, such as "Why do customers purchase the same product multiple times in an order?"

These types of questions naturally lead to investigating the relationship between products and customer behavior. Is purchasing some particular product or products an indicator that the purchaser will return? Conversely, do some products indicate that the customer will make no more purchases? Can we measure the contribution of a product to overall customer value? Answering this question leads to *residual value*, the value of everything else in orders containing a particular product. Residual value is a useful measure of how good products are for driving increased sales.

Products are related to other customer attributes as well. Some products have a wide geographic distribution; others may be more narrowly focused. One of the challenges in understanding products is that each product is on its own row in the database. This is true even for simple questions, such as which orders contain two or three specific products. This type of query is called a *set-within-a-set* query, and SQL offers several ways to approach this type of query.

The data for market basket analysis is more complex than for survival analysis because a single transaction is represented by multiple rows—each row containing a separate product. Analyzing such data introduces some new capabilities in SQL, including the ability to concatenate strings in an aggregation query.

Exploring the Products

This section explores the purchases database from the perspective of understanding the products in the orders.

Scatter Plot of Products

The Products table contains about 4,000 products, which are classified into nine product groups. Chapter 3 analyzed the orders and determined that the most popular group is BOOK.

Two of the most interesting features of products are price and popularity. Scatter plots are a good way to visualize this information, with different groups having different shapes and colors. The following query extracts the information for the scatter plot:

```
SELECT p.ProductId, p.GroupName, p.FullPrice, olp.numorders
FROM (SELECT ol.ProductId, COUNT(DISTINCT ol.OrderId) as numorders
      FROM OrderLines ol
      GROUP BY ol.ProductId
     ) olp JOIN
     Products p
     ON olp.ProductId = p.ProductId
```

This is a basic JOIN and aggregation query, providing the number of orders a product is in as well as its full price.

The scatter plot in Figure 9-1 shows relationships among these three features. Along the bottom of the chart are the few dozen products that have a price of $0. Most of these are, appropriately, in the FREEBIE category, along with a handful in the OTHER category. Although not obvious on the scatter plot, all FREEBIE products do, indeed, have a price of zero as their name suggests.

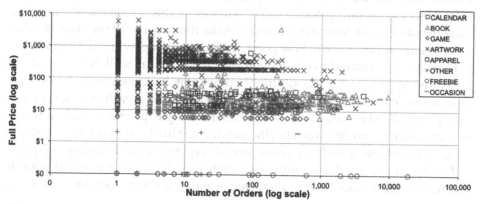

Figure 9-1: This scatter plot shows the relationship between product groups, price, and number of purchases.

The upper left-hand portion of the chart consists almost entirely of products in the ARTWORK product group. These products are expensive and rarely purchased. A few products in the ARTWORK group are quite popular (purchased by more than a thousand customers) and some that are relatively inexpensive (well under one hundred dollars), but these are exceptions within the category.

The most popular product group is BOOK, as seen by the abundance of triangles on the right side of the chart. Most are inexpensive, but one is among the most expensive products. This is, perhaps, an example of misclassification or perhaps the product is really a collection of books. The rest of the products tend to be in the middle, both in terms of pricing and popularity.

The scatter plot is a log-log plot, meaning that both the horizontal and vertical axes are on a logarithmic scale where one unit on either axis increases the axis value by a factor of ten. Log scales are useful when the values on an axis are all positive and have a wide range of values with a long tail.

Log-log plots are not able to plot zero because the logarithm of zero is undefined, and yet the chart shows the "0" value. The chart is using a trick: the "zero" value is really 0.1, which when formatted to have no decimal places looks like "0" instead of "0.1." To make this work, the zeros in the data have to be replaced by the value 0.1, either using SQL:

```
(CASE WHEN <value> = 0 THEN 0.1 ELSE <value> END) as <whatever>
```

Or using Excel:

```
=IF(<cellref>=0, 0.1, <cellref>)
```

The number format for the chart simply shows the value with no decimal places.

> **TIP** Use the log scale on axes where the values have a wide range and all values are positive. The log scale does not work when values are negative or zero; however, it is possible to show zero values by changing them to a small value and then using clever formatting.

Which Product Groups Are Shipped in Which Years?

This is a rather simple question about product groups and years. Yet, it introduces a subtly. *What if we are interested in product groups not shipped in particular years?* (The only reason for asking about the shipping date rather than the order date is to avoid the extra join back to `Orders`.)

An aggregation query readily answers the question about which product groups are shipped in each year:

```
SELECT YEAR(ol.ShipDate) as yr, p.GroupName, COUNT(*) as Count
FROM OrderLines ol JOIN
     Products p
     ON ol.ProductId = p.ProductId
GROUP BY YEAR(ol.ShipDate), p.GroupName
ORDER BY yr, GroupName
```

Table 9-1: Number of Orders with a Specific Product Group in 2009

YEAR	PRODUCT GROUP	COUNT
2009	APPAREL	15
2009	ARTWORK	4,835
2009	BOOK	3,917
2009	CALENDAR	15
2009	OCCASION	1,112

Table 9-1 shows the results for 2009.

But can we get the year/group name combinations with no orders? This question poses a fundamental challenge: SQL only operates on the data in the tables, but this question is asking about data that is not the table. SQL statements have no special clause that says, "include extra values that are not in the original table."

The solution lies in thinking about the problem a little bit differently. The key idea is to break the logic into three steps: First, get the combinations of all the years and all the product groups—a CROSS JOIN operator can generate these combinations. Then use LEFT JOIN to get the counts. Finally, use a WHERE clause to get the values that have no corresponding rows. That is, generate all possible combinations first, and then filter out the ones that are present. The query then returns the missing combinations.

The following query enhances the above results by including zeros for the year/group combinations that are not present:

```
SELECT y.yr, g.GroupName, COALESCE(cnt, 0) as cnt
FROM (SELECT DISTINCT YEAR(ShipDate) as yr FROM OrderLines ol
     ) y CROSS JOIN
     (SELECT DISTINCT GroupName FROM Products) g LEFT JOIN
     (SELECT YEAR(ol.ShipDate) as yr, p.GroupName, COUNT(*) as cnt
     FROM OrderLines ol JOIN
          Products p
          ON p.ProductId = ol.ProductId
     GROUP BY YEAR(ol.ShipDate), p.GroupName
     ) olp
     ON olp.yr = y.yr and olp.GroupName = g.GroupName
ORDER BY y.yr, g.GroupName
```

The FROM clause has three subqueries. The first extracts all the years of interest from OrderLines. The second extracts all the group names from Products. The CROSS JOIN creates a Cartesian product, which is all the combinations of product groups and years—all the possible rows that we could want.

Table 9-2: Number of Orders for All Product Groups in 2009

YEAR	GROUP NAME	NUMBER OF ORDERS
2009	#N/A	0
2009	APPAREL	15
2009	ARTWORK	4,835
2009	BOOK	3,917
2009	CALENDAR	15
2009	FREEBIE	0
2009	GAME	0
2009	OCCASION	1,112
2009	OTHER	0

The third subquery calculates the count where data *is* available (the first subquery in this section). The LEFT JOIN keeps all the combinations from the CROSS JOIN. The COALESCE() in the outer query turns the non-matching counts from NULL to zero. Table 9-2 shows the results for 2009. Notice that all product groups are now present.

Finding the product/year combinations that are missing uses a similar query; but this version can be simplified because the count is unnecessary. There are several approaches—using NOT EXISTS, for instance. Here is another method that uses LEFT JOIN and a WHERE clause:

```
SELECT y.yr, g.GroupName
FROM (SELECT DISTINCT YEAR(ShipDate) as yr FROM OrderLines ol
     ) y CROSS JOIN
     (SELECT DISTINCT GroupName FROM Products) g LEFT JOIN
     (SELECT YEAR(ol.ShipDate) as yr, p.GroupName
      FROM OrderLines ol JOIN
           Products p
           ON p.ProductId = ol.ProductId
     ) olp
     ON olp.yr = y.yr and olp.GroupName = g.GroupName
WHERE olp.yr IS NULL
ORDER BY y.yr, g.GroupName
```

Note that this query eliminates the count and even the aggregation in the third query. The count is unnecessary because it is always zero. If the count is unneeded, so is the aggregation.

> **TIP** When you have a question about combinations of things that are not in the data, think about using CROSS JOIN in combination with a LEFT JOIN.

Table 9-3: Years with No Shipments of Particular Product Groups

YEAR	PRODUCT GROUP
2009	#N/A
2009	FREEBIE
2009	GAME
2009	OTHER
2010	#N/A
2010	GAME
2011	#N/A
2012	#N/A
2012	FREEBIE
2013	#N/A
2013	FREEBIE
2015	#N/A
2016	#N/A

Table 9-3 shows the results, which are not particularly interesting. The group #N/A appears to be some sort of error in the data with only nine products in 2014. Freebies are part of marketing promotions, so are not under the control of customers. GAME and OTHER appear to have been introduced in 2010 and 2011.

Duplicate Products in Orders

Sometimes, the same product occurs multiple times in the same order. This is an anomaly because such orders should use the NumUnits column for multiple products rather than replicating the same product on multiple order lines. What is happening? Let's investigate this phenomenon and several hypotheses along the way.

Counting the number of orders with duplicate products is a good place to start:

```
SELECT numinorder, COUNT(*) as cnt, COUNT(DISTINCT ProductId) as numprods
FROM (SELECT ol.OrderId, ol.ProductId, COUNT(*) as numinorder
      FROM OrderLines ol
      GROUP BY ol.OrderId, ol.ProductId
     ) olp
GROUP BY numinorder
ORDER BY numinorder
```

The query counts the number of orders that have the same product on more than one order line, and the number of different products that appear on those orders.

Table 9-4 shows that almost 98% of the time products appear on only one order line, as expected. However, there are clearly exceptions. *What might be the cause of such duplicates?* The next few sections discuss different possibilities and how these can be investigated in SQL.

Are Duplicates Explained by the Product?

One possible explanation is that some small group of products is to blame. Perhaps some products just have a tendency to appear on multiple order lines. The following query counts the number of products that are duplicated in any order:

```
SELECT COUNT(DISTINCT ProductId)
FROM (SELECT ol.OrderId, ol.ProductId
      FROM OrderLines ol
      GROUP BY ol.OrderId, ol.ProductId
      HAVING COUNT(*) > 1
     ) op
```

There are 1,343 such products—about a third of all the products. With such a large number appearing multiple times, no particular products seem to explain the order line duplication.

Table 9-4: Number of Order Lines within an Order Having the Same Product

LINES IN ORDER WITH PRODUCT	NUMBER OF ORDERS	NUMBER OF PRODUCTS	% OF ORDERS
1	272,824	3,684	97.9%
2	5,009	1,143	1.8%
3	686	344	0.2%
4	155	101	0.1%
5	51	40	0.0%
6	20	14	0.0%
7	1	1	0.0%
8	4	3	0.0%
9	1	1	0.0%
11	2	2	0.0%
12	1	1	0.0%
40	1	1	0.0%

Are Duplicates Explained by the Product Group?

Perhaps some product groups are more likely to have duplicates than other product groups. This leads to the question: *What proportion of products is ever duplicated for each product group?* This query is a little challenging to answer because first we have to find the duplicated products, and then we need to summarize the products by their group:

```
SELECT p.GroupName,
       SUM(CASE WHEN maxnumol = 1 THEN 1 ELSE 0 END) as Singletons,
       SUM(CASE WHEN maxnumol > 1 THEN 1 ELSE 0 END) as Dups,
       AVG(CASE WHEN maxnumol > 1 THEN 1.0 ELSE 0 END) as DupRatio
FROM (SELECT olp.ProductId, MAX(numol) as maxnumol
      FROM (SELECT ol.OrderId, ol.ProductId, COUNT(*) as numol
            FROM OrderLines ol
            GROUP BY ol.OrderId, ol.ProductId
           ) olp
      GROUP BY olp.ProductId
     ) lp JOIN
     Products p
     ON lp.ProductId = p.ProductId
GROUP BY p.GroupName
ORDER BY DupRatio DESC
```

This query actually contains three levels of aggregations—not uncommon for some interesting questions. Of note are the nested aggregations. The innermost subquery aggregates by product and order, to gather the basic information about which products appear more than once. The next level aggregates by product, before joining in the Products table.

The query can actually be simplified by eliminating one level of aggregation. The key observation is that we can count the number of orders a product is in and the number of order lines—by using COUNT DISTINCT:

```
SELECT p.GroupName,
       SUM(CASE WHEN NumOrderLines = NumOrders THEN 1 ELSE 0
           END) as Singletons,
       SUM(CASE WHEN NumOrderLines > NumOrders THEN 1 ELSE 0 END) as Dups,
       AVG(CASE WHEN NumOrderLines > NumOrders THEN 1.0 ELSE 0
           END) as DupRatio
FROM (SELECT ol.ProductId, COUNT(DISTINCT ol.OrderId) as NumOrders,
             COUNT(*) as NumOrderLines
      FROM OrderLines ol
      GROUP BY ol.ProductId
     ) lp JOIN
     Products p
     ON lp.ProductId = p.ProductId
GROUP BY p.GroupName
ORDER BY DupRatio DESC
```

Table 9-5: Number of Products in a Group Having Multiple Order Lines

PRODUCT GROUP NAME	PRODUCTS NEVER DUPLICATED	PRODUCTS WITH SOME DUPLICATION	DUPLICATION RATIO
CALENDAR	9	22	71.0%
BOOK	112	128	53.3%
OCCASION	34	37	52.1%
APPAREL	43	43	50.0%
OTHER	31	24	43.6%
ARTWORK	2,254	1,046	31.7%
FREEBIE	19	6	24.0%
GAME	194	37	16.0%
#N/A	1	0	0.0%

This query compares the number of order lines to the number of orders for each product. If these are the same, then there are no duplicates.

Which approach is better, the extra subquery or COUNT(DISTINCT)? There is no right answer. The subquery is more versatile because the same logic can be used to count products that appear exactly twice in orders, exactly three times, and so on. From a performance perspective, the two are probably similar because COUNT(DISTINCT) is an expensive operation and similar, in a very broad sense, to doing another level of aggregation.

The results in Table 9-5 show a wide variation in the number of products that are duplicated. On the high side are CALENDAR and BOOK. On the low side are ARTWORK and GAME. This relationship is not particularly surprising. ARTWORK, for instance, has many more products than expected with a quantity of one in orders—and if only one of something is being ordered, then it is not duplicated.

Are Duplicates Explained by Timing?

The products do not seem to explain the duplication. What might be another explanation? A reasonable alternative hypothesis is that the duplicates come from a particular period of time. Perhaps there was a period of time when NumUnits was not used. Looking at the date of the first order containing each duplicate product sheds light on this:

```
SELECT YEAR(minshipdate) as year, COUNT(*) as cnt
FROM (SELECT ol.OrderId, ol.ProductId, MIN(ol.ShipDate) as minshipdate
      FROM OrderLines ol
      GROUP BY ol.OrderId, ol.ProductId
```

```
        HAVING COUNT(*) > 1
    ) olp
GROUP BY YEAR(minshipdate)
ORDER BY year
```

The query uses `ShipDate` instead of `OrderDate` simply to avoid joining in `Orders`. The `HAVING` clause chooses only those `OrderId` and `ProductId` pairs that appear more than once—the orders that have duplicates.

Some years have much higher occurrences of products on duplicate order lines, as shown in Table 9-6. However, the phenomenon has occurred in all years that have data. The reason for the duplicates is not a short-term change in policy.

Are Duplicates Explained by Multiple Ship Dates or Prices?

The duplicates seem to be due neither to products nor time. Perhaps in desperation, the next thing to consider is other data within `OrderLines`. Two columns of interest are `ShipDate` and `UnitPrice`. These columns suggest the question: *How often do multiple ship dates and unit prices occur for the same product within an order?*

The idea behind answering this question is to classify each occurrence of multiple lines into the following categories:

- "ONE" or "SOME" unit prices
- "ONE" or "SOME" shipping dates

Table 9-7 shows the results from such a classification. Having multiple values for `ShipDate` suggests an inventory issue. A customer orders multiple units of a particular item, but there is not enough in stock. Part of the order ships immediately, part ships at a later time.

Table 9-6: Number of Orders with Duplicate Products by Year

YEAR	NUMBER OF ORDERS WITH DUPLICATE PRODUCTS
2009	66
2010	186
2011	392
2012	181
2013	152
2014	1,433
2015	2,570
2016	951

Table 9-7: Classification of Duplicate Order Lines by Number of Shipping Dates and Prices within Order

PRICES	SHIP DATES	NUMBER OF PRODUCTS	NUMBER OF ORDERS
ONE	ONE	262	1,649
ONE	SOME	1,177	4,173
SOME	ONE	33	44
SOME	SOME	59	65

Having multiple values for UnitPrice suggests that a customer may be getting a discount on some of the units, but the discount is not available on all of them. And, over 1,000 orders still have duplicate products with the same ship date and unit price on all of them. These might be errors. Or, they might be related to data that is unavailable, such as orders going to multiple shipping addresses.

The following query was used to generate the table:

```
SELECT prices, ships, COUNT(DISTINCT ProductId) as numprods,
       COUNT(*) as numtimes
FROM (SELECT ol.OrderId, ol.ProductId,
             (CASE WHEN COUNT(DISTINCT UnitPrice) = 1 THEN 'ONE'
                   ELSE 'SOME' END) as prices,
             (CASE WHEN COUNT(DISTINCT ShipDate) = 1 THEN 'ONE'
                   ELSE 'SOME' END) as ships
      FROM OrderLines ol
      GROUP BY ol.OrderId, ol.ProductId
      HAVING COUNT(*) > 1
     ) olp
GROUP BY prices, ships
ORDER BY prices, ships
```

Figure 9-2 shows the dataflow diagram for this query. The order lines for each product are summarized, counting the number of different prices and ship dates on the lines. These are then classified as "ONE" or "SOME" and aggregated again. This query only uses GROUP BY to do the processing; it contains no joins at all.

Histogram of Number of Units

What is the average number of units by product group in a given order? It is tempting to answer this question using the following query:

```
SELECT p.GroupName, AVG(ol.NumUnits * 1.0) as avgnumunits
FROM OrderLines ol JOIN
     Products p
     ON ol.ProductId = p.ProductId
GROUP BY p.GroupName
ORDER BY p.GroupName
```

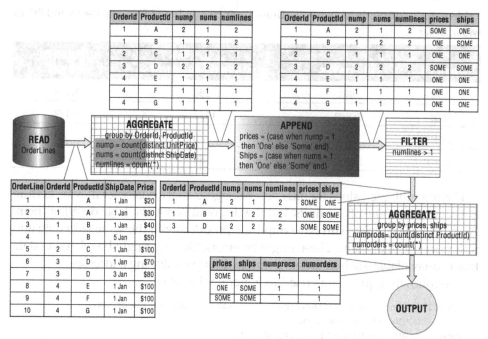

Figure 9-2: This dataflow diagram shows the processing for calculating the number of prices and of ship dates on order lines with the same product.

However, this query misses the important point that we just investigated: some products are split among multiple order lines in the data. Adding up NumUnits for each product in each order, and then taking the average solves this.

Both the correct average value and the incorrect value from the first query are in Table 9-8. The difference between these two values shows how often the product appears on multiple order lines in a single order. Some products, such as ARTWORK, are less likely to have multiple units in the same order. Other products, such as those in the OCCASION product group, are more likely to be ordered in multiple quantities.

Table 9-8: Number of Units by Order and by Order Line

PRODUCT GROUP	ORDER AVERAGE	ORDERLINE AVERAGE
#N/A	1.00	1.00
APPAREL	1.42	1.39
ARTWORK	1.26	1.20
BOOK	1.59	1.56
CALENDAR	1.67	1.64
FREEBIE	1.53	1.51
GAME	1.49	1.46
OCCASION	1.82	1.79
OTHER	2.44	2.30

For most of the product groups, the first method undercounts the number of units in an order by about 2%; this is consistent with the fact that about 2% of products in an order are on multiple lines. Some categories are affected more than others. The undercounting for ARTWORK is over 5%, for instance.

The following query generated the data for the table:

```
SELECT p.GroupName, AVG(ol.NumUnits) as orderaverage,
       SUM(ol.NumUnits) / SUM(ol.numlines) as orderlineaverage
FROM (SELECT ol.OrderId, ol.ProductId, SUM(ol.NumUnits) * 1.0 as numunits,
             COUNT(*) * 1.0 as numlines
      FROM OrderLines ol
      GROUP BY ol.OrderId, ol.ProductId
     ) ol JOIN
     Products p
     ON ol.ProductId = p.ProductId
GROUP BY p.GroupName
ORDER BY p.GroupName
```

This query summarizes the order lines, summing the NumUnits values for a given product in each order, and then taking the average. This is the real average of the number of products in an order. The query can also calculate the average number of products per order line by counting the total number of order lines for the product, and doing the division at the outer level. Both values can be calculated with a single query.

Which Products Tend to be Sold Multiple Times Within an Order?

Some products appear on multiple order lines; some do not. In fact, some products are never singletons. Table 9-9 shows the top ten products by the ratio of orders with the product with more than one unit.

This table highlights that these products tend to occur in few orders. Perhaps a threshold on the minimum number of orders where the product appears would produce more interesting results. Table 9-10 shows the results with a cut-off of 20 orders, meaning that a product needs to appear in at least 20 orders to be in the table (there are 788 such products). This table shows more variation. As expected, very few products typically appear multiple times in a single order. The exceptions are FREEBIE and OTHER products.

This type of analysis can suggest opportunities for cross-selling or bundling. Perhaps some products naturally sell in multiple quantities. These can be put into bundles to help consumers—and to increase overall product sales.

The query used to generate the second table is:

```
SELECT TOP 10 ol.ProductId, p.GroupName, COUNT(*) as NumOrders,
       AVG(CASE WHEN NumUnits > 1 THEN 1.0 ELSE 0 END) as MultiRatio
```

Table 9-9: Number of Units by Order and by Order Line

PRODUCT ID	PRODUCT GROUP	NUM ORDERS	MULTIPLE UNIT AVERAGE
10555	ARTWORK	1	100.0%
10830	APPAREL	2	100.0%
10831	APPAREL	2	100.0%
10832	APPAREL	2	100.0%
10833	APPAREL	1	100.0%
10876	GAME	1	100.0%
10969	OTHER	22	100.0%
10970	OTHER	11	100.0%
10998	OTHER	1	100.0%
10999	OTHER	1	100.0%

```
FROM (SELECT ol.OrderId, ol.ProductId, SUM(ol.NumUnits) as numunits
      FROM OrderLines ol
      GROUP BY ol.OrderId, ol.ProductId
     ) ol JOIN
     Products p
     ON ol.ProductId = p.ProductId
GROUP BY ol.ProductId, p.GroupName
HAVING COUNT(*) >= 20
ORDER BY MultiRatio DESC, ProductId
```

Table 9-10: Number of Units by Order and by Order Line

PRODUCT ID	PRODUCT GROUP	NUM ORDERS	MULTIPLE UNIT AVERAGE
10969	OTHER	22	100.0%
13323	FREEBIE	23	52.2%
12494	BOOK	253	48.2%
11047	ARTWORK	1,715	36.3%
10003	CALENDAR	168	34.5%
11090	OCCASION	32	34.4%
11009	ARTWORK	5,673	32.8%
12175	CALENDAR	216	32.4%
13297	CALENDAR	257	31.1%
12007	OTHER	235	30.6%

Notice the use of AVG() with CASE to calculate the ratio. To calculate a percentage (between 0 and 100) rather than a ratio, simply use THEN 100.0 instead of THEN 1.0.

Changes in Price

Products on different order lines sometimes have different prices. Many products also change prices throughout the historical data. *How many different prices do products have?* Actually, this question is interesting, but it is more feasible to answer a slightly simpler question: *What proportion of products in each product group has more than one price?*

```
SELECT GroupName, COUNT(*) as allproducts,
       SUM(CASE WHEN numprices > 1 THEN 1 ELSE 0 END) as morethan1price,
       SUM(CASE WHEN numol > 1 THEN 1 ELSE 0 END) as morethan1orderline
FROM (SELECT ol.ProductId, p.GroupName, COUNT(*) as numol,
             COUNT(DISTINCT ol.UnitPrice) as numprices
      FROM OrderLines ol JOIN
           Products p
           ON ol.ProductId = p.ProductId
      GROUP BY ol.ProductId, p.GroupName
     ) olp
GROUP BY GroupName
ORDER BY GroupName
```

This query does not do the division, but it calculates the numerator and the denominator.

Products must appear in more than one order line to have more than one price. Table 9-11 shows that 74.9% of products appearing more than once have multiple prices. In some product groups, such as APPAREL and CALENDARS, almost all the products have more than one price. Perhaps this is due to inventory control. Calendars, by their very nature, become outdated, so once the year covered by the calendar begins, the value decreases dramatically. APPAREL is also quite seasonal, with the same effect.

Figure 9-3 shows the average price by month for CALENDARs compared to BOOKs, for products costing less than $100 (expensive products appear for short periods, confusing the results). For most years, the average unit price for calendars increases in the late summer, and then decreases over the next few months.

By contrast, BOOKs tend to have their lowest price of the year in January, presumably representing after-holiday discounts. The peaks seem to appear randomly throughout the year, perhaps depending on when new books are released. Such charts suggest questions about price elasticity (whether changes in price for a product affects demand), which we'll discuss more in Chapter 12.

Table 9-11: Products by Product Groups That Have More Than One Price

PRODUCT GROUP	PRODUCTS WITH TWO OR MORE ORDERS	PRODUCTS WITH TWO OR MORE PRICES	PROPORTION
#N/A	0	1	0.0%
APPAREL	79	84	94.0%
ARTWORK	2,145	2,402	89.3%
BOOK	230	236	97.5%
CALENDAR	30	30	100.0%
FREEBIE	0	23	0.0%
GAME	176	211	83.4%
OCCASION	53	70	75.7%
OTHER	37	50	74.0%
TOTAL	**2,750**	**3,107**	**88.5%**

The query that generates the results for this chart is an aggregation query:

```
SELECT YEAR(o.OrderDate) as yr, MONTH(o.OrderDate) as mon,
       AVG(CASE WHEN p.GroupName = 'CALENDAR'
               THEN ol.UnitPrice END) as avgcallt100,
       AVG(CASE WHEN p.GroupName = 'BOOK'
               THEN ol.UnitPrice END) as avgbooklt100
FROM Orders o JOIN
     OrderLines ol
     ON o.OrderId = ol.OrderId JOIN
     Products p
     ON ol.ProductId = p.ProductId
WHERE p.GroupName IN ('CALENDAR', 'BOOK') AND p.FullPrice < 100
GROUP BY YEAR(o.OrderDate), MONTH(o.OrderDate)
ORDER BY yr, mon
```

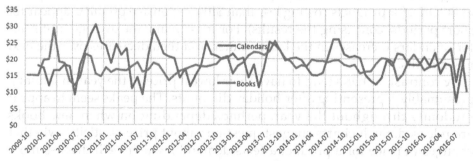

Figure 9-3: The average prices of calendars and books sold change during the year by month.

This query selects appropriate product groups and then does the conditional aggregation using a CASE expression. Notice that the condition on FullPrice is in the WHERE clause rather than the CASE. Having the condition in the WHERE clause reduces the amount of data processed by the query, which should make the query faster. In addition, the query can also make use of an appropriate index for further optimization. The CASE expression does not have an ELSE clause intentionally. Non-matching rows get NULL values, which do not affect the average.

Products and Customer Worth

This section investigates the relationship between products and customer worth. It starts with the question of whether good customers are consistent over time in their purchasing behavior. It then looks at the relationship between products on the one hand and good and bad customers on the other. Finally, this section defines and measures residual value.

Consistency of Order Size

Each order is a certain size, which can be defined in terms of its total value (amount paid). Over time some customers place multiple orders. *Are orders consistently about the same size for a given customer? Or do the orders for a given customer vary significantly in size?* The answers to these questions can give some indication of price sensitivity. For instance, if customers tend to have orders that are similar in size, we want to be cautious about recommending products that are either much more or much less expensive than the ones they have already ordered. On the other hand, if order sizes are not consistent, then this is less of a concern.

This analysis has several challenges, perhaps the hardest of which is framing the question so it can be answered analytically. It is tempting to look at the order size distribution for a given customer. The problem with this approach is that most customers only have a single order—so their distribution is one hundred percent pure. We might restrict the distribution only to customers who have made more than one order. But then the question arises: how do we compare customers who have two orders to customers who have three or four? Further complications arise because customers with more orders have many more possible comparisons.

Is there a way of comparing order sizes that is not biased by the number of orders that customers make? A reasonable approach is to re-phrase the question as: *What is the relationship of the next order size to the current order size?* A customer who has two orders has one comparison, which can be used to answer this question. A customer who has ten orders has nine comparisons, one for each order

Figure 9-4: The scatter plot of current order size to next order size shows little relationship.

except for the last one. The number of comparisons does not get out of hand. The approach still requires customers to have more than one order.

This relationship can be investigated in various ways. One method is to use a scatter plot of order size along with the next order size. With a bit over 30,000 such orders, this is just feasible in Excel. Figure 9-4 shows the results along with the best-fit line. With an R-square value of just 0.1078, the best-fit line suggests a weak relationship between one order amount and the next one. Very large values (outliers) can have a big impact on the best-fit line; and the largest orders have little correlation with the next order.

Binning the order sizes makes the results less sensitive to very large order sizes. Table 9-12 shows a relationship among order sizes when they are broken into quintiles. The first number, 47.1%, says that customers who have an order in the first quintile by value have their next order in the same quintile almost half the time. Similarly, 47.7% of orders in the top quintile have their next order (if there is one) in the top quintile. If there were no relationship, then the values would all be about 20%. The higher ratios on the diagonal suggest a reasonably strong relationship between the size of one order and the next.

Table 9-12: Previous and Next Order Size by Quintile

PREV QUINTILE	NEXT QUINTILE				
	1	2	3	4	5
1	47.1%	13.1%	14.2%	14.2%	11.4%
2	21.5%	29.6%	17.8%	19.4%	11.7%
3	20.4%	14.3%	33.6%	19.0%	12.7%
4	23.0%	12.9%	18.9%	27.7%	17.5%
5	20.7%	6.5%	10.9%	14.3%	47.7%

Binning the orders sizes shows a stronger relationship than a simple best-fit line. The difference in results between the best-fit line (very weak relationship) and binning (noticeable, relatively strong relationship) is the effect of very large orders. Even though two large orders can be in the same quintile, they can differ by thousands of dollars—a difference that has a large effect on the best-fit line and no effect on quintiles.

This calculation for the results in the table has two components: determining the quintiles for the orders and then determining the quintile for the next order. The goal is to produce a result set with three columns: current quintile, next quintile, and the number of orders. The pivoting and ratios can then be done in Excel (or with additional logic in SQL).

The following query does the work to calculate the quintiles of an order and the next order:

```
WITH oq as (
      SELECT o.*,
                CEILING((RANK() OVER (ORDER BY o.TotalPrice)) * 5.0 /
                      COUNT(*) OVER ()
                   ) as quintile
      FROM Orders o
     )
SELECT quintile, next_quintile, COUNT(*)
FROM (SELECT c.HouseholdId, oq.quintile,
             LEAD(oq.quintile) OVER (PARTITION BY c.HouseholdId
                            ORDER BY oq.OrderDate
                         ) as next_quintile
      FROM Customers c JOIN
           oq
           ON c.CustomerId = oq.CustomerId
     ) hq
WHERE next_quintile IS NOT NULL
GROUP BY quintile, next_quintile
ORDER BY quintile, next_quintile
```

The CTE oq calculates the quintile for the orders based on their size. It does this by ranking the price, multiplying by five, and dividing by the total number of rows. NTILE() could also be used.

The rest of the query follows simple logic. The subquery gets the next quintile using LEAD(). The outer query filters the results to include only those orders that have a next order. It then counts the values by the two quintiles. A very similar query, without the quintile calculation, can be used for the scatter plot.

Products Associated with One-Time Customers

Products associated with one-time customers pose a conundrum. They may be bad, in the sense that people purchase these products and never come back again—perhaps because the products fail to meet expectations. They may be good in the sense that people who would never make a purchase are attracted to these products, and what is missing are subsequent cross-sell opportunities to increase customer engagement. They may be neutral in the sense that some products might simply be very new, so first-time purchasers may not have had the opportunity to return.

The data sets do not have much information that can distinguish among these scenarios (except for the last which can use the first purchase date of each product)—other information, such as complaints, returns, and customer demographics would be helpful. Nevertheless, this turns into an interesting question: *How many products are purchased exactly once by a household that never purchases anything else?*

The following query returns the fact that 2,461 products have one-time purchasers:

```
SELECT COUNT(DISTINCT ProductId)
FROM (SELECT c.HouseholdId, MIN(o.ProductId) as ProductId
      FROM Customers c JOIN
           Orders o
           ON c.CustomerId = o.CustomerId JOIN
           OrderLines ol
           ON o.OrderId = ol.OrderId
      GROUP BY c.HouseholdId
      HAVING COUNT(DISTINCT ol.ProductId) = 1 AND
             COUNT(DISTINCT o.OrderId) = 1
     ) h
```

The HAVING clause does much of the work for this query. Of course, Customers, Orders, and OrderLines all need to be joined together and aggregated. Then, the HAVING clause chooses only those households that have exactly one order and exactly one product.

One nuance to the query is the MIN(ProductId) as ProductId in the subquery. Normally, this would be a strange construct. But, the HAVING clause limits the number of products in each group to just one. The minimum of a single product is that product—which is exactly the product that we want.

> **TIP** When bringing together data from different tables that have a one-to-many relationship, such as products, orders, and households, COUNT(DISTINCT) correctly counts the values at different levels. Use COUNT(DISTINCT OrderId) rather than COUNT(OrderId) to get the number of orders.

Many products are purchased only once by a household. More interesting are products that tend to be associated with one-time household purchasers: *Which products have a high proportion of their purchases associated with one-order households?* The answer to this question is the ratio of two numbers:

- The number of households where the product is the only product the household ever buys
- The total number of households that purchase the product

Both these numbers can be summarized from the data:

```
SELECT p.productid, numhouseholds, COALESCE(numuniques, 0) as
numuniques,
        COALESCE(numuniques * 1.0, 0.0) / numhouseholds as prodratio
FROM (SELECT ProductId, COUNT(*) as numhouseholds
      FROM (SELECT c.HouseholdId, ol.ProductId
            FROM Customers c JOIN
                 Orders o ON c.CustomerId = o.CustomerId JOIN
                 OrderLines ol ON o.OrderId = ol.OrderId
            GROUP BY c.HouseholdId, ol.ProductId
           ) hp
      GROUP BY ProductId
     ) p LEFT OUTER JOIN
     (SELECT ProductId, COUNT(*) as numuniques
      FROM (SELECT HouseholdId, MIN(ProductId) as ProductId
            FROM Customers c JOIN
                 Orders o ON c.CustomerId = o.CustomerId JOIN
                 OrderLines ol ON o.OrderId = ol.OrderId
            GROUP BY HouseholdId
            HAVING COUNT(DISTINCT ol.ProductId) = 1 AND
                   COUNT(DISTINCT o.Orderid) = 1) h
      GROUP BY ProductId
     ) hp
     ON hp.ProductId = p.ProductId
ORDER BY prodratio DESC, ProductId
```

This query aggregates the product and household information two ways. The first subquery calculates the total number of households that purchase each product. The second subquery calculates the total number of households whose only order is a one-time purchase of the product.

The results are somewhat expected. The products that have the highest ratios are the products that have only one order. In fact, of the 419 products where every order is the only household order, only one has more than ten purchases. The results highlight the fact that products have different behavior with respect to bringing in one-time households. And the category of the product makes a big difference. Of the 419 products that bring in exclusively one-time purchasers, 416 of them are in the ARTWORK category.

An entirely different way to approach this question uses window functions. For each order line, we can keep track of information about the households:

- Minimum order ID on the household
- Maximum order ID on the household

- Minimum product ID on the household
- Maximum product ID on the household

When the first two are equal and last two are equal, then the household meets the condition of being "unique."

This observation results in a simpler query for the same information:

```
SELECT ProductId, COUNT(DISTINCT HouseholdId) as numhouseholds,
       COUNT(DISTINCT (CASE WHEN minp = maxp AND mino = maxo
                            THEN HouseholdId END)) as numhouseholds,
       (COUNT(DISTINCT (CASE WHEN minp = maxp AND mino = maxo
                             THEN HouseholdId END)) * 1.0 /
        COUNT(DISTINCT HouseholdId)) as prodratio
FROM (SELECT ol.ProductId, c.HouseholdId,
             MIN(ol.Orderid) OVER (PARTITION BY c.HouseholdId) as mino,
             MAX(ol.OrderId) OVER (PARTITION BY c.HouseholdId) as maxo,
             MIN(ol.ProductId) OVER (PARTITION BY c.HouseholdId) as minp,
             MAX(ol.ProductId) OVER (PARTITION BY c.HouseholdId) as maxp
      FROM Customers c JOIN
           Orders o ON c.CustomerId = o.CustomerId JOIN
           OrderLines ol ON o.OrderId = ol.OrderId
     ) hp
GROUP BY ProductId
ORDER BY prodratio DESC, productid
```

Note the use of conditional aggregation with COUNT(DISTINCT). This counts the number of distinct households that meet the condition. It would seem unnecessary because the households are being restricted to one product and one order. However, there is the possibility of a household ordering the same product on multiple order lines within an order.

This query could replace each condition with something like COUNT(DISTINCT ol.Orderid) OVER (PARTITION BY c.HouseholdId) = 1. There are two reasons for preferring the version with MIN() and MAX(). First, not all databases support COUNT(DISTINCT) as a window function. Second, even if they do, the version with MIN() and MAX() is more efficient because of the overhead of keeping track of the distinct values.

This suggests a follow-up question: *For the different product groups, what is the proportion of one-time purchasing households?*

```
WITH ph as (
     SELECT ProductId, COUNT(DISTINCT HouseholdId) as numhouseholds,
            COUNT(DISTINCT (CASE WHEN minp = maxp AND mino = maxo
                                 THEN HouseholdId END)) as numuniques,
            (COUNT(DISTINCT (CASE WHEN minp = maxp AND mino = maxo
                                  THEN HouseholdId END)) * 1.0 /
             COUNT(DISTINCT HouseholdId)) as prodratio
     FROM (SELECT ol.ProductId, c.HouseholdId,
```

```
              MIN(ol.Orderid) OVER (PARTITION BY c.HouseholdId
                                    ) as mino,
              MAX(ol.OrderId) OVER (PARTITION BY c.HouseholdId
                                    ) as maxo,
              MIN(ol.ProductId) OVER (PARTITION BY c.HouseholdId
                                      ) as minp,
              MAX(ol.ProductId) OVER (PARTITION BY c.HouseholdId
                                      ) as maxp
         FROM Customers c JOIN
              Orders o
              ON c.CustomerId = o.CustomerId JOIN
              OrderLines ol
              ON o.OrderId = ol.OrderId
        ) hp
    GROUP BY ProductId
   )
SELECT p.GroupName, COUNT(*) as numprods,
       SUM(numhouseholds) as numhh, SUM(numuniques) as numuniques,
       SUM(numuniques * 1.0) / SUM(numhouseholds) as ratio
FROM ph JOIN
     Products p
     ON ph.ProductId = p.ProductId
GROUP BY p.GroupName
ORDER BY ratio DESC
```

This query uses the previous query (without the ORDER BY clause) as a subquery and joins it to Products to get the product group:

Figure 9-5 shows number of households that have made a purchase and the proportion that are one-time-only within each category. By this measure, the worst product group is APPAREL, where over half the purchasers are one-time only. The best is FREEBIE, with less than 1%. That is presumably because the FREEBIE products are typically included in bundles with other products.

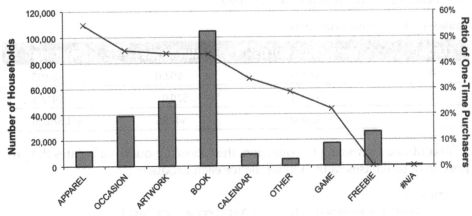

Figure 9-5: The proportion of households that purchase only one product varies considerably by product group. Some groups, such as APPAREL, are associated with such unique purchasers.

Products Associated with the Best Customer

The previous section asked about products associated with the worst (i.e., one-time) customers. The natural follow-on question is which products are associated with the best customers. Of course, this leads to the question of who are the best customers. Are they the ones who have the most orders? Purchased the most diverse items? Spent the most money? Or some combination of all three?

This investigation uses the total money spent to define the best customers, dividing the customers into roughly three equal-sized groups:

```
SELECT c.HouseholdId, SUM(o.TotalPrice) as Total,
       FLOOR((RANK() OVER (ORDER BY SUM(o.TotalPrice)) - 1) * 3.0 /
             COUNT(*) OVER ()
            ) as tercile
FROM Customers c JOIN
     Orders o
     ON c.CustomerId = o.CustomerId
GROUP BY c.HouseholdId
```

This query calculates the three groups by enumerating the households (by total amount spent) multiplying by three and dividing by the total number. Note that this calculation is slightly different from the calculation in the previous section for quintile. This uses `FLOOR()`, whereas the other uses `CEILING()`, for instance. The difference is strictly a matter of style—both methods produce equalish-sized groups. In this version, the numbering starts at zero; for the quintiles it starts at one. And, of course, `NTILE()` can be used for this calculation as well.

Table 9-13 shows the boundaries for the different groups and hints at a problem with this approach. The cutoff for the first group is $20 and for the second $41.95. Almost half the products (1,969 of them) never sell for less than $41.95. So, any customer who purchases one of these products is automatically considered the "best." For now, we'll ignore this issue.

Table 9-13: Total Spending by Tercile

TERCILE	NUM HOUSEHOLDS	MIN TOTAL	MAX TOTAL
0	52,477	$0.00	$20.00
1	51,721	$20.01	$41.95
2	52,060	$41.96	$11,670.00

To continue answering the question, the following query calculates the proportion of purchases in the top tercile for each product:

```
WITH hh as (
    SELECT c.HouseholdId, SUM(o.TotalPrice) as Total,
           FLOOR((RANK() OVER (ORDER BY SUM(o.TotalPrice)) - 1) * 3.0 /
                 COUNT(*) OVER ()
```

```
                ) as tercile
    FROM Customers c JOIN
         Orders o
         ON c.CustomerId = o.CustomerId
    GROUP BY c.HouseholdId
    )
SELECT ol.ProductId, COUNT(*) as cnt,
       AVG(CASE WHEN hh.tercile = 2 THEN 1.0 ELSE 0 END) as topratio
FROM Customers c JOIN
     Orders o
     ON o.CustomerId = c.CustomerId JOIN
     OrderLines ol
     ON ol.OrderId = o.Orderid JOIN
     hh
     ON c.HouseholdId = hh.HouseholdId
GROUP BY ol.ProductId
ORDER BY topratio DESC
```

This query basically just looks up the tercile for each product and then calculates the proportion.

The results are rather disappointing. Most of the products (3,280) are exclusively associated with the top third of the customers. Just 11 products are never purchased by the best customers.

It is, of course, possible to refine this analysis. Perhaps the definition of the best customer is not the best definition. They could be defined as the top fifth, or ten percent. Or, they could have to purchase a certain minimum number of products, or have at least a certain number of orders. The definition becomes rather ad hoc. Is there a better way to understand the relationship between product purchases and the best customers?

Residual Value

Once upon a time, in the 1990s, when bill-paying services were very expensive (because banks actually had to write checks and send them out), Fidelity Investments considered canceling its bill-paying service. After all, this service cost a lot of money and was provided free to qualified customers. Then someone in its special projects group noticed that customers who used the service had the largest balances and best retention. Customers who trust someone else to pay their bills are likely to be the very best customers. Cancelling the service might make these customers unhappy, and unhappy customers are more likely to leave, taking all their investments with them.

A similar moral comes from a very different business. A manager in a high-end grocery store decided to remove gourmet mustard from shelves to make room for other, faster moving items. Some of the mustard jars were actually gathering dust—anathema in the grocery business, which thrives on fast-moving merchandise. Further analysis showed that customers who purchased any of these gourmet mustards tended to do so in very large purchases. Without the mustard, the store feared losing the sales of everything else in those customers' carts.

Such insights (as well as our own personal experiences) illustrate that customers might make decisions about large purchases based on particular products—whether a bill-paying service or gourmet mustard. This observation leads to a question: *Which products have the largest remaining average value in the orders where they appear?* This remaining value, called *residual value,* is the value that remains in the order after said products are removed. An order containing only one product contributes no residual value for that product. A jar of gourmet mustard would contribute a large residual value. This section discusses an approach to residual value calculations, as well as certain biases in the calculation that are difficult to remove.

The following query calculates the average residual value for each product; that is, it calculates the average remaining value in orders that contain the product:

```
SELECT op.ProductId, COUNT(*) as numorders, AVG(ototal) as avgorder,
       AVG(prodprice) as avgprod, AVG(ototal - prodprice) as avgresidual
FROM (SELECT ol.OrderId, SUM(ol.TotalPrice) as ototal
      FROM OrderLines ol
      GROUP BY ol.OrderId
      HAVING COUNT(DISTINCT ol.ProductId) > 1
     ) o JOIN
     (SELECT ol.OrderId, ol.ProductId, SUM(ol.TotalPrice) as prodprice
      FROM OrderLines ol
      GROUP BY ol.OrderId, ol.ProductId
     ) op
     ON op.OrderId = o.OrderId
GROUP BY op.ProductId
ORDER BY avgresidual DESC
```

The first subquery summarizes orders with more than one product to calculate the total amount for the order. The second subquery summarizes the same orders by product as well. Note that this combines multiple order lines with the same product into a row for that product. The residual value for each product is the order total minus the amount for each product in the order—the sum of everything else in the order. The average of the residual is then calculated for each product across all orders.

This is a type of query we have seen before, where two aggregations of the same table are joined together. As you might expect, this query can be written more simply using analytic functions:

```
SELECT op.ProductId, COUNT(*) as numorders, AVG(ototal) as avgorder,
       AVG(prodprice) as avgprod, AVG(ototal - prodprice) as avgresidual
FROM (SELECT ol.OrderId, ol.ProductId, SUM(ol.TotalPrice) as prodprice,
             SUM(SUM(ol.TotalPrice)) OVER (PARTITION BY ol.OrderId
                                          ) as ototal,
             COUNT(*) OVER (PARTITION BY ol.OrderId) as cnt
      FROM OrderLines ol
      GROUP BY ol.OrderId, ol.ProductId
     ) op
```

```
WHERE cnt > 1
GROUP BY op.ProductId
ORDER BY avgresidual DESC
```

Notice the use of SUM(SUM()) to calculate the total value of each order, based on the order lines—the nesting of an aggregation function inside a window function. Also notice the use of COUNT(*) as a window function to count the number of products in each order. The outer WHERE clause has the same purpose as the HAVING clause in the previous query.

Summarizing by product group uses the previous query as a CTE called pp:

```
SELECT p.GroupName, COUNT(*) as numproducts,
       SUM(numorders) as numorders, AVG(avgresidual) as avgresidual
FROM pp JOIN
     Products p
     ON pp.ProductId = p.ProductId
GROUP BY p.GroupName
ORDER BY p.GroupName
```

This query calculates the average residual for each product and then returns the average for all products within a product group. This is different from calculating the average residual for a product group, which would require modifying the CTE to be at the product group level rather than the product level. Doing the calculation at the product group level would only calculate residuals that cross product boundaries, so two different books would not contribute to the residual for BOOK at the product group level (although it does for the above results).

Table 9-14 shows the average residual value by product group as well as the average price of items. Not surprisingly, the most expensive products—ARTWORK—have,

Table 9-14: Average Residual Value by Product Group

PRODUCT GROUP	NUMBER OF PRODUCTS	NUMBER OF ORDERS	AVERAGE ORDER RESIDUAL	AVERAGE HOUSEHOLD RESIDUAL
#N/A	1	9	$868.72	$658.40
APPAREL	85	4,030	$39.01	$618.88
ARTWORK	2,576	21,456	$1,032.24	$1,212.27
BOOK	236	48,852	$67.94	$365.06
CALENDAR	31	3,211	$37.01	$387.74
FREEBIE	25	27,708	$28.27	$1,584.93
GAME	230	12,844	$133.50	$732.72
OCCASION	71	16,757	$41.98	$719.87
OTHER	53	3,100	$36.49	$1,123.14

by far, the highest residual value. This suggests that customers are purchasing multiple expensive items at the same time, rather than mixing and matching less expensive items with more expensive ones.

Calculating the average residual at the household level requires joining in the household ID, using `Customers` and `Orders`. The household average residual is larger than the residual at the order level, even though most households are one-time purchasers. The reason points to a challenge when working with market basket data.

A handful of households have very many orders. As a result, these households have very large residual values for any product they purchase, and, they have generally purchased products from all product groups. In short, large households dominate the residual value calculation.

One way to remove the bias is to limit the calculations to households with only two purchases. Another way is to randomly choose one pair of products in each household, but such a technique is outside the scope of this book. The effect exists at the order level, but because there are many fewer humongous orders, the bias is smaller.

> **WARNING**   When analyzing market basket data, the size of orders (or of households) can introduce unexpected biases in results.

Product Geographic Distribution

As we saw in Chapter 4, geography is a key dimension for analysis. This is true at the product level as well. This section investigates some interactions between geography and products.

Most Common Product by State

One common question is what "thing" is most frequently associated with something else, such as the most common product in each state. The easiest approach to this type of question is to use window functions, particularly ROW_NUMBER():

```
SELECT sp.State, sp.ProductId, cnt, p.GroupName
FROM (SELECT o.State, ol.ProductId, COUNT(*) as cnt,
             ROW_NUMBER() OVER (PARTITION BY o.State
                                ORDER BY COUNT(*) DESC,
                                         ol.ProductId) as seqnum
      FROM Orders o JOIN
           OrderLines ol
           ON o.OrderId = ol.OrderId
      GROUP BY o.State, ol.ProductId
     ) sp JOIN
     Products p
     ON sp.ProductId = p.ProductId
WHERE seqnum = 1;
```

Table 9-15: Most Common Product by State (for Products That Appear More Than Once)

PRODUCT ID	GROUP	NUM STATES	MIN STATE	MAX STATE
12820	FREEBIE	59		WY
11009	ARTWORK	6	AA	SK
11016	APPAREL	3	NF	VC
11070	OCCASION	2	BD	SO
10005	BOOK	2	DF	NT

The COUNT(*) in the ORDER BY is another example of using window functions with aggregation functions. Notice that the ORDER BY clause also includes the ProductId. The row with the first sequence number is actually for the product with the highest count and, if there are ties, the one that has the lowest product ID. This ensures that the sort is *stable* and the result consistent, meaning that running the same query produces the same results, whether on the same database or on another database.

What do the results tell us? Table 9-15 shows the products that appear as the most popular product in more than one "state." There are 24 such products, but the top product appears in almost two-thirds of the "states." Interestingly, any state that has a reasonable number of purchases has product 12820 as the most common product. This is a freebie product given out with many different products.

The smaller areas—unrecognized state codes, that is—often have some other product as the most common one. These areas are associated with just one or a handful of orders. FREEBIEs are not given out with every order, so the particular orders for the "states" with few orders may not have the freebie. Hence, other products rise to the top. "States" have an unusual most common product because the "state" itself is unusual. The "state" may be a mistake, or it might be a foreign province or country placed in the state field.

Which Products Have Broad Appeal Versus Local Appeal

Which products sell in all the states? This can seem like an easy or a hard question to answer in SQL. One simple approach is to count the number of states where each product has been sold and to compare that to the total number of states.

The following query is a basic aggregation query with a join and a HAVING clause:

```
SELECT ol.ProductId, COUNT(DISTINCT o.State) as NumStates
FROM Orders o JOIN
     OrderLines ol
     ON o.OrderId = ol.OrderId
GROUP BY ol.ProductId
HAVING COUNT(DISTINCT o.State) = (SELECT COUNT(DISTINCT State)
                                  FROM Orders
                                 )
```

Notice that this query makes use of a subquery in the HAVING clause. The same logic could have been accomplished using a JOIN:

```
SELECT ol.ProductId, COUNT(DISTINCT o.State) as NumStates
FROM Orders o JOIN
     OrderLines ol
     ON o.OrderId = ol.OrderId CROSS JOIN
     (SELECT COUNT(DISTINCT State) as NumStates
      FROM Orders
     ) cnt
GROUP BY ol.ProductId
HAVING COUNT(DISTINCT o.State) = MAX(cnt.NumStates)
```

These two queries do the same thing. The difference is a matter of preference.

Sadly—or instructively—neither returns any products. The problem, as observed in the previous section, is that there are many more "states" than actual states. The extra "states" have just a small number of orders and hence a small number of products. So, let's limit the number of products to "states" that have at least 100 orders.

The interesting parts of this query are the changes from the first query in this section:

```
WITH states AS (
     SELECT State
     FROM Orders
     GROUP BY State
     HAVING COUNT(*) >= 100
     )
SELECT ol.ProductId, AVG(p.UnitPrice) as UnitPrice,
       COUNT(DISTINCT o.State) as NumStates, p.GroupName
FROM Orders o JOIN
     OrderLines ol
     ON o.OrderId = ol.OrderId JOIN
     Products p
     ON ol.ProductId = p.ProductId
WHERE o.state IN (SELECT state FROM states)
GROUP BY ol.ProductId, p.GroupName
HAVING COUNT(DISTINCT o.State) = (SELECT COUNT(*) FROM states)
```

This follows a similar form to the first query. The biggest addition is states, a CTE that provides the list of valid states (there are 55 of them). This is then used twice: once in the WHERE clause to filter the states being counted and the second time in the HAVING clause.

Table 9-16 shows the nine products that appear in all 55 such states. Three of these are freebies, but the other six are bona fide products. These products have wide geographic appeal.

Table 9-16: Products That Appear in All States with More Than 100 Orders

PRODUCT ID	UNIT PRICE	GROUP NAME
10005	$14.86	BOOK
11009	$9.61	ARTWORK
11016	$11.10	APPAREL
11107	$14.81	OCCASION
12139	$23.79	OCCASION
12819	$0.00	FREEBIE
12820	$0.00	FREEBIE
13190	$0.00	FREEBIE
13629	$28.28	BOOK

Understanding products with limited geographic appeal is actually much harder. The problem is that all the products that are purchased only once are necessarily purchased in only one geographic area.

Which Customers Have Particular Products?

This section moves from any product to particular products. It is also going to introduce aggregate string concatenation, an operation that is unfortunately not part of the SQL standard. So every database has a different method—with SQL Server's being the most arcane. Let's start with the most popular products and the customers who purchase them.

Which Customers Have the Most Popular Products?

It is easy to get the list of the most popular products by using an aggregation query. Let's ask a slight variation on this question: *How many customers purchase the ten most popular products?* As a further refinement, let's ask how many customers purchase one, two, three, and so on of these products.

The following query uses a subquery to identify the most popular products. This subquery is used in the WHERE clause in the subquery:

```
SELECT cnt, COUNT(*) as households
FROM (SELECT c.HouseholdId, COUNT(DISTINCT ol.ProductId) as cnt
      FROM Customers c JOIN
           Orders o
           ON c.CustomerId = o.CustomerId JOIN
           OrderLines ol
```

```
            ON ol.OrderId = o.OrderId
        WHERE ol.ProductId IN (SELECT TOP 10 ProductId
                               FROM OrderLines ol
                               GROUP BY ProductId
                               ORDER BY COUNT(*) DESC
                              )
        GROUP BY c.HouseholdId
      ) h
GROUP BY cnt
ORDER BY cnt
```

This is a basic histogram query with a twist. The WHERE clause selects only the ten most popular products.

Table 9-17 shows the results. Of households that have any of the products, most only have one or two. However, several hundred have three or more, with one household having nine of the most popular products.

Note that this table does not contain the number for zero products. There are 10,288 of these households. Perhaps the easiest way to find them is to use a LEFT JOIN for the filtering rather than IN:

```
SELECT cnt, COUNT(*)
FROM (SELECT c.HouseholdId, COUNT(DISTINCT popp.ProductId) as cnt
      FROM Customers c JOIN
           Orders o
           ON c.CustomerId = o.CustomerId JOIN
           OrderLines ol
           ON ol.OrderId = o.OrderId LEFT JOIN
           (SELECT TOP 10 ProductId
            FROM OrderLines ol
            GROUP BY ProductId
            ORDER BY COUNT(*) desc
           ) popp
           ON popp.ProductId = ol.ProductId
```

Table 9-17: Number of Households That Purchase Top 10 Products

NUMBER OF TOP 10 PRODUCTS	NUMBER OF HOUSEHOLDS
1	47,477
2	5,373
3	472
4	45
5	6
6	1
9	1

```
       GROUP BY c.HouseholdId
     ) h
GROUP BY cnt
ORDER BY cnt
```

One subtlety is the COUNT(DISTINCT). It uses the column from the second table, rather than the first. When there is no match, the column has NULL—and aggregation functions ignore NULL values. The count returns zero when there is no match.

Which Products Does a Customer Have?

This section starts with a simple question: *Of the ten most popular products, which has each household purchased?* This question has a simple answer, if we put the results into a table with multiple rows for each household, and one row per household and product:

```
SELECT DISTINCT c.HouseholdId, ol.ProductId
FROM Customers c JOIN
     Orders o
     ON c.CustomerId = o.CustomerId JOIN
     OrderLines ol
     ON ol.OrderId = o.OrderId
WHERE ol.ProductId IN (SELECT TOP 10 ProductId
                       FROM OrderLines ol
                       GROUP BY ProductId
                       ORDER BY COUNT(*) desc
                      )
ORDER BY c.HouseholdId, ol.ProductId
```

This query is a slight modification of the previous query. Note the use of SELECT DISTINCT to remove duplicates—households that purchased the same product multiple times.

This is all well and good. However, one row per household might be more useful than one row per household and product. One column with "10834, 11168, 12820" is often clearer than three rows with one value per row. Same information, different format.

Comma-delimited strings are a very reasonable format for humans to read. However, databases do not support such strings very well. There are at least four reasons why you do not want to store such values in a database column:

- Numbers should be stored in numeric columns, not as strings.
- SQL has a very good data structure for storing lists. It is called a table, not a string.
- Ids such as these should be declared as having foreign key references to another table. That is not possible when they are stored as strings.

▪ SQL has much better support for values stored in columns than in strings.

Although they are useful, comma-delimited strings can be difficult for SQL to generate. For an application being developed with a SQL back end, combining string values from multiple rows into a single value is often easier to do at the application layer. However, that solution is insufficient for mere analytic purposes, and it is possible to do this in SQL.

Lists Using Conditional Aggregation

When you know the maximum number of products, then you can approach this problem with conditional aggregation. For instance, the following query produces a comma-delimited list for households that purchased three or more of the top ten products:

```
WITH hp AS (
      SELECT DISTINCT c.HouseholdId,
             CAST(ol.ProductId as VARCHAR(255)) as ProductId
      FROM Customers c JOIN
           Orders o
           ON c.CustomerId = o.CustomerId JOIN
           OrderLines ol
           ON ol.OrderId = o.OrderId
      WHERE ol.ProductId IN (SELECT TOP 10 ProductId
                             FROM OrderLines ol
                             GROUP BY ProductId
                             ORDER BY COUNT(*) desc
                            )
     )
SELECT hp.HouseholdId, COUNT(*) as NumProducts,
       (MAX(CASE WHEN seqnum = 1 THEN ProductId ELSE '' END) +
        MAX(CASE WHEN seqnum = 2 THEN ',' + ProductId ELSE '' END) +
        . . .
        MAX(CASE WHEN seqnum = 10 THEN ',' + ProductId ELSE '' END)
       ) as Products
FROM (SELECT hp.*, ROW_NUMBER() OVER (PARTITION BY HouseholdId
                                      ORDER BY ProductId) as seqnum
      FROM hp
     ) hp
GROUP BY hp.HouseholdId
HAVING COUNT(*) >= 3
```

The CTE `hp` (which is used in other queries in this and the next section) simply gets the lists of products, with `ProductId` converted to a string because it will be used for concatenation. The subquery then enumerates each product in a household assigning a sequence number, and the sequence number is used for the conditional aggregation. Also note that the comma is put *before* the product ID for all but the first product.

This method is cumbersome because the list of products is constructed one element at a time, with a separate MAX(CASE . . .) expression for each element. Not only does this generate lots of repetitive code, it also requires knowing the maximum number of elements. For this example with ten products, the code is not too long. But, the SQL does not generalize very well.

When you only want a fixed number of items in the list—such as the top three products for each household—then string concatenation by conditional aggregation is reasonable. For a query such as this, the ORDER BY clause is quite important. You might use it to get the products with the largest count or with the highest price.

Aggregate String Concatenation in SQL Server

Because conditional aggregation does not generalize easily for string concatenation, another approach is needed. The idea is to use a string aggregation function that concatenates strings together. A function that does for strings what SUM() does for numbers: It combines multiple values into a single value.

Unfortunately, SQL does not have a standard function for this purpose. Oracle has a function called listagg(). Postgres has string_agg(). MySQL, group_concat(). All three have different syntax conventions. And, unfortunately, SQL Server does not offer such a simple function.

Instead, you can take the following approach, convert the query results to a format called XML for each row, and then extract the concatenated value from the XML. The aside "XML and String Aggregation" talks about this approach in more detail.

The place to start is with a single household. The following query produces XML that contains the concatenated values:

```
WITH hp AS ( <defined on page 454> )
SELECT ',' + ProductId
FROM hp
WHERE HouseholdId = 18147259
FOR XML PATH ('')
```

The expression FOR XML PATH is specific to SQL Server and it tells the engine to create an XML value for the result. The query returns a single row with one column: ",10834,12510,12820,13629"—the values concatenated together. Note that the separator is part of the SELECT statement. This is a super-simple version of XML because it contains no tags. Normally, each column name would have its own tag, but no column alias is defined, so the result has no tags.

When using this method, some special characters are treated in a funny way; for instance, ampersands are turned into "&". This conversion is due to the XML standard. Some characters, such as the ampersand, are used in a special way, so an alternative representation is needed for them.

The problem with these characters can be fixed using a slightly more complicated expression:

```
WITH hp AS ( <defined on page 454> )
SELECT (SELECT ',' + ProductId
        FROM hp
        WHERE HouseholdId = 18147259
        ORDER BY ProductId
        FOR XML PATH (''), TYPE
       ).VALUE('.', 'varchar(max)')
```

This query creates an XML value—one that looks like ",10834,12510,12820,13629". The result has a high-level tag that describes the record name and then values for the record. The TYPE keyword specifies that the return is an XML type (that is, a string that represents XML).

We want a string, not an XML type. The value is extracted in the last line of the query. The VALUE() function extracts a value from the XML representation as a string, specifically as varchar(max). The value being extracted is the element referred to using "." (meaning the entire value, in this case). The VALUE() function converts the XML to a string, which fixes the problem with "&" ">", and "<."

The result of either of the preceding queries is a list of products, prepended by a comma: ",10834,12510,12820,13629". The STUFF() function is the most convenient way of eliminating the leading comma; it replaces a particular substring with another. Unlike REPLACE() the substring is defined by position:

```
WITH hp AS ( <defined on page 454> )
SELECT STUFF((SELECT ',' + ProductId
              FROM hp
              WHERE HouseholdId = 18147259
              ORDER BY ProductId
              FOR XML PATH (''), TYPE
             ).VALUE('.', 'varchar(max)'),
             1, 1, '')
```

The arguments 1, 1, '' to STUFF() say to replace the characters starting at position one for one character with the empty string—exactly what is needed to get rid of the leading comma. Note that if the delimiter were a comma followed by a space, there would be two characters and the arguments would instead be 1, 2, ''.

Lists Using String Aggregation in SQL Server

The code from the previous section demonstrates string concatenation for a single household. This can be extended to all households, using a correlated subquery:

XML AND STRING AGGREGATION

XML stands for the Extensible Mark-up Language. It is a standardized way of describing complex data structures using text strings so structured data can be passed back and forth between different applications. An XML document stores both the data and its structure using tags and nested tags to define elements in the data structures. For instance, a row of data in a database can be represented as a record, with fields; the document also contains field names.

XML is a rich language that can express multiple levels of hierarchy. For more complicated data structures, the XML reference can be more complicated; for instance, the reference "/A[1]/B[3]/C[1]" would be to the first element of C nested in the third element of B nested in the first element of A.

XML can easily store much more complicated data than SQL. Not all records need to have the same fields, for instance. And, records can contain lists and other records—ad infinitum. The data itself is typically in a tree structure. So, if you stored the SQLBook database as an XML document, the top level would have the database, the next level would have each table in the database, and below that would be the fields in the tables, and finally the data being stored. The data structure could also have other information, describing tables, databases, indexes, and so on.

What does this have to do with databases? XML is a standard used for many applications. As a result, many databases now support reading and writing XML data (as well as JSON, another common data interchange format). SQL Server does this through an extensive interface that includes a built-in data type called XML and associated functions.

For instance, the following query returns an XML string:

```
WITH hp AS ( <defined on page 454> )
SELECT ',' + ProductId
FROM hp
WHERE HouseholdId = 18147259
ORDER BY ProductId
FOR XML PATH (''), TYPE
```

This string looks like: ",10834,12510,12820,13629".

Two key aspects of XML functionality are the VALUE() function, which extracts a particular value from an XML string, and the FOR XML clause, which creates an XML string. In addition, SQL Server supports indexes on the XML data type; these indexes can speed operations considerably when looking up fields in large XML values.

Because XML data is a long string of characters, creating an XML value necessarily requires creating a long string. Hence, XML requires a form of string concatenation—a form useful for aggregation as well as for its intended purpose.

As mentioned in the text, most other databases support built-in operations for string concatenation. These functions greatly simplify the process so aggregate string concatenation is as easy as any other aggregation.

```
WITH hp AS ( <defined on page 454> )
SELECT hp.HouseholdId,
       STUFF((SELECT ',' + ProductId
           FROM hp hp2
           WHERE hp2.HouseholdId = hp.HouseholdId
           ORDER BY ProductId
           FOR XML PATH (''), TYPE
           ).VALUE('.', 'varchar(max)'),
           1, 1, '') as Products
FROM hp
GROUP BY hp.HouseholdId
HAVING COUNT(*) >= 3
```

This query follows the general structure of string aggregation queries in SQL Server. They require a correlated subquery to implement the XML aggregation logic. The subquery does the aggregation for a single household. The STUFF() function then gets rid of the leading comma, and the outer query does an aggregation so each household has only one row in the result set.

The subquery can include an ORDER BY clause so the values are in a particular order. It can also include SELECT DISTINCT, to remove duplicates. Three tips on the subquery. First, be careful that all arguments to the + operator are strings, so it does not generate an error. Second, do not give the column a name (for this purpose) because the name turns into a tag in the XML. Third, a GROUP BY clause is unnecessary in the subquery.

Which Customers Have Three Particular Products?

Which households have all three products 12139, 12820, and 13190? This is one of the most common product combinations, so this is a natural question to ask. Even this simple question has two variations: which households have these products as well as others, perhaps, and which have these products but no others.

These questions are trickier than they first appear because they are not about values in a single row; they are about values in multiple rows. This section investigates three different ways of answering this question: using joins, using exists, and using aggregation. The latter generalizes most easily to many similar types of queries.

Three Products Using Joins

The first approach uses joins to answer the question:

```
WITH hp AS (
    SELECT DISTINCT c.HouseholdId, ol.ProductId
    FROM Customers c JOIN
         Orders o
```

```
            ON c.CustomerId = o.CustomerId JOIN
            OrderLines ol
            ON ol.OrderId = o.OrderId
    )
SELECT hp1.HouseholdId
FROM hp hp1 JOIN
     hp hp2
     ON hp2.HouseholdId = hp1.HouseholdId JOIN
     hp hp3
     ON hp3.HouseholdId = hp1.HouseholdId
WHERE hp1.ProductId = 12139 AND
      hp2.ProductId = 12820 AND
      hp3.ProductId = 13190
```

Each table reference in the FROM clause is for a different product. The first join is on HouseholdId, so only households that have both products match. The third join brings in the third product. The result is to get households that have all three products. Note that the definition of hp varies slightly from the proceeding query because the products are not limited to the ten most popular products.

This query does not need SELECT DISTINCT in the outer query because the CTE already selects distinct household product pairs. The joins cannot produce duplicates. For a given household, there is at most one row in hp for a product—regardless of the number of times the household purchased the product.

The result of this query is a list of 153 households that have all three products—and perhaps some others. Answering the related question of which households have these three products and no others requires an additional filter. This filter uses yet another self-join, a LEFT OUTER JOIN:

```
WITH hp AS (
        SELECT DISTINCT c.HouseholdId, ol.ProductId
        FROM Customers c JOIN
             Orders o
             ON c.CustomerId = o.CustomerId JOIN
             OrderLines ol
             ON ol.OrderId = o.OrderId
    )
SELECT hp1.HouseholdId
FROM hp hp1 JOIN
     hp hp2
     ON hp2.HouseholdId = hp1.HouseholdId JOIN
     hp hp3
     ON hp3.HouseholdId = hp1.HouseholdId LEFT JOIN
     hp hp4
     ON hp4.HouseholdId = hp1.HouseholdId AND
        hp4.ProductId NOT IN (12139, 12820, 13190)
WHERE hp1.ProductId = 12139 AND
```

```
            hp2.ProductId = 12820 AND
            hp3.ProductId = 13190 AND
            hp4.ProductId IS NULL
```

The extra join filters out households that have products other than the three of interest.

Three Products Using Exists

Another approach puts all the logic in the WHERE clause. In a sense, finding the households with all three products is a question about filtering, although the filter conditions are on different rows. The key to the filtering is multiple EXISTS expressions with correlated subqueries:

```
WITH hp AS (
        SELECT DISTINCT HouseholdId, ProductId
        FROM Customers c JOIN
             Orders o
             ON c.CustomerId = o.CustomerId JOIN
             OrderLines ol
             ON ol.OrderId = o.OrderId
     )
SELECT DISTINCT c.HouseholdId
FROM Customers c
WHERE EXISTS (SELECT 1 FROM hp hp1
              WHERE hp1.HouseholdId = c.HouseholdId AND
                    hp1.ProductId = 12139) AND
      EXISTS (SELECT 1 FROM hp hp2
              WHERE hp2.HouseholdId = c.HouseholdId AND
                    hp2.ProductId = 12820) AND
      EXISTS (SELECT 1 FROM hp hp3
              WHERE hp3.HouseholdId = c.HouseholdId AND
                    hp3.ProductId = 13190)
```

This version is actually quite similar to the version with the JOIN. Instead of a self-join, this checks for each product individually using EXISTS. In many database engines, the execution plan for these two versions would be quite similar.

One small comment about the use of SELECT DISTINCT in this query: What is really needed is just a list of households. However, the database does not have a table of just households. The DISTINCT is needed because households can appear multiple times in Customers. A table containing households would be a better choice, if one were available.

Getting households that have only these products and no other products can follow similar logic, using NOT EXISTS:

```
NOT EXISTS (SELECT 1 FROM hp hp4
            WHERE hp4.HouseholdId = c.HouseholdId AND
                  hp4.ProductId NOT IN (12139, 12820, 13190)
           )
```

This simply checks that matching households have no other products, apart from the three of interest.

Using Conditional Aggregation and Filtering

The third approach uses conditional aggregation. But, instead of the values going in the SELECT clause, they will be used for filtering in the HAVING clause:

```
WITH hp AS (
        SELECT DISTINCT HouseholdId, ProductId
        FROM Customers c JOIN
            Orders o
            ON c.CustomerId = o.CustomerId JOIN
            OrderLines ol
            ON ol.OrderId = o.OrderId
    )
SELECT hp.HouseholdId
FROM hp
GROUP BY hp.HouseholdId
HAVING SUM(CASE WHEN hp.ProductId = 12139 THEN 1 ELSE 0 END) > 0 AND
       SUM(CASE WHEN hp.ProductId = 12820 THEN 1 ELSE 0 END) > 0 AND
       SUM(CASE WHEN hp.ProductId = 13190 THEN 1 ELSE 0 END) > 0
```

This is a simpler query. But what is it doing?

The HAVING clause is doing the work. Each clause counts the number of rows that have one of the products. The >0 is simply requiring that the household have at least one row with the product. Voila! Only households that meet all three conditions satisfy the condition.

An alternative way of writing this query condenses the logic:

```
WITH hp AS (
        SELECT DISTINCT HouseholdId, ProductId
        FROM Customers c JOIN
            Orders o
            ON c.CustomerId = o.CustomerId JOIN
            OrderLines ol
            ON ol.OrderId = o.OrderId
    )
SELECT hp.HouseholdId
FROM hp
WHERE hp.ProductId IN (12139, 12820, 13190)
GROUP BY hp.HouseholdId
HAVING COUNT(*) = 3
```

This version uses a WHERE clause for filtering just for the three products. The HAVING clause checks for three matches. Note that no household has duplicate products because the definition of hp removes duplicates; otherwise, the condition would need to use COUNT(DISTINCT).

Getting households that have only these three products and no others can be handled in a variety of ways. Perhaps the simplest is this additional condition on the first query:

```
COUNT(hp.ProductId) = 3
```

This simply says that the household has three products, and because of the other conditions, we know what those products are.

Generalized Set-Within-a-Set Queries

The previous question about households having three products is an example of a *set-within-a-set* query. This is a type of question often asked of hierarchical data, when you want to filter by multiple conditions at lower levels of the hierarchy and the conditions are stored on separate rows. The previous question can be phrased as: *When does the set of products purchased in a household contain all three of these products?* The question is about the "set" of products for each household.

> **TIP** Aggregation and a smart HAVING clause are the most general way of solving set-within-set questions. For a particular question, joins may have better performance, but aggregation is flexible and can answer a very broad range of questions about hierarchical data.

A nice characteristic of the aggregation approach is that it is quite generalizable. Consider the following questions and the HAVING clause that implements the logic: *Which households have purchased none of the three products?*

```
HAVING SUM(CASE WHEN hp.ProductId = 12139 THEN 1 ELSE 0 END) = 0 AND
       SUM(CASE WHEN hp.ProductId = 12820 THEN 1 ELSE 0 END) = 0 AND
       SUM(CASE WHEN hp.ProductId = 13190 THEN 1 ELSE 0 END) = 0
```

The only difference here is that the comparisons are now =0 rather than >0. This is saying that none of the products are purchased, rather than all of them.
Which households have purchased these three products but not 13629? This is a combination of the two comparisons:

```
HAVING SUM(CASE WHEN hp.ProductId = 12139 THEN 1 ELSE 0 END) > 0 AND
       SUM(CASE WHEN hp.ProductId = 12820 THEN 1 ELSE 0 END) > 0 AND
       SUM(CASE WHEN hp.ProductId = 13190 THEN 1 ELSE 0 END) > 0 AND
       SUM(CASE WHEN hp.ProductId = 13629 THEN 1 ELSE 0 END) = 0
```

This adds a fourth condition, the comparison to zero for the additional product.
Which households have purchased at least two of the three products?

```
HAVING COUNT(DISTINCT CASE WHEN hp.ProductId IN (12139, 12820, 13190)
                 THEN hp.ProductId END) >= 2
```

The structure here consists of only one comparison. COUNT(DISTINCT) is used to count the number of products in the group.

Which households purchased 12139 with either 12820 or 13190?

```
HAVING SUM(CASE WHEN hp.ProductId = 12139 THEN 1 ELSE 0 END) > 0 AND
       (SUM(CASE WHEN hp.ProductId = 12820 THEN 1 ELSE 0 END) > 0 OR
        SUM(CASE WHEN hp.ProductId = 13190 THEN 1 ELSE 0 END) > 0
       )
```

Or equivalently:

```
HAVING SUM(CASE WHEN hp.ProductId = 12139 THEN 1 ELSE 0 END) > 0 AND
       SUM(CASE WHEN hp.ProductId IN (12820, 13190) THEN 1 ELSE 0 END) > 0
```

Which households purchased 12139 with either 12820 or 13190, but not both?

```
HAVING SUM(CASE WHEN hp.ProductId = 12139 THEN 1 ELSE 0 END) > 0 AND
       COUNT(DISTINCT CASE WHEN hp.ProductId IN (12820, 13190)
                           THEN hp.ProductId END) = 1
```

In this version, COUNT(DISTINCT) is used to be sure that only one of the two products passes the filter. Alternatively, this could be expressed using SUM() conditions, but the logic is a little more complicated.

These examples show that the use of conditional aggregation and a HAVING clause is a powerful way to implement many different types of set-within-a-set query logic.

Lessons Learned

This chapter looks at what customers purchase, rather than when or how they purchase, with an emphasis on exploratory data analysis. The contents of market baskets can be very interesting, providing information about both customers and products.

A good way to look at products is by using scatter plots and bubble charts to visualize relationships. A useful Excel trick makes it possible to see products along the X- and Y-axes for bubble charts and scatter plots.

Investigating products includes finding the products associated with the best customers, and finding the ones associated with the worst customers (those who only make one purchase). It is also interesting to explore other facets of products, such as the number of times a product changes price, the number of units in each order, the number of times products are repeated within an order, and how often customers purchase the same product again.

Exploratory data analysis goes beyond just these questions. Pricing is a very important aspect of products, and the price for a given product can vary over time. *Residual value* is the value of the rest of the stuff the customer purchases—and this can be a good indicator of products that drive additional value.

Sometimes, particular products are drivers of customer value. Some products are more frequently purchased by the best customers. Others tend to be only purchased once, perhaps indicating a poor customer experience with the product or an opportunity to broaden the customer relationship.

One important type of question about the products purchased by households is *set-within-a-set* queries. These queries can be solved using several methods, but aggregation with an intelligent HAVING clause is very versatile.

The next chapter extends these ideas by looking at products that tend to be purchased together. These are item sets and association rules that dive into the finest level of customer interactions.

Association Rules and Beyond

Association rules go beyond merely exploring products: They identify groups of products that tend to appear together. A big part of the allure and power of association rules is that they "discover" patterns automatically, rather than by the hypothesis testing methods used in the previous chapter.

A classical example of association rules is the beer and diapers story, which claims that the two items are purchased together late in the week. This makes for an appealing story. Young mom realizes that there are not enough diapers for the weekend. She calls young dad as he comes home from work, asking him to pick up diapers on the way home. He knows that if he gets beer (and drinks it), he won't have to change the diapers.

Although a colorful (and sexist) explanation, association rules were not used to find this "unexpected" pattern (the details were explained in a Forbes article in 1998). In fact, retailers already knew that these products sold together. The story itself has been traced to Shopko, a chain of retail stores based in Green Bay, Wisconsin. During the many icy winter months in northern Wisconsin, store managers would easily notice customers walking out with bulky items such as beer and diapers. The observation was verified in the data.

Association rules can reduce millions of transactions on thousands of items into easy-to-understand rules. This chapter introduces the techniques for discovering association rules using SQL. Some data mining software includes algorithms for association rules. However, such software does not provide the flexibility available when using SQL directly.

One advantage of using SQL for association rules is that the technique can be modified to fit particular needs. SQL can readily calculate the three traditional measures—support, confidence, and lift. SQL queries can also calculate an improved measure based on the chi-square metric.

Association rules can be about products purchased in a single order or about products purchased over time. A slight variation, called *sequential association rules*, finds the order in which products are purchased. And, finally, the "product" does not have to be an actual product ID. It can be attributes of the product, customer, or order.

The place to start with association rules is with combinations of items, which are also called item sets.

Item Sets

Item sets are combinations of products that appear together within an order. This section starts by considering items sets comprising two products, showing how to use SQL to generate all such combinations. It then moves to some interesting variations, especially combinations of products at the household level rather than the order level. The next sections apply these ideas to creating association rules.

Combinations of Two Products

Item sets with just one product are not particularly interesting, so this section starts by looking at pairs of products. An item set is unordered, so the combination consisting of products A and B is the same as B and A. This section counts the number of product pairs in orders and shows how to use SQL to generate them.

Number of Two-Way Combinations

If an order contains one product, how many two-way combinations of products does it have? The answer is easy. There are none, because the order has only one product. An order with two products has one combination: A and B is the same as B and A. And an order with three products? The answer happens to be three, but the situation is starting to get more complicated.

An easy formula calculates the number. Understanding the formula starts with the observation that the number of pairs of products is the number of products squared. Because pairs where the same product occurs twice are not interesting, subtract out the pairs consisting of identical products. And, because pairs are being counted twice this way (A and B as well as B and A), the difference needs to be divided in two. The number of two-way combinations in an order is half the difference between the number of products in the order and that number squared.

The following query calculates the number of two-way combinations among all orders in `OrderLines`:

```
SELECT SUM(numprods * (numprods - 1) / 2) as numcombo2
FROM (SELECT ol.OrderId, COUNT(DISTINCT ol.ProductId) as numprods
      FROM OrderLines ol
      GROUP BY ol.OrderId
     ) o
```

This query counts distinct products rather than order lines, so orders with the same product on multiple lines are not over counted.

The number of two-way combinations for all the orders is 185,791. This is useful because the number of combinations pretty much determines how quickly the query generating them runs. A single order with a large number of products can seriously degrade performance. For instance, if one order contained one thousand products, there would be about five hundred thousand two-way combinations in just that one order—versus 185,791 in all the orders. As the number of products in the largest order increases, the number of combinations increases faster.

> **WARNING**   Large orders that contain many items can seriously slow down queries for combinations and association rules. A particularly dangerous situation is when a "default" order ID, such as 0 or `NULL`, corresponds to many purchases.

Generating All Two-Way Combinations

To generate all the combinations do a self-join on `OrderLines`, with duplicate product pairs removed. The goal is to get all pairs of products, subject to the conditions:

- The two products in the pair are different.
- No two combinations have the same two products.

The first condition is easily met by filtering out any pairs where the two products are equal. The second condition is also easily met, by requiring that the first product ID be smaller than the second one.

These rules are combined in the following query, which counts the number of orders having any given pair of products:

```
SELECT p1, p2, COUNT(*) as numorders
FROM (SELECT op1.OrderId, op1.ProductId as p1, op2.ProductId as p2
      FROM (SELECT DISTINCT OrderId, ProductId FROM OrderLines) op1 JOIN
           (SELECT DISTINCT OrderId, ProductId FROM OrderLines) op2
          ON op1.OrderId = op2.OrderId AND
             op1.ProductId < op2.ProductId
     ) combinations
GROUP BY p1, p2
```

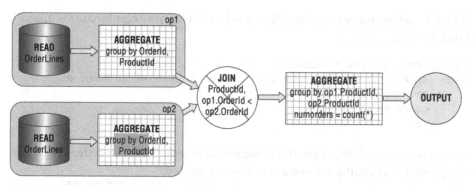

Figure 10-1: This dataflow generates all the two-way combinations of products in the Orders table.

Figure 10-1 shows the data flow for this query. The innermost subqueries, op1 and op2, are joined together to generate all pairs of products within each order. The JOIN condition restricts these pairs to those having different products, with the first smaller than the second. The outer query aggregates each pair of products, counting the number of orders along the way.

Sometimes, we do not want to include all orders. The most common reason is to limit the combinations to reasonable market baskets, such as those with between two and ten products. Other reasons are to use orders from a particular source, or a particular geographic region, or a particular time frame. Because the preceding query works directly on OrderLines, filtering by conditions on the orders requires additional joins. And, it would seem that both subqueries need the filtering logic.

An alternative solution is to use another subquery to define the population of orders and use join for the filtering:

```
SELECT p1, p2, COUNT(*) as numorders
FROM (SELECT op1.OrderId, op1.ProductId as p1, op2.ProductId as p2
      FROM (SELECT OrderId
            FROM OrderLines
            GROUP BY OrderId
            HAVING COUNT(DISTINCT OrderLineId) BETWEEN 2 and 10
           ) filter JOIN
           (SELECT DISTINCT OrderId, ProductId FROM OrderLines) op1
           ON filter.OrderId = op1.OrderId JOIN
           (SELECT DISTINCT OrderId, ProductId FROM OrderLines) op2
           ON op1.OrderId = op2.OrderId AND
              op1.ProductId < op2.ProductId
     ) combinations
GROUP BY p1, p2
```

The `filter` subquery chooses orders that have between two and ten orders. Here the subquery is really just an aggregation of `OrderLines`, but it could also be choosing orders based on characteristics in `Orders`, or even other tables such as `Customers` or `Campaigns`.

Examples of Item Sets

Generating hundreds of thousands of combinations is interesting. Looking at a few examples is informative. The following query fetches the top ten pairs of products in orders with two to ten products, along with the associated product groups:

```
SELECT TOP 10 p1, p2, COUNT(*) as numorders
FROM (SELECT op1.OrderId, op1.ProductId as p1, op2.ProductId as p2
      FROM (SELECT OrderId
            FROM OrderLines
            GROUP BY OrderId
            HAVING COUNT(DISTINCT OrderLineId) BETWEEN 2 and 10
           ) filter JOIN
           (SELECT DISTINCT OrderId, ProductId FROM OrderLines) op1
           ON filter.OrderId = op1.OrderId JOIN
           (SELECT DISTINCT OrderId, ProductId FROM OrderLines) op2
           ON op1.OrderId = op2.OrderId AND
              op1.ProductId < op2.ProductId
     ) combinations
GROUP BY p1, p2
ORDER BY numorders desc
```

This query is basically the same as the previous one, with the addition of TOP 10 and ORDER BY.

The ten most common product pairs are in Table 10-1. Of the ten, seven include FREEBIE products, which are usually part of some promotion. Sometimes more than one FREEBIE is included in the promotion or a given order may qualify for more than one promotion.

> **WARNING**   Association rules often reconstruct bundles of products that were sold together explicitly or sold via recommendation engines.

The three combinations that do not have a FREEBIE in them have ARTWORK and BOOK, BOOK and BOOK, and ARTWORK and OCCASION. These may be examples of products that customers purchase together on their own. On the other hand, these may be examples of product bundles: two or more products that are marketed together. The product-level combinations may have reconstructed the bundles. In fact, this is something that commonly happens when generating combinations of products.

Table 10-1: Pairs of Products Appearing Together in the Most Orders

PRODUCT 1	PRODUCT 2	NUMBER OF ORDERS	PRODUCT GROUP 1	PRODUCT GROUP 2
12820	13190	2,580	FREEBIE	FREEBIE
12819	12820	1,839	FREEBIE	FREEBIE
11048	11196	1,822	ARTWORK	BOOK
10956	12139	1,481	FREEBIE	OCCASION
12139	12820	1,239	OCCASION	FREEBIE
12820	12851	1,084	FREEBIE	OCCASION
11196	11197	667	BOOK	BOOK
12820	13254	592	FREEBIE	OCCASION
12820	12826	589	FREEBIE	ARTWORK
11053	11088	584	ARTWORK	OCCASION

More General Item Sets

There are two useful variations on the pair-wise item set. The first uses the product hierarchy to look at combinations of product groups. The second looks at adding more items into the combinations, moving beyond two-way combinations.

Combinations of Product Groups

Market basket analysis can be extended beyond products to product features. This example uses the product group rather than the product itself. An order with three books on three order lines becomes an order with one product group, BOOK. An order that has a CALENDAR and a BOOK has two product groups, regardless of the number of products in these groups in the order.

Fewer product groups means fewer combinations—just a few dozen. The following query generates the two-way product group combinations, as well as the number of orders having the combination:

```
WITH og as (
      SELECT DISTINCT ol.OrderId, p.GroupName
      FROM OrderLines ol JOIN Products p ON ol.ProductId = p.ProductId
    )
SELECT pg1, pg2, COUNT(*) as cnt
FROM (SELECT og1.OrderId, og1.GroupName as pg1, og2.GroupName as pg2
      FROM og og1 JOIN
           og og2
           ON og1.OrderId = og2.OrderId AND
           og1.GroupName < og2.GroupName
    ) combinations
GROUP BY pg1, pg2
ORDER BY cnt DESC
```

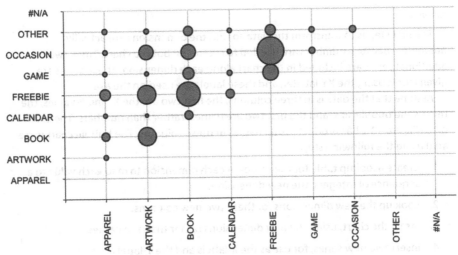

Figure 10-2: This bubble chart shows the most common product pairs. One product is along each dimension, with the bubble showing the number of orders containing the product.

This query is similar to the query for products. The subquery for generating the group name has been split out into a CTE.

Figure 10-2 shows a bubble chart of the results. The two most common product group pairs are FREEBIE with BOOK and FREEBIE with OCCASION. This is not surprising, because FREEBIE products are used as marketing incentives.

The two axes in the bubble chart are the two product groups in an order. Creating this bubble chart is challenging because Excel charting does not allow the axes of scatter plots and bubble charts to be names. The technical aside, "Bubble Charts and Scatter Plots with Non-Numeric Axes," explains one method for getting around this limitation.

Larger Item Sets

Two-way combinations are often sufficient; multi-way combinations can be more useful. Generating larger combinations in SQL requires an additional JOIN for each item in the combination. To keep the combinations distinct (that is, to avoid listing A, B, C and A, C, B as two different combinations), an additional comparison on the product ID needs to be added for each product.

BUBBLE CHARTS AND SCATTER PLOTS WITH NON-NUMERIC AXES

Unfortunately, bubble charts and scatter plots only allow numbers for the X- and Y-coordinates. Fortunately, the XY-labeler introduced in Chapter 4 can make scatter plots and bubble plots with non-numeric dimensions, such as product group names. As a reminder, the XY chart labeler is not part of Excel. It uses an add-in, written by Rob Bovey, and available for download at http://www.appspro.com/Utilities/ChartLabeler.htm.

Continues

continued

The first step is to transform the data so that the dimensions are actually numbers—because numbers are needed to create the bubble chart. Then, two additional series are included in the chart along each dimension. These series are given labels using the XY-labeler, and these labels are used on the axes.

Assume that the data is in three columns, the first two are the X- and Y-values, the third is the bubble size, and the first two are names, rather than numbers. The example in Figure 10-2 has product group names in these columns. The bubble chart is created using the following steps:

1. Create a lookup table for the values in each dimension to map each value to a sequence of integers, the new dimension.

2. Look up the new dimensions for these two new columns.

3. Insert the chart, using the new dimensions rather than the names.

4. Insert two new series, for use as the X-labels and the Y-labels.

5. Format the two series so they are invisible.

6. Use the XY-labeler to label the points with strings.

7. Format the chart as you wish.

This process starts by creating the lookup table. An alternative to manually typing it in is to take all the distinct values in the columns, sort them, and create the new dimension value in an adjacent column using the formula `"=<prev cell>+1"`.

To get the distinct values, copy both columns of product group names into one column, below the data. Filter out duplicates using the Data ➤ Filter ➤ Advanced menu option, and choose "Unique Records Only." Highlight the values using the mouse, copy the values in the cells (Ctrl+C), and paste them into another column (Ctrl+V). Remember to go the Data ➤ Filter ➤ Show All menu selection to undo the filtering, so you can see all the distinct values.

The next step is to lookup the values in the desired X- and Y-columns to get their lookup dimensions. Use `VLOOKUP()` to look up the appropriate values:

```
VLOOKUP(<column cell>, <lookup table>, 2, 0)
```

This provides the number column accepted by the bubble chart. Labeling the axes requires more information, so add two more columns to the lookup table, the first with values set to zero and the second with values set to 1000. The first is the coordinate position of the labels; the second is the width of the bubbles.

The axis labels are attached to two new series. Add the series by right-clicking in the chart and choosing "Source Data." Then choose "Add" and give it the name "X-labels." The X-values for this are the second column in the lookup table, the Y-values are the third column (which is all zeros), and the sizes are the fourth column (all 1000). Repeat for the Y-values, reversing the X- and Y-coordinates. To make the series invisible, left-click each one and select "None" for both the "Border" and "Area" on the "Patterns" tab.

Now, choose the menu option Tools ➤ XY Chart Labels ➤ Add Chart Labels. The "X-labels" are the values in the data series and the label range is the first column of the lookup table. Place the X-labels "Below" the data bubbles. Repeat for the "Y-labels," placing them to the "Left." The labels appear in the chart and can be formatted to any font or rotated by clicking them. It is also a good idea to adjust the scale of the axes to go from 0 to 9 in this case.

The following query is an example for three items:

```
WITH op as (
      SELECT DISTINCT OrderId, ProductId FROM OrderLines
      )
SELECT op1.ProductId as p1, op2.ProductId as p2,
      op3.ProductId as p3, COUNT(*) as cnt
FROM op op1 JOIN
      op op2
      ON op2.OrderId = op1.OrderId AND
         op1.ProductId < op2.ProductId JOIN
      op op3
      ON op3.OrderId = op1.OrderId AND op2.ProductId < op3.ProductId
GROUP BY op1.ProductId, op2.ProductId, op3.ProductId
ORDER BY cnt DESC
```

The results from this query are the combinations of items. The products are in numerical order because of the comparisons in the join conditions. This ordering ensures no duplicate sets of products among the different item sets.

For a particular order to be included in the result set, it needs to have at least three distinct products. We know that many orders have only one or two products, so filtering by the orders can improve performance. This filter can be added in the FROM clause:

```
FROM (SELECT OrderId, COUNT(DISTINCT ProductId) as numprods
      FROM OrderLines
      GROUP BY OrderId
      HAVING COUNT(DISTINCT ProductId) >= 3
      ) ofilter JOIN
      op op1
      ON op1.OrderId = ofilter.OrderId JOIN
      . . .
```

Filtering the orders reduces the amount of data generated by the intermediate joins; however, it does not affect the final result set, which has 1,163,893 rows.

Table 10-2 shows the top ten combinations of three products. The three-way combinations have lower counts than the two-way combinations. For instance, the top two-way combinations appeared in more than 2,000 orders. The top three-way combinations occur in fewer than 400. This is typical because the more products in the order, the fewer the customers who have ordered all of them at once.

All Item Sets Up to a Given Size

The previous example produced all item sets with three items. A natural extension is producing all the items sets with up to three items. Of course, one method is to use UNION ALL on the queries for one, two, and three items. And, UNION

Table 10-2: Top Ten Combinations of Three Products

PRODUCT 1	PRODUCT 2	PRODUCT 3	COUNT	GROUP 1	GROUP 2	GROUP 3
12506	12820	12830	399	FREEBIE	FREEBIE	GAME
12820	13144	13190	329	FREEBIE	APPAREL	FREEBIE
11052	11196	11197	275	ARTWORK	BOOK	BOOK
12139	12819	12820	253	OCCASION	FREEBIE	FREEBIE
12820	12823	12951	194	FREEBIE	OTHER	FREEBIE
10939	10940	10943	170	BOOK	BOOK	BOOK
12820	12851	13190	154	FREEBIE	OCCASION	FREEBIE
11093	12820	13190	142	OCCASION	FREEBIE	FREEBIE
12819	12820	12851	137	FREEBIE	FREEBIE	OCCASION
12005	12820	13190	125	BOOK	FREEBIE	FREEBIE

ALL can be the best method in terms of performance. On the other hand, the resulting queries are long and complicated, with logic such as filtering implemented multiple times.

It is tempting to generate all the items sets by replacing the JOIN with LEFT JOIN:

```
WITH op as (
     SELECT DISTINCT OrderId, ProductId FROM OrderLines
     )
SELECT op1.ProductId as p1, op2.ProductId as p2,
       op3.ProductId as p3, COUNT(*) as cnt
FROM op op1 LEFT JOIN
     op op2
     ON op2.OrderId = op1.OrderId AND
        op1.ProductId < op2.ProductId LEFT JOIN
     op op3
     ON op3.OrderId = op1.OrderId AND op2.ProductId < op3.ProductId
GROUP BY op1.ProductId, op2.ProductId, op3.ProductId
ORDER BY cnt DESC
```

Alas, this query is an example of hope over experience. It does return singletons, doubletons, and triples of products, along with the counts for them. (For singletons, the second and third columns are NULL.) However, the numbers are wrong. The most common product, 12821, appears in 18,441. However, the singleton has a count of only 9,229. Why the discrepancy? What is going on?

This query undercounts singletons and doubletons. The problem is the LEFT JOIN. When orders have more than one product, the LEFT JOIN always finds a matching product; no singleton is created: Products in orders with more than one product are never counted as singletons. Similarly, products in orders with more than two products are never counted as doubletons.

The way to fix this is to adjust the query by introducing a fake product ID into each order. A simple method is to have an ID larger than any existing product:

```
WITH op as (
        SELECT DISTINCT OrderId, ProductId FROM OrderLines UNION ALL
        SELECT DISTINCT OrderId, 9999999 FROM OrderLines
        )
SELECT op1.ProductId as p1, NULLIF(op2.ProductId, 9999999) as p2,
        NULLIF(op3.ProductId, 9999999) as p3, COUNT(*) as cnt
FROM op op1 LEFT JOIN
        op op2
        ON op2.OrderId = op1.OrderId AND
           op1.ProductId < op2.ProductId LEFT JOIN
        op op3
        ON op3.OrderId = op1.OrderId AND op2.ProductId < op3.ProductId
WHERE op1.ProductId <> 9999999
GROUP BY op1.ProductId, op2.ProductId, op3.ProductId
ORDER BY cnt DESC
```

The fake product ID is treated as NULL for output purposes. With this version, the LEFT JOIN keeps all the smaller orders, so the counts are correct.

A similar modification uses NULL for the additional product, changing the FROM clause to:

```
WITH op as (
        SELECT DISTINCT OrderId, ProductId FROM OrderLines UNION ALL
        SELECT DISTINCT OrderId, NULL FROM OrderLines
        )
SELECT op1.ProductId as p1, op2.ProductIdas p2,
        op3.ProductId as p3, COUNT(*) as cnt
FROM op op1 JOIN
        op op2
        ON op2.OrderId = op1.OrderId AND
           (op1.ProductId < op2.ProductId OR
            op2.ProductId IS NULL) LEFT JOIN
        op op3
        ON op3.OrderId = op1.OrderId AND
           (op2.ProductId < op3.ProductId OR
            op3.ProductId IS NULL)
WHERE op1.ProductId IS NOT NULL
GROUP BY op1.ProductId, op2.ProductId, op3.ProductId
ORDER BY cnt DESC
```

This version uses LEFT JOIN to prevent the second join from filtering out the singletons. All three of these methods generate item sets up to a given size; which method performs best depends on how the queries are optimized.

Households Not Orders

So far, we have considered only combinations of products within an order. Another possibility is to look at products that households purchase, even though the purchases occur at different times. One application is particularly interesting, looking at combinations that occur within a household but not within a particular order, because such combinations suggest opportunities for cross-selling.

Combinations within a Household

The following query extends two-way combinations to products in the same household:

```
WITH hp as (
        SELECT DISTINCT c.HouseholdId, ol.ProductId
        FROM OrderLines ol JOIN
             Orders o
             ON o.OrderId = ol.OrderId JOIN
             Customers c
             ON o.CustomerId = c.CustomerId
     )
SELECT hp1.ProductId as p1, hp2.ProductId as p2, COUNT(*) as cnt
FROM (SELECT HouseholdId
      FROM hp
      GROUP BY HouseholdId
      HAVING COUNT(DISTINCT ProductId) BETWEEN 2 AND 10
     ) hfilter JOIN
     hp hp1
     ON hp1.HouseholdId = hfilter.HouseholdId JOIN
     hp hp2
     ON hp2.HouseholdId = hfilter.HouseholdId AND
        hp1.ProductId < hp2.ProductId
GROUP BY hp1.ProductId, hp2.ProductId
ORDER BY COUNT(*) DESC
```

The CTE hp handles the logic to get the household ID along with the products purchased by that household. The structure of the rest of the query remains the same. This version has a filter on the households, limiting the number of products because a few households have a very large number of purchases, and those households both slow down the query and skew the results.

Investigating Products within Households but Not within Orders

The questions so far have all been within the realm of traditional association rules—just varying the unit of aggregation (order or household), the number of products being considered, or the definition of product (product ID or product group). The next question shows the power of doing this work in SQL: *What pairs of products occur frequently among household purchases but do not appear in the same order?* Such a question can provide very valuable information on potential cross-selling opportunities because such product pairs indicate affinities among products at different times.

Answering this question requires only minor modifications to the household query. This query had the following conditions:

- The household has two to ten products.

- Both products appear within the household.

- The first product in the pair has a lower product ID than the second product.

One more condition is needed:

- The products are in the same household but not in the same order.

SQL can readily handle all these conditions;

```
WITH hop as (
      SELECT DISTINCT c.HouseholdId, ol.OrderId, ol.ProductId,
             p.GroupName
      FROM OrderLines ol JOIN
           Orders o ON o.OrderId = ol.OrderId JOIN
           Customers c ON o.CustomerId = c.CustomerId JOIN
           Products p ON ol.ProductId = p.ProductId
     )
SELECT TOP 10 hop1.ProductId as p1, hop2.ProductId as p2,
       COUNT(DISTINCT hop1.HouseholdId) as cnt,
       hop1.GroupName as Group1, hop2.GroupName as Group2
FROM (SELECT HouseholdId
      FROM hop
      GROUP BY HouseholdId
      HAVING COUNT(DISTINCT ProductId) BETWEEN 2 AND 10
     ) hfilter JOIN
     hop hop1
     ON hop1.HouseholdId = hfilter.HouseholdId JOIN
     hop hop2
     ON hop2.HouseholdId = hfilter.HouseholdId AND
        hop1.ProductId < hop2.ProductId AND
        hop1.OrderId <> hop2.OrderId
GROUP BY hop1.ProductId, hop2.ProductId, hop1.GroupName, hop2.GroupName
ORDER BY cnt DESC
```

The differences between this query and the household query are instructive. The CTE hop now includes both the household and the order. As a consequence, the same product can appear multiple times for a household—in different orders.

Table 10-3: Top Ten Pairs of Products Purchased by Households At Different Times

PRODUCT1	PRODUCT2	COUNT	GROUP1	GROUP2
11196	11197	462	BOOK	BOOK
11111	11196	313	BOOK	BOOK
12139	12820	312	OCCASION	FREEBIE
12015	12176	299	CALENDAR	CALENDAR
11048	11196	294	ARTWORK	BOOK
12176	13298	279	CALENDAR	CALENDAR
10863	12015	255	CALENDAR	CALENDAR
11048	11052	253	ARTWORK	ARTWORK
11111	11197	246	BOOK	BOOK
11048	11197	232	ARTWORK	BOOK

Hence, `hfilter` uses `COUNT(DISTINCT)` instead of `COUNT()` to find households with between two and ten different products. And, the outer query also uses `COUNT(DISTINCT)`.

Table 10-3 shows the top ten results from this query. These results differ from the products within an order because the FREEBIE product group is much less common. Some of the combinations are not particularly surprising. For instance, customers who purchase calendars one year seem likely to purchase calendars in another year. This combination occurs three times in the top ten products.

Multiple Purchases of the Same Product

The previous example excluded from consideration the same product purchased at different times (that is, the query only considers two *different* products). This suggests another interesting question, although one that is not directly related to product combinations: *How often does a household purchase the same product in multiple orders?* The following query answers this question:

```
SELECT numprodinhh, COUNT(*) as numhouseholds
FROM (SELECT c.HouseholdId, ol.ProductId,
             COUNT(DISTINCT o.OrderId) as numprodinhh
      FROM Customers c JOIN
           Orders o ON c.CustomerId = o.CustomerId JOIN
           OrderLines ol ON o.OrderId = ol.OrderId
      GROUP BY c.HouseholdId, ol.ProductId
     ) h
GROUP BY numprodinhh
ORDER BY numprodinhh
```

The subquery aggregates the order lines by household ID and product, using COUNT(DISTINCT) to count the number of orders containing the product within a household. The outer query then creates a histogram of the counts.

More than 8,000 households have purchased the same product more than once. The most frequent ones purchase the same product more than 50 times. These very frequent purchases are possibly anomalous, perhaps a small businesses purchasing the same product multiple times.

One question often leads to another. *What are the top products appearing in these orders?* The following query shows which product groups have the most repeated products:

```
SELECT p.GroupName, COUNT(*) as numhouseholds
FROM (SELECT c.HouseholdId, ol.ProductId,
             COUNT(DISTINCT o.OrderId) as numorders
      FROM Customers c JOIN
           Orders o ON c.CustomerId = o.CustomerId JOIN
           OrderLines ol ON o.OrderId = ol.OrderId
      GROUP BY c.HouseholdId, ol.ProductId
     ) h JOIN
     Products p
     ON h.ProductId = p.ProductId
WHERE numorders > 1
GROUP BY p.GroupName
ORDER BY numhouseholds DESC
```

The subquery summarizes information for each household by product. The overall query is quite similar to the previous query, except the product information is being joined in, and then the outer query is aggregating by GroupName.

Table 10-4 shows that the three product groups with the most repeats are BOOK, ARTWORK, and OCCASION. This differs from the common combinations, which

Table 10-4: Products That Appear in More Than One Order, by Product Group

PRODUCT GROUP	NUMBER OF HOUSEHOLDS
BOOK	2,709
ARTWORK	2,101
OCCASION	1,212
FREEBIE	935
GAME	384
CALENDAR	353
APPAREL	309
OTHER	210

always include FREEBIE products. In fact, one FREEBIE product, whose ID is 12820, is the top product that appears in multiple orders within a household. Without this product, the FREEBIE category would have only 210 occurrences of the same product appearing in multiple orders, and would fall to the bottom of the table. This product is a catalog that was included in all shipments during a period of time. Customers who placed multiple orders during this period of time received the catalog with each purchase.

The Simplest Association Rules

Item sets are interesting. Association rules transform the item sets into rules. This section starts the discussion of association rules by calculating the proportion of orders that have a given product. These are the simplest, most basic type of association rule, one where the "if" clause is empty and the "then" clause contains one product: Given no information, what is the probability that a given product is an order? This idea of "zero-way" association rules is useful for two reasons. First, it provides a simple introduction to the ideas and terminology. Second, this overall probability is important for assessing more complex rules.

Associations and Rules

An *association* is a group of products that appear together—typically in an order, but the hierarchy could be at any level. The word "association" implies that the products have a relationship with each other based on the fact that they are found together. An *association rule* has the form:

    <left-hand side> ➢ <right-hand side>

The arrow in the rule means "implies," so this rule is read as "the presence of all the products on the left-hand side implies the presence of the products on the right-hand side in the same order." Of course, a rule is not always true, so there is a probability associated with it (called the *confidence*, which will be more formally defined later). The left- and right-hand sides are item sets that can be of any size, although typically the right-hand side consists of one product.

The automatic generation of association rules demonstrates the power of using detailed data. It must be admitted that the resulting rules are not always necessarily interesting. It is tempting to interpret the association rule as causality because of the "if"; but they do not show causal relationships. One early example, published in the 1990s by Sears, a large department store chain, was based on data from a multi-million dollar investment in a data warehousing system. They learned that customers who buy large appliance warranties are very likely to buy large appliances. No doubt, an affinity exists. Warranties are indeed sold with large appliances, but the causality goes in the other direction.

> **WARNING**   Association rules are not necessarily interesting. They are sometimes *trivial*, **telling us something we should already know.**

Such a rule is *trivial* because we should have known. Although trivial rules are not useful from a business perspective, they are resounding successes for the software—because the pattern is undeniably in the data. By the way, trivial rules can be useful. Exceptions to trivial rules that have a very high confidence might point to data quality or operational issues.

Zero-Way Association Rules

The zero-way association rule represents the idea that nothing else in an order implies that the order contains a given product:

> <nothing> ≽ <product ID>

It is "zero" way because the left-hand side has no products.

This rule is really just the probability that an order contains the product in question. The probability in turn is the number of orders containing a product divided by the total number of orders:

```
SELECT ProductId, COUNT(*) / MAX(numorders) as p
FROM (SELECT DISTINCT OrderId, ProductId FROM OrderLines) op CROSS JOIN
     (SELECT COUNT(*) * 1.0 as NumOrders FROM Orders) o
GROUP BY ProductId
ORDER BY p DESC
```

This query calculates the number of orders having any particular product, taking care to avoid double counting products on multiple order lines of the same order. The number of orders with the product is then divided by the total number of orders. A subquery, brought in using CROSS JOIN, calculates the total number of orders, which is converted to a real number by multiplying by 1.0 to avoid integer division.

The result is each product with the proportion of orders containing the product. For instance, the most popular product is product ID 12820, which is a FREEBIE product that occurs in about 9.6% of the orders.

What Is the Distribution of Probabilities?

With more than 4,000 products, looking at all the probabilities individually is cumbersome. What do these probabilities look like? The following query provides some information about the values:

```
SELECT COUNT(*) as numprods, MIN(p) as minp, MAX(p) as maxp,
       AVG(p) as avgp, COUNT(DISTINCT p) as nump
FROM (SELECT ol.ProductId,
             (COUNT(DISTINCT ol.OrderId) * 1.0 /
             (SELECT COUNT(*) FROM Orders)
             ) as p
      FROM OrderLines ol
      GROUP BY ol.productid
      ) op
```

This version of the calculation uses an in-line query, rather than the CROSS JOIN. Both methods work equally well, but the CROSS JOIN is actually better because you can add several variables at once and give them informative names. In addition, in some databases, the CROSS JOIN has performance advantages.

These probabilities have the following characteristics:

- The minimum value is 0.0005%.
- The maximum value is 9.6%.
- The average value is 0.036%.
- There are 385 different values.

This last number is curious. Why are there only a few hundred distinct values when there are thousands of products? The probabilities are ratios between two numbers, the number of times that a product appears, and the number of orders. For all products, the number of orders is the same, so the number of different probabilities is the number of different frequencies of products. There is much overlap, especially because over one thousand products appear only once.

Just a few hundred values can readily be plotted, as in Figure 10-3, which has both the histogram and the cumulative histogram. The histogram is on

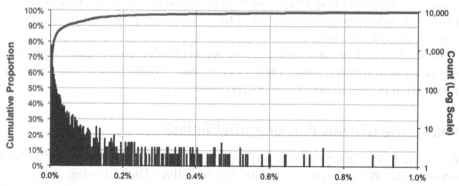

Figure 10-3: This chart shows the distribution of probabilities of an order containing a product.

the left-hand axis. However, this histogram is visually misleading because the points are not equally spaced.

The cumulative distribution is the other curve on the chart, and it provides more information. For instance, it says that half the products have a probability of less than about 0.0015%, so many products are quite rare indeed. Only half a percent of the products (23) occur in more than one percent of the orders.

What Do Zero-Way Associations Tell Us?

Zero-way association rules provide basic information about products. Given no other information about purchases, such rules give the probability of a given product being in an order. For instance, the top product, with ID 12820, occurs in about 9.6% of the orders. This is a FREEBIE product, which is not so interesting.

The second product is a book that occurs in 4.9% of orders; its product ID is 11168. An association rule predicting it has the form:

> <LHS> ➤ <product 11168>

If this more complex rule were accurate 50% of the time, then it is useful. If it were accurate 10% of the time, then it is useful. However, if it were accurate only 4.8% of the time, the rule does worse than an informed guess based on the zero-way rule. Such a rule is not useful, at least in the positive direction. The overall probability is a minimum level required for a rule to be useful (at least as a positive predictor of the right-hand side). This comparison is an important measure for the effectiveness of association rules.

One-Way Association Rules

This section moves from combinations of products to rules specifying that the presence of one product implies the presence of another. For many purposes, finding combinations of products that occur together is quite useful. However, these are still combinations, not rules.

Before investigating how to generate the rules, this section starts with the issue of evaluating rules. What makes one rule better than another?

Evaluating a One-Way Association Rule

The two most common products have IDs 12820 and 13190, suggesting the rule:

> Product 12820 ➤ Product 13190

The traditional ways of evaluating such a rule are called support, confidence, and lift.

Calculating these measures uses the following information:

- The total number of orders
- The number of orders that contain the left-hand side of the rule
- The number of orders that contain the right-hand side of the rule
- The number of orders that contain both the left- and right-hand sides

And these are calculated by the following query:

```
SELECT COUNT(*) as numorders, SUM(lhs) as numlhs, SUM(rhs) as numrhs,
       SUM(lhs * rhs) as numlhsrhs
FROM (SELECT OrderId,
             MAX(CASE WHEN ProductId = 12820 THEN 1 ELSE 0 END) as lhs,
             MAX(CASE WHEN ProductId = 13190 THEN 1 ELSE 0 END) as rhs
      FROM OrderLines ol
      GROUP BY OrderId) o
```

Notice that this query calculates the presence of the left-hand and right-hand products using conditional aggregation. Because the maximum function is used, the calculation counts only the presence of these products, ignoring NumUnits and counting duplicate products only once for each order. Also notice that the query has no WHERE clause. Filtering would work for all the calculations, except for the first one—the total number of orders.

The first evaluation measure in Table 10-5 is *support*. This is the proportion of orders where the rule is true. Support is the ratio of number of orders that have both the left side and right side to the total number of orders. For this rule, the support is 2,588 / 192,983 = 1.3%. Rules with higher support are more useful because they apply to more orders. A second measure is *confidence*, which is how often the rule is true, given that the left-hand side is true. Confidence is the ratio of orders that have both products to those that have the left-hand-side product. The confidence is 2,588 / 18,441 = 14.0%.

Table 10-5: Traditional Measures for the Rule Product 12820 ➤ Product 13190

MEASURE	VALUE
Number of Orders	192,983
Number of Orders with Left-Hand Side	18,441
Number of Orders with Right-Hand Side	3,404
Number of Orders with Both Sides	2,588
Support	1.3%
Confidence	14.0%
Lift	8.0

The third traditional measure is *lift*, which tells us how much better using the rule is than just guessing. Without the rule, we would expect 1.8% (3,404 / 192,983) of orders to have product 13190. When the rule is true, 14.0% have it. The rule does about eight times better than just guessing, so the rule has a high lift.

The following query calculates these values directly for this rule:

```
SELECT numlhsrhs / numorders as support, numlhsrhs / numlhs as confidence,
       (numlhsrhs / numlhs) / (numrhs / numorders) as lift
FROM (SELECT 1.0 * COUNT(*) as numorders, 1.0 * SUM(lhs) as numlhs,
             1.0 * SUM(rhs) as numrhs, 1.0 * SUM(lhs * rhs) as numlhsrhs
      FROM (SELECT orderid,
                   MAX(CASE WHEN ProductId = 12820 THEN 1 END) as lhs,
                   MAX(CASE WHEN ProductId = 13190 THEN 1 END) as rhs
            FROM OrderLines ol
            GROUP BY OrderId) o
     ) r
```

This query does the calculation for only one rule. The challenge in the next sections is to calculate these values for all possible rules.

Before looking at all rules, let's look at just one other, the inverse rule:

Product 13190 ≻ Product 12820

The support for the inverse rule is exactly the same as the support for the original rule because the two rules have the same combination of products.

Perhaps more surprising, the lift for the two rules is the same as well. This is not a coincidence; it comes from the definition of lift. The formula simplifies to:

```
(numlhsrsh * numorders) / (numlhs * numrhs)
```

Both the rule and its inverse have the same values of `numlhsrsh` and `numorders`, so the numerator is the same. The values of `numlhs` and `numrhs` are swapped, so the product of the two values remains the same. As a result the lift is the same for any rule and its inverse.

The confidence values for a rule and its inverse are different. However, there is a simple relationship between them. The product of the confidence values is the same as the product of the support and the lift. So, given the confidence, support, and lift for one rule, it is simple to calculate the confidence, support, and lift for the inverse rule.

Generating All One-Way Rules

The query to generate one-way association rules is similar to the query to calculate combinations, in that both involve self-joins on `OrderLines`. The query starts by enumerating all the possible rule combinations:

```
WITH items as (
     SELECT DISTINCT ol.OrderId as basket, ol.ProductId as Item
     FROM OrderLines ol
```

```
          )
    SELECT REPLACE(REPLACE('<lhs> -> <rhs>', '<lhs>', lhs),
                   '<rhs>', rhs) as therule,
           lhs, rhs, COUNT(*) as numlhsrhs
    FROM (SELECT lhs.basket, lhs.item as lhs, rhs.item as rhs
          FROM items lhs JOIN
               items rhs
               ON lhs.basket = rhs.basket AND
                  lhs.item <> rhs.item
         ) rules
    GROUP BY lhs, rhs
```

This query is similar to the previous queries, with some additions for actually generating the rule. First, notice that the query uses more generic names for columns and CTEs. This makes it easier to use almost the same code for different examples.

The rule itself is generated using REPLACE() to construct the rule as a single string from a template. An alternative to REPLACE() is to use string concatenation: (CAST(lhs as VARCHAR(255)) + ' -> ' + CAST(rhs as VARCHAR(255))). Changing the format of the string is easier with the version using REPLACE(). In addition, the use of the template gives a clearer idea of what the final result looks like. As a note, there is nothing special about the "255" in VARCHAR(255). When using VARCHAR() in SQL Server, you want an explicit length because the default length varies by context, and errors caused by leaving out a length can be quite hard to find. The value of 255 is more than long enough for this purpose.

One important difference from the combination query is that all pairs of products are being considered, rather than only unique pairs, because A ≻ B and B ≻ A are two different rules. The subquery Rules generates all candidate rules in Orders, instead of all pairs of items.

This form of the query does not restrict the orders, say, to orders that have between two and ten products. This condition can be added using the filter subquery as shown earlier.

One-Way Rules with Evaluation Information

The previous query generates all the possible one-way rules. Getting evaluation information is just a matter of calculating the right measures for each rule and then doing the necessary arithmetic, by modifying the previous query:

```
WITH items as (
     SELECT ol.OrderId as basket, ol.ProductId as item,
            COUNT(*) OVER (PARTITION BY ol.ProductId) as cnt,
            (SELECT COUNT(*) FROM Orders) as numbaskets
     FROM OrderLines ol
     GROUP BY ol.OrderId, ol.ProductId
     ),
     rules as (
```

```
        SELECT lhs, rhs, COUNT(*) as numlhsrhs, numlhs, numrhs,
               numbaskets
        FROM (SELECT lhs.basket, lhs.item as lhs, rhs.item as rhs,
                     lhs.cnt as numlhs, rhs.cnt as numrhs, lhs.numbaskets
              FROM items lhs JOIN
                   items rhs
                   ON lhs.basket = rhs.basket AND
                      lhs.item <> rhs.item
             ) rules
        GROUP BY lhs, rhs, numlhs, numrhs, numbaskets
       )
SELECT TOP 10 rules.lhs, rhs, numlhsrhs, numlhs, numrhs, numbaskets,
       numlhsrhs * 1.0 / numbaskets as support,
       numlhsrhs * 1.0 / numlhs as confidence,
       numlhsrhs * numbaskets * 1.0 / (numlhs * numrhs) as lift
FROM rules
ORDER BY lift DESC, lhs, rhs
```

The structure of the query is familiar. The subquery in `items` calculates the number of orders. An alternative is `COUNT(DISTINCT OrderId) OVER ()`. However, this window function is not supported by all databases that support window functions.

Table 10-6 shows the top few rules with the highest lift. These rules are rather uninteresting because the highest lift rules are the ones where two products appear together and the two products never appear without the other. This tends to occur somewhat randomly for the least common products.

Table 10-6: Top One-Way Rules with Highest Lift

RULE	NUM LHSRHS	NUM LHS	NUM RHS	NUM ORDERS	SUPPORT	CONFIDENCE	LIFT
10051 ➤ 10267	1	1	1	192,983	0.0%	100.0%	192,983.0
10058 ➤ 11794	1	1	1	192,983	0.0%	100.0%	192,983.0
10060 ➤ 12964	1	1	1	192,983	0.0%	100.0%	192,983.0
10097 ➤ 10529	1	1	1	192,983	0.0%	100.0%	192,983.0
10248 ➤ 12470	1	1	1	192,983	0.0%	100.0%	192,983.0
10248 ➤ 12703	1	1	1	192,983	0.0%	100.0%	192,983.0
10255 ➤ 11424	1	1	1	192,983	0.0%	100.0%	192,983.0
10263 ➤ 11711	1	1	1	192,983	0.0%	100.0%	192,983.0
10267 ➤ 10051	1	1	1	192,983	0.0%	100.0%	192,983.0
10294 ➤ 12211	1	1	1	192,983	0.0%	100.0%	192,983.0

One way to fix this is by putting in a threshold value for support. For instance, to consider only rules where the support is at least 0.1%:

```
WHERE numlhsrhs * 1.0 / numbaskets >= 0.001
```

126 rules meet this restriction. Almost all of them have a lift greater than one, but a small number have a lift less than one. Rules with high support do not necessarily have good lift, although they often do.

One-Way Rules on Product Groups

As another example of one-way association rules, let's consider rules about product groups. This is basically just a small change to the `items` CTE:

```
WITH items as (
      SELECT ol.OrderId as basket, p.GroupName as item,
             COUNT(*) OVER (PARTITION BY p.GroupName) as cnt,
             (SELECT COUNT(*) FROM Orders) as numbaskets
      FROM OrderLines ol JOIN
           Products p
           ON ol.ProductId = p.ProductId
      GROUP BY ol.OrderId, p.GroupName
     ),
     rules as (
      SELECT lhs, rhs, COUNT(*) as numlhsrhs, numlhs, numrhs,
             numbaskets
      FROM (SELECT lhs.basket, lhs.item as lhs, rhs.item as rhs,
                   lhs.cnt as numlhs, rhs.cnt as numrhs, lhs.numbaskets
            FROM items lhs JOIN
                 items rhs
                 ON lhs.basket = rhs.basket AND
                    lhs.item <> rhs.item
           ) rules
      GROUP BY lhs, rhs, numlhs, numrhs, numbaskets
     )
SELECT rules.lhs, rhs, numlhsrhs, numlhs, numrhs, numbaskets,
       numlhsrhs * 1.0 / numbaskets as support,
       numlhsrhs * 1.0 / numlhs as confidence,
       numlhsrhs * numbaskets * 1.0 / (1.0 * numlhs * numrhs) as lift
FROM rules
ORDER BY lift DESC
```

This query shows the power of having generic queries that use CTEs. Everything except the definition of `items` remains the same as in the query for products.

Figure 10-4 shows the results as a bubble plot. The bubble plot contains two series. One consists of pretty good rules where the lift is greater than one. The rest are grouped into not-good rules. This bubble chart uses the same tricks for labeling the axes that were discussed earlier.

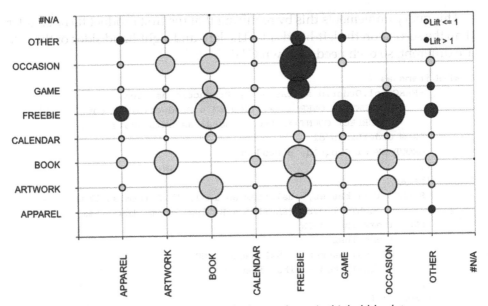

Figure 10-4: The good rules and not-so-good rules are shown in this bubble plot.

Not many of these rules have a good lift. One reason is that most orders have only one product and hence only one product group. These orders inflate the values of `numlhs` and `numrhs`, without contributing to the value of `numlhsrhs`.

Two-Way Associations

The calculation for two-way association rules follows the same logic as for the one-way rules. This section looks at the SQL for generating such rules, as well as some interesting extensions by extending the idea of item and the relationships among them.

Calculating Two-Way Associations

The basic query for calculating two-way associations is quite similar to the query for one-way associations. The difference is that the left-hand side has two products rather than one.

The following two rules are equivalent:

A and B ➤ C

B and A ➤ C

Hence, the products on the left-hand side are an item set, so the products should not be repeated.

This query implements this by requiring that the first product ID be smaller than the second on the left-hand side. The left- and right-hand sides of the rule are different, so each needs its own CTE:

```
WITH items as (
      SELECT ol.OrderId as basket, p.ProductId as item,
             COUNT(*) OVER (PARTITION BY p.ProductId) as cnt,
             (SELECT COUNT(*) FROM Orders) as numbaskets
      FROM OrderLines ol
      GROUP BY ol.OrderId, p.ProductId
      ),
      lhs as (
      SELECT lhs1.basket, lhs1.item as lhs1, lhs2.item as lhs2,
             COUNT(*) OVER (PARTITION BY lhs1.item, lhs2.item) as cnt
      FROM items lhs1 JOIN
           items lhs2
           ON lhs1.basket = lhs2.basket AND
              lhs1.item <> lhs2.item
      ),
      rules as (
      SELECT lhs1, lhs2, rhs, COUNT(*) as numlhsrhs,
             numlhs, numrhs, numbaskets
      FROM (SELECT lhs.basket, lhs.lhs1, lhs.lhs2, rhs.item as rhs,
                   lhs.cnt as numlhs, rhs.cnt as numrhs, rhs.numbaskets
            FROM lhs JOIN
                 items rhs
                 ON rhs.basket = lhs.basket AND
                    rhs.item NOT IN (lhs.lhs1, lhs.lhs2)
            ) rules
      GROUP BY lhs1, lhs2, rhs, numlhs, numrhs, numbaskets
      )
SELECT lhs1, lhs2, rhs, numbaskets, numlhs, numrhs,
       numlhsrhs * 1.0 / numbaskets as support,
       numlhsrhs * 1.0 / numlhs as confidence,
       numlhsrhs * numbaskets * 1.0 / (numlhs * numrhs) as lift
FROM rules
WHERE numlhsrhs * 1.0 / numbaskets >= 0.001
ORDER BY lift DESC
```

The CTE lhs calculates the two products for the left-hand side. Some extra logic is needed to ensure the right-hand side item differs from the left-hand side items (so the rule is not trivial). The overall flow of this query is remarkably similar to the previous query. And, the traditional measures are calculated in exactly the same way. By using careful naming conventions in the intermediate table, the same query can calculate support, confidence, and lift for one-way association rules and two-way association rules.

The results from this query are also rather similar to the results for the one-way associations. The rules with the highest lift are the extremely rare ones with three products. By the measure of lift, the best rules seem to be those that have products that only occur together and never separately.

Using Chi-Square to Find the Best Rules

Lift provides one measure of "best," but perhaps it is not the most practical. The rules with the best lift are those that have the least common products that happen to be purchased at the same time—this means that the rules with the highest lift have the lowest support. The typical way to get around this is by requiring a certain level of support for the rule. However, the rules with the highest lift are often still the ones with the rarest products that meet the support criterion. This section discusses an alternative measure, the chi-square measure. It produces a better subjective ordering of the rules, and one whose basis is in statistics.

Applying Chi-Square to Rules

The chi-square measure was introduced in Chapter 3 as a way to measure whether particular splits in data across multiple dimensions are due to chance. The higher the chi-square value for a particular set of splits, the less likely that observed data is happening due to chance. The measure can be used directly or it can be converted to a p-value based on the chi-square distribution.

Chi-square can also be applied to rules, and it provides a single value that determines whether or not the rule is reasonable. Lift, confidence, and support all measure how good a rule is, but they are three different measures. One warning, though: Chi-square does not work very well unless all cells have a minimum *expected* value. The usual value is a minimum of five.

The chi-square measure works on contingency tables, which—at first glance—do not have much to do with rules. But, they do. Start by considering a general rule:

LHS ≻ RHS

This rule divides all the orders into four discrete groups:

- LHS is TRUE and RHS is TRUE.
- LHS is TRUE and RHS is FALSE.
- LHS is FALSE and RHS is TRUE.
- LHS is FALSE and RHS is FALSE.

Table 10-7 shows the counts of orders that fall into each of these groups for the rule 12820 ≻ 13190. The rows indicate whether the orders contain the left-hand side of the rule. The columns are whether they contain the right-hand side. The 816, for instance, is the number of orders where the rule is true.

Table 10-7: Counts of Orders for Chi-Square Calculation for Rule 12820 ≻ 13190

	RHS TRUE	RHS FALSE
LHS TRUE	816	15,853
LHS FALSE	2,588	173,726

This matrix is a contingency table as described in Chapter 3. And the chi-square measure is a natural measure for determining whether the contingency table values are due to chance (uninteresting) or some other mechanism besides randomness (such as some underlying pattern captured by a rule). As described in Chapter 3, calculating the chi-square values is not difficult in Excel. Sum the rows and columns and then calculate an expected value matrix using these sums. The expected value is the product of the row sum times the column sum divided by the sum of all the cells in the table. The observed value minus the expected value is the variance. The chi-square value is then the sum of the variances squared divided by the expected values.

Chi-square has some nice properties compared to lift. It provides a measure of how unexpected the rule is rather than the improvement from using it. In one measure, it takes into account both the goodness and coverage of the rule. The standard measures of support and lift address these issues separately.

Applying Chi-Square to Rules in SQL

Excel is not sufficiently powerful to perform the chi-square calculation for millions of rules. As shown in Chapter 3, doing the chi-square calculation in SQL is also possible—it just requires a bunch of arithmetic.

Four counts have been used for calculating support, confidence, and lift:

- `numlhsrhs` is the number of orders where the entire rule is true.
- `numlhs` is the number of orders where the left-hand side is true.
- `numrhs` is the number of orders where the right-hand side is true.
- `numbaskets` is the total number of orders.

The chi-square calculation uses four slightly different counts, based on the contingency table for the rule:

- LHS true, RHS true: `numlhsrhs`
- LHS true, RHS false: `numlhs − numlhsrhs`
- LHS false, RHS true: `numrhs − numlhsrhs`
- LHS false, RHS false: `numorders − numlhs − numrhs + numlhsrhs`

With these values, the chi-square calculation can use the same query structure along with some additional arithmetic.

The following query calculates the traditional measures as well as the chi-square measure:

```
WITH items as (
    SELECT o.OrderId as basket, ol.ProductId as item,
        COUNT(*) OVER (PARTITION BY ProductId) as cnt,
        (SELECT COUNT(*) FROM Orders) as numbaskets
    FROM OrderLines ol
```

```
      GROUP BY o.OrderId, ol.ProductId
    ),
    rules as (
    SELECT lhs, rhs, COUNT(*) as numlhsrhs, numlhs, numrhs, numbaskets,
           numlhs - COUNT(*) as numlhsnorhs,
           numrhs - COUNT(*) as numnolhsrhs,
           numbaskets - numlhs - numrhs + COUNT(*) as numnolhsnorhs,
           numlhs * numrhs * 1.0 / numbaskets as explhsrhs,
           numlhs*(1.0*numbaskets - numrhs)*1.0 / numbaskets as explhsnorhs,
           (1.0*numbaskets - numlhs)*numrhs*1.0 / numbaskets as expnolhsrhs,
           ((1.0*numbaskets - numlhs)*(1.0*numbaskets - numrhs) / numbaskets
           ) as expnolhsnorhs,
           COUNT(*) * 1.0 / numbaskets as support,
           COUNT(*) * 1.0 / numlhs as confidence,
           COUNT(*) * numbaskets * 1.0 / (numlhs * numrhs) as lift
    FROM (SELECT lhs.basket, lhs.item as lhs, rhs.item as rhs,
                 lhs.cnt as numlhs, rhs.cnt as numrhs, lhs.numbaskets
          FROM items lhs JOIN
               items rhs
               ON lhs.basket = rhs.basket AND
                  lhs.item <> rhs.item
         ) rules
    GROUP BY lhs, rhs, numlhs, numrhs, numbaskets
    )
  SELECT (SQUARE(explhsrhs - numlhsrhs) / explhsrhs +
          SQUARE(explhsnorhs - numlhsnorhs) / explhsnorhs +
          SQUARE(expnolhsrhs - numnolhsrhs) / expnolhsrhs +
          SQUARE(expnolhsnorhs - numnolhsnorhs) / expnolhsnorhs
         ) as chisquare, rules.*
  FROM rules
  ORDER BY chisquare DESC
```

This follows the same structure as the previous queries; more columns are added to support the chi-square calculation.

Comparing Chi-Square Rules to Lift

At first glance, the rules with the highest chi-square values are the same as the rules with the highest lift. These are the rules consisting of products that appear in only one order. However, one of the conditions of the chi-square calculation is that the expected value of every cell should have a count of at least five.

This condition can be incorporated into the query using a WHERE condition:

```
WHERE explhsrhs > 5 AND explhsnorhs > 5 AND
      expnolhsrhs > 5 AND expnolhsnorhs > 5
```

Table 10-8 shows the top ten rules with the highest chi-square values and the highest lift values. The first thing to notice is that the two sets have some overlap—four of the ten rules are the same. Notice, further, that the rules all come in pairs. Both lift and chi-square have the property that A ≻ B and B ≻ A have the same values for the two measures.

Table 10-8: Top Rules by Lift and by Chi-Square Measures

	BEST CHI-SQUARE				BEST LIFT		
RULE	SUP-PORT	CHI-SQUARE	LIFT	RULE	SUP-PORT	CHI-SQUARE	LIFT
11048 ➤ 11196	0.95%	40,972.6	23.5	10940 ➤ 10943	0.21%	28,171.4	72.4
11196 ➤ 11048	0.95%	40,972.6	23.5	10943 ➤ 10940	0.21%	28,171.4	72.4
10940 ➤ 10943	0.21%	28,171.4	72.4	10939 ➤ 10943	0.17%	16,299.6	50.8
10943 ➤ 10940	0.21%	28,171.4	72.4	10943 ➤ 10939	0.17%	16,299.6	50.8
11052 ➤ 11197	0.28%	20,440.4	39.0	11052 ➤ 11197	0.28%	20,440.4	39.0
11197 ➤ 11052	0.28%	20,440.4	39.0	11197 ➤ 11052	0.28%	20,440.4	39.0
10956 ➤ 12139	0.77%	19,804.6	14.6	10939 ➤ 10942	0.17%	10,691.3	34.9
12139 ➤ 10956	0.77%	19,804.6	14.6	10942 ➤ 10939	0.17%	10,691.3	34.9
12820 ➤ 13190	1.34%	17,715.6	8.0	10939 ➤ 10940	0.12%	7,167.9	31.8
13190 ➤ 12820	1.34%	17,715.6	8.0	10940 ➤ 10939	0.12%	7,167.9	31.8

The rules with the highest lift are all similar: these rules all have low support and the products in the rules are quite rare. The average support for these rules is 0.19%, with the highest support at 0.28%. These rules do have reasonable confidence levels. What makes them good, though, is that the products are rare, so seeing them together in an order is quite unlikely. Most of the top rules by lift are about BOOKs, with one product being ARTWORK.

The rules with the highest chi-square values look more sensible. The top rule here has a support of over 1.34%, and the average support is 0.71%. The support is much better, and the confidence is also larger. The range of products is broader, including FREEBIE, BOOK, ARTWORK, and OCCASION.

> **TIP** The chi-square measure is better than support, confidence, or lift for choosing a good set of association rules.

The chi-square values and lift values are not totally independent. Figure 10-5 shows a bubble plot comparing decile values of chi-square with decile values of lift. The large bubbles along the axis show that lift and chi-square are correlated; overall, they put the rules in a similar order. However, the many smaller bubbles indicate that chi-square and lift disagree on how good many rules are.

Calculating the deciles for the lift and chi-square uses window functions:

```
SELECT chisquaredecile, liftdecile, COUNT(*), AVG(chisquare), AVG(lift)
FROM (SELECT NTILE(10) OVER (ORDER BY chisquare) as chisquaredecile,
```

```
                NTILE(10) OVER (ORDER BY lift) as liftdecile, a.*
        FROM (on page 492) a
        WHERE numlhsrhs >= 5 AND numlhsnorhs >= 5 AND numnolhsrhs >= 5) a
    GROUP BY chisquaredecile, liftdecile
```

Notice that this query requires a subquery because window functions cannot be used for aggregation. The results are plotted as a bubble chart in Excel.

Chi-Square for Negative Rules

The chi-square value measures how unexpected the rule is. However, a rule can be unexpected in two ways. It could be unexpected because the right-hand side occurs much more often when the left-hand side appears. Or, it could be unexpected because the right-hand side occurs much less often.

In the previous example, all the rules with the highest chi-square values have a lift greater than one (as seen in Table 10-8). In this case, the lift is saying that the right-hand size occurs more frequently than expected. For these rules, the chi-square value is indeed saying that the rule is a good rule.

What happens when the lift is less than one? Table 10-8 has no examples of this. However, this situation can occur. For instance, in a grocery store, a rule for "tofu ➤ meat" could have a high chi-square value but a negative lift—if we assume that many tofu eaters are vegetarians who never buy meat.

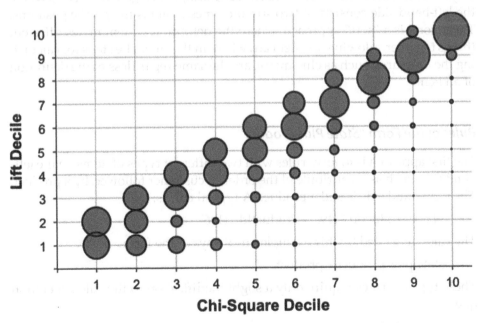

Figure 10-5: This bubble plot compares the values of lift and chi-square, by decile.

Lift less than one means that the negative rule is the stronger rule:

LHS ≻ NOT RHS

For our example, it would mean that the real rule is "tofu ≻ NOT meat." The chi-square value for this rule is the same as the chi-square value for the positive rule. On the other hand, the lift changes, so the lift for this rule is greater than one when the lift for the positive rule is less than one (and vice versa). In fact, the lift for a rule and its negative are multiplicative inverses—the product of the two values is one.

The chi-square value and lift can be used together. When the chi-square is high and the lift greater than one, then the resulting rule is the positive rule. When the chi-square value is high and the lift less than one, then the resulting rule is the negative rule. Using these values together makes it possible to look for both types of rules at the same time.

Heterogeneous Associations

The rules described so far have been about products or product groups, with the same items on both the left-hand and right-hand sides. This is traditional association rule analysis. Because we are building the rules ourselves, it is possible and feasible to extend the rules to include additional types of items.

The idea is to add other features into the rules. This section discusses two ways of doing this. The first is a "hard" approach, which generates rules where the left-hand side consists of two specific types of items in specific positions. The second is a "soft" approach, where the definition of item mixes different things together, allowing any item anywhere in the rule. The steps for calculating the measures, such as chi-square, are the same regardless of the definition of an item.

Rules of the Form "State Plus Product"

The first approach is to form rules with two different types of items on the left-hand side, such as an attribute of the order or customer followed by a product. The right-hand side is still a product. A typical rule is:

NY + ProductId 11197 ≻ ProductId 11196

The rules generated by this example are always of the form:

state plus product ≻ product

These types of rules require only a slight modification to the rule generation query.

The first item is the `State` column from `Orders`, rather than `ProductId` from `OrderLines`. The overall query is a bit more complicated because the left-hand side and right-hand side need separate CTEs:

```
WITH items as (
     SELECT ol.OrderId as basket, ol.ProductId as item,
            COUNT(*) OVER (PARTITION BY ol.ProductId) as cnt,
            (SELECT COUNT(*) FROM Orders) as numbaskets
     FROM OrderLines ol
     GROUP BY ol.OrderId, ol.ProductId
     ),
     lhs as (
     SELECT lhs.basket, o.State as lhs1, lhs.item as lhs2,
            COUNT(*) OVER (PARTITION BY o.State, lhs.item) as cnt
     FROM Orders o JOIN
          items lhs
          ON lhs.basket = o.OrderId
     ),
     rules as (
     SELECT lhs1, lhs2, rhs, COUNT(*) as numlhsrhs,
            numlhs, numrhs, numbaskets,
            numlhs - COUNT(*) as numlhsnorhs,
            numrhs - COUNT(*) as numnolhsrhs,
            numbaskets - numlhs - numrhs + COUNT(*) as numnolhsnorhs,
            numlhs * numrhs * 1.0 / numbaskets as explhsrhs,
            numlhs*(1.0*numbaskets - numrhs)*1.0 / numbaskets as explhsnorhs,
            (1.0*numbaskets - numlhs)*numrhs*1.0 / numbaskets as expnolhsrhs,
            ((1.0*numbaskets - numlhs)*(1.0*numbaskets - numrhs) / numbaskets
            ) as expnolhsnorhs,
            COUNT(*) * 1.0 / numbaskets as support,
            COUNT(*) * 1.0 / numlhs as confidence,
            COUNT(*) * numbaskets * 1.0 / (numlhs*numrhs) as lift
     FROM (SELECT lhs.basket, lhs.lhs1, lhs.lhs2, rhs.item as rhs,
                  lhs.cnt as numlhs, rhs.cnt as numrhs, rhs.numbaskets
           FROM lhs JOIN
                items rhs
                ON rhs.basket = lhs.basket AND
                   rhs.item NOT IN (lhs.lhs2)
          ) rules
     GROUP BY lhs1, lhs2, rhs, numlhs, numrhs, numbaskets
     )
SELECT (SQUARE(explhsrhs - numlhsrhs) / explhsrhs +
        SQUARE(explhsnorhs - numlhsnorhs) / explhsnorhs +
        SQUARE(expnolhsrhs - numnolhsrhs) / expnolhsrhs +
        SQUARE(expnolhsnorhs - numnolhsnorhs) / expnolhsnorhs
       ) as chisquare, rules.*
FROM rules
WHERE explhsrhs > 5 AND explhsnorhs > 5 AND expnolhsrhs > 5 AND
      expnolhsnorhs > 5
ORDER BY chisquare DESC
```

Table 10-9: Top Ten Rules with State and Product on Left-Hand Side

| | RULE COUNTS | | | | |
RULE	LHS	RHS	LHSRHS	CHI-SQUARE	LIFT
NY + 11196 ➤ 11048	2,193	3,166	848	18,847.5	23.6
NY + 11048 ➤ 11196	1,487	4,729	848	18,673.1	23.3
NY + 11052 ➤ 11197	644	1,900	280	11,968.8	44.2
NY + 11197 ➤ 11052	873	1,410	280	11,877.9	43.9
NJ + 11196 ➤ 11048	1,071	3,166	431	9,945.4	24.5
NJ + 11048 ➤ 11196	746	4,729	431	9,589.1	23.6
NY + 12820 ➤ 13190	4,442	3,404	769	6,343.2	9.8
NY + 13190 ➤ 12820	989	18,441	769	5,349.9	8.1
CT + 11196 ➤ 11048	468	3,166	208	5,326.7	27.1
CT + 11048 ➤ 11196	332	4,729	208	5,042.0	25.6

The structure of this query is quite similar to the structure for the two-way association rules, with the addition of the chi-square measure. Do note that removing duplicates is not necessary, because states are quite distinct from product IDs.

The resulting table has the same format as the earlier rule tables, so the same chi-square query can be used for choosing rules. Table 10-9 shows the top ten rules.

Rules Mixing Different Types of Products

Another method for adding different types of items is to expand the notion of item. By adding the state into the products, any of the following rules is possible:

- product plus product ➤ product
- product plus product ➤ state
- product plus state ➤ product
- state plus product ➤ product

In addition, the following rules are conceivable, but not possible, because there is only one state associated with each order:

- state plus state ➤ state
- state plus state ➤ product
- state plus product ➤ state
- product plus state ➤ state

These rules would be possible if an order could have more than one state.

Creating such rules is a simple matter of modifying the `items` CTE to include the state item, by using the UNION ALL operator.

```
WITH items as (
      SELECT OrderId as basket,
             CAST(ProductId as VARCHAR(255)) as item,
             COUNT(*) OVER (PARTITION BY ProductId) as cnt,
             (SELECT COUNT(*) FROM Orders) as numbaskets
      FROM OrderLines ol
      GROUP BY OrderId, ProductId
      UNION ALL
      SELECT OrderId, State,
             COUNT(*) OVER (PARTITION BY State) as cnt,
             (SELECT COUNT(*) FROM Orders) as numbaskets
      FROM Orders
      ),
      . . .
```

The only tricky part is handling the data types because `ProductId` is an integer and the state a string, so it needs to be cast to a character. The best rules have one state, so they are the same as the ones in Table 10-9.

Extending Association Rules

Association rule methods can be extended in several different ways. The most obvious extension is adding additional items on the left-hand side. Another extension is to have entirely different sets of items on the left-hand side and the right-hand side. And, perhaps the most interesting extension is the creation of sequential association rules, which look for patterns of items purchased in a particular order.

Multi-Way Associations

Association rules can have more than two items on the left-hand side. The mechanism is to continue adding in joins for every possible item, similar to the method for going from one item on the left-hand side to two items. As the number of items grows, the size of the intermediate results storing the candidate rules can get unmanageably large and take a long, long time to generate. The way to handle this is by adding restrictions so fewer candidate rules are considered.

TIP As the number of items in association rules gets larger, query performance can get worse. A filter subquery to limit the orders you are working on usually improves performance.

One obvious filter is to include only orders having at least as many items as used by the rule. Several examples in this chapter have used this restriction. A second restriction is to require a minimum support for the rule. This restriction also applies to products: Products that have less than the minimum support can be filtered out. A rule having a given level of support implies that each product in the rule has at least that level of support as well.

The third restriction is to remove the largest orders. Because large orders have many products, they result in very large numbers of combinations. These orders typically add very little information because there are few of them. However, they can contribute the vast bulk of processing time.

The following query combines these together for three-way combinations, with a minimum support of 20 and using orders with no more than ten products:

```
WITH filterorders as (
      SELECT OrderId
      FROM OrderLines
      GROUP BY OrderId
      HAVING COUNT(DISTINCT ProductId) BETWEEN 4 AND 10
      ),
      filterproducts as (
      SELECT ProductId
      FROM OrderLines
      GROUP BY ProductId
      HAVING COUNT(DISTINCT Orderid) >= 20
      ),
      items1 as (
      SELECT ol.OrderId as basket, ol.ProductId as item,
             COUNT(*) OVER (PARTITION BY ol.ProductId) as cnt,
             ROW_NUMBER() OVER (PARTITION BY ol.OrderId
                           ORDER BY ol.ProductId) as seqnum
      FROM filterorders fo JOIN
           OrderLines ol
           ON ol.OrderId = fo.OrderId JOIN
           filterproducts fp
           ON ol.ProductId = fp.ProductId
      GROUP BY ol.OrderId, ol.ProductId
      ),
      items as (
      SELECT i.*, SUM(CASE WHEN seqnum = 1 THEN 1 ELSE 0
                    END) OVER () as numbaskets
      FROM items1 i
      ),
      lhs as (
      SELECT lhs1.basket, lhs1.item as lhs1, lhs2.item as lhs2,
             lhs3.item as lhs3,
             COUNT(*) OVER (PARTITION BY lhs1.item, lhs2.item,
                                    lhs3.item) as cnt
      FROM items lhs1 JOIN
           items lhs2
```

```
        ON lhs2.basket = lhs1.basket AND
            lhs2.item > lhs1.item JOIN
      items lhs3
        ON lhs3.basket = lhs1.basket AND
            lhs3.item > lhs2.item
    ),
  . . .
```

The first two CTEs, `filterorders` and `filterproducts`, introduce the filters for orders and products. In this case, the filters are based on counts. These are then used in the `items` CTE. The `lhs` CTE has an additional join for the additional product. In addition, the subsequent code needs to change to handle the extra column.

Multi-Way Associations in One Query

The queries so far have done n-way associations in a single query for a given value of *n*. That is, the chapter has not presented a single query for both one- and two-way associations. This is intentional.

Association rules are part of exploratory data analysis. That is, humans generally need to evaluate whether the top performing rules make sense and are useful. As part of exploratory data analysis, it makes sense to start with one-way rules, then two-way rules, and so on. And, because no more than a handful of products typically make sense in such rules, only a handful of queries are needed.

It is simple enough to modify the logic for two-way queries to include one-way queries. In fact, the modifications are similar to generating item sets with up to a given number of items:

```
WITH items as (
      SELECT OrderId as basket, ProductId as item,
             COUNT(*) OVER (PARTITION BY ProductId) as cnt,
             (SELECT COUNT(*) FROM Orders) as numbaskets
      FROM OrderLines ol
      GROUP BY OrderId, ProductId
      UNION ALL
      SELECT o.OrderId, NULL as ProductId,
             COUNT(*) OVER () as cnt, COUNT(*) OVER () as numbaskets
      FROM Orders o
    ),
```

It would seem that the rest of the query remains basically the same. However, because all rules are being considered—including zero-way associations—some of the expected values for chi-square are zero. This poses a problem with divide-by-zero.

The arithmetic problems can be fixed. Two other important considerations arise. The first is filtering. This is used to make the query for n-way associations more efficient. However, it would have to work differently for a query that returned up-to-n-way rules. Second, the query itself becomes less efficient because the UNION ALL prevents certain optimizations.

So, if you want to generate all the rules up to a given value of n, the best way is to use UNION ALL to combine the results for one-way association rules, two-way association rules, and so on.

Rules Using Attributes of Products

So far, all the rules have been based on products or one attribute of products, the product group. Products could have different attributes assigned to them, such as:

- Whether the product is discounted in the order
- The manufacturer of the product
- The "subject" of the product, such as whether art is photography or painting, whether books are fiction or non-fiction
- The target market for the product (kids, adults, left-handers)

The idea is that attributes of the products are used for the rules instead of the products themselves. Adjusting the SQL to handle this is not difficult. It simply requires joining in the table containing the attributes when generating the item sets, similar to the way states were added in the examples in the previous section.

A problem is lurking with a naïve application of using attributes for rules. Each product would typically have the same set of attributes, wherever it appears. So, combinations are going to co-occur with each order, simply because they describe the same product. In other words, a rule specifying that certain attributes tend to occur together may only be telling us about a single product that has those attributes. This is not what we want, because we don't want rules on attributes to tell us what we already know.

Earlier, the section on item sets discussed a particular method for finding products that households purchase in different orders. The same idea can be used for categories. The approach is to find combinations that are in the same order, but not in the same product, in order to find the strength of affinities among the attributes.

Rules with Different Left- and Right-Hand Sides

Another variation on association rules is to have different types of items on the left- and right-hand sides of the rule. A small example of this was the use of state on the left-hand side, but not on the right-hand side. The implementation in SQL is a simple modification to the association rule query to generate the right item set for items on the left-hand side and the right-hand side.

Why would this be a good idea? One application is when customers are doing a variety of different things. For instance, customers may be visiting web pages and then clicking advertisements; or they may be visiting web pages and then making a purchase, or they may be receiving multiple marketing messages through different channels and then responding. In these cases, the left-hand side of the rule could be the advertising pages exposed, the web pages visited, or the campaigns sent out. The right-hand side could be the nature of the clicks or purchases or responses. The rules describe what combinations of actions are associated with the desired action.

This idea has other applications as well. When customizing banner ads or catalogs for particular types of products, the question might arise: *What items have customers purchased that suggest they are interested in these products?* Using association rules with purchases or visits on the left-hand side and banner clicks on the right-hand side is one possible way of approaching this question.

Such heterogeneous rules do bring up one technical issue. The question is whether to include customers who have no events on the right-hand side. Consider the situation where the left-hand side has pages on a website and the right-hand side has products purchased by customers. The purpose of the rules is to find which web pages lead to the purchase of particular products. Should the data used to generate these rules include customers who have never made a purchase?

This is an interesting question with no right answer, because the answer depends on the particular business needs. Using only customers who make purchases reduces the size of the data (since, presumably, many people do not make purchases). Perhaps the first step in approaching the problem is to ask which web pages lead to any purchase at all. The second step is to then find the product affinity based on the web pages.

Before and After: Sequential Associations

Sequential associations are quite similar to simple product associations. The difference is that the rule enforces the ordering of the products in purchases. So, a typical rule is:

Product 12175 ➢ Product 13297 will be purchased at a later time.

Such sequences can prove interesting, particularly when many customers have purchase histories. Sequential rules cannot be found within a single order, because all the products within an order are purchased at the same time. Instead, sequential rules need to consider all orders of products within a household.

The basic logic for generating sequential rules is quite similar to the logic for association rules. However, the calculation has some nuances. First, the household ID needs to be brought in along with the order date. This seems like a small change, but now households can qualify for the rule multiple times—there is no obvious way to restrict the data to one product per household because we need each order date.

This issue affects the calculations in the `rules` CTE. The number of "baskets" satisfying the rule has for the most part been calculating using `COUNT(*)`. This needs to change to `COUNT(DISTINCT basket)`. The following code shows the structure of the sequential rules query:

```
WITH items1 as (
      SELECT c.HouseholdId as basket, ol.ProductId as item,
              p.GroupName, o.OrderDate as basketdate
      FROM OrderLines ol JOIN
           Orders o
           ON o.OrderId = ol.OrderId JOIN
           Customers c
           ON c.CustomerId = o.CustomerId JOIN
           Products p
           ON ol.ProductId = p.ProductId
      GROUP BY c.HouseholdId, ol.ProductId, o.OrderDate, p.GroupName
),
     items as (
      SELECT i.*,
             SUM(CASE WHEN bi_seqnum = 1 THEN 1 ELSE 0
                 END) OVER () as cnt,
             SUM(CASE WHEN b_seqnum = 1 THEN 1 ELSE 0
                 END) OVER () as numbaskets
      FROM (SELECT i.*,
                   ROW_NUMBER() OVER (PARTITION BY item
                                      ORDER BY basket) as bi_seqnum,
                   ROW_NUMBER() OVER (PARTITION BY basket
                                      ORDER BY basket) as b_seqnum
            FROM items1 i
           ) i
),
     rules as (
      SELECT lhs, rhs, lhsGroup, rhsGroup,
             COUNT(DISTINCT basket) as numlhsrhs,
             numlhs, numrhs, numbaskets,
             numlhs - COUNT(DISTINCT basket) as numlhsnorhs,
             numrhs - COUNT(DISTINCT basket) as numnolhsrhs,
             (numbaskets - numlhs - numrhs +
              COUNT(DISTINCT basket) ) as numnolhsnorhs,
             numlhs * numrhs * 1.0 / numbaskets as explhsrhs,
             (numlhs * (1.0 * numbaskets - numrhs) * 1.0 /
              numbaskets) as explhsnorhs,
             (1.0 * numbaskets - numlhs) * numrhs * 1.0 /
              numbaskets) as expnolhsrhs,
             ((1.0 * numbaskets - numlhs)*
              (1.0 * numbaskets-numrhs) / numbaskets) as expnolhsnorhs,
             COUNT(DISTINCT basket) * 1.0 / numbaskets as support,
             COUNT(DISTINCT basket) * 1.0 / numlhs as confidence,
             (COUNT(DISTINCT basket) * numbaskets * 1.0 /
```

```
                    (numlhs * numrhs)) as lift
          FROM (SELECT lhs.basket, lhs.item as lhs, rhs.item as rhs,
                       lhs.cnt as numlhs, rhs.cnt as numrhs,
                       lhs.numbaskets,
                       lhs.GroupName as lhsGroup, rhs.GroupName as rhsGroup
                FROM items lhs JOIN
                     items rhs
                     ON lhs.basket = rhs.basket AND
                        lhs.basketdate < rhs.basketdate AND
                        lhs.item <> rhs.item
               ) rules
          GROUP BY lhs, rhs, numlhs, numrhs, numbaskets, lhsGroup, rhsGroup
         )
SELECT (SQUARE(explhsrhs - numlhsrhs) / explhsrhs +
        SQUARE(explhsnorhs - numlhsnorhs) / explhsnorhs +
        SQUARE(expnolhsrhs - numnolhsrhs) / expnolhsrhs +
        SQUARE(expnolhsnorhs - numnolhsnorhs) / expnolhsnorhs
       ) as chisquare, rules.*
FROM rules
WHERE explhsrhs > 5 AND explhsnorhs > 5 AND expnolhsrhs > 5 AND
      expnolhsnorhs > 5
ORDER BY chisquare DESC
```

This query also takes a different approach to calculating the number of products and the number of households—these calculations get confused because products can now appear multiple times in a household. Although the query could use COUNT(DISTINCT) in items, it opts for a slightly different approach. It uses ROW_NUMBER() to enumerate the rows, based on either basket or item. It then counts the number of times that the value is one—this counts the number of distinct values. Using a separate CTE is also more robust. When modifying a query based on orders to households, it is easy to miss that the subquery using Orders also has to change.

Apart from the subtlety about counting things, this structure of this query is very similar to the earlier queries.

Comparing all the products and orders in a household is a brute-force approach. There is an alternative. The calculation can use the minimum and maximum order date for each product within a household. These dates can then be used in rules to enforce the sequencing, without having to change the COUNT(*). However, this approach cannot be generalized for rules, such as products in the left-hand side occurring within three weeks before the products in the right-hand side.

Table 10-10 shows the resulting sequential association rules. These are interesting because they are intuitive. Three of the ten top rules (by the chi-square measure) are for calendars—which is quite reasonable. Customers who purchase calendars at one point in time are likely to purchase calendars later in time, probably about a year later.

Table 10-10: Top Ten Sequential Association Rules

RULE	PRODUCT GROUPS	SUPPORT	LIFT	CHI-SQUARE
11196 ➤ 11197	BOOK ➤ BOOK	0.2918%	4.5	1,296.2
12015 ➤ 12176	CALENDAR ➤ CALENDAR	0.2099%	3.2	528.5
11196 ➤ 11111	BOOK ➤ BOOK	0.2099%	3.2	528.5
12176 ➤ 13298	CALENDAR ➤ CALENDAR	0.1933%	3.0	413.9
10863 ➤ 12015	CALENDAR ➤ CALENDAR	0.1754%	2.7	306.2
11197 ➤ 11111	BOOK ➤ BOOK	0.1690%	2.6	271.7
11048 ➤ 11052	ARTWORK ➤ ARTWORK	0.1658%	2.5	255.2
11048 ➤ 11197	ARTWORK ➤ BOOK	0.1542%	2.4	200.0
11196 ➤ 11052	BOOK ➤ ARTWORK	0.1498%	2.3	180.4
12139 ➤ 12820	OCCASION ➤ FREEBIE	0.1466%	2.2	167.0

Lessons Learned

This chapter introduces association rules—automatically generated rules about the items most likely to appear together in an order. This is one of the most detailed ways of analyzing transaction information.

Simple one-way association rules specify that when a customer purchases one product (the left-hand side), then the customer is likely to purchase another product (the right-hand side) in the same order. The traditional way of measuring the goodness of these rules is with three measures: support, confidence, and lift. Support measures the proportion of orders where the rule is true. Confidence measures how often the rule is true when it applies. And lift specifies how much better the rule works rather than just guessing.

A better measure, however, is based on the chi-square value introduced in Chapter 3. This gives an indication of how likely it is that the rule is random—and when this likelihood is very small, then the rule is important.

Association rules are very powerful and extensible. Using SQL, the simple one-way associations can be extended to two-way rules and beyond. Non-product items, such as the state where the customer resides and other customer attributes, can be incorporated into the rules. With a relatively simple modification, the same mechanism can generate sequential rules, where products occur in a specific order.

With association rules we have dived into the finest details of customer purchase behavior. The next chapter moves back to the customer level, by using SQL to build basic data mining models on customers.

Data Mining Models in SQL

Data mining is the process of finding meaningful patterns in large quantities of data. Traditionally, the subject is introduced through statistics and statistical modeling. This chapter takes an alternative approach that introduces data mining concepts using databases. This perspective presents the important concepts, sidestepping the rigor of theoretical statistics to focus instead on the most important practical aspect: data.

The next two chapters extend the discussion that this chapter begins. Chapter 12 covers linear regression, a more traditional starting point for modeling and data mining. Chapter 13 focuses on data preparation, often the most challenging part of a data mining endeavor.

Earlier chapters have already shown some powerful techniques implemented using SQL. Snobs may feel that data mining is more advanced than mere SQL queries. This sentiment downplays the importance of data manipulation, which lies at the heart of even the most advanced techniques. Some powerful techniques adapt well to databases, and learning how they work—both in terms of their application to business problems and their implementation on real data—provides a good foundation for understanding modeling. Some techniques do not adapt as well to databases, so they require more specialized software. The fundamental ideas about how to use models and how to evaluate the results remain the same, regardless of the sophistication of the modeling technique.

Earlier chapters contain examples of models, without describing them as such. The RFM methodology introduced in Chapter 8 assigns an RFM bin to each customer; the estimated response rate of the RFM bin is a model score for estimating response. The expected remaining lifetime from a survival model is a model score. Even the expected value from the chi-square test is an example of a model score, produced by a basic statistics formula. What these have in common is that they all exploit patterns in data and apply the findings back to the original data or to new data, producing a meaningful result.

The first type of model in this chapter is the look-alike model, which takes an example—typically of something particularly good or bad—and finds other rows similar to the example. Look-alike models use a definition of similarity. Nearest-neighbor techniques are an extension of look-alike models that estimate a value by combining information from similar records where the value is already known.

The next type of model is the lookup model, which summarizes data along various dimensions to create a lookup table. These models are quite powerful and fit naturally in any discussion of data mining and databases. However, they are limited to at most a handful of dimensions. Lookup models lead to naïve Bayesian models, a powerful technique that combines information along any number of dimensions, using some interesting ideas from the area of probability.

Before talking about these techniques, the chapter introduces important data mining concepts and the processes of building and using models. There is an interesting analogy between these processes and SQL. Building models is analogous to aggregation because both are about bringing data together to identify patterns. Scoring models is like joining tables—applying the patterns to new rows of data.

Introduction to Directed Data Mining

Directed data mining is the most common type of data mining. "Directed" means that the historical data used for modeling contains examples of the target values, so the data mining techniques have examples to learn from. Directed data mining also makes the assumption that the patterns in historical data are applicable in the future.

Another type of data mining is undirected data mining, which uses sophisticated techniques to find patterns in the data without the guidance of a target. Without a target, the algorithm cannot determine if the results are good or bad; as a consequence, undirected data mining requires additional human judgment to assess the results. Association rules are one example of undirected data mining. Other undirected techniques are typically more specialized, so this chapter and the next two focus on directed techniques.

TIP The purpose of a directed model may be to apply model scores to new data or to gain better understanding of customers and what's happening in the business.

Directed Models

A directed model finds patterns in historical data by using examples where the answer is already known—how to take advantage of patterns in the input variables to approximate the target value. The process of finding the patterns is called *training* or *building* the model. The most common way to use the model is by *scoring* data to append a model score.

Sometimes, understanding gleaned from a model is more important than the model scores it generates. The models discussed in this book lend themselves to understanding, so they can contribute to exploratory data analysis as well as directed modeling. Other types of models, such as neural networks and support vector machines, are so complicated that they cannot readily explain how they arrive at their results. Such "black-box" models might do a good job of estimating values, but people cannot easily peek in and understand how they work or use them to learn about the data.

> **TIP** If understanding how a model works is important (which variables it is choosing, which variables are more important, and so on), then choose techniques that produce understandable models. The techniques discussed in this book fall in this category.

The models themselves take the form of formulas and auxiliary tables that are combined to generate scores for any given record. The process of training the model generates the information needed for scoring. This section explains important facets of modeling, in the areas of data and evaluation.

As a note, the word "model" has another sense in databases. As discussed in Chapter 1, a *data model* describes the contents of a database, the way that the data is structured. A *data mining* model, on the other hand, is the result of a process that analyzes data and produces useful information about the business. Both types of model are about patterns, one about the structure of the database and the other about patterns in the content of the data, but otherwise they are two very different things.

The Data in Modeling

Data is central to the data mining process. It is used to build models; it is used to assess models; and it is used for scoring models. This section discusses the different uses of data in modeling.

Model Set

The *model set*, which is sometimes also called the *training set*, consists of historical data with known outcomes. It generally has the form of a table, with rows for

These columns are input columns.

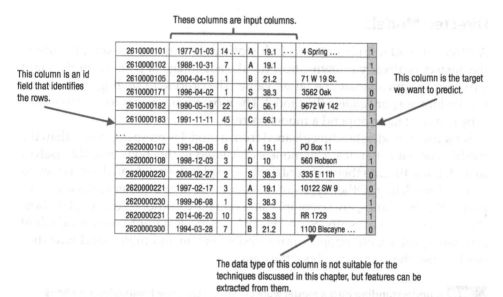

This column is an id field that identifies the rows.

2610000101	1977-01-03	14 . . .	A	19.1	. . .	4 Spring ...	1
2610000102	1988-10-31	7	A	19.1			1
2610000105	2004-04-15	1	B	21.2		71 W 19 St.	0
2610000171	1996-04-02	1	S	38.3		3562 Oak	0
2610000182	1990-05-19	22	C	56.1		9672 W 142	0
2610000183	1991-11-11	45	C	56.1			1
. . .							
2620000107	1991-08-08	6	A	19.1		PO Box 11	0
2620000108	1998-12-03	3	D	10		560 Robson	1
2620000220	2008-02-27	2	S	38.3		335 E 11th	0
2620000221	1997-02-17	3	A	19.1		10122 SW 9	0
2620000230	1999-06-08	1	S	38.3			1
2620000231	2014-06-20	10	S	38.3		RR 1729	1
2620000300	1994-03-28	7	B	21.2		1100 Biscayne ...	0

This column is the target we want to predict.

The data type of this column is not suitable for the techniques discussed in this chapter, but features can be extracted from them.

Figure 11-1: A model set consists of records with data where the outcome is already known. The process of training a model assigns a score or educated guess, estimating the target.

each example. Typically, each row is the granularity of what is being modeled, such as a customer.

The *target* is what we want to estimate; this is typically a value in one of the columns and is known for all the rows in the model set. Most of the remaining columns consist of input columns. Figure 11-1 illustrates data in a possible model set.

The goal of modeling is to intelligently and automatically assign values to the target column using the values in the input columns. The specific techniques used for this depend on the nature of the data in the input and target columns, and the data mining technique.

From the perspective of modeling, each column contains values that are one of a handful of types.

Binary columns (also called *flags*) contain one of two values. These typically describe specific aspects about a customer or a product. For instance, the subscription data consists of customers who are active (on the cutoff date) or stopped. This would lend itself naturally to a binary column.

Category columns contain one of multiple, known values. The subscription data, for instance, has several examples, including market, channel, and rate plan.

Numeric columns contain numbers, such as dollar amounts or tenures. Traditional statistical techniques work best on such columns.

Date-time columns contain dates and time stamps. These are often the most challenging type of data to work with. They are often converted to tenures and durations for data mining purposes.

Text columns (and other complex data types) contain important information. Some techniques are designed specifically for this type of data. However, these are not used directly in the process of modeling as described in this book. Instead, features of one of the other types are extracted, such as extracting the zip code from an address column.

Most of the techniques discussed in this chapter can handle missing values (represented as NULL). However, not all statistical and data mining techniques are able to handle missing values.

Score Set

Once a model has been built, the model can be applied to a *score set*, which has the same input columns as the model set, but does not necessarily have the target column. When the model is applied to the score set, the model processes the inputs to calculate the value of the target column, using formulas and auxiliary tables.

If the score set also has known target values, it can be used to determine how well the model is performing. The model set itself can be used as a score set. Note that models almost always perform better on the data used to build them than on unseen data, so performance on the model set is not indicative of performance on other data.

> **WARNING** A model almost always works best on the model set. Do not expect the performance on this data to match performance on other data.

Prediction Model Sets versus Profiling Model Sets

One very important distinction in data mining is the difference between profiling and prediction. This is a subtle concept because the process of building models and the applicable data mining techniques are the same for the two. The difference is solely in the data.

Each column describing a customer has a time frame associated with it, the "as-of" date when that datum becomes known. For some columns, such as market and channel in the subscription data, the "as-of" date is when the customer starts because these are the original channel and market. Other columns, such as the stop date and stop type, have an as-of date of when the customer stops. A column such as total amount spent is accurate as of some cutoff date when the value was calculated. Unfortunately, the as-of date is not normally stored in the database, although it can often be imputed from knowledge about how data is loaded.

In a profiling model set, the input and target columns come from the same time period. That is, the as-of date of the target is similar to some of the inputs. For a prediction model set, the as-of date of the target is strictly later than all the input columns. The input columns are "before" and the target is "after."

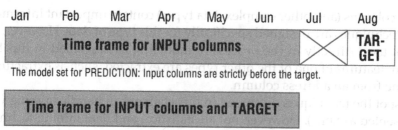

Figure 11-2: In a model set used for prediction, the target column represents data from a time frame strictly after the input columns. For a model set used for profiling, the target comes from the same time frame.

The upper part of Figure 11-2 shows a model set for prediction because the inputs come from an earlier time period than the target. The target might consist of customers who stopped during July or who purchased a particular product in July. The lower part of the chart shows a model set for profiling because the inputs and target all come from the same time period. The customers stopped during the same time period that the data comes from.

Building a model set for profiling, rather than for prediction, is usually easier because profiling does not care about the as-of date of the input columns. On the other hand, prediction model sets usually lead to better models. Because of the "before" and "after" structure of the data, they are less likely to find spurious correlations. An easy way to make prediction models is to limit the input columns to what is known when customers start. The downside is that such inputs are not as descriptive as customer behavior variables that use information during the customer relationship.

To illustrate the distinction between profiling and prediction, consider a bank that wants to estimate the probability of customers responding to an offer to open investment accounts. The bank has customer summaries stored in a table with various input columns describing the banking relationship—the balances in accounts of different types, dates when the accounts were opened, and so on. The bank also has a target column specifying which customers have an investment account.

The data contains at least one very strong pattern regarding investment accounts. Customers with investment accounts almost always have low savings account balances. On reflection, this is not so surprising. Customers with both investment accounts and savings accounts prefer to put their money in the higher yielding investment accounts. However, the reverse is not true. Targeting customers with low savings account balances to open investment accounts is a bad idea. Most such customers have few financial resources.

The problem is that the values in the input columns came from the same time period as the target, so the model is a profiling model. It would be better to take a snapshot of the customers *before* they opened an investment account, and to use this snapshot for the input columns—of course, the model set would need to contain customers that did not open accounts after the snapshot as well. The better approach uses a prediction model set, rather than a profiling model set.

Examples of Modeling Tasks

This section discusses several types of tasks that models might be used for.

Similarity Models

Sometimes, the purpose of mining data is to find more instances similar to a given target instance. In this case, an entire row is the target, and the score represents the similarity between any given row and the target instance.

The target may be a made up ideal, or it might be an actual example. For instance, the highest penetration zip code for the purchase data is 10007, a wealthy zip code in Manhattan. A similarity model might use census demographics to find similar zip codes from the perspective of the census data. The assumption is that if a wealthy zip code is working well, then other similar zip codes should also work well. Marketing efforts can be focused on similar areas. What constitutes a "good" area might include financial data, education data, home values, and other features gathered by the Census Bureau.

Yes-or-No Models (Binary Response Classification)

Perhaps the most common problem addressed by modeling is assigning "yes" or "no." This type of model addresses questions such as:

- Who is likely to respond to a particular marketing promotion?
- Who is likely to leave in the next three months?
- Who is likely to purchase a particular product?
- Who is likely to go bankrupt in the next year?
- Which transactions are likely to be fraud?
- Which visitors are likely to subscribe in the next day?

Each of these scenarios involves placing customers into one of two categories. Such a model can be used for:

- Saving money by contacting customers likely to respond to an offer
- Saving customers by offering an incentive to those likely to stop
- Optimizing campaigns by sending marketing messages to those likely to purchase a particular product
- Reducing risk by lowering the credit limit for those likely to go bankrupt

- Reducing losses by investigating transactions likely to be fraud

Yes-or-no models are also called *binary response models*.

Yes-or-No Models with Propensity Scores

A very useful variation on yes-or-no models assigns a propensity to each customer, rather than a specific classification. Everyone gets a "yes" score that varies from zero (definitely "no") to one (definitely "yes"). One reason why a propensity score is more useful is that any particular number of customers can be chosen for a campaign by adjusting the threshold value. Values on one side of the threshold are "no" and values on the other side are "yes." The model can choose the top 1%, or the top 40%, simply by varying the threshold.

Often, the propensity score is a probability estimate, which is even more useful. A probability can be combined with financial information to calculate an expected dollar amount. With such information, a campaign can be optimized to achieve particular financial and business results.

TIP When a model produces a probability estimate, the estimate can be multiplied by a monetary value to get an expected value for each customer/prospect being scored.

Consider a company that is sending customers an offer in the mail for a new product. From previous experience, the company knows that customers who order a new product generate an additional $200 during the first year, on average. Each item of direct mail costs $1 to print, mail out, and process. How can the company use modeling to optimize its business?

Let's assume that the company wants to invest in expanding its customer relationships, but not lose money during the first year. The campaign then needs to address the following constraints:

- Every customer contacted costs $1.
- Every customer who responds is worth $200 during the first year.
- The company wants to break even during the first year.

One responsive customer generates an excess value of $199 in the first year, which is enough money to contact an additional 199 customers. So, if one out of 200 customers (0.5%) respond, the campaign breaks even. To do this, the company looks at previous, similar campaigns and builds a model estimating the probability of response. The goal is to contact the customers whose expected response exceeds the break-even point of 0.5%.

Multiple Categories

Sometimes, two categories ("yes" and "no") are not enough. For instance, consider the next offer to make to each customer. Should this offer be in BOOKs or APPAREL or CALENDARs or something else?

For a handful of categories, building a separate propensity model for each category is a good way to handle this. But then the question arises of how to combine the different propensity scores. One method is to assign to each customer the product with the highest propensity score. Another approach is to multiply the propensity probabilities by the value of the product, and choose the product that has the highest expected value.

When the target category has many values, association rules (covered in Chapter 10) are probably a better place to start. Some of the most interesting information may be the products that have been purchased together.

Estimating Numeric Values

The final category is the traditional statistical problem of estimating numeric values. This might be a number at an aggregated level, such as the penetration within a particular area. Another example is the expected value of a customer over the next year. And yet another is tenure related, such as the number of days we expect a customer to be active over the next year.

There are many different methods to estimate real values, including regression and survival analysis.

Model Evaluation

Model evaluation is the process of measuring how well a model works. The best way is to compare the results of the model to actual results. How this comparison is made depends on the type of the target. This chapter covers several different methods of evaluating models.

When evaluating models, the choice of data used for the evaluation is very important. Models almost always perform better on the model set, the data used to build the model. Assuming that performance on the model set generalizes to other data is misleading. It is better to use a hold-out sample, called a *test set*, for model evaluation. For models built on prediction model sets, the best test set is an out-of-time sample; that is, data that is a bit more recent than the model set. However, such an out-of-time sample is often not available.

> **WARNING** Evaluating models on the data used to build the model is cheating. Use a hold-out sample for evaluation purposes.

Look-Alike Models

The first modeling technique is look-alike models, which are used to measure similarity to a known good or bad instance.

What Is the Model?

The look-alike model produces a similarity score. The model itself is a formula that describes the similarity, and this formula can be applied to new data. Typically, the purpose of a look-alike model is to choose some groups of customers or zip codes for further analysis or for a marketing effort.

The similarity measure cannot really be validated quantitatively. However, we can qualitatively evaluate the model by seeing if the rankings look reasonable and if the historical ranking of something we care about—such as response—is similar to the rankings provided by the similarity score.

What Is the Best Zip Code?

This example starts with the question: *Which zip codes have the highest penetration of orders and what are some of their demographic characteristics?* For practical purposes, the zip codes are limited to those with 1,000 or more households. The following query answers this question:

```
SELECT TOP 10 o.ZipCode, zc.Stab, zc.ZipName,
       COUNT(DISTINCT c.HouseholdId)/MAX(zc.tothhs*1.0) as penetration,
       MAX(zc.tothhs) as hh, MAX(zc.medianhhinc) as hhmedincome,
       MAX(zc.pctbachelorsormore) as collegep
FROM Orders o JOIN Customers c ON o.CustomerId = c.CustomerId JOIN
     ZipCensus zc ON o.ZipCode = zc.zcta5
WHERE zc.tothhs >= 1000
GROUP BY o.ZipCode, zc.Stab, zc.ZipName
ORDER BY penetration DESC
```

Penetration is defined at the household level, by counting distinct values of HouseholdId within a zip code.

The top ten zip codes by penetration are all well-educated and wealthy (see Table 11-1). *Which zip codes are similar to the zip code with the highest penetration?* This question suggests a look-alike model.

The first decision with a look-alike model is to decide on the dimensions used for the comparison. For the statistically inclined, one interesting method might be to use principal components. However, using the raw data has an advantage because human beings can then understand each dimension.

The approach described in this section uses only two attributes of the zip codes, the median household income and the proportion of the population with a college education. The limit to two variables is for didactic reasons. Two dimensions can be plotted on a scatter plot. In practice, using more attributes is a good idea.

Figure 11-3 shows a scatter plot of the approximately 10,000 largish zip codes that have orders. The scatter plot has three symbols. The diamonds are the zip codes with the highest number of orders, the squares are in the middle, and

Table 11-1: Ten Zip Codes with Highest Penetration

ZIP CODE	STATE	CITY	PENE-TRATION	HOUSE-HOLDS	HOUSEHOLD MEDIAN INCOME	COLLEGE %
10021	NY	New York	8.2%	23,377	$106,236	79.6%
07078	NJ	Short Hills	5.4%	3,942	$234,932	87.2%
10004	NY	New York	5.1%	1,469	$127,281	77.6%
10538	NY	Larchmont	5.0%	5,992	$155,000	78.4%
90067	CA	Los Angeles	5.0%	1,470	$82,714	53.6%
10504	NY	Armonk	5.0%	2,440	$178,409	67.5%
10022	NY	New York	4.8%	17,504	$106,888	79.5%
07043	NJ	Upper Montclair	4.8%	4,300	$159,712	79.3%
10506	NY	Bedford	4.8%	1,819	$173,625	71.7%
10514	NY	Chappaqua	4.8%	4,067	$213,750	81.5%

the triangles have the fewest orders. This scatter plot confirms that the highest penetration zip codes also seem to have high median household incomes and are well educated.

Alas, this scatter plot is potentially misleading because the three groups seem to differ in size. Many of the zip codes are in the big blob on the lower left-hand side of the chart—median income between $20,000 and $70,000 and college proportion between 20% and 50%. The three groups overlap significantly in this region. Because Excel draws one series at a time, a later series may hide the points in an earlier series, even when the symbols are hollow. The order of the

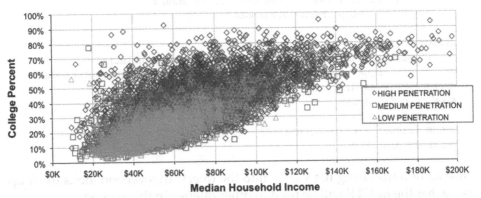

Figure 11-3: This scatter plot shows that the zip codes with the highest penetration do seem to have a higher median household income and higher education levels.

series affects how the chart looks. To change the order, select any of the series, right-click, and bring up the "Format Data Series" dialog box. The order of the series can be changed by selecting "Order" on the left pane.

> **WARNING** When plotting multiple series on a scatter plot, one series may overlap another, hiding some or many points. Use the "Series Order" option to rearrange the series and see the hidden points. Of course, changing the order may cause other points to be hidden.

A Basic Look-Alike Model

Zip code 10021 has the highest penetration and the following characteristics:

- Median household income is $106,236.
- College rate is 79.6%.

The first attempt at a look-alike model simply calculates the distance from each zip code to these values using the Euclidean distance formula:

```
SQRT(SQUARE(medianhhincome - 106236)+SQUARE(pctbachelorsormore - 0.796))
```

The lower the score the better (i.e., more similar).

This model can be used to assign a similarity measure to all zip codes using SQL:

```
WITH oz as (
      SELECT zc.zcta5,
             (COUNT(DISTINCT c.HouseholdId) /
              MAX(zc.tothhs*1.0) ) as penetration,
             zc.tothhs, zc.medianhhinc, zc.pctbachelorsormore
      FROM Orders o JOIN Customers c ON o.CustomerId = c.CustomerId JOIN
           ZipCensus zc ON o.ZipCode = zc.zcta5
      WHERE zc.tothhs >= 1000
      GROUP BY zc.zcta5, zc.tothhs, zc.medianhhinc,
               zc.pctbachelorsormore
     )
SELECT TOP 10
       SQRT(SQUARE(oz.medianhhinc - zc10021.medianhhinc)+
            SQUARE(oz.pctbachelorsormore - zc10021.pctbachelorsormore)
           ) as dist, oz.*
FROM oz CROSS JOIN
     ZipCensus zc10021
WHERE zc10021.zcta5 = '10021'
ORDER BY dist ASC
```

Instead of hardwiring the values into the query, this version looks them up. Note that the oz CTE will be used in other queries in this section.

Table 11-2: Ten Zip Codes Most Similar to 10021 (First Similarity Measure)

DISTANCE	ZIP CODE	PENETRATION	HOUSEHOLDS	HOUSEHOLD MEDIAN INCOME	COLLEGE %
0.0	10021	8.2%	23,377	$106,236	79.6%
2.0	55331	0.3%	6,801	$106,238	57.7%
12.0	20715	0.1%	8,707	$106,224	44.0%
14.0	23059	0.1%	11,736	$106,250	59.5%
14.0	11740	0.8%	3,393	$106,250	43.4%
17.0	01730	0.5%	4,971	$106,219	63.3%
61.0	60012	0.2%	3,776	$106,297	53.0%
74.0	19343	0.1%	2,761	$106,310	45.6%
82.0	91301	0.1%	9,209	$106,318	53.3%
82.0	96825	0.1%	10,699	$106,154	50.9%

Table 11-2 shows the ten closest zip codes by this measure. The median income for all these is right on the money, being very close to the value for 10021. On the other hand, the education levels vary rather widely. This is because the median income is measured in units of dollars with values going into the hundreds of thousands. The proportion of college educated is always less than one. The median household income dominates the calculation.

This is not a good thing. One variable is dominating the model. One way to fix this problem is to *normalize* values by subtracting the minimum from each value and dividing by the range (the difference between the maximum and the minimum). A better approach borrows an idea from Chapter 3.

Look-Alike Using Z-Scores

Z-scores replace numeric values that have wildly different ranges with values on the same scale. The z-score is the difference between a value and the average value for that column, measured in standard deviations.

The following query calculates the standard deviation and average value for the household median income and the proportion of college graduates:

```
WITH oz as (<defined on page 518>)
SELECT AVG(medianhhinc) as avghhmedinc, STDEV(medianhhinc) as stdhhmedinc,
       AVG(pctbachelorsormore) as avgpctbachelorsormore,
       STDEV(pctbachelorsormore) as stdpctbachelorsormore
FROM oz
```

This query uses the CTE oz defined in the previous query.

Because the model is restricted to zip codes that have at least 1,000 house-holds, the z-scores are restricted to this group of zip codes as well. The values are:

- HH median income: Average is $61,826; standard deviation is $25,866.50.

- Proportion College Grads: Average is 32.3%; standard deviation is 16.9%.

A scatter plot using the z-scores instead of the original values would look almost exactly the same as the scatter plot already seen in Figure 11-3; the only difference is that the X- and Y-axes would have different scales. Instead of going from $0 to $200,000, the range for median household income would go from about −3 to +6. For the proportion of college graduates, the z-scores would go from about −1.9 to 4.0, rather than from 0% to 100%.

To apply the z-score to a look-alike model, both the comparison values and the rows being scored need to be transformed into z-score values. The following query uses this same logic to calculate the similarity score:

```
WITH oz as (<defined on page 518>),
     ozm as (
      SELECT AVG(medianhhinc) as avgmedianhhinc,
             STDEV(medianhhinc) as stdmedianhhinc,
             AVG(pctbachelorsormore) as avgpctbachelorsormore,
             STDEV(pctbachelorsormore) as stdpctbachelorsormore
       FROM oz
      ),
     ozs as (
      SELECT oz.*,
             ((oz.medianhhinc - ozm.avgmedianhhinc) / ozm.stdmedianhhinc
             ) as z_medianhhinc,
             ((oz.pctbachelorsormore - ozm.avgpctbachelorsormore) /
              ozm.stdpctbachelorsormore) as z_pctbachelorsormore
       FROM oz CROSS JOIN ozm
      )
SELECT TOP 10 ozs.*,
       SQRT(SQUARE(ozs.z_medianhhinc - ozs10021.z_medianhhinc) +
            SQUARE(ozs.z_pctbachelorsormore -
                   ozs10021.z_pctbachelorsormore)
           ) as dist
 FROM ozs CROSS JOIN
      (SELECT ozs.* FROM ozs WHERE ozs.zcta5 = '10021') ozs10021
ORDER BY dist ASC
```

This query has a simple flow. The first CTE is the one we have already used. The second calculates the average and standard deviation for the variables. The third, ozs calculates the standardized values. These are then plugged into the distance formula to get the nearest values.

Table 11-3: Ten Zip Codes Most Similar to 10021 (Z-Score Measure)

DISTANCE	ZIP CODE	PENETRATION	HOUSEHOLDS	HOUSEHOLD MEDIAN INCOME	COLLEGE %
0.00	10021	8.2%	23,377	$106,236	79.6%
0.03	10022	4.8%	17,504	$106,888	79.5%
0.04	94123	0.9%	13,774	$107,226	79.7%
0.05	10023	3.2%	32,610	$105,311	79.1%
0.08	10017	3.9%	10,111	$108,250	79.2%
0.10	02445	1.1%	8,645	$104,069	78.7%
0.10	10028	3.1%	24,739	$107,976	80.9%
0.14	10014	2.5%	18,496	$105,144	81.9%
0.15	22202	0.6%	11,217	$109,006	81.3%
0.16	10065	0.0%	18,066	$109,960	78.3%

Table 11-3 shows the ten closest zip codes using the z-scores for distance. All the zip codes in this table have similar median incomes and proportions of college graduates. The college proportion now varies from 78.3% to 81.9%, rather than from 44.0% to 79.6%. The household median incomes still cluster around the value for 10021.

The look-alike model finds the zip codes that look like 10021 along both these dimensions, so the results are much more reasonable. However, the penetrations for similar zip codes vary from 0.0% to 4.8%. The 0.0% is an anomaly. 10065 is a new zip code and actually has a high penetration for the products—it was created in 2007 after the product data was generated. The wide range suggests that look-alike zip codes may not be similar in terms of penetration. On the other hand, perhaps the look-alike zip codes should be similar, and these other zip codes represent lost opportunity, perhaps because fewer households in those zip codes have been included in prospecting campaigns in the past.

Example of Nearest-Neighbor Model

Nearest-neighbor models are a variation on look-alike models. They use the measure of similarity to define a neighborhood of similar cases, and then summarize the cases to estimate a value.

As an example, the following query estimates the penetration for zip code 10021, using the similarity measure by median income and college proportion:

```
WITH oz as (<defined on page 518>),
     ozm as (<defined on page 520>),
     ozs as (<defined on page 520>)
SELECT AVG(penetration) as estpenetration
FROM (SELECT TOP 5 ozs.*,
             SQRT(SQUARE(ozs.z_medianhhinc - ozs10021.z_medianhhinc) +
                 SQUARE(ozs.z_pctbachelorsormore -
                        ozs10021.z_pctbachelorsormore)
                 ) as dist
      FROM ozs CROSS JOIN
           (SELECT ozs.* FROM ozs WHERE ozs.zcta5 = '10021') ozs10021
      WHERE ozs.zcta5 <> '10021'
      ORDER BY dist ASC
     ) neighbors
```

This query uses the same CTEs as the previous queries. The subquery pulls the five nearest neighbors and uses this information to calculate the estimated penetration.

A nearest-neighbor model consists of three things:

- The table of known instances

- A formula for calculating the distance from a new instance to the known values

- A formula for combining the information from the neighbors into an estimate of the target

The methodology is reasonably efficient for scoring one row at a time. However, for scoring large numbers of rows, every row in the score set has to be compared to every row in the training set (unless special-purpose software is used), which can result in long-running queries.

Lookup Model for Most Popular Product

A lookup model partitions the data into non-overlapping groups, and then assigns a constant value within each group. Lookup models do not look like fancy statistical models, because they pre-calculate all the possible scores, rather than estimating coefficients for a complicated equation.

The first example of a lookup model finds the most popular product group in a zip code using the purchases data. This model is a profiling model, as opposed to a predictive model.

Most Popular Product

The most popular product group in a zip code is easy to determine. The model itself is a lookup table with two columns: a zip code and a product group. Using the model simply requires looking up the appropriate value in the table, using the customer's zip code.

Once upon a time, a company was customizing its email offers. One of the things known about prospects was their zip codes. The marketing idea was to customize each email by including information about products of potential interest to that geographic area. Prospects were indeed more interested in the most popular product in their neighborhood (as defined by zip code) than in random products.

Calculating Most Popular Product Group

An earlier chapter noted that BOOKs is the most popular product group. The following query is one way to determine this information:

```
SELECT TOP 1 p.GroupName
FROM Orders o JOIN
     OrderLines ol
     ON o.OrderId = ol.OrderId JOIN
     Products p
     ON ol.ProductId = p.ProductId and
        p.GroupName <> 'FREEBIE'
GROUP BY p.GroupName
ORDER BY COUNT(*) DESC
```

This query aggregates the sales to get the count for each group. It then chooses the value with the highest count, using ORDER BY and TOP. This query does not include FREEBIE products, because they are not interesting for cross-selling purposes.

The most popular product is, in itself, a very simple model. However, we want to refine the model by zip code, resulting in a similar query:

```
SELECT ZipCode, GroupName
FROM (SELECT o.ZipCode, p.GroupName, COUNT(*) as cnt,
             ROW_NUMBER() OVER (PARTITION BY o.ZipCode
                                ORDER BY COUNT(*) DESC, p.GroupName
                               ) as seqnum
      FROM Orders o JOIN OrderLines ol ON o.OrderId = ol.OrderId JOIN
           Products p
           ON ol.ProductId = p.ProductId and
              p.GroupName <> 'FREEBIE'
      GROUP BY o.ZipCode, p.GroupName
     ) zg
WHERE seqnum = 1
```

This query aggregates the data by zip code and product group, and then assigns a sequential number using ROW_NUMBER(). This function assigns one to rows with the largest count for each zip code. If multiple groups are all equally the most common, then the query chooses the first one alphabetically. To get all of them, use RANK() or DENSE_RANK() instead of ROW_NUMBER().

> **TIP** When looking for rows containing the minimum and maximum values in a table, always consider that there might be more than one matching row.

The result contains two columns: the zip code and the most popular product group. This is the lookup table needed for the model. This model is a profiling model because the zip code and product group come from the same time frame. There is no "before" and "after." Note that, the most popular product group has been defined as the one with the most orders. Other definitions are possible, such as the one with the most households purchasing it or the largest dollar amount per household.

Table 11-4 shows each product group and the number of zip codes where that group is the most popular. Not surprisingly, BOOKs wins in over half the zip codes, as shown by the following query:

```
SELECT GroupName, COUNT(*) as cnt
FROM (SELECT o.ZipCode, p.GroupName, COUNT(*) as cnt,
             ROW_NUMBER() OVER (PARTITION BY o.ZipCode
                                ORDER BY COUNT(*) DESC, p.GroupName
                                ) as seqnum
      FROM Orders o JOIN OrderLines ol ON o.OrderId = ol.OrderId JOIN
           Products p
           ON ol.ProductId = p.ProductId and
              p.GroupName <> 'FREEBIE'
      GROUP BY o.ZipCode, p.GroupName
     ) zg
WHERE seqnum = 1
GROUP BY GroupName
ORDER BY cnt DESC
```

This query is quite similar to the previous query, with the addition of the GROUP BY and aggregation function.

Table 11-4: Number of Zip Codes Where Product Groups Are Most Popular

PRODUCT GROUP	NUMBER OF ZIPS	% OF ALL ZIPS
BOOK	8,409	53.9%
ARTWORK	2,922	18.7%
OCCASION	2,067	13.2%
GAME	900	5.8%
APPAREL	771	4.9%
CALENDAR	404	2.6%
OTHER	123	0.8%

Evaluating the Lookup Model

This model uses all the zip codes for determining the most popular product. There is no data left over to quantify how good the model is.

One idea for testing it would be to partition the data into two parts, one for determining the most popular product and the other for testing it. This strategy of testing a model on a separate set of data is a good idea and important to data mining. The next section describes an alternative approach that is often more useful.

Using a Profiling Lookup Model for Prediction

The "most popular product" model just created is a profiling model because the target (the most popular product group) comes from the same time frame as the input (the zip code). This is the nature of the model and the model set used to create it. However, it is possible to use a profiling model for prediction by making a small assumption.

The assumption is that the most popular product group prior to 2016 is the most popular after 2016. This assumption also requires building the model—still a profile model because of the dataset—using data prior to 2016. The only modification to the query is to add the following WHERE clause to the innermost subquery:

```
WHERE OrderDate < '2016-01-01'
```

The model now finds the most popular product group prior to the cutoff date.

A *correct classification matrix* is used to evaluate a model that classifies customers. It is simply a table where the modeled values are on the rows and the correct values are across the columns (or vice versa). Each cell in the table consists of the count (or proportion) of rows in the score set that have that particular combination of model prediction and actual result.

Figure 11-4 shows a classification matrix, where the rows contain the predicted product group (the most popular group prior to 2016) and the columns contain

		J	K	L	M	N	O	P
51					ACTUAL			
52		BOOK	OCCASION	ARTWORK	GAME	APPAREL	CALENDAR	OTHER
53	BOOK	1,406	483	938	303	149	30	38
54	OCCASION	138	89	84	35	16	6	5
55	ARTWORK	225	114	227	64	20	2	8
56	GAME	56	25	30	25	12	2	1
57	APPAREL	46	15	30	6	16	1	2
58	CALENDAR	26	11	10	4	4	4	3
59	OTHER	6	4	4	1	1	1	1

Figure 11-4: This classification matrix shows the number of zip codes by the predicted and actual most popular product group in 2016. The highlighted cells are where the prediction is correct.

the actual product group (the most popular after 2016). Each cell contains the number of zip codes with that particular combination of predicted and actual product groups. All the zip codes in the table have orders in the model set (prior to 2016) and the score set (after 2016). For 1,406 zip codes, BOOK is predicted to be the most popular product and it is actually BOOK. For an additional 1,941 zip codes (483 + 938 + 303 + 149 + 30 + 38), BOOK is predicted to be the most popular and it is not.

The cells in the table where the row and the column have the same value are shaded using Excel's conditional formatting capability, as explained in the aside "Conditional Formatting in Excel."

Although BOOK is still the most popular product group in 2016, its popularity is waning. If we totaled the values across the rows, BOOK consists of about 70% of the predicted values. However, if we total the rows across the columns, BOOK accounts for only about 40% of the actual values.

How well is the model doing? In this case, not so well. The model does well when its prediction agrees with what actually happens. So, there are 1,406 + 89 + 227 + 25 + 16 + 4 + 1 = 1,768 zip codes where the prediction matches what actually happened. This comes to 37.4% of the zip codes. This is much better than randomly guessing one out of seven categories. However, it is doing worse than just guessing that BOOK is going to be the most popular.

Using Binary Classification Instead

BOOK is so popular that we might tweak the model a bit, to look just for BOOK or NOT-BOOK as the most popular category, grouping all the non-book products together into a single value. To do this in SQL, replace the innermost references to product group with the following CASE statement:

```
(CASE WHEN GroupName = 'BOOK' THEN 'BOOK' ELSE 'NOT-BOOK' END) as GroupName
```

Not surprisingly, this model performs better than the categorical model, as shown in the classification matrix in Table 11-5. Now, the model is correct for 576 + 2,195 zip codes (58.4% versus 37.4%). In particular, the model does a better job predicting NOT-BOOK, where it is correct 73.6% of the time versus only 32.5% when it predicts BOOK.

Table 11-5: Classification Matrix for BOOK or NOT-BOOK

| | ACTUAL | |
PREDICTED	BOOK	NOT-BOOK
BOOK	567	1,179
NOT-BOOK	786	2,195

CONDITIONAL FORMATTING IN EXCEL

Excel has the ability to format each cell based on the value in the cell. That is, the border, color, and font in the cell can be controlled by the contents of the cell or even by a formula that refers to other cells. This *conditional formatting* can be used to highlight cells, as shown in Figure 11-4.

Conditional formatting comes in several flavors, the most common are formatting by the value in the cell or by a formula. The "Conditional Formatting" dialog box is accessed in one of three ways: using the Format ➢ Conditional Formatting menu option; using the Condition Formatting icon on the Home ribbon; or using the key sequence Alt+O, Alt+D.

To highlight cells with particular values, use formatting by a value. For instance, in a table showing chi-square values, the cells with a chi-square value exceeding a threshold can be given a different color. To do this, bring up the "Conditional Formatting" dialog box, click the "+" on the lower left to define a new rule. Then, choose the "Format only cells that contain" option, and set the condition. Then set the appropriate format.

Using a formula provides even more power. When the formula evaluates to true, the formatting gets applied. For instance, the shaded format in Figure 11-4 is when the name of the row and the name of the header have the same value:

```
=($I42 = J$41)
```

Where row 41 has the column names and column "I" has the row names. The formula uses "$" to ensure that the formula can be correctly copied to other cells. When copied, cell references in a conditional formatting formula change just like cell references for a regular formula.

Conditional formatting can be used for many things. For instance, to color every other row, use:

```
=MOD(ROW(), 2) = 0
```

To color every other column, use:

```
=MOD(COLUMN(), 2) = 0
```

To create a checkerboard pattern, use:

```
=MOD(ROW() + COLUMN(), 2) = 0
```

These formulas use the ROW() and COLUMN() functions, which return the current row and current column of the cell. To create a random pattern, with about 50% of the cells shaded, use:

```
=rand() < 0.5
```

Conditional formatting can also be used to put borders around regions in a table. Say column C has a key in a table that takes on repeated values and then changes. To put a line between blocks of similar values, use the following condition in the cells on row 10:

```
=($C10 <> $C11)
```

This says to apply the formatting when cell C11 has a different value from C10. If you make the formatting the bottom border and copy this over a range of cells, then horizontal lines appear between the different groups.

Using the paintbrush copies the conditional formatting as well as the overall formatting, so it is easy to copy formats from one cell to a group of cells.

The number of zip codes where BOOK is the most popular before and after has dropped from 1,406 to 576. These 576 zip codes are where the majority of orders are in BOOK. The rest are where BOOK has the most orders, but not over 50%.

This example shows a modeling challenge. When working with two categories of about the same size, binary models often do a pretty good job of distinguishing between them. When working with multiple categories, a single model can be less effective.

Another challenge in building a model is the fact that BOOK is becoming less popular as a category over time, relative to the other categories. (More optimistically, the other categories are growing in popularity.) There is a big word to describe this situation, *nonstationarity*, which means that patterns in the data change over time. Nonstationarity is the bane of data analysis, but is, alas, quite common in the real world.

> **WARNING**   When building models, we assume that the data used to build the model is representative of the data used when scoring the model. This is not always the case, due to changes in the market, in the customer base, in the economy, and so on.

Lookup Model for Order Size

The previous model was a lookup model for classification, both for multiple classification and binary classification. The lookup itself was along a single dimension. This section uses lookup models for estimating a real number. It starts with the very simplest case, no dimensions, and builds the model up from there.

Most Basic Example: No Dimensions

Another basic example of a lookup model is assigning an overall average value. For instance, we might ask the question: *Based on purchases in 2015, what do we expect the average order size to be in 2016?* The following query answers this question, by using the average of all purchases in 2015:

```
SELECT YEAR(o.OrderDate) as year, AVG(o.TotalPrice) as avgsize
FROM Orders o
WHERE YEAR(o.OrderDate) in (2015, 2016)
GROUP BY YEAR(o.OrderDate)
ORDER BY year
```

This query gives the estimate of $86.07. This is a reasonable estimate, but it is a bit off the mark because the actual average in 2016 is $113.19. The average could change for many reasons, perhaps all the prices went up, or customers ordered more expensive products, or customers ordered more products, or better customers placed orders, or for some other reason. Or, more likely, some combination of these.

This example is a predictive model. The average from 2015 is being used to estimate the value in 2016. This is a big assumption, but not unreasonable. Let's see what happens as we add more dimensions.

Adding One Dimension

The following query calculates the average by state:

```
SELECT State,
       AVG(CASE WHEN YEAR(OrderDate) = 2015 THEN TotalPrice END) as avg2015,
       AVG(CASE WHEN YEAR(OrderDate) = 2016 THEN TotalPrice END) as avg2016
FROM Orders o
WHERE YEAR(OrderDate) in (2015, 2016)
GROUP BY State
```

This query uses the AVG() function with a CASE statement to calculate the averages for 2015 and 2016. The CASE statement quite intentionally does not have an ELSE clause. Rows that do not match the WHEN condition are given a NULL value, which is ignored for the average. Of course, using ELSE NULL would have the same effect with more typing. The results from this query are a lookup table.

A good score set for evaluating the model is orders in 2016. Applying the model means joining the score set to the lookup table by state. One caveat is that some customers may be in states that did not place orders in 2015. These customers need a default value, and a suitable value is the overall average order size in 2015.

The following query attaches the estimated order size for 2016 onto each row in the score set:

```
SELECT toscore.*,
       COALESCE(statelu.avgamount, defaultlu.avgamount) as predamount
FROM (SELECT o.*
      FROM Orders o
      WHERE YEAR(o.OrderDate) = 2016) toscore LEFT OUTER JOIN
     (SELECT o.State, AVG(o.TotalPrice) as avgamount
      FROM Orders o
      WHERE YEAR(o.OrderDate) = 2015
      GROUP BY o.state) statelu
     ON o.State = statelu.State CROSS JOIN
     (SELECT AVG(o.TotalPrice) as avgamount
      FROM Orders o
      WHERE YEAR(o.OrderDate) = 2015) defaultlu
```

The dataflow diagram for this query, shown in Figure 11-5, has three subqueries. The first is for the score set that chooses orders from 2016. The second two are the lookup tables, one for state and one for the default value

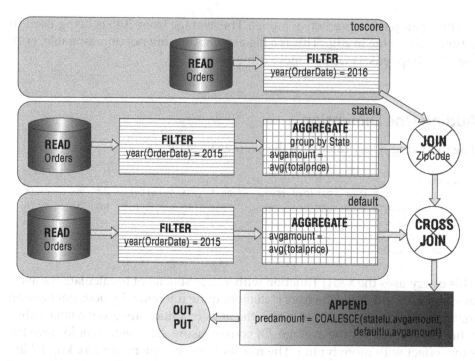

Figure 11-5: This dataflow diagram shows the processing needed for scoring a lookup model with one dimension.

(when no state matches). These lookup tables use the orders from 2015 to calculate values.

Comparing the average predicted amount to the average actual amount is an overall measure of how good the model is doing:

```
SELECT AVG(predamount) as avgpred, AVG(totalprice) as avgactual
FROM (<lookup-score-subquery>) subquery
```

This query uses the previous lookup score query as a subquery. The overall average by state is similar to the average overall. The structure of the query makes it easy to evaluate different dimensions by replacing state with another column name.

Table 11-6 shows the average amounts for various different dimensions, including channel, zip code, payment type, and month of order. What stands out is that the actual value is much larger than the predicted values—it appears that the order sizes are getting larger, and none of these variables explains what changed.

Table 11-6: Performance of Various One-Dimensional Lookup Models

DIMENSION	PREDICTED 2016	ACTUAL 2016
State	$85.89	$113.19
Zip Code	$88.21	$113.19
Channel	$86.49	$113.19
Month	$88.05	$113.19
Payment Type	$87.22	$113.19

Adding More Dimensions

Adding more dimensions is a simple modification to the basic query. The following query uses month and zip code as the dimensions:

```
SELECT toscore.*,
       COALESCE(dimllu.avgamount, defaultlu.avgamount) as predamount
FROM (SELECT o.*, MONTH(o.OrderDate) as mon
   FROM Orders o
   WHERE YEAR(o.OrderDate) = 2016
   ) toscore LEFT OUTER JOIN
   (SELECT MONTH(o.OrderDate) as mon, o.ZipCode,
        AVG(o.TotalPrice) as avgamount
   FROM Orders o
   WHERE YEAR(o.OrderDate) = 2015
   GROUP BY MONTH(o.OrderDate), o.ZipCode
   ) dimllu
ON toscore.mon = dimllu.mon AND
   toscore.ZipCode = dimllu.ZipCode CROSS JOIN
   (SELECT AVG(o.TotalPrice) as avgamount
   FROM Orders o
   WHERE YEAR(o.OrderDate) = 2015
   ) defaultlu
```

The structure of the query is the same as the query for one dimension. The only differences are changes related to the additional column in the dimllu subquery.

With the lookup table, the average rises to $90.76. The two-dimensional lookup table does a better job, but the average is still off from the actual value.

Examining Nonstationarity

As shown in Table 11-7, the average order size is increasing from year to year. Without taking into account this yearly increase, estimates based on the past are not going to work so well. This is an example of nonstationarity.

Table 11-7: Average Order Size Varies Over Time

YEAR	AVERAGE ORDER SIZE	CHANGE YEAR OVER YEAR
2009	$34.14	
2010	$52.24	53.0%
2011	$51.35	−1.7%
2012	$68.40	33.2%
2013	$74.98	9.6%
2014	$70.62	−5.8%
2015	$86.07	21.9%
2016	$113.19	31.5%

What is causing this change is perhaps a mystery. A likely reason is that prices increase from year to year. Alternatively, the product mix could be changing (more ARTWORK and fewer CALENDARs). Perhaps customers' initial orders are smaller than repeat orders, and the number of repeat orders (as a proportion of the total) increases from year to year. There are many possible reasons. So far, we have determined that variations in state, zip code, channel, price, and market from one year to the next only explain a small part of the difference from 2015 to 2016.

We could make an adjustment. For instance, note that the average purchase size increased by 22% from 2014 to 2015. If we increased the 2015 estimate by the same amount, the result would be much closer to the actual value.

Of course, to choose the appropriate factor it helps to understand what is happening. This requires additional understanding of the data and of the business.

Evaluating the Model Using an Average Value Chart

An average value chart is used to visualize model performance for a model with a numeric target, such as the look up models just created. The average value chart breaks customers into equal sized groups, based on the customers' predicted values. It might divide the customers into deciles, ten equal-sized groups, with the first one consisting of customers with the highest predicted order amounts, and the next highest in the second decile, and so on. The chart then shows the average of the predicted value and the average of the actual value for each decile.

Figure 11-6 shows an example for the lookup model using month and zip code as dimensions. The dotted line is the predicted average amount in each decile. It starts high and then decreases, although the values for deciles two through seven are flat.

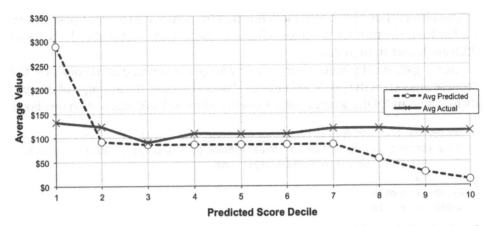

Figure 11-6: This average value chart is for a model that does not work for predicting the size of 2016 orders. This is apparent because the actual values are nearly a horizontal line.

The actual values look quite different. They are basically a horizontal line, indicating the lack of a relationship between the predicted amount and the actual amount. The average value chart shows visually that the model is doing a poor job of estimating the actual values because the actual values and the predicted values appear to have little relationship to each other.

The goal in the average value chart is for the actual values to correspond at least somewhat to the predicted values. Figure 11-7 shows a better model, which uses channel, payment type, and customer gender. Although the actual values are still (generally) higher than the predicted values, the deciles are generally doing what we expect. The actual values are higher when the predicted values are higher and lower when the predicted values are lower. Overall, this model does a much better job than the previous one.

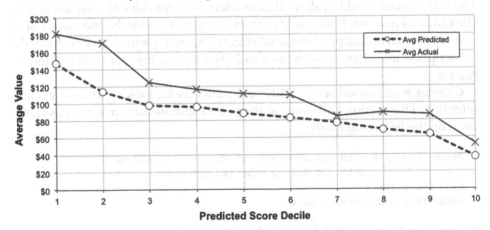

Figure 11-7: This average value chart uses channel, payment type, and customer gender. Here, the model is working better because the actual values are decreasing as the predicted values decrease.

One observation about both models is that the actual values are almost always higher than the predicted values. This is a result of the fact that order sizes in 2016 are larger than in 2015.

Creating an average value chart starts by assigning a decile to customers in the score set, based on the predicted amount. For each decile, the averages of the predicted value and of the actual value are calculated using basic aggregation functions:

```
SELECT decile, AVG(predamount) as avgpred, AVG(totalprice) as avgactual
FROM (SELECT lss.*, NTILE(10) OVER (ORDER BY predamount DESC) as decile
      FROM (<lookup-score-subquery>) lss
     ) s
GROUP BY decile
ORDER BY decile
```

This query uses the scoring subquery to get the predicted amount. The middle level uses the NTILE() window function to divide the scores into ten equal-sized groups (although this could use other window functions as well, as we have seen in other examples for creating quantiles). The outermost level calculates the average for the predicted amount and average amount for each of the groups.

Lookup Model for Probability of Response

This section considers a different sort of problem, related to the subscription data. *What is the probability that a customer who starts in 2005 is going to last for one year?*

The Overall Probability as a Model

The way to start thinking about this problem is to consider all customers who start in 2004 and ask how many of them survive for exactly one year. Using one year of starts dampens seasonal effects occurring within a year. Also, the subscription table has no stops prior to 2004, limiting how far back in time we can go.

Chapter 8 addressed several different methods for looking at survival and retention. This section looks only at the point estimate after one year, as calculated by the following query:

```
SELECT AVG(CASE WHEN Tenure < 365 AND StopType IS NOT NULL
                THEN 1.0 ELSE 0 END) as stoprate
FROM Subscribers
WHERE YEAR(StartDate) = 2004
```

Customers who stop within one year have tenures less than one year and a non-NULL stop type. Strictly speaking, the test for stop type is unnecessary, because all customers who both start in 2004 and have tenures less than 365 are stopped.

This query uses AVG() to calculate the proportion of customers who stop. The argument to the average is 1.0, rather than 1, because some databases return the average of an integer as an integer rather than as a real number. In such databases, the integer average would always be zero except when all customers stop within their first year.

Of the customers who start in 2004, 28.0% stop during the first year after they start. Given a new customer who starts in 2005, the best guess for that customer's stop rate during the first year is 28.0%.

The actual stop rate for 2005 starts is 26.6%, which is similar to the rate in 2004. This supports using the 2004 data to develop a model for 2005.

Exploring Different Dimensions

Five dimensions in the subscription data are known when customers start:

- Channel
- Market
- Rate Plan
- Initial Monthly Fee
- Date of Start

These are good candidates for modeling dimensions. Although the monthly fee is numeric, it only takes on a handful of values.

The following query calculates the stop rate by channel:

```
SELECT Channel,
       AVG(CASE WHEN Tenure < 365 AND StopType IS NOT NULL
               THEN 1.0 ELSE 0 END) as stoprate
FROM Subscribers
WHERE YEAR(StartDate) = 2004
GROUP BY Channel
```

The result is a lookup table that has the expected stop rate for different channels.

The lookup table is a model. To score data with the lookup table, it needs to be joined back to a score set. The following query calculates the probability that a customer who starts in 2005 is going to leave, using the channel for the lookup:

```
WITH toscore as (
    SELECT s.*,
           (CASE WHEN Tenure < 365 AND StopType IS NOT NULL
                THEN 1 ELSE 0 END) as is1yrstop
    FROM Subscribers s
    WHERE YEAR(StartDate) = 2005
),
lookup as (
    SELECT Channel,
```

```
            AVG(CASE WHEN Tenure < 365 AND StopType IS NOT NULL
                     THEN 1.0 ELSE 0 END) as stoprate
    FROM Subscribers
    WHERE YEAR(StartDate) = 2004
    GROUP BY Channel
    ),
    defaultlu as (
      SELECT AVG(CASE WHEN Tenure < 365 AND StopType IS NOT NULL
                      THEN 1.0 ELSE 0 END) as stoprate
      FROM Subscribers
      WHERE YEAR(StartDate) = 2004
      )
SELECT toscore.*, COALESCE(lookup.stoprate, defaultlu.stoprate) as predrate
FROM toscore LEFT OUTER JOIN
      lookup
      ON toscore.channel = lookup.channel CROSS JOIN
      defaultlu
```

The common table expressions define the three different result sets needed for the query: the records being scored, the lookup table by channel, and the default lookup value if the channel does not match. This query takes into account the fact that there might be no matching channel.

The process of scoring is the process of bringing this data together—using joins. The COALESCE() function chooses either the value from the channel lookup or the default value. In this case, the defaultlu is superfluous because all channels are represented in both years.

The following query calculates the overall stop rate and the predicted stop rate:

```
WITH . . .,
    Scored as (<previous query here>)
SELECT AVG(predrate) as predrate, AVG(1.0 * islyrstop) as actrate
FROM scored
```

In this query, the previous query is referred to as the CTE scored.

The model works very well overall. In fact, the query predicts an overall stop rate of 27.2%, which is quite close to the actual rate. However, Table 11-8 shows that the model does not work so well within each channel, especially for the chains.

Table 11-8: Actual and Predicted Stop Rates by Channel for 2005 Starts, Based on 2004 Starts

CHANNEL	PREDICTED	ACTUAL	DIFFERENCE
Store	16.3%	17.6%	−1.3%
Chain	41.0%	24.0%	17.0%
Mail	36.8%	34.6%	2.2%
Dealer	25.0%	27.0%	−2.1%

WARNING   Just because a model works well overall does not mean that the model works well on all subgroups of customers.

How Accurate Are the Models?

Table 11-9 compares the overall predicted stop rates and actual stop rates of one-dimensional lookup models, using each of five different dimensions. All the models do a reasonable job of estimating the overall stop rate. Notice that the accuracy of the models does not necessarily improve as the number of values in the dimension increases.

A reasonable business goal is to identify a group of customers that has a much greater chance of stopping than other customers, in order to offer them incentives to remain. Such incentives cost money, suggesting: *How many customers who actually stop are captured by the model in the top ten percent of model scores?*

This question motivates the *cumulative gains chart*, which is used to visualize model performance for models on binary targets. The cumulative gains chart provides a visual answer to the question. Its cousin, the ROC chart (described in the next section), also provides some very useful measures.

On a cumulative gains chart, the horizontal axis is a percentage of customers chosen based on the model score, ranging from 0% to 100%. The highest scoring customers are chosen first—in the left-most decile, so to speak—and the lower scoring customers are on the right. The vertical axis measures the proportion of the actual target found cumulatively in that group of customers, ranging from 0% (none of the desired target) to 100% (all of the desired target). The curves start at the lower left at 0% on both axes and rise to the upper right to 100% on both axes. If the model assigned a random score to customers, the cumulative gains chart is a diagonal line. The cumulative gains chart is useful because the horizontal axis measures the cost of a campaign (each person contacted costs money). The vertical axis measures the benefit (each responder is worth a certain amount of money).

Figure 11-8 shows a cumulative gains chart for the channel lookup model for stops. The horizontal axis is the percentage of customers with the highest scores.

Table 11-9: Actual and Predicted Stop Rates by Modeling Dimension for 2005 Starts, Based on 2004 Starts

DIMENSION	NUMBER OF VALUES	PREDICTED	ACTUAL	DIFFERENCE
Channel	4	27.2%	26.6%	0.58%
Market	3	27.1%	26.6%	0.54%
Rate Plan	3	27.8%	26.6%	1.27%
Monthly Fee	25	23.1%	26.6%	−3.46%
Month	12	29.0%	26.6%	2.40%

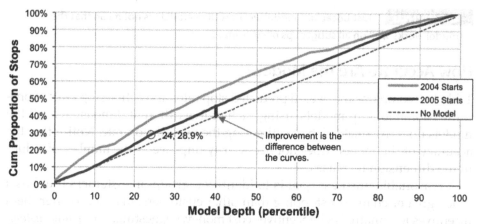

Figure 11-8: This cumulative gains chart shows the performance of the channel model on both the model set (2004 starts) and on the score set (2005 starts).

So, 10% represents the top decile of all customers; 20% represents the top two deciles. The vertical axis is the percentage of stoppers captured by that segment of customers. Sometimes this curve is called the *cumulative captured response curve*. This mouthful does a good job of expressing what the curve really is doing.

The chart has three curves. The best one, on the top, shows the performance of the model on the data used to build it. Models generally perform best on the model set. The middle curve is for the test set using 2005 starts, and the straight line is a reference assuming no model. For instance, the point at the 25% mark on the 2005 curve says that the top 25% of customers with the highest model score captures 28.6% of the customers who stop. *Lift* is one way to measure how well the model is working. At the 25% mark the lift is 28.6% / 25% = 114.4%. Note that lift always declines to one as the percentage moves toward 100%.

A cumulative gains chart is a good way to compare models. Figure 11-9 shows the chart for several lookup models on the test set of 2005 starts. The cumulative gains chart can also be used to select how many customers are needed to get a certain number of customers expected to have the target value.

The curves in these charts chart are based on a summary of the data, shown in Table 11-10:

- The quantile, which divides the customers into equal-sized groups based on the model score (the charts in the text divide the customers into percentiles)

- The predicted stop rate for the quantile (the average model score)

- The predicted number of stops (the average model score times the number of customers)

- The predicted and actual stop rate for the quantile

- The cumulative number of actual stops up to and including the quantile and the cumulative stop rate

- The lift of actual stops compared to no model

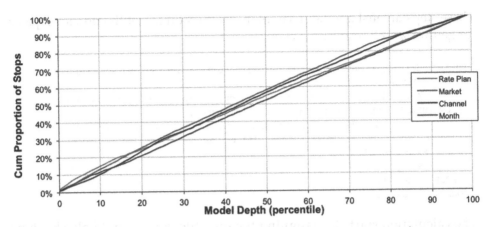

Figure 11-9: Cumulative gains charts for five models using 2005 charts are a good way to compare the performance of different models.

Only the first and last of these are used for the cumulative gains chart. The other information is helpful for understanding model performances and useful for creating other charts.

The following steps calculate the information in the table:

1. Apply the model to the score set to obtain the predicted stop rate.

2. Divide the scored customers into ten (or whatever) equal sized groups.

3. Calculate the summary information for each group.

Table 11-10: Summary Information for Cumulative Gains Chart

	NUM STOPS		STOP RATE		CUMULATIVE STOPS			
DECILE	PREDICTED	ACTUAL	PREDICTED	ACTUAL	NUMBER	RATE	PROP	LIFT
1	52,722.6	31,701	40.8%	24.5%	31,701	24.5%	9.2%	0.92
2	47,558.7	43,837	36.8%	33.9%	75,538	29.2%	22.0%	1.10
3	42,297.0	41,149	32.7%	31.8%	116,687	30.1%	34.0%	1.13
4	32,281.6	37,021	25.0%	28.6%	153,708	29.7%	44.7%	1.12
5	32,281.6	37,199	25.0%	28.8%	190,907	29.5%	55.6%	1.11
6	32,281.6	35,847	25.0%	27.7%	226,754	29.2%	66.0%	1.10
7	32,281.6	32,016	25.0%	24.8%	258,770	28.6%	75.3%	1.08
8	32,281.6	34,459	25.0%	26.7%	293,229	28.4%	85.3%	1.07
9	25,996.2	26,910	20.1%	20.8%	320,139	27.5%	93.2%	1.04
10	21,078.2	23,478	16.3%	18.2%	343,617	26.6%	100.0%	1.00

These steps are just another layer of query built on top of the previous query for getting scored results:

```
SELECT decile, COUNT(*) as numcustomers, SUM(is1yrstop) as numactualstops,
       SUM(predrate) as predactualstops,
       AVG(is1yrstop * 1.0) as actualstop, AVG(predrate) as predrate
FROM (SELECT SubscriberId, predrate, is1yrstop,
             CEILING(10 * (ROW_NUMBER() OVER (ORDER BY predrate DESC) - 1) /
                     COUNT(*) OVER ()) as decile
      FROM scored
     ) s
GROUP BY decile
ORDER BY decile
```

The calculation starts by assigning the quantile, which could also be done using the window ranking function NTILE(). Within each quantile, the query counts the number of customers who do actually stop and estimates the number of predicted stops by taking the average predicted stop rate and multiplying it by the number of customers in the quantile. The cumulative number of stops is calculated in Excel, although SQL can also do the calculation.

ROC Charts and AUC

These three-letter acronyms are another method for visualizing and measuring the effectiveness of models. The first, the ROC chart, is a cousin of the cumulative gains chart. The second acronym, AUC, stands for "area under the curve," the curve in question being the ROC curve. The technical aside "Receiver Operating Characteristics," discusses the naming and history for this chart.

The ROC curve has two advantages over the cumulative gains chart. The first is that the area under the curve is a good measurement of how well the model is performing. The second is that the ROC curve is independent of "oversampling." This means that the ROC curve should not change if the score set has a target density of 10%, 50%, or 90%. The cumulative gains chart (and the lift as well) shifts for different densities of the target.

Creating an ROC Chart

Perhaps the easiest way to understand the ROC chart is by comparison to the cumulative gains chart. The horizontal axis on the cumulative gains chart divides the entire score set into deciles based on the model score. The entire score set includes customers who both responded and did not respond—or who stopped and stayed active. The top decile is the decile of all customers with the top score.

The ROC chart is subtly different. The horizontal axis only considers the records that are classified as "no." So the top decile is the top ten percent of customers who have a "no" value—meaning that the model is wrong for these customers. The vertical point is the same as for the cumulative gains chart, which explains why the ROC chart and the cumulative gains chart look so similar.

The SQL to calculate the points on the ROC chart is quite similar to the SQL for the cumulative gains chart:

```
WITH . . .
     Scored (<defined on page 536>)
SELECT decile, COUNT(*) as numcustomers,
       SUM(is1yrstop) as numactualstops,
       SUM(predrate) as predactualstops,
       AVG(is1yrstop * 1.0) as actualstop, AVG(predrate) as predrate,
       (SUM(SUM(is1yrStop) * 1.0) OVER (ORDER BY decile) /
            SUM(SUM(is1yrStop)) OVER ()) as CumStops
FROM (SELECT SubscriberId, predrate, is1yrstop,
             CEILING(10 *
                  (SUM(1 - is1yrstop) OVER (ORDER BY predrate DESC,
                                            SubscriberId DESC) - 1) /
                   SUM(1 - is1yrstop) OVER ()
                  ) as decile
      FROM scored
     ) s
GROUP BY decile
ORDER BY decile
```

The main difference is the decile calculation, which for ROC curves is based only on the stops. Figure 11-10 shows the ROC curves for the five models shown in Figure 11-9.

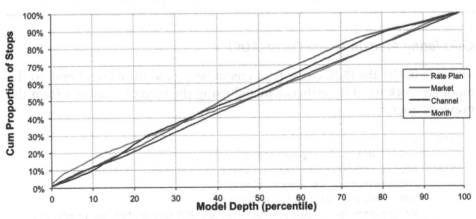

Figure 11-10: This chart shows the ROC curves for five models using one variable predicting stops on the survival data.

RECEIVER OPERATING CHARACTERISTICS

Radar was invented some time before World War II. During the war, it was refined and proved very valuable for detecting approaching aircraft. Alas, in those days, radars were also very good at detecting approaching flocks of birds. And, to further complicate things, the distinction between friendly airplanes and enemy aircraft was rather subtle.

So, the Department of Defense had a problem. How could it train radar operators to distinguish between the friendly, the benign, and the dangerous? And the training department had its own problem: How would it know if the trainings were effective?

This latter question is remarkably similar to the problem of measuring how good a model is—instead of a human operator marking incoming trails on a radar as "bad" (enemy aircraft) or "something else," a model does a similar assignment automatically. The same process can be used to measure how good the assignment is.

Two key characteristics for the operators were *sensitivity* and *specificity*:

- *Sensitivity* is the proportion of items of interest (enemy aircraft, in this case) correctly identified by the operator.

- *Specificity* is the proportion of items actually of interest out of all the items an operator identified.

Note that 100% sensitivity is possible, simply by identifying everything as enemy aircraft. But, this isn't a very good assignment, because the specificity is quite low.

Part of the evaluation plotted sensitivity against 1 – specificity. Not only is this hard to pronounce, but the language tends to obscure what is actually happening. Sensitivity is pretty easy to understand because it is the proportion of enemy aircraft that are assigned properly.

1 – specificity is also easy to understand, but in a different way. It measures negatives—the proportion of non-items of interest mislabeled by the process. That is, how often a flock of birds is labeled an enemy aircraft.

The ROC chart plots the proportion of "correct positive" predictions on the vertical axis for a given proportion of negative predictions on the horizontal axis. The result is something very similar to the cumulative gains chart, but with the advantages explained in the text.

Calculating Area under the Curve (AUC)

The area under the ROC curve happens to be a good measure of how well a model is working. It is easily calculated using the sum of `cumstops` from the previous query:

```
WITH . . .
     Scored (<defined on page 536>)
SELECT decile, COUNT(*) as numcustomers,
       SUM(is1yrstop) as numactualstops,
       SUM(predrate) as predactualstops,
       AVG(is1yrstop * 1.0) as actualstop, AVG(predrate) as predrate,
      (SUM(SUM(is1yrStop)) * 1.0) OVER (ORDER BY decile) /
          SUM(SUM(is1yrStop))) OVER ()) as CumStops
```

```
FROM (SELECT SubscriberId, predrate, is1yrstop,
             CEILING(10 *
                     (SUM(1 - is1yrstop) OVER (ORDER BY predrate DESC,
                                               SubscriberId DESC) - 1) /
                     SUM(1 - is1yrstop) OVER ()
                    ) as decile
      FROM scored
     ) s
GROUP BY decile
ORDER BY decile
```

The result varies from 0 (for a really bad model) to the number of deciles. The result should really be an average, divided by 10 in this case.

The exact value depends on the number of quantiles used for the calculation. An alternative method calculates the AUC without the intermediate calculation at the quantile level. The idea is to go to the finest level of granularity, which is a single non-stop. This following query uses this approach:

```
SELECT SUM(CumStopRate) / COUNT(*)
FROM (SELECT s.*,
             (SUM(is1yrStop * 1.0) OVER (ORDER BY actstopprop) /
              SUM(is1yrStop) OVER ()) as CumStopRate
      FROM (SELECT SubscriberId, predrate, is1yrstop,
                   ((SUM(1.0 - is1yrstop) OVER
                         (ORDER BY predrate DESC, SubscriberId DESC) - 1) /
                    SUM(1 - is1yrstop) OVER ()) as actstopprop
            FROM scored s
           ) s
     ) s
WHERE is1yrstop = 0
```

The structure of this query is similar to the previous one. The middle query, however, is not doing an aggregation, just cumulative sums. Notice that the WHERE clause is in the outermost query. Because the subqueries use the value of is1yrstop, we do not want to prematurely filter by that value.

Table 11-11 shows the AUC measurement for the five one-variable models, indicating that the Monthly Fee model is the best one.

Table 11-11: Summary Information for Area-Under-Curve (AUC) Measurement

MODEL	AUC
Channel	0.543
Market	0.558
Rate Plan	0.528
Monthly Fee	0.603
Month	0.511

Adding More Dimensions

A lookup model can have more than one dimension. Up to a point, increasing the number of dimensions usually improves the model. Figure 11-11 shows the cumulative gains chart for the model using three dimensions. This model does better than most of the models with one dimension. Interestingly, the model on MonthlyFee alone does a slightly better job by the AUC measure. The AUC for this model is 0.593 versus 0.602 for the one variable model. The MonthlyFee model does better in the first five deciles. This model does better in the lower five. Usually the top deciles are more important.

Generating such a model is simply a matter of replacing the lookup CTE with a more refined lookup table, resulting in a scoring query that starts:

```
WITH toscore as (
     SELECT s.*,
             (CASE WHEN Tenure < 365 AND StopType IS NOT NULL
                  THEN 1 ELSE 0 END) as is1yrstop
     FROM Subscribers s
     WHERE YEAR(StartDate) = 2005
    ),
    lookup as (
      SELECT Market, Channel, RatePlan,
             AVG(CASE WHEN Tenure < 365 AND StopType IS NOT NULL
                  THEN 1.0 ELSE 0 END) as stoprate
      FROM Subscribers
      WHERE YEAR(StartDate) = 2004
      GROUP BY Market, Channel, RatePlan
    ),
    defaultlu as (
      SELECT AVG(CASE WHEN Tenure < 365 AND StopType IS NOT NULL
                  THEN 1.0 ELSE 0 END) as stoprate
      FROM Subscribers
      WHERE YEAR(StartDate) = 2004
```

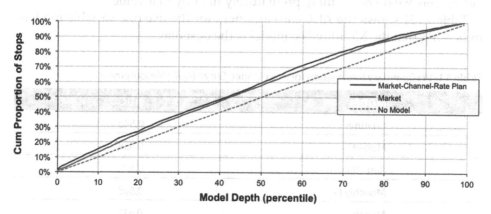

Figure 11-11: The lookup model with three dimensions does better than most of the models with one dimension.

```
    ),
    scored as (
     SELECT toscore.*,
           COALESCE(lookup.stoprate, defaultlu.stoprate) as predrate
     FROM toscore LEFT OUTER JOIN
          lookup
          ON toscore.Market = lookup.Market AND
            toscore.Channel = lookup.Channel AND
            toscore.RatePlan = lookup.RatePlan CROSS JOIN
          defaultlu
    )
```

This creates the scored data set, which can then be used for calculating lift and creating cumulative gains charts.

Adding more dimensions is beneficial because the lookup model captures more interactions among those features. However, as the number of dimensions increases, each cell has fewer and fewer customers. In fact, using `MonthlyFee` instead of `RatePlan` for the third dimension results in some of the combinations having no customers at all, and more than one in six cells having fewer than ten customers. The histogram in Figure 11-12 shows these cell sizes. The largest cell (for the market Gotham, the channel Dealer, and a monthly fee of $40) accounts for 15% of all customers.

Having large numbers of cells has another effect as well. The resulting estimate for the stop rate has a confidence interval, as discussed in Chapter 3. The fewer customers contributing to the proportion, the less confident we are in the result.

For this reason, cells in the lookup table should have some minimum size, such as a minimum of 500 customers. This is accomplished by including a `HAVING` clause in `lookup`:

```
HAVING COUNT(*) >= 500
```

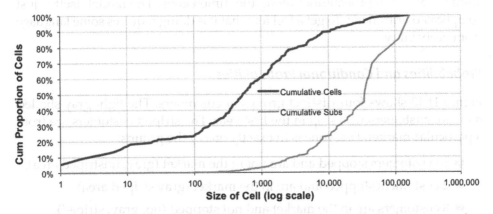

Figure 11-12: This histogram chart shows the cumulative number of cells that have up to each number of customers for the market, dealer, and monthly fee lookup model. Note that the horizontal axis uses a log scale because the range of cell sizes is very large.

Combinations of market, channel, and monthly fee that are not in the lookup table but are in the score set are then given the default value. Lookup models are useful, but they become less practical as the number of cells gets larger. The next section presents another method for bringing together data from many dimensions, a method that borrows ideas from probability.

Naïve Bayesian Models (Evidence Models)

Naïve Bayesian models extend the idea of lookup models for probabilities to the extreme. It is possible to have any number of dimensions and still use the information along each dimension to get sensible results, even when the corresponding lookup model would have an empty cell for that combination of values—or even for *all* combinations of values. Instead of creating ever smaller cells, naïve Bayesian models combine the information from each dimension, making a simple assumption.

The "naïve" part of the name is this assumption: The dimensions are independent of each other, statistically speaking. This makes it possible to combine information along the dimensions into a single score. The Bayesian part of the name refers to a simple idea from probability. Understanding this idea is a good place to start.

Some Ideas in Probability

The chi-square calculation uses expected values, and the calculation works for any number of dimensions, as explained in Chapter 3. The expected value is itself an estimate of the actual value. The chi-square test uses the expected value for another purpose, calculating the probability that the deviation from the expected values is due to chance.

In a similar way, naïve Bayesian models produce expected values based on summaries of the probabilities along the dimensions. The model itself is just complicated arithmetic. To get a feel for what it is doing requires some language from probability.

Probabilities and Conditional Probabilities

Figure 11-13 shows four distinct groups of customers. The light gray shaded ones are customers who stop in the first year. The striped customers are from a particular market. Everyone is in exactly one of the groups:

- 38 customers stopped and are not in the market (gray, unstriped area).
- 2 customers stopped and are in the market (gray striped area).
- 8 customers are in the market and not stopped (not gray, striped).
- 52 customers are not in the market and not stopped (not gray, not striped).

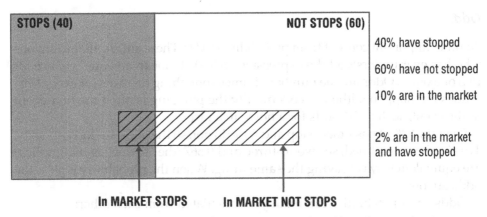

Figure 11-13: Four groups of customers here are represented as a Venn diagram, showing the overlaps between the customers in one market and the stopped and not stopped customers.

The purpose of the chart is to illustrate some ideas and vocabulary about probability. The chart itself is a Venn diagram, showing overlapping sets.

What is the probability that someone stops? (Strictly speaking, the question should be "If we choose one customer at random, what is the probability of choosing a customer who stops?") The answer is the number of customers who stop divided by the total number of customers. There are 40 customers who stop (38 + 2) out of 100 customers (38 + 2 + 8 + 52), so the probability is 40%. Similarly, the probability of someone being in the market shown in the chart is 10%.

It is worth pondering how useful this information is. If told that of 100 customers 40% stop and 10% are in a given market, what does this tell us about the relationship between stops and the market? The answer: very little. All the customers in the market could be stopped; all the customers in the market could be not stopped; or anything in between.

However, once the probability of stops within the market is known, then the various counts are all determined. The probability of stopping within the market is an example of a *conditional probability*. It is the number of customers in the market who stop divided by the number of customers in the market, or 20% (2 / 10).

When the conditional probability is the same as the overall probability, the two phenomena are said to be *independent*. Being independent simply means that knowing the market provides no additional information about stopping and vice versa. In this case, the probability of stopping is 40% and the probability of stopping for customers in the market is 20%, so the two are not independent: The market, either directly or indirectly, influences stopping behavior.

Odds

Another important concept from probability is *odds*. These are familiar to anyone who has ever understood the expression "50-50" to mean an equal chance for two outcomes. Odds are the number of times something happens for every time it does not happen (although colloquially the phrasing is often the non-event to the event, such as 7-1 odds for a horse in a race).

Overall, 40% of customers stop and 60% do not, so the odds are forty-to-sixty. This is often simplified, so two-to-three and 0.667 (the "to one" being implicit) are equivalent ways of saying the same thing. When the probability is 50%, the odds are one.

Odds and probabilities can readily be calculated from each other:

```
odds = probability / (1 - probability) =  -1 + 1 / (1 - probability)
probability = 1 - (1 / (1 + odds))
```

Given the probability it is easy to calculate the odds, and vice versa. Note that probabilities vary from zero to one whereas odds vary from zero to infinity.

Likelihood

The likelihood of someone in a market stopping is the ratio between two conditional probabilities: the probability of someone being in the market given that they stopped and the probability of someone being in the market given that they did not stop.

Figure 11-14 illustrates what this means. The probability of someone being in the market given they stopped is 2 divided by 40. The probability of someone being in the market given they did not stop is 8 divided by 60. The ratio is 3/8. This means that someone in the market has a 3/8 chance of stopping compared to not stopping.

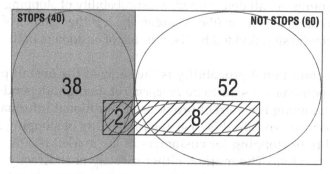

Figure 11-14: A likelihood is the ratio of two conditional probabilities.

An alternative way of expressing the likelihood is as the ratio of two odds. The first is the odds of stopping in the market and the second is the overall odds of stopping. The odds of stopping in the market are 2/8; the overall odds are 4/6. The ratio produces the same value: $(2 / 8) / (4 / 6) = (2 * 6) / (4 * 8) = 3 / 8$.

Calculating the Naïve Bayesian Model

This section moves from the simple ideas in probability to an intriguing observation by Thomas Bayes that motivates naïve Bayesian models. Although Bayes himself probably did not realize it, the observation also has philosophical implications, and it is the foundation of a branch of statistics called Bayesian statistics (which has little relationship to naïve Bayesian modeling). The aside "Bayes and Bayesian Statistics" discusses the man and the statistics.

An Intriguing Observation

Thomas Bayes made a key observation in the realm of statistics, which connects the following two probabilities:

- What is the probability of stopping for a customer in the particular market?
- What is the probability of being in the market for a customer who stops?

These are two ways of understanding the relationship between markets and stops, one focusing on what happens in the market and the other focusing on the customers who stop. Bayes proved that these probabilities are related to each other by a simple formula.

The two probabilities themselves are conditional probabilities. The first is the probability of stopping, given that a customer is in a market. The second is the probability of being in a market, given that a customer stops. In the example data, the first is 20% because two out of ten customers in the market stop. The second is 5% because two out of 40 stopped customers are in the market.

Simple enough. The ratio between these numbers is four (20% / 5% = 4). Remarkably, this is also the ratio between the overall stop rate (40%) and the overall proportion of customers in the given market (10%).

This observation is true in general. The ratio between two conditional probabilities that are the inverses of each other is the ratio between the two probabilities with no conditions. In a sense, the conditional parts of the probabilities cancel out. This is Bayes' Formula.

BAYES AND BAYESIAN STATISTICS

Rev. Thomas Bayes was born at the beginning of the 18th century to a family of Nonconformists. According to English law at the time, members of non-Anglican churches were officially classified as "nonconformist"; eventually, he took a ministering position in a Presbyterian church.

Bayes was quite interested in mathematics, yet he lived up to his religious affiliation in one striking way. His ideas in probability theory were published in 1763, three years after his death—distinctly nonconformist.

The paper, *An Essay Towards Solving a Problem in the Doctrine of Chances*, appeared in the *Philosophical Transactions of the Royal Society of London*. (The paper is available at `http://www.stat.ucla.edu/history/essay.pdf`.) For several decades the paper languished, until found and expounded upon by a French mathematician Pierre-Simon Laplace.

By the mid-20th century, statistics had two competing perspectives, the Frequentists and the Bayesians. To outsiders (and many insiders), this competition often looks like a religious debate, so it is perhaps fitting that Bayes himself was religiously ordained.

The primary difference between the two groups is how to deal with subjective information in probability theory. Both Bayesians and Frequentists would agree that the probability of a coin about to be flipped landing heads side up is 50% (because this is not a trick question).

Consider a slightly different scenario, though. Someone has flipped the coin, hidden it from view, and looked at whether the coin is heads or tails. Now, is the probability still 50% even though you cannot see the coin? Frequentists would say that probability does not apply because the event has occurred. The coin either is or is not heads, so the "probability" is either 0% or 100%. Bayesians are more comfortable saying that the probability is 50%. Which is true? There is no right answer. This is a question as much about philosophy as about probability.

Chapter 3 introduced the concept of the confidence interval and the p-value as a confidence. These are Frequentist notions. The Bayesian perspective has similar ideas, called "credible intervals" and Bayesians often treat p-values as actual probabilities. Thankfully, the mathematics is the same (or similar enough) for basic statistical measures.

The Bayesian perspective makes it possible to incorporate prior beliefs when analyzing data. This can be quite powerful and can simplify some very difficult problems, often using lots of computing power. Frequentists counter that any given outcome can be generated, just by choosing appropriate prior beliefs.

An old saying says that "statistics don't lie but statisticians do." Even without resorting to complex mathematical modeling, it is possible to mislead with statistics. Responsible analysts and statisticians—whether Bayesian or Frequentist—are not trying to mislead. They are trying to analyze data to increase understanding and provide useful results.

This history offers an important lesson. When analyzing data, the only responsible thing to do is to be explicit about assumptions being made. This is particularly important when working with databases, where business processes can result in unusual behavior. Be explicit about assumptions, so the results rest on a solid and credible foundation.

Bayesian Model of One Variable

The Bayesian model of one variable applies the formula in the following way: calculate the odds of stopping given that a customer is in the market by multiplying two numbers. The first is the overall odds of stopping; the second is the likelihood of the customer in the market stopping.

Let's work this out for the example. The probability of stopping given that a customer is in the market is 20%. Hence, the odds of a customer stopping are 20% / (1 – 20%) = 1 / 4. Is this the same as the product of the overall odds and the likelihood?

As observed earlier, the overall odds of stopping are 2/3. The likelihood of the customer stopping was also calculated as 3/8. Well, in this case, the result holds: 1/4 = (2 / 3) * (3 / 8).

The case with one dimension is trivially correct. Recall the alternative way of expressing the likelihood is the ratio of the odds of a customer stopping divided by the overall odds. The Bayesian model becomes the product of the overall odds times this ratio, and the overall odds cancel out. The result is what we were looking for.

Bayesian Model of One Variable in SQL

The goal of the Bayesian model is to calculate the conditional probability of a customer stopping. For the simple example in one dimension, the formula is not necessary. The following query calculates the odds by market:

```
SELECT Market,
       AVG(CASE WHEN Tenure < 365 AND StopType IS NOT NULL
                THEN 1.0 ELSE 0.0 END) as stoprate,
       (-1 + 1 / (1 - AVG(CASE WHEN tenure < 365 AND StopType IS NOT NULL
                               THEN 1.0 ELSE 0.0 END))) as stopodds,
       SUM(CASE WHEN Tenure < 365 AND StopType IS NOT NULL
                THEN 1 ELSE 0 END) as numstops,
       SUM(CASE WHEN Tenure < 365 AND StopType IS NOT NULL
                THEN 0 ELSE 1 END) as numnotstops
FROM Subscribers
WHERE YEAR(StartDate) = 2004
GROUP BY Market
```

The results are shown in Table 11-12.

Although the direct calculation is easy, it is instructive to show the alternative approach using the odds-times-likelihood approach, which uses the following:

- The overall odds
- The likelihood of a customer stopping given that the customer is in the market

The odds given the market are then the overall odds times the likelihood of stopping in the market. These odds can easily be converted to a probability.

Table 11-12: Results by Market for Bayesian Model of One Variable

MARKET	STOP RATE	STOP ODDS	NUMBER OF STOPS	NUMBER OF NOT STOPS
Gotham	33.0%	0.49	176,065	357,411
Metropolis	29.0%	0.41	117,695	288,809
Smallville	10.1%	0.11	17,365	155,362

Both of these values can readily be calculated in SQL because they are based on counting and dividing:

```
WITH dim1 as (
      SELECT Market,
            SUM(CASE WHEN Tenure < 365 AND StopType IS NOT NULL
                  THEN 1.0 ELSE 0 END) as numstop,
            SUM(CASE WHEN Tenure < 365 AND StopType IS NOT NULL
                  THEN 0.0 ELSE 1 END) as numnotstop
      FROM Subscribers
      WHERE YEAR(StartDate) = 2004
      GROUP BY Market
      ),
      overall as (
      SELECT SUM(CASE WHEN Tenure < 365 AND StopType IS NOT NULL
                  THEN 1.0 ELSE 0 END) as numstop,
            SUM(CASE WHEN Tenure < 365 AND StopType IS NOT NULL
                  THEN 0.0 ELSE 1 END) as numnotstop
      FROM Subscribers
      WHERE YEAR(StartDate) = 2004
      )
SELECT Market, (1 - (1 / (1 + overall_odds * likelihood))) as p,
      overall_odds * likelihood as odds, overall_odds, likelihood,
      numstop, numnotstop, overall_numstop, overall_numnotstop
FROM (SELECT dim1.Market,
            overall.numstop / overall.numnotstop as overall_odds,
            ((dim1.numstop / overall.numstop)/
            (dim1.numnotstop / overall.numnotstop)) as likelihood,
            dim1.numstop, dim1.numnotstop,
            overall.numstop as overall_numstop,
            overall.numnotstop as overall_numnotstop
      FROM dim1 CROSS JOIN overall
      ) d
GROUP BY Market
ORDER BY Market
```

The first CTE, `dim1`, calculates the number of customers who do and do not stop in each market. The second, `overall`, calculates the same values overall. The subquery in the outer query calculates the likelihood and overall odds, which are brought together in the outermost query.

Table 11-13: Results for the Naïve Bayesian Approach, with Intermediate Results

MARKET	P	ODDS	OVERALL ODDS	LIKELIHOOD
Gotham	33.0%	0.493	0.388	1.269
Metropolis	29.0%	0.408	0.388	1.050
Smallville	10.1%	0.112	0.388	0.288

The alternative formulation for odds changes the definition of likelihood to the arithmetically equivalent:

```
(dim1.numstop / dim1.numnotstop) / (overall.numstop / overall.numnotstop)
```

This formulation is easier to calculate in SQL.

The results in Table 11-13 are exactly the same as the results calculated directly. This is not a coincidence. With one variable, the Bayesian model is exact.

The "Naïve" Generalization

The "naïve" part of naïve Bayesian means "independent," in the sense of probability. This implies that each variable can be treated separately in the model. With this assumption, the formula for one dimension generalizes to any number of dimensions: The odds of stopping given several attributes in several dimensions are the overall odds of stopping times the product of the likelihoods for each attribute. What makes this powerful is the ease of calculating the overall odds and the individual likelihoods.

TIP Naïve Bayesian models can be applied to any number of inputs (dimensions). There are examples with hundreds of inputs.

Table 11-14 shows the actual probability and the estimated probability by channel and market for stopping in the first year. The estimates from the model are pretty close to the actual values. In particular, the ordering is quite similar. Unlike the one-attribute case, the estimate for two attributes is an approximation because the attributes are not strictly independent. This is okay; we should not expect modeled values to exactly match actual values.

The following query calculates the values in this table:

```
WITH dim1 as (
    SELECT Market,
           -1+1/(1-AVG(CASE WHEN Tenure < 365 AND StopType IS NOT NULL
                  THEN 1.0 ELSE 0 END)) as odds
    FROM Subscribers
```

Table 11-14: Results from Naïve Bayesian Model, Using Channel and Market for First Year Stops

MARKET	CHANNEL	PROBABILITY			RANK	
		PREDICTED	ACTUAL	DIFFERENCE	PREDICTED	ACTUAL
Gotham	Chain	46.9%	58.7%	−11.8%	1	1
Gotham	Dealer	29.7%	28.9%	0.8%	5	5
Gotham	Mail	42.5%	41.9%	0.6%	2	2
Gotham	Store	19.8%	21.3%	−1.5%	7	7
Metropolis	Chain	42.2%	38.2%	4.1%	3	4
Metropolis	Dealer	25.9%	23.1%	2.7%	6	6
Metropolis	Mail	37.9%	41.1%	−3.2%	4	3
Metropolis	Store	17.0%	17.9%	−0.9%	8	8
Smallville	Chain	16.7%	9.1%	7.6%	9	11
Smallville	Dealer	8.7%	9.7%	−1.0%	11	10
Smallville	Mail	14.4%	13.9%	0.4%	10	9
Smallville	Store	5.3%	8.5%	−3.2%	12	12

```
          WHERE YEAR(StartDate) = 2004
          GROUP BY Market
        ),
        dim2 as (
          SELECT Channel,
                 -1+1/(1-AVG(CASE WHEN Tenure < 365 AND StopType IS NOT NULL
                                  THEN 1.0 ELSE 0 END)) as odds
          FROM Subscribers
          WHERE YEAR(StartDate) = 2004
          GROUP BY Channel
        ),
        overall as (
          SELECT -1+1/(1-AVG(CASE WHEN Tenure < 365 AND StopType IS NOT NULL
                                  THEN 1.0 ELSE 0 END)) as odds
          FROM Subscribers
          WHERE YEAR(StartDate) = 2004
        ),
        actual as (
          SELECT Market, Channel,
                 -1+1/(1-AVG(CASE WHEN Tenure < 365 AND StopType IS NOT NULL
                                  THEN 1.0 ELSE 0 END)) as odds
          FROM Subscribers
          WHERE YEAR(StartDate) = 2004
          GROUP BY Market, Channel
        )
SELECT Market, Channel,
```

```
              1-1/(1+pred_odds) as predp, 1-1/(1+actual_odds) as actp,
              1-1/(1+market_odds) as marketp, 1-1/(1+channel_odds) as channelp,
              pred_odds, actual_odds, market_odds, channel_odds
       FROM (SELECT dim1.Market, dim2.Channel, actual.odds as actual_odds,
                    (overall.odds*(dim1.odds/overall.odds)*
                    (dim2.odds/overall.odds)) as pred_odds,
                 dim1.odds as market_odds, dim2.odds as channel_odds
             FROM dim1 CROSS JOIN dim2 CROSS JOIN overall JOIN
                  actual
                  ON dim1.Market = actual.Market AND
                     dim2.Channel = actual.Channel
            ) dims
       ORDER BY Market, Channel
```

This query has four CTEs. The first two calculate the odds for the market and channel separately. The third calculates the odds for the overall data. And the fourth calculates the actual odds, which are used only for comparison purposes. The middle subquery combines these into predicted odds, and the outermost query brings together the data needed for the full calculation.

The expression to estimate the odds multiplies the overall odds by several odds ratios. This can be simplified by combining the overall odds into one expression:

```
POWER(overall.odds, -1) * dim1.odds * dim2.odds as pred_odds
```

The simpler expression is helpful as the model incorporates more attributes.

Naïve Bayesian Model: Scoring and Lift

This section generates scores for the naïve Bayesian model, using the estimates from 2004 to apply to 2005.

Scoring with More Attributes

Adding more dimensions to the naïve Bayesian model is simple. The major change is adding a separate CTE for each dimension and then updating the expression for predicted odds:

```
POWER(overall.odds, 1 - <N>)*dim1.odds* . . . *dimN.odds as pred_odds
```

That is, the overall odds are raised to the power of one minus the number of dimensions and these are then multiplied by the odds along each dimension.

One complication arises when the score set has values with no corresponding odds. This can occur for two reasons. One is that new values appear, from one year to the next. The second is restricting the model to a minimum number of instances for the odds calculation, so some values are missing from the dimensional tables.

Naïve Bayesian models handle missing values quite well, theoretically. If a value is not available along a dimension, the likelihood value for the dimension is simply not used. As with many things, the practice is a bit more detailed than the theory.

A missing dimension is missed in two places:

- The likelihood value is NULL.

- The exponent used for the POWER() function needs to be decreased by one for each missing dimension.

Neither of these is insurmountable; they just require arithmetic and clever query logic.

The first thing is to use LEFT OUTER JOIN rather than JOIN for combining the dimensions tables with the score set. The second is to default the missing odds to one (rather than NULL or zero), so they do not affect the multiplication. The third is to count the number of dimensions that match.

The first is trivial. The second uses the COALESCE() function. The third could use a gargantuan, ugly nested CASE statement. But there is an alternative. Within each dimension subquery, a variable called n is given the value 1. The following expression calculates the number of matching dimensions:

```
COALESCE(dim1.n, 0) + COALESCE(dim2.n, 0) + . . . + COALESCE(dimn.n, 0)
```

Missing values are replaced by zeros, so the sum is the number of matching dimensions.

> **TIP** In a query that has several outer joins, you can count the number that succeed by adding a dummy variable in each subquery (let's call it N) and giving it a value of 1. Then, the expression COALESCE(q1.N, 0) + . . . + COALESCE(qn.N, 0) counts the number of successful joins.

The following query calculates the naïve Bayesian predicted score for two dimensions, channel and market:

```
WITH dim1 as (
    SELECT Market, 1 as n,
           -1 + 1 / (1 - (AVG(CASE WHEN Tenure < 365 AND StopType IS NOT NULL
                                   THEN 1.0 ELSE 0 END))) as odds
    FROM Subscribers
    WHERE YEAR(StartDate) = 2004
    GROUP BY Market
    ),
    dim2 as (
    SELECT Channel, 1 as n,
           -1 + 1 / (1 - (AVG(CASE WHEN Tenure < 365 AND StopType IS NOT NULL
                                   THEN 1.0 ELSE 0 END))) as odds
    FROM Subscribers
    WHERE YEAR(StartDate) = 2004
```

```
    GROUP BY Channel
    ),
    overall as (
    SELECT -1 + 1 / (1 - (AVG(CASE WHEN Tenure < 365 AND StopType IS NOT NULL
                                THEN 1.0 ELSE 0 END))) as odds
    FROM Subscribers
    WHERE YEAR(StartDate) = 2004
    ),
    score as (
    SELECT s.*,
            (CASE WHEN Tenure < 365 AND StopType IS NOT NULL THEN 1.0
                ELSE 0 END) as is1yrstop
    FROM Subscribers s
    WHERE YEAR(StartDate) = 2005
    )
SELECT score.SubscriberId, score.channel, score.market, is1yrstop,
        (POWER(overall.odds,
                1 - (COALESCE(dim1.n, 0) + COALESCE(dim2.n, 0))) *
        COALESCE(dim1.odds,0) * COALESCE(dim2.odds, 0)) as predodds
FROM score CROSS JOIN overall LEFT OUTER JOIN
    dim1
    ON score.Market = dim1.Market LEFT OUTER JOIN
    dim2
    ON score.Channel = dim2.Channel
```

The odds for each dimension use COALESCE(), so the query can handle values that don't match the dimension tables.

Creating a Cumulative Gains Chart

Creating a cumulative gains chart (or ROC chart or calculating AUC) uses the preceding query as a subquery, calculating the percentile based on the predicted odds. For this purpose, the predicted odds and predicted probability are interchangeable because they have the same ordering, and these charts only care about the relative ordering of the scores.

The resulting query is basically the same query used earlier for creating these charts:

```
SELECT percentile, COUNT(*) as numcustomers,
        SUM(is1yrstop) as numactualstops,
        SUM(predrate) as predactualstops,
        AVG(is1yrstop * 1.0) as actualstop, AVG(predrate) as predrate
FROM (SELECT SubscriberId, predrate, is1yrstop,
            CEILING(100 * (ROW_NUMBER() OVER (ORDER BY predrate DESC) - 1) /
                    COUNT(*) OVER ()) as percentile
    FROM (SELECT s.*, 1 - (1 / (1 + predodds)) as predrate
        FROM scored s
        ) s
    ) s
GROUP BY percentile
ORDER BY percentile
```

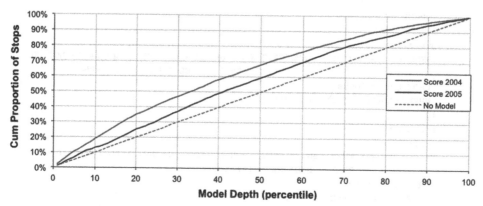

Figure 11-15: This chart shows cumulative gains charts for the naïve Bayesian model on the training set (2004 starts) and on the score set (2005 starts).

This query calculates the percentile based on the predicted score and counts the number of actual stops in each percentile. These are calculated in a CTE, scored, using the logic from the previous query.

The cumulative gains chart in Figure 11-15 shows the cumulative proportion of stops for two score sets. As expected, the better one is for the scores on the model set. The data from 2005 is a more reasonable score set. It demonstrates that the model does still work on data a year later, although not as well.

Comparison of Naïve Bayesian and Lookup Models

Both naïve Bayesian models and lookup models estimate probabilities based on values along dimensions. The two modeling techniques produce exactly the same results for one dimension; the results differ for multiple dimensions.

The lookup approach is a brute force approach that breaks the data into smaller and smaller cells. As the number of cells grows—either because there are more dimensions or because each dimension has more possible values—the cells become smaller and smaller. The data is literally partitioned among the cells. This means that the number of cells needs to be limited in some way, probably by using few dimensions that take on few values (as in the subscription data).

By contrast, naïve Bayesian models use all the data to estimate values for each dimension. The data is not divided and subdivided over and over. Instead, the approach uses probability theory and a reasonable assumption to combine the values along the dimensions into an estimated prediction. The assumption often works well in practice, despite the fact that dimensions are almost never completely independent.

Of course, both approaches are making another, unstated assumption. The assumption is that the past tells us about the future. As we saw in the cumulative gains charts that compare the two values, the models do work, but they do not work as well on the data being scored as they do on the data used to build the model.

Lessons Learned

A data mining model takes inputs and produces an output, which is typically a prediction or estimation of some value. There are two major processes involved with models. The first is training or building the model. The second is applying the model to new data.

SQL provides a good basis for learning the basics about data mining. Although this may seem surprising, some powerful techniques are really more about manipulating data than about fancy statistical techniques. The GROUP BY operation in SQL is analogous to creating a model (both summarize data). The JOIN operation is analogous to scoring a model.

This chapter discusses several different types of models. The first is a look-alike model, where the model score indicates how close one example is to another. For instance, the model score might indicate how similar zip codes are to the zip code that has highest market penetration.

Lookup models are another type. These create a lookup table, so the process of scoring the model is the process of looking up values. The values might be the most popular product, or the probability of someone stopping, or something else. Although any number of dimensions could be used to create the lookup table, the data gets partitioned into smaller and smaller pieces, meaning that the values in the table become more uncertain or even empty when there are more dimensions.

Naïve Bayesian models address this shortcoming. They use some basic probability theory along with Bayes' formula, an important formula in probability proven almost 300 years ago. This approach makes it possible to calculate lookup tables along each dimension separately, and then to combine the values together. The big advantage to the naïve Bayesian approach is the ability to handle many, many dimensions and missing values.

Naïve Bayesian models make an assumption about the data. This assumption is that the different dimensions are independent (in the probabilistic sense). Although this assumption is not true when working with business data, the results from the model are often still useful. In a sense, naïve Bayesian models produce an expected value for a probability, similar to the way that the chi-square approach calculates an expected value along the way to calculating the chi-square measure.

Evaluating models is as important as creating them. A cumulative gains chart shows how well a binary response model is performing. Its cousin, the ROC chart, has a similar shape. The area under the ROC curve, called AUC, is a valuable measure of how good a model is. An average value chart shows the performance of a model estimating a number. And a classification chart shows the performance of classification models.

This chapter has introduced modeling in the context of SQL and working with large databases. The traditional way of introducing modeling is through linear regression, covered in the next chapter.

CHAPTER

12

The Best-Fit Line: Linear Regression Models

The previous chapter introduced data mining ideas using various data mining techniques well suited to databases, such as look-alike models, lookup tables, and naïve Bayesian models. This chapter extends these ideas to the realm of the most traditional statistical modeling technique: linear regression and best-fit lines.

Unlike the techniques in the previous chapter, linear regression requires that input and target variables all be numeric. The results of the regression are coefficients in a mathematical formula. A formal treatment of linear regression involves lots of mathematics and proofs. This chapter steers away from an overly theoretical approach.

In addition to providing a basis for statistical modeling, linear regression has many applications. Regressions—especially best-fit lines—are a great way to investigate relationships between different numeric quantities. The examples in this chapter include estimating potential product penetration in zip codes, studying price elasticity (investigating the relationship between product prices and sales volumes), and quantifying the effect of the initial monthly fee on yearly stop rates.

The simplest linear regression models are best-fit lines that have one input and one target. Such two-variable models are readily understood visually, using scatter plots. In fact, Excel builds linear regression models into charts via the best-fit trend line, one of six built-in types of trend lines.

Excel can explicitly calculate best-fit lines in the spreadsheet as well as in the charts. The most general function introduces a new class of Excel functions that return multiple values in multiple cells—an extension of the array functions introduced in Chapter 4.

Apart from the built-in functions, Excel offers two other ways to calculate the linear regression formulas. These methods are more powerful than the built-in functions. One is a direct method, using somewhat complicated formulas for the parameters in the model. The other uses a capability provided by the Solver add-in to iteratively estimate the parameters. Solver is a general-purpose tool included with Excel that searches for optimal solutions to chains of calculations set up in a spreadsheet. Its ability to build linear regression models is just one example of its power.

Measuring how well the best-fit line fits the data introduces the idea of correlation, which fortunately is easy to calculate. As with many statistical measures, correlation does what it does well, but it comes with some warnings. Over-interpreting correlation values is easy but can lead to erroneous conclusions.

Multiple regression extends "best-fit line" regression by using more than one input variable. Fortunately, multiple regression is quite feasible in Excel. Unfortunately, it does not produce pretty scatter plots, because there are too many dimensions.

SQL can also be used to build basic linear regression models with one or even two input variables. Unfortunately, standard SQL does not have built-in functions to do this, so the equations have to be entered explicitly (and SQL has no equivalent of Solver). These equations become more and more complicated as more variables are added, as we'll see with the two-variable example at the end of this chapter. The chapter begins not with complicated SQL statements, but with the best-fit line, which enables us to visualize linear regression.

The Best-Fit Line

The simplest case of linear regression has one input variable and one target variable. This case is best illustrated with scatter plots, making it readily understandable visually and giving rise to the name "best-fit line."

Tenure and Amount Paid

The first example is for a set of customers in a subscription-based business, comparing the tenure of each customer with the total amount the customer has paid. The longer customers remain active, the more they pay—an evident relationship between the two values.

Figure 12-1 shows the resulting best-fit line, with the tenure on the X-axis and the amount paid on the Y-axis. The chart clearly shows a relationship; both the points and the best-fit line start low and rise upward to the right.

One way to use the best-fit line is to estimate how much a customer would pay if he or she survived to a given tenure. A typical customer with tenure of 360 days should pay about $192.30. This amount might influence acquisition budgets.

This simple example shows the virtues of the best-fit line. It is a good way to visualize data and to summarize the relationship between two variables. It can also be useful for estimating values.

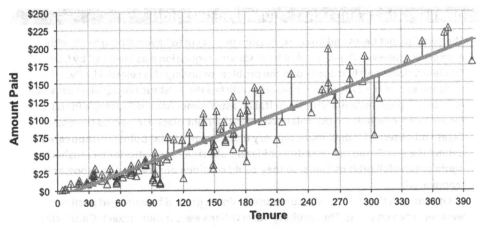

Figure 12-1: This chart shows the best-fit line for a set of data points showing the relationship between customers' tenures and the amount they have paid.

TIP   The best-fit line can be seen in an Excel chart by selecting a series, right-clicking the series, and adding a trend line. The linear best-fit line makes it possible to see trends in the data.

Properties of the Best-fit Line

Of all these possible lines that go near the data points, the best-fit line is a very specific one. Figure 12-1 shows the vertical line segments, connecting each observed data point to the point on the line directly above or beneath it. The best-fit line is the one where the vertical distances between the observed point and the line are as small as possible—for some definition of "small."

What Does Best-Fit Mean?

The specific definition of best-fit is that the line minimizes the sum of the squares of the distances between the observed data points and the line, along the vertical dimension. This type of regression is also called *ordinary least squares* (OLS) regression.

The sum of squares results in relatively simple calculations for the coefficients of the line. These simpler calculations were feasible before the era of computers, as explained in the aside "Dwarf Planets and Least Squares Regression." After centuries of use, the technique and models are well understood. There are a plethora of measures to understand the models and to determine when and whether they are working.

The definition of the best-fit line uses the distance along the Y-dimension (all the line segments are vertical instead of being horizontal, for instance). Why the Y-dimension? The simple answer is almost obvious: the Y-value is the target, the thing we are trying to estimate.

DWARF PLANETS AND LEAST SQUARES REGRESSION

The dwarf planet Ceres and linear regression may seem to have nothing to do with each other. However, the method of least squares regression was invented by Carl Friederich Gauss and first applied to the problem of finding this celestial body.

At the end of the 1700s, astronomers predicted the existence of a planet between Mars and Jupiter. In January 1801, an Italian astronomer named Giuseppe Piazzi discovered a new body in the solar system in the right place. He named the object Ceres and observed it until mid-February of that year. At that point it disappeared behind the sun. Based on a handful of Piazzi's observations, astronomers rushed to figure out the full orbit of Ceres, so they could continue observations as soon as it reappeared.

Of course, in those days, telescopes used mirrors ground by hand and positions were recorded on paper. The resulting observations were rather inexact. Gauss, who was just starting his career, recognized several key aspects of the problem, some involving astronomy and physics. The most innovative part dealt with the inaccuracy in the measurements: Gauss found the orbit (an ellipse) that was closest to the observed positions, defining closest as the sum of the squares of the distances from the orbit to the observed positions.

Based on the observed positions, Gauss correctly estimated the orbit and accurately predicted when and where Ceres would reappear. By the fall of 1801, it did reappear, very close to where Gauss predicted—and his prediction was better than the predictions of much more established astronomers. This reinforced the strength of Gauss's methods.

This history is interesting for several reasons. First, Gauss is considered by some to be the greatest mathematician ever, for his contributions to a wide range of subjects, including statistics. It is also interesting because the first problem was not a linear regression problem as explained in the text. Gauss was trying to estimate an ellipse rather than a line.

The third reason is practical. Ordinary least squares regression uses the sum of the distances from the line, rather than the distances themselves. Perhaps this is because the distance is the square root of some quantity. Hence, calculating the distance squared is easier than calculating distance. In a world where all calculations have to be done by hand, Gauss may have preferred the simpler calculation that ignores taking the final square root.

Although the best-fit line is (almost always) unique, it is worth pointing out that slight variations in the definition result in different lines. If another distance were used, such as the horizontal distance, the resulting "best-fit" line would be different. If the lengths of the line segments were combined in a way other than by taking the sum of the squares, say by taking the sum of the distances instead, the resulting line would also be different. The traditional definition of the best-fit line is quite useful because it is so well understood, is calculated relatively easily, and captures important features of data.

Formula for Line

The best-fit line is a line, and lines are defined by a formula that readers may recall from high school math:

```
Y = m * X + b
```

In this equation, m is the slope of the line and b is the Y-intercept, which is where the line crosses the Y-axis. When the slope is positive, the values of Y increase as the values of X increase (positive correlation). When the slope is negative, the line goes down instead (negative correlation). When the slope is zero, the line is horizontal. The goal of linear regression is to find the values of m and b that minimize the sum of the squares of vertical distance between the line and the observed points.

The best-fit line in Figure 12-1 has a formula:

```
<amount paid> = $0.5512 * <tenure> - $8.8558
```

This line defines a simple relationship between the two variables: tenure and amount paid. They are positively correlated (meaning that amount paid goes up as tenure goes up) because the coefficient on tenure is positive. One easy way to calculate the values m and b in Excel is using the SLOPE() and INTERCEPT() functions.

There is nothing special about calling the slope m and the intercept b. In fact, statisticians have different names for them. They use the Greek letter beta for the coefficients, calling the Y-intercept ß$_0$ and the slope ß$_1$. This notation has the advantage of being readily extensible to more coefficients.

Renaming the coefficients (albeit for a good reason) is not the only oddity in standard statistical terminology. From perspective of statistics, the Xs and Ys are constants, the betas are variables, and lines do not have to be straight. The aside "Some Strange Statistical Terminology" explains this in more detail.

Expected Value

For a given value of X, the equation for the line can be used to calculate a value of Y. This *expected value* represents what the model "knows" about the relationship between X and Y, applied to a particular value of X.

Table 12-1 shows the expected values for various tenure values shown in Figure 12-1. The expected values can be higher or lower than the actual values. They can also be out-of-range, in the sense that a negative amount paid makes no sense (and the expected values for small tenures are negative). On the other hand, all values of tenure have expected values, making it possible to use the line to estimate the value of a customer at any tenure.

SOME STRANGE STATISTICAL TERMINOLOGY

In the equation for the line, the Xs and Ys are normally thought of as being variables and the coefficients as being constants. That is because we are thinking of using the line to estimate a Y-value given an X-value.

In statistics, the problem is estimating the coefficients, so the language of statistical modeling turns this terminology upside down. The Xs and Ys are constants because they refer to known data points (perhaps with an uncertainty in the measurement). The data may have two data points or two million, but for all of them the X- and Y-values are known. On the other hand, the challenge in statistical modeling is to find the line, by calculating coefficients that minimize the sum of the squares of the distances between the points and the line. The coefficients need to be solved for; hence, they are the "variables."

This inverse terminology actually explains why the following are also examples of "linear" models although the formulas do not look like the formula for a line:

$$Y = ß_1 * X^2 + ß_0$$
$$\ln(Y) = ß_1 * X + ß_0$$
$$\ln(Y) = ß_1 * X^2 + ß_0$$

These are linear because they are linear in the coefficients. The funky functions of Xs and Ys do not make a difference. The coefficients are the important part. We know the values of X and Y; the coefficients are unknown.

A good way to think about this is that all the observed data could be transformed. For example, in the first example, the X-value could be squared and called Z:

$$Z = X^2$$

In terms of Y and Z, the first equation becomes:

$$Y = ß_1 * Z + ß_0$$

This is a linear relationship between Y and Z. And Z is just as known as X is because it is the square of the X value.

Table 12-1: Some Expected Values for Best-Fit Line in Figure 12-1

TENURE	EXPECTED $$ (0.55*TENURE − $8.86)	ACTUAL $$	DIFFERENCE
5	−$6.10	$1.65	$7.75
8	−$4.45	$0.90	$5.35
70	$29.72	$15.75	−$13.97
140	$68.30	$91.78	$23.48
210	$106.88	$71.45	−$35.43
365	$192.30	None	N/A

The expected value can be calculated directly from two columns of X- and Y-values using the FORECAST() function in Excel. This function takes three arguments: the value to make the estimate for, and ranges for the Y-values and the X-values. It returns the expected value, using a linear regression formula. FORECAST() applies the model, without producing any other information to determine how good the model is or what the model looks like.

One rule of thumb when using best-fit lines is to use the line for interpolation rather than extrapolation. In English, this means calculating expected values only for values of X that are in the range of the data used to calculate the line.

Error (Residuals)

The expected value generally differs from the actual value because the line does not perfectly fit the data. The difference between the two is called the *error* or *residual*. When the residuals are calculated for the best-fit line using the data used to define the line, their sum is zero. The best-fit line is not the only line with this property, but it also has the property that the sum of the squares of the residuals is as small as possible.

There is a wealth of statistical theory about residuals. For instance, a model is considered a good fit on data when the residuals follow a normal distribution (which was discussed in Chapter 3). The residuals should be independent with respect to the X-values.

Figure 12-2 plots the residuals from the data in Figure 12-1 against the X-values. As a general rule, the residuals should not exhibit any particular pattern. In particular, long sequences of positive or negative residuals indicate that the model is missing something. Also, the residuals should not get bigger as the X-values get bigger.

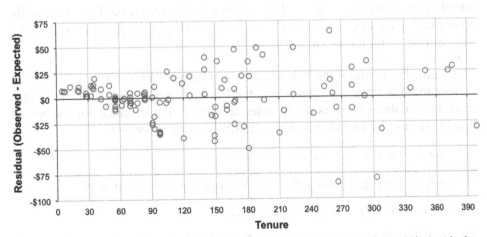

Figure 12-2: This chart shows the residuals for the data in Figure 12-1. Notice that the residuals tend to get larger as the X-values get larger.

These residuals are pretty good, but not perfect. For instance, the initial residuals are almost all positive and relatively small. This is because the expected values are negative for small values of X, but actual values are never negative. That the model is not perfect should not be surprising because it takes only one variable into account. Although important, other things also affect customers' total payments.

TIP Creating a scatter plot of the residuals and the X-values in the model is one way to see if the model is doing a good job. In general, the scatter plot should look random, with no long sequences of positive or negative values.

Preserving Averages

One very nice characteristic of best-fit lines (and linear regression models in general) is that they preserve averages: The average of the expected values of the original data is the same as the average of the observed values. Geometrically, this implies that all best-fit lines go through a particular point. This point is the average of the X-values and the average of the Y-values of the data used to build the model.

In practical terms, this property means that best-fit lines preserve some key characteristics of the data used to build them. Applying the model does not "move" the center of the data. So, taking the average of a large number of expected values (such as for all customers) is usually a fairly accurate estimate of the average of the actual values, even if the individual estimates vary significantly from the actual values.

Inverse Model

Another nice feature of best-fit lines is that the inverse model can be readily constructed. That is, given a value of Y, the corresponding value of X can be determined using the following formula:

```
X = (Y - b) / m
```

This formula calculates the value of X for any given value of Y.

Note that the inverse model calculated this way is different from the inverse model calculated by reversing the roles of X and Y. For instance, for the best-fit line in Figure 12-1 (on page 563), the "mathematical" inverse is:

```
<tenure> = 1.8145 * <tenure> + 16.0687
```

However, reversing the roles of X and Y generates a different line:

```
<tenure> = 1.5029 * <tenure> + 35.6518
```

The fact that these two lines are different is interesting from a theoretical perspective. Reversing the roles of X and Y is equivalent to using the horizontal distance, rather than the vertical distance to calculate the best-fit line. For practical purposes, if we need the inverse relationship, then either works well enough.

WARNING   The inverse relationship for a linear regression model is easy to calculate from the model equation. However, this is not the same as building another model by swapping the X-values and the Y-values.

Beware of the Data

A model is only as good as the data used to build it. There are many ways of understanding how well a model fits a particular set of data. Alas, there are many fewer ways of determining whether the right data is being used for the model.

The data used for the scatter plot in Figure 12-1 (on page 563) is missing an important subset of customers; the data excludes customers who never paid. Hence, the relationship between payment and tenure is only for the customers who make a payment, not for everyone.

Almost half the customers in this sample never make a payment, because the customers come from the worst channel. When these freeloading customers are included, they have a small effect on the best-fit line, as shown in Figure 12-3. The non-payers are shown as the circles along the X-axis, and the best-fit line is the dashed line. The line has shifted a bit downward and become a bit steeper as it attempts to get closer to the zero values on the left.

Before diving into the contents of the chart, it is worth commenting on how this chart is created. Although only two series are visible, the chart has three. One is for all customers and is used to generate the dotted best-fit line. The

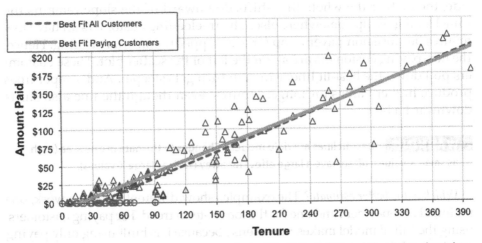

Figure 12-3: When non-paying customers are included, the best-fit line shifts a bit to the right and becomes a bit steeper.

trend line for this series is visible, although the points are not. Another series is for the paying customers, shown in Figure 12-1. The best-fit line for this dataset is the solid gray line. Then, the third series is the non-payers, and is used to show the customers who never paid. The best-fit lines are also given names, to make them clearer in the legend.

The chart has 226 customers, of whom 108 are non-payers (48%), and, of course, including them changes the line. *What is the expected revenue for a new customer who survives for one year?* For the original data, the answer was $192.30. When all customers including non-payers are included, the value goes up slightly to $194.41.

Huh? The expected value has gone up by including customers *who did not pay*. This is counterintuitive. One could argue that linear regressions are not good for extrapolation. However, this example does not extrapolate beyond the range of the data because the data extends beyond 365 days (although 365 days is among the higher tenure values). One could argue that the values are close and within some margin of error, which is undoubtedly true for just a couple of hundred data points. The irony is that we could add more and more non-paying customers to obtain almost any value at the one-year mark.

With a bit more thought, the issue goes from counterintuitive to absurd. Consider using the model to estimate revenue for customers who survive for one year. If one hundred customers start and are expected to stay for one year, what is their expected revenue during the first year? Using the model that includes all customers—payers and non-payers—the estimate is $19,441. However, building the model only on customers who pay reduces the estimate to $19,230. Although the difference is small, it raises the question: How does including non-paying customers increase the one-year estimated revenue? And, as noted earlier, additional non-paying customers could push the estimate up even more.

Something curious is happening. A line is rigid. If it goes down on one side, then either the whole line shifts downward (if the slope remains the same), or it goes up somewhere else. The freeloading customers all have low tenures because non-payers stop (or are stopped) soon after starting. Hence, the non-paying customers are all on the left of the scatter plot. These customers pull down the best-fit line, which in turn gets steeper. And steeper lines produce higher values for longer tenures, even though the line also shifts downward a bit.

WARNING Best-fit lines are rigid models. Changes to the data in one area (such as small X-values) often have a large effect far away (such as large X-values).

Which is the better estimate? The examples show different factors at work, one for initial non-payment and one for the longer-term trend. For paying customers, using the initial model makes more sense because it is built using only paying customers. It is not distracted by the non-payers.

The purpose of this example is to stress the importance of choosing the right data for modeling. Be aware of local effects of data on the resulting model.

Trend Lines in Charts

Best-fit lines are one of several types of trend lines supported in Excel's charts. The purpose of trend lines is to see patterns that may not be apparent when looking at disparate points. Trend lines are only available in Excel when the data has one input and one target variable. Nevertheless, they can be quite useful.

Best-Fit Line in Scatter Plots

A powerful and simple way to calculate a linear regression is directly within a chart using the best-fit trend line, as already shown in Figures 12-1 and 12-3. To add the best-fit trend line:

1. Left-click the series to select it.
2. Right-click and choose "Add Trendline …." to bring up the "Format Trendline" dialog box.
3. Choose the "Linear" option on the upper-left side.

At this point, you can exit the dialog box, and the best-fit line appears between the first and the last X-values.

The line appears in the chart as a solid black line. Because the trend line is generally less important than the data, change its format to a lighter color or dotted pattern. When the chart has more than one series, make the color of the trend line similar to the color of the series. As with any other series, just right-click the line to change its format.

TIP When placing a trend line in a scatter plot or a bubble plot, change its format to be lighter than the data points but similar in color, so the trend line is visible but does not dominate the chart.

The "Options" tab of the "Format Trendline" dialog box has several useful options:

- To give the trend line a name that appears in the chart legend, click by "Custom" and type in the name.
- By default, the trend line is only for the range of X-values in the data. To extend beyond this range, use the "Forecast" area and specify the number of units "Forward" after the last data point.
- To extend the range to values before the first data point, use the "Forecast" area and specify the number of units "Backward" before the first data point.
- To see the formula, choose "Display equation on chart." Once the equation appears, it is easy to modify the font and move it around.
- To see how well the model fits the data, choose "Display R-squared value on chart." The R^2 value is discussed later in this chapter.

If you forget to add options when the trend line is created, double-click the trend line and choose "Format Trendline" to bring up the dialog box. One nifty feature is that the trend line itself can be formatted to be invisible, so only the equation appears on the chart. Also note that when the data in the chart changes (even just by using a data filter), the trend line changes as well.

Logarithmic, Power, and Exponential Trend Curves

Three types of trend curves are variations on the best-fit line, the difference being the shape used for the curve is not a line:

- Logarithmic: $Y = \ln(\beta_1 * X + \beta_0)$
- Power: $Y = \beta_0 * X^{\beta_1}$
- Exponential: $Y = \exp(\beta_1 * X + \beta_0)$

Fitting these curves has the same spirit as linear regression because all three formulas have two coefficients that are analogous to the slope and intercept values for a line. Each of these curves has its own particular properties. The first two, the logarithmic and power curves, require that the X-values be positive. The second two always produce Y-values that are positive (Excel does not allow the coefficient β_0 to be negative for the power trend line).

The logarithmic curve decreases slowly, much more slowly than a line does. So, doubling the X-value only increases the Y-value by a constant. The left side of Figure 12-4 shows the logarithmic trend line for the payment data. Because the data has a linear relationship, the logarithmic curve is not a particularly good fit.

The logarithmic trend line and the best-fit line are related to each other. Changing the X-axis to be on a "logarithmic" scale (by clicking the "Logarithmic Scale" button on the "Scale" tab of the "Format axis" dialog box) makes the logarithmic curve look like a line. Figure 12-4 shows a side-by-side comparison of the same data, with one chart having the normal scale on the X-axis and the other, the logarithmic scale.

The exponential curve increases very rapidly, much more rapidly than a line. Its behavior is similar to the logarithmic trend line, but with respect to the Y-axis rather than the X-axis. That is, when the Y-axis has a logarithmic scale, the exponential curve looks like a line.

The power curve increases more slowly than the exponential. It looks like a line when both the X-axis and the Y-axis have a logarithmic scale. It also looks like a line under normal scaling when $\beta 1$ is close to one.

One way of thinking about these trend lines is that they are best-fit lines, but the data is transformed. This is, in fact, the method used to calculate the curves in Excel. As we'll see the later in the chapter, this method is useful practically, but it is an approximation. The results are a bit different from directly calculating

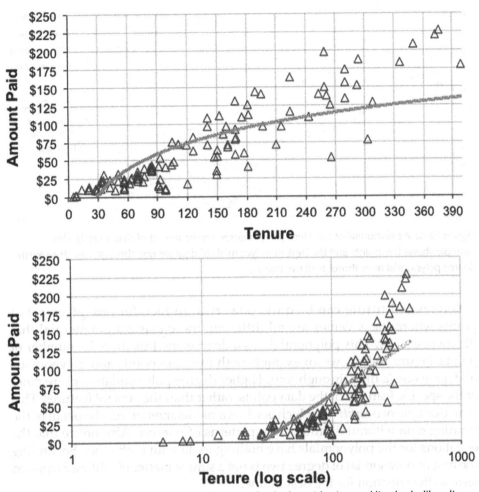

Figure 12-4: When the X-axis has a logarithmic scale, the logarithmic trend line looks like a line.

the actual best-fit curves. Excel's trend curves are good, but not the theoretically correct best-fit curves.

Polynomial Trend Curves

The polynomial curve is a bit more complicated because polynomial curves can have more than two coefficients. The form for these curves is:

- Polynomial: $Y = \beta_n * X^n + \ldots + \beta_2 * X^2 + \beta_1 * X + \beta_0$

The degree of the polynomial is the largest value of *n* in the equation, which is input into the box labeled "Order" on the "Type" tab of the "Format Trendline" dialog box.

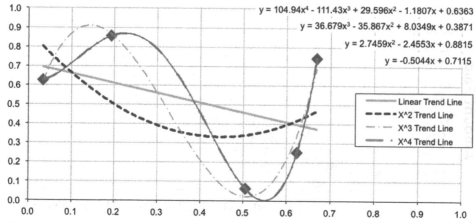

$y = 104.94x^4 - 111.43x^3 + 29.596x^2 - 1.1807x + 0.6363$

$y = 36.679x^3 - 35.867x^2 + 8.0349x + 0.3871$

$y = 2.7459x^2 - 2.4553x + 0.8815$

$y = -0.5044x + 0.7115$

Linear Trend Line
X^2 Trend Line
X^3 Trend Line
X^4 Trend Line

Figure 12-5: A polynomial of sufficiently high degree can fit any set of data exactly. This example shows five points and the best-fit polynomials of degrees one through four. The fourth degree polynomial goes through all five points.

Polynomial fitting can be quite powerful. In fact, for any given set of points where the X-values are all different, there exists a polynomial that fits them exactly. This polynomial has a degree one less than the number of points. Figure 12-5 shows an example with five data points and polynomials of degree one (a line) through four. Higher degree polynomials capture more of the specific features of the data points, rather than the general features. This is an example of *overfitting*, which is when a model memorizes the detail of the training data without finding larger patterns of interest. Also notice that the equations for the polynomials have nothing to do with each other. So, finding the best-fit polynomial of degree two is not a simple matter of adding a squared term to the equation for the best-fit line.

When the order of the polynomial is odd, the curve starts high and goes low or starts low and goes high. The typical example is the line, which either slants upward or downward, but all odd degree polynomials have this property.

Polynomials of even degree either start and end high or start and end low. These have the property that there is either a minimum or maximum value, among the values. For some optimization applications, having a minimum or maximum is a very useful property.

> **TIP** When fitting polynomial trend curve to data points, be sure that the degree of the polynomial is much smaller than the number of data points. This reduces the likelihood of overfitting.

Moving Average

After the best-fit line, probably the most common type of trend line is the moving average. These are often used when the horizontal axis is time because they wash away variation within a week or within a month.

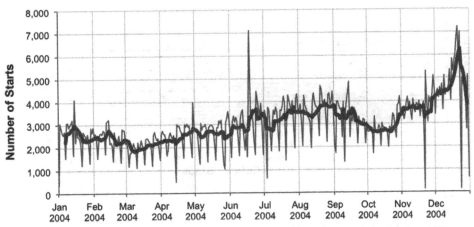

Figure 12-6: Starts by day are very jagged, because there are few starts on the weekend. The 7-day moving average does a better job of showing the trend during the year.

Figure 12-6 shows starts by day for the subscription data. Weekly variation dominates the chart because human eyes tend to follow the maximum and minimum values. The peaks might obscure what's really happening. The trend line shows the 7-day moving average, in order to eliminate the within-week variation and highlight the longer-term trend.

Moving averages can sometimes be used to spot subtle patterns. This example looks at the relationship between the proportion of a zip code that has graduated from college and the proportion on public assistance, for zip codes in Minnesota. This data comes from ZipCensus, using the following query:

```
SELECT zcta5, pctbachelorsormore, pctnumhhpubassist
FROM ZipCensus
WHERE stab = 'MN' AND pctbachelorsormore IS NOT NULL AND
      pctnumhhpubassist IS NOT NULL
ORDER BY zcta5
```

The scatter plot in Figure 12-7 does not show an obvious pattern, although it does seem that zip codes where most adults have a college degree have relatively few residents on public assistance.

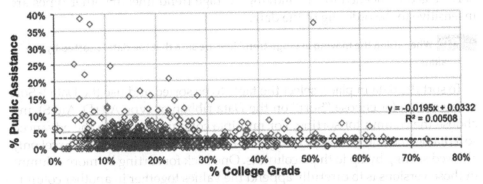

Figure 12-7: The relationship between the proportion of a zip code with a college education and the proportion on public assistance in the state of Minnesota is not obvious.

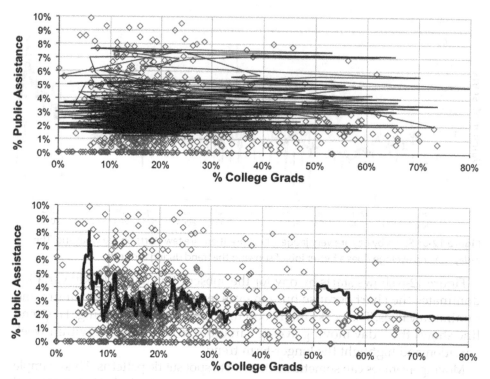

Figure 12-8: A moving average can find patterns in the data, as shown in the lower chart where the X-values are sorted. However, if the data is not sorted, the moving average can be a meaningless scribble.

The top chart in Figure 12-8 shows one of the dangers when adding a moving average trend line. This chart applies the moving average directly to the data as pulled from the database, producing a zigzag line that bounces back and forth and makes no sense. The lower chart fixes this problem by sorting the data by the X-values. A pattern is visible, although the relationship is not a line. As zip codes have more college graduates, they seem to have fewer households on public assistance.

In general, when using moving averages, make sure that the data is sorted. Sorting is only needed for the moving average trend line; the other types are insensitive to the ordering of the data.

TIP When using the moving average trend line, be sure that the data is sorted by the X-values.

To sort the data in place, select the table to be sorted and use the Data ➤ Sort menu option (or choose "Sort" on the Data ribbon or type Alt+D, Alt+S) and choose the column for sorting. For multiple columns, bring up the advanced sort dialog and add new keys using the "+" option. Older versions of Excel only allowed sorting by up to three columns. One trick for sorting by more columns in those versions is to carefully append the values together in another column.

Best-Fit Using the LINEST() Function

Trend lines are not the only way to do linear regression in Excel. The function LINEST() provides the full functionality of linear regression, including calculating various statistics that describe the goodness of fit, such as:

- The R^2 value
- The standard error for the coefficients
- The standard error for the Y-estimate
- The degrees of freedom
- The sum of squares
- The sum of the squares of the residuals

This chapter discusses the first of these because it is the most practical. The remaining are more advanced statistical measures, which are more appropriately discussed in a statistics book.

Returning Values in Multiple Cells

Before moving to the statistics and the calculation of these values, a question arises: How can a single function such as LINEST() can return more than one value? All the functions we have seen so far reside in only a single cell and the return value goes into the cell. In fact, this seems like the intuitive behavior of what a "function" does.

The answer is array functions, as discussed in the aside "Excel Functions Returning More Than One Value." The call to an array function that returns multiple values looks like other function calls:

```
= LINEST(<y - values>, <x - values>, TRUE, TRUE)
```

The first argument is the range of cells containing the target (typically a column of values); the second argument is the range containing the input values (typically one or more adjacent columns). The final two arguments are flags. The first flag says to do a normal linear regression (when FALSE or zero, this would force the constant β_0 to have the value of zero, which is sometimes useful). The final flag says to calculate various statistics along with the coefficients.

Although this is an Excel formula, it is not entered in quite the same way as other Excel formulas. First, the formula is entered for multiple cells rather than just one, so select the cells and then type in the formula. In this particular case, the resulting values are in ten cells, two across by five down. The function always returns values in five rows (when the last argument is TRUE) and one column for each coefficient. With one column of X-values, there are two coefficients, one for the X and one for the constant.

Array formulas are entered using Ctrl+Shift+Enter rather than just Enter. Excel shows the formula surrounded by curly braces ("{" and "}") to indicate that it is an array formula. These curly braces are not typed in when the formula is entered.

Once the formula is in place, it can only be modified by highlighting all the cells where it is defined. Attempts to modify a single cell in the array cause an error: "You cannot change part of an array." Similarly, removing the formula requires selecting all the cells in the formula and then hitting the Delete key or right clicking and choosing "Clear Contents."

> **WARNING**   When you try to change one cell in an array of cells that has an array function, Excel returns an error. Select the whole array of cells to delete or modify the formula.

Calculating Expected Values

Although staring at the coefficients and statistics that describe a linear regression model may be interesting and informative, probably the most important thing to do with a model is to apply it to new data. Because `LINEST()` produces coefficients for a line, it is simple enough to apply the model using the formula:

```
= $D$2 * A2 + $D$3
```

where `$D$2` and `$D$3` contain the coefficients calculated by `LINEST()`. Notice that the last coefficient is the constant.

Excel offers several other ways of calculating the coefficients. For instance, the formula produced in a chart for the best-fit line is the same as the one calculated by `LINEST()`. In addition, the following formulas also calculate the expected value for a line that has one input variable:

```
= SLOPE(<y - values>, <x - values>) * A2 + INTERCEPT(<y - values>, <x - values>)
= FORECAST(A2, <y - values>, <x - values>)
= TREND(<y - values>, <x - values>, A2, TRUE)
```

The first method calculates the slope and intercept separately, using the appropriately named functions `SLOPE()` and `INTERCEPT()`. The second and third use two functions that are almost equivalent. The only difference is that `TREND()` takes a final argument specifying whether or not to force the Y-intercept to be zero. The advantage of using the formula explicitly with `LINEST()` is that it generalizes to more variables. The advantage to the other methods is that all the calculations fit in one cell.

EXCEL FUNCTIONS RETURNING MORE THAN ONE VALUE

Chapter 4 introduced array functions as a way of performing complicated arithmetic on columns of numbers. For instance, array functions can combine the functionality of IF() and SUM(). Array functions not only have the ability to accept arrays of cells as inputs, they can also return arrays of values. In fact, almost any Excel function can be used in this fashion.

Consider a simple situation, where columns A and B each contain 100 numbers and each cell in column C contains a formula that adds the values in the same row in columns A and B. Cells in column C have formulas that look like:

```
= A1 + B1
= A2 + B2
. . .
= A100 + B100
```

The formula is repeated on every row; typically, the first formula is typed on the first row and then copied down using Ctrl+D.

An alternative method of expressing this calculation is to use an array function. After selecting the first 100 rows in column C, the array function can be entered as:

```
= A1:A100 + B1:B100
```

And then completed using Ctrl+Shift+Enter, rather than just Enter. Excel recognizes this as an array function and puts curly braces around the formula:

```
{= A1:A100 + B1:B100}
```

All 100 cells have exactly the same function.

Excel figures out that the range of 100 cells in the A column matches the 100 cells in the B column and this also matches the 100 cells in the C column containing the array formula. Because all these ranges match, Excel iterates over the values in the cell ranges. So the formula is equivalent to C1 containing A1 + B1 and C2 containing A2 + B2 and so on to C100.

This simple example of an array formula is not particularly useful, because in this case (and many similar cases), the appropriate formula can simply be copied down the column. One advantage of array formulas is that the formula is only stored once rather than once for each cell. This can make a difference when the function is being applied to thousands of rows and the overall size of the Excel file is an issue.

A handful of functions are designed to work as array functions because they return values in arrays of cells. This chapter discusses LINEST(), which is one such function. A similar function, LOGEST(), is also an array function. It fits an exponential curve to data, rather than a line.

Other examples of array functions are those that operate on matrixes, such as TRANSPOSE(), MINVERSE(), and MMULT().

LINEST() for Logarithmic, Exponential, and Power Curves

The logarithmic, exponential, and power curves are three types of trend lines related to the best-fit line, and these formulas can be approximated using LINEST() as well. The results are not exact, but they are useful.

The key is to transform the X-values, Y-values, or both using logs and exponential functions. To understand how this works, recall how logarithms and exponentiation work. These functions are inverses of each other, so EXP(LN(<any number>)) is the original number (when the number is positive). A useful property of logarithms is that the sum of the logs of two numbers is the same as the log of the product of the numbers.

The first example shows how to calculate the coefficients for the logarithmic curve by transforming the variables. The idea is to calculate the best-fit line for the X-values and the exponentiation of the Y-values. The resulting equation is:

```
EXP(Y) = ß₁ * X + ß₀
```

By taking the logarithm of both sides, this equation is equivalent to the following:

```
Y = LN(ß₁ * X + ß₀)
```

This is the formula for the logarithmic trend line. The coefficients calculated with the transformed Y-values are the same as the coefficients calculated in the chart.

The transformation for the exponential is similar. Instead of using EXP(Y), use LN(Y), so the resulting best-fit equation is for:

```
LN(Y) = ß₁ * X + ß₀
```

When "undoing" the log by taking the exponential, the formula is very similar to the formula for the exponential trend line:

```
Y = EXP(ß₁ * X + ß₀) = EXP(ß₀) * EXP(ß₁ * X)
```

The difference is that the $ß_0$ coefficient produced this way is the log of the coefficient given in the chart.

Finally, the transformation for the power curve uses the log of both the X-values and the Y-values:

```
LN(Y) = ß₁ * LN(X) + ß₀ = LN(EXP(ß₀) * X^ß₁)
```

Undoing the log on both sides produces:

```
Y = EXP(ß₀) * X^ß₁
```

The only difference between these coefficients and the ones in the chart is that the $ß_0$ calculated using LINEST() is the logarithm of the value calculated in the chart.

The Excel function LOGEST() fits the exponential curve directly. The coefficients are related to the coefficients in the charts. The $ß_0$ is the same, but log of $ß_1$ is the corresponding coefficient in the chart.

When calculated using any of these methods—in the charts, using LOGEST(), or by transforming the original data—the resulting coefficients are only approximations of the correct values. The problem is that transforming the Y-value also changes the distance metric. Hence, what is the "best-fit" for the transformed data may not quite be the "best-fit" on the original data, although the results are usually similar enough. The transformation method does make it possible to fit these curves in a "quick and dirty" way. To obtain more exact answers in Excel, use the Solver method (described later in this chapter) or a statistics tool.

> **WARNING**   In Excel, the exponential, logarithmic, and power curve trend lines, as well as LOGEST(), are approximately correct. The coefficients are not optimal, but they are generally close enough.

Measuring Goodness of Fit Using R^2

How good is the best-fit line? Understanding how well a model works can be as important as building the model in the first place. Scatter plots of some data look a lot like a line; in such cases, the best-fit line fits the data quite well. In other cases, the data looks like a big blob, and the best-fit line is not very descriptive. The R^2 value provides a measure to distinguish these situations.

The R^2 Value

R^2 measures how well the best-fit line fits the data. When the line does not fit the data at all, the value is zero. When the line is a perfect fit, the value is one.

The best way to understand this measure is to see it in action. Figure 12-9 shows four sets of data artificially created to illustrate different scenarios. The two on the top have an R^2 value of 0.9; the two on the bottom have an R^2 value of 0.1. The two on the left have positive correlation, and the two on the right have negative correlation.

Visually, when the R^2 value is close to one, the points are quite close to the best-fit line. They differ a little bit here and there, but the best-fit line does a good job of capturing the trend. When the R^2 value is close to one, the model is stable in the sense that removing a few points has a negligible effect on the best-fit line.

On the other hand, when the R^2 value is close to zero, the resulting line does not have much to do with the data (at least visually). This is probably because the X-values do not contain enough information to estimate the Y-values very

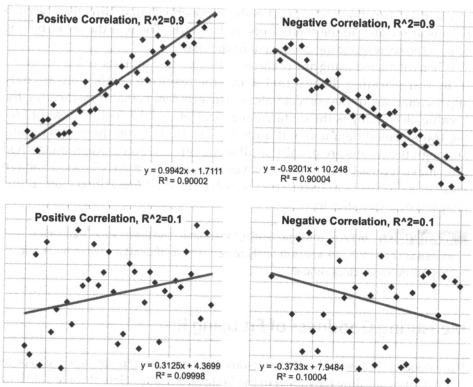

Figure 12-9: The four examples here show the different scenarios of positive and negative correlation among the data points, and examples with R^2 of 0.1 (loose fit) and 0.9 (tight fit).

well, or because there is enough information, but the relationship is not linear. Removing a few data points could have a big impact on the best-fit line.

In short, the R^2 tells us how tightly the data points fit around the best-fit line, which is a good description of how well the best-fit line fits the data.

Limitations of R^2

R^2 does not tell us whether a relationship exists between the X- and Y-values; it only tells us how good the best-fit line is. This is an important distinction. There may be an obvious relationship, even when the R^2 value is zero.

Figure 12-10 shows two such cases. In the chart on the left, the data forms a U-shape. The relationship is obvious, and yet the best-fit line has an R^2 value of zero. This is actually true for any symmetric pattern flipped around a vertical line. The pattern is obvious, but the best-fit line does not capture it.

The chart on the right side of Figure 12-10 shows what can happen with outliers. For any given set of data, it is possible to add one data point that makes the R^2 value be zero. This occurs when the additional data point causes the best-fit line to be horizontal.

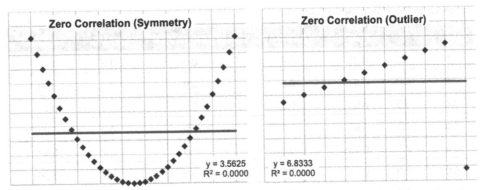

Figure 12-10: There may be an obvious relationship between the X and Y values even when the R^2 value is zero. The relationship is not the best-fit line, however.

These examples are intended to show the limits of R^2. When the value is close to one, the regression line explains the data well. When the value is close to zero, the best-fit line does not explain what is happening.

> **TIP** When the R^2 value is close to one, the particular model explains the relationship between the input variables and the target. When the value is close to zero, the particular model does not explain the relationship, but there may be some other relationship between the variables.

What R^2 Really Means

The R^2 value is the ratio of two values. The numerator is the total variation of the Y-values explained by the model. The denominator is the total variation of the Y-values. The ratio measures how much of the total variation in the data is explained by the model.

Simple enough. Excel can calculate the value using the CORREL() function. This function calculates the Pearson correlation coefficient, which is called r. As its name implies, R^2 is the square of r.

The R^2 value can also be calculated directly from the data. The numerator is the sum of the squares of the differences between the expected Y-values and the average Y-value; that is, the numerator measures how far the expected values are from the overall average. The denominator is the sum of the squares of the differences between the observed Y-values and the average Y-value. The denominator measures how far the observed values are from the overall average.

Table 12-2 walks through the calculation for the example on the right of Figure 12-10 where the R^2 value is zero. Columns two and three have the observed Y-value and the expected Y-value. Columns four and six have the differences between these and the average. Columns five and seven have the squares. The R^2 value is then the ratio of the sums of these squared values.

Table 12-2: Example of an R^2 Calculation

X	Y	YEXP	YEXP-YAVG	(YEXP-YAVG)²	Y-YAVG	(Y-YAVG)²
1.0	5.5	6.83	0.0	0.0	−1.3	1.78
2.0	6.0	6.83	0.0	0.0	−0.8	0.69
3.0	6.5	6.83	0.0	0.0	−0.3	0.11
4.0	7.0	6.83	0.0	0.0	0.2	0.03
5.0	7.5	6.83	0.0	0.0	0.7	0.44
6.0	8.0	6.83	0.0	0.0	1.2	1.36
7.0	8.5	6.83	0.0	0.0	1.7	2.78
8.0	9.0	6.83	0.0	0.0	2.2	4.69
9.0	9.5	6.83	0.0	0.0	2.7	7.11
10.0	0.8	6.83	0.0	0.0	−6.0	36.00
Sum				0.0		55.0
R²						0.0

This table shows what happens when the R^2 value is zero. The expected value is a constant, which is the average of the Y-values (remember that one of the properties of the best-fit line is that it goes through the point that is the average of the X-values and the average of the Y-values). The R^2 value can only be zero when the expected value is always constant. Similarly, when the R^2 value is small, the expected values do not vary very much.

Notice that the R^2 value can never be negative, because the sums of squares are never negative. However, the Pearson correlation (r) can be negative, with the sign indicating whether the relationship is positive correlation (as X gets bigger, Y gets bigger) or negative correlation (as X gets bigger, Y gets smaller).

The R^2 value only makes sense for the best-fit line. For an arbitrary line, the value can be greater than one, although this never happens for the best-fit line.

Direct Calculation of Best-Fit Line Coefficients

There are two reasons for explaining the arithmetic for calculating the coefficients of the best-fit line. Directly calculating the coefficients makes it possible to do the calculation in SQL as well as Excel. More importantly, though, Excel is missing a bit of useful functionality: the ability to do a weighted best-fit line, which is addressed later in this chapter.

Calculating the Coefficients

Calculating the best-fit line means finding the values of the coefficients $ß_1$ and $ß_0$ in the equation for the line. The mathematics needed for the calculation is simple addition, multiplication, and division. There is nothing magical about the calculation itself, although the proof that it works is beyond the scope of this book.

The calculation uses the following easily calculated intermediate results:

- Sx is the sum of the X-values.
- Sy is the sum of the Y-values.
- Sxx is the sum of the squares of the X-values.
- Sxy is the sum of each X-value multiplied by the corresponding Y-value.

The first coefficient, ß1, is calculated from these values using the formula:

```
ß₁ = (n*Sxy - Sx*Sy) / (n*Sxx - Sx*Sx)
```

The second coefficient has the formula:

```
ß₀ = (Sy/n) - beta1*Sx/n
```

Table 12-3 shows the calculation for the data used in the R^2 example. The top portion of this table contains the data points, along with the squares and products needed. The sums and subsequent calculation are at the bottom of the table.

Table 12-3: Direct Calculation of the Coefficients

X	Y	X^2	X*Y
1.0	5.5	1.00	5.5
2.0	6.0	4.00	12.0
3.0	6.5	9.00	19.5
4.0	7.0	16.00	28.0
5.0	7.5	25.00	37.5
6.0	8.0	36.00	48.0
7.0	8.5	49.00	59.5
8.0	9.0	64.00	72.0
9.0	9.5	81.00	85.5
10.0	0.8	100.00	8.3
VARIABLE	Sx	Sy	Sxx	Sxy
Sum	55.0	68.3	385.0	375.8
n * Sxy - Sx * Sy	0.00			
n * Sxx - Sx * Sx	825.00			
Beta1	0.00			
Beta0	6.83			

Calculating the Best-Fit Line in SQL

Unlike Excel, SQL does not generally have functions to calculate the coefficients for a linear regression formula (although some databases such as Postgres and Oracle do have such functions). For the simple case of one variable, the calculations can be done explicitly, using the preceding formulas. For the Minnesota example in Figure 12-7:

```
SELECT (1.0*n*Sxy - Sx*Sy) / (n*Sxx - Sx*Sx) as beta1,
       (1.0*Sy - Sx*(1.0*n*Sxy - Sx*Sy) / (n*Sxx - Sx*Sx)) / n as beta0,
       POWER(1.0*n*Sxy - Sx*Sy, 2) / ((n*Sxx-Sx*Sx)*(n*Syy-Sy*Sy)) as r2,
       s.*
FROM (SELECT COUNT(*) as n, SUM(x) as Sx, SUM(y) as Sy,
             SUM(x*x) as Sxx, SUM(x*y) as Sxy, SUM(y*y) as Syy
      FROM (SELECT pctbachelorsormore as x, pctnumhhpubassist as y
            FROM ZipCensus
            WHERE stab = 'MN'
           ) z
     ) s
```

The innermost subquery defines x and y variables. The middle subquery calculates Sx, Sy, Sxx, Sxy, and Syy (the latter is needed for R^2). These are then combined in the next level into the coefficients. This query also calculates the R^2 value, using an alternative formula that does the calculation directly, rather than by first calculating expected values.

Table 12-4 contains the resulting values. Although the moving average suggests a relationship, the very low R^2 value suggests that the relationship is not a line.

Table 12-4: Coefficients for Relationship College Education and Public Assistance in Minnesota Zip Codes

COEFFICIENT/STATISTIC	VALUE
N	885
Sx	185.0340
Sy	25.6020
Sxx	53.9560
Sxy	5.0619
Syy	1.8146
Beta1	−0.0190
Beta0	0.0329
R^2	0.0052

Price Elasticity

Price elasticity is the economic notion that product prices and product sales are inversely related to each other. As prices go up, sales go down, and vice versa. In practice, price elasticity provides information about the impact of raising or lowering prices. Although the economic relationship is approximate, and sometimes quite weak, price elasticity is useful for what-if analyses that investigate the effects of changing prices.

The subject of price elasticity opens up the subject of prices in general. Typically, a product has a full price. Customers may pay the full price or a discounted price—the product may be on sale, the customer may have a loyalty relationship that offers discounts, the product may be bundled with other products, the customer may have a group discount, and so on.

This section starts by investigating prices, first by product group and then more specifically for books whose full price is $20. It then shows how basic regression analysis can be used to estimate elasticity effects. These effects are only approximate, because demand is based on more than pricing (what competitors are doing, marketing programs, and so on). Even so, regression analysis sheds some light on the subject.

Price Frequency

Visualizing the relationship is a good place to start. A price frequency chart shows how often products are sold at a given price. The horizontal axis is the price; the vertical axis is the frequency, so each point shows the number of products sold at a particular price. A price frequency chart might use the full price, the average price, or a bar showing the range of prices.

Figure 12-11 shows a full price frequency chart broken out by product groups. Because the range of values is so large and values are always positive, both axes use a logarithmic scale. The seven symbols represent the seven product groups of interest. Each point in the chart is an instance of products in the product group having a particular full price.

As a whole, the chart gives an idea of the relationship between full prices, product groups, and demand. The circled point at the top, for instance, indicates that 17,517 orders contain ARTWORK products whose full price is $195. Although not shown on the chart, this point actually corresponds to 670 different products in the product table, all in the ARTWORK group and all having the same full price.

The pricing frequency chart has other interesting information. The most commonly sold items are ARTWORK products having a full price of $195 (the circled point is the highest point in the chart). Although relatively expensive, the ARTWORK products selling at this price are inexpensive relative to other ARTWORK products. The products in this category typically cost more, as seen by the fact that the ARTWORK products (labeled with "x"s) are to the right of the circled marker.

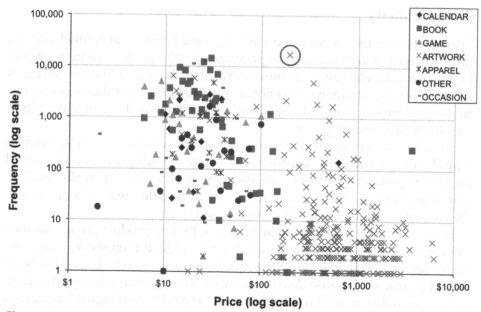

Figure 12-11: This pricing frequency chart shows the relationship between sales volume and full price by product group.

Almost all the expensive products are ARTWORK, with the exception of one BOOK and one CALENDAR (and these may be examples of misclassification). On the other hand, the BOOK group is quite well represented as having many products selling in more than one thousand orders—these are the solid squares on the upper left of the chart. Books are also generally moderately priced. The least expensive products further to the left include many GAMEs and CALENDARs. FREEBIEs, which are by definition free, are not included in the chart.

The pricing frequency chart is a good way to visualize the relationship between pricing and sales. With respect to price elasticity, its use is limited. The best-selling books, for instance, have a price point pretty much in the middle of the book prices. Books that are more expensive sell fewer copies. But also, books that are less expensive sell fewer copies. Unsurprisingly, something besides price is important for book sales.

The following query gathers the data for the chart:

```
SELECT p.GroupName, p.FullPrice, COUNT(*) as cnt
FROM OrderLines ol JOIN Products p ON ol.ProductId = p.ProductId
WHERE p.FullPrice > 0
GROUP BY p.GroupName, p.FullPrice
ORDER BY cnt DESC
```

This query uses `OrderLines` to calculate the total number of orders and `Products` to get `FullPrice` and the group name. This query counts the number of lines in orders for the frequency, which is reasonable. Another reasonable alternative would be counting the number of units.

The results are broken out by product group—a natural way to compare products. To create the chart, the data needs to have a separate column for each product group. `FullPrice` is placed in the appropriate column for each row, with `NA()` going in the other columns. A scatter plot is created from the pivoted data.

Price Frequency for $20 Books

The range of prices and sales volumes is interesting. For elasticity, though, it is better to focus on a single product or group of similar products. This section investigates products in the BOOK category whose full price is $20. Even though the full price is $20, these are often discounted, using marketing techniques such as coupons, clearance offers, product bundles, and customer loyalty discounts.

Price elasticity suggests that when prices are lower, sales should be higher and when prices are higher, sales should be lower. Of course, this is economic theory, and a lot of things get in the way in the real world. Prices lower than the full price may indicate special promotions for the product that further increase demand, beyond the change in price. Or, low prices may indicate inventory clearance sales for the last few copies of otherwise popular books. In such a case, demand might be relatively high, but because inventory is not sufficient to fulfill all demand, sales are relatively low.

This investigation assumes that most of the discounts are available for all customers, and the discounts are available for a certain period of time. The price elasticity question is then one about the relationship of volume and average prices by month, suggesting the following summary:

- The average price of $20 full-price books sold in the month
- The total units sold in the month for these products

Just to be clear, the full price is $20, but customers may be getting a discount. Also, a given book always has the same full price, which is in `Products`, not `Orders`. In the real world, products may have different full prices at different times. If this is the case, `OrderLines` should include the full price as well as the price the customer pays (or the table containing the product pricing should be designed as a slowly changing dimension, meaning that time frames are included in the pricing table).

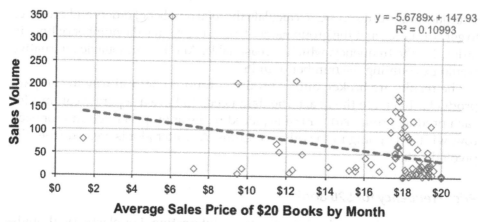

Figure 12-12: This scatter plot shows the actual prices of books whose full price is $20. Each point is the average price by month and the average sales by month.

The following query summarizes the data for the scatter plot in Figure 12-12:

```
SELECT YEAR(o.OrderDate) as year, MONTH(o.OrderDate) as mon,
       COUNT(DISTINCT ol.ProductId) as numprods,
       AVG(ol.UnitPrice) as avgprice, SUM(ol.NumUnits) as numunits
FROM Orders o JOIN
     OrderLines ol
     ON o.OrderId = ol.OrderId JOIN
     Products p
     ON ol.ProductId = p.ProductId
WHERE p.GroupName = 'BOOK' and p.FullPrice = 20
GROUP BY YEAR(o.OrderDate), MONTH(o.OrderDate)
ORDER BY year, mon
```

The horizontal axis in the plot is the price in the month and the vertical axis is the total units sold. Each point in the scatter plot is the summary of one month of data for $20 books. The chart does not show which point corresponds to which month, because the purpose is to determine the relationship between average price and volume, not to see trends over time.

In most months, the average price of these books is over $17, as seen by the prevalence of points on the lower right. During these months, the sales are often on the low side, particularly as the average increases toward $20. This does suggest a relationship between price and demand. During some months, the average price is absurdly low, less than $10, suggesting that $20 books are sometimes sold at a hefty discount.

The best-fit line is also shown in the chart. This line is not a particularly good fit, but it does suggest that as the price increases, demand decreases. The slope of the line is minus 5.7, which means that for every dollar increase in price, the demand decreases by 5.7 units per month.

There is no *a priori* reason to believe that the relationship is a simple line, so more sophisticated models might be needed. On the other hand, a line produces a very handy number—minus 5.7—that can be used to inform pricing and discounting efforts.

The analysis is complicated by the real world. Any given month has different numbers of products for sale at that price and different amounts of inventory for those products. When inventory is an issue, customers may try to purchase the product and fail because of a lack of inventory. The relationship between price and demand is interesting to investigate; it is also related to many other factors that can make it challenging to tease out a particular formula.

Price Elasticity Model in SQL

The coefficients for the line can also be calculated in SQL. The following query performs the same analysis, finding the relationship between the price of $20 full-price books and the volume of sales on a monthly basis:

```
SELECT (1.0*n*Sxy - Sx*Sy) / (n*Sxx - Sx*Sx) as beta1,
       (1.0*Sy - Sx*(1.0*n*Sxy - Sx*Sy) / (n*Sxx - Sx*Sx)) / n as beta0,
       POWER(1.0*n*Sxy - Sx*Sy, 2) / ((n*Sxx-Sx*Sx)*(n*Syy - Sy*Sy)) as R2
FROM (SELECT COUNT(*) as n, SUM(x) as Sx, SUM(y) as Sy,
             SUM(x*x) as Sxx, SUM(x*y) as Sxy, SUM(y*y) as Syy
      FROM (SELECT YEAR(o.OrderDate) as year, MONTH(o.OrderDate) as mon,
                   AVG(ol.UnitPrice) as x, 1.0*SUM(ol.NumUnits) as y
            FROM Orders o JOIN
                 OrderLines ol
                 ON o.OrderId = ol.OrderId JOIN
                 Products p
                 ON ol.ProductId = p.ProductId
            WHERE p.GroupName = 'BOOK' and p.FullPrice = 20
            GROUP BY YEAR(o.OrderDate), Text MONTH(o.OrderDate)
           ) ym
     ) s
```

The innermost query summarizes the appropriate orders by month. The rest of the query we have seen earlier as the logic for calculating the coefficients and R-square value. Note that the Y-value is multiplied by 1.0, so it is not treated as an integer in the calculation. Reassuringly, this SQL calculates the same coefficients as the best-fit line in Excel's charts.

Price Elasticity Average Value Chart

As explained in the previous chapter, the average value chart is a good way to evaluate a model whose target is numeric. This chart divides the estimates of the target into ten deciles, and compares the actual target and the expected value within each decile. Figure 12-13 shows such a chart for comparing the actual demand and the estimated demand based on the best-fit line for price.

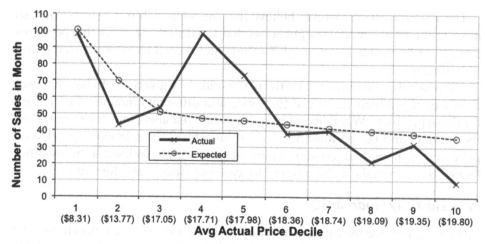

Figure 12-13: This average value chart shows the relationship between the expected number of sales and the actual number of sales by sales price for books whose full price is $20.

The chart emphasizes that the model simply does not work well (which we already suspected because of the low R^2 value). The expected sales generally decrease as the deciles increase, although it gets rather flat after the first three deciles. The actual sales have a different pattern, starting high, dipping, and then going up again. The top two deciles also have much lower average prices than the rest of the deciles ($8.31 and $13.77 versus over $17 in the remaining ones).

Deciles 4 and 5 are particularly problematic because the actual sales are noticeably bigger than the expected sales—or alternatively the demand for the first three deciles is much lower than it should be. Despite the low R^2 value, there does seem to be a relationship between price and sales, albeit with exceptions, suggesting that pricing discounts on the books are not the only factor driving sales. Some discounts seem to drive sales of popular books even higher. Other discounts seem designed to sell the last available copies books. When it comes to estimating sales volume, price is only one factor.

Weighted Linear Regression

Bubble charts are a natural way to visualize many types of summarized data. The data is located on the chart according to X- and Y-values, and the size of each bubble is the frequency count. Alas, when Excel calculates the best-fit line in a bubble chart, it does not take into account the sizes of bubbles. The resulting best-fit line does a poor job showing trends in the data.

> **WARNING**   When Excel calculates best-fit lines in bubble charts, it does not take the size of the groups into account. This can significantly skew the resulting line. The desired line requires doing a weighted linear regression.

The way to solve this problem is by using weighted linear regression to take the sizes of the bubbles into account. Unfortunately, this capability is not built into Excel directly. There are two ways to do the calculation. One is to apply the formulas from the previous section, adjusting the various intermediate sums for the frequencies. The other uses special functionality in Excel called Solver, which is a general-purpose tool that can be used for this specific need.

This section starts with a basic business problem where weighted linear regression is needed. It then discusses various ways to address the problem in Excel and SQL.

Customer Stops during the First Year

In the subscriptions data, is there a relationship between the monthly fee and the stops during the first year? The hypothesis is that each increment in the monthly fee increases the overall stop rate.

The bubble chart in Figure 12-14 shows the monthly fee on the horizontal axis and the proportion of customers who stop during the first year on the vertical axis. The size of each bubble is the number of customers in the group. Many bubbles are so small that they do not appear in the chart. For instance, two customers started with a monthly fee of $3, and one of them stopped. However, they are not visible because a bubble for two customers is simply too small to see on a chart where the largest bubbles represent hundreds of thousands of customers.

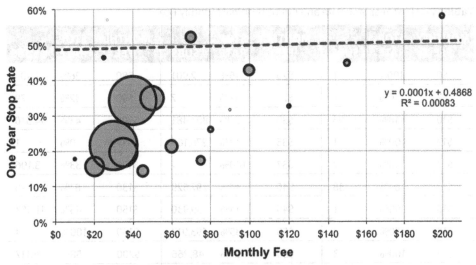

Figure 12-14: This bubble chart shows the relationship between the initial monthly fee (horizontal axis) and the stop rate during the first year for customers who started in 2004 and 2005. The size of the bubble represents the number of customers.

The chart itself includes the best-fit line for the data, as produced in Excel. This line is almost horizontal, suggesting almost no relationship between the monthly fee and the stop rate. The lack of relationship is corroborated by the miniscule R^2 value, which suggests that any relationship that might exist is not a line.

The following query provides the data for the bubble chart:

```
SELECT MonthlyFee,
       AVG(CASE WHEN tenure < 365 AND StopType IS NOT NULL THEN 1.0
               ELSE 0 END) as stoprate,
       COUNT(*) as numsubs
FROM Subscribers
WHERE StartDate BETWEEN '2004-01-01' and '2005-12-31'
GROUP BY MonthlyFee
ORDER BY MonthlyFee
```

This query simply aggregates all the customers who started in 2004 and 2005, keeping track of those who stopped during the first year.

Weighted Best Fit

Table 12-5 shows the data used to create the bubble chart. Notice that most of the groups are quite small. Over half have fewer than three hundred customers, and these do not even show up on the chart. When Excel calculates the best-fit line, it does not take the size of the bubbles into account, so these invisible points are worth as much as the visible ones, which have 99.9% of the customers. This is true both for the best-fit line in the charts and for the LINEST() function.

Table 12-5: First Year Stop Rate and Count by Initial Monthly Fee

MONTHLY FEE	STOP RATE	# SUBS	MONTHLY FEE	STOP RATE	# SUBS	MONTHLY FEE	STOP RATE	# SUBS
$0	100%	1	$25	46%	2,901	$80	26%	7,903
$7	0%	1	$27	57%	7	$90	32%	79
$10	18%	1,296	$30	21%	803,481	$100	43%	34,510
$12	100%	1	$35	19%	276,166	$117	0%	1
$13	50%	2	$37	100%	1	$120	33%	3,106
$15	89%	38	$40	34%	797,629	$130	81%	26
$16	100%	1	$45	14%	39,930	$150	45%	11,557
$18	50%	2	$50	35%	193,917	$160	100%	4
$19	100%	3	$60	21%	48,266	$200	58%	6,117
$20	15%	120,785	$70	52%	35,379	$300	10%	241
$22	67%	9	$75	17%	22,160	$360	100%	6

This is a problem; some bubbles are clearly more important than others. One approach is to filter the data, and choose only the bubbles that exceed a certain size. To do this, select the cells and turn on filtering using the Data ➤ Filter menu option (or the sequence of three keys: Alt+D, Alt+F, Alt+F). When the filter appears, apply a "(Custom…)" filter in the numsubs column to select the rows that have a count greater than, say, 1,000. When the data is filtered, the chart automatically updates both the data and the best-fit line. The resulting R^2 value increases to 0.4088, suggesting a relationship between monthly fee and surviving the first year.

TIP When filtering rows of data that have an associated chart on the same worksheet, be sure that the chart is either above or below the data. Otherwise, the filters might reduce the height of the chart, or cause it to disappear altogether.

Using filters is an ad hoc approach, depending on the choice of an arbitrary threshold. And, the resulting line is still giving all bubbles the same weight. A better approach is to use all the data to calculate a weighted best-fit line. The weighted best-fit is used when data is summarized, and the groups have different sizes. This is a common occurrence, particularly when summarizing data from large databases and analyzing the data in Excel.

The calculations take the weights into account for all the various intermediate sums. Table 12-6 shows the calculation of β_1, β_0, and R^2 for the best-fit line with and without weights. The calculation of N, the total number of points, shows the difference. The unweighted case has 33 points because monthly fee takes on 33 different values. These groups correspond to 2.4 million customers, which is the value of N using the weights. The 1,296 customers who initially paid \$10 and have a stop rate of 17.6% are instead treated as 1,296 rows with the same information.

Table 12-6: Comparison of Calculations with and without Weights

COEFFICIENT/STATISTIC	UNWEIGHTED	WEIGHTED
N	33.00	2,405,526.00
Sx	2,453.00	94,203,540.00
Sy	16.33	647,635.68
Sxx	404,799.00	4,394,117,810.00
Sxy	1,241.02	27,310,559.03
Syy	11.68	190,438.85
Beta1	0.00	0.00
Beta0	0.49	0.16
R^2	0.0009	0.3349

The resulting best-fit line now has the following characteristics:

- slope = 0.0028
- intercept = 0.2665
- R^2 = 0.3349

The slope indicates that for each dollar that the monthly fee increases, the stop rate increases by 0.28%. Without the weighting, the increase was a negligible 0.01%. The R^2 value suggests that the pattern is of medium strength, not dominant, but potentially informative. Doing the analysis with the weights changes the results from no pattern to one of medium strength.

Based on this analysis, if the company were to raise the monthly fee by $10 for new customers, it would expect an additional 2.8% of them to leave during the first year.

Weighted Best-Fit Line in a Chart

Being able to plot the weighted best-fit line in a chart is useful. Even though Excel's charts do not support this functionality directly, we can trick it into doing what we want.

The idea is to insert another series in the chart corresponding to the best-fit line, add the line for the series, and make the new series invisible so only the line is visible:

1. For each monthly fee, apply the weighted best-fit formula to get the expected value.
2. Add a new data series to the chart with the monthly fee and the expected value. Because this is a bubble chart, be sure to include a size for the bubbles as well.
3. Add the trend line for the new monthly fee series. This line perfectly fits the data.
4. Format the series so it is invisible, either by making the pattern and area be transparent or by making the width of the bubbles equal to zero.

Figure 12-15 shows the original data with the two trend lines. The sloping trend line that takes into account the sizes of the bubbles does a better job of capturing the information in the chart.

Weighted Best-Fit in SQL

The following query uses the same ideas to calculate the coefficients and R^2 value directly in SQL for a weighted linear regression:

```
SELECT (1.0*n*Sxy - Sx*Sy) / (n*Sxx - Sx*Sx) as beta1,
       (1.0*Sy - Sx*(1.0*n*Sxy - Sx*Sy) / (n*Sxx - Sx*Sx)) / n as beta0,
```

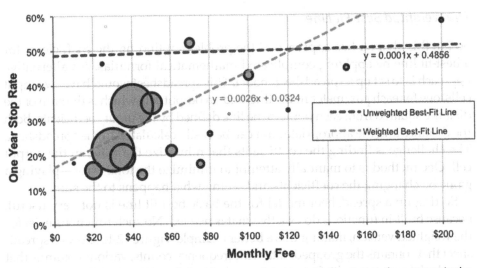

Figure 12-15: The weighted best-fit line does a much better job of capturing the patterns in the data points.

```
        (POWER(1.0*n*Sxy - Sx*Sy, 2) / ((n*Sxx-Sx*Sx)*(n*Syy - Sy*Sy))
        ) as Rsquare
FROM (SELECT SUM(cnt) as n, SUM(x*cnt) as Sx, SUM(y*cnt) as Sy,
             SUM(x*x*cnt) as Sxx, SUM(x*y*cnt) as Sxy,
             SUM(y*y*cnt) as Syy
      FROM (SELECT MonthlyFee as x,
                   AVG(CASE WHEN tenure < 364 THEN 1.0 ELSE 0 END) as y,
                   COUNT(*) as cnt
            FROM Subscribers
            WHERE StartDate BETWEEN '2004-01-01' AND '2005-12-31'
            GROUP BY MonthlyFee
           ) xy
     ) s
```

The only difference between this query and the unweighted query is the calculation of the intermediate values in the middle subquery. This query returns the same results at the Excel calculation.

Weighted Best-Fit Using Solver

Using the formulas is one way to calculate the coefficients of the weighted best-fit line. However, this works only for one input variable, not to mention the fact that remembering and typing the formulas is onerous.

This section describes an alternative approach using an Excel add-in called Solver (included for free with Excel). Solver allows you to set up a spreadsheet model, where certain cells are inputs and one cell is an output. Solver then finds the right set of inputs to obtain the desired output—very powerful functionality. The question is how to set up a spreadsheet model that does the weighted best-fit line.

The Weighted Best-Fit Line

So far, this chapter has approached the problem of finding the coefficients for a best-fit line by applying complicated mathematical formulas. An alternative approach is to set up a spreadsheet model. This spreadsheet would have two input cells, one for each parameter in the line, and an output cell, which is the sum of the distance squared from each point to the line defined by the input coefficients. Both the distance and the appropriate sum can be easily calculated in the spreadsheet. The challenge is finding the coefficients that minimize the value in the output cell. One method is to manually attempt to minimize the total error—playing a game by changing the coefficients and seeing what happens to the sum.

Setting up a spreadsheet model for the basic best-fit line is not very useful, because built-in functions do exactly what is needed. No such functions exist for the weighted version, making this a better example. Figure 12-16 shows a spreadsheet that contains the grouped data with frequency counts, various columns that do calculations, two cells for input (I3 and I4), and one that has the error (I5).

The first of the additional columns contains the expected value, which is calculated using the input cells:

```
=<beta1> * <monthly_fee> + <beta0>
```

The next column has the error, which is the absolute value of the difference between the expected value and the actual value, and the column after that, the error squared. The final column calculates the square of the error times the count. The total error cell contains the sum of these squares, which the best-fit line minimizes.

Modifying the values in cells I3 and I4 changes the error value. One way to minimize the error is to manually try different combinations of values. The spreadsheet recalculates very quickly and with only two input cells, a person can get reasonably close to the minimum value.

	G	H	I	J	K	L	M
7	INPUT	Beta1	0.002763607807				
8	INPUT	Beta0	0.161001811113				
9	OUTPUT	Sum Dist^2	=SUM(M13:M45				
10							
11		**FROM SQL**					
12	Monthly Fee	Stop Rate	Count	Expected	Error	Squared	Weighted
13	0	1	1	=G13*$I$7+$I$8	=ABS(H13-J13)	=K13*K13	=L13*I13
14	7	0	1	=G14*$I$7+$I$8	=ABS(H14-J14)	=K14*K14	=L14*I14
15	10	0.175925	1296	=G15*$I$7+$I$8	=ABS(H15-J15)	=K15*K15	=L15*I15
16	12	1	1	=G16*$I$7+$I$8	=ABS(H16-J16)	=K16*K16	=L16*I16
17	13	0.5	2	=G17*$I$7+$I$8	=ABS(H17-J17)	=K17*K17	=L17*I17
18	15	0.894736	38	=G18*$I$7+$I$8	=ABS(H18-J18)	=K18*K18	=L18*I18
19	16	1	1	=G19*$I$7+$I$8	=ABS(H19-J19)	=K19*K19	=L19*I19
20	18	0.5	2	=G20*$I$7+$I$8	=ABS(H20-J20)	=K20*K20	=L20*I20

Figure 12-16: This is a spreadsheet model for calculating the error between a given line and the data points (taking the weight into account).

Solver Is More Accurate Than a Guessing Game

Solver uses the same spreadsheet model. However, instead of guessing the values of the coefficients that minimize the error, Solver finds the coefficients automatically. But first, it has to be loaded in using the menu item Tools ➤ AddIns (Alt+T then Alt+I). Then click "Solver," and "OK." Once installed, Solver is available under the menu Tools ➤ Solver or using the keystrokes Alt+T then Alt+V.

The "Solver Parameters" dialog box, shown in Figure 12-17, has several prompts for information. At the top is the entry "Set Objective" to specify the target cell. The goal can be to minimize, maximize, or to set the target cell to a particular value.

The list of cells that Solver can change is in the area called "By Changing Variable Cells." In addition, Solver allows you to set constraints on the cells, such as requiring that all values be positive or in some range. This functionality is not needed for finding the weighted best-fit line. Solver also allows you to choose the optimization method. The default method is quite suitable for weighted regression.

Clicking "Solve" causes Excel to try many different combinations of coefficients looking for the optimal value. This problem is not particularly complicated, and Solver finds the right solution quickly, placing the optimal coefficients in the input cells. The aside "Discussion of Solver" discusses this add-in in a bit more detail.

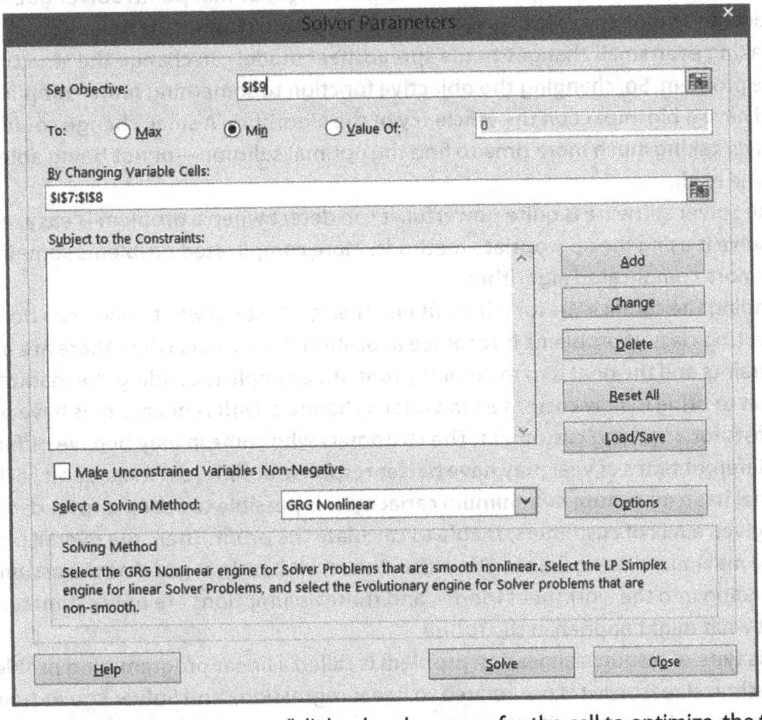

Figure 12-17: The "Solver Parameters" dialog box has areas for the cell to optimize, the type of optimization, the cells whose values can change, and any constraints on the problem.

More Than One Input Variable

Linear regression has been introduced using the best-fit line, which has one input and one target variable. In practice, more than one possible input variable is typically of interest. This section touches on the topic. So-called *multiple regression* pushes the abilities of SQL. In general, such problems are better solved with statistics tools rather than Excel.

DISCUSSION OF SOLVER

Solver is an add-in developed by the company Frontline Systems (www.solver.com). A basic version of Solver has been bundled with Excel since 1991. More advanced versions are offered by Frontline Systems.

Finding the optimal value is determining the coefficients that minimize or maximize some *objective function*. For our purposes, the objective function simply means the value in the target cell, such as the example in the text for the total error for the weighted best-fit line. The objective function can be quite complicated because it can depend directly on the input cells or the spreadsheet could have many intermediate calculations.

The weighted best-fit line is a simple type of problem to solve because it is in a class called *convex conic quadratics*. The simplest example of this, a parabola, has a single minimum value. By analyzing information at any point along the curve, it is possible to determine whether the minimum is to the left or right of that point. Solver guesses the solution and then refines the guess, getting closer and closer each time.

Making even small changes to the spreadsheet model can change the structure of the problem. So, changing the objective function to something more complicated could have a big impact on the efficiency of the algorithm. A small change could result in Solver taking much more time to find the optimal solution—or not being able to find one at all.

The Solver software is quite powerful. It can detect when a problem is easy to solve and solve it using the appropriate methods. More complicated problems sometimes need more complicated algorithms.

Finding the coefficients for a best-fit line is only a taste of what Solver can do. One interesting class of problems is resource allocation. This occurs when there are many constraints and the goal is to maximize profit. An example is dividing the marketing budget to bring in new customers in various channels. Different channels have different costs for acquiring customers. The customers who come in may behave differently, and different times of year may have better response or different mixes, and each channel has a maximum or minimum capacity. It is possible to set up a spreadsheet that, given a mix of customers, is able to calculate the profit. Then, the overall profit can be maximized using Solver. Of course, the result is only as good as the assumptions going into the worksheet model, and these assumptions are only estimates about what might happen in the future.

This type of resource allocation problem is called a linear programming problem (for technical reasons; it is not related to linear regression), and Solver knows how to solve such problems as well.

Multiple Regression in Excel

The function LINEST() can take more than one input column, as long as the input columns are adjacent. The function call is the same, except for the size of the array containing the returned values. The width of this array should be the number of different input variables plus one. It always has five rows.

Getting the Data

The penetration of a zip code in the orders data is related to the average household income, the proportion that have graduated from college and the proportion of people on public assistance. Such relationships can be investigated further using multiple regression.

This example uses zip codes that have more than one thousand households and at least one order:

```
SELECT o.zipcode, (numorders * 1.0 / tothhs) as pen,
       Zc.medianhhinc, zc.pctnumhhpubassist, zc.pctbachelorsormore
FROM ZipCensus zc JOIN
     (SELECT o.ZipCode, COUNT(*) as numorders
      FROM Orders o
      GROUP BY o.ZipCode
     ) o
     ON zc.zcta5 = o.ZipCode
WHERE zc.tothhs >= 1000
```

The returned data has 10,175 rows. The second column pen is the Y-value. The last three columns are X-values.

Investigating Each Variable Separately

A good first step is to investigate each of the variables one-by-one. The best-fit-line and R2 values for each variable can be calculated using the functions SLOPE(), INTERCEPT(), and CORREL().

Table 12-7 shows this information. Note that the best variable is the proportion of the zip code in college. This is the best because it has the highest R^2 value.

Table 12-7: Relationship between Three Variables Independently and Product Penetration

	SLOPE	INTERCEPT	R-SQUARE
HH Median Income	0.0000	−0.0041	0.2512
% HH On Public Assistance	−0.0466	0.0036	0.0357
College Percent	0.0169	−0.0031	0.2726

The signs of the slope are interesting. Positive slope means that as the input value increases, the target value increases. So, penetration increases as median income goes up and as the proportion graduating from college goes up. On the other hand, penetration decreases as a greater proportion of the population is on public assistance.

It would seem that variables with larger slope (steeper lines) would have a bigger impact on the target. Unfortunately, the sizes of the slope provide no information about which variables are better or which have a bigger impact on the target. The reason is that the original variables have very different ranges. The median income is measured in thousands of dollars, so its coefficient is going to be very close to zero. The other two are ratios and vary between zero and one, so their coefficients are higher.

This is unfortunate because it is useful to know which variables have greater effects on the target. Standardizing the inputs fixes this problem. As explained in Chapter 3, the standardized value is the number of standard deviations of a value from the average. The Excel formula looks like:

```
=(A1 - AVERAGE($A1:$A10176)/STDEV($A1:$A10176)
```

This formula is then copied down the column to get standardized value for all inputs.

TIP If you want to compare the effects of a variable on the target (in a linear regression), standardize the input value before calculating the coefficients.

Table 12-8 shows the results with the standardized values. The R^2 values remain the same. The slopes and intercepts change. Standardizing the inputs has no impact on how good the resulting line is.

The constant in the formula (β_0) is the same for all three formulas. This is not a coincidence. When doing the linear regression on standardized input values, the constant is always the average of the Y-values. The converse is not true. If the intercept happens to be the average, this does not mean that the X-values are standardized.

The bigger the slope (either positive or negative) on the standardized values, the bigger the impact on the predicted penetration.

Table 12-8: Relationship between Standardized Values and Product Penetration

	SLOPE	INTERCEPT	R-SQUARE
HH Median Income	0.0027	0.0024	0.2512
% HH On Public Assistance	−0.0010	0.0024	0.0357
College Percent	0.0028	0.0024	0.2726

Building a Model with Three Input Variables

Building a model with all three input variables is as easy as building a model with one. The call to LINEST() looks like:

```
=LINEST('T11-07'!D14:D10188, 'T11-07'!E14:G10188, TRUE, TRUE)
```

Remember, this is an array function. The three input variables mean that the function needs to be entered into an array of four cells across and five cells down, as shown in the screen shot in Figure 12-18. All the cells in the array have the same formula, shown in the formula bar. Remember that Excel adds the curly braces to indicate that the formula is an array formula.

How does this model compare to the models with a single variable? The R^2 value is in the middle cell in the first column. The value is higher, so by that measure the model is better. The R^2 value is 0.312, which is not a big increase over the best single variable model, which had an R^2 value of 0.273. Adding new variables should not make the model worse, but it may not make the model much better.

The coefficients for this model are all positive, which is interesting—because this is not true of the models for each variable individually. The coefficient for the proportion of the population on public assistance is negative when it is the only variable in the model. With other variables in the model, this variable becomes positively correlated. Whatever else, this illustrates that the coefficients can change dramatically as new variables are added into the regression. How and why does this happen?

The answer is at once simple and rather profound. The simple answer is that the other variables overcompensate for the proportion of the population on public assistance. That is, all the variables are trying to determine what makes a good zip code for penetration, and it seems to be wealthier, better educated zip codes. The other variables do a better job of finding these, so when they are included, the effect of the public assistance variable changes dramatically.

More formally, the mathematics of multiple regression assume that the variables are independent. This has a specific meaning. It basically means that the correlation coefficient—the CORREL() function in Excel—is zero (or very close to

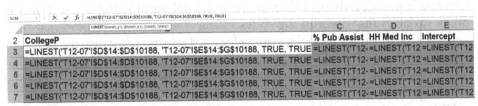

Figure 12-18: The call to LINEST() with three input columns requires entering the formula in an array four columns wide and five rows down.

zero) for any two input variables. The correlation between the household median income and the proportion of the population on public assistance is −0.55. It is negative because as one goes up the other goes down (wealthier people tend to have fewer neighbors on public assistance; people on public assistance tend to have fewer wealthy neighbors). The correlation is rather strong, so the variables are somewhat redundant.

In fact, when doing linear regression, it is easy to forget that the technique works best when the variables are independent. This is because, in practice, input variables are rarely independent unless we make them so. One way of doing that is by using a technique called *principal components,* which is beyond the scope of this book, although it is included in most statistics packages.

Using Solver for Multiple Regression

Just as Solver was used for weighted regression, Solver can also be used for multiple regression. The coefficients are entered into one area of the spreadsheet. The spreadsheet calculates the expected values and total error. Solver can be used to minimize the total error to find the optimal coefficients.

This is useful for at least two important reasons. First, Solver allows you to create more complicated expressions, such as ones using logarithms, or exponentials, or other fancy mathematical functions. Second, Solver allows you to incorporate weights, which is just as useful for multiple regression as for the one-input variety.

As an example, when the multiple regression is run on the standardized inputs, Solver and LINEST() calculate the same coefficients. In some earlier versions of Excel, LINEST() used a different method for calculating the coefficients, one that was numerically unstable. A numerically unstable algorithm means that intermediate values might get very large, so the results are prone to errors caused by the computer not being able to keep enough significant digits during the computation. In those versions, Solver provided better estimates than the built-in functions.

Choosing Input Variables One-By-One

One powerful way of using regression is to choose the variables one at a time, first the best variable, then the next best, and so on. This is called forward selection and is particularly useful for many potential input variables, such as the many variables that describe zip codes.

Excel is not the optimal tool for doing forward selection, because the LINEST() function requires that the X-values be in adjacent columns. This means that essentially every combination of variables needs to be placed into a separate set of adjacent columns.

Different pairs of variables can be tested manually. Create a regression with two columns for the input variables. Then, copy two original columns into these columns for the regression. You can copy different columns in for another regression.

A similar but easier method uses the OFFSET() function along with a column offset in another cell. Changing the value of the column offset cell has the effect of copying data from one of the original columns into the input column for the regression.

With this set up, it is easy to try different pairs of columns by changing the offset values and looking at the resulting R^2 value. It would be convenient to find the optimal offsets using Solver. Unfortunately, the version of Solver provided with Excel cannot handle this type of optimization. Frontline Systems does offer other versions that do.

Multiple Regression in SQL

As more variables are added into the regression formula, it becomes more and more complicated. The problem is that solving the regression requires matrix algebra, in particular, calculating the determinant of a matrix. With one input variable, the problem is a two-by-two matrix, which is pretty easy to solve. Two input variables require a three-by-three matrix, which is at the edge of solving explicitly. And for larger numbers of variables, standard SQL is simply not the best tool, unless the database has built-in functions for this purpose.

This section demonstrates how the logic can be implemented in SQL, even though the resulting queries are complicated and very prone to error. This method is not recommended, because special purpose tools do a much better job.

Solving the equation for two input variables (X1 and X2) requires quite a bit more arithmetic than for one. Two input variables require three coefficients ($ß_0$, $ß_1$, and $ß_2$), and more intermediate sums. The following combinations are needed to calculate the coefficients:

- Sx1, which is the sum of the X1-values
- Sx2, which is the sum of the X2-values
- Sx1x1, which is the sum of the squares of the X1-values
- Sx2x2, which is the sum of the product of X1-values and X2-values
- Sx2x2, which is the sum of the squares of X2 values
- Sx1y, which is the sum of the products of the X1-values and Y-values
- Sx2y, which is the sum of the products of X2-values and Y-values
- Sy, which is the sum of the Y-values

A few more similar variables are needed for R^2. These then need to be combined in rather complicated ways.

The following example calculates the coefficients for penetration, using MedianHHIncome and PctBachelorsOrMore as the two input variables. The CTE renames the input variables to `y`, `x1`, and `x2`, so the arithmetic in the outer subqueries is generic.

```
WITH xy as (
        SELECT o.ZipCode, numorders * 1.0/tothhs as y,
               CAST(medianhhinc as FLOAT) as x1, pctbachelorsormore as x2
        FROM ZipCensus zc JOIN
             (SELECT ZipCode, COUNT(*) as numorders
              FROM Orders o
              GROUP BY ZipCode
             ) o
             ON zc.zcta5 = o.ZipCode
        WHERE tothhs >= 1000
     )
SELECT beta0, beta1, beta2,
       (1 - (Syy - 2*(beta1*Sx1y+beta2*Sx2y + beta0*Sy) +
        beta1*beta1*Sx1x1 + beta2*beta2*Sx2x2 + beta0*beta0*n +
        2*(beta1*beta2*Sx1x2 + beta1*beta0*Sx1 + beta2*beta0*Sx2)) /
        (Syy-Sy*Sy / n)) as rsquare
FROM (SELECT (a11*Sy + a12*Sx1y + a13*Sx2y) / det as beta0,
             (a21*Sy + a22*Sx1y + a23*Sx2y) / det as beta1,
             (a31*Sy + a32*Sx1y + a33*Sx2y) / det as beta2, s.*
      FROM (SELECT (n*(Sx1x1*Sx2x2 - Sx1x2*Sx1x2) -
                   Sx1*(Sx1*Sx2x2 - Sx1x2*Sx2) +
                   Sx2*(Sx1*Sx1x2 - Sx1x1*Sx2)) as det,
                   (Sx1x1*Sx2x2 - Sx1x2*Sx1x2) as a11,
                   (Sx2*Sx1x2 - Sx1*Sx2x2) as a12,
                   (Sx1*Sx1x2 - Sx2*Sx1x1) as a13,
                   (Sx1x2*Sx2 - Sx1*Sx2x2) as a21,
                   (n*Sx2x2 - Sx2*Sx2) as a22, (Sx2*Sx1 - n*Sx1x2) as a23,
                   (Sx1*Sx1x2 - Sx1x1*Sx2) as a31,
                   (Sx1*Sx2 - n*Sx1x2) as a32,
                   (n*Sx1x1 - Sx1*Sx1) as a33,
                   s.*
            FROM (SELECT COUNT(*) as n, SUM(x1) as Sx1, SUM(x2) as Sx2,
                         SUM(y) as Sy, SUM(x1*x1) as Sx1x1,
                         SUM(x1*x2) as Sx1x2, SUM(x2*x2) as Sx2x2,
                         SUM(x1*y) as Sx1y, SUM(x2*y) as Sx2y,
                         SUM(y*y) as Syy
                  FROM xy
                 ) s
           ) s
     ) s
```

Embedded within the query are aliases such as `a11` and `a12`. These values represent cells in a matrix. In any case, after all the arithmetic, the results are in Table 12-9. These results match the results in Excel using the same two variables. Note: The median income is an important variable, but because it is not standardized, the coefficient looks like it is zero.

Table 12-9: Coefficients for Regression of HHMEDINCOME, PCOLL, to Predict Penetration, Calculated Using SQL

COEFFICIENT/STATISTIC	VARIABLE	VALUE
beta0	Intercept	−0.004463
beta1	MedianHHInc	0.000000
beta2	PctBachersOrMore	0.010819
R^2	R-square	0.304130

Understanding the particular arithmetic is not important. At this point, though, we have clearly pushed the limits of what can be accomplished with SQL, and adding more variables is not feasible. Doing more complicated regressions requires the use of statistics tools that support such functionality or Excel.

Lessons Learned

This chapter introduces linear regression (best-fit lines) from the perspective of SQL and Excel. Linear regression is an example of a statistical model and is similar to the models discussed in the previous chapter.

There are several ways to approach linear regressions using SQL and Excel. Excel has at least four ways to create such models for a given set of data. Excel charting has a very nice feature where a trend line can be added to a chart. One of the types of trend lines is the best-fit line, which can be included on a chart along with its equation and statistics describing the line. Other types of trend lines—polynomial fits, exponential curves, power curves, logarithmic curves, and moving averages—are also useful for capturing and visualizing patterns in data.

A second way to estimate coefficients for a linear regression is with the array function LINEST() and various other functions that return individual coefficients, such as SLOPE() and INTERCEPT(). LINEST() is more powerful than the best-fit line in charts because it can support more than one X-variable.

Calculating the coefficients explicitly, using the formulas from mathematics, is the third approach. And, the fourth way is to set up the linear regression problem as an optimization problem using a spreadsheet model. The coefficients are in input calls and the target cell has the sum of the squares of the differences between the expected values and the actual values. The coefficients that minimize the sum define the model. An Excel add-in called Solver finds the optimal set of coefficients to minimize the error. The advantage to this approach is that it supports regressions on summarized data by doing weighted regressions. This is quite powerful, and not otherwise supported in Excel.

Regression has many variations besides weighted regression. Multiple regression handles more than one input variable. A good way to choose variables is using forward selection—that is, selecting one variable at a time to maximize the R^2 value (or more formally something called the *f-statistic*).

For one or two input variables, the calculations can be set up in SQL as well as Excel. This has the advantage of overcoming the limits of the spreadsheet. However, the arithmetic quickly becomes too complicated to express in SQL, and only a few databases do have built-in support for multiple regression.

Although Excel is quite useful for getting started, the serious user will want to use statistical packages for this type of work. The next chapter of this book recognizes that SQL and Excel cannot solve all problems. Some problems require more powerful tools. Setting up the data for these tools—the topic in the next chapter—is an area that takes advantage of the power of SQL.

Building Customer Signatures for Further Analysis

The combination of SQL and Excel is powerful for manipulating data, visualizing trends, exploring interesting features, and finding patterns. However, SQL is still a language designed for data access, and Excel is still a spreadsheet designed for investigating relatively small amounts of data. Although powerful, the combination has its limits.

The solution is to use more powerful data mining and statistical tools, such as SAS, SPSS, R, and Python (among others) or even special purpose code. Assuming that the source data resides in a relational database, SQL still plays an important role in transforming it into the format needed for further analysis. Even NoSQL databases often use SQL-like syntax for accessing and processing data.

Preparing data for such applications is where customer signatures fit in. A customer signature contains summarized attributes of customers, putting important information in one place. This is useful both for building models and for scoring them, as well as for reporting and ad hoc analyses. The model sets discussed in the previous two chapters are examples of customer signature tables.

Signatures are useful beyond sophisticated modeling, having their roots in customer information files developed for reporting purposes. However, signatures are summaries designed for analytic purposes rather than reporting purposes, taking special care with regards to the naming of columns, the time frame of the data going into the signature, and similar considerations.

Customer signatures are powerful because they include both behavior and demographics in one place. The term "customer" should not be taken too literally. In some businesses, for instance, prospects are more important than customers. So, the "customer" may be a prospect and "behavior" may be exposure to marketing campaigns. Or, the level of modeling may be at the zip code level, so the signatures represent zip codes rather than specific customers.

The word "signature" arises from the notion that customers are unique in the specific behavioral and demographic traces that each leaves behind in databases. This is an intriguing notion of human individuality. Unlike human signatures, unique identification is not the purpose; bringing information to the surface for analysis is.

Even though other tools offer more advanced analytics, SQL has an advantage for data preparation: databases exploit parallel processing. In simple terms, this means that database engines can keep multiple disks spinning, multiple processors active, and lots of memory filled while working on a single query. And SQL is quite scalable. So a query that works on a smaller sample is re-optimized for processing larger amounts of data or on different hardware. Another advantage of SQL is that a single query often suffices for all the data processing for customer signatures, eliminating the need for intermediate tables.

Many of the ideas in this chapter have been discussed in earlier chapters. This chapter brings these ideas together around the concept of the customer signature, information that summarizes customers along multiple dimensions. This chapter starts by explaining customer signatures and time frames in more detail. It then discusses the technical operations for building signatures, and interesting attributes to include in them.

What Is a Customer Signature?

A customer signature is a row in a table that describes many aspects of customers—behavior, demographics, neighborhoods, and so on. This section introduces customer signatures, how they are used, and why they are important. The process of building them should make it possible to reconstruct what customers look like at any point in the past. This may be a snapshot on the same date for all customers, or a different date for each customer, such as one year after the customer starts, when the customer makes a second visit, when the customer purchases a particular product, or when the customer enrolls in the loyalty program.

> **TIP** The process for creating customer signatures should be customizable to take a snapshot of customers any point in time or relative to events during the customer tenure. The process for building a customer signature table is as important as the table itself.

Customer signatures summarize *longitudinal* information as a snapshot. In this context, longitudinal does not mean the distance east or west of Greenwich, England. Longitudinal is a word borrowed from medical research where it describes keeping track of patients over time including all the treatments, measurements, and things that happen to the patients. Almost everything is of interest to medical researchers because they are dealing with life and death issues. Although information about customers is not typically quite so detailed and personal, customer signatures serve a similar purpose in the business world by combining many features of customers over time to understand particular outcomes.

What Is a Customer?

The definition of customer permeates the earlier chapters. Chapter 1 brings up the difficulties of identifying customers; Chapter 8 discusses challenges in tracking them over time; and Chapter 10 describes association rules at different levels of the customer relationship (orders and households).

What is a customer? As we've seen, the question can have multiple answers. Four typical ones are:

- An anonymous transaction
- An account, cookie, or device ID
- An individual
- A household

From the perspective of identifying customers in a database over time, accounts and anonymous transactions are usually easy; individuals and households require more work.

At the account/cookie level, one quickly discovers that individuals and households can have multiple relationships. Multiple accounts belonging to the same customer result in operational inefficiencies—multiple contacts to the same household, for instance. These multiple accounts can interfere with analysis. For instance, when trying to understand why customers stop, summaries at the account level may miss the fact that some people have remained customers—on another account. The same problem arises when using cookies or device IDs to identify users.

On the other hand, the identification of individuals and households over time requires a lot of work to identify the same person across multiple transactions, accounts, channels, and devices. Households pose acute problems because their composition changes over time. These changes represent potential marketing opportunities: marriage, divorce, cohabitation, children moving in, children moving out, and so on.

Tracking households and individuals over time also presents a challenge. For instance, users may use a site anonymously from different devices. Then, when the user does identify him or herself (by making a purchase or logging in), should you go back and add the identifier to earlier anonymous sessions that have the same cookie/device ID? This question has no right answer; it depends on the business requirements for customer identification.

The purchases dataset contains a customer ID table that provides lookups for the household for any account. These IDs tie disparate transactions together over time. Such customer IDs are often assigned by matching names, addresses, phone numbers, email addresses, and credit cards on the transactions. These are then grouped together into households, typically assigned by a third-party vendor. If more complete data were available, these household IDs would have effective dates on them, identifying when the household information is active and when the information changes.

Sources of Data for the Customer Signature

In a typical database, data about customers is spread though many different tables, some of which do not even know that they help describe customers. Products is intended to describe products, not customers. Yet, when combined with transaction information, this table helps answer questions such as:

- Which customers only purchase products at discounted prices?
- Does a customer have an affinity with a particular product group?
- Does this affinity change over time?

These questions highlight the interplay between different types of data.

Information about customers comes from diverse subject areas, as shown in Figure 13-1. One particularly important attribute is the time frame for each item of data. The time frame is when the data becomes known for analytic purposes.

Current Customer Snapshot

Sometimes, a table is already available that describes the current customers (and perhaps former customers as well), containing information such as:

- Customer ID
- Customer name
- Original start date or first purchase date
- Current product or most recent purchase date
- Total spending
- Current contact information

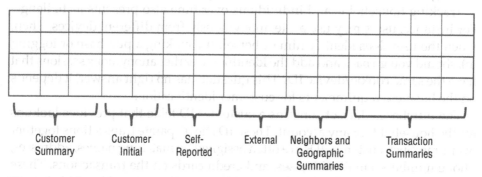

Customer Summary | Customer Initial | Self-Reported | External | Neighbors and Geographic Summaries | Transaction Summaries

Figure 13-1: Customer signatures are records that describe customers, containing information from different subject areas.

This information is a snapshot of what customers look like at the time the snapshot is created. Such a snapshot is a good starting point for a customer signature. It has useful information and is at the right level of granularity. The most useful columns are the ones that do not change over time, because these can be used to create a snapshot of customers at any point in time.

For instance, the customer ID and original start date do not change. The contact information can change over time, although slowly. Total spending, most recent product, and most recent purchase date all change frequently. "Frequently," of course, depends on the business. Updates on automobile purchases might change over a period of years; updates on electricity usage, every month or even more frequently. Updates on web visits or phone usage, every day or even more often.

In a poorly designed data warehouse or data mart, snapshot information might contain data elements that are not otherwise available in transaction tables. Once upon a time, a company had a customer snapshot with the *dunning level*, a field that described how late customers were in paying their bills: The higher the dunning level, the later the customer payment, until the account was suspended. This information was only kept current in the snapshot information, with no historical transaction table. Although quite important for understanding customers and a driver of important behaviors, the dunning level could not be used for analysis, because the values could not be reconstructed in the past.

The solution was simple enough. On the analysis side, we could capture the dunning level periodically from the current snapshot, and create a dunning transaction table for analysis purposes.

Initial Customer Information

Initial customer information remains constant for the duration of the customer relationship (except when households merge or split). This information includes:

- The customer start date
- Initial products and spending amounts
- Channel and marketing promotions that led to the initial relationship
- Other relevant information (underwriting, credit scores, and so on)

The initial customer relationship describes the expectations when a customer starts. Exceeding expectations can result in delighted customers who survive for long periods of time. On the other hand, unfulfilled expectations can lead to disappointed customers who were, perhaps, never in the target market in the first place, but were led to start by aggressive marketing tactics.

TIP Initial customer information, both demographic and behavioral, is quite valuable for understanding customers because the initial interactions set customers' longer term expectations.

Self-Reported Information

Customers explicitly provide some valuable data. Basic contact information, such as name, address, telephone number, and email address is provided when they start. Addresses used for billing and delivery lead to geocoding and associated geographic information. Email addresses contain domain information. Names suggest gender and ethnicity. Credit cards provide credit card types.

In addition, customers may complete application forms, provide information for credit checks, and respond to questionnaires and surveys. These additional sources of self-reported information are often available only for the few rather than the many. One challenge is to extend learnings from this subset to all customers. A survey might find an interesting subset of customers; the next problem is to find similar customers in the overall data. Similarity models described in Chapter 11 are one way to approach this.

Self-reported information has a time frame associated with it. Some is available at the beginning of the customer relationship because such information is part of the application process. Some is only available sporadically after customers begin. The information itself is current as of the date it is collected.

External Data (Demographic and So On)

External data is typically purchased from outside bureaus that specialize in demographic data or from business partners who share similar information. Such information is usually a current snapshot of customers. Unfortunately, reconstructing what a customer used to look like is difficult.

Changes in such information can be quite informative. When a couple marries in the United States, one spouse often legally changes his or her name. After a period of time, the newlyweds often unify their financial accounts into a single household account. This offers an opportunity to the bank of the name-changing spouse because it receives notice of the name change. More often than not, a name change gets recorded in a database as the current name, and the previous name is simply forgotten, or at least unavailable outside operational systems.

When a customer moves from one neighborhood to another, the neighborhood demographics change. The address is updated, and the old address forgotten (or at least not readily available for analysis). Without the ability to compare neighborhood demographics, it is not possible to know if the customer is moving up or moving down, into a great school district or into a peaceful retirement community.

TIP Changes in demographic information can be very informative, particularly because such changes can reveal information about the customer's life stages.

Banks usually know when customers reach retirement age. Do the banks cease marketing to customers who are no longer eligible to contribute to individual retirement accounts (IRAs)? Customers are no longer eligible for these once they reach a certain age.

The time frame for demographic information usually represents a compromise because the information is not maintained over time. Only the current snapshot of data is available for current customers, and the last snapshot for stopped customers.

About Their Neighbors

Some information does not tell us directly about customers, but instead about the neighborhoods where they live. The Census Bureau for instance provides detailed information for free. Other "neighborhood" information consists of dynamic summaries of customer behavior, projected onto the neighborhood level. Although "neighborhood" usually refers to geography, it could refer to other types of similarity, such as all customers who arrived via a particular marketing campaign or who have the same email domain.

Using geographic data requires geocoding addresses or GPS coordinates—typically identifying the census block groups or census tracts where individuals or addresses are located. Zip codes are a poor man's geocoding. They often work well enough but the census geographies are better designed for characterizing neighborhoods.

Census blocks change periodically as populations shift. If you are looking at customers over long periods of time, maintaining the history of the census variables can be useful for understanding how neighborhoods and customers are evolving.

Census information is also used for developing marketing clusters, of which the best known are probably Claritas's Prizm codes. These are descriptions of the people living in particular areas using catchy names such as "Young Digerati," "Kids & Cul-de-Sacs," "Shotguns and Pickups," and "Park Bench Seniors," that are based primarily on census data augmented with market research data (you can look up any U.S. zip code by choosing zip code lookup at http://www.claritas.com/MyBestSegments/Default.jsp).

Transaction Summaries and Behavioral Data

Transactions, web logs, online behavior, historical marketing contacts—these are typically the most voluminous of the data sources, at least by number of rows of data. This type of data describes customers' behaviors. The useful attributes in the torrents of records are not always obvious.

The key to effectively using such information is summarization and feature extraction. Some basic methods of summarization are taking sums and averages and counts. More advanced methods identify the presence, absence, or extent of particular behaviors.

Customer interactions, particularly on-line, provide additional information that customers may not even be aware that they are sharing. For instance, you can determine the browser preference, mobile device type, language preference, and time zone simply by collecting the right information from online interactions. This can be quite useful—perhaps iPhone users are different from other mobile customers.

Transaction history and online behavior is quite amenable to the use of time frames, assuming that enough data is available. Shifting the time frame is simply a matter of taking transactions before a certain date and then summarizing them appropriately.

Using Customer Signatures

Customer signatures have a variety of uses, as discussed in this section.

Data Mining Modeling

Customer signatures provide the inputs to models, including predictive models and profiling models. These models use most of the columns as input variables to estimate values in one or more target columns. Chapters 11 and 12 discuss several different types of models. More advanced data mining and statistical tools can access the signatures directly in a table or perhaps via files of exported data.

Scoring Models

Customer signatures are also used for scoring models, although only a subset of the columns are typically needed for any given model. The data can be kept up to date perhaps by using daily processes to update the signature or even real-time processes for key fields. If so, model scores can be updated in real time or close to real time.

Ad Hoc Analysis

Reporting systems do a good job of slicing and dicing business information along important dimensions, such as geography, customer type, department, product, and so on. Because the volume of data is so large and the data is quite complex, signatures can be a convenient way to approach ad hoc analysis.

Repository of Customer-Centric Business Metrics

Columns in a customer signature can go beyond merely gathering data from other tables. Customer signatures are a place to put interesting metrics, particularly those derived from customer behavior information.

For instance, the history of marketing efforts might include attempted contacts by email, telephone, direct mail, and other channels. One of the attributes in the signature might be "email responsiveness." Customers who responded to email offers in the past would have higher email responsiveness scores. Customers who have been contacted many times and never responded would have low scores.

This idea can extend beyond the channel preference, of course. The times when customers shop might be summarized to define who is a "weekend" shopper, who is a "weekday" shopper, who is an "after-work" shopper. The times when customers go to the web site might distinguish between "work browsers" and "home browsers." Customers who buy the newest products without a discount might be "leading edge" shoppers. Credit card customers might be classified as revolvers (keep a high balance and pay interest), transactors (pay off the bill every month), or convenience users (charge up for a vacation or furniture or something and then pay the balance over several months). A customer signature is a good place to publish these types of business metrics and make them available for a wide range of analytic purposes.

TIP Customer signatures are a good place to publish important measures about customers that might otherwise go undocumented and be forgotten.

Designing Customer Signatures

Before going into the details of the data manipulations, let's cover some key ideas concerning the design of customer signatures. These ideas ensure that they work well for analytic purposes, and that they can be generated to be as-of arbitrary points in time.

Profiling versus Prediction

Chapter 11 introduces the distinction between a profiling model set and a prediction model set. In a profiling model set, the inputs and the targets come from the same time frame. In a prediction model set, the inputs are known before the target. The same ideas hold for customer signatures.

This chapter focuses on prediction model sets because they are more powerful. In a profiling model set, the target variables can simply be created in the same way as the input variables. In a prediction model set, the cutoff date is for the input variables, and the target comes from a time frame after the cutoff date.

Column Roles

Columns in a customer signature have various roles, related to how the columns are used in modeling. The roles are important because they affect how the columns are created.

Identification Columns

Some columns uniquely identify each customer. *Identification columns* are important because they provide a link back to the detailed customer data in other databases. Customers often have more than one method of identification. For instance, the customer ID in the data warehouse could be different from the customer ID in the operational systems; the on-line registration ID is probably different from the account number. Sometimes external vendors return match keys, which are different from the keys used internally.

What is important about identification columns is that they uniquely identify each customer—or at least that customer's records in a particular system—for the duration of the data in the customer signature. The identification column prevents customers from being confused with each other.

Input Columns

Most columns in the customer signature are *input columns*. These columns describe customer characteristics and are intended for use as inputs in modeling. Input columns are all defined by a cutoff date. No information from after the cutoff date should be included in the inputs.

This date may be a single date for the entire customer signature, so the customer signature is a snapshot of what all customers look like on that date. Alternatively, the cutoff date could be defined individually for each customer. For instance, it could be one year after the customer starts, or when the customer adds a particular product, or the first time that the customer complains.

Target Columns

Target columns are added to the customer signature during the analysis phase for predictive modeling. For such models, the target columns come from a later time frame than the input columns. Target columns already present in the signature (as opposed to being added in a subsequent step) usually imply a customer signature for profiling rather than prediction.

Foreign Key Columns

Some columns are used to look up additional information. Usually, the additional information is simply added in by joining other tables or subqueries. The key used for the join can remain in the signature, although it is not usually as useful as the data brought in.

Cutoff Date

The cutoff date should be included in each customer signature record. This date may be fixed for all customers, or it may vary. The purpose of including the cutoff date is to inform subsequent analysis, for instance, to convert dates into tenures. It should not be used as an input column for modeling. The cutoff date refers to the cutoff date for the input columns; target information may come from after the cutoff.

Time Frames

One key question in designing customer signatures is: "What do we know and when did we know it?" All the inputs in the signature come from a time frame before the cutoff date. Each column has a time frame associated with it because each value in a database becomes known at some point in time and the value in the column may be replaced at a later point in time. Columns are only available for analysis when the cutoff date for the customer signature is on or after the time frame for the values in those columns.

> **TIP** "What do we know?" and "When do we know it?" are key questions about columns going into customer signatures.

The goal of using time frames is to be able to create the customer signature with arbitrary cutoff dates. This goal has some consequences in terms of naming columns, handling dates and times, and incorporating seasonality.

Naming of Columns

Column names should respect the cutoff date. So, the names should not be tied to particular dates or date ranges. Instead, they should be relative. Good examples of such columns are:

- Sales in the customer's first year
- Average number of weekend visits to a website
- Most recent month billing invoice

On the other hand, bad examples of columns specify particular dates (such as months and years) that would not be relevant in another time frame.

Eliminating Seasonality

Columns that include data from explicit dates and times cause problems because they interfere with generating the signatures for different time frames. Tenures and time spans are better than including explicit dates:

- Instead of the start date, include the number of days before the cutoff date when the customer started.
- Instead of the date of the first purchase and the second purchase, include the number of days from one to the next.
- Instead of the date when a customer enrolled in a program, include the tenure of the customer at that time.

- ▪ Instead of the date of the most recent complaint, include the tenure of the customer on the first complaint and on the most recent complaint.

As a general rule, specific dates are less important relative to the calendar time line than relative to the customer life cycle time line. Dates on the calendar time line should be turned into numbers of days before the cutoff date for the signature.

This also eliminates many effects of seasonality. For instance, many cell phone customers sign up around Christmas. As a result, many pre-paid customers stop in May—four or five months after the phones are activated. These are customers who never replenish their phone account.

This peak in May is not really related to the month of May. Instead, it is related to the peak in starts during the preceding December and January and the business rules that define churn for pre-paid customers. On the customer timeline, the same proportion stops after four or five months regardless of when they started. A peak in starts, though, does result in a peak of stops several months later.

Having the tenure of the customer in the customer signature rather than the dates themselves makes signatures independent of such inadvertent seasonality effects.

Adding Seasonality Back In

Of course, seasonality is useful and informative. For instance, purchases in August may be related to students starting a new school year (in the United States). Students behave differently from other customers. They may be more likely to change brands, more responsive to certain types of promotions, and have fewer financial resources.

Some of this information can be captured in the customer signature by including information such as the season when a customer started. The average customer who starts during the back-to-school season may be different from the average customer who starts at other times. In fact, the subscription data has slight difference in survival for customers who start in August and September versus December, as shown in Figure 13-2. The important point is that customers who

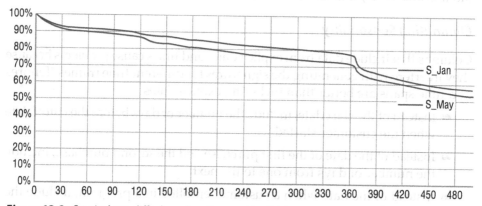

Figure 13-2: Survival can differ based on the month when customers start.

start at different times throughout the year may behave differently because the mix of different customer segments changes throughout the year.

The following are some examples of seasonality variables that might be included to capture possibly interesting characteristics:

- Quarter of the year when a customer started
- Proportion of transactions on the weekend
- Website visits during the traditional work day
- Volume of purchases during the preceding holiday season
- Day of the week of the start and stop

The idea is to first wash seasonality out of the data, to get a better picture of what customers are doing independently of the calendar. This makes it easier to focus on customers, rather than on extraneous events. Of course, seasonality is so important that such effects should go into the customer signature intentionally rather than accidentally. For this reason, separate out variables that capture seasonality information, so it is purposefully in the signature.

TIP Remove inadvertent seasonality from the customer signature by looking at complete years of data and time frames relative to the customer life cycle. Then explicitly add important variables describing seasonality, such as purchases in the last holiday season as a proportion of one year's purchases.

Multiple Time Frames

For predictive modeling purposes, model sets are more powerful when they contain records with different time frames. This prevents the models from "memorizing" one particular time frame. Figure 13-3 shows an example.

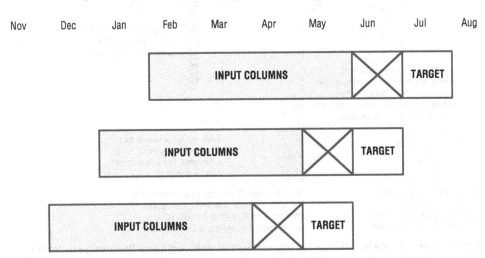

Figure 13-3: Model sets can mix customer signatures from different time frames. Having multiple time frames is actually a best practice for prediction model sets.

When using a model set with multiple time frames, the same customer can appear more than once. In general, this is not a big problem when most of the columns are based on transactions and behavior. If most are based on more static information, then the overlap can be an issue. In general, it is better to not have too many duplicates in a model set.

Operations to Build Customer Signatures

Customer signatures bring data together from disparate data sources, as suggested in Figure 13-4. Some data is already in the right format, and at the right granularity. This data merely needs to be copied. Some fields are keys into other tables, where information can be looked up. Other data is in the format of regular time series that can be pivoted. Irregular time series, such as transactions, need to be summarized. This section describes these operations in the context of building customer signatures.

Driving Table

The first step in building customer signatures is identifying the correct group of customers and the appropriate cutoff date. A customer signature has a set of conditions that determine whether any given customer should be in the

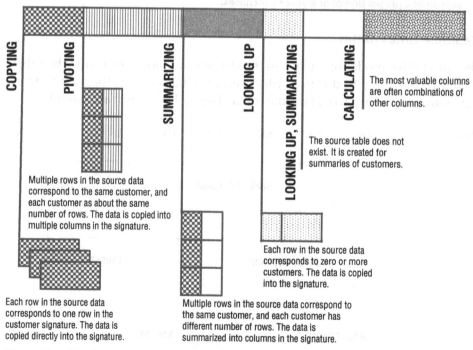

Figure 13-4: The data in customer signatures needs to be brought together using a variety of processing methods.

signature. The table that defines these customers is the *driving table*, which may be an actual table or a subquery.

The driving table defines the population for the signatures and the cut off date. If the signatures are built only for customers who have been around for one year, then the driving table defines this population. Sometimes, filtering can be done after the customer signature has been created for all customers. Sometimes it is simpler to do it when building the signatures.

In an ideal situation, all other subqueries would simply be joined into the driving table using LEFT OUTER JOINs. Important parameters such as the cutoff date (if constant) can be defined using a CTE, resulting in a query like:

```
WITH params as (
      SELECT <custoffdate> as CutoffDate
      )
SELECT *
FROM (<driving table>) dt LEFT OUTER JOIN
      (SELECT CustomerId, <summary information>
       FROM params CROSS JOIN <other table>
       GROUP BY CustomerId
      ) t1
      ON dt.CustomerId = t1.CustomerId LEFT OUTER JOIN
      <ref table> rt
      ON rt.<key> = dt.<key>
```

That is, the driving table would be joined to summaries (typically at the customer level) and reference tables to calculate the columns in the customer signature. This ensures the correct population in the customer signature and that rows do not get inadvertently duplicated.

Using an Existing Table as the Driving Table

Sometimes a table with the right level of granularity can be used for the driving table, although not all its columns are necessarily appropriate for the signature.

Consider Subscribers. The most useful columns in this table describe customers when they start, such as start date, channel, and market. Information that occurs after the customer start date is not appropriate, so the resulting query might be:

```
WITH params as (
      SELECT CAST('2005-01-01' as DATE) as CutoffDate
      )
SELECT SubscriberId, RatePlan as initial_rate_plan,
       MonthlyFee as initial_monthly_fee,
       Market as initial_market, Channel as initial_channel,
       DATEDIFF(day, StartDate, CutoffDate) as days_ago_start,
       CutoffDate
FROM params CROSS JOIN Subscribers s
WHERE StartDate < CutoffDate
```

Only customers who started before the cutoff date are included. This is handled through the use of the `params` CTE. Start dates are transformed into tenures, as of the cutoff date. And, only columns whose value is known at the beginning of the customer relationship are included in the query.

> **TIP** The `CROSS JOIN` operation is a convenient way to incorporate constants into queries, by using a subquery or CTE that defines the constants and returns one row.

Often, an existing table is really a snapshot of a customer at a given point in time. Some columns may still be usable for the driving table, assuming they are modified for different cutoff dates. For instance, the `Tenure` and `StopType` columns could also be included, but they have to be modified to take the cutoff date into account:

```
WITH params as (
     SELECT CAST('2005-01-01' as DATE) as CutoffDate
     )
SELECT SubscriberId, RatePlan as initial_rate_plan,
     MonthlyFee as initial_monthly_fee,
     Market as initial_market, Channel as initial_channel,
     DATEDIFF(day, StartDate, CustoffDate) as days_ago_start,
     DATEDIFF(day, StartDate,
          (CASE WHEN StopDate IS NOT NULL AND
                    StopDate < CutoffDate
               THEN StopDate ELSE CutoffDate END)) as tenure,
     (CASE WHEN StopDate IS NOT NULL AND StopDate < CutoffDate
          THEN StopType END) as StopType,
     CutoffDate
FROM params CROSS JOIN Subscribers s
WHERE StartDate < CutoffDate
```

The logic says that customers who stopped on or after the cutoff date are considered active as of the cutoff date, and customers who stopped before the cutoff date are considered stopped. For the customers who are stopped, the stop type does not change.

Some columns in a snapshot table cannot be used directly in the customer signature. These columns contain information that cannot be rolled back in time, such as total number of purchases, the date of the last complaint, and the customer's billing status. These have to be derived again from transaction tables.

Derived Table as the Driving Table

Sometimes, the appropriate table is not available. In this case, the driving table is a subquery. For instance, consider customer signatures at the household level for the purchases dataset. The database does not have a household table (although perhaps it should). Relevant information can be derived from other tables.

The following query provides a basic summary of households, based on `Customers` and `Orders`:

```
WITH params as (
      SELECT CAST('2016-01-01' as DATE) as CutoffDate
      )
SELECT HouseholdId, COUNT(DISTINCT c.CustomerId) as numcustomers,
       SUM(CASE WHEN Gender = 'M' THEN 1 ELSE 0 END) as nummales,
       SUM(CASE WHEN Gender = 'F' THEN 1 ELSE 0 END) as numfemales,
       MIN(first_orderdate) as first_orderdate,
       DATEDIFF(day, MIN(first_orderdate),
              MIN(cutoff_date)) as days_since_first_order,
       MIN(CutoffDate) as CutoffDate
FROM params CROSS JOIN Customers c JOIN
     (SELECT CustomerId, MIN(OrderDate) as first_orderdate
      FROM Orders o
      GROUP BY CustomerId) o
     ON c.CustomerId = o.CustomerId
WHERE o.first_orderdate < params.CutoffDate
GROUP BY HouseholdId
```

This query looks up the earliest order date for customers. Only customers with an order before the cutoff date are included in the driving table.

Looking Up Data

A lookup table can either be a fixed table that describes features that do not change or a dynamic summary of customer data. Such historical summaries along business dimensions can be very valuable, but they need to take the cutoff date into account.

Fixed Lookup Tables

Fixed lookup tables contain information that does not change over time. These tables can be included without reference to the cutoff date. The classic example is census information. The data from the 2010 Census does not change. However subsequent Census data will supersede it, just as the 2010 Census data superseded the 2000 data.

Census data can be useful in a customer signature, such as:

- Household median income
- Education variables
- Number of households in the zip code

Looking up the values requires a zip code for each customer. Often, the zip code (and other geocoded information) would be a column in a household table and hence part of the driving table.

This example gets the most recent valid-looking zip code in each household:

```
WITH params as (
      SELECT CAST('2016-01-01' as DATE) as CutoffDate
    )
SELECT HouseholdId, ZipCode as first_zip
FROM (SELECT c.HouseholdId, o.ZipCode,
             ROW_NUMBER() OVER (PARTITION BY c.HouseholdId
                                ORDER BY o.OrderDate DESC) as seqnum
      FROM params CROSS JOIN Customers c JOIN
           Orders o
           ON o.CustomerId = c.CustomerId
      WHERE SUBSTRING(o.ZipCode, 1, 1) BETWEEN '0' AND '9' AND
            SUBSTRING(o.ZipCode, 2, 1) BETWEEN '0' AND '9' AND
            SUBSTRING(o.ZipCode, 3, 1) BETWEEN '0' AND '9' AND
            SUBSTRING(o.ZipCode, 4, 1) BETWEEN '0' AND '9' AND
            SUBSTRING(o.ZipCode, 5, 1) BETWEEN '0' AND '9' AND
            LEN(o.ZipCode) = 5 AND
            OrderDate < CutoffDate
     ) h
WHERE seqnum = 1
```

This uses the typical method of getting the most recent value by using `ROW_NUMBER()` and conditional aggregation. Note that the window function `FIRST_VALUE()` can also be used.

The expression in the WHERE clause that chooses the appropriate zip codes is not:

```
ZipCode BETWEEN '00000' AND '99999'
```

The problem is that poorly formed zip codes such as '1ABC9' would fall into this range. Each digit needs to be tested separately. SQL Server offers an extension to LIKE, so this could be written as:

```
ZipCode LIKE '[0-9][0-9][0-9][0-9][0-9]'
```

This syntax is specific to SQL Server. Other databases support regular expressions, and the regular expression pattern would be similar to this pattern.

With the appropriate zip code, the lookup then takes the form:

```
SELECT HouseholdId, zc.*
FROM (<hh first zip subquery>) hhzip LEFT OUTER JOIN
     ZipCensus zc
     ON hhzip.firstzip = zc.zipcode
```

This query looks up the zip in `ZipCensus` and extracts the columns of interest.

Customer Dimension Lookup Tables

Some very powerful lookup tables are summaries of customer behavior along various dimensions. For example, the following might be interesting:

- Penetration by zip code
- Response rate by device type
- Average transaction amount by channel
- Average transaction amount in the state
- Stop rate by channel, market, and monthly fee

This process is sometimes described as projecting one or more measures onto a dimension.

It is tempting to create summaries using simple aggregations. Resist this temptation. All the data in the summaries have to be from a period before the cutoff date to meet the requirements of the input variables. A simple aggregation over all the data might include information from the same time frame as the target—creating customer signatures that cheat.

> **WARNING** When summarizing variables for customer signatures (such as historical churn rates by handset type or historical purchases by zip code), be sure that the data in the summary table comes from a time frame *before* the target variables'.

As an example, consider penetration by zip code, which is the number of households in a zip code with an order divided by the number of households in the zip code. The first number is calculated from the orders data. The second comes from census information.

The following query is the basic query to retrieve the counts:

```
SELECT o.ZipCode, COUNT(DISTINCT c.HouseholdId) as numhhwithorder
FROM Customers c JOIN
     Orders o
     ON c.CustomerId = o.CustomerId
GROUP BY o.ZipCode
```

This summary has two problems, one obvious and one subtle. The obvious problem is that it does not use the cutoff date, so the resulting columns include information from the target time frame. The subtle problem is that as the cutoff date moves into the future, larger amounts of time are used for the calculation. As a result, customer signatures with more recent cutoff dates necessarily have larger penetrations than customer signatures with earlier cutoff dates. Penetration can only grow over time.

The following version solves both these problems:

```
WITH params AS (
     SELECT CAST('2016-01-01' as DATE) as CutoffDate
     )
```

```
SELECT o.ZipCode, COUNT(DISTINCT c.HouseholdId) as numhh
FROM params CROSS JOIN Customers c JOIN
    Orders o
    ON c.CustomerId = o.CustomerId
WHERE DATEDIFF(day, o.OrderDate, CutoffDate) BETWEEN 0 AND 365
GROUP BY o.ZipCode
```

This query uses a fixed period of one year before the cutoff date for the calculation of penetration. Using a fixed period makes the variable more compatible with different cutoff dates.

When the cutoff date differs for each household, the driving table is needed to get the date:

```
SELECT o.ZipCode, COUNT(DISTINCT c.HouseholdId) as numhh
FROM <driving table> dt JOIN
    Customers c
    ON c.HouseholdId = dt.HouseholdId JOIN
    Orders o
    ON c.CustomerId = o.CustomerId
WHERE DATEDIFF(day, o.OrderDate, CutoffDate) BETWEEN 0 AND 365
GROUP BY o.ZipCode
```

In this version, the cutoff date comes from the driving table rather than from a constant subquery. Using the cutoff date ensures that future information is not inadvertently incorporated into the signature.

Initial Transaction

The first transaction provides a lot of information about a customer. This information might include the sections of a web site visited on the first visit, the referral URL, the browser type, and the amount of time spent on the site; or, the contents of the market basket on the first purchase, discounts applied, and the payment type.

As an example, let's gather information from the first purchase in `Orders`. Unfortunately, SQL does not have direct support for joining in just the first transaction. Because the driving table for the purchases data includes the customer start date, which is also the first order date, we can get pretty close:

```
SELECT dt.HouseholdId, firsto.*
FROM (<driving table>) dt LEFT OUTER JOIN
    (SELECT c.HouseholdId, o.*
    FROM Customers c JOIN
        Orders o
        ON c.CustomerId = o.CustomerId) firsto
    ON firsto.HouseholdId = dt.HouseholdId AND
        firsto.OrderDate = dt.first_orderdate
```

Although this looks like a good idea, some customers have multiple orders on the first day.

Some solutions to this problem include:

- Fix the orders so the order date has a time stamp in addition to a date stamp.
- Treat all orders on the first day as a single order.
- Choose a single, reasonable first day transaction.

The first possibility is generally a non-starter. Data analysis projects often find opportunities to improve source data. Alas, fixing data problems is usually outside the scope of such projects.

The second approach requires combining multiple orders on the same day. Some attributes, such as the original channel and the original payment type, need to be combined from more than one order. There is no obvious way to do this consistently.

The preferred solution is to choose a single, reasonable first day transaction. We have already encountered the problem of having multiple transactions on the same date in Chapter 8. This is easily solved using ROW_NUMBER():

```
SELECT h.*
FROM (SELECT HouseholdId, o.*,
             ROW_NUMBER() OVER (PARTITION BY HouseholdId
                                ORDER BY OrderDate, OrderId) as seqnum
      FROM Customers c JOIN
           Orders o
           ON o.CustomerId = c.CustomerId) h
WHERE seqnum = 1
```

ROW_NUMBER() assigns a sequence number to the orders within each household, starting with the earliest OrderDate and smallest OrderId on that date. The first order is simply the one whose sequence number is one.

Sequence numbers can be quite convenient for analytic purposes. They make it easier to determine what happens first and next and right before something else (as well as the window functions LAG() and LEAD()). If these values are not included in the data warehouse, then window functions can calculate them.

> **TIP** Sequence numbers on transactions are useful for finding the first transaction (as well as the next and previous ones). They can be added easily using the ROW_NUMBER() window function.

Pivoting

Pivoting is a common way to summarize data. It is the process of taking customer transactions that follow a regular pattern and summarizing multiple transactions into a single row with columns describing them. Each pivot column corresponds to a particular value or group of values, such as transactions during a month or transactions containing a particular product. The columns themselves contain basic summaries, such as:

- Counts of orders
- Sum of dollar amounts
- Average of dollar amounts
- Counts of some distinguishing feature (such as counts of distinct orders)

The examples in this section calculate the first of these.

The purchases dataset has several obvious dimensions for pivoting:

- Payment type pivot—Summarizing the transactions by payment type
- Campaign pivot—Summarizing the transactions by campaign
- Time pivot—Summarizing the transactions by time period
- Product pivot—Summarizing the transactions by product information

This section walks through the process of adding these pivots to the customer signature.

Conditional aggregation for pivoting creates multiple columns independently. Although this is a hassle, it only needs to be done once. When there are large numbers of columns, Excel can be used to automatically generate the code, as discussed in the aside "Using Excel to Generate SQL Code." Some databases support the PIVOT or CROSSTAB keyword; although this keyword simplifies the code a little, it is not as flexible as conditional aggregation.

Payment Type Pivot

The first example of a pivot is by payment type. This is the simplest because payment type is an attribute of Orders. Table 13-1 shows the six different payment types.

Table 13-1: Payment Types in Orders Table

PAYMENT TYPE	# ORDERS	DESCRIPTION
??	313	Unknown
AE	47,382	American Express
DB	12,739	Debit Card
MC	47,318	MasterCard
OC	8,214	Other Credit Card
VI	77,017	Visa

USING EXCEL TO GENERATE SQL CODE

Creating pivot columns requires repetitive code that can be cumbersome to type in. Earlier chapters (2 and 12 in particular) contain examples of using SQL to generate code. Excel can also be used to generate SQL statements.

For example, the payment type pivot contains several SELECT statements similar to:

```
SUM(CASE WHEN paymenttype = 'VI' THEN 1 ELSE 0 END) as pt_vi,
```

Assume that the various payment type values are in one column (for instance, the column B) and the preceding statement is in cell $A$1. To get the appropriate statement in column C, use the following formula:

```
=SUBSTITUTE($A$1, "VI", $B2)
```

And copy this formula down column C. The results can be copied into the SQL expression to add the appropriate columns.

Extra spaces before the SUM() cause the resulting expressions to "line up," making the query much easier to read. Also, the final comma needs to be removed from the last expression to prevent a syntax error in the SQL.

The ability to generate code in Excel is useful for other purposes as well. For instance, sometimes character strings contain unrecognized characters and we might want to look at the numeric values of each character. For this, the SELECT statement might look like:

```
SELECT ASCII(SUBSTRING(<str>, 1, 1)), SUBSTRING(<str>, 1, 1),
       ASCII(SUBSTRING(<str>, 2, 1)), SUBSTRING(<str>, 2, 1)
    . . .
```

Each expression extracts one character from the string and converts it to its ASCII code. The character itself is also included after the code.

Generating all these SELECT statements is cumbersome. Excel can simplify this task. The only difference is that column B contains the numbers 1, 2, 3, and so on, rather than values from the database.

The two smallest groups, "OC" and "??," can be combined into a single group, indicating some other credit card. The following query does the pivot:

```
WITH params as (
      SELECT CAST('2016-01-01' as DATE) as CutoffDate
      )
SELECT HouseholdId,
       SUM(CASE WHEN PaymentType = 'VI' THEN 1 ELSE 0 END) as pt_vi,
       SUM(CASE WHEN PaymentType = 'MC' THEN 1 ELSE 0 END) as pt_mc,
       SUM(CASE WHEN PaymentType = 'AX' THEN 1 ELSE 0 END) as pt_ax,
       SUM(CASE WHEN PaymentType = 'DB' THEN 1 ELSE 0 END) as pt_db,
       SUM(CASE WHEN PaymentType IN ('??', 'OC') THEN 1 ELSE 0 END
          ) as pt_oc
```

```
FROM params CROSS JOIN Orders o JOIN
     Customers c
     ON o.CustomerId = c.CustomerId
WHERE o.OrderDate < params.CutoffDate
GROUP BY c.HouseholdId
```

The pivoting uses the CASE statement nested in SUM() to calculate counts based on the payment type. Because the results are for the customer signature, the aggregation is at the household level. The query restricts orders to those before the cutoff date.

Channel Pivot

The next step is to include the channel pivot into the same query. This is only slightly more complicated because the channel is in Campaigns, so an additional join is needed. Table 13-2 shows the campaigns with the number of orders.

As with many categorical columns, a small number are quite common and many are uncommon. The first three values will go into their own columns, with the remaining going into an "OTHER" column.

The columns for the channels can be added directly into the query for the payment type pivot:

Table 13-2: Channels in Orders Table

CHANNEL	COUNT
PARTNER	84,518
WEB	53,362
AD	40,652
INSERT	7,333
REFERRAL	2,550
MAIL	1,755
BULK	1,295
CATALOG	710
EMPLOYEE	642
EMAIL	128
INTERNAL	34
CONFERENCE	3
SURVEY	1

```
WITH params as (
       SELECT CAST('2016-01-01' as DATE) as CutoffDate
     )
SELECT HouseholdId,
     . . .
       SUM(CASE WHEN channel = 'PARTNER' THEN 1 ELSE 0 END) as ca_partner,
       SUM(CASE WHEN channel = 'WEB' THEN 1 ELSE 0 END) as ca_web,
       SUM(CASE WHEN channel = 'AD' THEN 1 ELSE 0 END) as ca_ad,
       SUM(CASE WHEN channel NOT IN ('PARTNER', 'WEB', 'AD') THEN 1
             ELSE 0 END) as ca_other
FROM params CROSS JOIN Orders o JOIN
     Campaigns ca
     ON o.CampaignId = ca.CampaignId JOIN
     Customers c
     ON o.CustomerId = c.CustomerId
WHERE o.OrderDate < params.CutoffDate
GROUP BY c.HouseholdId
```

This query joins in `Campaigns` to get the channel code. It would be more fitting to use `LEFT OUTER JOIN` rather than a regular `JOIN` because this explicitly preserves all the rows in `Orders`. In this case, the `JOIN` never has an unmatched value, because all campaign IDs in the orders table are present in the lookup table.

Year Pivot

The next example is pivoting by time. The cutoff date used for the driving table is 2016-01-01. The idea is to summarize the number of orders placed in each year. A first attempt might have column names such as `Orders2013`, `Orders2014`, and `Orders2015`. This works when the cutoff date is in 2016, but not for other cutoff dates. For instance, if the cutoff date were in 2014, then the last two variables would not make sense.

Instead, the column names should be relative to the cutoff date. The following query adds the appropriate `SELECT` clauses onto the payment type/channel pivot:

```
WITH params as (
       SELECT CAST('2016-01-01' as DATE) as CutoffDate
     )
SELECT HouseholdId,
     . . .,
       SUM(CASE WHEN DATEDIFF(year, OrderDate, CutoffDate) = 0 THEN 1
             ELSE 0 END) as yr_1,
       SUM(CASE WHEN DATEDIFF(year, OrderDate, CutoffDate) = 1 THEN 1
             ELSE 0 END) as yr_2,
       SUM(CASE WHEN DATEDIFF(year, OrderDate, CutoffDate) = 2 THEN 1
             ELSE 0 END) as yr_3,
```

```
            SUM(CASE WHEN DATEDIFF(year, OrderDate, CutoffDate) = 3 THEN 1
                     ELSE 0 END) as yr_4
FROM params CROSS JOIN Orders o JOIN
     Campaigns ca
     ON o.CampaignId = ca.CampaignId JOIN
     Customers c
     ON o.CustomerId = c.CustomerId
WHERE o.OrderDate < params.CutoffDate
GROUP BY c.HouseholdId
```

This pivot calculates the number of years before the cutoff date using the DATEDIFF() function with the year argument.

Note that this works because the cutoff date is the first date of the year. DATEDIFF() counts the number of year boundaries between two dates, so 2015-12-31 and 2016-01-1 are one year apart. Chapter 5 discusses other ways to do this calculation.

Order Line Information Pivot

The product pivot counts the number of orders having a product in each of the eight product groups, as shown in Table 13-3.

This information can be calculated in the same subquery as the order information because order lines are logically related to orders. This also limits the number of places where the query needs to look up HouseholdId and apply the date restriction.

Table 13-3: Product Group Information in Orders

PRODUCT GROUP	NUMBER OF ORDER LINES	NUMBER OF ORDERS
BOOK	113,210	86,564
ARTWORK	56,498	45,430
OCCASION	41,713	37,898
FREEBIE	28,073	22,261
GAME	18,469	11,972
APPAREL	12,348	10,976
CALENDAR	9,872	8,983
OTHER	5,825	5,002
#N/A	9	9

A basic version is:

```
WITH params as (
        SELECT CAST('2016-01-01' as DATE) as CutoffDate
     )
SELECT HouseholdId,
        SUM(CASE WHEN p.GroupName = 'BOOK' THEN 1 ELSE 0
            END) as pg_book,
        SUM(CASE WHEN p.GroupName = 'ARTWORK' THEN 1 ELSE 0
            END) as pg_artwork,
        SUM(CASE WHEN p.GroupName = 'OCCASION' THEN 1 ELSE 0
            END) as pg_occasion,
        SUM(CASE WHEN p.GroupName = 'FREEBIE' THEN 1 ELSE 0
            END) as pg_freebie,
        SUM(CASE WHEN p.GroupName = 'GAME' THEN 1 ELSE 0
            END) as pg_game,
        SUM(CASE WHEN p.GroupName = 'APPAREL' THEN 1 ELSE 0
            END) as pg_apparel,
        SUM(CASE WHEN p.GroupName = 'CALENDAR' THEN 1 ELSE 0
            END) as pg_calendar,
        SUM(CASE WHEN p.GroupName = 'OTHER' THEN 1 ELSE 0
            END) as pg_other
 FROM params CROSS JOIN OrderLines ol JOIN
        Products p
        ON ol.ProductId = p.ProductId JOIN
        Orders o
        ON ol.OrderId = o.OrderId JOIN
        Customers c
        ON c.CustomerId = o.CustomerId
 WHERE o.OrderDate < params.CutoffDate
 GROUP BY c.HouseholdId
```

The SUM(CASE . . .) statements count order lines instead of orders, which is not quite the intention, but possibly close enough.

There are two ways to calculate a count of orders rather than order lines in this pivot query: One uses a single subquery for all the information from the order lines and the second uses multiple subqueries. The first approach basically changes all the previous SUM(CASE . . .) expressions to COUNT(DISTINCT CASE . . . OrderId END) in order to count the distinct order IDs rather than order lines.

This is a clever solution, and it works for a handful of columns. However, counting distinct order IDs is slower than simply adding up a bunch of ones and zeros.

The second approach is to summarize the order line data twice, once at the orders level and then again at the household level. The summary at the order lines level looks like:

```
SELECT ol.OrderId,
        MAX(CASE WHEN p.GroupName = 'BOOK' THEN 1 ELSE 0
            END) as pg_book,
```

```
        MAX(CASE WHEN p.GroupName = 'ARTWORK' THEN 1 ELSE 0
            END) as pg_artwork,
        MAX(CASE WHEN p.GroupName = 'OCCASION' THEN 1 ELSE 0
            END) as pg_occasion,
        MAX(CASE WHEN p.GroupName = 'FREEBIE' THEN 1 ELSE 0
            END) as pg_freebie,
        MAX(CASE WHEN p.GroupName = 'GAME' THEN 1 ELSE 0
            END) as pg_game,
        MAX(CASE WHEN p.GroupName = 'APPAREL' THEN 1 ELSE 0
            END) as pg_apparel,
        MAX(CASE WHEN p.GroupName = 'CALENDAR' THEN 1 ELSE 0
            END) as pg_calendar,
        MAX(CASE WHEN p.GroupName = 'OTHER' THEN 1 ELSE 0
            END) as pg_other
FROM params CROSS JOIN OrderLines ol JOIN
     Products p
     ON ol.ProductId = p.ProductId
GROUP BY ol.OrderId
```

This query uses MAX() to create an indicator variable for each product group in the order. This query does not join in the HouseholdId, nor does it apply the restriction on OrderDate. These restrictions can be applied at the next level to the order. The database does some unnecessary calculations (summarizing the order lines for orders that are not part of the final result). Sometimes including the restrictions at this level can improve performance, although the query is a bit more complicated.

Summarizing the order lines at the order level is only half the work. This order summary needs to be summarized again at the household level:

```
WITH params as (. . .),
     os as (previous query here)
SELECT HouseholdId, . . .,
       SUM(pg_book) as pg_book,
       SUM(pg_artwork) as pg_artwork,
       SUM(pg_occasion) as pg_occasion,
       SUM(pg_freebie) as pg_freebie,
       SUM(pg_game) as pg_game,
       SUM(pg_apparel) as pg_apparel,
       SUM(pg_calendar) as pg_calendar,
       SUM(pg_other) as pg_other
FROM params CROSS JOIN Orders o LEFT OUTER JOIN
     Campaigns ca
     ON o.CampaignId = ca.CampaignId LEFT JOIN
     os
     ON os.OrderId = o.OrderId JOIN
     Customers c
     ON o.CustomerId = c.CustomerId
WHERE o.OrderDate < params.CutoffDate
GROUP BY c.HouseholdId
```

The order line subquery is joined in using a LEFT OUTER JOIN to ensure that orders are not lost, even orders having no order lines. This is good practice, even though all orders do in fact have order lines in this database.

The subquery that summarizes the order lines could use SUM() to count order lines rather than MAX() to create an indicator flag. The outer query would then use a slightly different expression to count orders:

```
SUM(CASE WHEN pg_book > 0 THEN 1 ELSE 0 END) as pg_book
```

These two forms are equivalent, but the first has slightly simpler code. On the other hand, the second produces an intermediate result that could be used for other purposes.

Although this query looks complicated, it is composed of well-defined pieces, carefully sewn together and made visible by the use of indentation and CTEs. This structure works for a couple of reasons. First, each subquery is created subject to the constraints of the customer signature. Also, each table and subquery is carefully joined in with consideration of how it affects the number of rows in the final result. Care is taken not to lose rows or to multiply rows inadvertently.

> **WARNING**   When joining tables together for a customer signature, be very careful that there are no duplicate rows in the tables being joined into the driving table. Duplicate rows can inadvertently multiply the number of rows in the customer signature table.

Summarizing

Pivoting data summarizes transactions by aggregating information along various dimensions. There are other ways to summarize data. Some fit directly into the pivoting query built in the previous section. Some are a bit more complicated and provide an opportunity to add in customer-centric business measures.

Basic Summaries

Basic summaries of the orders data include information such as:

- Total number of orders
- Total number of units ordered
- Total dollar amount of orders
- Average dollar amount

These summaries can be calculated in the same way as the pivoted data. The only difference is the particular expressions used for calculating the values.

More Complex Summaries

Interesting indicators of customer behavior lurk inside customer transactions. One credit card company, for instance, tracks how often a customer spends more than $100 at a restaurant more than 50 miles from the customer's home.

In the purchases data, the following are potentially interesting questions:

- How many of the customer's orders are over $200?
- What is the maximum number of different products in any one order?
- How many different products has the customer ordered over time?
- What is the longest duration between the order date and the ship date?
- How often has the ship date been more than one week after the order date?

Each of these questions suggests a particular measure that might be useful for the customer signature.

The following query calculates the answers as measures for each customer:

```
SELECT HouseholdId,
       COUNT(DISTINCT CASE WHEN o.TotalPrice > 200 THEN o.OrderId END
            ) as numgt2000,
       COUNT(DISTINCT ol.ProductId) as numhhprods,
       MAX(op.numproducts) as maxnumordprods,
       MAX(DATEDIFF(day, o.OrderDate, ol.ShipDate)) as maxshipdelay,
       COUNT(DISTINCT CASE WHEN DATEDIFF(day, o.OrderDate, ol.ShipDate) > 7
                   THEN o.OrderId END)
FROM Customers c JOIN
     Orders o
     ON c.CustomerId = o.CustomerId JOIN
     OrderLines ol
     ON o.OrderId = ol.OrderId JOIN
     (SELECT ol.OrderId, COUNT(DISTINCT ol.ProductId) as numproducts
      FROM OrderLines ol
      GROUP BY ol.OrderId) op
     ON o.OrderId = op.OrderId
GROUP BY c.HouseholdId
```

This version of the query has the same problem as some of the earlier queries. It does not take the cutoff date into account. To fix this:

```
WITH params as (
     SELECT CAST('2016-01-01' as DATE) as CutoffDate
     )
SELECT HouseholdId,
       COUNT(DISTINCT CASE WHEN o.TotalPrice > 200 THEN o.OrderId END
            ) as numgt2000,
       COUNT(DISTINCT ol.ProductId) as numhhprods,

       MAX(op.numproducts) as maxnumordprods,
       MAX(DATEDIFF(day, o.OrderDate, ol.ShipDate)) as maxshipdelay,
       COUNT(DISTINCT CASE WHEN DATEDIFF(day, o.OrderDate, ol.ShipDate) > 7
                   THEN o.OrderId END)
FROM params CROSS JOIN Customers c JOIN
     Orders o
     ON c.CustomerId = o.CustomerId JOIN
     OrderLines ol
```

```
    ON o.OrderId = ol.OrderId JOIN
    (SELECT ol.OrderId, COUNT(DISTINCT ol.ProductId) as numproducts
     FROM OrderLines ol
     GROUP BY ol.OrderId) op
    ON o.OrderId = op.OrderId
 WHERE o.OrderDate < params.CutoffDate AND ol.ShipDate < params.CutoffDate
 GROUP BY c.HouseholdId
```

The WHERE clause requires that both OrderDate and ShipDate be before the cutoff date.

Clearly, only orders whose order date precedes the cutoff date should be included in the customer signature. It is not clear if the ship date should have this restriction. The decision depends on how data is loaded into the database. The following are some possibilities:

- Only completed orders are loaded in the database. An order is completed when the last item is shipped.

- All orders are in the database; ship dates in order lines are updated as new information is available.

- All orders are in the data, but order lines are available only after they ship.

These different scenarios affect the relationship between the ship date and the cutoff date. If the first is true, then orders are only available after the last ship date, so the signature should only include orders whose last ship date is before the cutoff date. If the second scenario is true, then it is okay to ignore the ship date. Future ship dates are "intended ship dates." If the third is true, then very recent orders should be smaller than orders even a week old. In addition, some orders might have no order lines.

Understanding when data is loaded is important. We could imagine a scenario where order lines are only available after they ship, although the corresponding orders are already in the database. An analysis might "discover" that the most recent orders are smaller than older orders. This fact would merely be an artifact of how the data is loaded because the most recent orders might not have all their order lines.

TIP Understanding the process of loading the database is important. This process leaves artifacts in the data that might be "discovered" when analyzing the data.

Extracting Features

Sometimes, the most interesting features are the descriptions of products and channels, markets and retailers. These descriptions include more complex data types, such as text and geographic position. This section discusses some ideas about extracting information for geographic and character data types.

Geographic Location Information

Geographic location information is represented as latitudes and longitudes, and perhaps as geographic hierarchies. When mapped, this information is quite interesting. However, maps do not fit well into customer signatures nor are they well-suited for most statistical and data mining algorithms.

Longitudes and latitudes are generated by geocoding addresses or by reading positioning information on a mobile device. The most obvious address is the customer address. However, there are addresses for retailers, and ATM machines, and mobile phones, and city centers, and Internet service provider points-of-presence, and so on. Such geocoding leads to questions such as:

- How far is a customer from the center of the nearest MSA (metropolitan statistical area)?

- How many purchases were made more than 100 miles from home?

- What proportion of ATM transactions is within 10 miles of home?

- What is the direction from the customer to the nearest MSA center?

These questions readily turn into customer attributes.

Geographic positions typically have two types of information. The most common is distance, which was discussed in Chapter 4, along with formulas for calculating the distance between two geographic points.

The other type of information is directional, calculated using a basic trigonometric formula:

```
direction = ATAN(vertical distance / horizontal distance)) * 180 / PI()
```

This formula is very similar in both Excel and SQL.

Date Time Columns

Customer behavior varies by time of day, by day of week, by season of the year. Some businesses classify their customers as "weekday lunch buyers" or "weekend shoppers" or "Monday complainers." These are examples of business classifications that can be captured in the customer signature.

> **TIP** The timing of customer interactions is a good example of a business metric to incorporate in the customer signature.

The customer signature can capture the raw information by pivoting date and time information. For instance, the following SELECT statement can be added to the pivot query to add up the number of orders made on each day of the week:

```
WITH params as (
    SELECT CAST('2016-01-01' as DATE) as CutoffDate)
```

```
         )
SELECT HouseholdId, . . .
        SUM(CASE WHEN cal.dow = 'Mon' THEN 1 ELSE 0 END) as dw_mon,
        SUM(CASE WHEN cal.dow = 'Tue' THEN 1 ELSE 0 END) as dw_tue,
        . . .
        SUM(CASE WHEN cal.dow = 'Sun' THEN 1 ELSE 0 END) as dw_sun,
        . . .
FROM params CROSS JOIN Orders o JOIN
        Campaigns ca
        ON o.CampaignId = ca.CampaignId JOIN
        Calendar cal
        ON o.OrderDate = cal.Date JOIN
        Customers c
        ON o.CustomerId = c.CustomerId
WHERE o.OrderDate < params.CutoffDate
GROUP BY c.HouseholdId
```

This query uses `Calendar` to find the day of the week. An alternative is to use a database function, such as `DATENAME(weekday, <col>)`. Using `Calendar` makes further refinements possible, such as distinguishing holidays from non-holidays. And, a calendar table has another advantage because internationalization settings in a database can affect the names of weekdays and months.

If `OrderDate` had a time component, the following `SELECT` statement would add up the number of orders during from midnight to 3:59:59.999 a.m.:

```
SELECT SUM(CASE WHEN DATEPART(hour, o.OrderDate) BETWEEN 0 AND 3
                THEN 1 ELSE 0 END) as hh00_03
```

This is the same structure as the earlier pivot statements, but applied to times.

Patterns in Strings

Traditionally, SQL has only rudimentary string manipulation functions, but these are often sufficient for extracting interesting features. More recently, databases have started to provide better string functions, such as regular expressions, and support for XML and JSON data types. Unfortunately, these functions are database specific.

TIP Descriptions and names often contain very interesting information. However, the information needs to be extracted feature by feature into the customer signature.

Email Addresses

An email address has the form "<user name>@<domain name>", where the domain name has an extension, such as .com, .edu, .uk, or .gov. The domain name and domain name extension can be interesting features about users.

The following code extracts these features from an email address:

```
SELECT LEFT(emailaddress, CHARINDEX('@', emailaddress) - 1) as username,
       SUBSTRING(emailaddress, CHARINDEX('@', emailaddress) + 1, 1000
              ) as domain,
       RIGHT(emailaddress, CHARINDEX('.', REVERSE(emailaddress))
            ) as extension
```

The user name takes all characters up to the "@," and the domain is all characters after it. The domain extension is everything after the last period. This expression uses a trick to find the position of the last period by finding the position of the first period in the reversed string.

Addresses

Addresses are complicated strings that are difficult to use directly for data mining purposes. Geocoding converts them to latitudes and longitudes, and the associated census descriptors of the location.

The address line itself might provide information about customers:

- Is the address for an apartment?
- Is the address for a PO Box?

The following code identifies whether a column called `address` contains an apartment number or a post office box:

```
SELECT (CASE WHEN address LIKE '%#%' OR
                  LOWER(address) LIKE '%apt.%' OR
                  LOWER(address) LIKE '% apt %' OR
                  LOWER(address) LIKE '% unit %'
             THEN 1 ELSE 0 END) as hasapt,
       (CASE WHEN REPLACE(REPLACE(UPPER(address), '.', ''), 6),
                   ' ', '') LIKE 'POBOX%'
             THEN 1 ELSE 0 END) as haspobox
```

The apartment indicator is defined by the presence of " apt." or " apt " (rather than just "apt") to avoid matching street names such as "Sanibel-Captiva Road," "Captains Court," and "Baptist Camp Road." For post office boxes, the address should start with "PO BOX", "P.O. Box.", or "POBOX".

Product Descriptions

Product descriptions often contain useful information such as:

- Color
- Flavor
- Special attributes (such as organic, all cotton, and so on)

Interesting attributes can be turned into flags:

```
(CASE WHEN LOWER(description) LIKE '%diet%' THEN 1 ELSE 0 END) as is_diet,
(CASE WHEN LOWER(description) LIKE '%red%' THEN 1 ELSE 0 END) as is_red,
(CASE WHEN LOWER(description) LIKE '%organic%' THEN 1 ELSE 0 END) as is_org
```

These cases look for particular substrings in the description.

A product description might have a specific format. For instance, the first word may be the product group name. It can be extracted using:

```
SUBSTRING(description, CHARINDEX(' ', description), 1000) as productgroup
```

Or, the last word might be something interesting such as the price:

```
RIGHT(description, CHARINDEX(' ', REVERSE(description))) as price
```

Discovering what is interesting is a manual process that often involves reading through the descriptions and making judgments as to what is important for distinguishing among customers.

Credit Card Numbers

Credit card numbers are useful for analysis in two ways. The first is by identifying the type of credit card. The second is by identifying whether the same card is being used over time. Chapter 2 has both the table mapping the initial digits of credit card numbers to credit card types and a SQL query for transforming the information.

Comparing credit card numbers on different payment transactions is as easy as comparing two columns. However, storing credit card numbers in analytic databases poses a security risk, so storing them explicitly is a bad idea.

An alternative is to convert the credit card number to something unrecognizable as a credit card number. One way is to have a master table that contains credit card numbers, with no duplicates. The row number from this table replaces the credit card number, and very few people have access to the master table. This approach just shifts the security risk to another system.

Another approach uses *hashing*. There are many different hashing algorithms. One very simple algorithm that is often sufficient is:

1. Treat the credit card number as a number.
2. Multiply the number by a large prime number.
3. Add another large prime number.
4. Divide by yet another and take the remainder.

This works because two different numbers very, very rarely get mapped to the same number. Extracting the original credit card number is difficult unless you know the specific primes used in the formula. Databases also have hash functions built in. (In SQL Server two such functions are CHECKSUM() and HASHBYTES().)

> **TIP** When storing sensitive customer information in a database, consider hashing it so that the analysis database doesn't store the real value.

Summarizing Customer Behaviors

The customer signature has been presented as a place to put lots of data elements and basic summaries. It is also a place to put more complex measures of customer behaviors that rise to being customer-centric business metrics.

This section has three examples. The first is calculating the slope, the beta value, for series of transactions. The second is identifying weekend shoppers, and the third is applying metrics to identify customers whose usage is decreasing.

Calculating Slope for Time Series

Pivoting numeric values creates a time series, such as the dollar amount of purchases in a series of months. Using the ideas from Chapter 12, we can calculate the slope for these numbers.

Most households in the purchases data have one order, which does not provide a good example for finding a trend. Instead, let's look at the zip-code level: *Which zip codes have seen an increase in customers in the years before the cutoff date?* Notice that this question is still about what happens before the cutoff date, so the resulting measures can be included in a customer signature.

This section answers the question three different ways. The first is to use the pivoted values to calculate the slope—but the SQL is messy. The second way is to summarize each year of data for the zip codes. The third method generalizes the second for any series of values.

Calculating Slope from Pivoted Time Series

The following query calculates the number of households who place an order in each year for each zip code.

```
WITH params as (
      SELECT CAST('2016-01-01' as DATE) as CutoffDate)
      )
SELECT o.ZipCode, COUNT(*) as cnt,
      FLOOR(DATEDIFF(year, '2009-01-01', MIN(CutoffDate))) as numyears,
```

```
       COUNT(DISTINCT (CASE WHEN DATEDIFF(year, OrderDate, CutoffDate) = 1
                      THEN c.HouseholdId END)) as year1,
       COUNT(DISTINCT (CASE WHEN DATEDIFF(year, OrderDate, CutoffDate) = 2
                      THEN c.HouseholdId END)) as year2,
       . . .
       COUNT(DISTINCT (CASE WHEN DATEDIFF(year, OrderDate, CutoffDate) = 7
                      THEN c.HouseholdId END)) as year7
FROM params CROSS JOIN Orders o JOIN
     Customers c
     ON o.CustomerId = c.CustomerId
GROUP BY o.ZipCode
```

This query is carefully dependent on the cutoff date, so the results can be used in the customer signature. The number of years of data is contained in the column numyears. The remaining columns contain the summaries by year.

The query uses `DATEDIFF(year, . . .)`. This works because the cutoff date is on the first of the year. As already noted, in SQL Server this function does not calculate the number of years between two dates; it calculates the number of year boundaries—the number of times the ball drops in Times Square at the end of New Year's Eve between two dates. A more accurate function for any cutoff date would be something like: `FLOOR(DATEDIFF(day, OrderDate, CutoffDate) / 365.25)` or one of the methods described in Chapter 5.

Chapter 12 has the formula for the slope:

```
slope = (n*Sxy - Sx*Sy) / (n*Sxx - Sx*Sx)
```

The pivoted data has no explicit X-values. They can be assumed to be a sequence of numbers starting with one for the oldest value. The resulting slope can be interpreted as the average number of additional households that make a purchase in each succeeding year.

The following query calculates the intermediate values and then the slope:

```
WITH zsum AS (<previous query>)
SELECT (n*Sxy - Sx*Sy) / (n*Sxx - Sx*Sx), z.*
FROM (SELECT zipcode, cnt,
             numyears*1.0 as n,
             numyears*(numyears + 1) / 2 as Sx,
             numyears*(numyears + 1)*(2*numyears + 1) / 6 as Sxx,
             (CASE WHEN numyears < 2 THEN NULL
                   WHEN numyears = 3 THEN year3 + year2 + year1
                   WHEN numyears = 4 THEN year4 + year3 + year2 + year1
                   WHEN numyears = 5 THEN year5 + year4 + year3 + year2 +
                        year1
                   WHEN numyears = 6 THEN year6 + year5 + year4 + year3 +
                        year2 + year1
                   ELSE year7 + year6 + year5 + year4 + year3 + year2 +
                        year1 END) as Sy,
```

```
                    (CASE WHEN numyears < 2 THEN NULL
                          WHEN numyears = 3 THEN 1*year3 + 2*year2 + 3*year1
                          WHEN numyears = 4 THEN 1*year4 + 2*year3 + 3*year2 +
                                                 4*year1
                          WHEN numyears = 5 THEN 1*year5 + 2*year4 + 3*year3 +
                                                 4*year2 + 5*year1
                          WHEN numyears = 6 THEN 1*year6 + 2*year5 + 3*year4 +
                                                 4*year3 + 5*year2 + 6*year1
                          ELSE 1*year7 + 2*year6 + 3*year5 + 4*year4 + 5*year3 +
                               6*year2 + 7*year1 END) as Sxy
          FROM zsum z) z
```

This follows the logic from Chapter 12. The slope represents the growth in terms of the number of additional customers who make purchases each year in a zip code.

Eliminating the intermediate sums makes the query even more cumbersome and prone to error:

```
SELECT (CASE WHEN numyears < 2 THEN NULL
             WHEN numyears = 3
             THEN numyears*(1*year3 + 2*year2 + 3*year1)-
                  (numyears*(numyears + 1) / 2)*(year3 + year2 + year1)
             WHEN numyears = 4
             THEN numyears*(1*year4 + 2*year3 + 3*year2 + 4*year1)-
                  (numyears*(numyears + 1) / 2)*(year4 + year3 + year2 + year1)
             WHEN numyears = 5
             THEN numyears*(1*year5 + 2*year4 + 3*year3 + 4*year2 +
                  5*year1) - (numyears*(numyears + 1) / 2)*(year5 + year4 +
                  year3 + year2 + year1)
             WHEN numyears = 6
             THEN numyears*(1*year6 + 2*year5 + 3*year4 + 4*year3 +
                  5*year2 + 6*year1) -
                  (numyears*(numyears + 1)/2)*(year6 + year5 + year4 +
                  year3 + year2 + year1)
             ELSE numyears*(1*year7 + 2*year6 + 3*year5 + 4*year4 +
                  5*year3 + 6*year2 + 7*year1) -
                  (numyears*(numyears + 1) / 2)*(year7 + year6 + year5 +
                  year4 + year3 + year2 + year1)
             END) / (1.0*numyears * numyears*(numyears + 1)*(2*numyears + 1) / 6
                  - ((numyears*(numyears + 1) / 2))*(numyears*(numyears + 1) / 2)
         ) as slope, z.*
   FROM zsum
```

Under these circumstances, keeping the intermediate sums is preferable, even though they are not otherwise useful. One simplification is to remove the complicated CASE statement by assuming that all the pivot columns have data, but this assumption may not be true.

Calculating Slope for a Regular Time Series

An alternative approach does not use the pivot columns, instead using an intermediate result set with a separate row for each zip code and year:

```
WITH params as (
     SELECT CAST('2016-01-01' as DATE) as CutoffDate)
     )
SELECT o.ZipCode, DATEDIFF(year, o.OrderDate, CutoffDate) as yearsago,
       DATEDIFF(year, '2009-01-01', MIN(CutoffDate)) as numyears,
       (DATEDIFF(year, '2009-01-01', MAX(CutoffDate)) -
        DATEDIFF(year, o.OrderDate, CutoffDate)) as x,
       COUNT(DISTINCT HouseholdId) as y
FROM params CROSS JOIN Orders o JOIN
     Customers c
     ON o.CustomerId = c.CustomerId
WHERE o.OrderDate < CutoffDate
GROUP BY o.ZipCode, DATEDIFF(year, o.OrderDate, CutoffDate)
```

When a given year has no orders, the data is simply missing from the summary. For zip codes that have years with no customers, the slope calculated this way is going to be different from the slope calculated on the pivoted data.

The following query calculates the intermediate values and slope:

```
WITH zysm as (<previous query>)
SELECT (CASE WHEN n = 1 THEN 0
             ELSE (n*Sxy - Sx*Sy) / (n*Sxx - Sx*Sx) END) as slope, zy.*
FROM (SELECT zipcode, MAX(numyears) as numyears, COUNT(*)*1.0 as n,
             SUM(x) as Sx,
             SUM(x*x) as Sxx,
             SUM(x*y) as Sxy,
             SUM(y) as Sy
      FROM zysum
      GROUP BY zipcode
     ) zy
ORDER BY n DESC
```

This query is simpler than the previous version. Instead of using the pivoted time series, it calculates the X-value implicitly from the years before the cutoff date. The CASE statement in the SELECT assigns a value for slope when only one year has purchases; otherwise, the formula would result in a divide-by-zero error. The results from this query are slightly different from the pivoted version because the pivoted version treats years with no data as having zero sales, whereas this excludes such years from the calculation.

Calculating Slope for an Irregular Time Series

The previous calculation can be extended to irregular time series as well as regular time series. An irregular time series is one where the spacing between the X-values is not constant. Purchases for customers are a typical example, and determining the trend can be quite useful.

The query for this is essentially the same as the previous example, except the X-values would come from some other value in the data.

Weekend Shoppers

A "perfect" weekend shopper has the following characteristics:

- All their shopping by number of orders is on Saturday or Sunday.
- All their shopping by dollar value is on Saturday or Sunday.
- All their shopping by number of units is on Saturday or Sunday.

For the perfect weekender, these are all equivalent because all shopping on the weekends implies that all units, orders, and dollars are spent on the weekends. They also suggest defining a metric that defines how close a customer is to being a "perfect" weekender.

Table 13-4 shows some examples of customers with multiple orders: one is a perfect weekender, one a partial weekender, and one a never weekender.

Table 13-4: Examples of Transactions for Weekend and Non-Weekend Shoppers

HOUSEHOLD ID	ORDER ID	ORDER DATE	DAY OF WEEK	DOLLARS	UNITS
21159179	1102013	2013-08-17	Sat	$40.00	3
21159179	1107588	2013-09-16	Mon	$67.00	5
21159179	1143702	2014-08-03	Sun	$90.00	6
36207142	1089881	2013-06-13	Thu	$10.00	1
36207142	1092505	2013-11-27	Wed	$8.00	1
36207142	1084048	2013-12-23	Mon	$49.00	3
36207142	1186443	2014-12-05	Fri	$5.00	2
36207142	1206093	2014-12-31	Wed	$7.00	1
36528618	1013609	2011-01-29	Sat	$182.00	2
36528618	1057400	2012-11-25	Sun	$195.00	1
36528618	1059424	2012-11-25	Sun	$195.00	1
36528618	1074857	2013-12-14	Sat	$570.00	2

The following ratios help distinguish among these groups:

- Proportion of all orders that are on weekends
- Proportion of all dollars spent on weekends
- Proportion of all units on weekends

These all vary from zero (no evidence of weekend shopping behavior) to one (always a weekend shopper). Table 13-5 shows the summaries with this information.

Recalling some ideas from probability, these can be combined into a single likelihood measure, as in the following query:

```
WITH params as (
        SELECT CAST('2016-01-01' as DATE) as CutoffDate)
    )
SELECT h.*,
       (CASE WHEN weekend_orders = 1 OR weekend_units = 1 OR
                  weekend_dollars = 1 THEN 1
             ELSE (weekend_orders / (1 - weekend_orders))*
                  (weekend_units / (1 - weekend_units))*
                  (weekend_dollars / (1 - weekend_dollars)) END) as weekendp
FROM (SELECT HouseholdId,
             SUM(CASE WHEN cal.dow IN ('Sat', 'Sun') THEN 1.0
                      ELSE 0 END) / COUNT(*) as weekend_orders,
             SUM(CASE WHEN cal.dow IN ('Sat', 'Sun') THEN NumUnits*1.0
                      ELSE 0 END) / SUM(numunits) as weekend_units,
             SUM(CASE WHEN cal.dow IN ('Sat', 'Sun') THEN TotalPrice
                      ELSE 0 END) / SUM(TotalPrice) as weekend_dollars
      FROM params CROSS JOIN Orders o JOIN
           Calendar cal
           ON o.OrderDate = cal.Date JOIN
           Customers c
           ON o.CustomerId = c.CustomerId
      WHERE o.OrderDate < CutoffDate AND
            o.NumUnits > 0 AND o.TotalPrice > 0
      GROUP BY c.HouseholdId) h
```

Table 13-5: Some Shoppers and Their Weekend Shopping Behavior

	# ORDERS		DOLLARS		# UNITS	
HOUSEHOLD	ALL	WEEKEND	ALL	WEEKEND	ALL	WEEKEND
21159179	3	66.7%	$197	66.0%	14	64.3%
36207142	5	0.0%	$79	0.0%	8	0.0%
36528618	4	100.0%	$1,142	100.0%	6	100.0%

INCORPORATING PRIOR INFORMATION

The definition of weekend shopper works well for customers who have lots of data. However, it does not work well for only a few transactions. For instance, should the score of someone who has made exactly one purchase that is on the weekend be the same as someone who has made one hundred purchases, all on the weekend?

Intuitively, the answer is no because much more evidence has accumulated for the second customer. How can the weekend shopper score reflect this intuition?

One method from Chapter 3 is to subtract one standard deviation from the score and use this as the bound; however, that still does not work for a customer with only one purchase, because the standard deviation is not defined. A more interesting way is to assume that everyone has a score between zero and one of being a weekend shopper—and this score starts out with some value for everyone, even before they have made a purchase. Such an assumption is called a *prior*, which is a central notion in Bayesian statistics.

For this discussion, let's consider using only the proportion of transactions as the indicator for a weekend shopper (rather than the combined likelihood value). What is an appropriate value for the prior? The appropriate prior is the overall proportion of weekend orders in the data, which is 21.6%. Given no other information, this says that someone has a weekend shopper score of 21.6%, even before they make any purchases.

The next question is how to combine information from `Orders` with the prior. What is the estimate for being a weekend shopper for someone who has exactly one purchase on the weekend? Remember, the method in the text gives this person a perfect 100% score, which seems a bit too high.

The idea is to combine the prior estimate with the new evidence, using a weighted average:

```
new estimate = ((prior * K) + 1) / (K + 1)
```

The value `K` represents how much weight we put on the prior. If the value is zero, the result is the same as in the text. A reasonable value is one, which results in the score of 60.8% for the customer with one weekend purchase.

Continues

This query calculates three measures of being a weekend shopper along the dimensions of orders, units, and price. The likelihood of someone being a weekend shopper is one minus the product of one minus each of these proportions, a method of combining probabilities discussed in Chapter 11 in the context of naïve Bayesian models. Although these are not independent, the combination still gives an overall measure of being a weekend shopper.

This method for calculating the weekend shoppers has a problem when customers have very few purchases; a more intuitive calculation is discussed in the aside "Incorporating Prior Information."

Declining Usage Behavior

Declining usage is often a precursor to customers stopping. One way to quantify declining usage is to use the beta value (slope) of a usage measure, such as dollars spent per month or web visits per week.

INCORPORATING PRIOR INFORMATION (*continued*)

What happens for the next purchase? The reasoning is the same, except the value of K is incremented by one, because of the additional observation.

The following table shows the scores for customers who make only weekend purchases and no weekend purchases:

ONLY WEEKEND SHOPPER			NON-WEEKEND SHOPPER		
# ORDERS	K	SCORE	# ORDERS	K	SCORE
0	1	21.6%	0	1	21.6%
1	2	60.8%	1	2	10.8%
2	3	73.9%	2	3	7.2%
3	4	80.4%	3	4	5.4%
4	5	84.3%	4	5	4.3%
5	6	86.9%	5	6	3.6%

A customer with five weekend purchases (and no others) has a score of 86.9%. A customer who has made five weekday purchases (and no others) has a score of 3.6%. These seem reasonable.

The following formula allows you to adjust the weight of the prior, using the number of observations and the average observed value:

```
Est = (K * prior + number * average) / (K + number)
```

What happens to a customer who has 100 purchases all on the weekend? The calculation is simple: The number is 100 and the average is 1, resulting in a score of 99.2%.

This method of incorporating priors requires both finding an appropriate prior estimate to use when no evidence is available, and a way of combining new evidence with the prior. The use of priors produces more intuitive scores than directly using the proportion.

The beta value can be misleading because it fits a long-term trend to the data. Often, customer behaviors are relatively steady (varying within a range) and then declining. Other measures of declining behavior include:

- Ratio of recent activity to historical activity, such as most recent month of usage divided by usage twelve months ago

- Number of recent months where usage is less than the month before

- Ratio of the most recent month to the average over the previous year

- Difference between recent values and the longer term trend, measured in standard deviations

These are all reasonable measures of declining usage and all are possible to implement in SQL.

We'll investigate the first three by looking at the corresponding quantities for zip codes by year:

- Ratio of most recent number of customers to the year before
- Ratio of the most recent number of customers to the average of preceding years (the index value)
- Number of recent years where the number of customers is declining

The following query calculates these quantities from the pivoted zip code columns:

```
WITH zsum as (<zip code summary query>)
SELECT zsum.*,
       NULLIF(year2, 0)  as year1_2_growth,
       (CASE WHEN (COALESCE(year1, 0) + COALESCE(year2, 0) +
                   COALESCE(year3, 0) + COALESCE(year4, 0) +
                   COALESCE(year5, 0) + COALESCE(year6, 0) +
                   COALESCE(year7, 0)) = 0 THEN 1
             ELSE year1 / ((COALESCE(year1, 0) + COALESCE(year2, 0) +
                            COALESCE(year3, 0) + COALESCE(year4, 0) +
                            COALESCE(year5, 0) + COALESCE(year6, 0) +
                            COALESCE(year7, 0)) / 7.0) END) as year1_index,
       COALESCE(CASE WHEN numyears < 2 OR year1 >= year2 THEN 0 END,
                CASE WHEN numyears < 3 OR year2 >= year3 THEN 1 END,
                CASE WHEN numyears < 4 OR year3 >= year4 THEN 2 END,
                CASE WHEN numyears < 5 OR year4 >= year5 THEN 3 END,
                CASE WHEN numyears < 6 OR year5 >= year6 THEN 4 END,
                CASE WHEN numyears < 7 OR year6 >= year7 THEN 5 END,
                6) as years_of_declining_sales
FROM zsum
```

The calculation for growth is fairly obvious; the NULLIF() expression handles division by zero. If the previous year had no customers, the growth is undefined.

The index calculation does a direct calculation of the average over the previous seven years. A simpler approach would calculate the sum or average in the subquery. However, this version uses the zip code summary subquery exactly as originally written.

The number of years of declining sales uses the COALESCE() function extensively. This function returns the first non-null value. So, the logic proceeds as follows:

1. If the year1 >= year2, then the first value is zero and COALESCE() returns this value; otherwise, the value is NULL, indicating at least one year of declining usages, and processing continues.

2. Then, if year2 >= year3, the decline is only from last year. So, the most recent two years show a decline but none before that; otherwise, the value is NULL, indicating at least two years of declining usage, and processing continues.

3. And so on.

An alternative to the COALESCE() function is a more complicated CASE statement. These values can then be included in the customer signature as indicators of declining usage.

TIP The COALESCE() function can be very useful for calculating indexes, counts, and averages in sets of columns where some of the values may be NULL.

Lessons Learned

When analytic needs go beyond the capabilities of SQL and Excel, customer signatures can be used to store summarized behavior and demographic information for other tools. SQL has an advantage for building customer signatures because it has powerful and scalable data manipulation capabilities—and databases often contain the data that is ultimately going to be scored.

The customer signature should be based on a cutoff date, only incorporating input columns from before the date. For predictive modeling, the targets come from a time frame after the cutoff date. A customer signature has columns coming from many different tables. Most columns are input columns. The customer signature might also include target columns, identification columns, and the cutoff date.

Creating customer signatures requires gathering information from different sources. Some columns might be copied directly. Others might come from fixed lookup tables. Yet others might come from dynamic lookup tables that summarize customer behavior along various dimensions. And others come from pivoting and summarizing the most voluminous part of the data, customer transactions. These operations can be combined to create very powerful features for data mining purposes.

Combining information from multiple columns can lead to very powerful features. For instance, trends over time can be added by incorporating the slope of the best-fit line, an idea discussed in the previous chapter.

The customer signature provides a structure for understanding customers and using many of the techniques described in earlier chapters. Much of the effort in data analysis is in bringing the data together and understanding it. The ability of SQL to express very complex data manipulations, and the ability to optimize the resulting queries on large hardware, makes relational databases a powerful choice for creating customer signatures.

As earlier chapters have shown, the combination of SQL and Excel is a powerful analysis tool itself for understanding customers. When the combination is not powerful enough, they provide the foundation for bringing the right data into even more sophisticated tools. Queries that build customer signatures are another example of complex queries. As SQL queries become more complex, the performance of SQL becomes more important—a topic that brings us to the final chapter of the book.

Performance *Is* the Issue: Using SQL Effectively

This chapter differs from the earlier chapters by shifting the focus from functionality to performance. The subject of performance can be highly database specific. Fortunately (and perhaps surprisingly), some general rules and considerations apply to most if not all databases. Some of these rules are based on general principles of how database engines are designed; others are based on how SQL is written; and still others on how the data is represented in the database. This chapter covers these general principles rather than database-specific optimizations.

The power of SQL arises from several factors. First, SQL can express many important data manipulations needed for analysis—the use of common table expressions and subqueries gives the language a lot of power. Second, the database engine optimizes the queries for available hardware and data. This optimization is very important: The same SQL query that runs on a small table on an Android device can run on a giant table on a massive server with many processors. The SQL statement remains the same, even though the underlying algorithms may change dramatically. Users do not have to fully understand the underlying algorithms to use SQL effectively, any more than commuters need to understand mechanics or the physics of the internal combustion engine to drive their cars to work.

This chapter discusses different ways that a simple query might be executed, to give a flavor of the optimization component of the SQL compiler. This overview glosses over the underlying algorithms used for things like joins and aggregations. It does introduce key ideas about performance, such as the difference between full table scans and index lookups and the ability of the database engine to take advantage of parallelism.

The most important feature in SQL for improving performance is the index, a topic that has so far been studiously avoided in order to focus on *what* SQL can do rather than *how* the engine works. Indexes are often the key to getting good performance from a database, but they do not provide any new functionality. Fortunately, some handy rules help determine the best index for a given query.

The final part of the chapter presents multiple ways of doing the same thing. SQL is a very expressive language and often more than one query returns a particular result set. Surprisingly, one method can be significantly more efficient than other methods—and the more efficient methods are often the best regardless of the database.

Each database offers opportunities for further optimizations specific to that database; these are not covered here. For instance, sometimes, using temporary tables is better than writing a more complicated query (although this is rarer than one might expect). However, that type of optimization is highly database-specific. Because databases have a similar underlying architecture, some common principles work across all, or almost all, databases. This chapter starts by discussing these commonalities.

Query Engines and Performance

A SQL query describes the result set but does not specify the particular steps or algorithms used for generating the results. This allows the SQL optimizer to produce the best query plan—at least in theory.

By contrast, most computer languages are *procedural*. A command that says "sort the data" generally implements a particular algorithm for the sort—bubble sort, merge sort, quicksort, or perhaps some fancy parallel out-of-memory sort. The SQL statement ORDER BY simply says that the result set will be in a particular order. The statement does not specify exactly how that should be done. And, different databases take different approaches. For instance, in SQL Server, if the statement accesses only a single table and the ORDER BY key is the clustered index for the table, then an additional sorting step is generally unnecessary.

This section starts by introducing "order notation" from computer science as a way of characterizing query performance. After all, if we want to talk about performance, then understanding a measure—independent of hardware and database versions—is helpful. A simple example then illustrates what this really means, before we move on to more interesting examples.

Order Notation for Understanding Performance

Computer scientists have a way of measuring the "complexity" of an algorithm. In the language of databases, this measures how much longer it takes a query to run as the size of the data increases. Order notation—not to be confused with

ORDER BY—is written as a capital letter "O" followed by a simple expression in parentheses and often called *big-O notation*.

A place to start with understanding the concept is O(1), which means that the time to run the query is bounded by a constant. Running the query on larger tables does not affect the running time. Such queries are not common, but here is an example:

```
SELECT TOP 1 t.*
FROM t
```

This selects one (arbitrary) row from a table. Because only one row needs to be read, the length of time should be independent of the size of table. This notation is not saying whether this time is long or short, simply that the time does not increase with larger data.

More common is O(n), meaning that the time for the query grows as the number of rows in the table grows (the "n" refers to the size of something, typically the number of rows in the table). A typical example is reading all the rows in the table—say to count the number of rows. If the number of rows doubles, the amount of time needed to count them also doubles, assuming each row needs to be read.

As the function of "n" gets bigger, performance gets worse. For example, $O(n^2)$ means that the time for the query grows as the square of the number of rows. This is the performance of naïve sorting algorithms and unoptimized self-joins.

Order notation is useful for understanding how the underlying algorithms scale as the data gets larger. O(n) is better than $O(n^2)$, particularly as the data size increases. As we will see, there are other considerations in databases—such as memory usage and disk reads—which can be more important for practical problems, but order notation captures a key aspect of performance.

A Simple Example

What is the maximum value of a particular column in a table? Let's step outside the world of databases for a moment, and imagine the table printed out neatly on sheets of paper. This idea of working with paper can be a useful analogy for understanding some of the methods used by databases. A real database has numerous advantages over working with paper—particularly for tables that have millions of rows.

The SQL query to answer the question is quite simple:

```
SELECT MAX(t.col)
FROM table t
```

What are different ways that a database might actually execute this query? This is an introduction to several (but by no means all) of the algorithms that a database could use.

Full Table Scan

The most obvious way of finding the maximum value is to read the table, row by row, keeping track of the largest value encountered. The analogous method using paper is to read the table manually, keeping track of the maximum value as you read. This is also the approach that a programmer would typically take if the table were stored in a file or in an array in memory.

In terms of order notation, this method is $O(n)$. As the size of the table grows, the work needed for the query grows by the same amount. Doubling the size of the data roughly doubles the amount of work.

A full table scan can be the best way to answer this question—particularly when the table is small. If all the rows fit on one sheet of paper, for instance, then scanning down one column might be the fastest way to get the maximum. For larger amounts of data, full table scans are usually not the most efficient method.

Parallel Full Table Scan

One way to speed the execution of the query is to break it down into pieces that can run simultaneously. After all, modern computers support multiple processors with multiple cores and they can run multiple threads of processing at the same time.

In the world of paper, this is equivalent to parceling out sheets to several colleagues. Each colleague goes through his or her sheets and calculates the maximum on that portion. In the end, the colleagues have looked through all the rows and found their own maximum value. You still need to combine their intermediate results together, but that should be a fast process.

Taking advantage of parallelism can substantially increase the speed of many queries, including this one. How much improvement depends on "how parallel" the system is—and for a given query, this is generally a combination of available hardware, configuration parameters, data size, and query complexity. For this type of query, having ten threads running simultaneously would cause the query to finish in about one-tenth the time.

Running operations in parallel incurs some additional overhead, such as the need to gather the intermediate results together. This overhead, as well as the overhead for setting up the problem, is usually much, much smaller than the efficiencies gained by processing large quantities of data in parallel.

Parallelism has its limits. For instance, if you are processing paper and you have more colleagues than sheets of paper, the additional colleagues really don't help (unless ripping sheets in half is allowed).

Although queries run faster in parallel, the processing is still $O(n)$—for a given number of parallel threads. All the rows still need to be read, even if multiple processors are reading them. However, because each processor finishes faster, the query would still finish faster. This explains why throwing more hardware at a problem can speed things up—even when the underlying algorithms are not particularly scalable.

Index Lookup

At this point, you might be thinking: "Gosh, wouldn't it just be easier if the column was sorted to begin with?" If that were the case, choosing the maximum price would be simple—just go to the first or last row in the table (depending on the direction of the sort) and get the value. Can't SQL do the same thing?

Well, the answer is no and yes. SQL tables represent *unordered* sets: tables have no inherent ordering. And, even if there were an ordering, how would we access a particular row, without knowing the values in the row? There are ways around both of these issues, but let's stay true to the relational model for now.

> **TIP** SQL tables represent unordered sets, so queries should not assume that the data is in any particular order. However, indexes are (generally) ordered and can speed up queries by allowing algorithms that take advantage of ordering.

Indexes, which are described in more detail later in this chapter, are the solution. You can think of these like the index in the back of a book: values from one or more columns in the table (called *keys*) are sorted, along with a reference to the original row in the table. Figure 14-1 shows an example.

Because the index is sorted, it is almost trivial to pull out the one with the maximum value.

How long does this operation take in terms of order notation? The index contains the maximum value, so this is just asking how long it takes to find it. The answer depends on the underlying data structure for the index, but typically this would be O(log n). That means that doubling number of rows only

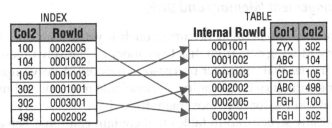

Figure 14-1: Indexes are a lookup table that (essentially) stores the columns in sorted order with reference back to an internal address to locate any particular row.

increases the running time by a constant. For instance, the log of 8 is 3, which is 1 more than the log of 4; similarly, the log of 1,024 is 10, which is 1 more than the log of 512. An index lookup on one million rows is only about ten times as long as an index lookup on one thousand rows. For practical purposes of using databases, this is very similar to constant time.

Performance of the Query

This simple query has touched on three different execution methods—a full table scan, a parallel full table scan, and an index lookup. In any given environment, the query optimizer can choose the best of these and other methods. The database, which in theory understands the details about the data being stored, can decide the best method for executing the query based on the query, the data, and the available computing resources.

A database engine has many, many different ways to optimize joins, aggregations, and other SQL operations. A major power of SQL is that the same query can be optimized for its environment, to run as effectively as possible.

> **TIP** SQL engines have an optimization step that considers many different ways of creating the result set. The engine chooses the best method for the query, data, and processing resources available.

Considerations When Thinking About Performance

Relational databases are powerful tools for storing and processing data. Query optimization takes advantage of available resources, which include:

- Storage management (memory and disk)
- Indexes
- Parallel processing

These three components provide SQL with much of its processing power. They also provide a framework for understanding some key performance considerations.

Storage Management (Memory and Disk)

Databases store tables in permanent storage, on disk, yet do their actually processing in memory. Moving data from disk to memory is relatively time-consuming (on the time frames that computer processors work on). A very important part of database performance is managing the available memory and minimizing the time spent waiting for data movement from disk.

Data is logically structured in tables that contain columns. The actual unit of storage, on the other hand, is the data page. These are of a fixed size (such as

8,192 bytes in SQL Server), and a given data page contains rows from a single table. (If necessary, rows with very large columns can span multiple pages.) A table, then, consists of a collection of pages that stores its rows. Figure 14-2 shows a schematic diagram of this structure.

One fundamental performance question is: *How many pages need to be read from (and written to) disk?* If you know the number of pages that a query must read you have a pretty good idea of the query's overall performance. If a query reads all the rows in a table, then—in general—it needs to read each page once from disk. This process is called a *full table scan.*

To make queries more efficient, the database manages pages in a special part of memory called the *page cache.* The page cache (along with caches for other objects) typically occupies most of the memory used by the database server. Sometimes, the pages needed by a query are already available in the page cache; in this case, the query runs faster because the pages do not need to be loaded from disk. For this reason, running a query for the first time after a database starts often takes longer than running it a second time. The second time, the needed data is already in the page cache and does not have to be fetched from disk.

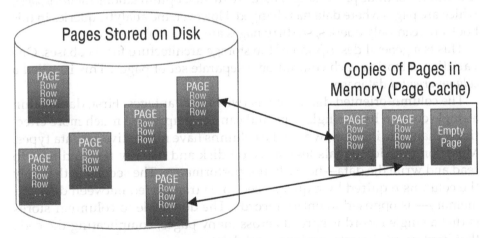

Pages are stored on disk. As they are needed by the database engine, they are loaded into the page cache.
The page manager typically implements optimizations such as:
- Reading multiple pages at one time
- Loading pages in anticipation of being needed
- Keeping pages in the cache in case they are needed later
- Reading and writing pages while the engine is processing data ("asynchronous reads and writes")

Figure 14-2: Pages are stored in memory and disk and the page cache manages pages for the database.

When the database first starts, nothing is in memory. The empty page cache is referred to as being "cold." When the page cache has data of interest, it is referred to as "warm." Proper timings for a query usually clear the page cache, so the timings run on a cold cache. Note that this only affects the page cache managed by the database. The operating system and network may have additional caching mechanisms that can also affect database performance.

TIP A page cache efficiently manages the interface between memory and disk—so efficiently that sometimes the data needed for a query is already in memory, making the query run faster than it would on a cold cache.

Database engines are smart about how they use data pages. Data pages are typically allocated in adjacent disk blocks because reading adjacent data from disk in one large read is faster than reading smaller amounts of data scattered over the disk. Databases also implement a *look-ahead* optimization, where the database engine reads pages for a table before it needs them. Modern computers can read from disk and process data at the same time, which is a big improvement over earlier generations of processors that had to wait until the read was finished to continue processing. There are further optimizations for *dirty pages*, which are pages where data has changed. However, the analytic queries in this book are read-only queries, so dirty pages are not a major concern.

This is a general description of the storage architecture for databases. One variation is storing each column on a separate set of pages. This is called a *column-oriented* database.

The column-oriented database has two big advantages. First, data within a single column has a single type and can be compressed much more effectively than data in a row, where the columns have many diverse data types. More compression equals less space on disk and usually reduced time to read and write the data—hence better performance. The second is that only the columns required by a query need to be transferred between disk and memory—as opposed to entire records. The downside to columnar stores is that a single record is spread across many pages, complicating the code that implements inserts, updates, and deletes.

Another tweak to the architecture is in-memory databases and—almost the equivalent—disk technology (such as solid state) that is almost as fast as memory. These technologies generally greatly improve database performance.

Indexes

Indexes, which are described in more detail in the next section, are another capability for improving performance. In all databases, indexes can improve the performance of JOINs, filters in the WHERE clause (including correlated subqueries), and the ORDER BY clause. Most database engines can also take advantage of them (in the right circumstances) for GROUP BY and window functions.

Processing Engine and Parallel Processing

Another important component of database performance is parallelism and the processing engine. For most users, this is an invisible layer in the database. The question is: Will the SQL engine take advantage of all available hardware for a given query?

Most of the queries in this book can readily take advantage of parallel hardware. The underlying algorithms for reading data, writing data, joins, aggregations, and sorting can all be implemented in parallel—and are, in any serious database.

Some SQL constructs can significantly impede performance. Cursors are one of them. This is a part of the SQL language that allows you to pass data back one row at a time to a scripting language (such as T-SQL for SQL Server). There is even an acronym for this type of processing: RBAR (row by agonizing row). This book has focused on set-based queries, which take better advantage of available hardware. Cursors are almost never needed for analytic data processing, because set-based operations work better. However, they are useful under some circumstances, such as calling a stored procedure for each row.

A separate processing issue is user-defined functions. These tend to incur more overhead than built-in functions. And, if a query uses these extensively, then performance may be slower than alternative solutions. Once again, this can depend on the particular database and version.

Performance: Its Meaning and Measurement

Generally, *performance* refers to the time taken to run a query—a simple idea, but the concept is more complicated than it sounds.

Performance depends not only on the data and the query, but also on the system running the database. Of course, more and/or better hardware—more memory, more processors, more disks, more I/O bandwidth—usually results in better performance.

Even a simple hardware system has many factors that might affect performance:

- Are other queries running on the database system, using hardware resources?
- Are other queries running on the database system, locking tables and rows, slowing things down?
- Are other processes running on the database server, perhaps using memory and processing time?
- Is network traffic interfering with communication from the disk to the database machine?

In other words, databases are complex systems that exist in complex technical ecosystems. The overall environment can affect query performance.

If you are concerned about the performance of one or more queries, find a system that has minimal other stuff on it and start testing. The first thing you

DATABASES REALLY ARE DIFFERENT

Although this book has used SQL Server as a reference database, the queries presented should be able to run on almost any recent version of most databases with minor tweaks. (One important exception is the use of window functions, which are not supported by MySQL and MS Access.) This aside points out some significant performance differences among different databases.

Consider common table expressions. There are basically two approaches to handling these. One is to materialize the CTE, meaning that the results from the CTE are placed in a temporary table. The second is to simply incorporate the CTE logic into the overall query—treating it as a subquery.

Each of these methods is potentially useful. If the CTE is really complicated, then you only want to run it one time: Reusing the results is a performance win. Materializing the CTE as a temporary table is a good idea.

On the other hand, sometimes the CTEs might have more efficient paths if they can be incorporated into the larger query, particularly because indexes on the underlying tables are available for filtering. As an example, consider the following query and assume an index exists on `State`:

```
WITH o as (
     SELECT o.*, DATEDIFF(day, OrderDate, GETDATE()) as recency
     FROM Orders o
     )
SELECT o.*
FROM o
WHERE recency < 100 AND State = 'FL'
```

Materializing the CTE creates an intermediate table with all orders, but no available indexes.

The second method processes the query by substitution, so it is equivalent to:

```
SELECT o.*, DATEDIFF(day, OrderDate, GETDATE()) as recency
FROM Orders o
WHERE "recency" < 100 AND State = 'FL'
```

(Continues)

might discover is that the query runs slower the first time and then picks up speed—like many of us in the morning before coffee. As mentioned earlier in this chapter, the increased speed is quite possibly due to data being cached in memory. Queries run faster when data is already available in memory.

So, find the "cold cache" option on your database. This option ensures that each time the query runs, it has to read all the data from the tables. Then you proceed. What do you measure?

The most obvious is elapsed time. Other measures can also be useful, such as the number of pages read and written to the disk, the total time spent reading/

DATABASES REALLY ARE DIFFERENT *(Continued)*

(Regarding the quotes around "recency": This syntax is not quite valid SQL, but it gets the idea across—the value from the `SELECT` is used for filtering.) This version can take advantage of the existing index on `State`.

How do different database engines handle this? Up through SQL Server 2014 (at least), SQL Server implements only the second method. Up through Postgres 9.4, Postgres uses only the first method. Oracle uses the second method, but can sometimes take advantage of materialized intermediate results. In other words, there are two possible approaches and three databases manage to find three different ways to handle the construct.

Another example is `IN` with a long list of constant values. Most databases treat the values as a sequence of "OR" expressions, searching through the list one at a time. MySQL has a more intelligent approach. It transforms the list into an internal sorted list, and then uses a binary search—speeding up the comparison.

For a third example, consider the following query:

```
SELECT OrderDate, COUNT(DISTINCT PaymentType)
FROM Orders
GROUP BY OrderDate
```

There are basically two ways to approach an aggregation—by sorting all the data or by using an algorithm called *hash aggregate*. Usually, the hash aggregate is faster, unless the data is already sorted. Postgres generates a plan that uses sorting for this query. However, remove the distinct, and Postgres generates a much better plan using hash aggregate. Oracle and SQL Server generate more efficient plans using hash aggregate in both cases.

Different databases have numerous other differences, in the naming of functions (`SUBSTR()` or `SUBSTRING()`? `CHARINDEX()` or `INSTR()` or `POSITION()` or `LOCATE()`? And so on). The functions for handling dates and times vary. Some databases support regular expressions, and some don't. Sometimes, syntax varies as well. Optimizers differ. And, other aspects of the database—from replication to backup and recovery to syntax for stored procedures—all differ.

Nevertheless, relational databases all implement systems inspired by the ANSI SQL standard. Focusing on the differences misses the many opportunities for writing efficient queries across databases.

writing from disk, and the total time used by the processors. The exact measures, of course, differ from one database to the next.

Performance Improvement 101

A good place to get started is with some basic rules for good performance. These rules are basically: Don't do more than you have to, and express things concisely.

The technical aside "Databases Really Are Different" highlights some of the issues with discussing performance in general—as opposed to performance for a specific database engine. Fortunately, databases have a lot in common, despite their differences.

Ensure that Types are Consistent

When doing a comparison, either for filtering or for a JOIN, make sure that the types on the two sides are the same. Avoid:

- WHERE intcol = '123'
- WHERE stringcol = 123
- A JOIN B ON A.intcol = B.stringcol

At the very least, writing conditions using mixed types relies on implicit type conversion, and when one of the values is a constant, the code is also misleading. Code that is hard to understand or at all misleading is a potential maintenance problem.

Although databases sometimes handle these situations well, mismatched types can confuse the optimizer. The wrong choice of algorithm for a join has a large impact on query performance. Properly declared foreign key relationships help avoid this problem because the foreign key declarations ensure that the types are correct.

Reference Only the Columns and Tables That Are Needed by the Query

SQL optimizers can be both really smart and really dumb. A query such as the following counts the number of rows in Orders:

```
SELECT COUNT(*) as NumOrders
FROM Orders o JOIN
     Customers c
     ON o.CustomerId = c.CustomerId
```

However, the JOIN is unnecessary because all orders have a valid customer ID. Alas, the SQL optimizer probably doesn't know this. So, just do:

```
SELECT COUNT(*) as NumOrders
FROM Orders o
```

This version returns the same value and does not require the extra effort for the join.

Use DISTINCT Only When Necessary

The DISTINCT keyword can easily be put in a SELECT clause or COUNT() expression. Alas, DISTINCT almost always implies more work for the SQL engine—and in some cases, the use of DISTINCT can radically change the query plan for the worse. Even if the optimizer is smart enough to figure out that the rows are unique, the code is misleading to anyone who later reads it.

In short, DISTINCT almost always causes extra work. If it is not really needed, then leave it out. Of course, do use it when it is the right thing to do.

UNION ALL: 1, UNION: 0

Always prefer UNION ALL to UNION because UNION incurs the added cost of removing duplicates. The SQL engine does this work, even when the rows are already distinct. On occasion, removing duplicates is desirable, and this is when UNION should be used intentionally.

When using UNION, the subqueries do not generally need SELECT DISTINCT, because the UNION removes duplicates anyway. The one exception is when the columns in the SELECT are part of an index that can be used for the SELECT DISTINCT. SELECT DISTINCT in the subquery allows the index to be used, which typically improves overall performance.

Put Conditions in WHERE Rather Than HAVING

Consider the following query to get the number of zip codes in states that start with "A":

```
SELECT stab, COUNT(*)
FROM ZipCensus zc
GROUP BY stab
HAVING stab LIKE 'A%'
```

This is a reasonable query, but it does more work than necessary. The query aggregates the results for all the states, then it filters the results.

An equivalent query filters the results first, so the data being aggregated is smaller:

```
SELECT stab, COUNT(*)
FROM ZipCensus zc
WHERE stab LIKE 'A%'
GROUP BY stab
```

In addition, this version can better use an index on stab.

From a performance perspective, reduce the volume of data using filtering as "early" as possible. This means putting conditions in a WHERE clause in the deepest possible subquery.

Use OUTER JOINs Only When Needed

The SQL optimizer has more options with inner joins than with outer joins. More options generally mean that the resulting query will run faster as an inner join than as an outer join—even when the result sets are exactly the same.

Of course, when the query logic requires an outer join, don't hesitate to use it! Just do not use outer joins unnecessarily. For instance, outer joins are often not needed when joining on foreign keys in a well-designed database.

Using Indexes Effectively

Indexes are the single most important part of a relational database for improving query performance. The subject of indexes in databases is very broad. This section starts with a discussion of different types of indexes. It then moves on to the types of queries that can benefit from indexes and how to look at a query from the perspective of "what is the best index."

What Are Indexes?

An *index* is a supporting data structure that speeds access to specific rows in a table. You do not query indexes directly. Instead, the query optimizer knows about them and decides when to use one in addition to—or even instead of—the original table.

Earlier, this chapter discussed a simple way to think of an index: as a table with columns sorted along with a row identifier. By providing additional information about where values are located, indexes can radically speed up queries.

The syntax for creating an index is:

```
CREATE INDEX <index name> ON <table name>(<column>, . . .)
```

For instance, to create an index on OrderId in OrderLines:

```
CREATE INDEX idx_OrderLines_OrderId ON OrderLines(OrderId)
```

The basic syntax is sufficient for many purposes. There are additional options, some of which are specific to particular databases. The index can be removed using DROP INDEX idx_OrderLines_OrderId.

The standard index in SQL is the B-tree index. This is the default but is only one type of index that is available. The following describes some of the types of indexes, starting with the most common type.

B-Trees

Figure 14-3 shows an example B-tree with one key. The tree consists of nodes, which have one or more children. The children are ordered, based on values of the keys, with smaller values going to the left children and larger values to the right children. Accessing a particular value in the tree requires descending through the index tree structure, comparing the value to find with the values for the children, and then choosing the correct branch at each intermediate node. B-trees can have multiple keys. In such cases, the first key has priority, then the second key, and so on.

This process is much, much faster than scanning all the data. In order notation, it is O(log n). Once the first value is found, subsequent values can easily be located, by traversing the tree from the first value. Although most easily shown as a binary tree, such an index does not require that nodes have only two children.

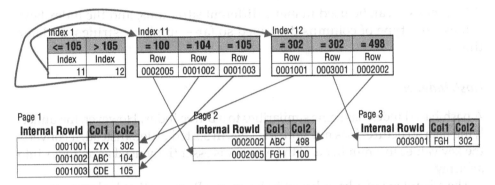

B-trees are a balanced index structure, but the nodes do not have a maximum number of children. This example uses a B-tree that supports up to three children. The tree has a constant depth, maintained as new records are inserted, updated, and deleted.

In this example, the top level of the index has two children (11 and 12). The children are defined by inequalities on the key values. Each of these have three children. The index has a depth of two, so the grandchildren point to rows in a table.

In a *clustered index*, the actual rows are stored at the lowest level of the index.

Figure 14-3: In practice, indexes are usually stored as B-trees with references to pages containing records.

The *B* in B-tree stands for balanced, meaning that all the leaves in the tree have the same depth. A balanced tree has nice properties when looking up values. However, maintaining the balance requires additional overhead on inserts, updates, and deletes.

B-tree indexes readily support two types of operations for finding data. An *index lookup* goes directly into the index and finds an exact match for given key values (or the minimum or maximum value). An *index scan* matches all the records between two values—and this might be the entire index—returning them in sorted order.

Here are some examples of how a B-tree index can be used:

- When the query has a WHERE clause containing an equality condition on all keys used in the index, the index can be used to quickly find the rows that match the condition. This is an example of an index lookup.

- When the query has an ORDER BY clause, the index can be used to fetch the records in the right order. This is an example of an index scan on the entire table.

- When the query has a GROUP BY clause on the keys in the index, the index can be used to find the records in each group.

- When the query has a JOIN/ON clause, the index can be used to easily find matching records.

- When the query uses window functions and the PARTITION BY columns (and perhaps ORDER BY as well) are in the index, then the index can be used for the calculation.

B-tree indexes can be used in many different situations, and the index keys can use any type of columns described so far—numbers, strings, or date/times.

Hash Indexes

A hash-based index has some similarities to a B-tree index. However, the underlying data structure does not store the keys in sorted order. Instead, it converts the key values to a number and the number is essentially used as an index into an array.

The advantage of a hash-based index over a B-tree is that lookups are even faster. The process is simply converting the keys to the number (called *hashing*) and then using the resulting hash value to locate matching record locators in the hash array. A lookup in a hash index is typically O(1) rather than the O(log n) for a B-tree.

Hash indexes support only index lookups. They do not support index scans. So, hash indexes are less useful than B-tree indexes. The limitation means that a hash index can be used in fewer cases, such as:

- Equality conditions on all keys in the index (in either a WHERE clause or JOIN clause)
- Aggregation that uses all keys in the index
- Window functions where the PARTITION BY clause uses all the keys in the index

By contrast, B-tree indexes are more versatile and can be used under more circumstances.

Spatial Indexes (R-Trees)

Many databases also support special indexes for different types of data. One of these is the spatial index, which is structurally related to B-trees. These indexes are used to efficiently find geographic objects that are close to each other spatially.

The most important operation supported by these indexes is finding the geographic areas that are "next" to each other—think about a zooming out on a map and determining what the adjacent areas are so they can be included in the next map image. They also enable operations such as determining the overlap of two regions or what regions are within a specific distance.

Spatial indexes use a data structure similar to B-trees, extending the idea to support multiple dimensions. Figure 14-4 gives an example. Basically, the index divides space into little squares (or cubes). It then keeps track of what is next to each square, north, south, east, and west of the square. Then, the tree also keeps track of groups of squares at different levels.

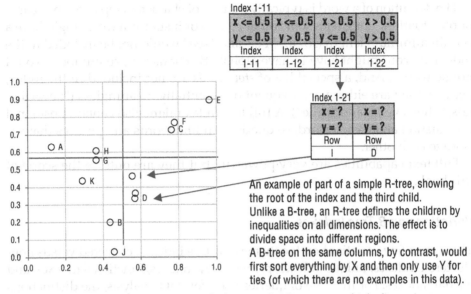

Figure 14-4: Spatial indexes use R-trees, which generalize B-trees to multiple dimensions.

Full Text Indexes (Inverted Indexes)

Full text indexes are another powerful index structure specialized for a particular type of data. The index itself consists of words in the text, along with the list of records where they appear. This type of index is an example of an *inverted index*. Instead of words being stored in a document, this index stores individual words along with their locations, as shown in Figure 14-5.

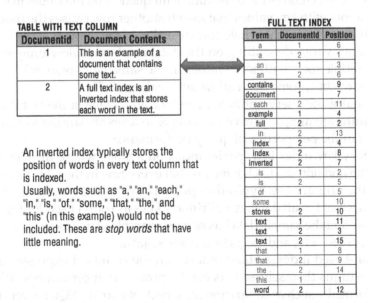

Figure 14-5: A full text index keeps track of words in documents, along with their positions.

The definition of a word is typically a string of characters separated by spaces or punctuation, along with some other rules. For instance, a word might have a certain minimum length (so "a," "be," and "see" would not be included in the index). A word might have to have alphabetic characters, so numbers would not be words. And, a special list of *stop words* are not included in the index, because they are either very frequent or essentially meaningless ("nevertheless," "however," "and," "the"). A full text index might also contain positional information about each word, so queries can find words and phrases that are close to each other.

Full text capabilities are very powerful, but they are outside the scope of this book.

Variations on B-Tree Indexes

There are a few variations on the theme of B-tree indexes: clustered versus non-clustered indexes, unique indexes, primary key indexes, functional indexes, and partial indexes. For the type of queries used for data analysis, the distinctions between the first three are usually not very important, but they are worth describing.

A *clustered* index means that the rows in the table are physically ordered by the key or keys. Without such an index, a new row can be inserted into a table anywhere free space is available. This is typically—but not necessarily—on the last page allocated to the table. If the table has a clustered index (and at most one is allowed), then the record is inserted in the appropriate location to keep the rows ordered by the primary key. Occasionally, a clustered index is helpful for certain types of queries. Generally they are just a slightly more efficient version of a B-tree.

A unique index enforces the constraint of uniqueness on the values in the index. Inserting a row with key values that match another row causes the index insertion to fail—and hence the whole row insertion to fail. Note that the treatment of NULL values varies depending on the database. Some allow unique indexes to have multiple rows with NULL values in the same key; some only allow one occurrence of NULL, some don't allow NULL values at all.

Occasionally, the query optimizer can take advantage of the fact that one or more columns are unique; otherwise, unique indexes are similar to non-unique indexes from the perspective of query performance.

A primary key index is a special index on a table, where the columns are both unique and non-NULL. That means that every row in the table has a unique value for the primary key. Typically a primary key is also clustered, but that is not a requirement in all databases. Primary keys are often used for foreign key references—and the sample data has several examples, such as `Orders.OrderId`, `Products.ProductId`, and `Campaigns.CampaignId`.

Function-based indexes allow indexes on the results of expressions rather than on columns themselves. This can be powerful, if certain operations are often performed—such as comparing the length of a string. SQL Server supports function-based indexes in an indirect manner. The expression itself can be added to a table as a computed column, and the index is built on the computed column.

Finally, partial indexes are indexes built on a subset of data. In databases that support them, they are often defined by adding a WHERE clause to the CREATE INDEX statement. The most important use of these indexes is to enforce a unique constraint on a subset of rows, although they can also be used for queries that have matching conditions in the query's WHERE clause.

Simple Examples of Indexes

At this point, the discussion moves to "standard" indexes, which are B-tree indexes. As an example, you can create an index on the TotalPrice column in OrderLines using:

```
CREATE INDEX idx_OrderLines_TotalPrice ON OrderLines(TotalPrice)
```

This section discusses some simple queries and how the database engine would process the query with and without the index.

Equality in a Where Clause

The following query returns one order whose price is zero:

```
SELECT TOP 1 ol.*
FROM OrderLines ol
WHERE ol.TotalPrice = 0
```

The result set consists of an arbitrary row where the total price is zero because the query lacks an ORDER BY clause, which you would normally use with TOP. This query is for discussion only.

Without an index, the database engine reads the entire OrderLines table, one row at a time, checking the TotalPrice column until it finds a row where the value is zero. The engine returns the values from that row and stops reading the table. Of course, database engines are powerful, so millions of rows can be read in a relatively short amount of time (say, a few seconds). And the query could be lucky or unlucky. Perhaps the first row read has TotalPrice equal to zero. Or perhaps only the last row.

An index allows the database engine to quickly find all the rows where the TotalPrice is zero. Instead of reading the entire table, the database engine goes to the index and quickly fetches the row identifier for the first row that matches the condition. It then looks up that row in the data pages and returns the row. The index lookup and fetch should be much faster than reading the table— assuming the table is large enough. However, on a very small table, scanning the table might actually be faster than using the index. This is particularly true if all the records in the table fit on a single data page.

Variations on the Theme of Equality

Let's consider some related queries and how the engine processes them. The first is:

```
SELECT ol.*
FROM OrderLines ol
WHERE ol.TotalPrice = 0
```

The variation here is that the query returns all rows that match the condition, rather than just one.

The processing is similar to the previous query. Without an index, the engine needs to read the entire table. It cannot stop at the first row that matches the condition. It must go to the last row because even that could have a zero price.

With an index, the database engine finds the first entry in the index where `TotalPrice` is zero. It fetches the data for the corresponding row, placing it in the result set. The engine then moves to the next entry in the index to get the next row where `TotalPrice` is zero, adding that to the result set. And so on.

The rows themselves may be spread out through the table, each located on its own page. However, their row identifiers are all adjacent in the index, so the group of rows is easy to find quickly.

This variation has a more complicated WHERE clause with two conditions, one in the index and one not:

```
SELECT ol.*
FROM OrderLines ol
WHERE ol.TotalPrice = 0 AND ol.NumUnits > 1
```

The SQL engine can use the index to find all rows where the first condition is met. However, the information in the index is not sufficient to determine if the rows pass both conditions. So, the engine fetches the rows from the data pages and uses this information for the second condition. In other words, database engines are powerful enough to use indexes for some of the conditions when necessary.

In this case, the index can be used because the conditions are connect by AND. If the connector were OR, then the SQL optimizer would probably not use the index.

The next example is one where the actual data for the records is not needed. Only the index is needed for the following query:

```
SELECT COUNT(*)
FROM OrderLines ol
WHERE ol.TotalPrice = 0
```

When an index can be used to generate the result set without accessing the data pages, the index is said to be a *covering index* for the query. In general, a covering index contains all the columns referenced anywhere in the query, although the index may have additional columns beyond these.

> **TIP** When an index contains all the columns used in a query, in the right order for processing, then the index is said to "cover" the query. Such covering indexes typically provide the best performance.

Inequality in a WHERE Clause

Indexes can also be used for inequalities in the WHERE clause. So, the SQL optimizer can take advantage of an index for the following clauses:

```
WHERE TotalPrice > 0
WHERE TotalPrice BETWEEN 100 and 200
WHERE TotalPrice IN (0, 20, 100)
```

The first two would use index scans. The third would use multiple index lookups. Inequalities generally return more rows than equality conditions, so scanning the data pages can sometimes be more efficient than using an index.

For example, the first condition returns about 84% of the rows in OrderLines. Just scanning the table is likely to be faster than going through the index to read almost all the rows; after all, the query probably has to read all the data pages either way. A later section discusses some serious performance implications of using an index in this case.

ORDER BY

Which two order lines have the highest total prices? This query can also use an index:

```
SELECT TOP 2 ol.*
FROM OrderLines ol
ORDER BY ol.TotalPrice DESC
```

The database engine starts at the end of the index—the highest priced order line. And it then get scans backwards to get the two rows with the highest price and return the information from those two rows.

Of course, some rows may have the same total price on them. If we wanted all the rows, including ties, the query might use a subquery, such as:

```
SELECT ol.*
FROM OrderLines ol
WHERE ol.TotalPrice IN (SELECT TOP 2 ol.TotalPrice
                        FROM OrderLines ol
                        ORDER BY ol.TotalPrice DESC
                       )
```

The index would get used twice for this query. First, the database engine uses it to find the two records with the highest total price for the subquery. Then the query engine uses the index again to fetch all rows with the same values.

SQL Server offers a simpler syntax for this type of query:

```
SELECT TOP 2 WITH TIES ol.*
FROM OrderLines ol
ORDER BY ol.TotalPrice DESC
```

The keywords WITH TIES instruct the query engine to keep returning rows as long as the rows have the same values (based on the ORDER BY) as the preceding row.

The index can also be used when a WHERE clause is included in the query. For instance, the following query gets all the lines with the lowest priced products:

```
SELECT TOP 1 WITH TIES ol.*
FROM OrderLines ol
WHERE ol.TotalPrice > 0
ORDER BY ol.TotalPrice ASC
```

The engine can find the first non-zero value for TotalPrice in the index. It can then start scanning from there.

Aggregation

Indexes can also be used for aggregation (by most databases):

```
SELECT ol.TotalPrice, COUNT(*)
FROM OrderLines ol
GROUP BY ol.TotalPrice
```

This query can clearly be processed using only the index. In the index, the prices with the same value are next to each other, so they are easy to count.

The same query processed without an index requires reading the table, bringing similar values together, and then doing the count—much more work than scanning the index.

This also applies to aggregation queries without GROUP BY. For instance:

```
SELECT MIN(ol.TotalPrice)
FROM OrderLines ol
```

This query can take advantage of the index to get the smallest value.

Limitations on Indexes

Although indexes are usually beneficial for performance, there are some cases where they can actually make things worse, as discussed in the aside "Thrashing: When Indexes Go Bad."

Indexes do have quirks. SQL optimizers often only consider using an index for columns that are being compared to constants (or query parameters), that do not require type conversion, and that are not modified by functions or operators. Although some engines do occasionally relax some of these rules it is a good idea to keep them in mind.

Consider a date comparison on a date time field to get all values from today:

```
WHERE CAST(dte as DATE) = CAST(GETDATE() as DATE)
```

The optimizer may not be able to use an index on `dte`. But, the following version can:

```
WHERE dte < CAST(GETDATE() as DATE) AND dte >= CAST(GETDATE() - 1 AS DATE)
```

These two versions do the same thing, but the second version has no functions operating on the column, so it is safer for index use. (Note: SQL Server is smart enough to use an index in this case, despite the `CAST()` function; however, this is a rare exception to the rule about indexes and functions.) As a general rule, apply functions to query constants rather than columns if you want the query to take advantage of indexes.

Comparisons to the beginning of a string provide another example. Both these return zip codes in counties that start with the letter Q:

```
WHERE County LIKE 'Q%'
WHERE LEFT(County) = 'Q'
```

However, the second version would not use an index because of the function call. `LIKE` is smart enough to use an index when the pattern starts with constant characters. It cannot use an index when the pattern starts with a wildcard.

WARNING   In a `WHERE` clause, avoid using functions and operators on columns that are included in indexes. Modifying the column value often prevents the use of an index.

The same thing happens with type conversions and even trivial operations:

```
WHERE TotalPrice + 0 = 0
WHERE TotalPrice = '0'
```

Modifications to the column, even type conversions and adding zero, usually prevent the use of an index.

The same consideration applies to comparisons between columns in an `ON` clause—you want to be sure that these have the same type. Fortunately, most joins use primary keys and foreign keys. And, a well-designed database would have the foreign key references defined in the table definitions—so the database would guarantee that the types are compatible.

THRASHING: WHEN INDEXES GO BAD

Consider the following simple query:

```
SELECT t.*
FROM table t
ORDER BY t.col
```

And also assume that the table has an index on `t.col`.

The SQL optimizer basically has two choices on how to run this query. The first method is to read the data, then sort it and return the results. The alternative is to use the index to read the data in the proper order. The engine can then fetch the rows in order and return the results.

The second method seems so reasonable that some database engines always use the index for this type of query. What could be wrong with that?

This is a case where intuition on smaller amounts of data does not scale to large data. Consider the simple case, where the table fits into memory. The database engine goes to the index and finds the location of the first row—nicely ordered to be the first in the result set. It then goes to fetch the rest of the columns for the row by loading the data into the page cache. Remember, the row could be anywhere in the table.

The engine then goes to the next row in the index. It then fetches the additional columns in the row. It is highly unlikely that the second row is on the page containing the first row, so the engine loads another page.

This process continues for subsequent records. Sometimes the record is found in the page cache because the page has already been loaded for an earlier record (this is called a *cache hit*). Sometimes a new page has to be loaded (called a *cache miss*). Eventually, the entire table is in memory, so cache misses cannot occur. All subsequent reads hit the cache. The query goes pretty fast from this point.

When the table is larger than memory, something more ominous happens. The page cache eventually fills up. Then another record is located in the index, and the page is not in the cache. To make room for the new page, an arbitrary page is removed from the cache and the page with the newly located record replaces it. This continues, with old pages being overwritten in memory to make room for the new.

Then, a record is needed from one of those old pages. So, it has to be re-read into memory—and another arbitrary page removed. In other words, a single page gets loaded into the cache multiple times. In the worst case, a page is loaded for each record on the page. This continual loading of pages over and over into memory is called *thrashing*. And, it is the bane of systems working with random-access data larger than memory.

Remember the alternative execution plan. That plan just reads the data and sorts it without using the index. One method of sorting data requires reading it three times and writing it twice. Under some circumstances—for tables too big to fit in the page cache—doing the sort is much more efficient than using an index because the latter results in thrashing.

Effectively Using Composite Indexes

The basics of indexes are pretty easy. However, as queries get more complicated it can be more challenging to figure out how to define effective indexes.

Often the best index for a query is a single index that contains multiple columns. Such an index is called a *composite index*. Defining the right composite index has some nuances.

Composite Indexes for a Query with One Table

For a query on only one table, some rules specify the columns to put into the index and the order of these columns in the index:

1. Assuming the WHERE clause consists of conditions connected by AND with comparisons to constants (or fixed parameters), then index the columns used in the WHERE clause. Columns used for equality conditions go first, followed by columns used for inequality conditions (such as <, <=, >, >=, <>, IS NOT NULL, IN, NOT IN). The index will directly use only one column with an inequality condition.

2. For an aggregation query, then index the columns used for aggregation.

3. For an order by query, then index the columns in the ORDER BY clause.

4. If you want a covering index, then include the rest of the columns from the SELECT.

The ordering of columns in the index is very important. The correct ordering can greatly improve performance for a given query. Conversely, the same columns in a different order may render the index unusable for the same query.

For example, consider:

```
SELECT ol.*
FROM OrderLines ol
WHERE ol.TotalPrice = 0 AND ol.NumUnits = 2
```

The best index is either on `OrderLines(TotalPrice, NumUnits)` or `OrderLines(NumUnits, TotalPrice)`. Either index should be equally efficient. This is a case where the ordering does not matter because both columns have equality conditions.

Modifying the second condition to an inequality means that one index is better than the other:

```
SELECT ol.*
FROM OrderLines ol
WHERE ol.TotalPrice = 0 AND ol.NumUnits >= 2
```

The best index for this query is `OrderLines(TotalPrice, NumUnits)`. This index allows the database engine to immediately find the first row with TotalPrice of zero and NumUnits equal to two. From that row, the other records meeting the condition are located sequentially after that row.

An index with NumUnits as the first key and TotalPrice as the second is less effective. The engine uses the index to readily find rows where the second condition is met. It finds the first row where the number of units is two and scans from that point on. Then the values with total price of zero would be scattered through the index. The engine is able to use the index for the entire WHERE clause—because both values are in the index—but it must read unnecessary entries. This execution plan makes some use of the index, but it is less efficient than the version with the correct ordering of the columns in the index.

Another example is this aggregation query:

```
SELECT ol.TotalPrice, COUNT(*)
FROM OrderLines ol
GROUP BY ol.TotalPrice
```

The best index for this is on TotalPrice. However, not all database optimizers use indexes for aggregation.

Changing the query to have a WHERE clause affects the indexing strategy. Remember that the best index starts with the columns in the WHERE.

```
SELECT ol.NumUnits, COUNT(*)
FROM OrderLines ol
WHERE ol.TotalPrice = 0
GROUP BY ol.NumUnits
```

For this query, the best index is OrderLines(TotalPrice, NumUnits). Reversing the columns would probably prevent the index from being used at all.

The related query:

```
SELECT ol.NumUnits, COUNT(*)
FROM OrderLines ol
WHERE ol.TotalPrice > 0
GROUP BY ol.NumUnits
```

cannot use the NumUnits part of the index for the aggregation, because of the inequality condition.

Similar considerations apply for the ORDER BY clause, so the best index for this query:

```
SELECT ol.*
FROM OrderLines ol
WHERE ol.TotalPrice = 0
ORDER BY ol.NumUnits DESC
```

is an index on OrderLines(TotalPrice, NumUnits). But this query:

```
SELECT ol.*
FROM OrderLines ol
WHERE ol.TotalPrice > 0
ORDER BY ol.NumUnits DESC
```

cannot use an index for both the WHERE clause and the ORDER BY.

The following query from Chapter 3 is a bit more complicated than the basic examples so far discussed:

```
SELECT Market, stoprate - 1.96 * stderr as conflower,
       stoprate + 1.96 * stderr as confupper,
       stoprate, stderr, numstarts, numstops
FROM (SELECT Market,
             SQRT(stoprate * (1 - stoprate) / numstarts) as stderr,
             stoprate, numstarts, numstops
      FROM (SELECT Market, COUNT(*) as numstarts,
                   SUM(CASE WHEN StopType IS NOT NULL THEN 1 ELSE 0
                       END) as numstops,
                   AVG(CASE WHEN StopType IS NOT NULL THEN 1.0 ELSE 0
                       END) as stoprate
            FROM Subscribers
            WHERE StartDate in ('2005-12-26')
            GROUP BY Market
           ) s
     ) s
```

The best index is not hard to figure out. The place to start is the innermost sub-query. It has a WHERE clause and GROUP BY so that is where the processing starts.

The best index for this subquery is Subscribers(StartDate, Market). In addition, the SELECT clause uses the column StopType. If this is included in the index, then the index is a covering index for the query: Subscribers(StartDate, Market, StopType). Note that the extra column should be the last column in the index.

Composite Indexes for a Query with Joins

Joins with equality conditions complicate the use of indexes by introducing a wider range of possible execution plans. In general, when the join condition has no equals sign, then indexes cannot help the query. On the other hand, a simple equijoin query has multiple ways of taking advantage of an index:

```
SELECT *
FROM A JOIN
     B
     ON A.col = B.col
```

The query optimizer might consider three broad strategies for executing the query. The first is to use A as the *driving* table. That is, the engine would read A and find the matching record(s) in B. For this situation, an index on B(col) is the best index.

The optimizer could decide to use B as the driving table instead of A. The best index is then A(col). Or, the engine could use a different algorithm such as a merge join or hash join algorithm, which does not have a driving table. A merge join first sorts each of the tables and then matches them row by row. Of course, the "sort-and-compare" could make use of both indexes at the same time.

As a general rule, having indexes on the columns used for joins is a good idea. Fortunately, many such queries use primary keys for the join, and these automatically have an index.

If the join query has a WHERE clause that mentions only one table, then that table is an excellent candidate for the driving table. For instance, consider a query like this:

```
SELECT *
FROM A JOIN B ON A.Col = B.Col
WHERE A.OtherCol = 0
```

If A is used as the driving table, then the best indexes are A(OtherCol, Col) and B(Col). The query engine uses the index on A to find all the rows that match the WHERE condition. Because A.Col is already in the index, it can readily locate the matching rows in B. Then, the engine fetches those rows from the data pages.

An alternative method would use B for the driving table. In this case the best indexes are A(Col, OtherCol) and an index on B does not really help. The engine would scan the B table, and use the index to find the matching rows in A. Because OtherCol is also in the index, it can do the WHERE filtering before fetching the actual data.

For a LEFT OUTER JOIN, the driving table is going to be the first table because all the rows from that table are in the result set. Similarly, for RIGHT OUTER JOIN, the second table is the driving table. A FULL OUTER JOIN requires a somewhat different approach to guarantee that all rows from both tables are in the result set.

This query from Chapter 10 joins three tables:

```
SELECT YEAR(o.OrderDate) as yr, MONTH(o.OrderDate) as mon,
       AVG(CASE WHEN p.GroupName = 'CALENDAR' AND p.FullPrice < 100
                THEN ol.UnitPrice END) as avgcallt100,
       AVG(CASE WHEN p.GroupName = 'BOOK' AND p.FullPrice < 100
                THEN ol.UnitPrice END) as avgbooklt100
FROM Orders o JOIN
     OrderLines ol
     ON o.OrderId = ol.OrderId JOIN
     Products p
     ON ol.ProductId = p.ProductId
```

```
WHERE p.GroupName IN ('CALENDAR', 'BOOK')
GROUP BY YEAR(o.OrderDate), MONTH(o.OrderDate)
ORDER BY yr, mon
```

The columns `Orders(Orderid)` and `Products(ProductId)` are primary keys. Absent any other indexes, the query would generate all combinations of orders, order lines, and products, filtering the results either while it generates the combinations or just before doing the aggregation.

An index on `Products(GroupName, ProductId)` might not help this query. Although this would filter on the WHERE clause, consider the condition ON `ol.ProductId = p.ProductId`. The join to `OrderLines` would not have an index available, and that might be computationally expensive. Fortunately, another index fixes this problem: `OrderLines(ProductId, OrderId)`. The second column is a convenience to handle the join to `Orders` without reading the data pages for `OrderLines`.

When you have a GROUP BY with a JOIN, then the query engine probably cannot use an index for the aggregation. An ORDER BY on the driving table in a query with no GROUP BY can sometimes use an index.

Most correlated subqueries can be written as joins. Hence, correlated subqueries with equality conditions and no aggregation follow basically the same rules as those outlined for joins.

When OR Is a Bad Thing

OR is a very powerful construct in databases. Unfortunately, it is one that optimizers often do not handle well, at least with respect to indexes.

Simple WHERE clauses with conditions on only a single column generally do not pose a problem. SQL optimizers are smart enough to use an index on `Orders(State)` for a query such as:

```
SELECT o.*
FROM Orders o
WHERE State = 'MA' OR State = 'NY'
```

Note that this would be better written with IN. The two constructs are usually identical with respect to optimization.

Sometimes UNION ALL Is Better Than OR

Consider an index on `Orders(State, City)` and a query to fetch orders from Boston and Miami:

```
SELECT o.*
FROM Orders o
WHERE (o.State = 'MA' AND o.City = 'BOSTON') OR
      (o.State = 'FL' AND o.City = 'MIAMI')
```

SQL optimizers may not recognize the opportunity to use the index because of the OR. Even if the optimizer is smart enough in this case, it may miss the opportunity for a modification like: *Get me all order lines from Boston and Miami that have a non-free product*:

```
SELECT ol.*
FROM Orders o JOIN
     OrderLines ol
     ON o.OrderId = ol.OrderId
WHERE ((o.State = 'MA' AND o.City = 'BOSTON') OR
       (o.State = 'FL' AND o.City = 'MIAMI')
     ) AND
     ol.TotalPrice > 0
```

What can be done?

This is one of the situations when a more complicated query might produce a more efficient execution plan. The problem with the previous query is that the conditions are complicated—from the perspective of optimization. Some databases have optimizers smart enough to catch this, but even the best optimizer can miss opportunities.

There is more than one way to write this query to ensure better performance. Once method is to put the constant values in a derived table and use JOIN. Another is to use UNION ALL:

```
SELECT ol.*
FROM Orders o JOIN
     OrderLines ol
     ON o.OrderId = ol.OrderId
WHERE o.State = 'MA' AND o.City = 'BOSTON' AND ol.TotalPrice > 0
UNION ALL
SELECT ol.*
FROM Orders o JOIN
     OrderLines ol
     ON o.OrderId = ol.OrderId
WHERE o.State = 'FL' AND o.City = 'MIAMI' AND ol.TotalPrice > 0
```

Each subquery uses only AND conditions. That means that the optimizer can easily choose to use the index, greatly reducing the effort for each subquery. Having to run the two queries twice does not really effect performance because each subquery is just looking up rows using an index.

Note the use of UNION ALL here instead of UNION. Remember that UNION goes through extra effort to remove duplicates. Hence, you should always use UNION ALL, unless you specifically want that extra work to be done.

Sometimes LEFT OUTER JOIN Is Better Than OR

What order lines have been either shipped or billed on national holidays and what is the holiday? This is a rather simple question whose answer can readily be turned into SQL. It is just a complicated JOIN between OrderLines and Calendar:

```
SELECT c.hol_national, ol.*
FROM OrderLines ol JOIN
     Calendar c
     ON (ol.ShipDate = c.Date OR ol.BillDate = c.Date) AND
        c.hol_national <> ''
```

The logic is easy to follow: match one of the two dates to the calendar table and check to see if the date is a national holiday.

The query is easy enough, but the OR might prevent the database optimizer from using an index—after all, two indexes would be needed for this part of the query, one for ShipDate and one for BillDate. One solution is to use UNION ALL as described in the previous section. However, this can be cumbersome. UNION ALL doubles the length of the query.

An alternative approach is to replace the single JOIN with two JOINs, one for each of the dates. Because only one condition might match, the one JOIN becomes two LEFT JOINs:

```
SELECT COALESCE(cs.hol_national, cb.hol_national) as hol_national, ol.*
FROM OrderLines ol LEFT JOIN
     Calendar cs
     ON ol.ShipDate = cs.Date AND cs.hol_national <> '' LEFT JOIN
     Calendar cb
     ON ol.BillDate = cb.Date AND cb.hol_national <> ''
WHERE cs.Date IS NOT NULL OR cb.Date IS NOT NULL
```

The query has three important changes. First the LEFT JOIN is now used twice, once for each date. Although this version has two joins, each can efficiently take advantage of an appropriate index.

The second change is the WHERE clause. The left outer join keeps everything in OrderLines, so the joins are not filtering the data. Hence, the need for the WHERE clause to see if either JOIN found a match.

Finally, the SELECT clause returns the holiday name. However, the holiday could come from either the ship date or the bill date. COALESCE() allows the query to put the values in a single column.

This query is not exactly the same as the original query. The difference occurs when ShipDate and BillDate both fall on holidays. The first version returns two rows. This version returns only one row, with the holiday from the ShipDate (although the query could be modified to return both holidays). If needed, the values from this query could be pivoted to get two rows; however, only one holiday per order might be the right answer to the question.

Sometimes Multiple Conditional Expressions Are Better

We might ask a relatively simple question about orders and zip code: *What orders come from zip codes whose median family or household income is more than $250,000?* The following query answers this question:

```
SELECT o.*
FROM Orders o
WHERE o.ZipCode IN (SELECT zcta5
                    FROM ZipCensus zc
                    WHERE MedianHHInc > 250000 OR
                          MedianFamInc > 250000
                   )
```

Note the use of OR in the subquery. Because of the OR, the query engine would probably scan all the rows of ZipCensus to find the matching zip codes, even when MedianHHInc and MedianFamInc are both indexed. Some databases have a capability called *index merge* to handle two indexes on different variables in this case. However, optimizers have a hard time determining when this operation is better than just scanning the table.

If each column has an index, the following produces an efficient execution plan:

```
SELECT *
FROM Orders o
WHERE o.ZipCode IN (SELECT zcta5
                    FROM ZipCensus
                    WHERE MedianHHInc > 250000
                   ) OR
      o.ZipCode IN (SELECT zcta5
                    FROM ZipCensus
                    WHERE MedianFamInc > 250000
                   )
```

Each of the conditional expressions can use an index, which should make the query run faster if the indexes are available.

Pros and Cons: Different Ways of Expressing the Same Thing

SQL is supposed to be descriptive, in the sense that a SQL query describes the result set rather than specify the exact steps for creating it (hence the need for compiling and optimizing the query). SQL is so descriptive, in fact, that it often offers more than one way to express a given result set. The SQL optimizer is supposed to "understand" the query and find the best way to execute it.

That's the theory. The practice is rather different. Often, one way of writing a query is more efficient than other equivalent ways. Of course, sometimes the differences depend on the database engine. Perhaps surprisingly, in many situations the same construct works best across many databases.

What States Are Not Recognized in Orders?

This section investigates the simple question: *What states are in* Orders *but not in* ZipCensus?

The Most Obvious Query

A simple query answers the question:

```
SELECT DISTINCT o.State
From Orders o
WHERE o.State NOT IN (SELECT stab FROM ZipCensus)
```

This query has the advantage of being almost a direct translation of the question. However, it is not good from a performance perspective.

The problem is that the WHERE clause is executed before the SELECT DISTINCT, so this query tests every state in Orders. There are 192,983 rows in Orders, but only 92 distinct state abbreviations. That means that the SQL statement is going to check the state code against ZipCensus.stab way more times than necessary— and then go through additional effort to remove the duplicates.

A Simple Modification

A simple modification of the query should be about 2,000 times faster (192,983÷92):

```
SELECT o.State
FROM (SELECT DISTINCT o.State FROM Orders o) o
WHERE o.State NOT IN (SELECT stab FROM ZipCensus)
```

The strategy here is to get the distinct values for State before looking them up in ZipCensus. Instead of doing the comparison on 192,983 rows, this query only does the comparison on 92 rows. That part of the query should be 2,000 times faster—and as an added bonus the SELECT DISTINCT can also make use of an index on Orders(State).

A Better Version

The basic query has another potential problem, which is fixed by this version:

```
SELECT o.State
FROM (SELECT DISTINCT o.State FROM Orders o) o
WHERE NOT EXISTS (SELECT 1 FROM ZipCensus zc WHERE zc.stab = o.State)
```

The difference is the use of NOT EXISTS rather than NOT IN. The two versions are not exactly the same, because they treat NULL values differently. If ZipCensus ever had even a single NULL value for stab, then the NOT IN query would return no rows at all. The semantics of NOT IN cause it to return NULL or false when any of the list values are NULL—never returning true. The version using NOT EXISTS has more intuitive behavior, which is the primary reason to prefer it to NOT IN.

> **TIP** Instead of using NOT IN with a subquery, use EXISTS. NOT IN will never return true if even one of the values in the subquery is NULL, sometimes leading to unexpected behavior.

This version has another advantage. The use of NOT IN with a subquery can mean that the entire subquery list is generated first, and then the comparison made to that list. Although some database engines do optimize the code correctly, the NOT EXISTS version often has equivalent or better performance. It can stop at the first matching value and return false.

An Alternative Using LEFT JOIN

The same query can also be expressed using LEFT JOIN:

```
SELECT o.State
FROM (SELECT DISTINCT o.State FROM Orders o) o LEFT JOIN
     (SELECT DISTINCT zc.stab
      FROM ZipCensus zc
     ) zc
     ON o.State = zc.stab
WHERE stab IS NULL
```

In most databases, this has the same performance as the previous version.

Technically, this type of join is called a *left anti-join* because rows from the first table are kept only when no row matches in the second table (an "anti-join"). Most databases recognize this construct and are able to process it efficiently.

Note that the processing is efficient even when the corresponding join might produce a gazillion rows in the logical intermediate results. Consider the following version of the above query:

```
SELECT DISTINCT o.State
FROM Orders o LEFT JOIN
     ZipCensus zc
     ON o.State = zc.stab
WHERE stab IS NULL
```

A lot of states match both tables. So, if a state has 100 orders and 500 zip codes, then—without the WHERE clause—this query would have an intermediate table of 50,000 rows, just for that one state. However, when the query engine recognizes the query as an anti-join, the matching values do not need to be generated—the query only cares about the non-matches. This leads to the next question.

How Big Would That Intermediate Table Be?

The previous query—if it were done naïvely—would have an intermediate result set with hundreds of millions of rows. This entire result set is not generated, if the database knows what it is doing.

One way to calculate the exact number of rows produced by the query without the WHERE clause is to generate and then count them:

```
SELECT COUNT(*)
FROM Orders o LEFT JOIN
     ZipCensus zc
     ON o.State = zc.stab
```

However, this is quite inefficient because it has to generate the intermediate rows. And there are 223,242,930 to be precise.

The following version does the same calculation much more efficiently:

```
SELECT SUM(os.cnt * COALESCE(zcs.cnt, 1))
FROM (SELECT o.State, COUNT(*) as cnt
      FROM Orders o
      GROUP BY o.State
     ) os LEFT JOIN
     (SELECT zc.stab, COUNT(*) as cnt
      FROM ZipCensus zc
      GROUP BY zc.stab
     ) zcs
     ON os.State = zcs.stab
```

Pre-aggregation reduces the number of rows to at most one in each table for each state. And then the sum of the product of the counts gives the number of rows. Note that the COALESCE() is needed because the second table has a value of NULL for non-matching rows.

A GROUP BY Conundrum

The last query leads to a question: *For states with at least one order, what is the number of orders and valid zip codes?* Once again, there are various ways of approaching this question.

A Basic Query

It is tempting to answer this question with this query:

```
SELECT o.State, COUNT(o.OrderId) as NumOrders, COUNT(zc.zcta5) as NumZip
FROM Orders o LEFT JOIN
```

```
        ZipCensus zc
        ON zc.stab = o.State
    GROUP BY o.State
```

However, COUNT()—as we know—counts the number of non-NULL values, not the number of distinct values. So this produces incorrect results.

The right function to use is COUNT(DISTINCT):

```
SELECT o.State, COUNT(DISTINCT o.OrderId) as NumOrders,
       COUNT(DISTINCT zc.zcta5) as NumZip
FROM Orders o LEFT JOIN
     ZipCensus zc
     ON zc.stab = o.State
GROUP BY o.State
```

This generates the full intermediate table. The query then does additional work for each of the distinct counts. This query has poor performance.

Pre-aggregation Fixes the Performance Problem

Notice that this query uses a left outer join, so the result set needs to have everything in the first table. The values from the first table can be aggregated before the join (so indexes can be used for the join to the second table):

```
SELECT o.State, o.NumOrders, COUNT(zc.zcta5) as NumZips
FROM (SELECT o.State, COUNT(*) as NumOrders
      FROM Orders o
      GROUP BY o.State
     ) o LEFT JOIN
     ZipCensus zc
     ON zc.stab = o.State
GROUP BY o.State, o.NumOrders
```

Notice two small tweaks to the query structure. First, COUNT() is used instead of COUNT(DISTINCT) because unwanted duplication of rows is no longer a problem. Also NumOrders is included in the GROUP BY clause.

Another approach pre-aggregates along both dimensions:

```
SELECT o.State, o.NumOrders, COALESCE(zc.NumZips, 0) as NumZips
FROM (SELECT o.State, COUNT(*) as NumOrders
      FROM Orders o
      GROUP BY o.State
     ) o LEFT JOIN
     (SELECT zc.stab, COUNT(*) as NumZips
      FROM ZipCensus zc
      GROUP BY zc.stab
     ) zc
     ON zc.stab = o.State
```

With this version, the outer aggregation is not needed. However, COALESCE() is needed because NumZips could be zero.

Which of these versions is faster? That actually depends on the database and data. The second version can take advantage of indexes and statistics on each table to optimize the aggregation. But the join cannot make use of indexes (because it is on the results of aggregations). The first version can use indexes effectively for the join, but the outer aggregation is more complicated.

Correlated Subqueries Can Be a Reasonable Alternative

A very different approach uses correlated subqueries. The idea is to do the aggregation for the orders, and then use a correlated subquery for the zip codes:

```
SELECT o.State, COUNT(*) as NumOrders,
       (SELECT COUNT(*)
        FROM ZipCensus zc
        WHERE zc.stab = o.State
       ) as NumZips
FROM Orders o
GROUP BY o.State
```

For this to work well, the table in the subquery needs an index on the fields used for the comparison—ZipCensus(stab).

One situation where the correlated subquery has a major performance advantage over the previous versions is when a WHERE clause restricts the number of rows returned by the query. For instance, if we only wanted this information for states that begin with the letter "N," then we can add the filter:

```
WHERE o.State LIKE 'N%'
```

This reduces the number of rows returned by the query, and the subquery only runs once for each returned row. Note that a HAVING clause would produce the same result set but without the performance gain because all the data is aggregated before the filtering takes place.

For the previous queries to be equally efficient, you need to include the filtering condition in the subqueries (and often the outer query as well). That is, the condition needs to be included twice, once for each table. Using a correlated subquery simplifies the filtering.

Be Careful With COUNT(*) = 0

Consider the question: *Which states have no orders with the most common product?* This section is going to start with a naïve approach for answering the question and then build up to a more efficient query.

A Naïve Approach

This query to answer this question seems to have three components:

- Some way of identifying the most popular product
- Counting up the number of that product in each state
- Choosing the states that have no occurrences of the product

The first is an aggregation subquery or CTE. The second is some sort of join and aggregation. And the third can be implemented in various different ways. The following query answers the question following these three steps:

```
WITH MostPopular as (
     SELECT TOP 1 ProductId
     FROM OrderLines ol
     GROUP BY ProductId
     ORDER BY COUNT(*) DESC, ProductId DESC
     )
SELECT DISTINCT o.State
FROM Orders o
WHERE (SELECT COUNT(*)
       FROM OrderLines ol
       WHERE o.OrderId = ol.OrderId AND
             ol.ProductId IN (SELECT p.ProductId FROM MostPouplar p)
       ) = 0
```

The CTE `MostPopular` finds the most popular product—as measured by the number of rows containing the product in `OrderLines`. The subquery counts the number of orders in each state that have the product and the `WHERE` clause chooses those where the count is zero.

What is the problem with this query? Basically, the correlated subquery needs to be executed for every row in `Orders`—and that is a lot of joining and aggregating. This query can take a long, long time to execute. Despite the performance problem, the structure of this query has the advantage of also being able to return the states that have a particular number of orders, just by changing the comparison to some other number.

NOT EXISTS Is Better

The construct `(SELECT COUNT() . . . .) = 0` is almost never the right construct. Why? Because the count requires processing all the data. This is overkill; the comparison to zero just determines whether something exists. The better approach is to use `NOT EXISTS`. (If the comparison were not equals, the right logic would be `EXISTS`.) The resulting query should execute much faster:

```
WITH MostPop as (
     SELECT TOP 1 ProductId
     FROM OrderLines ol
```

```
        GROUP BY ProductId
        ORDER BY COUNT(*) DESC, ProductId
 )
 SELECT DISTINCT o.State
 FROM Orders o
 WHERE NOT EXISTS (SELECT 1
                   FROM OrderLines ol
                   WHERE o.OrderId = ol.OrderId AND
                         ol.ProductId IN (SELECT p.ProductId FROM MostPop p)
                   )
```

The engine can stop processing the subquery at the first order that contains the most popular product. For a state that has many thousands of orders, this can reduce the number of records processed by a factor of thousands.

Note that this query is still a correlated subquery—so correlation is not specifically the performance problem. The problem with the first version is the aggregation, not the correlation.

Using Aggregation and Joins

The query can also be expressed only using aggregation and joins:

```
 WITH MostPopular as (
        SELECT TOP 1 ProductId
        FROM OrderLines ol
        GROUP BY ProductId
        ORDER BY COUNT(*) DESC, ProductId
        )
 SELECT o.State
 FROM Orders o JOIN
      OrderLines ol
      ON o.OrderId = ol.OrderId LEFT JOIN
      MostPopular p
      ON p.ProductId = ol.ProductId
 GROUP BY State
 HAVING COUNT(p.ProductId) = 0
```

The performance of this version is a bit worse than the version using NOT EXISTS because of the lack of filtering before the aggregation. More intermediate data processed by the query means lesser performance.

Nevertheless, this version does have an advantage because the number of products can be counted. So, this version—unlike the version with NOT EXISTS—can find the number of states that have exactly one such order.

A Slight Variation

A slight variation on the previous query further improves performance. The final aggregation is on all order lines. However, only orders with the most popular product need to be included. How can others be filtered out before the aggregation?

The answer uses a subquery to fetch only the orders that have the most common product:

```
WITH MostPopular as (
        SELECT TOP 1 ProductId
        FROM OrderLines ol
        GROUP BY ProductId
        ORDER BY COUNT(*) DESC, ProductId
        )
SELECT o.State
FROM Orders o LEFT JOIN
        (SELECT ol.OrderId
        FROM OrderLines ol JOIN
            MostPopular p
            ON p.ProductId = ol.ProductId
        ) ol
    ON o.OrderId = ol.OrderId
GROUP BY o.State
HAVING MAX(ol.OrderId) IS NULL
```

The subquery summarizes the orders to get only the ones containing the most popular product. Note that this subquery uses JOIN rather than LEFT JOIN because JOIN does this filtering. The outer query then uses a LEFT JOIN in order to find the states with no such orders.

Window Functions

Window functions are a very powerful part of the SQL language. They are often the most efficient way to solve problems—this is especially true when the window function is the "natural" method for doing a calculation. They can also be used in clever ways.

Where Window Functions Are Appropriate

What proportion of a state's population lives in each zip code? This query can be answered using "traditional" SQL using a join and an aggregation:

```
SELECT zc.zcta5, zc.TotPop / s.StatePop
FROM ZipCensus zc JOIN
        (SELECT zc.Stab, SUM(1.0 * zc.TotPop) as StatePop
        FROM ZipCensus zc
        GROUP BY zc.Stab
        ) s
    ON zc.Stab = s.Stab
```

Although readily expressed in traditional SQL, this is not the best way to answer this question.

One problem with this approach is evident if filtering is needed. Say we were to add a WHERE clause to choose a single state: WHERE stab = 'MA'. The subquery would still process the data for all the states. From a performance perspective, this query performs the aggregation before the join, and it might not make optimal use of available indexes.

The version using window functions fixes both these problems:

```
SELECT zc.zcta5,
       zc.TotPop * 1.0 / SUM(zc.TotPop) OVER (PARTITION BY zc.Stab)
FROM ZipCensus zc
```

Filtering in a WHERE clause occurs before the work is done to calculate the total population in the state—this reduces the volume of data and should speed such a query. Similarly, the window function can take direct advantage of an index on Stab or on (Stab, TotPop).

This example shows a canonical use of window functions. To a large extent, this is how they are defined and they work very well in this situation.

Clever Use of Window Functions

Window functions can be used in some unexpected ways, allowing SQL to answer some interesting questions.

Number of Active Subscribers

Chapter 5 showed a clever use of window functions to calculate the number of active subscribers on each day. One approach to this problem uses a calendar table:

```
SELECT c.date,
       (SELECT COUNT(*)
        FROM Subscribers s
        WHERE StartDate <= c.Date AND
              (StopDate > c.Date OR StopDate IS NULL)
       ) as NumActives
FROM Calendar c
WHERE c.Date BETWEEN '2006-01-01' and '2006-01-07'
```

This query—even for only a week of actives—is painfully slow. In essence, the query has to count every subscriber on every day that she or he is active.

A clever approach realizes that you can count the subscribers only when they start and then subtract them out when they stop. Window functions then accumulate the counts in-between:

```
SELECT s.*
FROM (SELECT s.date,
```

```
            SUM(SUM(inc)) OVER (ORDER BY s.Date) as NumActives
    FROM (SELECT StartDate as date, 1 as inc
          FROM Subscribers
          UNION ALL
          SELECT COALESCE(StopDate, '2006-12-31'), -1 as inc
          FROM Subscribers
         ) s
    GROUP BY s.Date
   ) s
WHERE s.Date BETWEEN '2006-01-01' and '2006-01-07'
```

Note that the WHERE clause is in the outer query, not the subquery. It is tempting to use a WHERE or HAVING clause with no subquery. Alas, these filter the dates *before* window function SUM() is executed—so only start dates and stop dates in the date range are considered for the calculation. Instead, the subquery calculates the results for all dates, so they can be appropriately added together and then the totals are limited to the correct range.

The filtering outside the subquery does mean that extra work is being done, for customers who start and stop either before the period begins or after the period ends. We can fix this by adding the following code to each subquery:

```
WHERE StartDate <= '2006-01-07' AND
      (StopDate >= '2006-01-01' OR StopDate IS NULL)
```

This arranges for the calculation to use only customers that are active during at least one day during the period of interest, which reduces the size of data being processed, and increases performance.

Number of Active Households with a Twist

The orders business has a rule for counting active households. A household remains active for one year after a purchase. This is important for marketing purposes for distinguishing between active and lapsed customers. *How many active households are there on each day?*

It is quite tempting to use the calendar table for this:

```
SELECT d.Date,
       (SELECT COUNT(DISTINCT c.HouseholdId)
        FROM Orders o JOIN Customers c ON o.CustomerId = c.CustomerId
        WHERE d.Date BETWEEN o.OrderDate AND o.OrderDate + 365
       ) as NumActives
FROM Calendar d
WHERE d.Date BETWEEN '2009-10-04' AND '2009-10-10'
```

However, this suffers from the same performance problem that was discussed in the previous section: Each order is counted once for every day in the year—about 365 times.

A different idea is to figure out when to add in a new household and when to remove one. A household starts being counted when it has no orders in the preceding year. Similarly, it is counted until one year has elapsed with no orders. Both of these can be determined using LAG(), LEAD(), and simple logic. The rest is a cumulative sum.

The following query shows the SQL query:

```
WITH oc as (
    SELECT o.*, c.HouseholdId,
           LAG(o.OrderDate) OVER (PARTITION BY c.HouseholdId
                                       ORDER BY o.OrderDate) as prev_OrderDate,
           LEAD(o.OrderDate) OVER (PARTITION BY c.HouseholdId
                                        ORDER BY o.OrderDate) as next_OrderDate
      FROM Orders o JOIN Customers c ON o.CustomerId = c.CustomerId
    )
SELECT thedate, SUM(inc), SUM(SUM(inc)) OVER (ORDER BY thedate)
FROM ((SELECT oc.OrderDate as thedate, 1 as inc
       FROM oc
       WHERE prev_OrderDate IS NULL OR prev_OrderDate + 365 < OrderDate
      ) UNION ALL
      (SELECT oc.OrderDate + 365, -1 as inc
       FROM oc
       WHERE next_OrderDate IS NULL OR next_OrderDate - 365 > OrderDate
      )
     ) d
GROUP BY thedate
```

The CTE combines Orders and Customers and calculates the next and previous dates. The subquery calculates when households become active. Notice that a household could be counted more than once, if it has orders with gaps of more than one year. The query then gets households that cease being active. The cumulative sum uses the start and stop information to calculate the total at any given time.

When using the calendar table, you can ensure that you get all the dates, even those with no orders. This method might have missing dates. If such "holes" in the resulting dates are a problem, then add the appropriate calendar range to the UNION ALL subquery, giving these dates an inc value of zero. These dates do not contribute to the overall sums, but the dates would then appear in the result set.

Number of Maximum Prices

The orders data has products with their prices. Any given time, each product has a most expensive price paid for the product, up to that time. *How many different maximum prices has a product had?* Let's simplify this to a histogram—the number that have had only one, two, and so on. For convenience, this query uses the shipping date instead of the ordering date, simply to avoid the join to the Orders table.

This is an example of a snapshotting query because it is capturing information that is true at a given point in time, but the information might subsequently change. Changes over time suggest using window functions.

> **TIP** Window functions are very handy for understanding changes over time.

One approach uses a subquery to determine if the current price is larger than any previous price. The subquery keeps only rows that have a new maximum price:

```
SELECT ol.ProductId, COUNT(DISTINCT ol.ShipDate)
FROM OrderLines ol
WHERE ol.UnitPrice > (SELECT MAX(ol2.UnitPrice)
                      FROM OrderLines ol2
                      WHERE ol2.ProductId = ol.ProductId AND
                            ol2.ShipDate < ol.ShipDate
                     )
GROUP BY ol.ProductId
```

This query does a reasonable job of getting the counts for each product. But, the subquery has to process a lot of data, slowing it down.

Window functions provide an alternative—if we think about the problem a bit differently. For each day, get the cumulative maximum. Then, check the cumulative maximum on the previous day. The query looks for changes in the maximum price on consecutive days:

```
WITH ps AS (
     SELECT ProductId, ShipDate,
            MAX(MAX(UnitPrice)) OVER (PARTITION BY ProductId
                                      ORDER BY ShipDate) as maxup
     FROM OrderLines ol
     GROUP BY ProductId, ShipDate
    )
SELECT cnt, COUNT(*), MIN(ProductId), MAX(ProductId)
FROM (SELECT ProductId, COUNT(*) as cnt
      FROM (SELECT ps.*,
                   LAG(maxup) OVER (PARTITION BY ProductId
                                    ORDER BY ShipDate) as prev_maxup
            FROM ps
           ) ps
      WHERE prev_maxup IS NULL OR prev_maxup <> maxup
      GROUP BY ProductId
     ) ps
GROUP BY cnt
ORDER BY cnt
```

The CTE calculates the maximum unit price up to a given shipping date. The innermost subquery gets the maximum from the previous day, and the WHERE clause uses this information to select rows where the maximum has changed. The outermost query does an aggregation.

There is one small subtlety. The CTE does the aggregation by product-day. Why? The problem is that each product could be shipped multiple times on a given day—and hence the product could have multiple maximum prices even within a single day. The maximum of these values is fine; it gets the maximum including all shipments on that day.

The problem comes with the LAG(). Without the aggregation by day, it might end up choosing a row from the same day as the given row. A problem arises if two orders have different prices that are both bigger than the previous maximum. Then the day could end up being counted twice. In any case, because the intent of the LAG() is for an offset by at least one day, it is best to aggregate at that level.

Most Recent Holiday

What is the most recent national holiday before each order? This simple question results in a complicated join between Orders and Calendar. One approach is to get the date of the holiday and then join in the rest of the information.

The following query can get the date of the most recent holiday:

```
SELECT o.OrderId, o.OrderDate,
       (SELECT TOP 1 c.HolidayName
        FROM Calendar c
        WHERE c.Date <= o.OrderDate and
              c.HolidayType = 'national'
        ORDER BY c.date DESC
       ) as HolidayName
FROM Orders o
WHERE o.OrderDate BETWEEN '2015-01-01' and '2015-12-31'
```

Sadly, this correlated subquery is very bad performance-wise. It requires getting all the holidays before the given date, sorting them, and choosing the most recent—and all that work is just for one order. Filtering the calendar rows to holidays just in the right period of time for the data would make this a bit more efficient.

A better way uses window functions. The idea is to interleave the calendar data with the orders and then use cumulative functions to fill in the unknown values. Figure 14-6 illustrates the idea on a small amount of data.

The following query is the equivalent of the previous query, with the caveat that the extra rows from Calendar for holidays are in the result set.

```
WITH oc as (
     SELECT o.OrderId, o.OrderDate, NULL as HolidayDate,
            NULL as HolidayName
     FROM Orders o
     UNION ALL
     SELECT NULL, Date, Date as HolidayDate, HolidayName
```

```
       FROM Calendar c
       WHERE c.HolidayTYpe = 'national'
    )
SELECT oc.OrderId, oc.OrderDate,
       MAX(oc.HolidayDate) OVER (ORDER BY oc.OrderDate) as HolidayDate
FROM oc
```

This query takes advantage of window functions to accumulate information—and the performance is much better than the version using the correlated subquery. In the oc CTE, HolidayDate is uniformly NULL for the orders. It gets filled in with the cumulative maximum value. The way that the cumulative max works, all records with the same date get the same value for cumulative max. So, the maximum is not affected by how the orders and calendar records are interleaved on any given day.

Note that this approach works for the date, but it does not work for the holiday name, because they are not in alphabetical order. So, if we put in the maximum holiday, it quickly becomes "Thanksgiving" for all holiday names. "Thanksgiving" is the last national holiday, alphabetically.

HOLIDAYS

DATE	HOLIDAY	TYPE
December 25	Christmas	National
January 1	New Years	National

DATA

DATE	...
December 18	
December 20	
December 21	
December 30	
December 31	
January 1	
January 2	

Two tables have data by dates.
We want to get the most recent holiday date for each record in the second table
Combine the records using UNION ALL.

COMBINED

DATE	HOLIDAY	...
December 18		
December 20		
December 21		
December 25	December 25	NULL
December 30		
December 31		
January 1	January 1	NULL
January 1		
January 2		

INTERLEAVED WITH CUMULATIVE MAXIMUM

DATE	HOLIDAY	HOLIDAY_CUME	...
December 18			
December 20			
December 21			
December 25	December 25	December 25	NULL
December 30		December 25	
December 31		December 25	
January 1	January 1	January 1	NULL
January 1		January 1	
January 2		January 1	

Calculate the maximum date using MAX(HolidayDate) OVER (ORDER BY DATE).
This assigns the maximum date from HOLIDAYS to each record.
Finally, filter out the records that contain the data. (This step is not shown.)
A subsequent join can bring in the holiday name.

Figure 14-6: Sometimes interleaving data and using windows functions can be a big win performance-wise.

The following assigns the holiday name by using the holiday date as a "group" and just taking the maximum value over the group.

```
WITH oc as (
      SELECT o.OrderId, o.OrderDate, NULL as HolidayDate,
             NULL as HolidayName
      FROM Orders o
      UNION ALL
      SELECT NULL, Date, Date as HolidayDate, HolidayName
      FROM Calendar c
      WHERE c.HolidayTYpe = 'national'
      )
SELECT oc.*
FROM (SELECT Orderid, OrderDate, HolidayDate,
             MAX(HolidayName) OVER (PARTITION BY HolidayDate
                                   ) as HolidayName
      FROM (SELECT oc.OrderId, oc.OrderDate,
                   MAX(oc.HolidayDate) OVER (ORDER BY oc.OrderDate
                                            ) as HolidayDate,
                   oc.HolidayName
            FROM oc
           ) oc
     ) oc
WHERE OrderId IS NOT NULL
```

These steps could also be done using joins back to the Calendar table.

This method of interleaving records from multiple tables can be quite powerful. The approach works for a single dimension—in this case date. Another problem where this can be very practical is looking up IP address information in an IP table. Once upon a time, using this technique reduced the running time of a query from over 17 hours to under three minutes—a 99.7% reduction in query time simply by using a smarter querying method.

Lessons Learned

The power of SQL comes from its being a *descriptive* language rather than a *procedural* language. A SQL query describes the result set, rather than the specific algorithms used to create it. Database engines support many different algorithms, so even a simple query can have multiple implementation choices, as complicated as out-of-memory parallel algorithms or as simple as just scanning all the rows in the table as if it were a file.

From a performance perspective, indexes are the most important component of relational databases. Indexes do not change SQL queries at all, because the optimizer does the work of figuring out how to use them. For the problems discussed in this book, B-tree indexes are the most appropriate. Other types of indexes exist, such as inverted indexes for text, R-trees for spatial data, and even more esoteric types.

Despite the many implementations of relational databases, there are common themes for writing good queries that perform well. Of course, indentation and naming conventions are important for reading and maintaining SQL code. It is also important to avoid mixing types in expressions, to avoid DISTINCT where possible (but not if necessary), and to favor UNION ALL over UNION.

Another very important feature is window functions, which allow SQL to answer some very complicated questions—quite efficiently. Window functions often appear in SQL statements, sometimes significantly improving performance.

One very imporant purpose of using relational databases is to store data and analyze it. Performance is necessarily a major consideration when using SQL. As examples throughout this book have shown, SQL can answer many interesting questions, providing a strong foundation for data analysis. It can also take advantage of the most powerful computers and grid computing for answering these questions, providing a scalable solution to the problems of data big and small.

Equivalent Constructs Among Databases

Relational databases support SQL in the same way that English is the language of Great Britain, the United States, India, and Jamaica. Although there is much in common among the databases, each dialect has its own vocabulary and accents.

Throughout the book, the SQL examples have used Microsoft T-SQL as the dialect of choice. The purpose of this appendix is to show equivalent SQL constructs in different databases for many of the capabilities used throughout the chapters.

The six database engines, in alphabetical order, are:

- IBM DB2 version 9 and above
- MySQL version 5 and above
- Oracle version 9 and above
- Postgres version 9 and above
- SAS proc sql
- SQL Server version 2012 and above

The databases from IBM, Microsoft, and Oracle are commercial products, although functional versions can often be downloaded for free. MySQL and Postgres are free database engines, and Postgres syntax is used for many commercial products, such as Netezza, Vertica, Amazon Redshift, ParAccel, and more. SAS proc sql is the SQL engine within the SAS language (the most popular commercial statistical software). When using SAS, proc sql can be used in two different modes. In one, it communicates directly to a database, and supports the language of the database. In the other, it runs within SAS and uses SAS's particular constructs.

This appendix is provided as is, without any guarantees that the software has not changed for whatever reason.

This appendix is organized by the following topics:

- String functions
- Date/time functions
- Mathematical functions
- Other functions and features

Within each topic, specific functions are in subsections. Within each subsection, the structure for each database is shown.

String Functions

This section includes functions that operate on string values.

Searching for Position of One String within Another

Which function searches for one string inside another string? The arguments are:

- `<search string>`: The string to be searched
- `<pattern>`: The string to look for
- `<occurrence>`: Which occurrence
- `<offset>`: Where to start searching

IBM DB2

```
LOCATE(<pattern>, <search string>, <offset>)
```

The argument `<offset>` is optional and defaults to 1. The function returns the position in the search string where the pattern is found and 0 if the pattern is not found.

An alternative method:

```
POSSTR(<search string>, <pattern>)
```

The function returns the position in the search string where the pattern is found and 0 if the pattern is not found.

MySQL

```
INSTR(<search string>, <pattern>)
```

The function returns the position in the search string where the pattern is found and 0 if the pattern is not found.

An alternative method:

```
LOCATE(<pattern>, <search string>, <offset>)
```

The argument `<offset>` is optional and defaults to 1. The function returns the position in the search string where the pattern is found and 0 if the pattern is not found.

Oracle

```
INSTR(<search string>, <pattern>, <occurrence>)
```

The argument `<occurrence>` is optional and defaults to 1. The function returns the position in the search string where the pattern is found and 0 if the pattern is not found.

Postgres

```
POSITION(<pattern IN <search string>)
```

The argument `<occurrence>` is optional and defaults to 1. The function returns the position in the search string where the pattern is found and 0 if the pattern is not found.

SAS proc sql

```
FIND(<search string>, <pattern>)
```

The function returns the position in `<search string>` where the pattern is found, and 0 if the pattern is not found.

SQL Server

```
CHARINDEX(<pattern>, <search string>, <offset>)
```

The argument `<offset>` is optional and defaults to 1. The function returns the position in the search string where the pattern is found and 0 if the pattern is not found.

String Concatenation

Which function and operator append strings together?

IBM DB2

```
CONCAT(<string 1>, <string 2>)
```

Note: This function only takes two arguments, but the function can be nested. In addition, the operator || also concatenates strings.

MySQL

```
CONCAT(<string 1>, <string 2>, . . .)
```

Note: This function can take two or more arguments.

Oracle

```
<string 1> || <string 2>
```

In addition, Oracle supports CONCAT() with only two arguments.

Postgres

```
<string 1> || <string 2>
```

In addition, Postgres supports CONCAT() with any number of arguments.

SAS proc sql

```
CAT(<string 1>, <string 2>, . . .)
```

Note: This function can take two or more arguments.

SQL Server

```
<string 1> + <string 2>
```

The concatenation operator is an overloaded "+" operator. When mixing character and numeric types, be sure to cast the numeric values to strings. SQL Server also supports CONCAT() with an arbitrary number of arguments.

String Length Function

Which function returns the length of a string?

IBM DB2

```
LENGTH(<string>)
```

MySQL

```
LENGTH(<string>)
```

Oracle

```
LENGTH(<string>)
```

Postgres

```
LENGTH(<string>)
```

SAS proc sql

```
LENGTH(<string>)
```

Note: This function ignores trailing blanks.

SQL Server

```
LEN(<string>)
```

Substring Function

Which function returns a substring?

IBM DB2

```
SUBSTRING(<string>, <positive offset>, <len>)
```

The argument `<len>` is optional; when missing, the function returns the rest of the string. The argument `<offset>` must be non-negative.

MySQL

```
SUBSTRING(<string>, <offset>, <len>)
```

The argument `<len>` is optional; when missing, the function returns the rest of the string. If `<offset>` is negative, the function counts from the end of the string rather than the beginning. MySQL also supports `SUBSTR()`.

Oracle

```
SUBSTR(<string>, <offset>, <len>)
```

The argument `<len>` is optional; when missing, the function returns the rest of the string. If `<offset>` is negative, the function counts from the end of the string rather than the beginning.

Postgres

```
SUBSTR(<string>, <positive offset>, <len>)
```

The argument `<len>` is optional; when missing, the function returns the rest of the string.

SAS proc sql

```
SUBSTRN(<string>, <offset>, <len>)
```

The argument `<len>` is optional; when missing, the function returns the rest of the string. Note: `SUBSTRN()` is preferable to `SUBSTR()` because it does not produce errors or warnings when `<offset>+<len>` extends beyond the length of `<string>`.

SQL Server

```
SUBSTRING(<string>, <positive offset>, <len>)
```

All arguments are required and the last two must be non-negative.

Replace One Substring with Another

Which function replaces one substring with another? The `REPLACE()` function is the same across all databases except SAS.

IBM DB2

```
REPLACE(<string>, <from>, <to>)
```

MySQL

```
REPLACE(<string>, <from>, <to>)
```

Oracle

```
REPLACE(<string>, <from>, <to>)
```

Postgres

```
REPLACE(<string>, <from>, <to>)
```

SAS proc sql

```
RXCHANGE(RXPARSE('<from> to <to>'), 999, <string>))
```

SQL Server

```
REPLACE(<string>, <from>, <to>)
```

Remove Leading and Trailing Blanks

How can spaces at the beginning and end of a string be removed?

IBM DB2

```
LTRIM(RTRIM(<string>))
```

MySQL

```
TRIM(<string>)
```

Oracle

```
TRIM(<string>)
```

Note: `LTRIM()` and `RTRIM()` are also supported.

Postgres

```
TRIM(LEADING | TRAILING | BOTH FROM <string>)
```

SAS proc sql

```
BTRIM(<string>)
```

SQL Server

```
LTRIM(RTRIM(<string>))
```

RIGHT Function

Which function and operator return a substring of length `<len>` from the end of a string?

IBM DB2

```
RIGHT(<string>, <len>)
```

MySQL

```
RIGHT(<string>, <len>)
```

Oracle

```
SUBSTR(<string>, - <len>)>
```

Postgres

```
RIGHT(<string>, <len>)
```

SAS proc sql

```
SUBSTR(<string>, LENGTH(<string>) + 1 - <len>, <len>)
```

SQL Server

```
RIGHT(<string>, <len>)
```

LEFT Function

Which function and operator return a substring from the beginning of a string with length `<len>`?

IBM DB2

```
LEFT(<string>, <len>)
```

MySQL

```
LEFT(<string>, <len>)
```

Oracle

```
SUBSTR(<string>, 1, <len>)
```

Postgres

```
LEFT(<string>, <len>)
```

SAS proc sql

```
SUBSTRN(<string>, 1, <len>)
```

SQL Server

```
LEFT(<string>, <len>)
```

ASCII Function

Which functions return the ASCII value of an 8-bit character?

IBM DB2

```
ASCII(<char>)
```

MySQL

```
ASCII(<char>)
```

Oracle

```
ASCII(<char>)
```

Postgres

```
ASCII(<char>)
```

SAS proc sql

```
RANK(<char>)
```

SQL Server

```
ASCII(<char>)
```

Date/Time Functions

This section has functions that deal with dates and times.

Date Constant

How is a date constant represented in code?

IBM DB2

```
DATE(<string as YYYY-MM-DD>)
```

MySQL

```
DATE(<string as YYYY-MM-DD> )
```

Strings of the form YYYY-MM-DD are interpreted as dates when a date is expected.

Oracle

```
DATE <string as YYYY-MM-DD>
```

Postgres

```
<string as YYYY-MM-DD>::DATE
```

The ::DATE converts the string to a date. Strings of the form YYYY-MM-DD are interpreted as dates when a date is expected.

SAS proc sql

```
<string as ddMmmyyyy>d
```

SQL Server

```
CAST(<string as YYYY-MM-DD> as DATE)
```

Strings of the form YYYY-MM-DD are also recognized as date constants for almost all settings. (There is one arcane internationalization setting where this is not true.)

Current Date and Time

What is the current date and time?

IBM DB2

CURRENT_DATE (for date), CURRENT_TIMESTAMP (for date/time)

MySQL

CURDATE() (for date), NOW() (for date/time)

Oracle

```
TRUNC(sysdate) (for date), SYSDATE (for date/time)
```

Postgres

```
CURRENT_DATE) (for date), CURRENT_TIMESTAMP (for date/time)
```

SAS proc sql

```
TODAY()
```

SQL Server

```
CAST(GETDATE() as DATE) (for date),
GETDATE() or CURRENT_TIMESTAMP (for date/time)
```

Convert to YYYYMMDD String

How can a date be converted to the format YYYYMMDD?

IBM DB2

```
REPLACE(LEFT(CHAR(<date>, ISO), 10), '-', '')))
```

MySQL

```
DATE_FORMAT(<date>, '%Y%m%d')
```

Oracle

```
TO_CHAR(<date>, 'YYYYMMDD')
```

Postgres

```
TO_CHAR(<date>, 'YYYYMMDD')
```

SAS proc sql

```
PUT(<date>, YYMMDD10.)
```

This returns a string of the form YYYY-MM-DD. This format is usually sufficient, and removing the hyphens in SAS is cumbersome.

SQL Server

```
CONVERT(VARCHAR(8), <date>, 112)
```

Year, Month, and Day of Month

Which functions extract the year, month, and day from a date as numbers?

IBM DB2

```
YEAR(date)
MONTH(date)
DAY(date)
```

MySQL

```
EXTRACT(YEAR FROM <date>) or YEAR(date)
EXTRACT(MONTH FROM <date>) or MONTH(date)
EXTRACT(DAY FROM <date>) or DAY(date)
```

Oracle

```
EXTRACT(YEAR FROM <date>) or TO_CHAR(<date>, 'YYYY')
EXTRACT(MONTH FROM <date>) or TO_CHAR(<date>, 'MM')
EXTRACT(DAY FROM <date>) or TO_CHAR(<date>, 'DD')
```

Postgres

```
EXTRACT(YEAR FROM <date>) or TO_CHAR(<date>, 'YYYY')
EXTRACT(MONTH FROM <date>) or TO_CHAR(<date>, 'MM')
EXTRACT(DAY FROM <date>) or TO_CHAR(<date>, 'DD')
```

SAS proc sql

```
YEAR(date)
MONTH(date)
DAY(date)
```

SQL Server

```
YEAR(date) or DATEPART(year, <date>)
MONTH(date) or DATEPART(month, <date>)
DAY(date) or DATEPART(day, <date>)
```

Day of Week (Integer and String)

Which functions extract the day of the week as a day number (starting with 1 for Sunday) and as a name?

IBM DB2

```
DAYOFWEEK(<date>)
DAYNAME(<date>)
```

MySQL

```
DAYOFWEEK(<date>)
DAYNAME(<date>)
```

Oracle

```
TO_CHAR(<date>, 'D')
TO_CHAR(<date>, 'DY')
```

Postgres

```
EXTRACT(dow FROM <date>)
TO_CHAR(<date>, 'Day')
```

SAS proc sql

```
WEEKDAY(<date>)
PUT(<date>, weekdate3.)
```

SQL Server

```
DATEPART(dayofweek, <date>)
DATENAME(dayofweek, <date>)
```

Adding (or Subtracting) Days from a Date

How is a given number of days added to or subtracted from a date?

IBM DB2

```
<date> + <days> DAYS
```

MySQL

```
DATE_ADD(<date>, INTERVAL <days> DAY)
```

Oracle

```
<date> + <days>
```

Postgres

```
<date> + <days> * interval '1 day'
```

SAS proc sql

```
<date> + <days>
```

SQL Server

```
DATEADD(day, <days>, <date>)
```

Adding (or Subtracting) Months from a Date

How is a given number of months added to or subtracted from a date?

IBM DB2

```
ADD_MONTHS(<date>, <months>)
```

MySQL

```
DATE_ADD(<date>, INTERVAL <months> MONTH)
```

Oracle

```
ADD_MONTHS(<date>, <months>)
```

Postgres

```
<date> + <months> * INTERVAL '1 month'
```

SAS proc sql

```
INTNX('MONTH', <date>, <months>)
```

SQL Server

```
DATEADD(month, <months>, <date>)
```

Difference between Two Dates in Days

How is the difference between two dates in days calculated?

IBM DB2

```
DAYS(<datelater>) - DAYS(<dateearlier>)
```

MySQL

```
DATEDIFF(<datelater>, <dateearlier>)
```

Oracle

```
<datelater> - <dateearlier>
```

Postgres

```
<datelater> - <dateearlier>
```

SAS proc sql

```
<datelater> - <dateearlier>
```

SQL Server

```
DATEDIFF(day, <dateearlier>, <datelater>)
```

Difference between Two Dates in Months

How is the difference between two dates in months calculated? Note that the definition of "month" is not precise, so the following are not all equivalent.

IBM DB2

```
MONTHS_BETWEEN(<datelater>, <dateearlier>)
```

Note: This returns a floating-point number, not an integer.

MySQL

```
TIMESTAMPDIFF(month, <dateearlier>, <datelater>)
```

Oracle

```
MONTHS_BETWEEN(<datelater>, <dateearlier>)
```

Note: This returns a floating-point number, not an integer.

Postgres

```
EXTRACT(YEAR FROM AGE(<datelater>, <dateearlier>))*12
+ EXTRACT(MONTH FROM AGE(<datelater>, <dateearlier>))
```

SAS proc sql

```
INTCK('MONTH', <dateearlier>, <datelater>)
```

Note: This counts the number of month boundaries between two values, rather than the number of full months.

SQL Server

```
DATEDIFF(month, <dateearlier>, <datelater>)
```

Note: This counts the number of month boundaries between two values, rather than the number of full months.

Extracting Date from Date Time

How is a date extracted from a date time value, removing the time component?

IBM DB2

```
DATE(<date>)
```

MySQL

```
DATE(<date>)
```

Postgres

```
DATE_TRUNC('day', <date>)
```

Oracle

```
TRUNC(<date>)
```

SAS proc sql

```
DATEPART(<date>)
```

SQL Server

```
CAST(<date> as DATE)
```

Mathematical Functions

These functions operate on numeric values.

Remainder/Modulo

Which function returns the remainder when one number, <num>, is divided by another, <base>?

IBM DB2

```
MOD(<num>, <base>)
```

MySQL

```
MOD(<num>, <base>) or <num> MOD <base> or <num> % <base>
```

Oracle

```
MOD(<num>, <base>)
```

Postgres

```
<num> % <base> or MOD(<num>, <base>)
```

SAS proc sql

```
MOD(<num>, <base>)
```

SQL Server

```
<num> % <base>
```

Power

How do you raise one number, `<base>`, to another number, `<exp>`?

IBM DB2

```
POWER(<base>, <exp>)
```

MySQL

```
POWER(<base>, <exp>)
```

Oracle

```
POWER(<base>, <exp>)
```

Postgres

```
POWER(<base>, <exp>) or <base>^<exp>
```

SAS proc SQL

```
<base>**<exp>
```

SQL Server

```
POWER(<base>, <exp>)
```

Natural Logs and Exponential Function

What are the functions for the natural log and exponential function?

IBM DB2

```
EXP(LN(<number>))
```

MySQL

```
EXP(LN(<number>)) or EXP(LOG(<number>))
```

Oracle

```
EXP(LN(<number>))
```

Postgres

```
EXP(LN(<number>))
```

SAS proc SQL

```
EXP(LN(<number>))
```

SQL Server

```
EXP(LOG(<number>))
```

Floor

Which function removes the fractional part of a number?

IBM DB2

```
FLOOR(<number>)
```

MySQL

```
FLOOR(<number>)
```

Oracle

```
FLOOR(<number>)
```

Postgres

```
FLOOR(<number>)
```

SAS proc sql

```
FLOOR(<number>)
```

SQL Server

```
FLOOR(<number>)
```

"Random" Numbers

How can we get random numbers between 0 and 1? This is useful, for instance, for returning a randomized set of rows. For random number generators that accept a seed as an argument, the sequence is always the same for a given seed.

IBM DB2

```
RAND()
```

MySQL

```
RAND()
RAND(<seed>)
```

Oracle

```
DBMS_RANDOM.VALUE()
```

Postgres

```
RANDOM()
```

SAS proc sql

```
RAND('UNIFORM')
```

Note: SAS has a wide variety of random number generators that pull numbers from many different distributions.

SQL Server

```
RAND(CHECKSUM(NEWID()))
```

Note: The RAND() function returns a single value for the entire query. However, by providing a varying seed, this returns a different value for each row. When using a random number for ORDER BY, NEWID() is sufficient.

Left Padding an Integer with Zeros

How can an integer value be converted to a string of a fixed length and padded with zeros on the left?

IBM DB2

```
RIGHT(CONCAT(REPEAT('0', <len>), CAST(<num> as CHAR)), <len>)
                        or
LPAD(<num>, <len>, '0')
```

MySQL

```
LPAD(<num>, <len>, '0')
```

Oracle

```
LPAD(<num>, <len>, '0')
```

Postgres

```
LPAD(<num>, <len>, '0')
```

SAS proc sql

```
PUTN(<num>, Z<len>.)
```

SQL SERVER

```
RIGHT(REPLICATE('0', <len>) + CAST(<num> as VARCHAR(32)), <len>)
```

Conversion from Number to String

How is a number converted to a string?

IBM DB2

```
CAST(<arg> as CHAR)
```

MySQL

```
CAST(<arg> as CHAR) or FORMAT(<arg>, <decimal points>)
```

Note: VARCHAR does not work.

Oracle

```
TO_CHAR(<arg>)
```

Postgres

```
TO_CHAR(<arg>)
```

SAS proc sql

```
PUT(<arg>, BEST.)
```

The default puts the number into 12 characters. For a wider format, use BEST<width> (such as BEST20.) for the second argument.

SQL Server

```
CAST(<arg> as VARCHAR(32)) or STR(<arg>, <decimal points>)
```

Other Functions and Features

These are miscellaneous functions and features that do not fall into any of the previous categories.

Least and Greatest

How do you get the smallest and largest values from a list?

IBM DB2

```
(CASE WHEN <arg1> < <arg2> THEN <arg1> ELSE <arg2> END)
(CASE WHEN <arg1> > <arg2> THEN <arg1> ELSE <arg2> END)
```

If you have to worry about NULL values:

```
(CASE WHEN <arg2> IS NULL OR <arg1> < <arg2> THEN <arg1>
     ELSE <arg2> END)
(CASE WHEN <arg2> IS NULL or <arg1> > <arg2> THEN <arg1>
     ELSE <arg2> END)
```

MySQL

```
LEAST(<arg1>, <arg2>)
GREATEST(<arg1>, <arg2>)
```

For NULL values use a CASE statement.

Oracle

```
LEAST(<arg1>, <arg2>)
GREATEST(<arg1>, <arg2>)
```

For NULL values use a CASE statement.

Postgres

```
LEAST(<arg1>, <arg2>)
GREATEST(<arg1>, <arg2>)
```

SAS proc sql

```
(CASE WHEN <arg1> < <arg2> THEN <arg1> ELSE <arg2> END)
(CASE WHEN <arg1> > <arg2> THEN <arg1> ELSE <arg2> END)
```

If you have to worry about NULL values:
```
(CASE WHEN <arg2> IS NULL OR <arg1> < <arg2> THEN <arg1>
      ELSE <arg2> END)
(CASE WHEN <arg2> IS NULL OR <arg1> > <arg2> THEN <arg1>
      ELSE <arg2> END)
```

SQL Server

```
(CASE WHEN <arg1> < <arg2> THEN <arg1> ELSE <arg2> END)
(CASE WHEN <arg1> > <arg2> THEN <arg1> ELSE <arg2> END)
```

If you have to worry about NULL values:
```
(CASE WHEN <arg2> IS NULL OR <arg1> < <arg2> THEN <arg1>
      ELSE <arg2> END)
(CASE WHEN <arg2> IS NULL OR <arg1> > <arg2> THEN <arg1>
      ELSE <arg2> END)
```

Return Result with One Row

How can a query return a value with only one row? This is useful for testing syntax and for incorporating subqueries for constants.

IBM DB2

```
SELECT <whatever>
FROM SYSIBM.SYSDUMMY1
```

MySQL

```
SELECT <whatever>
```

Oracle

```
SELECT <whatever>
FROM dual
```

Postgres

```
SELECT <whatever>
```

SAS proc sql

Does not seem to support this; can be implemented by creating a dataset with one row or by using aggregation functions.

SQL Server

```
SELECT <whatever>
```

Return a Handful of Rows

How can a query return just a handful of rows? This is useful to see a few results without returning all of them.

IBM DB2

```
SELECT . . .
FROM . . .
FETCH FIRST <num> ROWS ONLY
```

MySQL

```
SELECT . . .
FROM . . .
LIMIT <num>
```

Oracle

```
SELECT . . .
FROM . . .
WHERE ROWNUM < <num>
```

or

```
SELECT . . .
FROM . . .
FETCH FIRST <num> ROWS ONLY
```

Postgres

```
SELECT . . .
FROM . . .
LIMIT <num>
```

or

```
SELECT . . .
FROM . . .
FETCH FIRST <num> ROWS ONLY
```

SAS proc sql

```
proc sql outobs=2;
    SELECT . . .;
```

SQL Server

```
SELECT TOP <num> . . .
FROM . . .
or
SELECT . . .
FROM . . .
FETCH FIRST <num> ROWS ONLY
```

Get List of Columns in a Table

How can a query return a list of columns in a table?

IBM DB2

```
SELECT colname
FROM syscat.columns
WHERE tabname = <tablename> AND
      tabschema = <tableschema>
```

MySQL

```
SELECT column_name
FROM information_schema.columns
WHERE table_name = <tablename> AND
      table_schema = <tableschema>
```

Oracle

```
SELECT column_name
FROM all_tab_columns
WHERE table_name =<tablename> AND
      owner = <owner>
```

Postgres

```
SELECT column_name
FROM information_schema.columns
WHERE table_name =
<tablename> AND table_catalog = <databasename>
```

SAS proc sql

```
SELECT name
FROM dictionary.columns
WHERE UPPER(memname) = <tablename> AND
      UPPER(libname) = <tableschema>
```

SQL Server

```
SELECT column_name
FROM information_schema.columns
WHERE table_name = <tablename> AND
      table_schema = <tableschema>
```

Note: This needs to be run in the database where the table is defined or using `<database>.information_schema.columns`.

Window Functions

Does the database support window functions, such as `ROW_NUMBER()`?

IBM DB2

Supported

MySQL

Not supported

Oracle

Supported; called analytic functions

Postgres

Supported

SAS proc sql

Not supported

SQL Server

Supported

Average of Integers

Is the average of a set of integers, using the AVG() function, an integer or a floating-point number?

IBM DB2

Integer

MySQL

Floating-point

Oracle

Floating-point

Postgres

Floating point

SAS proc sql

Floating-point

SQL Server

Integer

Index